HOLT
ALGEBRA
1

Eugene D. Nichols

Mervine L. Edwards

E. Henry Garland

Sylvia A. Hoffman

Albert Mamary

William F. Palmer

HOLT ALGEBRA 1

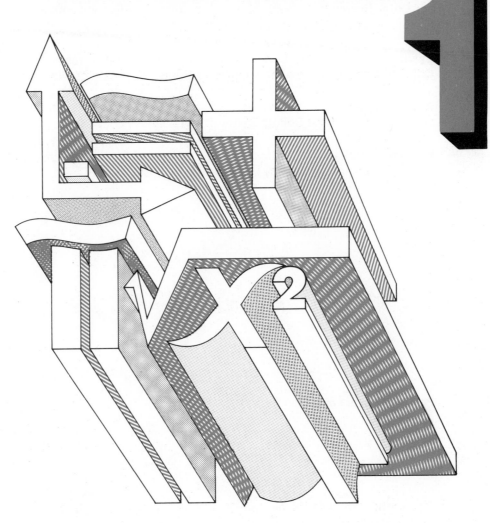

HOLT, RINEHART AND WINSTON, PUBLISHERS
New York · Toronto · London · Sydney

About the Authors

Eugene D. Nichols is Professor of Mathematics Education and Lecturer in the Department of Mathematics at Florida State University, Tallahassee, Florida.

Mervine L. Edwards is Chairman of the Mathematics Department, Shore Regional High School, West Long Branch, New Jersey.

E. Henry Garland is Head of the Mathematics Department at the Developmental Research School, and Associate Professor of Mathematics Education at Florida State University, Tallahassee, Florida.

Sylvia A. Hoffman is Curriculum Coordinator for the Metropolitan Chicago Region of the Illinois Office of Education, State of Illinois.

Albert Mamary is Assistant Superintendent of Schools for Instruction, Johnson City Central School District, Johnson City, New York.

William F. Palmer is Professor and Chairman of the Department of Education, Catawba College, Salisbury, North Carolina.

Photo credits are on page viii.

Copyright © 1978, 1974 by Holt, Rinehart and Winston, Publishers
All Rights Reserved
Printed in the United States of America

ISBN: 0-03-018901-2

23456 071 987

CONTENTS

SPECIAL TOPICS

ACKNOWLEDGEMENTS FOR PHOTOGRAPHS

Page   3   Top: SAS Photo
            Bottom: © Betty Medsger
Page   87   Top and Bottom: Irene Fertik
Page 202   Top Left: HRW Photo by Russell
            Dian
            Top Right: Courtesy of *Flooring
            Magazine*
            Bottom: Courtesy of the DuPont
            Co.

Page 260   Irene Fertik
Page 303   Courtesy of Pfizer, Inc.
Page 340   HRW Photo by Russell Dian
Page 413   HRW Photo by Russell Dian

SYMBOL LIST

1 BASIC OPERATIONS

Puzzles

PUZZLE 1.

Start with a pile of 15 tooth-picks. Each player in turn may take 1, 2, or 3 toothpicks from the pile. The player who must take the last toothpick is the loser.

PUZZLE 2.

Arrange the numbers 1, 2, 3, 4, 5, 6, 7, 8, 9 so that they meet these conditions:
(1) There are exactly three numbers in each circle.
(2) The sum of the numbers in each circle is 15.

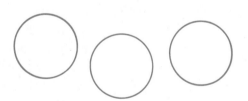

PUZZLE 3.

All you have is a 3-minute hourglass and an 8-minute hourglass. How can you cook an egg for exactly 13 minutes?

Order of Operations

 REVIEW CAPSULE

Ways to show multiplication:

times sign	raised dot	parentheses
↓	↓	↙ ↘
2×5	$2 \cdot 5$	(2)(5), or 2(5)

Read each as 2 times 5.

EXAMPLE 1   What does this mean? (2)(5) + 3

There are two possibilities.

$$(2)(5) + 3 \qquad\qquad (2)(5) + 3$$

Multiply first. ⟶   10 +3   (2)(8) ← Add first.
Then add. ⟶   13   16   ← Then multiply.

Two different answers ⟶   13 or 16?

Order of Operations
When both multiplications and additions occur, we multiply first and then add.

We make this agreement to avoid confusion. ⟶

Thus, in Example 1,   (2)(5) + 3
Multiply first. ⟶   10 +3
Then add. ⟶   13

EXAMPLE 2   Compute 6 + (3)(4).

Multiply first. ⟶   6 + (3)(4)
Then add. ⟶   6 +   12
                                18

Thus, 6 + 3(4) = 18.

EXAMPLE 3 Compute (4) (2) + (3) (1).

$$(4) (2) + (3) (1)$$
$$8 \ + \ 3$$
$$11$$

EXAMPLE 4 Compute $7 + 4 \cdot 2 + 1 + 6 \cdot 5$.

Remember the order of operations. $\longrightarrow$

$$7 + \underbrace{4 \cdot 2} + 1 + \underbrace{6 \cdot 5}$$

$$7 + \ \ 8 \ \ + 1 + \ \ 30$$
$$46$$

EXERCISES

PART A

Compute.

1. (4) (6) + 1

2. (7) (5) + 8

3. $6 \cdot 3 + 12$

4. $7 + 5 \cdot 8$

5. 8(3) + 5

6. 6 + (4) (11)

7. 8 + (3) (9)

8. (9) (1) + 12

9. 10 + (8) (1)

10. (3) (9) + 13

11. $6 \cdot 11 + 2$

12. 8 + (3) (9)

13. $14 + 12 \cdot 1$

14. 5(0) + 0

15. 3(2) + 4(1)

16. (6) (5) + (8) (3)

17. (7) (9) + (10) (1)

18. (6) (2) + (5) (0)

19. (4) (8) + (0) (7)

20. (6) (3) + (17) (2)

21. $5 \cdot 8 + 4 \cdot 9$

22. (6) (9) + 1 + (8) (2)

23. (7) (5) + (4) (8) + 2

24. $0 \cdot 8 + 5 + 0 \cdot 9$

PART B

Compute.

25. 1 + (0) (18) + (2) (9)

26. 6 + (4) (13) + 12

27. 7(9) + 8 + 4(2)

28. (3) (9) + (2) (12) + 8

29. (7) (4) + 8 + 10 + (9) (3)

30. 2 + (6) (7) + (3) (5) + 4

31. $6 + 2 \cdot 9 + 4 \cdot 6 + 5$

32. (1) (8) + 7 + (0) (3) + (2) (4)

33. (0) (8) + 2 + (9) (4) + (3) (5) + 4

34. 7 + (2) (13) + (5) (7) + 1 + (4) (5)

35. (2) (36) + 15 + (9) (14) + 7

36. $28 \cdot 5 + 4 \cdot 16 + 17 + 8 \cdot 3$

PART C

Compute.

37. (.5) (.007) + 1.18

38. .15 + (2.18) (.004)

39. (.15) (.6) + .004 + (1.1) (.007)

Mathematics in Aviation

Airplane pilots make careful checks of the instrument panel before and during flights.

Air traffic is monitored by traffic controllers in control towers of airports. They carefully calculate the flight patterns of arriving and departing planes.

Variables

REVIEW CAPSULE

Order of Operations
Multiply first. Then add.

$$7 + 5(8)$$
$$7 + \ \ 40 \quad \leftarrow \text{Multiply } 5(8) \text{ first.}$$
$$47 \qquad \leftarrow \text{Then add.}$$

Think of a number. — Multiply 5 by the number. — Then add 2 to the result.

$$5(\text{number}) + 2$$
$$5n \qquad + 2$$
$$\uparrow$$
$$\text{variable}$$

$5n$ means $5(n)$. ⟶

A *variable* takes the place of a number. ⟶

EXAMPLE 1 Evaluate $5n + 2$ for the values of n shown.

To evaluate means to find the value.
Substitute the values for the variable. ⟶

Let n be 3.	Let n be 8.	Let n be 20.
$5n + 2$	$5n + 2$	$5n + 2$
$5(3) + 2$	$5(8) + 2$	$5(20) + 2$
$15 + 2$	$40 + 2$	$100 + 2$
17	42	102

EXAMPLE 2 Evaluate $5 + 8a + 2b$ if $a = 7$ and $b = 4$.

$$5 + 8(7) + 2(4)$$
$$5 + \ \ 56 \ \ + \ \ 8$$
$$69$$

Terms are added.

Order of operations:
Multiply first.
Then add.

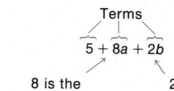

Terms

$$5 + 8a + 2b$$

A coefficient is the multiplier of a variable.

8 is the coefficient of a.   2 is the coefficient of b.

EXAMPLE 3 Name the terms and the variables in $3w + 8z + 2$.
Then name the coefficient of each variable.

Terms are added.
Variables are letters which take the
place of numbers.

The terms are $3w$, $8z$, and 2.
The variables are w and z.

$3w + 8z + 2$

3 is the
coefficient of w.

8 is the
coefficient of z.

ORAL EXERCISES

Name the terms and the variables. Then name the coefficient of each variable.

1. $6x + 1$

2. $4 + 3c$

3. $2y + 5$

4. $5a + 6 + 4b$

5. $7 + 3x + 8y$

6. $9m + 1 + 2n$

7. $3c + 2d + 6$

8. $7g + 3h + 12k$

9. $4y + 12z + 5w$

EXERCISES

PART A

Evaluate.

1. $2x + 3$ if $x = 5$

2. $5 + 3y$ if $y = 4$

3. $7 + 6a$ if $a = 7$

4. $7y + 3$ if $y = 2$

5. $9a + 1$ if $a = 6$

6. $5 + 6z$ if $z = 1$

7. $3x + 9$ if $x = 3$

8. $7 + 4c$ if $c = 8$

9. $2m + 6$ if $m = 4$

10. $5x + 4 + 2y$ if $x = 2, y = 4$

11. $3a + 6b + 1$ if $a = 3, b = 6$

12. $4m + 8 + 7n$ if $m = 6, n = 1$

13. $2k + 8 + 5t$ if $k = 9, t = 1$

14. $2 + 4y + 5z$ if $y = 7, z = 8$

15. $8g + 5 + 3e$ if $g = 8, e = 3$

16. $4p + 9 + 3q$ if $p = 9, q = 2$

17. $6r + 7s + 2$ if $r = 6, s = 5$

PART B

EXAMPLE Evaluate $xz + 7y$ if $x = 3, y = 5$, and $z = 2$.

$3(2) + 7(5)$

$6 \; + \; 35$, or 41

Evaluate if $x = 3, y = 8$, and $z = 5$.

18. $3x + 2y + 4z$

19. $5z + 4x + 7y$

20. $8y + 3z + 7x$

21. $2yz + xz$

22. $yz + 5xy$

23. $4xy + 8zy$

24. $6xy + 3yz + 1$

25. $9y + 5xy + 2zx$

26. $2xy + 6xz + 4yz$

Commutative and Associative Properties

▶ *REVIEW CAPSULE*

$4 + 7 = 11$ and $7 + 4 = 11$

Thus, $4 + 7 = 7 + 4.$

$5 \cdot 6 = 30$ and $6 \cdot 5 = 30$

Thus, $5 \cdot 6 = 6 \cdot 5.$

When adding or multiplying two numbers, we can change the order.

The Review suggests this. ──────────→

Commutative Property

Addition: $a + b = b + a$, for all numbers a and b.

Multiplication: $a \cdot b = b \cdot a$, for all numbers a and b.

EXAMPLE 1   Is this statement true? $(3 + 1) + 9 = 3 + (1 + 9)$

$(3 + 1) + 9$	$3 + (1 + 9)$
$4 \quad + 9$	$3 + \quad 10$
13	13

Add inside the parentheses first. ──────→
Answers are the same. ──────→

Yes, $(3 + 1) + 9 = 3 + (1 + 9)$ is a true statement.

EXAMPLE 2   Is this statement true? $(5 \cdot 2) \cdot 4 = 5 \cdot (2 \cdot 4)$

$(5 \cdot 2) \cdot 4$	$5 \cdot (2 \cdot 4)$
$10 \quad \cdot 4$	$5 \cdot \quad 8$
40	40

Multiply inside the parentheses first. ──────→
Answers are the same. ──────→

Yes, $(5 \cdot 2) \cdot 4 = 5 \cdot (2 \cdot 4)$ is a true statement.

Examples 1 and 2 suggest this. ──────→

When adding or multiplying, we can change the grouping.

Associative Property

Addition: $(a + b) + c = a + (b + c)$, for all numbers a, b, and c.

Multiplication: $(a \cdot b) \cdot c = a \cdot (b \cdot c)$, for all numbers a, b, and c.

EXAMPLE 3 Rewrite $295 + 42 + 5$ by using the commutative and associative properties. Then compute.

Associative property of addition

Commutative property of addition ──────→
Associative property of addition ──────→

$$
\begin{aligned}
295 + 42 + 5 &= (295 + 42) + 5 \\
&= 295 + (42 + 5) \\
&= 295 + (5 + 42) \\
&= (295 + 5) + 42 \\
&= \underbrace{300} + 42 \\
&= 342
\end{aligned}
$$

Thus, $295 + 42 + 5 = 342$.

EXAMPLE 4 Rewrite $25 \cdot 7 \cdot 4$ by using the commutative and associative properties. Then compute.

Associative property of multiplication

Commutative property of multiplication ──────→

Associative property ──────→

$$
\begin{aligned}
25 \cdot 7 \cdot 4 &= (25 \cdot 7) \cdot 4 \\
&= 25 \cdot (7 \cdot 4) \\
&= 25 \cdot (4 \cdot 7) \\
&= (25 \cdot 4) \cdot 7 \\
&= \underbrace{100} \cdot 7 \\
&= 700
\end{aligned}
$$

Thus, $25 \cdot 7 \cdot 4 = 700$.

SUMMARY   **Addition can be done in any order. Multiplication can be done in any order. The commutative and associative properties make this possible.**

EXAMPLE 5 Which property is illustrated by each equation?

Comm. is short for commutative.
Assoc. is short for associative.

$6x + 8y = 8y + 6x$
$(4 \cdot r)s = 4(rs)$
$3x(8) = 8(3x)$

Answers
Comm. Prop. Add.
Assoc. Prop. Mult.
Comm. Prop. Mult.

EXERCISES

PART A

Rewrite by using the commutative and associative properties. Then compute.

1. $17 + 4 + 56$

2. $49 + 16 + 1$

3. $2 + 56 + 38$

4. $27 + 2 + 98$

5. $67 + 35 + 3$

6. $25 + 47 + 5$

7. $4 \cdot 17 \cdot 25$

8. $50 \cdot 23 \cdot 2$

9. $5 \cdot 164 \cdot 2$

10. $20 \cdot 39 \cdot 5$

11. $250 \cdot 49 \cdot 4$

12. $2 \cdot 78 \cdot 50$

Which property is illustrated?

13. $8 + 2 = 2 + 8$

14. $(4 \cdot 5) \cdot 7 = 4 \cdot (5 \cdot 7)$

15. $(2 + 8) + 1 = 2 + (8 + 1)$

16. $9 \cdot 4 = 4 \cdot 9$

17. $(xy)z = x(yz)$

18. $5 + (8 + x) = (5 + 8) + x$

19. $4c + 8d = 8d + 4c$

20. $7(5b) = (7 \cdot 5)b$

21. $4y(9) = 9(4y)$

PART B

Rewrite by using the commutative and associative properties. Then compute.

22. $29 + 44 + 6 + 1$

23. $2 + 167 + 38 + 3$

24. $121 + 136 + 4 + 9$

25. $522 + 7 + 28 + 43$

26. $632 + 271 + 29 + 68$

27. $285 + 24 + 15 + 66$

28. $8 \cdot 56 \cdot 125$

29. $2 \cdot 187 \cdot 25 \cdot 2$

30. $20 \cdot 36 \cdot 2 \cdot 5$

PART C

EXAMPLE Is division commutative?
(Is $a \div b = b \div a$ always true?)

Let's try $6 \div 2$ and $2 \div 6$.

$6 \div 2 = 3$ and $2 \div 6 = \dfrac{2}{6}$, or $\dfrac{1}{3}$. So, $6 \div 2 \neq 2 \div 6$.

Thus, division is not commutative.

31. Is subtraction commutative?
Is subtraction associative?
Illustrate your answer.

32. Is division associative?
Illustrate your answer.

Distributive Property

EXAMPLE 1 Show that $5(6+3) = 5 \cdot 6 + 5 \cdot 3$.

Compute $5(6+3)$ and $5 \cdot 6 + 5 \cdot 3$.

$5(6+3)$	$5 \cdot 6 + 5 \cdot 3$
$5(9)$	$30 + 15$
45	45

Answers are the same. ⟶

Thus, $5(6+3) = 5 \cdot 6 + 5 \cdot 3$.

EXAMPLE 2 Show that $(5+3)4 = 5 \cdot 4 + 3 \cdot 4$.

$(5+3)4$	$5 \cdot 4 + 3 \cdot 4$
$8(4)$	$20 + 12$
32	32

Answers are the same. ⟶

Thus, $(5+3)4 = 5 \cdot 4 + 3 \cdot 4$.

Examples 1 and 2 suggest this. ⟶

Distributive Property of Multiplication over Addition

$a(b+c) = a \cdot b + a \cdot c$ and $(b+c)a = b \cdot a + c \cdot a$, for all numbers a, b, and c.

EXAMPLE 3 Rewrite $5(4+7)$ by using the distributive property. Then compute both expressions.

Distribute 5. ⟶

$$5(4+7) = 5 \cdot 4 + 5 \cdot 7$$

Compute $5(4+7)$ and $5 \cdot 4 + 5 \cdot 7$.

$5(4+7)$	$5 \cdot 4 + 5 \cdot 7$
$5(11)$	$20 + 35$
55	55

Answers are the same. ⟶

EXAMPLE 4 Rewrite $(8 + 3)\,5$ by using the distributive property.

$$(8 + 3)\,5 = 8 \cdot 5 + 3 \cdot 5$$

EXAMPLE 5 Show that $3(7 + 4 + 2) = 3 \cdot 7 + 3 \cdot 4 + 3 \cdot 2$.

$3(7 + 4 + 2)$	$3 \cdot 7 + 3 \cdot 4 + 3 \cdot 2$
$3(13)$	$21 + 12 + 6$
39	39

Answers are the same. ⟶

The distributive property may be used with three or more terms.

Thus, $3(7 + 4 + 2) = 3 \cdot 7 + 3 \cdot 4 + 3 \cdot 2$.

EXAMPLE 6 Rewrite $3(8) + 3(1)$ by using the distributive property.

3 is distributed.
Use the property "in reverse."

$$3(8) + 3(1) = 3(8 + 1)$$

EXAMPLE 7 Rewrite $5 \cdot 10 + 5 \cdot 2 + 5 \cdot 3 + 5 \cdot 5$ by using the distributive property.

$$5 \cdot 10 + 5 \cdot 2 + 5 \cdot 3 + 5 \cdot 5 = 5\,(10 + 2 + 3 + 5)$$

EXAMPLE 8 Rewrite $6(2) + 9(2)$ by using the distributive property.

2 is distributed. ⟶

$$6(2) + 9(2) = (6 + 9)\,2$$

EXAMPLE 9 Rewrite $6(3) + 1(3) + 8(3)$ by using the distributive property.

$$6(3) + 1(3) + 8(3) = (6 + 1 + 8)\,3$$

EXAMPLE 10 Rewrite $(6)\,(5) + (4)\,(6) + (6)\,(8)$ by using the distributive property.

$$(6)\,(5) + (4)\,(6) + (6)\,(8)$$

$$(6)\,(5) + (6)\,(4) + (6)\,(8)$$
$$6(5 + 4 + 8)$$

Thus, $(6)\,(5) + (4)\,(6) + (6)\,(8) = 6(5 + 4 + 8)$.

EXERCISES

PART A

Rewrite by using the distributive property. Then compute both expressions.

1. $4(6 + 2)$ **2.** $5(3 + 8)$ **3.** $2(9 + 4)$

4. $(9 + 7)1$ **5.** $(2 + 9)6$ **6.** $(3 + 7)5$

7. Show that $7(4 + 8 + 2) = 7 \cdot 4 + 7 \cdot 8 + 7 \cdot 2$.   **8.** Show that $(9 + 4 + 1)6 = 9 \cdot 6 + 4 \cdot 6 + 1 \cdot 6$.

Rewrite by using the distributive property.

9. $6(3 + 5)$ **10.** $8(4 + 9)$ **11.** $3(8 + 1)$

12. $(8 + 1 + 9)5$ **13.** $4(2 + 7 + 6)$ **14.** $(5 + 4 + 9)3$

15. $4(6) + 4(2)$ **16.** $7(3) + 7(9)$

17. $(5)(6) + (9)(6)$ **18.** $(1)(5) + (9)(5)$

19. $3 \cdot 8 + 8 \cdot 7$ **20.** $9 \cdot 2 + 4 \cdot 9$

21. $5 \cdot 4 + 5 \cdot 2 + 5 \cdot 7$ **22.** $1 \cdot 3 + 2 \cdot 3 + 8 \cdot 3$

23. $(6)(8) + (4)(8) + (7)(8)$ **24.** $2(9) + 2(4) + 2(6)$

25. $(4)(3) + (7)(4) + (4)(1)$ **26.** $(6)(5) + (4)(6) + (9)(6)$

27. $8 \cdot 7 + 7 \cdot 4 + 7 \cdot 2$ **28.** $1(9) + 5(9) + 9(3)$

PART B

Rewrite by using the distributive property.

29. $7(5 + 1 + 9 + 2)$ **30.** $(6 + 8 + 4 + 3)5$ **31.** $(1 + 9 + 7 + 2)4$

32. $3(2 + 6 + 4 + 8)$ **33.** $7(8 + 4 + 3 + 5)$ **34.** $(5 + 2 + 6 + 5)5$

35. $4(8 + 1 + 3 + 5 + 9)$ **36.** $(2 + 7 + 1 + 6 + 3)7$ **37.** $(8 + 9 + 1 + 4 + 6)3$

38. $6(3) + 4(6) + 6(1) + 2(6)$ **39.** $(7)(4) + (4)(7) + (2)(4) + (7)(4)$

PART C

EXAMPLE   Is subtraction distributive over multiplication? [Is it always true that $a - (b \cdot c) = (a - b) \cdot (a - c)$?]

Let's try $12 - (2 \cdot 4)$ and $(12 - 2)(12 - 4)$.

$12 - (2 \cdot 4)$	$(12 - 2)(12 - 4)$
$12 - 8$	$10(8)$
4	80

Two different answers $\longrightarrow$

Subtraction is not distributive over multiplication.

40. Is multiplication distributive over subtraction? Illustrate your answer.

41. Is addition distributive over multiplication? Illustrate your answer.

42. Is division distributive over addition from the left? Illustrate your answer.

43. Is division distributive over addition from the right? Illustrate your answer.

The Metric System

The metric system of measurement is based on ten, just as our numeration system is based on ten. The commonly-used units are screened.

Place name	thousands	hundreds	tens	units	tenths	hundredths	thousandths
	1,000	100	10	1	.1	.01	.001
Unit of length / Symbol	kilometer / km	hectometer / hm	dekameter / dam	meter / m	decimeter / dm	centimeter / cm	millimeter / mm
Value	1,000 m	100 m	10 m	1 m	.1 m	.01 m	.001 m
Prefix	kilo	hecto	deka		deci	centi	milli
Meaning	1,000	100	10		.1	.01	.001

PROBLEM

Change 5 km to cm.

One Way

Think: To get from km to cm, move 5 places to the right. So, move the decimal point 5 places to the right.

5.00000.

Thus, 5 km = 500,000 cm.

Another Way

$$\frac{5 \text{ km}}{1} \cdot \frac{100 \text{ cm}}{1 \text{ m}}$$

$$\frac{5 \, (1{,}000)\,(\cancel{1 \text{ m}}) \cdot 100 \text{ cm}}{\cancel{1 \text{ m}}}$$

$$5{,}000 \cdot 100 \text{ cm} = 500{,}000 \text{ cm}$$

PROJECT

Change as indicated. Use either method.

1. 3 m to mm   2. 6 hm to cm   3. 7 km to dm

4. 5 m to km   5. 8 cm to m   6. 4 mm to km

CAPACITY

The units of capacity are related in the same way as the units of length. The commonly-used units are screened.

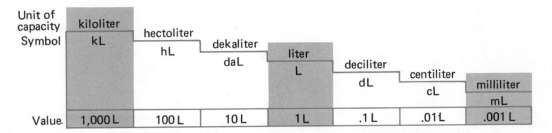

Unit of capacity Symbol	kiloliter kL	hectoliter hL	dekaliter daL	liter L	deciliter dL	centiliter cL	milliliter mL
Value.	1,000 L	100 L	10 L	1 L	.1 L	.01 L	.001 L

PROJECT Change as indicated.

7. 3L to cL   **8.** 5 daL to cL   **9.** 6 kL to mL

10. 7 dL to hL   **11.** 8L to kL   **12.** 9 mL to kL

WEIGHT (MASS)

The commonly used units are screened.

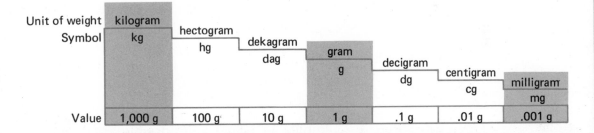

Unit of weight Symbol	kilogram kg	hectogram hg	dekagram dag	gram g	decigram dg	centigram cg	milligram mg
Value	1,000 g	100 g	10 g	1 g	.1 g	.01 g	.001 g

PROJECT Change as indicated.

13. 5 g to mg   **14.** 3 dag to cg   **15.** 8 kg to mg

16. 2 dg to dag   **17.** 7 g to kg   **18.** 6 mg to kg

Distributive Property and Variables

 REVIEW CAPSULE

Rewrite $7(4) + 2(4)$ by using the distributive property.

$$7(4) + 2(4) = (7 + 2)4$$

EXAMPLE 1   Rewrite $6y + 7y$ by using the distributive property. Simplify the result.

y is distributed. ────────────────→

$$6y + 7y = (6 + 7)y$$
$$= (13)y$$
$$= 13y$$

Thus, $6y + 7y = 13y$.

$6y + 7y$
like terms

$x + 9y + 4$
unlike terms

To *simplify* an expression, we combine like terms.

EXAMPLE 2   Simplify $5x + 7x$.

Combine like terms. ────────────────→

$$5x + 7x = 12x$$

EXAMPLE 3   Simplify $4a + 5b + 2$, if possible.

$4a$, $5b$, and 2 are unlike terms. ──────→ $4a + 5b + 2$ cannot be simplified.

EXAMPLE 4   Simplify $9x + 8y + 5x + 1 + 9$, if possible.

$9x$ and $5x$ are like terms.
Rearrange terms to group
$9x$ and $5x$ together.

$$9x + 8y + 5x + 1 + 9$$
$$9x + 5x + 8y + 1 + 9$$

$$14x \quad + 8y + \quad 10$$

ORAL EXERCISES

Simplify, if possible.

1. $2x + 3x$
2. $4p + 7p$
3. $2a + 3$
4. $6b + 7b$
5. $5y + 6y$
6. $5a + 8b$
7. $6r + 9r$
8. $8 + 3y$
9. $2m + 8m$
10. $7x + 9x$
11. $4y + 8z$
12. $5c + 8c$
13. $4 + 9y$
14. $2x + 5x$
15. $9w + 4w$
16. $7e + 8f$
17. $2z + 6z$
18. $8x + 9y$
19. $3g + 7g$
20. $5 + 5e$

EXERCISES

PART A

Simplify, if possible.

1. $6x + 3 + 4x$
2. $6 + 8x + 7$
3. $5y + 9 + 2y$
4. $3m + 2 + 5m$
5. $3a + 8a + 9$
6. $2r + 8 + 6r$
7. $7 + 6z + 5$
8. $9 + 5z + 8z$
9. $4b + 7 + 5b$
10. $8 + 6x + 3$
11. $5k + 7 + 4k$
12. $9 + 6x + 8$
13. $2y + 1 + 3y$
14. $2a + 7 + 5$
15. $3z + 8z + 4$
16. $2m + 3m + 8 + 1$
17. $6t + 7 + 4t + 9$
18. $7y + 3 + 7 + 3y$
19. $9 + 5z + 4 + 3z$
20. $5 + 4x + 3 + 8x$
21. $5x + 2y + 4x + 7y$
22. $6a + 7b + 8b + 2a$
23. $4m + 2q + 3m + 7q$
24. $3c + 5d + 9c + 4d$
25. $7x + 8y + 4x + 1$
26. $2 + 3z + 5 + 4y$
27. $7a + 8b + 9a + 6$
28. $5a + 4b + 9c + 5a$
29. $7x + 2y + 5z + 1$
30. $6g + 4 + 5h + 9g$

PART B

EXAMPLE   Simplify $5x + 9y + 3x + 2y$. Then evaluate if $x = 6$ and $y = 1$.

Group x terms together
and y terms together. $\longrightarrow$

$$5x + 9y + 3x + 2y$$
$$5x + 3x + 9y + 2y$$
$$8x \;\; + \;\; 11y$$

Substitute 6 for x, 1 for y. $\longrightarrow$

$$8(6) + 11(1)$$
$$48 \;\; + \;\; 11, \text{ or } 59$$

Simplify. Then evaluate for the given values of the variables.

31. $4a + 6a + 5$ if $a = 2$
32. $9 + 5r + 7r$ if $r = 3$
33. $2y + 8 + 5y$ if $y = 8$
34. $8 + 4k + 7$ if $k = 9$
35. $9 + 4y + 3 + 2y$ if $y = 7$
36. $6x + 4 + 9 + 3x$ if $x = 3$.
37. $4z + 2 + 3w + 8z$ if $z = 6, w = 4$
38. $5a + 6b + 4 + 3b + 7a$ if $a = 4, b = 5$

Applying the Distributive Property

OBJECTIVE
■ To simplify expressions like $6(4x + 3) + 5x + 9$

 REVIEW CAPSULE

Simplify $4x + 3 + 2x + 9$.

Group like terms. → $(4x + 2x) + (3 + 9)$
Combine like terms. → $\quad 6x \quad + \quad 12$

EXAMPLE 1   Simplify $7(5x)$.

Associative property ────────────→

$$7(5x) = (7 \cdot 5)x$$
$$= \quad 35x$$

EXAMPLE 2   Simplify $(9y)3$.

Rearrange and regroup. ────────→

$$(9y)3 = (9 \cdot 3)y$$
$$= \quad 27y$$

EXAMPLE 3   Simplify $7(4x + 5)$.

Distribute 7. ────────────────→
$7(4x) = (7 \cdot 4)x = 28x$ ──────→

$$7(4x + 5) = 7(4x) + 7(5)$$
$$= \quad 28x \quad + \quad 35$$

EXAMPLE 4   Simplify $6 + 7(3c + 2) + 4c$.

$$6 + 7(3c + 2) + 4c = 6 + 7(3c) + 7(2) + 4c$$
$$= 6 + \quad 21c \quad + \quad 14 \quad + 4c$$
$$= (21c + 4c) + (6 + 14)$$
$$= 25c + 20$$

EXAMPLE 5   Simplify $8 + (2y + 5)3 + 7y$.

$(2y + 5)3 = (2y)3 + (5)3$ ──────→

$$8 + (2y + 5)3 + 7y$$
$$8 + (2y)3 + (5)3 + 7y$$
$$8 + 6y + 15 + 7y$$
$$(6y + 7y) + (8 + 15)$$
$$13y + 23$$

Thus, $8 + (2y + 5)3 + 7y = 13y + 23$.

ORAL EXERCISES

Simplify.

1. $8(3x)$ **2.** $7(9r)$ **3.** $5(4y)$ **4.** $3(9z)$ **5.** $7(4a)$ **6.** $8(7x)$
7. $3(2a + 5)$ **8.** $4(3x + 2)$ **9.** $7(5c + 4)$ **10.** $(1 + 9a)5$

EXERCISES

PART A

Simplify.

1. $7(1 + 5y) + 8y$

3. $(6m + 9)4 + 5m$

5. $8c + 7(2 + 4c)$

7. $3(9x + 4) + 2x$

9. $2r + 8(7 + 5r)$

11. $5(6 + 4y) + 7y$

13. $(1 + 7c)5 + 4c$

15. $9 + 2(4x + 1)$

17. $2x + 4(6 + 2x) + 3x$

19. $5 + (4c + 2)3 + 6c$

21. $2x + 6 + (5 + 3x)4$

2. $4z + (2z + 5)3$

4. $9 + 3(2m + 8)$

6. $7b + (1 + 8b)6$

8. $(5 + 2d)4 + 9$

10. $4 + (7n + 8)2$

12. $(2d + 8)7 + 9d$

14. $3z + 6(4 + 8z)$

16. $6(7a + 2) + 5a$

18. $5 + 7(4y + 3) + 5y$

20. $3g + 5(7 + 4g) + 8$

22. $4z + 8(7 + 3z) + 5$

PART B

Simplify.

23. $(5 + 6r)3 + (7 + 2r)2$

25. $4(6e + 5) + 2(7e + 9)$

24. $5(7y + 3) + 9(1 + 2y)$

26. $(8a + 9)3 + (4a + 2)7$

PART C

EXAMPLE   Simplify $2[5x + 4(2x + 3)]$.

Remove inner parentheses first by
distributing 4. $\longrightarrow$

$$
\begin{aligned}
2[5x + 4(2x + 3)] &= 2[5x + 4(2x) + 4(3)] \\
&= 2(5x + \quad 8x \quad + \quad 12) \\
&= 2(13x + 12) \\
&= 2(13x) + 2(12) \\
&= 26x + 24
\end{aligned}
$$

Now distribute 2. $\longrightarrow$

Simplify.

27. $5[6c + 7(4c + 2)]$

29. $7x + 4[2x + (5 + 3x)6]$

28. $2a + 5[(6a + 8)2 + 3a]$

30. $6[2y + 3(2y + 4) + 1] + 3(5 + 8y)$

Chapter One Review

Compute. $[p.\ 1]$

1. $(7)(2) + 8$

2. $9 + (3)(4)$

3. $4 + (9)(0)$

4. $0 \cdot 4 + 6 + 8 \cdot 1$

5. $6 + 2(1) + 5 + 4(3)$

6. $5 + 2 \cdot 8 + 3 \cdot 2 + 6 + 5 \cdot 2$

Evaluate for the given values of the variables. $[p.\ 4]$

7. $9 + 7r$ if $r = 8$

8. $2d + 9$ if $d = 9$

9. $6 + 5x + 3y$ if $x = 4$, $y = 6$

10. $7a + 8 + 5b$ if $a = 1$, $b = 9$

11. $4g + 9h + 2$ if $g = 5$, $h = 7$

12. $8 + 4x + 7y$ if $x = 2$, $y = 8$

Name the terms and the variables. Then name the coefficient of each variable. $[p.\ 4]$

13. $5 + 9x$

14. $5y + 1 + 4z$

15. $8a + 7b + 2c$

Rewrite by using the commutative and associative properties. Then compute. $[p.\ 6]$

16. $2 + 57 + 28$

17. $23 + 9 + 7 + 41$

18. $422 + 36 + 24 + 38$

19. $(50)(47)(2)$

20. $97 \cdot 125 \cdot 8$

21. $(25)(41)(4)(2)$

Which property is illustrated? $[p.\ 6]$

22. $6 + 5 = 5 + 6$

23. $(7 \cdot 2) \cdot 6 = 7 \cdot (2 \cdot 6)$

24. $9 + (4 + x) = (9 + 4) + x$

25. $3(x + y) = (x + y)3$

Rewrite by using the distributive property. $[p.\ 9]$

26. $7(4 + 9)$

27. $(6 + 8)3$

28. $(5 + 2 + 6)9$

29. $8(3 + 7 + 5)$

30. $5(6) + 5(3)$

31. $(8)(9) + (9)(2)$

32. $(6)(7) + (7)(1) + (7)(6)$

33. $(4)(5) + (8)(4) + (3)(4) + (1)(4)$

34. Show $5(4 + 3 + 2) = 5 \cdot 4 + 5 \cdot 3 + 5 \cdot 2$.

35. Show $(1 + 5 + 9)3 = 1 \cdot 3 + 5 \cdot 3 + 9 \cdot 3$.

Simplify. $[p.\ 14,\ 16]$

36. $3x + 8 + 7x$

37. $9 + 4y + 8y$

38. $3t + 7 + 5t + 9$

39. $4p + 6q + 7p + 8q + 3$

40. $5r + 6(1 + 3r)$

41. $(6y + 8)3 + 2y$

42. $9(5p + 2) + 4p$

43. $8 + 2(7z + 3)$

44. $(3x + 5)4 + (8x + 7)6$

45. $5(9 + 3y) + 7(8 + 6y)$

Simplify. Then evaluate for the given values of the variables. $[p.\ 14]$

46. $7x + 9 + 3x$ if $x = 8$

47. $5 + 3y + 8 + 6y$ if $y = 2$

48. $4a + 3b + 6a + 7b$ if $a = 2$, $b = 1$

49. $4 + 3x + 7y + 9x + 4y$ if $x = 8$, $y = 6$

Chapter One Test

Compute.

1. $8 + (5)(6)$

2. $0 \cdot 4 + 7 + 5 \cdot 6$

3. $7(1) + 8 + 4(6)$

4. $7 + 3 \cdot 9 + 5 + 4 \cdot 6$

Evaluate for the given values of the variables.

5. $4 + 9y$ if $y = 7$

6. $2d + 12$ if $d = 7$

7. $6a + 2b + 4$ if $a = 3$, $b = 8$

Name the terms and the variables. Then name the coefficient of each variable.

8. $4 + 7x + 9y$

Rewrite by using the commutative and associative properties. Then compute.

9. $5 + 67 + 15$

10. $25 \cdot 58 \cdot 4$

11. $47 + 21 + 3 + 39$

12. $(50)(31)(2)(6)$

Which property is illustrated?

13. $(x + y) + z = x + (y + z)$

14. $12 + y = y + 12$

15. $b(5a) = (5a)b$

16. $(4 \cdot c) \cdot d = 4 \cdot (c \cdot d)$

Rewrite by using the distributive property.

17. $6(4 + 9)$

18. $(8 + 1 + 7)3$

19. $9(7) + 9(2)$

20. $(4)(5) + (5)(6) + (7)(5)$

21. Show $3(8 + 2 + 5) = 3 \cdot 8 + 3 \cdot 2 + 3 \cdot 5$.

22. Show $(4 + 1 + 6)7 = 4 \cdot 7 + 1 \cdot 7 + 6 \cdot 7$.

Simplify.

23. $6x + 7 + 3x$

24. $5y + 8 + 4z + 7y + 3z$

25. $2a + 4(7 + 5a)$

26. $7r + (6 + 2r)3 + 9$

27. $4(3x + 2) + 5(7x + 5)$

28. $(8y + 4)5 + (2y + 9)3$

Simplify. Then evaluate for the given values of the variables.

29. $3x + 7 + 9x$ if $x = 4$

30. $5a + 9 + 6b + 4a + 8b$ if $a = 5$, $b = 2$

Temperature

Temperature is measured in degrees Celsius (°C) in the metric system.

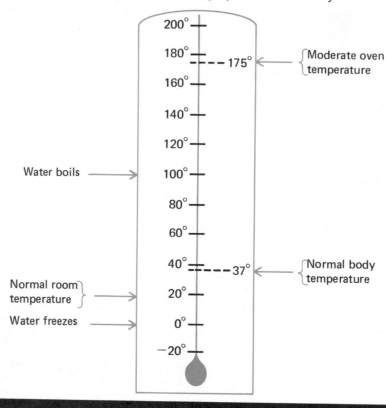

What is a good estimate of the temperature for the activity?

1. Wearing a sweater in the house   **2.** Swimming outdoors

3. Wearing woolen gloves   **4.** Burning toast

Adding Integers

OBJECTIVE
■ To add two integers

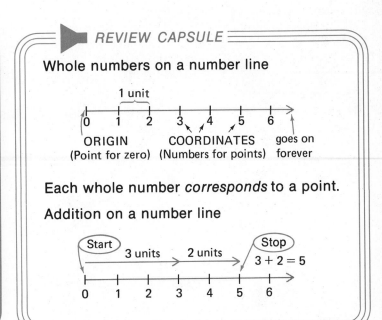

REVIEW CAPSULE

Whole numbers on a number line

1 unit

0 1 2 3 4 5 6

ORIGIN
(Point for zero)

COORDINATES
(Numbers for points)

goes on
forever

Each whole number *corresponds* to a point.

Addition on a number line

Start   3 units   2 units   Stop
3 + 2 = 5

0 1 2 3 4 5 6

We can extend a number line to the left of 0.

Integers on a number line ──────→

−4 −3 −2 −1 0 +1 +2 +3 +4

negative numbers   zero   positive numbers

. . . means the numbers go
on forever.

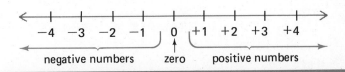

The numbers, . . . , −3, −2, −1, 0, +1, +2, +· · ·
are *integers*.

Positive integers ──────→
Read. ──────→

+1,   +2,   +3, . . .
positive 1,   positive 2,   positive 3, and so on

Zero ──────→

0 Zero is neither positive nor negative.

Negative integers ──────→
Read. ──────→

−1,   −2,   −3, . . .
negative 1,   negative 2,   negative 3, and so on

The regular sign + will be used
for positive integers.

To avoid confusion, we will use a heavy plus
sign **+** to show addition.

Adding positive integers is like adding whole numbers. For example,

Positive plus positive
Read. ————————————————————→
$+8 + +3 = +11$
Positive 8 plus positive 3 equals positive 11.

EXAMPLE 1   Add $-4 + -2$.

Negative plus negative
Read. ————————————————————→
Negative 4 plus negative 2

Start at 0. Move 4 units to the *left* to -4.
Then move 2 more units to the *left*.
The sum is -6.

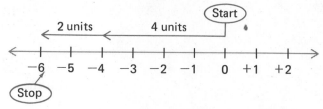

$$-4 + -2 = -6$$

EXAMPLE 2   Add $+4 + -5$.

Positive plus negative
Start at 0. Move 4 units to the *right* to $+4$.
Then move 5 units to the *left*.
The sum is -1.

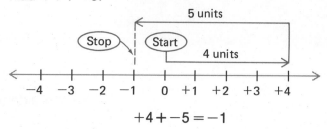

$$+4 + -5 = -1$$

EXAMPLE 3   Add $+5 + -3$.

Positive plus negative
Start at 0.
Move 5 right to $+5$.
Move 3 left.
The sum is $+2$.

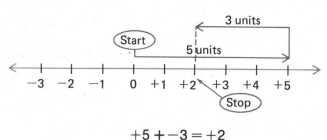

$$+5 + -3 = +2$$

EXAMPLE 4   Add $-3 + +7$.

Negative plus positive
Start at 0.
Move 3 left to -3.
Move 7 right.
The sum is $+4$.

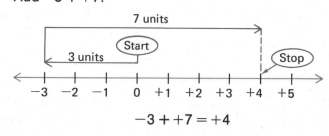

$$-3 + +7 = +4$$

EXERCISES

Add.

1. $+3 + +7$
2. $+8 + +5$
3. $-6 + -8$
4. $+4 + -2$
5. $-6 + -4$
6. $-1 + +7$
7. $+9 + -2$
8. $-5 + -3$
9. $+7 + -2$
10. $+4 + +4$
11. $+6 + -9$
12. $-3 + -7$
13. $+8 + -9$
14. $+6 + -2$
15. $-4 + -5$
16. $+6 + +1$
17. $-4 + -6$
18. $-6 + +2$
19. $+5 + -9$
20. $+3 + +6$
21. $-10 + -3$
22. $+11 + +5$
23. $+12 + -9$
24. $-3 + +15$
25. $+13 + -8$
26. $-17 + -2$
27. $-16 + +5$
28. $+8 + -19$
29. $-14 + -9$
30. $-6 + +17$
31. $+13 + +7$
32. $-18 + -8$

Add.

33. $+4 + +5$
34. $+5 + +4$
35. $-6 + -1$
36. $-1 + -6$
37. $-3 + +8$
38. $+8 + -3$
39. $+2 + -6$
40. $-6 + +2$
41. $+9 + -3$
42. $-3 + +9$
43. $-8 + -2$
44. $-2 + -8$
45. $-2 + 0$
46. $0 + -2$
47. $+8 + 0$
48. $0 + +8$

Add.

49. $+6 + -6$
50. $-3 + +3$
51. $+8 + -8$
52. $-6 + +6$
53. $-5 + +5$
54. $+8 + -8$
55. $+3 + -3$
56. $-9 + +9$

Add.

57. $+10 + -32$
58. $-27 + -31$
59. $+46 + -22$
60. $-38 + +28$
61. $+46 + +21$
62. $-37 + +56$
63. $-62 + -19$
64. $+45 + -45$
65. $-28 + +36$
66. $+59 + -63$
67. $+12 + -87$
68. $-56 + -23$
69. $-96 + -35$
70. $+48 + -37$
71. $-56 + +56$
72. $+43 + -39$
73. $+158 + -136$
74. $+279 + +346$
75. $-458 + -329$
76. $+728 + -958$
77. $-379 + +247$
78. $-586 + -431$
79. $+372 + +622$
80. $-489 + +262$

For each case below, state a rule for addition of integers.

81. positive plus positive
82. negative plus negative
83. positive plus negative
84. negative plus positive

Add.

85. $+.03 + -.86$
86. $-1.07 + +.83$
87. $-1.12 + +.046$
88. $-2.03 + +1.42$
89. $-.16 + +2.03$
90. $+2.06 + -6.04$
91. $-28.4 + +114.03$
92. $-.0004 + +1.703$

Properties of Addition of Integers

OBJECTIVES
- To identify the properties of addition of integers
- To determine the opposite of an integer
- To read and interpret the symbol $-a$

 REVIEW CAPSULE

Adding Integers

Signs the same	Signs different
$+5 + +9 = +14$	$+8 + -3 = +5$
$-8 + -9 = -17$	$-6 + +4 = -2$

Commutative Property of Addition
$8 + 3 = 3 + 8$ ← Whole numbers
$-8 + +3 = +3 + -8$ ← Integers

EXAMPLE 1 Show that $(+4 + -6) + -3 = +4 + (-6 + -3)$.

$(+4 + -6) + -3$	$+4 + (-6 + -3)$
$-2 + -3$	$+4 + -9$
-5	-5

Add inside parentheses first. ⟶

Answers are the same. ⟶

Thus, $(+4 + -6) + -3 = +4 + (-6 + -3)$.

EXAMPLE 2 Draw a conclusion from these additions.

$+6 + 0 = +6$ | $-4 + 0 = -4$ | $0 + -6 = -6$

Adding zero gives the same number.

The sum of any integer and zero is that integer.

Example 2 suggests this. ⟶
Zero is the additive identity.

Property of Additive Identity
$a + 0 = a$ and $0 + a = a$, for each number a.

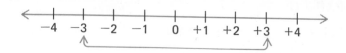

Opposites are the same distance from 0 on a number line.

-3 and $+3$ are opposites. 0 is its own opposite.

Read $-a$ as the opposite of a, or as the additive inverse of a.

The symbol $-a$ means the opposite of a, or the additive inverse of a.

EXAMPLE 3   For each value of *a*, give the value of −*a*.

−*a* (the opposite of *a*) can be positive, negative, or zero, depending upon the value of *a*.

a	Answers	−*a*
+6		−6
−2		+2
0		0

EXAMPLE 4   Draw a conclusion from these additions.

$$+4 + -4 = 0 \quad | \quad -2 + +2 = 0$$

The sum of any integer and its opposite is zero.

> **Property of Additive Inverses**
> $a + -a = 0$, for each number *a*.

SUMMARY

Commutative Property: $a + b = b + a$
Associative Property: $(a + b) + c = a + (b + c)$
Property of Additive Identity: $a + 0 = a$ and $0 + a = a$
Property of Additive Inverses: $a + -a = 0$

EXAMPLE 5   Which property of addition of integers is illustrated?

	Answers
$-6 + +6 = 0$	Additive Inverses
$0 + +8 = +8$	Additive Identity
$-7 + +2 = +2 + -7$	Commutative
$(-8 + -3) + +3$	
$\quad = -8 + (-3 + +3)$	Associative

ORAL EXERCISES

Give the opposite of each.

1. +2   **2.** −6   **3.** +10   **4.** 0   **5.** −1   **6.** −9
7. +7   **8.** −5   **9.** +18   **10.** −93   **11.** +87   **12.** −125
13. −50   **14.** +233   **15.** −424   **16.** *a*   **17.** −*x*   **18.** −*n*
19. Tell how to read the symbol −*x*.
20. Explain why the symbol −*a* should not be read as negative *a*.

EXERCISES

Compute to show that each statement is true.

1. $(+6 + -2) + -3 = +6 + (-2 + -3)$
2. $(-7 + +4) + +8 = -7 + (+4 + +8)$
3. $-10 + (-8 + +5) = (-10 + -8) + +5$
4. $(-8 + +16) + -16 = -8 + (+16 + -16)$

Which property of addition of integers is illustrated?

5. $+5 + -2 = -2 + +5$
6. $-6 + +6 = 0$
7. $0 + +8 = +8$
8. $(+2 + -5) + +7 = +2 + (-5 + +7)$
9. $-9 + 0 = -9$
10. $+4 + -4 = 0$
11. $-7 + -4 = -4 + -7$
12. $-8 + +3 = +3 + -8$
13. $(-8 + +6) + +3 = -8 + (+6 + +3)$
14. $+15 + -15 = 0$
15. $x + -x = 0$
16. $y + 0 = y$
17. $c + d = d + c$
18. $(x + y) + z = x + (y + z)$

PART B

Find the value of each.

19. $-x$ if $x = 3$
20. $-b$ if $b = -5$
21. a if $-a = -2$
22. y if $-y = 8$
23. z if $z = -7$
24. n if $-n = 0$

Explain why each statement is true.

25. If x is negative, then $-x$ is positive.
26. If $-x$ is negative, then $-(-x)$ is positive.

PART C

EXAMPLE Prove $(-3 + +5) + -7 = (-7 + +5) + -3$.

Expression	Reason
$(-3 + +5) + -7$	Given
$-7 + (-3 + +5)$	Commutative Property
$-7 + (+5 + -3)$	Commutative Property
$(-7 + +5) + -3$	Associative Property

Prove.

27. $(-9 + +4) + -8 = (-8 + +4) + -9$
28. $(-6 + +7) + -5 = (-5 + +7) + -6$
29. $(-3 + +5) + +3 = +5$
30. $(-8 + -3) + +8 = -3$
31. $(x + y) + z = (z + y) + x$
32. $(-x + -y) + x = -y$

Probability

The set S of all possibilities for an experiment is called the *sample space*.

$$P(A) = \frac{\text{number of times } A \text{ appears in sample space}}{\text{total number of elements in sample space}}$$

Read: the probability of A

In tossing 3 coins $S = \{HHH, HHT, HTH, HTT, THH, THT, TTH, TTT\}$ and $P(2H) = \frac{3}{8}$.

PROBLEM

In tossing 2 dice, what is the probability that the sum is 7?

Sample Space for 2 dice

FIRST DIE

	1	2	3	4	5	6
1	2	3	4	5	6	⑦
2	3	4	5	6	⑦	8
3	4	5	6	⑦	8	9
4	5	6	⑦	8	9	10
5	6	⑦	8	9	10	11
6	⑦	8	9	10	11	12

SECOND DIE

Sum of dice

$$P(\text{sum } 7) = \frac{6}{36}, \text{ or } \frac{1}{6}$$

PROJECT

1. A coin and a die are tossed. Find the sample space.

2. A die is rolled once. Find the sample space and $P(\text{even})$.

3. In tossing 2 dice, what is $P(\text{sum 8})$? $P(\text{sum even})$?

4. In tossing 2 dice, what is $P(\text{both dice are same})$? $P(\text{sum 0})$?

Multiplying Integers

 REVIEW CAPSULE

Multiplying positive integers is like multiplying whole numbers.

Whole numbers	Positive integers
$(3)\,(4) = 12$	$(+3)\,(+4) = +12$
$(1)\,(7) = 7$	$(+1)\,(+7) = +7$
$(8)\,(2) = 16$	$(+8)\,(+2) = +16$

The Review Capsule suggests this rule. →
$(+)\,(+) = +$ —————————————→

The product of two positive numbers is a positive number.
$$\text{positive} \times \text{positive} = \text{positive}$$

EXAMPLE 1   Draw a conclusion from these multiplications.

$(+3)\,(0) = 0 \qquad (0)\,(-4) = 0 \qquad (0)\,(0) = 0$
The product of any number and 0 is 0.

Example 1 suggests this. —————————→

Property of Zero for Multiplication
$a \cdot 0 = 0$ and $0 \cdot a = 0$, for each number a.

EXAMPLE 2   Determine a logical answer for the product $(+5)\,(-3)$.

Start with this expression: $(+5)\,(-3 + +3)$.
Simplify it.

$-3 + +3 = 0$ —————————————→

$$+5\,(-3 + +3)$$
$$+5\,(0)$$
$$0$$

So, $\qquad +5\,(-3 + +3) = 0.$
$(+5)\,(-3) + (+5)\,(+3) = 0$

Distribute +5. —————————→
The result is still 0.
What number plus +15 equals 0?
Answer: −15 —————————————→

$\boxed{} + +15 = 0$
$\boxed{-15} + +15 = 0$

Thus, $(+5)\,(-3) = -15.$

EXAMPLE 3 Determine a logical answer for the product
$(-3)(+5)$.

Use the commutative property.

$$(-3)(+5) = (+5)(-3)$$
$$= -15 \qquad \textbf{Thus, } (-3)(+5) = -15$$

Examples 2 and 3 suggest this rule. ⟶
$(+)(-) = -$ ——————————
$(-)(+) = -$ ——————————

> The product of a positive number and a
> negative number is a negative number.
> positive × negative = negative
> negative × positive = negative

EXAMPLE 4 Multiply $(+8)(-4)$.   Multiply $(-5)(+7)$.

$(+)(-) = -$ $(-)(+) = -$ $(+8)(-4) = -32$ $(-5)(+7) = -35$

EXAMPLE 5 Determine a logical answer for the product
$(-4)(-9)$.

Start with this expression: $-4(-9 + +9)$.
Simplify it.

$$-4(-9 + +9)$$
$$-4(0)$$
$$0$$

So, $-4(-9 + +9) = 0$.

Distribute -4. ⟶ $(-4)(-9) + (-4)(+9) = 0$

What number plus -36 equals 0? ⟶ $\boxed{} + -36 = 0$
Answer: $+36$ $\boxed{+36} + -36 = 0$

Thus, $(-4)(-9) = +36$.

Example 5 suggests this rule. ⟶

$(-)(-) = +$ ——————————

> The product of two negative numbers is
> a positive number.
> negative × negative = positive

EXAMPLE 6 Multiply $(-8)(-7)$.

$(-)(-) = +$ ⟶ $(-8)(-7) = +56$

SUMMARY   **Like signs give a** | **Unlike signs give a**
                positive product. | **negative product.**
    $(+)(+) = +$ $(-)(-) = +$ | $(+)(-) = -$ $(-)(+) = -$

ORAL EXERCISES

Is the product positive or negative?

1. $(+100)(-25)$ **2.** $(-80)(-90)$ **3.** $(+15)(+15)$ **4.** $(-37)(+83)$

EXERCISES

PART A

Multiply.

1. $(+3)(+7)$	**2.** $(-2)(+4)$	**3.** $(+6)(-8)$	**4.** $(-3)(-1)$
5. $(-5)(+9)$	**6.** $(-1)(0)$	**7.** $(+7)(-4)$	**8.** $(0)(+6)$
9. $(+7)(-1)$	**10.** $(-5)(-6)$	**11.** $(-8)(+2)$	**12.** $(-9)(0)$
13. $(+3)(+9)$	**14.** $(-7)(+6)$	**15.** $(0)(-4)$	**16.** $(-6)(-1)$
17. $(+1)(-8)$	**18.** $(-3)(-9)$	**19.** $(+6)(+10)$	**20.** $(+5)(-12)$
21. $(-9)(-8)$	**22.** $(0)(-12)$	**23.** $(+3)(-6)$	**24.** $(+10)(+13)$
25. $(-20)(0)$	**26.** $(-5)(+14)$	**27.** $(-25)(-4)$	**28.** $(-7)(-11)$
29. $(0)(+36)$	**30.** $(-6)(+6)$	**31.** $(+10)(-10)$	**32.** $(-8)(+12)$
33. $(+13)(-3)$	**34.** $(-12)(+4)$	**35.** $(+15)(-8)$	**36.** $(-26)(0)$
37. $(+16)(-2)$	**38.** $(-15)(+5)$	**39.** $(-36)(-2)$	**40.** $(0)(-40)$
41. $(+5)(+50)$	**42.** $(-30)(-4)$	**43.** $(+60)(-8)$	**44.** $(-65)(-2)$
45. $(+80)(-9)$	**46.** $(+41)(+1)$	**47.** $(-40)(+40)$	**48.** $(-1)(-89)$
49. $(-18)(-50)$	**50.** $(+42)(-13)$	**51.** $(0)(+72)$	**52.** $(+63)(-63)$

PART B

EXAMPLE   Multiply $(-2)(+8)(-5)(+6)$.

Multiplication can be done in any order. $\longrightarrow$

$$
\begin{aligned}
(-2)(+8)(-5)(+6) &= (-2)(-5)(+8)(+6) \\
&= \quad (+10) \quad (+48) \\
&= \quad +480
\end{aligned}
$$

Multiply.

53. $(-6)(+3)(-5)$ **54.** $(+8)(-2)(-3)$

55. $(-6)(+8)(+3)(-1)$ **56.** $(+9)(-7)(-3)(+5)$

57. $(+3)(-7)(+8)(-9)$ **58.** $(+6)(0)(-7)(-9)$

59. $(-3)(+8)(-5)(+6)(-7)$ **60.** $(+8)(+3)(-9)(-1)(+5)$

PART C

Give two examples to illustrate each property for integers.

61. Commutative property of multiplication

62. Associative property of multiplication

63. Distributive property of multiplication over addition

Dividing Integers

OBJECTIVES
- To divide one integer by another
- To compute expressions like $-18 \div (-6 \div -3)$

REVIEW CAPSULE

Multiplication and division are related operations.

Multiplication	*Division*
(3) (2) = 6	$6 \div 2 = 3$, or $\dfrac{6}{2} = 3$
(5) (9) = 45	$45 \div 9 = 5$, or $\dfrac{45}{9} = 5$
(6) (8) = 48	$48 \div 8 = 6$, or $\dfrac{48}{8} = 6$

The product 3 times 2 is 6.

The quotient 6 divided by 2 is 3.

EXAMPLE 1   Divide $+8 \div +2$.   Divide $-10 \div -5$.

Start with this division sentence.
Write a related multiplication. $\longrightarrow$
Replace the □ to make the sentence true. $\longrightarrow$

$$+8 \div +2 = \square$$
$$(\square)\,(+2) = +8$$
$$\downarrow$$
$$(+4)\,(+2) = +8$$
Thus, $+8 \div +2 = +4$,
or $\dfrac{+8}{+2} = +4$.

$$-10 \div -5 = \square$$
$$(\square)\,(-5) = -10$$
$$\downarrow$$
$$(+2)\,(-5) = -10$$
Thus, $-10 \div -5 = +2$,
or $\dfrac{-10}{-5} = +2$.

Example 1 suggests this rule. $\longrightarrow$

$\dfrac{(+)}{(+)} = +; \dfrac{(-)}{(-)} = +$ $\longrightarrow$

The quotient of two numbers with like signs is a positive number.

$$\dfrac{\text{positive}}{\text{positive}} = \text{positive} \qquad \dfrac{\text{negative}}{\text{negative}} = \text{positive}$$

EXAMPLE 2   Divide $\dfrac{+15}{+3}$.   Divide $-16 \div -2$.

$$\dfrac{+15}{+3} = +5$$

$$-16 \div -2 = +8$$

EXAMPLE 3 Divide $-18 \div +3$.   Divide $+24 \div -6$.

Start with this division sentence.
Write a related multiplication. $\longrightarrow$

$$-18 \div +3 = \square \qquad\qquad +24 \div -6 = \square$$
$$(\square)\,(+3) = -18 \qquad\qquad (\square)\,(-6) = +24$$
$$\downarrow \qquad\qquad\qquad\qquad\qquad \downarrow$$

Replace the $\square$. $\longrightarrow$

$$(-6)\,(+3) = -18 \qquad\qquad (-4)\,(-6) = +24$$

Thus, $-18 \div +3 = -6,$ **Thus,** $+24 \div -6 = -4,$

or $\dfrac{-18}{+3} = -6.$ or $\dfrac{+24}{-6} = -4.$

Example 3 suggests this rule. $\longrightarrow$

$\dfrac{(-)}{(+)} = -; \dfrac{(+)}{(-)} = - \longrightarrow$

The quotient of two numbers with unlike signs is a negative number.

$\dfrac{\text{negative}}{\text{positive}} = \text{negative}$ $\qquad\qquad$ $\dfrac{\text{positive}}{\text{negative}} = \text{negative}$

EXAMPLE 4 Divide $\dfrac{-20}{+4}$.   Divide $+21 \div -7$.

$$\frac{-20}{+4} = -5 \qquad\qquad\qquad +21 \div -7 = -3$$

SUMMARY

Like signs give a positive quotient.
$$\frac{(+)}{(+)} = + \qquad \frac{(-)}{(-)} = +$$

Unlike signs give a negative quotient.
$$\frac{(+)}{(-)} = - \qquad \frac{(-)}{(+)} = -$$

The rules for division of integers are the same as for multiplication.

ORAL EXERCISES

Is the quotient positive or negative?

1. $+76 \div +19$ **2.** $-84 \div -21$ **3.** $-75 \div +25$ **4.** $+100 \div -20$ **5.** $-800 \div -400$

6. $\dfrac{+125}{-25}$ **7.** $\dfrac{-216}{-24}$ **8.** $\dfrac{-527}{+527}$ **9.** $\dfrac{+800}{+200}$ **10.** $\dfrac{-1,926}{-18}$

EXERCISES

PART A

Divide.

1. $\dfrac{+8}{+4}$ 2. $\dfrac{-12}{+3}$ 3. $\dfrac{+35}{-7}$ 4. $\dfrac{-72}{-9}$ 5. $\dfrac{+28}{+4}$ 6. $\dfrac{-46}{+2}$

7. $\dfrac{-45}{-5}$ 8. $\dfrac{+8}{-8}$ 9. $\dfrac{-81}{+9}$ 10. $\dfrac{+100}{-25}$ 11. $\dfrac{0}{+9}$ 12. $\dfrac{+85}{+5}$

13. $\dfrac{-60}{-10}$ 14. $\dfrac{-56}{+8}$ 15. $\dfrac{+21}{+7}$ 16. $\dfrac{-25}{-5}$ 17. $\dfrac{+44}{+11}$ 18. $\dfrac{-80}{+16}$

19. $\dfrac{-72}{+24}$ 20. $\dfrac{+45}{-9}$ 21. $\dfrac{-30}{-30}$ 22. $\dfrac{-42}{+7}$ 23. $\dfrac{+60}{+12}$ 24. $\dfrac{-32}{-8}$

25. $\dfrac{+42}{-1}$ 26. $\dfrac{-36}{+6}$ 27. $\dfrac{-52}{+13}$ 28. $\dfrac{-48}{-6}$ 29. $\dfrac{+49}{+7}$ 30. $\dfrac{+38}{-19}$

Divide.

31. $-63 \div +7$ 32. $+48 \div -12$ 33. $-72 \div +9$ 34. $-64 \div -8$
35. $+45 \div +3$ 36. $-50 \div +5$ 37. $-65 \div -13$ 38. $-49 \div +7$

Divide.

39. $+6 \div +1$ 40. $-8 \div +1$ 41. $-32 \div +1$ 42. $+46 \div +1$
43. $+9 \div +9$ 44. $-7 \div -7$ 45. $+12 \div +12$ 46. $-38 \div -38$

PART B

EXAMPLE   Compute $-72 \div (+24 \div -3)$.

Divide within the parentheses first. ———→
$$-72 \div (+24 \div -3)$$
$$-72 \div -8$$
$$+9$$

Compute.

47. $-27 \div (-18 \div +6)$ 48. $-32 \div (-28 \div +7)$
49. $(+10 \div -2) \div -5$ 50. $-60 \div (+48 \div -4)$
51. $(-36 \div -4) \div -3$ 52. $+72 \div (-12 \div +3)$
53. $(+100 \div -5) \div +4$ 54. $(+90 \div +3) \div -10$
55. $-16 \div (-32 \div -4)$ 56. $+56 \div (+35 \div -5)$

PART C

Compute.

57. $-.42 \div (+21 \div -.01)$ 58. $(+8.1 \div -.003) \div +.09$

Using Integers

Integers can be used to describe many everyday situations.

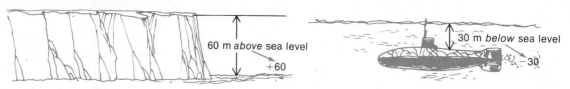

60 m *above* sea level
+60

30 m *below* sea level
-30

Deposit of $300
+300

50 soldiers discharged from the Army
-50

$5,000 loss in sales
-5,000

PROBLEM 1.

A submarine, located 60 meters below sea level, rose 15 meters. It then fired a rocket that climbed 240 meters. Find the level reached by the rocket.

To find the level reached by the rocket, add integers.

Begin with the location of the submarine.

Below   rose   rocket climbed

$$-60 + {}^+15 + {}^+240$$
$$-60 + {}^+255$$
$$+195$$

+195 means above sea level. ⟶

Thus, the rocket reached a level of 195 meters above sea level.

PROJECT

1. A submarine, located 80 m below sea level, rose 40 m. It then fired a rocket that climbed 100 m. Find the level reached by the rocket.

2. One month Lee's weight changes were a gain of 3 kg, a loss of 2 kg, a gain of 4 kg, and a loss of 5 kg. What was the net change?

34

PROBLEM 2.

The Shinskis had $175 in a checking account. They made deposits of $15, $45, and $60. They need to write checks for $100, $85, and $205. Can they do this?

Balance   deposit   withdrawal

$+175 +$ $+15 + +45 + +60$ $+$ $-100 + -85 + -205$

$+175 +$ $+120$ $+$ -390

$+295 + -390$
-95

-95 means the account would be overdrawn.

Thus, they cannot write the checks.

PROJECT

3. The Carlsons had $300 in a checking account. They made deposits of $30, $70, and $100. They need to write checks for $200, $125, $20, and $130. Can they do this?

4. The population of a city was 32,000. Over the next 4 years, a planning committee recorded these population changes: gain of 3,000, loss of 4,000, gain of 6,000, loss of 5,000. Find the net change in population.

5. Several months ago, a certain bread sold for $.65 a loaf. In the meantime, the bread underwent several price changes: dropped $.04, rose $.03, rose $.02, dropped $.04. What is the current price of the bread?

6. A plane was flying at an altitude of 8,000 m. During the next 4 hours, these altitude changes were recorded: dropped 1,000 m, rose 2,000 m, dropped 500 m, rose 1,500 m. At what altitude was the plane flying then?

A New Look at Addition

EXAMPLE 1   Add $6 + -13$.

6 is like $+6$. ← (positive 6)
Read $6 + -13$ as
↗ ↑ ↑
positive 6 plus negative 13.

Thus, $6 + -13 = -7$.

EXAMPLE 2   Add $-9 + 12$.

12 is like $+12$. ← (positive 12)

Thus, $-9 + 12 = 3$. ← (positive 3)

EXAMPLE 3   Add $(-18 + +25) + -2$.

Associative property ⟶
Commutative property ⟶
Associative property ⟶

$$(-18 + +25) + -2 = -18 + (+25 + -2)$$
$$= -18 + (-2 + +25)$$
$$= (-18 + -2) + +25$$
$$= \quad -20 \quad + +25$$
$$= +5, \text{ or } 5$$

We can shorten our work in Example 3.

Use the associative and commutative
properties to group negatives together. ⟶

$$(-18 + +25) + -2$$

$$(-18 + -2) \quad + +25$$
$$-20 \quad + +25$$
$$+5, \text{ or } 5$$

Magic Squares

In ancient China and India the people often wore jewelry which was assumed to contain mystical powers. One such ornament was the magic square.

8	1	6
3	5	7
4	9	2

The sum of the numbers along any row, column, or diagonal is 15.

PROJECT Arrange the numbers 1 to 16 in each of these 4 × 4 squares to make magic squares.

1.

1		7	
	13		11
10		16	
	6		4

2.

16			
			8
		7	
4			1

Evaluating Expressions

▶ *REVIEW CAPSULE*

$4 - 7$ means $+4 + -7$
$7 - 6 + 2$ means $+7 + -6 + +2$
$-3 + 8 - 6$ means $-3 + +8 + -6$
$4x - 5$ means $(+4)(x) + -5$
$6 - 5a$ means $+6 + (-5)(a)$
$2x - 6y$ means $(+2)(x) + (-6)(y)$

EXAMPLE 1   Evaluate $4x - 3$ if $x = 7$.

Read: positive 4 times x plus negative 3. ⟶
Substitute $+7$ for x. ⟶
Multiply first. Then add. ⟶
We can omit the $+$. ⟶

$$
\begin{aligned}
4x - 3 &= (+4)(x) \quad + -3 \\
&= (+4)(+7) + -3 \\
&= \quad +28 \quad + -3 \\
&= \quad\quad +28 - 3 \\
&= \quad\quad\quad +25
\end{aligned}
$$

EXAMPLE 2   Evaluate $-6 + 5a$ if $a = 3$.

$5a$ means $(+5)(a)$. ⟶

$(+)(+) = (+)$ ⟶
$-6 + 15 = +9$, or 9 ⟶

$$
\begin{aligned}
-6 + 5a &= -6 + (5)(a) \\
&= -6 + (5)(3) \\
&= -6 \quad + 15 \\
&= \quad\quad 9
\end{aligned}
$$

EXAMPLE 3   Evaluate $2x - 6y$ if $x = -3$ and $y = -1$.

$2x$ means $(+2)(x)$. ⟶

$(+)(-) = (-)$ $(-)(-) = (+)$ ⟶

$$
\begin{aligned}
2x - 6y &= (2)(x) \quad + (-6)(y) \\
&= (2)(-3) + (-6)(-1) \\
&= \quad -6 \quad\quad + 6 \\
&= \quad\quad 0
\end{aligned}
$$

EXAMPLE 4   Evaluate $-5a - 8b + 7c$ if $a = -1$, $b = -3$, $c = -4$.

$$
\begin{aligned}
-5a - 8b + 7c &= (-5)(a) \quad + (-8)(b) \quad + (7)(c) \\
&= (-5)(-1) + (-8)(-3) + (7)(-4) \\
&= \quad 5 \quad\quad + 24 \quad\quad - 28 \\
&= \quad 1
\end{aligned}
$$

Add 5 and 24 first, then add -28.

EXERCISES

Evaluate for the given values of the variables.

1. $6x + 2$ if $x = 2$
2. $7g + 9$ if $g = 5$
3. $5a + 3$ if $a = -1$
4. $-3x - 5$ if $x = -2$
5. $7c - 2d$ if $c = 3, d = 5$
6. $8r - 7s$ if $r = 7, s = 7$
7. $-5y + 4z$ if $y = -4, z = -2$
8. $-2k - 5t$ if $k = -4, t = -6$
9. $7e - 3f$ if $e = 6, f = -7$
10. $-5m + 3n$ if $m = -5, n = 1$
11. $4x + 5y + 3z$ if $x = 1, y = -2, z = 3$
12. $6r - 9s - 5t$ if $r = 6, s = -2, t = -8$
13. $-8e + 7f - 4g$ if $e = 3, f = -4, g = -5$
14. $-2p - 8q + 6r$ if $p = -2, q = -9, r = -6$
15. $4f + 7g - 2h$ if $f = -5, g = -8, h = -4$
16. $-7d + 8e - 3f$ if $d = -3, e = 7, f = -6$
17. $7a - 2b + 9c$ if $a = -1, b = -7, c = -9$

PART B

EXAMPLE   Simplify $(6x + 3y)2 + 7x + 4$. Then evaluate if $x = -3$ and $y = -7$.

$$(6x + 3y)2 + 7x + 4$$

Distribute 2. $\longrightarrow$ $(6x)(2) + (3y)(2) + 7x + 4$

$$12x + 6y + 7x + 4$$

Combine like terms. $\longrightarrow$ $19x + 6y + 4$

Substitute -3 for x, -7 for y. $\longrightarrow$ $(19)(-3) + 6(-7) + 4$

$$-57 - 42 + 4$$
$$-99 + 4$$
$$-95$$

Simplify. Then evaluate if $x = -5$, $y = 3$, and $z = -1$.

18. $4(7x + 3y) + 6x + 2$
19. $9 + 3(5x + 2y) + 7$
20. $8 + 4z + 2(3x + 5z)$
21. $(4y + 3z)8 + 7y + 1$
22. $(7x + 3y)4 + 8x + 9y$
23. $6z + 2(9y + 3z) + 8y + 5$
24. $2(6x + 3y + 2z) + 8y + 4z$
25. $(6x + 9z)4 + 5(7x + 8y)$

PART C

Simplify. Then evaluate if $x = -2$ and $y = 3$. [Hint: Work within brackets first.]

26. $3[2x + 4(3y + 8)]$
27. $7x + 2[4 + 3(x + 6y)]$

Combining Like Terms

REVIEW CAPSULE

Combine like terms.

$$3x + 5x = 8x$$
$$6a + 3a = 9a$$
$$5c + 2 + 8c = 13c + 2$$

EXAMPLE 1 Simplify $-2x + 5x$.

$-2x$ and $+5x$ are like terms.
Use the distributive property. ⟶

$$-2x + 5x = (-2 + 5)x$$
$$= 3x$$

Thus, $-2x + 5x = 3x$.

EXAMPLE 2 Simplify $8a - 3a$.

To combine like terms,
add the coefficients. ⟶

$$8a - 3a = (8 - 3)a$$
$$= 5a$$

EXAMPLE 3 Simplify $-5b - 9b$.

$$-5b - 9b = -14b$$

EXAMPLE 4 Simplify $4y - 9 - 7y + 14$.

Group like terms. ⟶

$$4y - 9 - 7y + 14 = \underbrace{4y - 7y} \; \underbrace{- 9 + 14}$$
$$= \quad -3y \; + \quad 5$$

EXAMPLE 5 Simplify $6x - 4 - 2y - 9x + 7y - 8$.

$$6x - 4 - 2y - 9x + 7y - 8$$
$$\underbrace{6x - 9x} \; \underbrace{- 2y + 7y} \; \underbrace{- 4 - 8}$$
$$-3x \; + \quad 5y \quad - \quad 12$$

EXERCISES

PART A

Simplify.

1. $-3y + 8y$
2. $4a - 7a$
3. $-6b + 8b$
4. $-9x - 2x$
5. $-7z + 5z$
6. $-4c - 7c$
7. $-8r + 3r$
8. $-5y - 5y$
9. $2r - 9r$
10. $4x - 5 - 2x$
11. $5z - 8 - 9z$
12. $-7c - 8 - 5c$
13. $-5q - 9 + 3q$
14. $8x - 4 - 3x$
15. $-6y - 4 - 3y$
16. $7 - 5t + 9 + 7t$
17. $-4x + 3 - 8x - 2$
18. $-6y + 3 + 8 - 7y$

Simplify.

19. $6x - 2y - 4x + 3 + 8y$
20. $5a + 3b - 4 - 7a - 6b$
21. $-5r - 9s + 9r + 3s - 6$
22. $3p - 7q - 5 + 9q - 7p$
23. $-9x + 8 - 3y - 5x + 7y$
24. $4d - 5 - 8d + 3e - 6$
25. $-6x + 9y - 4 - 4x - 6y$
26. $4j - 7k + 2 - 9j - 8$
27. $-9 + 8a - 4c - 7 + 5a$
28. $-8q + 9s - 2 + 6q - 4s$
29. $6b - 7 - 4a + 8 - 3b - 2a$
30. $-7a + 4 - 5a + 6b + 4a - 2b$

PART B

EXAMPLE Simplify $-3x - 5 + 8y - 4x - 4y$. Then evaluate if $x = -4$ and $y = -9$.

$$-3x - 5 + 8y - 4x - 4y$$

Regroup. $\longrightarrow$
$$\underbrace{-3x - 4x} + \underbrace{8y - 4y} - 5$$

Combine like terms. $\longrightarrow$
$$-7x \qquad +4y \quad -5$$

Substitute -4 for x, -9 for y. $\longrightarrow$
$$-7(-4) + 4(-9) - 5$$
$$28 \qquad -36 \quad -5$$
$$28 - 41$$
$$-13$$

Simplify. Then evaluate for $x = -2$, $y = -3$, and $z = 8$.

31. $5x - 3 + 8y - 2y - 3x$
32. $-4z + 8 - 2x - 9z + 8x$
33. $-3x + 7y - 4z + 9x - 3y$
34. $-7z - 8y - 3x - 4y + 5z$
35. $-6x + 3 + 2y - 9 - 5x + 4y$
36. $-8y + 4z + 2y - 7 - 9z - 2y$

PART C

Simplify. Then evaluate for $x = -.3$, $y = 2.5$, and $z = .004$.

37. $1.5x - 4 + .007y - 1.2y - .3x$
38. $2.4 - .08x + .3y - .1 + 3.02z - .7x$

$(1)(a) = a$ and $(-1)(a) = -a$

OBJECTIVE

■ To simplify expressions like $7c - c + 9n + n$ by applying the properties $(1)(a) = a$; $(-1)(a) = -a$

REVIEW CAPSULE

Simplify $4x - 7 + 5x$.

$$4x - 7 + 5x = 4x + 5x - 7$$
$$= 9x - 7$$

EXAMPLE 1 Draw a conclusion from these multiplications.

$(1)(6) = 6$ ┆ $(1)(-2) = -2$ ┆ $(8)(1) = 8$

The product of one and any number is that number.

Example 1 suggests this.
One is the multiplicative identity.

Property of Multiplicative Identity

$(1)(a) = a$ and $(a)(1) = a$, for each number a.

EXAMPLE 2 Draw a conclusion from these multiplications.

-5 is the opposite of 5.

$(-1)(5) = -5$ ┆ $(-1)(-4) = 4$ ┆ $(7)(-1) = -7$

The product of negative one and any number is the opposite (additive inverse) of the number.

Example 2 suggests this.

Multiplication Property of -1

$(-1)(a) = -a$ and $(a)(-1) = -a$,

for each number a.

EXAMPLE 3 Simplify $6a + 2a + a$.

Replace a with $1a$.

$$6a + 2a + 1a = 9a$$

EXAMPLE 4 Simplify $-9 + 3b + 4 - b$.

Replace $-b$ with $-1b$.
Rearrange terms.
Combine like terms.

$$-9 + 3b + 4 - 1b$$
$$3b - 1b - 9 + 4$$
$$2b - 5$$

EXAMPLE 5   Simplify $3m - 9 + 4m + 7 - 8m$.

Rearrange terms. ⟶

$$\underbrace{3m + 4m - 8m}_{-1m} \underbrace{- 9 + 7}_{-2}$$

Replace $-1m$ with $-m$. ⟶ $-m - 2$

ORAL EXERCISES

Which property is illustrated?

1. $(-1)(-8) = 8$ **2.** $(x)(1) = x$ **3.** $(-y)(1) = -y$ **4.** $-c = (-1)(c)$

EXERCISES

PART A

Simplify.

1. $4x - 5x + x$
3. $6b - 4b + b$
5. $5r - r + 8r$
7. $a - 4 - 2a + 6$
9. $7c + 8 - 6c - 9$
11. $4e - 9 - 5e + 6$
13. $9 - q + 6 - 8q$
15. $3p - 2 - 5 - p$
17. $-7 + d - 8 - 6d + 5$
19. $-5a + 9 - a - 7 + 3a$
21. $5 - 4z + 7 - 2z + 4 - z$
23. $8b - 9 - b + 7b + 4 - 9$

2. $a + 4a - 7a$
4. $-c + 8c - 2c$
6. $6y - y - 6y$
8. $7 - z - 3z + 4$
10. $9d - 4 - d + 8$
12. $2 + 3x - 7 - 2x$
14. $2s - 9 - s + 5$
16. $7a - 5 - a + 6$
18. $4z - 8 + z - 6 - 5z$
20. $3r - 5 - 7r - 8 + r$
22. $4y - 5 - 6y + 8 - y + 7$
24. $-f + 4 - 7f - 8 + 2f + 6$

PART B

Simplify. Then evaluate if $x = -2$, $y = 6$, and $z = -3$.

25. $3x - 4y - x - 8$
27. $7x - y + 8z - 8x$
29. $6z - 8y + x - 7z$
31. $-8y - 4z + x - y - 2z + 1$

26. $6y + z - 7y - 5$
28. $5x + z - 6x + 3y$
30. $-y + 8x - z - 2x$
32. $4z - y - 7x - 2z - 8x + 3 + y$

PART C

Simplify. Then evaluate if $x = .03$, $y = 1.04$, and $z = 2.01$.

33. $-.7x + 5z + .002y - 6z + 1.4x$

34. $-x + 2.04y + 3.1x - .05y - z$

Removing Parentheses

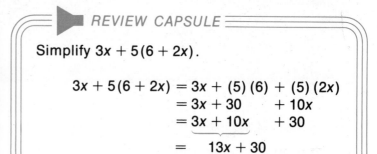

▶ REVIEW CAPSULE

Simplify $3x + 5(6 + 2x)$.

$$3x + 5(6 + 2x) = 3x + (5)(6) + (5)(2x)$$
$$= 3x + 30 \quad\;\; + 10x$$
$$= 3x + 10x \quad + 30$$
$$= \quad 13x + 30$$

EXAMPLE 1 Simplify $4a - 5(7 + 3a)$.

Read: $4a$ plus -5 times the quantity 7 plus $3a$. ⟶
Distribute -5. ⟶
Omit the $+$ signs. ⟶
Rearrange terms. ⟶

$$4a - 5(7 + 3a) = 4a + -5(7 + 3a)$$
$$= 4a + (-5)(7) + (-5)(3a)$$
$$= 4a - 35 - 15a$$
$$= 4a - 15a - 35$$
$$= \;\; -11a - 35$$

EXAMPLE 2 Simplify $3n - 6(4 - 5n)$.

$$3n - 6(4 - 5n)$$

Distribute -6. Omit the $+$ signs. ⟶
Combine like terms. ⟶

$$3n - 24 + 30n$$
$$33n - 24$$

EXAMPLE 3 Simplify $-2(7x + 3) - 8x$. Then evaluate the result if $x = -3$.

$$-2(7x + 3) - 8x$$

$$-14x - 6 - 8x$$
$$-22x - 6$$
$$\downarrow$$

Substitute -3 for x. ⟶
Multiply first. ⟶
Then add. ⟶

$$-22(-3) - 6$$
$$66 - 6$$
$$60$$

EXERCISES

Simplify.

1. $5x - 8(2 - 3x)$
2. $4 - 3(7 - 9z)$
3. $4y - 2(7 - 5y)$
4. $6b - 8(3b + 7)$
5. $6 - 4(2a - 8)$
6. $5c - 6(8 - 4c)$
7. $3(2x - 9) - 4x$
8. $-7(3 - 2x) + 8x$
9. $-9(4a + 7) - 3a$
10. $-6(-5d - 8) + 2d$
11. $-7(5a + 3) + 6a$
12. $7c - 2(3c - 5)$
13. $2x - 2(4x + 3) - 5$
14. $6y - 8(4 + 7y) - 3y$
15. $8 - 7(5 - 3c) + 4c$
16. $-7r + 6 - 3(4r - 2)$
17. $5x - 2(4 - 6x) + 8$
18. $-3(8 - 5z) + 2 - 6z$
19. $-5 - 9(4y + 8) - 2y + 3$
20. $7x - 8 - 5(4x - 9) + 2x$

Simplify. Then evaluate the result for the given value of the variable.

21. $4(5y - 8) - 3y$ if $y = 8$
22. $8 - 5(4 - 3c)$ if $c = -5$
23. $-6(7x + 1) + 5x$ if $x = -4$
24. $7x - 2(4x - 6)$ if $x = 6$
25. $9 - 2(-5x + 8)$ if $x = -9$
26. $-5y - 4(8 - 9y)$ if $y = -6$
27. $7d - 8(4 - 3d) + 6$ if $d = 3$
28. $-6r + 5 - 3(2r - 1)$ if $r = -7$
29. $4(-3x + 2) - 5x - 9$ if $x = -1$
30. $9 - 2(8g + 7) + 2g$ if $g = -3$

EXAMPLE   Simplify $-3(5x - 7) - 6(4 + 2x)$.

$$-3(5x - 7) - 6(4 + 2x)$$

Distribute -3. Then distribute -6.

$$-15x + 21 - 24 - 12x$$
$$-15x - 12x + 21 - 24$$
$$-27x - 3$$

Simplify.

31. $-4(3x - 5) - 3(2 + 7x)$
32. $-5(3y - 7) - 2(6 + 4y)$
33. $-5(6 + 3y) - 7(2y - 9)$
34. $-3(5x - 4) + 8(-3x + 2)$
35. $5(3z - 7) - 9(-8z - 6)$
36. $-4(7 - 8d) - 2(-6d + 5)$
37. $7x - 3(5x + 2) - 6(7 + 2x)$
38. $-3(8 - 7z) + 6z - 9(4 - 3z)$

Simplify. [Hint: Work within brackets first.]

39. $4 - 2[7 - 2(3 - 5x)]$
40. $6x - 3[8 + 3x - 4(5 - 2x)]$

Applying the Property $-a = -1(a)$

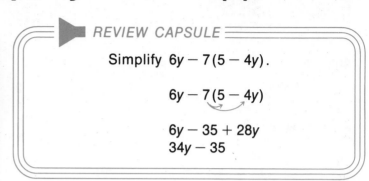

REVIEW CAPSULE

Simplify $6y - 7(5 - 4y)$.

$6y - 7(5 - 4y)$

$6y - 35 + 28y$
$34y - 35$

EXAMPLE 1 Simplify $5x - (4 + 3x)$.

$-(a) = -1a$, so
$-(4 + 3x) = -1(4 + 3x)$

$5x - (4 + 3x) = 5x - 1(4 + 3x)$

Distribute -1. ────────→ $= 5x - 4 - 3x$
Combine like terms. ────────→ $= 2x - 4$

EXAMPLE 2 Simplify $-6b - (8 - 7b)$.

Replace $-(8 - 7b)$ with $-1(8 - 7b)$. ──→ $-6b - (8 - 7b) = -6b - 1(8 - 7b)$

$= -6b - 8 + 7b$
$= 1b - 8$
Replace $1b$ with b. ────────→ $= b - 8$

EXAMPLE 3 Simplify $2 - (9 - c) + 5c$. Then evaluate the result if $c = -4$.

$-a = -1a$ ────────→ $2 - (9 - c) + 5c = 2 - 1(9 - 1c) + 5c$

$= 2 - 9 + 1c + 5c$
$= -7 + 6c$
$\downarrow$
Replace c with -4. ────────→ $-7 + 6(-4)$
Multiply first. ────────→ $= -7 - 24$
Then add. ────────→ $= -31$

EXERCISES

Simplify.

  1. $-5y - (6y + 2)$ **2.** $3 - (6x - 9)$
  3. $-8 - (5z + 4)$ **4.** $-6x - (3 + 5x)$
  5. $7c + (8 - 9c)$ **6.** $-(4x - 3) + 2x$
  7. $-(8 - 6f) - 3f$ **8.** $-(7z + 8) - 9z$
  9. $6y - (7 - 3y) - 2$ **10.** $-8 + (-4p + 7) - 9p$
11. $y - (9 - 7y) - 8$ **12.** $6r - (3r - 21) + 8r$
13. $-(e + 7) - 5e - 6$ **14.** $4c - (3c + 2) - 10c$
15. $-5d + (8 - d) - 9$ **16.** $7x - 8 - (5x + 6)$
17. $-(3y - 8) + 7y - 12$ **18.** $9q + (8 - 3q) + 16$
19. $3z + 8 - (5z + 2) - 9z$ **20.** $5x - (2 - 4x) + 8x - 7$
21. $-9b - 4 - (7b + 6) - 3b$ **22.** $-(-5c - 8) + 6 - 9c - c$

Simplify. Then evaluate the result for the given value of the variable.

23. $-4x - (6 - 3x)$ if $x = 6$ **24.** $-9z - (8 + z)$ if $z = -7$
25. $-(c + 8) + 6c$ if $c = -3$ **26.** $-(4y - 6) + 3y$ if $y = 9$
27. $5r - (-7 + 2r) + 8$ if $r = 8$ **28.** $-6 - (3b - 2) + 5b$ if $b = -4$
29. $-(-7x + 2) - 8x + 1$ if $x = 6$ **30.** $-8z - (5z + 6) + 3z$ if $z = -9$
31. $5y - 9 - (7y - 6)$ if $y = 2$ **32.** $7r - (8 - r) + 12$ if $r = -8$

                          EXAMPLE   Simplify $-4(7 - x) - (5x + 3)$.

$-a = -1a$ ⟶ $-4(7 - x) - (5x + 3) = -4(7 - 1x) - 1(5x + 3)$

Distribute -4. Then distribute -1.   ⟶ $= -28 + 4x - 5x - 3$
                                                 $= -1x - 31$
Replace $-1x$ with $-x$.   ⟶ $= -x - 31$

Simplify.

33. $-(7 + 3y) - 5(4y - 8)$ **34.** $-6(7x - 5) - (4 - x)$
35. $-(5z - 7) - (9 - z)$ **36.** $-(a + 4) - 3(7 - a)$
37. $-(-6r + 9) - (-7 - 3r)$ **38.** $-(-5 + c) - (-8 - c)$

Simplify. [Hint: Work within the brackets first.]

39. $-[3(x - 2) - (4 - 5x)]$ **40.** $-2a - [-2(1 - 7a) - (5 - 3a)]$

Subtracting Integers

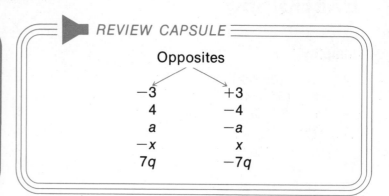

REVIEW CAPSULE

Opposites

-3	$+3$
4	-4
a	$-a$
$-x$	x
$7q$	$-7q$

EXAMPLE 1   Subtract 3 from 8.

$$\overbrace{8 \quad \text{subtract} \quad 3}$$

8 subtract 3 is
8 plus the opposite of 3. ⟶

$$8 \quad - \quad 3$$
$$8 \quad + \quad -3$$
$$5$$

Subtract b *from* a means

a subtract b
a plus the opposite of b.

$a - b = a + -1(b)$, or $a + -b$, for all numbers a and b.

EXAMPLE 2   Subtract 6 from 4.

$$4 \quad \text{subtract} \quad 6$$

4 subtract 6 is
4 plus the opposite of 6. ⟶

$$4 \quad - \quad 6$$
$$4 \quad + \quad -6$$
$$-2$$

EXAMPLE 3   Subtract −9 from 7.

$$7 \quad \text{subtract} \quad -9$$

7 subtract −9 is
7 plus the opposite of −9. ⟶

$$7 \quad - \quad (-9)$$
$$7 \quad + \quad +9$$
$$16$$

Recall the Property of -1. $\longrightarrow$ The opposite of a is equal to -1 times a.
$$-a = (-1)(a)$$

EXAMPLE 4   Subtract $-7a + 5$ from $3a - 2$.

$$3a - 2 \text{ subtract} \qquad -7a + 5$$
$$3a - 2 \qquad - \qquad (-7a + 5)$$

Add the opposite of $(-7a + 5)$. $\longrightarrow$ $\qquad 3a - 2 \qquad + \qquad -(-7a + 5)$
$-(-7a + 5) = (-1)(-7a + 5)$ $\longrightarrow$ $\qquad 3a - 2 \qquad + \qquad -1(-7a + 5)$
Distribute -1. $\longrightarrow$ $\qquad 3a - 2 + 7a - 5$
$$\qquad 10a - 7$$

EXERCISES

PART A

1. Subtract 2 from 5.
2. Subtract -1 from 6.
3. Subtract -5 from -7.
4. Subtract 5 from -8.
5. Subtract 4 from -10.
6. Subtract -7 from 0.
7. Subtract -12 from -3.
8. Subtract -10 from 10.
9. Subtract 17 from -1.

10. Subtract $4x - 3$ from $6x - 4$.
11. Subtract $b - 7$ from $4b + 1$.
12. Subtract -5 from $5y + 3$.
13. Subtract $3x + 7$ from $2x - 5$.
14. Subtract $-2x - 5$ from $x + 4$.
15. Subtract $-4y - 9$ from $-2y + 8$.
16. Subtract $-x - 8$ from $7x + 9$.
17. Subtract $3x - 4$ from $-2x - 1$.

PART B

EXAMPLE   From $3a - 4$, subtract $-5a + 2$.

$$3a - 4 \text{ subtract} \qquad -5a + 2$$
$$3a - 4 \qquad - \qquad (-5a + 2)$$

Add the opposite of $(-5a + 2)$
which is $(-1)(-5a + 2)$. $\longrightarrow$ $\qquad 3a - 4 \qquad + \qquad (-1)(-5a + 2)$
Distribute -1. $\longrightarrow$ $\qquad 3a - 4 + 5a - 2$
$$\qquad 8a - 6$$

18. From $-12y - 1$, subtract $8y + 2$.
19. From $16z + 3$, subtract $-7 - 4z$.
20. From $-4a - 5$, subtract $-7a - 8$.
21. From $y - 18$, subtract $-2y + 9$.
22. From $-1 - x$, subtract $-5x + 3$.
23. From $9z - 3$, subtract $-9z + 3$.
24. From $-y + 18$, subtract $2y - 9$.
25. From -9, subtract $3x + 2$.

PART C

26. Show that $a - b = a + (-1)b$. Justify each step.

Chapter Two Review

Add. [*p. 21*]

1. $+3 + +7$
2. $+6 + -2$
3. $-5 + +8$
4. $+4 + -9$
5. $-3 + -15$
6. $-7 + 0$

Compute. [*p. 36*]

7. $-9 + 7 - 3$
8. $6 + 7 - 4$
9. $-8 - 3 + 2$
10. $-16 + 8 - 15$
11. $-5 - 9 + 22$
12. $36 - 21 - 4$
13. $-12 + 14 - 18 + 22$
14. $31 - 55 + 14 - 18$
15. $-104 + 54 + 62 - 21$

Multiply. [*p. 28*]

16. $(-9)(+7)$
17. $(+8)(-2)$
18. $(+6)(+4)$
19. $(-21)(-5)$
20. $(0)(-7)$
21. $(-5)(-3)(-5)$
22. $(-7)(+3)(-4)$
23. $(-5)(-4)(+3)(-2)$
24. $(-8)(+2)(-5)(+4)$

Divide. [*p. 31*]

25. $\dfrac{+14}{+2}$
26. $\dfrac{-49}{+7}$
27. $\dfrac{+36}{-6}$
28. $-52 \div -4$
29. $+45 \div -9$
30. $(-63 \div +7) \div -3$

Evaluate for the given values of the variables. [*p. 40*]

31. $5r + 7s$ if $r = 3$, $s = -6$
32. $-2x + 7y$ if $x = 4$, $y = 9$
33. $6x + 7y - 9z$ if $x = 3$, $y = -2$, $z = -5$

Simplify. [*p. 42, 44, 48*]

34. $3y - 8y + 6y$
35. $x + 5x - 9x$
36. $5d - 8 - d + 6$
37. $-4p + 7 + 13 - p$
38. $4c - 2(3 - 2c)$
39. $-a + 4 - 3(-4 - 2a)$
40. $6 - (5 - x) - 4x$
41. $-(z - 2) - 8z - 7$

Simplify. Then evaluate the result for the given value of the variable. [*p. 46, 48*]

42. $5(6x - 7) - 3x$ if $x = 4$
43. $-6k - 8(3k - 2)$ if $k = -5$

[*p. 50*]

44. Subtract 5 from -8.
45. Subtract -9 from 6.
46. Subtract -4 from -1.
47. Subtract $3x - 10$ from $7x + 2$.
48. Subtract $-7a + 8$ from $4a - 2$.
49. From $4a - 3$, subtract $2a + 5$.
50. From $-3a - 4$, subtract $-2a + 5$.

Which property of addition of integers is illustrated? [*p. 24*]

51. $-2 + -7 = -7 + -2$
52. $0 + x = x$

Chapter Two Test

Add.

1. $+9 + -4$

2. $-6 + -7$

3. $-12 + +7$

Compute.

4. $8 - 3 - 19$

5. $-5 + 12 - 81$

6. $16 - 14 + 5$

Multiply.

7. $(-8)(-2)$

8. $(+7)(-3)$

9. $(-9)(+6)$

10. $(-7)(0)$

11. $(-5)(-9)$

12. $(+8)(+7)(-2)$

Divide.

13. $\dfrac{-24}{+6}$

14. $\dfrac{-18}{-3}$

15. $\dfrac{+42}{-3}$

16. $-9 \div -1$

17. $+56 \div +14$

18. $-72 \div (-8 \div +4)$

Evaluate for the given values of the variables.

19. $6x + 8y$ if $x = 3, y = -5$
20. $-7a - 9 + 8b$ if $a = -2, b = -8$

Simplify.

21. $-4x - 2x$

22. $6 + 8c - 2c$

23. $5a + 2b - 9 - 3a - 7b$

24. $4z + 8 - z - 3$

25. $-y + 7 - 9y - 8 + 2y$

26. $-5(3x - 2) - 5x$

27. $-4a - 8(2 - 3a) - 9$

28. $4y - (7 - 2y)$

29. $-(7b + 8) - 6b - 2$

30. $4p - (8 - p) + 5 - p$

Simplify. Then evaluate for the given value of the variable.

31. $-5r - 2(6 + 3r)$ if $r = -3$

32. $-(5y - 3) - 7y + 8$ if $y = -9$

33. Subtract -12 from -7.

34. Subtract 4 from -9.

35. Subtract $-8y + 6$ from $5y - 2$.

36. From $-2a + 3$, subtract $-4a + 6$.

Which property of addition of integers is illustrated?

37. $(-7 + +3) + -5 = -7 + (+3 + -5)$

38. $+8 + -3 = -3 + +8$

3 LINEAR EQUATIONS

Computer Programs: Flow Charts

Instructions are given to a computer by means of a program.

PROBLEM 1.

Write a flow chart to show how to cross from corner A to corner B.

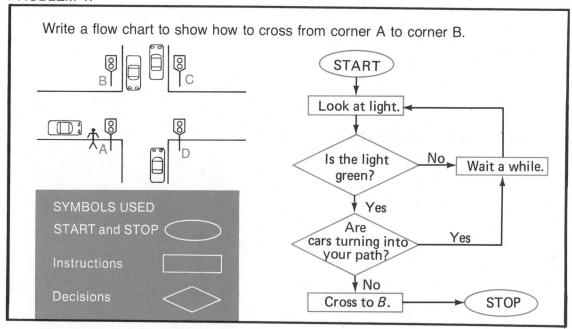

The two loops in the flow chart call for instructions to be repeated.

FIRST LOOP

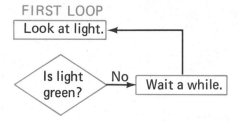

SECOND LOOP

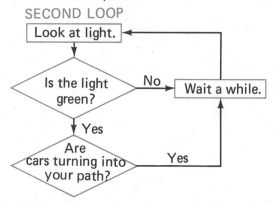

PROBLEM 2.

Write a flow chart to show how to cross from corner A to corner C.
The traffic is eliminated to simplify matters.

```
                          ( START )
                              │
                              ▼
                    ┌──────────────────┐
                    │   Look at light. │
                    └──────────────────┘
                              │
                              ▼
   Yes                 ◇ Is           No
  ┌────────────── light green from ──────────────┐
  │                    A to B? ◇                  │
  │                                               │
  ▼                                               ▼
┌──────────────┐                          ┌──────────────┐
│ Cross to B.  │                          │ Cross to D.  │
└──────────────┘                          └──────────────┘
  │                                               │
  ▼                                               ▼
 ◇ Is         Yes                    Yes     ◇ Is
light green from ────┐              ┌──── light green from
  B to C? ◇          │              │        D to C? ◇
  │  No              │              │          │  No
  ▼                  ▼              ▼          ▼
┌──────────────┐  ┌──────────────┐     ┌──────────────┐
│ Wait a while.│  │  Cross to C. │     │ Wait a while.│
└──────────────┘  └──────────────┘     └──────────────┘
                         │
                         ▼
                     ( STOP )
```

How many loops can you identify in the flow chart?

PROJECT

Draw a flow chart to show all of the steps for each process.

1. Unlocking a certain door with a choice of three keys.

2. Changing a burnt-out light bulb. (Start with an unused bulb.)

Open Sentences

OBJECTIVE
■ To determine which members of a set like {3, 2, 1} are solutions of a sentence like
$$2x - 6 = x + 3$$

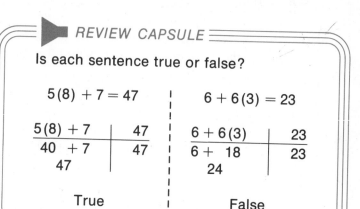

▶ *REVIEW CAPSULE*

Is each sentence true or false?

$$5(8) + 7 = 47$$

$5(8) + 7$	47
$40 + 7$	47
47	

True

$$6 + 6(3) = 23$$

$6 + 6(3)$	23
$6 + 18$	23
24	

False

A sentence like $8x + 3 = 35$ is an open sentence. It contains a variable, x.

EXAMPLE 1 In the sentence $8x + 3 = 35$, replace x with 3. Is the resulting sentence true or false? Then replace x with 4. True or false?

Replace x with 3.

$8x + 3$	35
$8(3) + 3$	35
$24 + 3$	
27	

False

Replace x with 4.

$8x + 3$	35
$8(4) + 3$	35
$32 + 3$	
35	

True

EXAMPLE 2 The sentence below is an open English sentence.

Neither true nor false ⟶ It is the shortest month of the year.

Replace "It" with the name of a month to make a true sentence. Then replace "It" to make a false sentence.

Replace "It" with any month except February. ⟶ February is the shortest month of the year. — True
May is the shortest month of the year. — False

A solution of an open sentence is a replacement which makes it true.

EXAMPLE 3

Which members of the replacement set $\{1, 2, 3\}$ are solutions of $4x + 3 = x + 9$?

Replace x with each member of the set $\{1, 2, 3\}$.

Replace x with 1.

$4x + 3$	$x + 9$
$4(1) + 3$	$1 + 9$
$4 + 3$	10
7	

False

Replace x with 2.

$4x + 3$	$x + 9$
$4(2) + 3$	$2 + 9$
$8 + 3$	11
11	

True

Replace x with 3.

$4x + 3$	$x + 9$
$4(3) + 3$	$3 + 9$
$12 + 3$	12
15	

False

2 is the only member of the replacement set which makes the sentence true. ⟶ **Thus, 2 is the solution of $4x + 3 = x + 9$.**

EXAMPLE 4

Which members of the replacement set $\{2, 0, -1, -2\}$ are solutions of $23 - 6c = 15 - 10c$?

Replace c with each member of $\{2, 0, -1, -2\}$

Replace c with 2.

$23 - 6c$	$15 - 10c$
$23 - 6(2)$	$15 - 10(2)$
$23 - 12$	$15 - 20$
11	-5

False

Replace c with 0.

$23 - 6c$	$15 - 10c$
$23 - 6(0)$	$15 - 10(0)$
$23 - 0$	$15 - 0$
23	15

False

$(-)(-) = (+)$

Replace c with -1.

$23 - 6c$	$15 - 10c$
$23 - 6(-1)$	$15 - 10(-1)$
$23 + 6$	$15 + 10$
29	25

False

Replace c with -2.

$23 - 6c$	$15 - 10c$
$23 - 6(-2)$	$15 - 10(-2)$
$23 + 12$	$15 + 20$
35	35

True

-2 is the only member which makes the sentence true. ⟶ **Thus, -2 is the solution of $23 - 6c = 15 - 10c$.**

ORAL EXERCISES

Which are open sentences?

1. $5x + 6 = 22$
2. $13 = (6)(2) + 1$
3. $14 - 2y = 8$
4. $7(5) + 8 = c$
5. $6x = 9 + 2y$
6. $4 + 9 = 2 + 11$
7. $5(9) - 12 = 17$
8. $8 + 9x = 36$
9. $2(4 + 5) = 20$
10. $3(7 + 2a) = 4$
11. $23 = 3(5) + 8$
12. $8 + 3(7) = 9d$
13. He is president of his class.
14. Texas is the smallest state in the U.S.A.
15. It is the largest planet in the solar system.

For each sentence above which is *not* an open sentence, tell whether it is true or false.

EXERCISES

Part A

Which members of the given replacement set are solutions of the sentence?

1. $6x + 5 = 35$ $\{1, 5\}$
2. $47 = 5y + 7$ $\{4, 8, 12\}$
3. $9 + 4z = 45$ $\{4, 2, 9\}$
4. $22 = 8 + 2d$ $\{7, 8\}$
5. $5r - 1 = 24$ $\{1, 3, 5\}$
6. $29 - 4g = 21$ $\{2, 5, 8\}$
7. $58 - 5x = 13$ $\{3, 4, 9\}$
8. $56 = 29 + 9b$ $\{1, 3, 5, 7\}$
9. $39 = 7y - 10$ $\{4, 7, 10\}$
10. $8r - 38 = 26$ $\{4, 6, 8\}$
11. $12x + 8 = 56$ $\{2, 4, 6, 8\}$
12. $7m - 32 = 31$ $\{1, 5, 9, 10, 12\}$
13. $5 + 6z = 35$ $\{5, 6, 7\}$
14. $68 = 9x - 85$ $\{17, 19, 21\}$
15. $10r = 7r + 21$ $\{3, 7\}$
16. $6a - 48 = 6$ $\{9, 10, 11\}$
17. $8d - 32 = 0$ $\{1, 4, 9\}$
18. $70 = 2y + 56$ $\{5, 7, 9\}$
19. $15 + y = 5y + 3$ $\{3, 4, 5, 6, 7\}$
20. $4x - 3 = 3x - 1$ $\{1, 2, 3, 4, 5\}$
21. $9c - 5 = 7c + 3$ $\{2, 4, 6\}$
22. $2r - 6 = r + 3$ $\{2, 5, 9\}$
23. $18 - 5r = 2r + 4$ $\{1, 2, 3, 4\}$
24. $40 - 9a = 13a - 26$ $\{3, 4, 5\}$
25. $10y - 22 = 8y - 10$ $\{12, 14, 6\}$
26. $4z + 2 = -z + 27$ $\{5, 8, 9\}$
27. $8x - 13 = 21x - 52$ $\{3, 8, 11\}$
28. $5y + 2 = 8y - 10$ $\{1, 2, 4, 8\}$

PART B

Which members of the given replacement set are solutions of the sentence?

29. $7y + 6 = 6 - y$ $\{0, 1, 2\}$
30. $24 - 5t = 19 - 10t$ $\{-3, -2, -1\}$
31. $6d + 7 = 2d + 8$ $\{\frac{1}{2}, \frac{1}{3}, \frac{1}{4}\}$
32. $1 + 5x = 9 - x$ $\{\frac{3}{2}, \frac{4}{3}, \frac{3}{4}\}$
33. $9a - 2 = 3a - 20$ $\{-1, -3, -5\}$
34. $2x + 2 = 4x + 2$ $\{-1, 0, 1, 2\}$
35. $5y + 12 = 3 + y$ $\{1, 2, 3, 4\}$
36. $-8z - 46 = 7z - 1$ $\{-3, -2, -1\}$
37. $8r + 4 = 7 + 2r$ $\{\frac{1}{2}, \frac{1}{3}, \frac{1}{4}\}$
38. $5x + 8 = x - 6$ $\{2, 3, 4, 5, 6\}$

Solving Equations

REVIEW CAPSULE

Additive Inverses, or Opposites

6	−6	$6 + -6 = 0$
−3	3	$-3 + 3 = 0$
x	$-x$	$x + -x = 0$

A sentence with $=$ is an equation. To solve
an equation means to find all of its solutions.
We will assume that the replacement set is the
set of all numbers.

EXAMPLE 1   Add 8 to each side of the equation $n = 3$.
Then find the solution.

The solution of $n = 3$ is 3.

$$
\begin{aligned}
n &= 3 \\
n + 8 &= 3 + 8 \\
\text{or} \quad n + 8 &= 11
\end{aligned}
$$

3 is the solution of both equations.

The solution of $n + 8 = 11$ is 3, since $3 + 8 = 11$.

Example 1 suggests this.
We can add the same number to each
side of an equation.

Addition Property for Equations

If $a = b$ is true, then $a + c = b + c$ is also true,
for all numbers a, b, and c.

EXAMPLE 2   Multiply each side of the equation $x = 5$
by 2. Then find the solution.

The solution of $x = 5$ is 5.

$$
\begin{aligned}
x &= 5 \\
2(x) &= 2(5) \\
2x &= 10
\end{aligned}
$$

5 is the solution of both equations.

The solution of $2x = 10$ is 5, since $2(5) = 10$.

Example 2 suggests this. ──────────→

We can multiply each side of an equation by the same number.

Multiplication Property for Equations

If $a = b$ is true, then $a(c) = b(c)$ is also true, for all numbers a, b, and c.

EXAMPLE 3   Divide each side of the equation $7x = 42$ by 7. Is the solution of the resulting equation the same as the solution of $7x = 42$?

$\frac{7}{7} = 1$ ──────────────────→

The solution of $x = 6$ is 6.

$$7x = 42$$
$$\frac{7x}{7} = \frac{42}{7}$$
$$1x = 6$$
$$x = 6$$

$7x = 42$

The solution of $7x = 42$ is 6, since $7(6) = 42$.

Yes, 6 is the solution of both equations.

Example 3 suggests this. ──────────→

We can divide each side of an equation by the same nonzero number.

Division Property for Equations

If $a = b$ is true, then $\frac{a}{c} = \frac{b}{c}$ is also true, for all numbers, a, b, and c $[c \neq 0]$.

EXAMPLE 4   Solve $3c + 5 = 17$. Then check your solution.

Get $3c$ alone; (alone if no $+5$).

-5 is the additive inverse of 5.

Add -5 to each side. ──────────→

Now $3c$ is alone. ──────────→

Divide each side by 3. ──────────→

$\frac{3}{3} = 1$ ──────────────────→

Now c is alone. ──────────→

$$\begin{array}{r} 3c + 5 = 17 \\ -5 \quad -5 \\ \hline 3c + 0 = 12 \\ 3c = 12 \end{array}$$ $\begin{cases} \text{Addition Property} \\ \text{for Equations} \end{cases}$

$$\frac{3c}{3} = \frac{12}{3}$$ $\begin{cases} \text{Division Property} \\ \text{for Equations} \end{cases}$
$$1c = 4$$
$$c = 4$$

Check. ──────────────────→

Replace c with 4. ──────────→

$$\begin{array}{c|c} 3c + 5 & 17 \\ \hline 3(4) + 5 & 17 \\ 12 + 5 & \\ 17 & \end{array}$$

True

Thus, 4 is the solution of $3c + 5 = 17$.

EXAMPLE 5   Solve $6x - 7 = 11$. Then check your solution.

Get $6x$ alone; (alone if no -7).
7 is the additive inverse of -7.
Add 7 to each side. —————————→

$$\begin{array}{rl} 6x - 7 &= 11 \\ +7 \quad &+7 \\ \hline 6x + 0 &= 18 \end{array}$$ $\left\{\begin{array}{l}\text{Addition Property}\\\text{for Equations}\end{array}\right.$

Now $6x$ is alone. —————————→
Divide each side by 6. —————————→

$$6x = 18$$
$$\frac{6x}{6} = \frac{18}{6}$$ $\left\{\begin{array}{l}\text{Division Property}\\\text{for Equations}\end{array}\right.$

Now x is alone. —————————→

$$1x = 3$$
$$x = 3$$

Check. —————————→
Replace x with 3. —————————→

$6x - 7$	11
$6(3) - 7$	11
$18 - 7$	
11	

True

Thus, 3 is the solution of $6x - 7 = 11$.

EXAMPLE 6   Solve $8 = -12 - 4a$.

Get $-4a$ alone; (alone if no -12).

Add 12 to each side. —————————→

$$\begin{array}{rl} 8 &= -12 - 4a \\ +12 \quad &+12 \\ \hline 20 &= \quad 0 - 4a \end{array}$$ $\left\{\begin{array}{l}\text{Addition Property}\\\text{for Equations}\end{array}\right.$

Now $-4a$ is alone. —————————→

$$20 = -4a$$

Divide each side by -4. —————————→

$$\frac{20}{-4} = \frac{-4a}{-4}$$ $\left\{\begin{array}{l}\text{Division Property}\\\text{for Equations}\end{array}\right.$

$\dfrac{20}{-4} = -5 \qquad \dfrac{-4}{-4} = 1$

Now a is alone. —————————→

$$-5 = 1a$$
$$-5 = a$$

Check -5 in $8 = -12 - 4a$. —————————→   **Thus,** -5 is the solution of $8 = -12 - 4a$.

SUMMARY   **To solve $ax + b = c$ for x:**

Add the additive inverse of b to each side. ——→

$$\begin{array}{rl} ax + b &= \quad c \\ -b \quad &-b \\ \hline ax + 0 &= \quad c - b \end{array}$$

Divide each side by a. ————————→

$$\frac{ax}{a} = \frac{c - b}{a}$$

$$x = \frac{c - b}{a}$$

ORAL EXERCISES

**To solve each equation, what number would you add to each side?
By what number would you divide each side?**

1. $2x + 9 = 17$
2. $-8 = 2 + 5z$
3. $-6c + 30 = -6$
4. $14 - 3y = -13$
5. $4d - 7 = -11$
6. $40 - 8x = -16$
7. $7 = 19 + 4c$
8. $3z - 7 = 8$
9. $7y + 20 = 6$
10. $8 = 10d - 32$
11. $-58 - 9r = 14$
12. $62 = 20 + 7x$
13. $4z - 5 = -9$
14. $8p - 42 = 38$
15. $-36 = 10y + 14$
16. $24 = 2 + 11q$
17. $-41 = 12z - 5$
18. $9c + 8 = 8$
19. $10x - 17 = -7$
20. $-16 = 62 + 13y$
21. $15g - 7 = -37$
22. $73 - 20r = -27$
23. $10c - 9 = -9$
24. $87 = 51 - 9b$

EXERCISES

PART A

Solve each equation in Exercises 1–24 above.

PART B

EXAMPLE   Solve $2x - 8 = -7$.

Add 8 to each side. ———————————→

$$\begin{array}{r} 2x - 8 = -7 \\ +8 \quad +8 \\ \hline 2x \quad = 1 \end{array}$$

Divide each side by 2. ———————→

$$\frac{2x}{2} = \frac{1}{2}$$

The solution is a fraction. ————→

$$x = \frac{1}{2}$$

Check on your own. ———————————→ **Thus,** $\frac{1}{2}$ is the solution of $2x - 8 = -7$.

Solve.

25. $5r + 8 = 9$
26. $12 = 4y + 9$
27. $8 = 6r + 7$
28. $9 + 3x = 10$
29. $18 = 19 - 8d$
30. $17 = 20 - 4x$
31. $13 - 5z = 11$
32. $17 - 3a = 15$
33. $4x + 19 = 20$
34. $14 - 6y = 9$
35. $8x = 22 - 19$
36. $5 = 9 - 7x$

PART C

Solve.

37. $3x - .02 = -.548$
38. $6.2 - 2x = 3.4$
39. $-.07 - 5x = -2.1$

Algebra and Commissions

It is a common practice in business to encourage sales people to sell more by giving them extra money, a commission, for each item they sell.

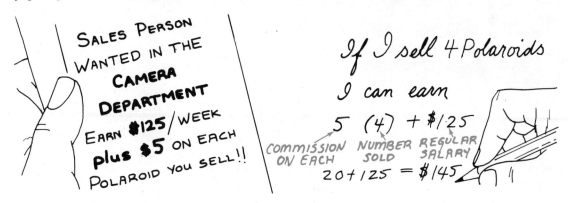

SALES PERSON WANTED IN THE **CAMERA DEPARTMENT** EARN $125/WEEK **plus $5** ON EACH POLAROID YOU SELL!!

If I sell 4 Polaroids I can earn

5 (4) + $125

COMMISSION ON EACH   NUMBER SOLD   REGULAR SALARY

20 + 125 = $145

PROBLEM

Jill earns $160 a week plus a commission of $15 for each portable TV she sells. How many must she sell to earn a total of $250?

Let n = the number she must sell

(Commission on each) (number sold) + (regular salary) = total

$$(15) \qquad (n) \qquad + \qquad 160 \qquad = 250$$
$$15n + 160 = 250$$
$$15n = 90$$
$$n = 6$$

Thus, she must sell 6 portable TV's.

PROJECT

1. Mary earns $155 a week plus a commission of $4 for each mower she sells. How many must she sell to make $183?

2. Harry earns $150 a week plus a commission of $5 for each radio he sells. How many must he sell to make $190?

Equations: The Variable on Both Sides

<table>
<tr><td>

OBJECTIVE

■ To solve an equation like $5x - 8 = 3x + 12$

</td><td>

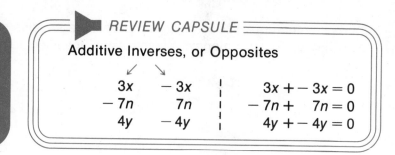

▶ *REVIEW CAPSULE*

Additive Inverses, or Opposites

$3x$	$-3x$		$3x + -3x = 0$
$-7n$	$7n$		$-7n + 7n = 0$
$4y$	$-4y$		$4y + -4y = 0$

</td></tr>
</table>

EXAMPLE 1   Solve $5n - 4 = 3n + 18$. Check your solution.

$-3n$ is the additive inverse of $3n$.
Add $-3n$ to each side. ⟶

Now the variable term is on one side only. ⟶

Add 4 to each side. ⟶

Divide each side by 2. ⟶

$$
\begin{array}{rcl}
5n - 4 = & 3n + 18 \\
-3n & -3n \\
\hline
2n - 4 = & 0 + 18 \\
2n - 4 = & 18 \\
+4 & +4 \\
\hline
2n + 0 = & 22 \\
2n = & 22 \\
\dfrac{2n}{2} & = \dfrac{22}{2} \\
n = 11
\end{array}
$$

Check.

$5n$ -4	$3n$ $+18$
$5(11) - 4$	$3(11) + 18$
$55 - 4$	$33 + 18$
51	51

Thus, 11 is the solution of $5n - 4 = 3n + 18$.

EXAMPLE 2   Solve the equation in Example 1 by adding $-5n$, rather than $-3n$, to each side.

$-5n$ is the additive inverse of $5n$.
Add $-5n$ to each side. ⟶
Now the variable term is on one side only.

Add -18 to each side. ⟶

Divide each side by -2. ⟶

$$
\begin{array}{rcl}
5n - 4 = & 3n + 18 \\
-5n & -5n \\
\hline
-4 = & -2n + 18 \\
-18 & -18 \\
\hline
-22 = & -2n + 0 \\
-22 = & -2n \\
\dfrac{-22}{-2} & = \dfrac{-2n}{-2} \\
11 = n
\end{array}
$$

Thus, 11 is the solution of $5n - 4 = 3n + 18$.

EXAMPLE 3   Solve $4y - 21 = 9y - 16$.

Add $-9y$ to each side. $\longrightarrow$
(We could have added $-4y$ to each side.)

$$
\begin{array}{r}
4y - 21 = 9y - 16 \\
-9y -9y \\
\hline
-5y - 21 = 0 - 16 \\
-5y - 21 = -16
\end{array}
$$

Add 21 to each side. $\longrightarrow$

$$
\begin{array}{r}
+21 +21 \\
\hline
-5y + 0 = 5 \\
-5y = 5
\end{array}
$$

Divide each side by -5. $\longrightarrow$

$$
\frac{-5y}{-5} = \frac{5}{-5}
$$

$$
y = -1
$$

Check on your own. $\longrightarrow$ **Thus,** -1 is the solution of $4y - 21 = 9y - 16$.

EXAMPLE 4   Solve $5x - 7 = x + 9$.

x means $1x$. $\longrightarrow$
Add $-1x$ to each side. $\longrightarrow$
(We could have added $-5x$ to each side.)

$$
\begin{array}{r}
5x - 7 = 1x + 9 \\
-1x -1x \\
\hline
4x - 7 = 0 + 9 \\
4x - 7 = 9
\end{array}
$$

Add 7 to each side. $\longrightarrow$

$$
\begin{array}{r}
+7 +7 \\
\hline
4x + 0 = 16 \\
4x = 16
\end{array}
$$

Divide each side by 4. $\longrightarrow$

$$
\frac{4x}{4} = \frac{16}{4}
$$

$$
x = 4
$$

Check on your own. $\longrightarrow$ **Thus,** 4 is the solution of $5x - 7 = x + 9$.

EXAMPLE 5   Solve $8x - 12 = 15x - 4x$.

$15x - 4x = 11x$ $\longrightarrow$
Add $-11x$ to each side. $\longrightarrow$

$$
\begin{array}{r}
8x - 12 = 15x - 4x \\
8x - 12 = 11x \\
-11x -11x \\
\hline
-3x - 12 = 0
\end{array}
$$

Add 12 to each side. $\longrightarrow$

$$
\begin{array}{r}
+12 +12 \\
\hline
-3x + 0 = 12 \\
-3x = 12
\end{array}
$$

Divide each side by -3. $\longrightarrow$

$$
\frac{-3x}{-3} = \frac{12}{-3}
$$

$$
x = -4
$$

Check on your own. $\longrightarrow$ **Thus,** -4 is the solution of $8x - 12 = 15x - 4x$.

EXERCISES

PART A

Solve.

1. $5x + 6 = 2x + 15$
2. $6y - 8 = 20 + 2y$
3. $5 + 9x = 7x + 11$
4. $3z + 10 = 2 + 5z$
5. $4a - 9 = 3a - 1$
6. $21r - 26 = 8r - 13$
7. $2x - 12 = x + 3$
8. $5d + 11 = 8d - 7$
9. $-x + 22 = 4x + 2$
10. $6c - 20 = 2c$
11. $9e + 14 = 11e$
12. $7c = -24 + c$
13. $8y + 11 = 7y$
14. $17x - 8 = 5x + 4$
15. $3y = 15y - 72$
16. $7 + 11z = 97 - 7z$
17. $18 - 9x = 2x + 7$
18. $3r - 2 = -9 + 2r$
19. $10g - 22 = 8g - 14$
20. $7z + 8 = -16 + 3z$
21. $x - 3 = 22 - 4x$
22. $20x - 16x = 6x - 8$
23. $5x - 2x = 24 - 9x$
24. $13x - 4x = 10x - 21$
25. $-x + 3x = 6 + x$
26. $4y - 3y = 18 - 2y$
27. $4z - 5z = -28 + 3z$
28. $27 - 6y = 4y - 7y$
29. $3x + 8 = 2x - x$
30. $x + x + 18 = 30$
31. $2y + 5y + 3 = 10y$
32. $8 + 2x = 5x - 13$
33. $25 - 4y = 1 + 4y$
34. $13x + 11 = 10x - 7$
35. $7x - 8x = 4 - 2x$
36. $13y - 4y = -14 + 2y$

PART B

EXAMPLE   Solve $7x + 8 = 5 + 3x$.

	$7x + 8 = 5 + 3x$
Add $-3x$ to each side. $\longrightarrow$	$4x + 8 = 5$
Add -8 to each side. $\longrightarrow$	$4x = -3$
Divide each side by 4. $\longrightarrow$	$x = \frac{-3}{4}$

Thus, $\frac{-3}{4}$ is the solution.

Solve.

37. $7x + 6 = 9 + 8x$
38. $3y + 9 = -2y + 7$
39. $y + 6 = 7 - 3y$
40. $-6a - 15 = -17 - 9a$
41. $2 + 6c = -1 + 11c$
42. $10x - 5 = -9 + 3x$
43. $2x + 13 = -4x + 18$
44. $-11 + 4x = -13 - 3x$
45. $12 - 5y = 7 - y$
46. $13z - 3 = 8z + 6$
47. $2y - 15 = -3y - 22$
48. $a + 11 = -2a + 7$

PART C

Solve.

49. $3x + x - 2 = 7 - 2x$
50. $7c + 4 - c = 2c - 3$
51. $6a + 8 = 19 + 9a + 7 - 15a$
52. $-4 - d + 2d = 3 + 4d$
53. $8y + 7 = 22 - y + 3y$
54. $3x + 6x + 2 = 4x - 3 - 2x$
55. $12x - 1.2 = 3x + 1.5$
56. $.04 - 3x = -5x - .002$
57. $7x - .05 = 3.15 + 2x$

Number Mysteries

GAME

Play this game with a friend. You can always tell what your friend's starting number was. Here's how.

Ask your friend to do the following:
1. Choose a number.
2. Add 2.
3. Multiply by 8.
4. Subtract 10.
5. Divide by 2.
6. Add 9.
7. Divide by 4.
8. Give the result.

You think:
1. x
2. $x + 2$
3. $8x + 16$
4. $8x + 6$
5. $4x + 3$
6. $4x + 12$
7. $x + 3$
8. $x + 3$

The result will always be 3 more than the starting digit.

PROJECT

1. Now try this. Explain how to find the mystery number.
    Choose a mystery number.
    Double it.
    Add 6.
    Add the mystery number.
    Divide by 3.
    Give the result.

2. Make up some mystery numbers of your own.

Equations with Parentheses

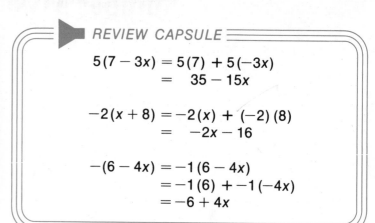

REVIEW CAPSULE

$$5(7 - 3x) = 5(7) + 5(-3x)$$
$$= 35 - 15x$$

$$-2(x + 8) = -2(x) + (-2)(8)$$
$$= -2x - 16$$

$$-(6 - 4x) = -1(6 - 4x)$$
$$= -1(6) + -1(-4x)$$
$$= -6 + 4x$$

EXAMPLE 1   Solve $10x - 3(5 - 3x) = 23$. Then check your solution.

Check.

$-3(5 - 3x) = -15 + 9x$

$10x + 9x = 19x$ ⟶

Add 15 to each side. ⟶

Divide each side by 19. ⟶

$10x - 3(5 - 3x) = 23$	$10x - 3(5 - 3x)$ 23
$10x - 15 + 9x = 23$	$10(2) - 3[5 - 3(2)]$ 23
$19x - 15 = 23$	$20 - 3(5 - 6)$
$\underline{+15 \quad +15}$	$20 - 3(-1)$
$19x = 38$	$20 + 3$
$x = 2$	23

Thus, 2 is the solution.

EXAMPLE 2   Solve $7x - (9 - 4x) = 3(x - 11)$.

$-(9 - 4x) = -1(9 - 4x)$ ⟶

$-1(9 - 4x) = -9 + 4x; 3(x - 11) = 3x - 33$

$7x + 4x = 11x$ ⟶

Add $-3x$ to each side. ⟶

Add 9 to each side. ⟶

Divide each side by 8. ⟶

$$7x - (9 - 4x) = 3(x - 11)$$
$$7x - 1(9 - 4x) = 3(x - 11)$$
$$7x - 9 + 4x = 3x - 33$$
$$11x - 9 = 3x - 33$$
$$\underline{-3x \qquad\quad -3x}$$
$$8x - 9 = -33$$
$$\underline{+9 \qquad + 9}$$
$$8x = -24$$
$$x = -3$$

Check on your own. ⟶ **Thus,** -3 is the solution.

EXERCISES

Solve.

1. $4(x - 2) = 20$
2. $2(5 + x) = 22$
3. $-5(x + 4) = 15$
4. $8 - 4(y - 1) = -36$
5. $5(z - 6) = 10$
6. $3(c - 1) + 8 = -10$
7. $2(2s + 3) = -18$
8. $-4(2x + 6) = 16$
9. $y - (8 - y) = 32$
10. $(50 - x) - (3x + 2) = 0$
11. $20 - (8 + x) = -(1 - x) + 29$
12. $3c + 2(c + 2) = 13 - (2c - 5)$
13. $5z + 10(-z + 14) = 95$
14. $x + (x + 1) + (x + 2) = 15$
15. $2(c + 3) + 5c = 15 - (2c + 18)$
16. $5d - (d + 3) = (d + 2) + 7$
17. $(x + 4) - (x - 6) = 5(x - 8)$
18. $5 + 7x = -(3 - 2x) - 3x$
19. $3y - (4 - 2y) = 3(y + 2)$
20. $6(x + 2) = 4 - (3 - 2x) - 1$
21. $2(2 - 3z) = 8 - 2(4z + 5)$
22. $7y - (4 - 2y) = 3(y + 3) - 1$
23. $5 - 3(4 - 2x) = 4(x - 3) - 3$
24. $2(x + 1) + 15x = -(3x - 17) + 5x$
25. $7y - 2(3 - y) = 4(y + 1)$
26. $7(x - 1) + 5 = -2(3 - 4x) + 5$
27. $2(3 - z) = 16 - 2(3 + 2z)$
28. $8y - 3(4 - 2y) = 6(y + 1) - 2$
29. $3 + 7(x + 1) = 6 - (5 + 2x)$
30. $7(a - 1) + 4 = -(2a - 4) + 6a + 2$
31. $-2(3 - 4z) + 7z = 13z - 4$
32. $-4(2x - 5) + 3x = x - 28$
33. $5 - (x + 8) + 6x = 4(x + 2)$
34. $7 - 3(y + 1) + 8 = 4 - 5(y - 2)$
35. $-(2x + 6) + 3x = 1 + 2(4 - 2x)$
36. $5 - 3(x + 1) = -(x - 9) + 5x$
37. $6y + 3(4 - y) = 8 - 2(y + 3)$
38. $-(6 - 4c) + 3c = 10 - 2(c - 1)$
39. $16 - 4(2a + 1) = 6a + (1 - 3a)$
40. $7 - 2(4 - 3x) + 8x = -(x + 31)$

Solve.

41. $7(2x - 2) - 5x = 4x + 2$
42. $4z - 3 - 7(z + 1) = 6z$
43. $-5y - 2(y + 4) = 6y - 9$
44. $8y + 5(1 - y) = 4y - 6$
45. $3(-2x + 1) = 4(1 + 3x) + 2$
46. $5r + 3(r - 7) = -(r + 8)$
47. $7(1 - 3a) + a = 6 - (a - 4)$
48. $2z - 8(z + 1) = 6z + (3z - 4)$
49. $9 - 4(2 - y) = 7y - (3 + y)$
50. $6(r - 2) - 3r - 1 = 8(5r + 1) - 10r$
51. $5z + 3(z - 2) - 6z = 12$
52. $-3(6 - 2x) + 4x = -(2x - 8)$

Solve.

53. $6[5 - 3(x - 4)] = 4x + 18$
54. $3 - 2x = -[4 + 5(2x - 1)]$
55. $-7x - [2(3x + 1) + 4] = 3x$
56. $-2[4 - (2 + 3x)] = 4x + 5$
57. $-[-7 + 2(1 - 2x)] = 1 - 5x$
58. $4x - 2[5(x + 1) + 3] = 8x$

English Phrases to Algebra

REVIEW CAPSULE

English phrase: 6 decreased by 2

Mathematical terms: 6   —   2
    6 decreased by 2 means 6 made smaller by 2, or 6 − 2

English phrase: 8 increased by 3

Mathematical terms: 8   +   3
    8 increased by 3 means 8 made greater by 3, or 8 + 3

EXAMPLE 1   Write in mathematical terms.

Decreased by means made smaller by. Use −.

7 decreased by 5   9 increased by 4
7   —   5   9   +   4

EXAMPLE 2   Write in mathematical terms.

The value of *x* is not known.

3 decreased by *x*
3   —   *x*

EXAMPLE 3   Write in mathematical terms.

Let a variable represent the number.

12 increased by 4 times a number
12   + $(4)(y)$, or $12 + 4y$

EXAMPLE 4   Write in mathematical terms.

7 less than 10 does not mean 7 − 10. It means 10 − 7.

7 less than 10
10   —   7

EXAMPLE 5

9 more than 5 means 5 made greater by 9.

Write in mathematical terms.

9 more than 5

5 + 9

EXAMPLE 6

Write in mathematical terms.

5 less than 3 times a number

Let n represent the number.

$(3)(n)$ $-$ 5, or $3n - 5$

EXAMPLE 7

Write in mathematical terms.

8 more than twice x

Twice x means 2 times x.

$(2)(x)$ $+$ 8, or $2x + 8$

EXERCISES

PART A

Write in mathematical terms.

1. 8 decreased by 5
2. 9 increased by 7
3. 12 increased by 6
4. 8 less than 15
5. 2 more than 23
6. 15 decreased by x
7. y increased by 4
8. 7 more than x
9. 8 less than n
10. 8 decreased by twice x
11. 3 more than 5 times y
12. 7 times a number, decreased by 2
13. 6 less than 3 times a number
14. 5 decreased by twice n
15. 25 decreased by 4 times a number
16. 8 more than 7 times a number
17. 4 times x, increased by 8
18. 12 less than 3 times a number
19. 14 increased by twice a number
20. 2 times n, decreased by 4
21. 9 times a number, decreased by 7
22. twice a number, increased by 1

PART B

Write in mathematical terms.

23. x increased by y
24. x more than y
25. 7 times x, decreased by twice y
26. m less than 3 times n
27. 9 more than x times y
28. m times n less than 20
29. y decreased by 5 times x
30. 6 times x, increased by 5 times y
31. 5 increased by 8 more than 7 times y
32. 7 more than twice a number, increased by 6
33. 2 less than 5 times a number, increased by 9
34. x more than 8 times y, decreased by twice x

Number Problems

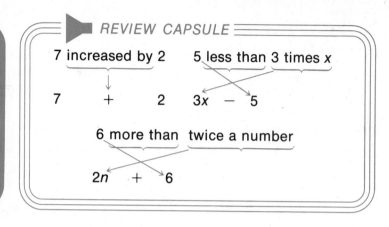

REVIEW CAPSULE

7 increased by 2   5 less than 3 times x

7   +   2 $3x$ $-$ 5

6 more than twice a number

$2n$ +   6

EXAMPLE 1   Write an equation for each sentence.

Three more than a number is 9.

$$n + 3 = 9$$

A number decreased by 7 is 8 times the number.

$$n - 7 = 8n$$

EXAMPLE 2   Seven more than 4 times a number is 31. Find the number.

Let n = the number

7 more than 4 times n is 31.

Write an equation. ⟶
Add −7 to each side. ⟶

$$4n + 7 = 31$$
$$\; -7 \quad -7$$
$$\overline{4n \qquad = 24}$$

Divide each side by 4. ⟶

$$n = 6$$

Check 6 in the problem. ⟶

7 more than 4 times 6 is 31.

$4(6) + 7$	31
$24 + 7$	
31	

Thus, the number is 6.

EXAMPLE 3 A number decreased by 14 is the same as 8 times the number. Find the number.

Let n = the number

n decreased by 14 is the same as 8 times n.

Write an equation. $\longrightarrow$

$n = 1n$ $\longrightarrow$

Add $-1n$ to each side. $\longrightarrow$

Divide each side by 7. $\longrightarrow$

$$
\begin{aligned}
n - 14 &= 8n \\
1n - 14 &= 8n \\
-1n \quad\quad &\;\; -1n \\
\hline
-14 &= 7n \\
-2 &= n
\end{aligned}
$$

Check -2 in the problem. $\longrightarrow$

n decreased by 14 is 8 times n.

$-2 - 14$	$8\,(-2)$
-16	-16

Thus, the number is -2.

EXAMPLE 4 Three less than twice a number is the same as the number increased by 8. Find the number.

Let x = the number

Twice x is $2x$.

3 less than $2x$ is the same as x increased by 8.

$$
\begin{aligned}
2x - 3 &= x + 8 \\
2x - 3 &= 1x + 8 \\
-1x \quad\quad &\;\; -1x \\
\hline
1x - 3 &= 8 \\
+3 \quad\quad &\;\; +3 \\
\hline
x &= 11
\end{aligned}
$$

$1x = x$ $\longrightarrow$

Check 11 in the problem. $\longrightarrow$ **Thus,** the number is 11.

EXAMPLE 5 A number increased by 6 times the number is -63. Find the number.

Let n = the number

$$
\begin{aligned}
n + 6n &= -63 \\
7n &= -63 \\
n &= -9
\end{aligned}
$$

$n + 6n = 1n + 6n = 7n$ $\longrightarrow$

Check -9 in the problem. $\longrightarrow$ **Thus,** the number is -9.

ORAL EXERCISES

Give an equation for each sentence.

1. Five more than twice x is 14.
2. Six decreased by 4 times n is 18.
3. Seven times n is 3 more than n.
4. Two less than a number is 20.
5. Eight more than twice a number is 2.
6. The sum of x and 6 is 8 times x.
7. Two decreased by 4 times x is 15.
8. Twelve is 5 more than 6 times x.
9. Sixteen less than twice x is 32.
10. Nine increased by 5 times n is 18.

EXERCISES

PART A

1. Nine more than a number is 13. Find the number.
2. A number decreased by 10 is 16. Find the number.
3. Eleven increased by twice a number is 17. Find the number.
4. Eight less than 5 times a number is 22. Find the number.
5. Twelve decreased by 3 times a number is 9. Find the number.
6. Three more than 8 times a number is −29. Find the number.
7. Sixteen is 5 less than 7 times a number. Find the number.
8. Thirteen increased by 9 times a number is 4. Find the number.
9. Ten less than twice a number is the same as 7 times the number. Find the number.
10. A number increased by 30 is 14 decreased by 3 times the number. Find the number.
11. Nine more than 5 times a number is the same as 2 times the number. Find the number.
12. Twice a number is the same as 6 more than 8 times the number. Find the number.
13. Seven less than 6 times a number is the same as the number decreased by 2. Find the number.
14. Five times a number is the same as 30 more than 8 times the number. Find the number.
15. Two less than 2 times a number is the same as the number decreased by 38. Find the number.
16. A number increased by 5 is the same as 37 decreased by 7 times the number. Find the number.
17. Eight times a number decreased by the number is 35. Find the number.
18. Twice a number plus 4 times the number is −54. Find the number.
19. A number plus 3 more than the number is 17. Find the number.
20. Six more than a number increased by the number is 40. Find the number.
21. Seven times a number decreased by the number is −48. Find the number.
22. Five less than 3 times a number is −20. Find the number.
23. Eight times a number is the same as 30 less than 5 times the number. Find the number.
24. Three less than 3 times a number is the same as 5 less than twice the number. Find the number.

PART B

EXAMPLE Three times the sum of a number and 2 is the same as 8 increased by the number. Find the number.

Let $x =$ the number

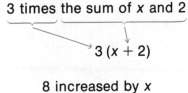

3 times the sum of x and 2

$3(x + 2)$

8 increased by x

$8 \ + \ x$

$3(x + 2)$ is the same as $8 + x$

$3(x + 2) = 8 + x$

Remove parentheses. ⟶ $3x + 6 = 8 + x$
Add $-1x$ to each side. ⟶ $2x + 6 = 8$
Add -6 to each side. ⟶ $2x = 2$
Divide each side by 2. $x = 1$

Check 1 in the problem. ⟶ **Thus,** the number is 1.

---

25. Five times the sum of a number and 2 is 45. Find the number.

26. Six times the sum of a number and -4 is 30. Find the number.

27. Five more than a number is 4 times the sum of the number and 8. Find the number.

28. Three times the sum of 4 and a number is the same as 18 increased by the number. Find the number.

29. Twice the sum of 6 and a number is the same as 15 decreased by the number. Find the number.

30. Eight more than three times a number is the same as twice the number decreased by 6. Find the number.

PART C

31. If 6 times the sum of twice a number and 8 is decreased by 4, the result is 1 less than 3 times the sum of the number and 6. Find the number.

32. If 15 is decreased by 7 times the sum of 5 and 3 times a number, the result is 12 more than twice the sum of the number and 7. Find the number.

More Number Problems

OBJECTIVES
■ To solve word problems involving two or more numbers

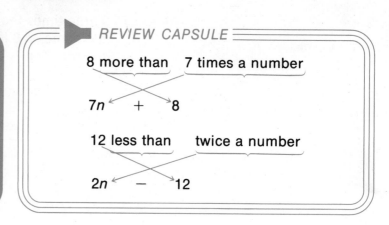

REVIEW CAPSULE

8 more than   7 times a number

$7n$ +   8

12 less than   twice a number

$2n$ −   12

EXAMPLE 1 Clyde is thinking of two numbers. The second number is 5 more than twice the first. Repesent the two numbers.

5 more than twice the first ⟶

Let f = first number
$2f + 5$ = second number

Thus, f and $2f + 5$ represent the two numbers.

EXAMPLE 2 The greater of two numbers is 8 less than 4 times the smaller. Represent the two numbers.

Let s = smaller number
$4s - 8$ = greater number

Thus, s and $4s - 8$ represent the two numbers.

EXAMPLE 3 The second of three numbers is 6 times the first. The third is 1 more than the second. Represent the three numbers.

6 times the first ⟶
1 more than the second ⟶

Let f = first number
$6f$ = second number
$6f + 1$ = third number

Thus, f, $6f$, and $6f + 1$ represent the three numbers.

EXAMPLE 4 The greater of two numbers is 12 more than 8 times the smaller. Their sum is 21. Find the numbers.

Represent the two numbers.

Let s = smaller number
$8s + 12$ = greater number

Smaller + greater = 21. ———————→
Write an equation and solve it.

$$s + (8s + 12) = 21$$
$$9s + 12 = 21$$
$$9s = 9$$
$$s = 1$$

Find both numbers.

Smaller number, s is 1.
Greater number, $8s + 12$ is $8(1) + 12$, or 20.

Check 1 and 20 in the first part of the problem.

Greater is 12 more than 8 times smaller.

20	$8(1) + 12$
20	20

Check 1 and 20 in the second part of the problem.

Their sum is 21.

$1 + 20$	21
21	

Thus, 1 and 20 are the two numbers.

EXAMPLE 5 The second of two numbers is 16 less than 3 times the first. Their sum is 24. Find the two numbers.

Let f = first number
$3f - 16$ = second number

First + second = 24. ———————→

$$f + (3f - 16) = 24$$
$$4f - 16 = 24$$
$$4f = 40$$
$$f = 10$$

Find both numbers. $3(10) - 16 = 30 - 16$, or 14

First number, f is 10.
Second number, $3f - 16$ is $3(10) - 16$, or 14.

Check. ———————————→

The sum is 24.

$10 + 14$	24
24	

Second is 16 less than 3 times first.

14	$3(10) - 16$
	14

Thus, 10 and 14 are the two numbers.

EXAMPLE 6	Separate $90 into two parts so that the first part is $30 less than twice the second part.

Let s = second part
$2s - 30$ = first part

First is 30 less than twice second.
Their sum is 90. ⟶
Separate 90 into two parts means the sum of the parts is 90.

$$s + (2s - 30) = 90$$
$$3s - 30 = 90$$
$$3s = 120$$
$$s = 40$$

Find both parts.
$2(40) - 30 = 80 - 30$, or 50 ⎫
⎭

Second part, s is 40.
First part, $2s - 30$ is $2(40) - 30$, or 50.

Thus, $50 and $40 are the two parts.

EXAMPLE 7	The second of three numbers is 6 times the first. The third is 1 more than the second. Their sum is 27. Find the three numbers.

Let f = first number
$6f$ = second number

1 more than second ⟶ $6f + 1$ = third number
Their sum is 27. ⟶

$$f + 6f + 6f + 1 = 27$$
$$13f + 1 = 27$$
$$13f = 26$$
$$f = 2$$

First, f is 2.
Second, $6f$ is $6(2)$, or 12.

$6(2) + 1 = 12 + 1 = 13$ ⟶ Third, $6f + 1$ is $6(2) + 1$, or 13.

Thus, 2, 12, and 13 are the three numbers.

EXERCISES

PART A

1. The second of two numbers is 5 times the first. Their sum is 42. Find the numbers.
2. The greater of two numbers is 3 more than twice the smaller. Their sum is 24. Find the numbers.
3. The sum of two numbers is 50. The first is 5 less than 4 times the second. Find the numbers.
4. Find two numbers whose sum is 55 if the second is 7 more than 5 times the first.

5. The greater of two numbers is 9 more than the smaller. Their sum is 83. Find the numbers.

6. The sum of two numbers is 19. The second is 8 less than twice the first. Find the numbers.

7. Sixty-eight students are separated into two groups. The first group is 3 times as large as the second. How many students are in each group?

8. Separate $115 into two parts so that the greater part is $12 more than the smaller part.

9. Separate $89 into two parts so that the second part is $4 less than twice the first part.

10. Separate 43 people into two groups so that the first group is 5 less than 3 times the second.

11. The sum of three numbers is 34. The first is 3 less than the second, while the third is 4 more than the second. Find the numbers.

12. The sum of three numbers is 26. The second number is twice the first, and the third is 6 more than the second. Find the numbers.

PART B

EXAMPLE The smaller of two numbers is 3 less than the greater. If the greater is decreased by twice the smaller, the result is -5. Find the numbers.

Let g = greater number
$g - 3$ = smaller number
greater decreased by twice smaller is -5

$-2(g - 3) = -2g + 6$ $\longrightarrow$

$$g \quad - \quad 2(g - 3) \quad = -5$$
$$g - 2g + 6 = -5$$
$$1g - 2g + 6 = -5$$
$$-1g + 6 = -5$$
$$-1g = -11$$
$$g = 11$$

Greater number, g is 11.
Smaller number, $g - 3$ is $11 - 3$, or 8.
Thus, the numbers are 11 and 8.

13. The greater of two numbers is 3 more than the smaller. If twice the smaller is added to the greater, the result is 30. Find the numbers.

14. The second of two numbers is 4 more than the first. If the second is increased by 1, the result is twice the first. Find the numbers.

15. The first of two numbers is twice the second. Seven more than the second number is equal to the first number decreased by 6. Find the numbers.

16. The second of two numbers is 3 more than the first. If 4 times the first is increased by the second, the result is 73. Find the numbers.

Coin Problems

OBJECTIVE

■ To solve problems about coins

▶ REVIEW CAPSULE

Number of dimes	Value in cents	Number of quarters	Value in cents
1	10	1	25
3	30	3	75
d	$10d$	q	$25q$
$4x$	$10(4x)$, or $40x$	$x + 2$	$25(x + 2)$

EXAMPLE 1 Find the total value in cents.
3 nickels and 7 dimes

$$\text{Total value} = 3\,(5) + 7\,(10)$$
$$= 15 \quad + 70, \quad \text{or } 85 \text{ cents}$$

EXAMPLE 2 Represent the total value in cents.
d dimes and q quarters

Number of coins ⟶
Value in cents ⟶

	Dimes	Quarters
Number	d	q
Value	$10d$	$25q$

Thus, the total value in cents is $10d + 25q$.

EXAMPLE 3 Represent the total value in cents.
x quarters and $15 - x$ nickels

	Quarters	Nickels
Number	x	$15 - x$
Value	$25x$	$5(15 - x)$

$$\text{Total value} = 25x + 5\,(15 - x)$$
$$= 25x + 75 - 5x$$
$$= 20x + 75$$

Thus, the total value in cents is $20x + 75$.

EXAMPLE 4 Eleanor had three times as many quarters as nickels. She had $1.60 in all. How many nickels and how many quarters did she have?

	Nickels	Quarters
Number	n	$3n$
Value	$5n$	$25(3n)$

Let n = number of nickels
$3n$ = number of quarters

$$5n + 25(3n) = 160$$
$$5n + \quad 75n = 160$$
$$80n = 160$$
$$n = 2$$

$1.60 = 160 cents
total value = 160 cents

Find both numbers.

Number of nickels, n is 2.
Number of quarters, $3n$ is $3(2)$, or 6.

Check 2 and 6 in the first part of the problem.

Number of quarters is 3 times number of nickels.

6	$3(2)$
	6

Check 2 and 6 in the second part of the problem.

Total value	is 160 cents.
$5(2) + 25(6)$	160
$10 + 150$	
160	

Thus, she had 2 nickels and 6 quarters.

EXAMPLE 5 Paul had 23 coins in nickels and dimes. Their total value was $1.55. How many were nickels and how many were dimes?

	Nickels	Dimes
Number	n	$23 - n$
Value	$5n$	$10(23 - n)$

23 coins in all.
Let n = number of nickels
$23 - n$ = number of dimes

$$5n + 10(23 - n) = 155$$
$$5n + \quad 230 - 10n = 155$$
$$230 - 5n = 155$$
$$-5n = -75$$
$$n = 15$$

$1.55 = 155 cents
total value = 155 cents

Find both numbers.

Number of nickels, n is 15.
Number of dimes, $23 - n$ is $23 - 15$, or 8.

Check 15 and 8 in the problem.

Thus, he had 15 nickels and 8 dimes.

EXAMPLE 6 Bob has 4 more dimes than nickels. He has $1.45 in all. Write an equation to find the number of nickels he has.

Let n = number of nickels.

4 more than n

$n + 4$ = number of dimes.

	Nickels	Dimes
Number	n	$n + 4$
Value	$5n$	$10(n + 4)$

Equation ————————————————→ $5n + 10(n + 4) = 145$

EXERCISES

PART A

1. John has 4 times as many nickels as dimes. He has $.90 in all. How many coins of each type does he have?

2. Chris has 5 times as many nickels as quarters. Their value is $1.50. How many nickels does she have?

3. Gladys has $.85. She has 3 times as many quarters as dimes. How many coins of each type does she have?

4. Jose has 7 times as many dimes as nickels. Their value is $3.00. How many dimes does he have?

5. Jim has 11 coins in dimes and quarters. Their value is $1.70. How many of each does he have?

6. A collection of 24 dimes and half dollars amounts to $3.60. How many dimes are there?

7. Beth has 7 more nickels than pennies. She has $1.19 in all. How many of each does she have?

8. The number of dimes is 5 less than the number of quarters. The total value is $2.30. How many dimes are there?

PART B

9. For a school play, 738 tickets valued at $856 were sold. Some cost $1 and some cost $1.50. How many $1 tickets were sold?

10. Angelo has $6.25 in dimes and quarters. The number of dimes is 2 more than 3 times the number of quarters. How many of each does he have?

11. Bill has 6 times as many dimes as nickels and 2 more pennies than dimes. He has $2.15 in all. How many of each does he have?

12. Mary has $3.41. She has 2 more dimes than half dollars and 3 times as many pennies as dimes. How many pennies does she have?

PART C

13. Kay has 5 more nickels than pennies, twice as many dimes as nickels, and 2 more quarters than dimes. She has $17.17 in all. How many dimes does she have?

14. In changing a $5 bill, Sarah received 9 more dimes than nickels and 7 fewer quarters than dimes. How many coins of each type did she receive?

Vacationing by Rental Car

Many people fly to a resort and then rent a car for touring.

CHAN'S
CAR RENTALS
$75/wk plus 9¢/km

THE TRIP IS 450 KM.
THAT WOULD COST
$75 + $.09(450) =
$75 + $40.50
FLAT + COST/KM = $115.50
RATE

PROBLEM

A car renting agency charges $85/week plus 8¢/km. How far can you travel, to the nearest km, on a maximum budget of $200?

Let n = the number of km you can travel

Use the formula. ———————→ flat rate plus $(.08)$ (number of km)

$(.08)(n) = .08n$

Add -85 to each side. ———————→

Divide each side by .08. ———————→

$$85 + .08n = 200$$
$$.08n = 115$$
$$n = 1,437.5$$

$$.08 \overline{)115.00\,0} \quad \frac{1,437.5}{}$$

Thus, you can travel 1,438 km.

PROJECT

Round answers to the nearest unit.

1. Earl budgeted $150 for renting a car. How far can he travel if the charges are $75 plus 23¢/km?

2. Jill budgeted $250 for renting a car. How far can she travel if the charges are $90 plus 18¢/km?

3. Which is more economical? A 200-km bus tour for $85, or renting a car for $75 plus 8¢/km?

4. The Byrnes budgeted $240 for renting a car. The charges are $16.45/day plus 13¢/km. How far can they travel in a week?

Perimeter Problems

OBJECTIVE

■ To solve problems about perimeters

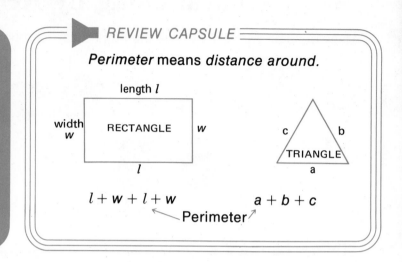

EXAMPLE 1   The length of a rectangle is 5 meters (m) greater than the width. The perimeter is 38 meters. Find the length and the width.

Length is 5 greater than width. ————→   Let w = width
$w + 5$ = length

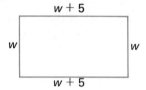

Formula for perimeter ————————→
Substitute $w + 5$ for l. ————————→

$$2l + 2w = \text{perimeter}$$
$$2(w + 5) + 2w = 38$$
$$2w + 10 + 2w = 38$$
$$4w + 10 = 38$$
$$4w = 28$$
$$w = 7$$

Width, w is 7.
Length, $w + 5$ is $7 + 5$, or 12.

Check 7 and 12 in the problem.

Length is 5 greater than width.

12	$7 + 5$
12	12

Perimeter   is 38.

$2(12) + 2(7)$	38
38	

Thus, the length is 12 m and the width is 7 m.

EXAMPLE 2   The length of a rectangle is 8 kilometers (km) more than 6 times the width. The perimeter is 156 km. Find the length and the width.

Let w = width
$6w + 8$ = length

$6w + 8$
w | | w
$6w + 8$

$$2l + 2w = \text{perimeter}$$

Substitute $6w + 8$ for l. ⟶

$$2(6w + 8) + 2w = 156$$
$$12w + 16 + 2w = 156$$
$$14w + 16 = 156$$
$$14w = 140$$
$$w = 10$$

Width, *w* is 10.
Length, $6w + 8$ is $6(10) + 8$, or 68.

Check.
Perimeter $= 2l + 2w$
$\quad = 2(68) + 2(10)$
$\quad = 136 + 20$
$\quad = 156$ km

Thus, the length is 68 km and the width is 10 km.

EXAMPLE 3   Side *b* of a triangle is twice as long as side *c*. Side *a* is 3 meters longer than side *b*. The perimeter is 48 meters. Find the length of each side.

Let *c* = side *c*
$2c$ = side *b*
$2c + 3$ = side *a*

It is easy to represent *a* and *b* in terms of *c*.

c b $(2c)$
a
$(2c + 3)$

$$a \quad + \ b \ + c = \text{perimeter}$$
$$(2c + 3) + 2c + c = 48$$
$$5c + 3 = 48$$
$$5c = 45$$
$$c = 9$$

Side *c* is 9.
Side *b*, $2c$ is $2(9)$, or 18.
Side *a*, $2c + 3$ is $2(9) + 3$, or 21.

Check.
Perimeter $= a + b + c$
$\quad = 21 + 18 + 9$
$\quad = 48$ meters

Thus, the lengths of the sides are 21 meters, 18 meters, and 9 meters.

EXERCISES

1. The length of a rectangle is 6 m greater than the width. The perimeter is 40 m. Find the length and the width.

2. The length of a rectangle is twice the width. The perimeter is 42 cm. Find the length and the width.

3. The length of a rectangle is 3 km more than twice the width. The perimeter is 54 km. Find the length and the width.

4. The length of a rectangle is 2 m less than 3 times the width. The perimeter is 68 m. Find the length and the width.

5. Side x of a triangle is 2 cm longer than side y. Side z is 5 cm shorter than twice side y. The perimeter is 49 cm. Find the length of each side.

6. The perimeter of a triangle is 40 m. The first side is twice the second. The third side is 5 m more than the first. Find the length of each side.

7. The perimeter of a triangle is 38 cm. The first side is 3 cm less than the second, and the third is 5 cm more than the second. Find the lengths of the three sides.

8. The perimeter of a triangle is 47 km. The first side is 5 km less than twice the second, and the third is 2 km more than the first. Find the lengths of the sides.

9. The base of an isosceles triangle is 8 m. The perimeter is 30 m. Find the lengths of the two congruent sides.

10. One of the two congruent sides of an isosceles triangle is 7 cm. The perimeter is 24 cm. Find the base.

PART B

11. A square and an equilateral triangle have the same perimeter. Each side of the square is 12 m. Find the length of each side of the triangle.

12. A square and an equilateral triangle have the same perimeter. Each side of the triangle is 20 cm. Find the length of each side of the square.

13. A rectangle and an equilateral triangle have the same perimeter. The length of the rectangle is twice the width. Each side of the triangle is 18 cm. Find the length and width of the rectangle.

14. Each side of an equilateral triangle is 2 m more than each side of a square. Their perimeters are the same. Find the length of each side of the triangle.

PART C

15. The length of a rectangle is 3 cm less than twice the width. If the length is decreased by 2 cm and the width by 1 cm, the perimeter will be 24 cm. Find the dimensions of the original rectangle.

16. A rectangular field is 4 times as long as it is wide. If the length is decreased by 10 m and the width is increased by 2 m, the perimeter will be 64 m. Find the dimensions of the original field.

Mathematics in the Hospital

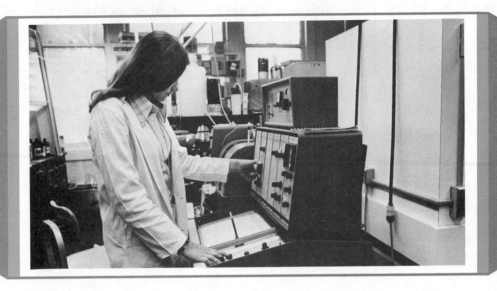

Many important jobs are done in hospitals by technicians and lab specialists. Pictured above is a technician setting up one of the many machines that are used to monitor a patient's health. Below is a lab specialist analyzing blood samples.

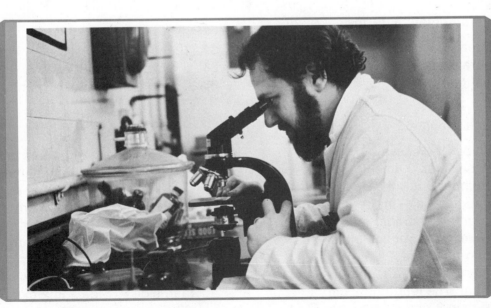

Chapter Three Review

Which members of the given replacement set are solutions of the sentence? $[p.\ 56]$

1. $20 = 2x + 6$ {7, 8, 9}

2. $13 + 2x = 3 + 6x$ {1, 2, 3, 4, 5}

3. $23 + 9y = 50$ {1, 3, 5, 7}

4. $7x - 21 = 5x - 9$ {5, 6}

5. $8y - 36 = 24$ {4, 6, 8}

6. $6y - 13 = -52 + 19y$ {3, 8, 11}

7. $-4c - 46 = -2$ {-9, -10, -11}

8. $4x - 4 = 3x - 2$ {1, 2, 3, 4}

Solve. $[p.\ 59,\ 64,\ 68]$

9. $-7 = 5x + 1$

10. $8r - 22 = 58$

11. $3y - 6 = 9$

12. $-39 = -3 + 12y$

13. $10c - 15 = -5$

14. $5x - 8 = -8$

15. $1 + 4x = 55 - 8$

16. $-42 + 39 = 11 - 2z$

17. $5 + 8x = 6x + 11$

18. $3c + 2 = -70 + 15c$

19. $9x - 20 = 8x + 2$

20. $27 - 5y = 4y - 6y$

21. $3z - 2z = -8 - z$

22. $33 - 4x = 1 + 4x$

23. $x + 12 + x = -14$

24. $16 - 9 = 5x - 8$

25. $-4(2x + 6) = -3x + 1$

26. $5 - 10x = -(3 - 2x)$

27. $6(y + 3) = 9 - (3 - 2y)$

28. $7(x - 1) = -2(-4x + 3)$

29. $5x - 4(2x - 6) = 3x - 24$

30. $-3(2x + 1) + 5 = -(4x - 9) + 5x$

31. $8y - 2(-3y + 4) = -(y + 38)$

32. $12 - 3(y + 1) = 1 - 5(y - 2)$

Write in mathematical terms. $[p.\ 70]$

33. 6 increased by x

34. 12 less than y

35. n decreased by 3

36. 6 more than 3 times x

37. 5 less than twice y

38. 7 less than 9 times a number

Solve each problem. $[p.\ 72,\ 76,\ 80,\ 84]$

39. A number increased by 8 is the same as 3 times the number. Find the number.

40. The sum of two numbers is 26. The second is 2 less than 3 times the first. Find the two numbers.

41. One number is 17 more than another. If the greater number is increased by 3, the result is 5 times the smaller. Find the two numbers.

42. Paula had 7 times as many nickels as quarters. Their value was $1.80. How many quarters did she have?

43. The perimeter of a rectangle is 68 cm. The length is 2 cm more than 3 times the width. Find the length and the width.

44. Side x of a triangle is 3 m longer than side y. Side z is 2 m shorter than twice side y. The perimeter is 17 m. Find the lengths of the three sides.

Chapter Three Test

Which members of the given replacement set are solutions of the sentence?

1. $13 + x = 5x + 1$ $\{3, 4\}$
2. $9y - 7 = 11 + 7y$ $\{7, 8, 9\}$
3. $5x + 2 = 8x - 10$ $\{1, 2, 4, 5\}$
4. $-6 + 8z = 21z - 45$ $\{3, 8, 11\}$
5. $5x - 7 = 4x - 12$ $\{-4, -5, -6\}$
6. $8y - 9 = 5y + 3$ $\{1, 2, 4, 5\}$

Solve.

7. $38 - 8x = -18$
8. $6y + 7 = 7$
9. $15r - 5 = -35$
10. $8c - 9 = -2c - 9$
11. $9 + 15 = 10z - 7$
12. $-2 + 5x = 38 - 10$
13. $3(x + 5) = x + 21$
14. $-(3x + 2) = x - 50$
15. $6y + (1 - 3y) = 16 - 4(2y + 1)$
16. $7(x + 1) - 1 = 2 - (5 + 2x)$
17. $2(3 - x) - 7 = 9 - 2(3 + 2x)$
18. $(x + 2) + (x + 4) = 42 - (x + 6)$

Write in mathematical terms.

19. 7 decreased by 2
20. 5 increased by x
21. x less than twice y
22. 8 more than 3 times a number

Solve each problem.

23. Seven less than 4 times a number is the same as the number increased by 8. Find the number.

24. The greater of two numbers is 8 less than 3 times the smaller. Their sum is 36. Find the two numbers.

25. A collection of 25 dimes and quarters amounts to $5.05. How many of each kind of coin are there?

26. The length of a rectangle is 3 m less than 3 times the width. The perimeter is 66 m. Find the length and the width.

Sequences

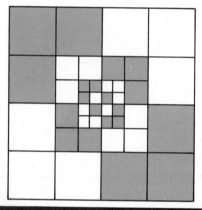

Mathematics is concerned with patterns formed by numbers. A pattern is displayed in each sequence of numbers below.

PROJECT

See if you can find the pattern. Then give the next three numbers in the sequence.

1. −6, −7, −8, −9, −10, . . .

2. 3, 9, 27, 81, . . .

3. −3, −3, −3, −3, . . .

4. 2, −2, 2, −2, 2, . . .

5. .1, .01, .001, .0001, . . .

6. 3, −6, 12, −24, . . .

7. 1, 2, 4, 5, 7, 8, 10, 11, . . .

8. 1, 4, 9, 16, 25, . . .

9. 1, 8, 27, 64, . . .

10. −6, −2, 2, 6, 10, . . .

11. $\dfrac{1}{2}, \dfrac{2}{3}, \dfrac{3}{4}, \dfrac{4}{5}, \ldots$

12. $\dfrac{1}{2}$, 2, 8, 32, . . .

13. 0, 3, 8, 15, . . .

14. $\dfrac{1}{2}, \dfrac{4}{3}, \dfrac{9}{4}, \dfrac{16}{5}, \ldots$

15. 0, 7, 26, 63, . . .

16. 0, 1, 1, 2, 3, 5, 8, 13, . . .

Sets

 REVIEW CAPSULE

A *set* is a collection of objects. The objects are *members,* or *elements* of the set. Braces are used to enclose the names of the elements of a set.

Set A   Set B
↓   ↓
$A = \{2, 4, 6\}$ $B = \{-2, -1, 0, 1, 2\}$

elements of A   elements of B

Definition of equal sets ⟶ | Two sets are *equal* if they have the same elements.

Examples of equal sets

The order of listing the elements does not matter. ⟶ $\{-1, 3, 8\} = \{3, 8, -1\}$ $\{1, 2, 3\} = \{1, 1+1, 1+2\}$

Finite sets		Infinite sets	
✓ ↘		✓ ↘	
$\{1, 2, 3\}$	$\{-1, 0, 1, 2\}$	$\{1, 2, 3, 4, \ldots\}$	$\{\text{integers}\}$
A definite number of elements		No definite number of elements	

The three dots mean the pattern continues forever.

It is not possible to list all the members of an infinite set.

EXAMPLE 1 Tell whether each set is finite or infinite. Then describe each set in words.

$\{5, 6, 7\}$ finite
$\{2, 4, 6, 8, \ldots\}$ infinite

Between 4 and 8 means *not* including 4 and 8. Other descriptions are possible.

$\{5, 6, 7\}$ is the set of whole numbers between 4 and 8.
$\{2, 4, 6, 8, \ldots\}$ is the set of positive even integers.

EXAMPLE 2 $C = \{$integers between -3 and $2\}$. Describe set C by listing its elements.

Examine the integers on a number line.

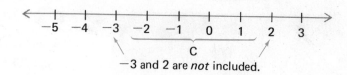

-3 and 2 are *not* included.

Thus, $C = \{-2, -1, 0, 1\}$.

EXAMPLE 3 $A = \{$integers between 5 and $6\}$. Describe set A by listing its elements.

There are no integers between 5 and 6. A set can have no elements. ⟶ Thus, $A = \phi$ (the set with no elements).

Definition of empty set ⟶

> The set with no elements is the empty set.
>
> Symbol for the empty set: ϕ

EXAMPLE 4 Find the set of all solutions of $6x - 9 = 2x + 19$. Then graph the set.

The replacement set is $\{$all numbers$\}$.

$$6x - 9 = 2x + 19$$
$$4x - 9 = 19$$
$$4x = 28$$
$$x = 7$$

7 is the solution. ⟶

A set can have only 1 element. ⟶ Thus, $\{7\}$ is the set of all solutions.

To graph $\{7\}$, place a dot at 7 on a number line.

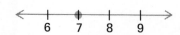

Definition of solution set ⟶
For Example 4, the solution set is $\{7\}$.

> The *solution set* of an open sentence is the set of all members of the replacement set which are solutions of the sentence.

EXAMPLE 5 Find the solution set of $x + 5 = x + 2$.

Add $-x$ to each side. ⟶

$$x + 5 = x + 2$$
$$\underline{-x \qquad -x}$$
$$5 = \quad 2 \quad \leftarrow \text{ False sentence}$$

There is no number which makes $x + 5 = x + 2$ true. ⟶ Thus, the solution set of $x + 5 = x + 2$ is ϕ.

EXERCISES

PART A

Which sets are equal to $\{1, 3, 5, 6\}$?

1. $\{1, 6, 3, 5\}$

2. $\{1, 3, 7, 6\}$

3. $\{5, 2, 1, 6\}$

4. $\{6, 3, 1, 5\}$

5. $\{1, 1 + 2, 1 + 4, 1 + 5\}$

6. $\{3, 8 - 1, 7 - 1, 1\}$

For each set, tell whether it is finite or infinite. Then describe the set in words.

7. $\{0, 1, 2, 3, 4\}$

8. $\{0, 1, 2, 3, 4, \ldots\}$

9. $\{1, 3, 5, 7, \ldots\}$

10. $\{-1, -2, -3, -4\}$

11. ϕ

12. $\{\ldots -2, -1, 0, 1, 2, \ldots\}$

Describe each set by listing its elements.

13. $A = \{$positive integers less than 6$\}$

14. $B = \{$positive integers greater than 8$\}$

15. $C = \{$negative integers between -4 and $-1\}$

16. $D = \{$integers between 8 and 9$\}$

Find the solution set of each sentence. Then graph it.

17. $5y - 8 = 20 + y$

18. $3x - 5 = 7 + 3x$

19. $9z + 17 = 11z + 3$

20. $9 + 4y = 4y - 12$

21. $8y - 22 = -14 + 6y$

22. $3x + 4 = -68 + 15x$

23. $-8y + 7y = 4 - 2y$

24. $13 + 20 = 10x - 7$

25. $27 - 6y = -8y + 5y$

26. $-3x + 2 = x - 8 - 4x$

27. $x + x + 5x = -7$

28. $6x + 8 + x = -4 + 7x$

PART B

EXAMPLE Find the solution set of $7x + 2 = 2 + 3x + 4x$. Then graph it.

$$7x + 2 = 2 + \underline{3x + 4x}$$
$$7x + 2 = 2 + \quad 7x$$
$$7x = 7x$$
$$x = x$$

Add -2 to each side. ⟶

Divide each side by 7. ⟶

Every number also makes $7x + 2 = 2 + 3x + 4x$ true.

Every number makes $x = x$ true.

Thus, the solution set is $\{$all numbers$\}$.

Graph of $\{$all numbers$\}$ ⟶

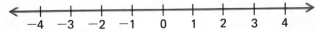

Find the solution set of each sentence. Then graph it.

29. $3x - 6 = -6 + 3x$

30. $x + x - 2x = -12$

31. $4x + 7 + 5x = 7 + 9x$

PART C

Graph the solution set of each.

32. $8 - [5 - (4 + x)] = 8 - (6 - x)$

33. $8x - 3[4 - (2 - x)] = 5x - 6$

Inequalities

▶ REVIEW CAPSULE

SENTENCES

Types & Symbols		Examples	
EQUATIONS	True	False	Open
= is equal to	$2+3=5$	$4+6=9$	$x+3=8$
INEQUALITIES	True	False	Open
≠ is not equal to	$5 \neq 7$	$1+2 \neq 3$	$y \neq 6$
< is less than	$4 < 8$	$10 < 7$	$x < 2$
> is greater than	$7 > 2$	$3 > 9$	$c+2 > 4$

$a < b$ means $b > a$.

EXAMPLE 1   Graph the solution set of $x < 4$.

Read: x is less than 4. ⟶
Many numbers make $x < 4$ true.

$$
\begin{array}{r}
x < 4 \\
\hline
3\tfrac{1}{2} < 4 \\
3 < 4 \\
1 < 4 \\
0 < 4 \\
-2 < 4 \\
-4\tfrac{1}{3} < 4 \\
-5 < 4
\end{array}
$$

We could go on forever. ⟶

Mark the points with the ⟶
coordinates listed above.

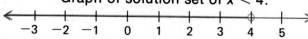

Any point to the left of the point with coordinate 4 has a coordinate less than 4. We draw an arrow to show all such points.

Graph of solution set of $x < 4$:

Note the circle around 4.
4 is not in the solution set.

Read: the set of all numbers x, such that x is less than 4. ————————→

The solution set of $x < 4$ is an infinite set.
$$\{x \mid x < 4\}$$

EXAMPLE 2   Graph the solution set of $x > -2$.

Read: x is greater than −2. ————————→
Substitute numbers for x. ————————→

We could go on forever. ————————→

$$
\begin{array}{rcl}
x & > & -2 \\
\hline
-1 & > & -2 \\
-\dfrac{1}{2} & > & -2 \\
0 & > & -2 \\
3 & > & -2 \\
20 & > & -2 \\
\end{array}
$$

Graph of $\{x \mid x > -2\}$ ————————→
−2 is not in the solution set.

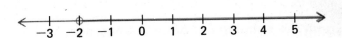

−1 >−2. For example, a temperature of 1° below 0° is warmer than a temperature of 2° below 0°.

Any point to the right of the point with coordinate −2 has a coordinate greater than −2.

EXAMPLE 3   Graph the solution set of $x \le 1$.
$x \le 1$ means x is less than or equal to 1.

Graph of $\{x \mid x \le 1\}$ ————————→
The dot shows that 1 is in the solution set.

Any number which is less than or equal to 1 makes $x \le 1$ true. **Thus,** the graph includes 1 and all points to the left.

EXAMPLE 4   Graph the solution set of $-3 \le x$.

$$-3 \le x \text{ means } x \ge -3$$
x is greater than or equal to −3

Read the variable first. ————————→

Graph of $\{x \mid x \ge -3\}$ ————————→
−3 is in the solution set.

Any number which is greater than or equal to −3 makes $x \ge -3$ true. **Thus,** the graph includes −3 and all points to the right.

ORAL EXERCISES

Tell which inequality symbol, > or <, will make the sentence true.

1. 5 ? 8   **2.** 9 ? 6   **3.** −5 ? −2   **4.** −3 ? −5   **5.** −4 ? −1

6. −13 ? −18   **7.** −5 ? 1   **8.** −6 ? 14   **9.** 5 ? −3   **10.** −8 ? −12

Read each inequality. [Hint: Read the variable first.]
Then replace x with a number that will make the inequality true.

11. $x > -5$ **12.** $-8 \leq x$ **13.** $x < +3$ **14.** $-6 \geq x$ **15.** $-4 < x$ **16.** $x \leq -8$

EXERCISES

PART A

Graph the solution set of each sentence.

1. $b < 3$ **2.** $y > 1$ **3.** $x \leq 5$ **4.** $d \geq -5$

5. $x \leq -2$ **6.** $y > -4$ **7.** $2 < c$ **8.** $r < 4$

9. $-6 \leq y$ **10.** $x > -5$ **11.** $2 > g$ **12.** $x \leq 0$

13. $4 < y$ **14.** $z \geq 4$ **15.** $r \geq 4$ **16.** $y < -1$

17. $a < -3$ **18.** $r > 0$ **19.** $x \geq 1$ **20.** $a \leq 3$

21. $b \leq -3$ **22.** $1 > z$ **23.** $y < -2$ **24.** $3 \leq c$

25. $c \geq -1$ **26.** $-2 \geq x$ **27.** $r \leq -4$ **28.** $x < -5$

29. $x > -2$ **30.** $x > -1$ **31.** $a \geq 2$ **32.** $y \leq 2$

33. $1 \leq b$ **34.** $y < -3$ **35.** $5 \geq g$ **36.** $r < -4$

PART B

EXAMPLE   Graph the solution set of $y \neq -\frac{1}{3}$.

Every number except $-\frac{1}{3}$
is in the solution set. ⟶

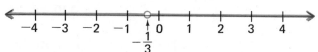

Graph the solution set of each sentence.

37. $x \neq 2\frac{1}{2}$ **38.** $-\frac{1}{4} > y$ **39.** $x < \frac{5}{4}$ **40.** $-\frac{3}{2} \leq x$

41. $\frac{1}{2} \geq y$ **42.** $0 \neq x$ **43.** $x \geq -\frac{2}{3}$ **44.** $0 \geq y$

PART C

Graph the solution set of each sentence.

45. $x \not\geq 5$ **46.** $-8 \not> x$ **47.** $-2.5 \not\neq x$ **48.** $x \not< -8.1$

Computer Programs: Input and Output

Some computer programs call for information to be entered into the machine before calculations can be done and the answer printed out.

PROBLEM

Write a flow chart to evaluate $4x + 3y - 5$ for given values of x and y.

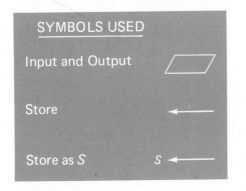

SYMBOLS USED

Input and Output

Store

Store as S $S \leftarrow$

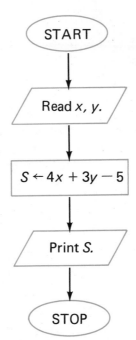

START

Read x, y.

Input: Feed the values of x and y into the machine.

$S \leftarrow 4x + 3y - 5$

Replace x and y with input values. Compute. Store as S.

Print S.

Output: Print the result.

STOP

Evaluate $4x + 3y - 5$ for the given values of x and y. Use the flow chart above.

1. $x = 2$, $y = -3$ **2.** $x = 5$, $y = 4$ **3.** $x = -1$, $y = 5$

4. Write a flow chart to show how to find the average of three numbers.

Properties for Inequalities

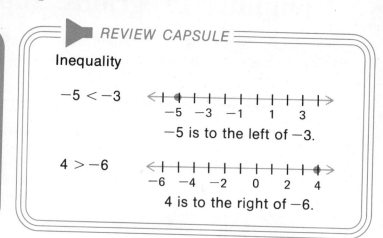

▶ REVIEW CAPSULE

Inequality

$-5 < -3$

-5 is to the left of -3.

$4 > -6$

4 is to the right of -6.

EXAMPLE 1   Consider the inequality $4 < 7$. Add 2 to each side. Use the symbol, $<$ or $>$, to write a true inequality.

Different numbers ⟶
Same number ⟶
Different numbers ⟶

$$\begin{array}{r} 4 < 7 \\ +2 \quad +2 \\ \hline 6 < 9 \end{array}$$ same order

EXAMPLE 2   Consider $-6 < -1$. Add -3 to each side. Write a true inequality.

$$\begin{array}{r} -6 < -1 \\ -3 \quad -3 \\ \hline -9 < -4 \end{array}$$ same order

EXAMPLE 3   Consider $4 \geq -2$. Add 7 to each side. Write a true inequality.

$$\begin{array}{r} 4 \geq -2 \\ +7 \quad +7 \\ \hline 11 \geq 5 \end{array}$$ same order

EXAMPLE 4   Consider $8 > -1$. Add -10 to each side. Write a true inequality.

$$\begin{array}{r} 8 > -1 \\ -10 \quad -10 \\ \hline -2 > -11 \end{array}$$ same order

Addition Property for Inequalities

If $a < b,$ If $a > b,$
then $a + c < b + c.$ then $a + c > b + c.$
Adding the same number to each side of an inequality does not change the order.

EXAMPLE 5 Consider $2 < 7$. Multiply each side by 3 and write a true inequality. Then multiply each side by -3 and write a true inequality.

Multiplying by a negative number reverses the order.

$$
\begin{array}{c}
2 < 7 \\
2(3) \ ? \ 7(3) \\
6 < 21
\end{array}
\begin{array}{c}
\text{same} \\
\text{order}
\end{array}
\qquad
\begin{array}{c}
2 < 7 \\
2(-3) \ ? \ 7(-3) \\
-6 > -21
\end{array}
\begin{array}{c}
\text{reverse} \\
\text{order}
\end{array}
$$

EXAMPLE 6 Consider $3 \geq -5$. Multiply each side by 2 and write a true inequality. Then multiply each side by -2 and write a true inequality.

Multiplying by a negative number reverses the order.

$$
\begin{array}{c}
3 \geq -5 \\
3(2) \ ? \ -5(2) \\
6 \geq -10
\end{array}
\begin{array}{c}
\text{same} \\
\text{order}
\end{array}
\qquad
\begin{array}{c}
3 \geq -5 \\
3(-2) \ ? \ -5(-2) \\
-6 \leq 10
\end{array}
\begin{array}{c}
\text{reverse} \\
\text{order}
\end{array}
$$

Examples 5 and 6 suggest this property.

Multiplication Property for Inequalities

If $a < b$ and $c > 0,$ c is positive. The order of the inequality is the same.
then $ac < bc.$

If $a < b$ and $c < 0,$ c is negative. The order of the inequality is reversed.
then $ac > bc.$

EXAMPLE 7

Consider $9 > 6$. Divide each side by 3 and write a true inequality. Then divide each side by -3 and write a true inequality.

$$
\begin{array}{c}
9 > 6 \\
\dfrac{9}{3} \ ? \ \dfrac{6}{3} \\
3 > 2
\end{array}
\quad \text{same order}
\qquad
\begin{array}{c}
9 > 6 \\
\dfrac{9}{-3} \ ? \ \dfrac{6}{-3} \\
-3 < -2
\end{array}
\quad \text{reverse order}
$$

EXAMPLE 8

Consider $-4 \le 12$. Divide each side by 4 and write a true inequality. Then divide each side by -4 and write a true inequality.

$$
\begin{array}{c}
-4 \le 12 \\
\dfrac{-4}{4} \ ? \ \dfrac{12}{4} \\
-1 \le 3
\end{array}
\quad \text{same order}
\qquad
\begin{array}{c}
-4 \le 12 \\
\dfrac{-4}{-4} \ ? \ \dfrac{12}{-4} \\
1 \ge -3
\end{array}
\quad \text{reverse order}
$$

Examples 7 and 8 suggest this property.

Division Property for Inequalities

If $a < b$ and $c > 0$, then $\dfrac{a}{c} < \dfrac{b}{c}$. | c is positive. The order of the inequality is the same.

If $a < b$ and $c < 0$, then $\dfrac{a}{c} > \dfrac{b}{c}$. | c is negative. The order of the inequality is reversed.

EXAMPLE 9

Tell what operation was performed on each side of the first inequality to give the second inequality.

$$-21 < 14 \qquad 3 > -2$$

$$
\left.
\begin{array}{cc}
\dfrac{-21}{-7}; & \dfrac{14}{-7} \\
\downarrow & \downarrow \\
3 & -2
\end{array}
\right\}
$$

Thus, each side of $-21 < 14$ was divided by -7 to give $3 > -2$.

SUMMARY Properties for Inequalities

ORAL EXERCISES

If the indicated operation is performed, will the order of the inequality change?

1. $4 > 3$ Add 6.
2. $-6 < -2$ Divide by -2.
3. $6 > -1$ Multiply by -4.
4. $8 > -4$ Divide by 4.
5. $-8 < -2$ Divide by 2.
6. $9 > -2$ Add -5.
7. $-3 < 2$ Multiply by 7.
8. $4 > 0$ Multiply by 5.
9. $0 < 5$ Multiply by -3.
10. $-9 \leq -3$ Divide by -3.
11. $-24 < 12$ Divide by 3.
12. $-8 < 1$ Add 7.
13. $7 > -1$ Multiply by -6.
14. $-6 \leq 2$ Divide by -2.
15. $2 \leq 3$ Divide by 1.
16. $-5 \leq 0$ Add -4.
17. $0 > -4$ Add 2.
18. $6 \geq 3$ Divide by -3.
19. $9 \geq -4$ Add -6.
20. $0 < 8$ Multiply by 6.
21. $0 \leq 5$ Multiply by 3.
22. $-4 < 0$ Multiply by -5.
23. $3 \leq 7$ Add 4.
24. $-8 < 6$ Multiply by -1.
25. $-2 > -3$ Add 8.
26. $-6 > -7$ Multiply by 4.

EXERCISES

PART A

For each inequality in Exercises 1–26 above, write a true inequality by performing the indicated operation on each side.

PART B

Tell what operation was performed on each side of the first inequality to give the second inequality.

27. $5 > 3$ $2 > 0$
28. $4 \leq 7$ $8 \leq 14$
29. $-6 < 2$ $18 > -6$
30. $8 > 4$ $2 > 1$
31. $-2 \geq -3$ $3 \geq 2$
32. $3 \geq -1$ $12 \geq -4$
33. $-9 < -6$ $3 > 2$
34. $-8 < 2$ $-5 < 5$
35. $2 > 0$ $-6 < 0$
36. $-7 < 14$ $1 > -2$

Solving Inequalities

EXAMPLE 1 Find and graph the solution set of
$4x + 7 > 3x + 10$.

Add $-3x$ to each side. ⟶

The order is the same. ⟶

Add -7 to each side. ⟶

Same order ⟶

$$4x + 7 > \quad 3x + 10$$
$$\underline{-3x \qquad\quad -3x}$$
$$1x + 7 > \qquad\quad 10$$
$$\underline{\qquad -7 \qquad\qquad -7}$$
$$1x \quad > \qquad 3, \text{ or } x > 3$$

Any number greater than 3 should make
$4x + 7 > 3x + 10$ true.

Check two numbers greater than 3.

Try 4.

$4x + 7 > 3x + 10$	
$4(4) + 7$	$3(4) + 10$
$16 + 7$	$12 + 10$
23	22
23 > 22 True	

Try 7.

$4x + 7 > 3x + 10$	
$4(7) + 7$	$3(7) + 10$
$28 + 7$	$21 + 10$
35	31
35 > 31 True	

Check two numbers *not* greater than 3.

Try 3.

$4x + 7 > 3x + 10$	
$4(3) + 7$	$3(3) + 10$
$12 + 7$	$9 + 10$
19	19
19 > 19	
	False

Try -2.

$4x + 7 > 3x + 10$	
$4(-2) + 7$	$3(-2) + 10$
$-8 + 7$	$-6 + 10$
-1	4
$-1 > 4$	
	False

We could check numbers forever!

It appears that any number greater than 3 makes the sentence true. Any number less than or equal to 3 makes the sentence false.

Thus, the solution set of $4x + 7 > 3x + 10$ is
$$\{x \mid x > 3\}.$$

3 is not a solution.

Graph of $\{x \mid x > 3\}$ ——————

EXAMPLE 2 Find and graph the solution set of
$5x - 10 \leq 6x - 8.$

$$
\begin{array}{r}
5x - 10 \leq 6x - 8 \\
-5x -5x \\
\hline
-10 \leq 1x - 8 \\
+8 +8 \\
\hline
-2 \leq x \\
x \geq -2
\end{array}
$$

$-2 \leq x$ means $x \geq -2$. ——————→

Check -2 and several numbers greater than -2.

Thus, the solution set is $\{x \mid x \geq -2\}$.

-2 is a solution.

Graph of $\{x \mid x \geq -2\}$ ——————

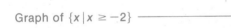

EXAMPLE 3 Find and graph the solution set of
$10x + 3 < 7x - 9.$

$$
\begin{array}{r}
10x + 3 < 7x - 9 \\
-7x \phantom{+ 3 <} -7x \\
\hline
3x + 3 < -9 \\
-3 \phantom{x + 3 <} -3 \\
\hline
3x < -12
\end{array}
$$

$$\frac{3x}{3} < \frac{-12}{3}$$

$$x < -4$$

Divide each side by 3. ——————→

The order is the same since 3 is positive.

Thus, the solution set is $\{x \mid x < -4\}$.

Graph of $\{x \mid x < -4\}$ ——————

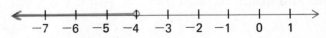

EXAMPLE 4 Solve $10x + 3 < 7x - 9$ again. This time add $-10x$ to each side rather than $-7x$. Is the result the same?

Add $-10x$ to each side. ──────────────→

Add 9 to each side. ──────────────→

Divide each side by -3.

Reverse the order, since -3 is ──────→
negative.

$-4 > x$ means $x < -4$. ──────────────→

$$\begin{array}{r} 10x + 3 < \quad 7x - 9 \\ -10x \qquad -10x \\ \hline 3 < -3x \; - 9 \\ +9 \qquad\quad +9 \\ \hline 12 < -3x \\ \dfrac{12}{-3} > \dfrac{-3x}{-3} \\ -4 > x \\ x < -4 \end{array}$$

Yes, the result is the same.

EXERCISES

PART A

Find and graph the solution set.

1. $2 + 5x > -8$

2. $10x + 14 \geq -36$

3. $-17 < 9y - 8$

4. $7 > 3x - 8$

5. $-2x - 28 > -5x - 7$

6. $5y + 8 < -4 + 17y$

7. $4a + 1 \leq 3a + 9$

8. $8x - 11 \geq 5x + 7$

9. $7d - 6 < -24 + d$

10. $7y + 3 > 10y - 12$

11. $-3r + 13 \leq 2r - 7$

12. $-22 + 10x > -14 + 8x$

13. $25 - 4x \geq 4x + 1$

14. $8 - 7y < y + 8$

15. $-x + 12 > 3x - 4$

16. $8 - 3x < -4x + 7$

17. $9x - 5 \leq 25 + 4x$

18. $9y + 7 \geq 13 + 11y$

19. $10y - 24 > 3y - 3$

20. $6x - 18 \leq 3x - 6$

21. $6x + 3 \geq 91 - 5x$

22. $4y + 3 > 9y - 17$

23. $12y - 8 > 55 + 5y$

24. $4x + 8 > -9 + 5x$

PART B

Find and graph the solution set. [Hint: Remove parentheses first.]

25. $2(x + 5) > x + 15$

26. $4(y + 1) < 7y - 2(3 - y)$

PART C

Find and graph the solution set. [Hint: Work within brackets first.]

27. $7 - [4 - (3x - 2)] < 13 + 3x$

28. $2x - [8 - (3 - x)] > 2 - (5 - x)$

Intersection and Union of Sets

▶ REVIEW CAPSULE

$A = \{1, 2, 3\}$ $B = \{1, 2, 3, 4, 5\}$

A is a subset of *B*
means
every element of *A* is also in *B*.

Write $A \subseteq B$ to mean *A* is a subset of *B*.

EXAMPLE 1 Consider sets *A* and *B* above. Is *B* a subset of *A*?

Think: Is every element of *B* also an element of *A*? $B \not\subseteq A$ means *B* is not a subset of *A*. —————→ *B* contains the elements 4 and 5, which are not in *A*. **Thus, $B \not\subseteq A$.**

We make these agreements about subsets.

> Every set is a subset of itself.
> The empty set is a subset of every set.

EXAMPLE 2 List all the subsets of *C*. How many are there?
$C = \{5, 7, 9\}$

Subsets of *C*:

Every set is a subset of itself. —————→ $\{5, 7, 9\}$
$\{5, 7\}$
$\{5, 9\}$
$\{7, 9\}$
$\{5\}$
$\{7\}$
The empty set is a subset of every set. —————→ $\{9\}$
ϕ

Thus, *C* has 8 subsets.

Consider sets R and S.

$$R = \{2, 4, 6, 8\} \quad S = \{2, 6, 10\}$$

$$\{2, 6\}$$

The *intersection* of two sets contains all the elements common to *both* sets.

The *intersection* of sets R and S is $\{2, 6\}$.

$\cap$ is the symbol for intersection.

We write $\{2, 4, 6, 8\} \cap \{2, 6, 10\} = \{2, 6\}$,

or $\quad R \quad \cap \quad S \quad = \{2, 6\}$.

EXAMPLE 3 $X = \{-3, -2, 0, 1, 2\}$ and $Y = \{-2, 1, 2, 3\}$.
Find $X \cap Y$.

-2, 1, and 2 are common to sets X and Y.

$$X \cap Y = \{-2, 1, 2\}.$$

Consider sets P and Q.

$$P = \{1, 2, 3, 7\} \quad Q = \{2, 3, 4\}$$

$$\{1, 2, 3, 4, 7\}$$

The *union* of two sets contains the elements which are in the 1st set, or 2nd set, or in both sets.

The *union* of sets P and Q is $\{1, 2, 3, 4, 7\}$.

$\cup$ is the symbol for union.

We write $\{1, 2, 3, 7\} \cup \{2, 3, 4\} = \{1, 2, 3, 4, 7\}$

or $\quad P \quad \cup \quad Q \quad = \{1, 2, 3, 4, 7\}$

EXAMPLE 4 $A = \{2, 4, 6\}$ and $B = \{5, 7, 9, 10\}$. Find $A \cap B$.

There are no elements common to both sets.

$$A \cap B = \{\ \}, \text{ or } \phi$$

EXAMPLE 5 $C = \{0, 2, 4, 6\}$ and $D = \{0, 1, 2\}$. Find $C \cup D$.

Each element in $C \cup D$ is in C, or in D, or in both.

$$C \cup D = \{0, 1, 2, 4, 6\}.$$

SUMMARY

Intersection
$A \cap B$ **is the set of all elements common to both set** A **and set** B.

Union
$A \cup B$ **is the set of elements belonging to set** A **or set** B **or both set** A **and set** B.

EXERCISES

PART A

For each pair of sets, determine if $A \subseteq B$. Then determine if $B \subseteq A$.

1. $A = \{0, 2, 4\}$ $B = \{0, 4\}$
2. $A = \{1, 2, 3\}$ $B = \{2, 3, 4\}$
3. $A = \{-1, -2\}$ $B = \{-3, -2, -1\}$
4. $A = \{4, 5, 6\}$ $B = \{6, 4, 5\}$
5. $A = \{2, 4, 6\}$ $B = \{2, 4, 6, 8, 10\}$
6. $A = \{-6, 0, 6\}$ $B = \{-7, 0, 7\}$
7. $A = \phi$ $B = \{2, 3, 6\}$
8. $A = \{1, 2, 3, 4\}$ $B = \{1, 3\}$
9. $A = \{1, 2, 3\}$ $B = \{1, 1 + 1, 1 + 2\}$
10. $A = \{-1, 0, 1\}$ $B = \{-2, -1, 0, 1, 2\}$
11. $A = \{5\}$ $B = \{6, 7, 8\}$
12. $A = \{0\}$ $B = \phi$
13. $A = \{\text{integers}\}$ $B = \{\text{negative integers}\}$
14. $A = \{0\}$ $B = \{\text{integers}\}$
15. $A = \{\text{positive integers}\}$
    $B = \{\text{whole numbers}\}$
16. $A = \{\text{negative integers}\}$
    $B = \{\text{positive integers}\}$

List all the subsets of each set. Then give the number of subsets.

17. $\{1, 2\}$
18. $\{2, 4, 6\}$
19. $\{8\}$
20. ϕ
21. $\{-1, 0\}$
22. $\{1, 3, 5, 7\}$

For each pair of sets, find the intersection. Then find the union.

23. $\{1, 3, 5\}$ $\{3, 5\}$
24. $\{2, 4, 6\}$ $\{6, 4, 2\}$
25. $\{4, 5, 6\}$ $\{7\}$
26. $\{1, 4, 5, 9\}$ $\{1, 2, 5\}$
27. ϕ $\{0, 2, 4\}$
28. $\{-4, 0, 4\}$ $\{-8, 0, 8\}$
29. $\{-1, -2, -3\}$ $\{1, 2, 3\}$
30. $\{1, 2, -1, -2\}$ $\{0, -1, -2\}$
31. $\{1, 4, 5\}$ $\{1, 2, 3, 4, 5\}$
32. $\{0\}$ ϕ
33. $\{2, 4, 6\}$ $\{6, 8, 10\}$
34. $\{1, 3, 5, 7\}$ $\{2, 4, 6, 8\}$
35. $\{5, 8, 9, 2\}$ $\{2, 5, 8, 9\}$
36. $\{0, 2, 4, 6\}$ $\{0, 3, 6, 9\}$

PART B

For each pair of sets, find the intersection. Then find the union.

37. $\{0, 2, 4, 6, 8, \ldots\}$ $\{1, 3, 5, 7, 9, \ldots\}$
38. $\{0, -1, -2, -3, \ldots\}$ $\{0, 1, 2, 3, \ldots\}$
39. $\{0, 2, 4, 6, 8, \ldots\}$ $\{0, 3, 6, 9, 12, \ldots\}$
40. $\{0, -2, -4, -6, -8, \ldots\}$
    $\{0, -4, -8, -12, -16, \ldots\}$
41. $\{0\}$ $\{\text{integers}\}$
42. $\{\text{negative integers}\}$ $\{\text{positive integers}\}$
43. $\{\text{positive integers}\}$ $\{\text{whole numbers}\}$
44. $\{\text{integers}\}$ $\{\text{negative integers}\}$

PART C

$A = \{0, 1, 2, 3, 4\}$ $B = \{1, 3, 5\}$, and $C = \{0, 2, 4, 6\}$. **List each set.**

45. $(A \cup B) \cup C$
46. $A \cup (B \cup C)$
47. $(A \cap B) \cap C$
48. $A \cap (B \cap C)$
49. $(A \cup B) \cap C$
50. $(A \cap B) \cup C$

Motion Problems

OBJECTIVE

■ To solve problems about motion

REVIEW CAPSULE

A bus traveled at a speed of 80 km/h. How far did it travel in 3 hours?

|—80—+—80—+—80—| $d = rt$
|———240———| $= 80(3)$, or 240

Thus, it traveled 240 kilometers.

EXAMPLE 1

Read 10 km/h as 10 km per hour.

Two cars traveled in opposite directions from the same point. The rate of one car was 10 km/h less than the rate of the other car. After 10 hours, the cars were 900 kilometers apart. Find the rate of each car.

Draw a diagram. ⟶

Represent the rates algebraically. ⟶ Let x = rate of faster car in km/h
$x - 10$ = rate of slower car in km/h

Make a chart. ⟶

	Rate	Time	Distance ($d = rt$)
Faster car	x	10	$10x$
Slower car	$x - 10$	10	$10(x - 10)$

Write an equation. ⟶ $\begin{pmatrix}\text{Distance of} \\ \text{faster car}\end{pmatrix} + \begin{pmatrix}\text{Distance of} \\ \text{slower car}\end{pmatrix} = \begin{pmatrix}\text{Total} \\ \text{distance}\end{pmatrix}$

Substitute. ⟶
Solve the equation.

$$10x \quad + \quad 10(x - 10) \quad = \quad 900$$
$$10x + 10x - 100 = 900$$
$$20x = 1{,}000$$
$$x = 50$$

Rate of faster car, x is 50 km/h.
Rate of slower car, $x - 10$ is 40 km/h.

Thus, the faster car traveled at 50 km/h and the slower car traveled at 40 km/h.

EXAMPLE 2   Two trains left the same station at the same time but traveled in opposite directions. The E train averaged 120 km/h. The A train averaged 130 km/h. In how many hours were they 750 km apart?

Draw a diagram. ————————→

Represent the time algebraically. ————→ Let x = number of hours when they were 750 km apart

Make a chart. ————————→

	Rate	Time	Distance ($d = rt$)
E train	120	x	$120x$
A train	130	x	$130x$

Write an equation. ————————→ $\left(\begin{array}{c}\text{Distance of}\\ \text{E train}\end{array}\right) + \left(\begin{array}{c}\text{Distance of}\\ \text{A train}\end{array}\right) = \left(\begin{array}{c}\text{Total}\\ \text{Distance}\end{array}\right)$

Substitute. ————————→ $\qquad\qquad 120x \qquad + \qquad 130x \qquad = \qquad 750$

Solve the equation.

$$250x = 750$$
$$x = 3$$

Thus, in 3 hours the trains were 750 km apart.

EXAMPLE 3   The Dawns drove to the beach at 50 km/h. On their return trip they averaged 40 km/h. The total trip took 9 hours. How far was it to the beach?

Draw a diagram. ————————→

Home — To → Beach — From

Represent the times algebraically. ————→ Let x = time in hours of trip to the beach
$9 - x$ = times in hours of return trip

Make a chart. ————————→

	Rate	Time	Distance ($d = rt$)
To beach	50	x	$50x$
Return trip	40	$9 - x$	$40(9 - x)$

Write an equation. ————————→ (Distance to beach) = (Distance of return trip)

Substitute. ————————→ $\qquad 50x = 40(9 - x)$

Solve. $\left(\begin{array}{c}50x = 360 - 40x\\ 90x = 360\end{array}\right)$ $\qquad 50x = 360 - 40x$

$$x = 4$$

Thus, it was 50(4), or 200 km to the beach.

EXAMPLE 4 Abe started out in his car at a rate of 40 km/h. Two hours later, Carla left from the same point. She drove along the same road at 50 km/h. How many hours had Carla driven when she caught up up with Abe?

Draw a diagram. ──────────→

Start

Abe ────────────────────→ Point where Carla caught up

Carla ───────────────→

Represent the times algebraically. ──→ Let x = time Carla traveled
$x + 2$ = time Abe traveled

Make a chart. ──────────────→

	Rate	Time	Distance ($d = rt$)
Abe	40	$x + 2$	$40(x + 2)$
Carla	50	x	$50x$

Write an equation. ──────────→ (Abe's distance) = (Carla's distance)
Substitute. ─────────────→ $40(x + 2) = 50x$
Solve. $\left(\begin{array}{l} 40x + 80 = 50x \\ \quad\quad 80 = 10x \end{array}\right)$ $40x + 80 = 50x$
$80 = 10x$
$8 = x$

Thus, it took Carla 8 hours to catch up with Abe.

EXAMPLE 5   A train left a station at 3:00 pm and traveled at 100 km/h. Another train left the station at 4:00 pm and traveled in the same direction at 125 km/h. At what time did it overtake the first train?

Draw a diagram. ──────────→

Start

First train ────────────→ Point where second train overtakes first

Second train ──────────→

Represent the times algebraically. ──→ Let x = time second train traveled
$x + 1$ = time first train traveled

Make a chart. ──────────────→

	Rate	Time	Distance ($d = rt$)
First train	100	$x + 1$	$100(x + 1)$
Second train	125	x	$125x$

Write an equation. ──────────→ (First train's distance) = (Second train's distance)
Substitute. ─────────────→ $100(x + 1) = 125x$
Solve. $\left(\begin{array}{l} 100x + 100 = 125x \\ \quad\quad\; 100 = 25x \end{array}\right)$ $100(x + 1) = 125x$
$100x + 100 = 125x$
$4 = x$

4:00 + 4 hr = 8:00 ──────────→ **Thus,** the second train overtook the first at 8:00 pm.

EXERCISES

1. Two trucks started toward each other at the same time from towns 500 km apart. One truck traveled at a rate of 65 km/h, the other at 60 km/h. After how many hours did they meet?

2. The Foys rode at 40 km/h to a bus stop where they boarded a chartered bus. The bus traveled at 80 km/h. Their total trip was 280 km and took 4 hours. How long were the Foys on the bus?

3. Jan and Joel started from the same point at the same time. They traveled in opposite directions on their bicycles. Jan traveled at 8 km/h and Joel at 7 km/h. In how many hours were they 45 km apart?

4. A car and a truck were traveling in opposite directions. They passed each other at a crossroad in the country. The car was traveling at 75 km/h and the truck at 50 km/h. In how many hours were they 375 km apart?

5. A train left a station and traveled north at 110 km/h. Two hours later, another train left the station and traveled south at 90 km/h. How many hours had the first train traveled when they were 420 km apart?

6. A train left a station and traveled south at 100 km/h. Two hours later, another train left the station and traveled in the same direction at 110 km/h. How many hours had the first train traveled when the second train overtook it?

7. Sheila and Kevin drove to the service station at 60 km/h. They returned home by bicycle at 15 km/h. The entire trip took 4 hours. How far was it from their home to the service station?

8. Dick and Roby left home for a fishing trip at 8:30 am. They were traveling at 30 km/h. Part of the way there, their car broke down. They walked back at a rate of 10 km/h and returned home at 10:30 am. How far from home were they when the car broke down?

9. An airplane left an airport and traveled due north at 1,200 km/h. Two hours later, another plane left the airport and traveled due south at 1,000 km/h. How many hours had the first plane flown when they were 9,000 km apart?

10. Amos and Russ were walking toward town at 3 km/h. Half an hour later, Theresa and Claire left from the same point and walked in the same direction at 4 km/h. For how many hours had the boys walked when the girls caught up with them?

Graphing Intersections and Unions

▶ REVIEW CAPSULE

$$A = \{-4, -1, 0, 1\}$$
$$B = \{-4, -3, 0, 2\}$$
$$A \cap B = \{-4, 0\}$$
$$A \cup B = \{-4, -3, -1, 0, 1, 2\}$$

EXAMPLE 1 $P = \{x \mid x \geq -2\}$ and $Q = \{x \mid x < 3\}$. Graph P, Q, and $P \cap Q$. Then describe the intersection.

Graph of $P = \{x \mid x \geq -2\}$ ⟶

Graph of $Q = \{x \mid x < 3\}$ ⟶

Graph of $P \cap Q$ ⟶

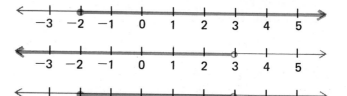

$P \cap Q$ contains all numbers common to sets P and Q.

Description of $P \cap Q$ ⟶
x is between -2 and 3. ⟶

Thus, $P \cap Q = \{x \mid x \geq -2 \text{ and } x < 3\}$.
We may also write $P \cap Q = \{x \mid -2 \leq x < 3\}$.

EXAMPLE 2 $P = \{x \mid x \geq -2\}$ and $Q = \{x \mid x < 3\}$. Graph P, Q, and $P \cup Q$. Then describe the union.

Graph of $P = \{x \mid x \geq -2\}$ ⟶

Graph of $Q = \{x \mid x < 3\}$ ⟶

Graph of $P \cup Q$ ⟶

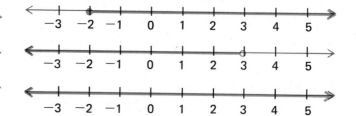

$P \cup Q$ contains all numbers belonging to P, or Q, or both P and Q.

We may also write
$P \cup Q = \{x \mid x \geq -2 \text{ or } x < 3\}$. ⟶   **Thus,** $P \cup Q = \{\text{all numbers}\}$.

EXAMPLE 3 $R = \{x \mid x < -1\}$ and $S = \{x \mid x \geq 2\}$. Graph $R, S,$ and $R \cap S$. Then describe the intersection.

Graph of $R = \{x \mid x < -1\}$ ⟶

Graph of $S = \{x \mid x \geq 2\}$ ⟶

Graph of $R \cap S$ ⟶

There are no numbers common to sets R and S.

Description of $R \cap S$ ⟶ **Thus, $R \cap S = \phi$, or**

$$R \cap S = \{x \mid x < -1 \ and \ x \geq 2\}.$$

EXAMPLE 4   Consider sets R and S graphed in Example 3. Graph $R \cup S$. Then describe the union.

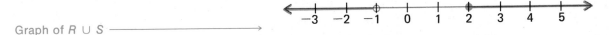

Graph of $R \cup S$ ⟶

$R \cup S$ contains all numbers belonging to R, or S, or both R and S.

Description of $R \cup S$ ⟶ **Thus, $R \cup S = \{x \mid x < -1 \ or \ x \geq 2\}.$**

EXAMPLE 5 $C = \{x \mid x < 4\}$ and $D = \{x \mid x \leq -1\}$. Graph $C, D, C \cap D,$ and $C \cup D$. Then describe the intersection and the union.

Graph of $C = \{x \mid x < 4\}$ ⟶

Graph of $D = \{x \mid x \leq -1\}$ ⟶

Graph of $C \cap D = \{x \mid x \leq -1\}$ ⟶

Graph of $C \cup D = \{x \mid x < 4\}$ ⟶

Description of $C \cap D$;
actually, $C \cap D = D$. ⟶ **Thus, $C \cap D = \{x \mid x \leq -1\}$**

Description of $C \cup D$;
actually, $C \cup D = C$. ⟶ **and $C \cup D = \{x \mid x < 4\}.$**

EXERCISES

PART A

Graph A, B, $A \cap B$, and $A \cup B$ on four separate number lines. Then describe the intersection and the union.

1. $A = \{x \mid x > -2\}$ $B = \{x \mid x < 5\}$ 2. $A = \{x \mid x > 3\}$ $B = \{x \mid x < -1\}$
3. $A = \{x \mid x \geq -4\}$ $B = \{x \mid x < 2\}$ 4. $A = \{x \mid x > 4\}$ $B = \{x \mid x \leq 0\}$
5. $A = \{x \mid x > -3\}$ $B = \{x \mid x \geq -1\}$ 6. $A = \{x \mid x \leq 5\}$ $B = \{x \mid x < 3\}$
7. $A = \{x \mid x \geq -1\}$ $B = \{x \mid x \leq 3\}$ 8. $A = \{x \mid x \leq 1\}$ $B = \{x \mid x \geq 4\}$
9. $A = \{x \mid x < 4\}$ $B = \{x \mid x < 0\}$ 10. $A = \{x \mid x > -1\}$ $B = \{x \mid x > -7\}$
11. $A = \{x \mid x \geq 1\}$ $B = \{x \mid x \leq 1\}$ 12. $A = \{x \mid x > 3\}$ $B = \{x \mid x \leq 3\}$
13. $A = \{x \mid x > -5\}$ $B = \{x \mid x > -4\}$ 14. $A = \{x \mid x > -1\}$ $B = \{x \mid x \leq 0\}$
15. $A = \{x \mid x \leq 2\}$ $B = \{x \mid x > -1\}$ 16. $A = \{x \mid x < -3\}$ $B = \{x \mid x > -3\}$
17. $A = \{x \mid x > 3\}$ $B = \{x \mid x \geq 3\}$ 18. $A = \{x \mid x > 2\}$ $B = \{x \mid x < -2\}$
19. $A = \{x \mid x \geq 0\}$ $B = \{x \mid x < 0\}$ 20. $A = \{x \mid x < -2\}$ $B = \{x \mid x \leq -2\}$
21. $A = \{x \mid x = 5\}$ $B = \{x \mid x > 5\}$ 22. $A = \{x \mid x \geq 3\}$ $B = \{x \mid x \leq -3\}$
23. $A = \{x \mid x \geq -3\}$ $B = \{x \mid x \leq 3\}$ 24. $A = \{x \mid x = 0\}$ $B = \{x \mid x \geq 0\}$
25. $A = \{x \mid x = -3\}$ $B = \{x \mid x \leq -3\}$ 26. $A = \{x \mid x > 0\}$ $B = \{x \mid x = 0\}$
27. $A = \{x \mid x > 3\}$ $B = \{x \mid x \leq 4\}$ 28. $A = \{x \mid x \leq 1\}$ $B = \{x \mid x > 2\}$
29. $A = \{\text{all numbers}\}$ $B = \{x \mid x > 2\}$ 30. $A = \{\text{all numbers}\}$ $B = \{x \mid x = -1\}$

PART B

       EXAMPLE   Describe the set graphed.   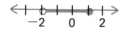

Also written $\{x \mid -2 < x \leq 1\}$ ⟶   The set graphed is $\{x \mid x > -2 \text{ and } x \leq 1\}$.

Describe the set graphed.

31.

32.

33.

34.

35.

36.

37.

38.

PART C

If $A = \{x \mid x > -4\}$, $B = \{x \mid x \leq 5\}$, and $C = \{x \mid x \geq 0\}$, graph the following.

39. $(A \cap B) \cap C$ 40. $(A \cup B) \cup C$ 41. $(A \cap B) \cup C$ 42. $(A \cup B) \cap C$

René Descartes

René Descartes
(1596–1650)

René Descartes was known not only as a great mathematician but as a great scientist and philosopher as well. He was very sickly as a child and throughout his life. Because of his condition, he would spend the morning hours in bed and would often use this time to think. Sometimes he would watch a fly walking on the ceiling and try to derive a mathematical equation for its path. Descartes, also called Cartesius, is regarded as the founder of analytic geometry which defines geometric functions using algebraic expressions. Whenever ordered pairs of real numbers are assigned to points in the plane, we have a Cartesian coordinate system.

Descartes was a founder of modern philosophy and one of the Western world's most influential thinkers. His famous statement, "Cogito, ergo sum" (I think, therefore I am), provided a basis for his philosophical system, Cartesianism.

PROJECT

You might be interested in learning more about Descartes. One reference that we suggest is E. T. Bell's *Men of Mathematics*.

Chapter Four Review

Which sets are equal to $\{2, 5, 8, 9\}$? $[p.\,91]$
1. $\{8, 9, 5, 2\}$ **2.** $\{2, 9, 6, 5\}$ **3.** $\{5, 8, 3, 9\}$ **4.** $\{2, 2+3, 2+6, 2+7\}$

For each set, tell whether it is finite or infinite. The describe the set in words. $[p.\,91]$
5. $\{1, 3, 5, 7, \ldots\}$ **6.** $\{2, 4, 6, 8\}$ **7.** $\{-1, -2, -3, -4, \ldots\}$

Describe each set by listing its elements. $[p.\,91]$
8. {negative integers greater than -5}   **9.** {positive integers less than 1}

Find the solution set of each sentence. Then graph it. $[p.\,91]$
10. $6x - 3 = 8 + 6x$ **11.** $10z + 17 = -9 + 8z$ **12.** $3x - 8 + 4x = -8 + 7x$

Graph the solution set of each sentence. $[p.\,94]$
13. $x > -2$ **14.** $y \le 5$ **15.** $y \ne -\frac{1}{2}$ **16.** $y < -4$ **17.** $2 < y$ **18.** $-3 \ge x$

For each inequality, write a true inequality by performing the indicated operation on each side. $[p.\,98]$
19. $-3 \le 9$ Divide by -3.   **20.** $-7 \ge -8$ Multiply by -8.   **21.** $8 > -1$ Add -5.

What operation was performed on each side of the first inequality to give the second inequality? $[p.\,98]$
22. $-18 < -6$ $6 > 2$ **23.** $6 > 2$ $4 > 0$ **24.** $-3 < -1$ $6 > 2$

Find and graph the solution set. $[p.\,102]$
25. $11x + 8 \le -14$ **26.** $24 - 4x \ge -16 + 4x$ **27.** $6 - (4 - x) > 2x + 1$

For each pair of sets, determine if $A \subseteq B$. Then determine if $B \subseteq A$. $[p.\,105]$
28. $A = \{2, 4\}$ $B = \{6, 4, 2\}$ **29.** $A = \phi$ $B = \{0, 1\}$ **30.** $A = \{6, 10, 12\}$ $B = \{10, 6, 12\}$

List all the subsets of each set. Then give the number of subsets. $[p.\,105]$
31. $\{3\}$ **32.** $\{4, 1\}$ **33.** $\{9, 8, 7\}$

For each pair of sets, find the intersection. Then find the union. $[p.\,105]$
34. $\{4, 5, 9\}$ $\{9, 5\}$ **35.** $\{1, 3, 5\}$ $\{2, 4, 6\}$ **36.** $\{-2, 0, 2\}$ $\{-1, 0, 1\}$

Graph A, B, $A \cap B$, and $A \cup B$ on four separate number lines. Then describe the intersection and the union. $[p.\,112]$
37. $A = \{x \mid x > 3\}$ $B = \{x \mid x \le 4\}$ **38.** $A = \{x \mid x \ge -4\}$ $B = \{x \mid x < 1\}$

Describe the set graphed. $[p.\,112]$

39.

40.

Chapter Four Test

Which sets are equal to $\{3, 6, 8, 9\}$?

1. $\{6, 3, 9, 8\}$

2. $\{9, 8, 3, 7\}$

3. $\{1 + 2, 7 + 1, 7 - 1, 8 + 1\}$

For each set, tell whether it is finite or infinite. Then describe the set in words.

4. $\{5, 6, 7, 8, \ldots\}$

5. $\{1, 3, 5, 7\}$

6. $\{-2, -4, -6, -8, \ldots\}$

Describe each set by listing its elements.

7. {integers between -3 and 2}

8. {positive integers less than 4}

Find the solution set of each sentence. Then graph it.

9. $4y + 9 = -17 + 4y$

10. $3x + 8 = -3x - 16$

11. $8r + 12 = 15r - 9 - 7r$

Graph the solution set of each sentence.

12. $x \geq -3$

13. $4 < y$

14. $x \neq 5$

For each inequality, write a true inequality by performing the indicated operation on each side.

15. $6 > -5$ Add -8.

16. $-12 \leq -8$ Divide by -4.

What operation was performed on each side of the first inequality to give the second inequality?

17. $-4 < 8 \quad 16 > -32$

18. $7 < 9 \quad 4 < 6$

Find and graph the solution set.

19. $6 - 9x < -21$

20. $x - 2x \geq 18 + 2x$

21. $4 - (3 - y) < 3y + 9$

For each pair of sets, determine if $A \subseteq B$. Then determine if $B \subseteq A$.

22. $A = \{3, 5, 7, 9\} \ B = \{9, 5\}$

23. $A = \{1, 6, 8\} \ B = \{8, 1, 6\}$

List all the subsets of each set. Then give the number of subsets.

24. $\{7\}$

25. $\{1, 3, 5\}$

For each pair of sets, find the intersection. Then find the union.

26. $\{-5, 0, 5\} \ \{-4, 0, 4\}$

27. $\{0, 2, 4\} \ \{1, 3, 5\}$

Graph A, B, $A \cap B$, and $A \cup B$ on four separate number lines. Then describe the intersection and the union.

28. $A = \{x \,|\, x \geq -3\} \ B = \{x \,|\, x < 1\}$

29. $A = \{x \,|\, x < -4\} \ B = \{x \,|\, x \geq -1\}$

Describe the set graphed.

30.

31.

5 FACTORING

Sophie Germain

Sophie Germain
(1776–1831)

Sophie Germain was born in Paris on the brink of the French Revolution. Confined to her house, Sophie amused herself by spending long hours in her father's library. Here, she read of the violent death of Archimedes as he contemplated a mathematical figure in the sand. Impressed by this, Sophie decided to study mathematics, much against the wishes of her parents.

Germain would get up at night and study the language of analysis until dawn. During the reign of terror, she studied differential calculus. She was able to get the lecture notes of various professors from the École Polytechnique, even though the school did not accept women. She began a correspondence with the famous mathematician Lagrange but signed herself M. Leblanc. Lagrange was very impressed with this young mathematician. He eventually learned of her identity and openly praised her work. Germain began to think of herself as a mathematician.

Most of her work was in the fields of number theory and mathematical analysis. In 1815, she was awarded a prize by the Institut de France. She was also recommended for an honorary degree from the University of Gottingen. Unfortunately, she died before the degree could be awarded.

Exponents

▶ REVIEW CAPSULE

(3) (3) (3) (3)

3^4 — Exponent

Base — 3^4

3^4
Fourth power of 3

A positive integer exponent tells the number of times the base is used as a factor.

x^1 means x, for each number x.

EXAMPLE 1   Find the value of 2^5.

Use 2 as a factor 5 times. 2^5 does not mean $2(5)$.

$$2^5 = \underbrace{(2)\,(2)\,(2)\,(2)\,(2)}$$
$$= \quad 32$$

EXAMPLE 2   Rewrite x^3 without an exponent.

Write x as a factor 3 times.

$$x^3 \quad = (x)\,(x)\,(x)$$

EXAMPLE 3   Evaluate a^5 if $a = -2$.

Write a as a factor 5 times.

$$(a)\quad(a)\quad(a)\quad(a)\quad(a)$$

Substitute -2 for a.

$$(-2)\,(-2)\,(-2)\,(-2)\,(-2)$$

$$\underbrace{(4)}\quad\underbrace{(4)}\quad(-2)$$

Multiply.

$$(16)\,(-2)$$
$$-32$$

EXAMPLE 4   Evaluate $-2a^3$ if $a = -3$.

Use a as a factor 3 times.
Substitute -3 for a.

$$-2a^3 = (-2)\,(a)\,(a)\,(a)$$
$$(-2)\,\underbrace{(-3)\,(-3)\,(-3)}$$
$$= (-2)\quad(-27)$$
$$= \quad 54$$

EXAMPLE 5 Evaluate $-m^2b^3$ if $m=-2$, $b=3$.

Replace $-m^2b^3$ with $-1m^2b^3$. $\longrightarrow$

$m^2=(m)(m)$; $b^3=(b)(b)(b)$ $\longrightarrow$

Substitute -2 for m, 3 for b. $\longrightarrow$

$$
\begin{aligned}
-m^2b^3 &= -1m^2b^3 \\
&= -1(m)(m)(b)(b)(b) \\
&= -1(-2)(-2)(3)(3)(3) \\
&= -1 \quad (4) \qquad (27) \\
&= -1 \quad (108) \\
&= -108
\end{aligned}
$$

EXERCISES

PART A

Rewrite without exponents.

1. x^5 **2.** x^3 **3.** a^4 **4.** a^2 **5.** $4n^3$ **6.** m^6 **7.** $-3a^2$ **8.** a^3b^2

Evaluate for the given values of the variables.

9. a^3 if $a=-3$ **10.** b^5 if $b=-2$ **11.** m^4 if $m=2$

12. $-2m^2$ if $m=-3$ **13.** $-3x^3$ if $x=2$ **14.** $2a^5$ if $a=-2$

15. $-x^3$ if $x=-4$ **16.** $-a^2$ if $a=5$ **17.** $-x^5$ if $x=-3$

18. $2ab^4$ if $a=-1$, $b=2$ **19.** $-3x^3y^2$ if $x=-2$, $y=-1$ **20.** $-xy^5$ if $x=-2$, $y=-2$

21. $-x^3y^3$ if $x=-1$, $y=-3$ **22.** $-a^3b^2c$ if $a=-4$, $b=2$, $c=-1$ **23.** $-2x^3yz$ if $x=1$, $y=1$, $z=2$

PART B

EXAMPLE Evaluate $(5b)^2$ if $b=4$.

$$
\begin{aligned}
[(5)(4)]^2 &= (20)^2 \\
&= (20)(20) \\
&= 400
\end{aligned}
$$

Evaluate for the given values of the variables.

24. $(4a)^3$ if $a=-1$ **25.** $(-2m)^3$ if $m=-2$ **26.** $(-4a)^2$ if $a=-2$

27. $(x^2y^3)^2$ if $x=-2$, $y=3$ **28.** $(x^3y^2)^3$ if $x=-1$, $y=4$ **29.** $(-x^3y^4)^5$ if $x=-1$, $y=2$

PART C

Evaluate for the given values of the variables.

30. $-x^my^n$ if $x=-2$, $m=3$, $y=5$, $n=2$ **31.** $(kb)^m$ if $k=-2$, $b=3$, $m=3$

Properties of Exponents

▶ *REVIEW CAPSULE*

Evaluate $-4a^3$ if $a = -2$.

$$-4a^3 = (-4)(a)(a)(a)$$
$$= (-4)(-2)(-2)(-2)$$
$$= 32$$

EXAMPLE 1   Simplify $a^3 \cdot a^4$.

Same base
$\underbrace{(3 \text{ factors, } a) + (4 \text{ factors, } a)}$
7 factors, a

$\underbrace{a \cdot a \cdot a \cdot a \cdot a \cdot a \cdot a}$
a^7

Example 1 suggests this.
Add exponents.

Product of Powers
$$x^m \cdot x^n = x^{m+n}$$

EXAMPLE 2   Simplify $y^2 \cdot y^7$.   Simplify $x^5 \cdot x^4$.

$x^m \cdot x^n = x^{m+n}$

y^{2+7} x^{5+4}
y^9 x^9

EXAMPLE 3   Simplify $(-5t^3)(-3t)$.   Simplify $(4a^3)(-6a^4)$.

t means t^1.

Group like factors.

$(-5t^3)(-3t^1)$ $4 \cdot -6 \cdot a^3 \cdot a^4$
$-5 \cdot -3 \cdot t^3 \cdot t^1$ $-24 \cdot a^{3+4}$
$15 \quad \cdot t^{3+1}$ $-24a^7$
$15t^4$

EXAMPLE 4   Simplify $x^2 \cdot y^3$.

Different bases

$$x^2 \cdot y^3 = x \cdot x \cdot y \cdot y \cdot y$$
$$x^2 \quad \cdot \quad y^3$$

Thus, $x^2 \cdot y^3$ cannot be simplified.

EXAMPLE 5   Show that $(x^4)^3 = x^{4 \cdot 3}$.

$(x^4)^3$	$x^{4 \cdot 3}$
$x^4 \cdot x^4 \cdot x^4$	x^{12}
x^{4+4+4}	
x^{12}	

Use x^4 as a factor three times.

Same answers

Thus, $(x^4)^3 = x^{4 \cdot 3}$.

Example 5 suggests this.
$(x^4)^3 = x^{4 \cdot 3} = x^{12}$

Power of a Power
$$(x^m)^n = x^{m \cdot n}$$

EXAMPLE 6   Simplify $(x^3)^2$.   Simplify $(a^8)^3$.

$(x^3)^2$ Multiply exponents.

$$(x^3)^2 = x^{3 \cdot 2} \qquad (a^8)^3 = a^{8 \cdot 3}$$
$$= x^6 \qquad\qquad = a^{24}$$

EXAMPLE 7   Show that $(a^3b^2)^4 = a^{3 \cdot 4}b^{2 \cdot 4}$.

$(a^3b^2)^4$	$a^{3 \cdot 4}b^{2 \cdot 4}$
$a^3b^2 \cdot a^3b^2 \cdot a^3b^2 \cdot a^3b^2$	$a^{3 \cdot 4}b^{2 \cdot 4}$
$a^3 \cdot a^3 \cdot a^3 \cdot a^3 \cdot b^2 \cdot b^2 \cdot b^2 \cdot b^2$	
$a^{3+3+3+3} \qquad b^{2+2+2+2}$	
$a^{3 \cdot 4} \qquad\qquad b^{2 \cdot 4}$	

Use a^3b^2 as a factor 4 times.

$3 + 3 + 3 + 3$ means $4 \cdot 3$, or $3 \cdot 4$.

Thus, $(a^3b^2)^4 = a^{3 \cdot 4}b^{2 \cdot 4}$, or $a^{12}b^8$.

Example 7 suggests this.
$(a^3b^2)^4 = a^{3 \cdot 4} \cdot b^{2 \cdot 4}$

Power of a Product
$$(x^m \cdot y^n)^p = x^{m \cdot p} \cdot y^{n \cdot p}$$

EXAMPLE 8   Simplify $(2a^2b^4)^3$.

$2 = 2^1$

Multiply exponents.

$$(2a^2b^4)^3 = (2^1 a^2 b^4)^3$$
$$= 2^{1 \cdot 3} \cdot a^{2 \cdot 3} \cdot b^{4 \cdot 3}$$
$$= 2^3 \cdot \quad a^6 \cdot \quad b^{12}$$
$$= 8a^6b^{12}$$

2^3 is $2 \cdot 2 \cdot 2$, or 8.

EXAMPLE 9   Simplify $(-3x^3y^5)^3$.

$-3 = 3^1$

Multiply exponents.

$$(-3x^3y^5)^3 = (-3^1 x^3 y^5)^3$$
$$= (-3)^{1 \cdot 3} \cdot x^{3 \cdot 3} \cdot y^{5 \cdot 3}$$
$$= (-3)^3 \cdot \quad x^9 \quad \cdot \quad y^{15}$$
$$= -27x^9y^{15}$$

$(-3)^3$ is $(-3)(-3)(-3)$, or -27.

ORAL EXERCISES

Simplify.

1. $(m^3)(m^2)$ **2.** $(b^3)(b^7)$ **3.** $(b^2)(b^5)$ **4.** $(c^6)(c^5)$ **5.** $(b^5)(b)$

6. $(m^4)(m)$ **7.** $(b)(b)$ **8.** $(a)(a^6)$ **9.** $(x)(x^3)$ **10.** $(m)(m^9)$

11. $(c^2)^3$ **12.** $(a^4)^5$ **13.** $(x^8)^2$ **14.** $(y^3)^4$ **15.** $(x^6)^3$

EXERCISES

PART A

Simplify.

1. $(3a^2)(4a^6)$ **2.** $(5a^4)(3a^7)$ **3.** $(2m^5)(3m^6)$ **4.** $(2b^3)(3b^4)$

5. $(4x^2)(7x^{10})$ **6.** $(2n^5)(4n^2)$ **7.** $(5a^4)(3a^5)$ **8.** $(2y^3)(5y^4)$

9. $(a^2)(4a^3)$ **10.** $(3b^5)(b^2)$ **11.** $(6a^5)(a^6)$ **12.** $(m^5)(3m^5)$

13. $(-4a^3)(2a^5)$ **14.** $(-6b^5)(-2b^7)$ **15.** $(4m^3)(-2m^5)$ **16.** $(a^7)(-3a^8)$

17. $(4a^3)(2a)$ **18.** $(5b^2)(-4b)$ **19.** $(-3b)(5b^7)$ **20.** $(4b^4)(-3b)$

21. $(3a^3b^2)(4a^2b^4)$ **22.** $(4x^2y^3)(2x^3y^4)$ **23.** $(5m^2n^3)(-4m^2n^4)$

24. $(-2a^2b^3)(4ab^5)$ **25.** $(-2ab^3)(-3a^4b)$ **26.** $(ab)(ab)$

27. $(a^2)^3$ **28.** $(b^3)^4$ **29.** $(x^2)^6$ **30.** $(y^5)^3$ **31.** $(z^6)^5$ **32.** $(c^9)^3$

33. $(r^3)^{10}$ **34.** $(f^7)^7$ **35.** $(g^{15})^3$ **36.** $(d^{25})^4$ **37.** $(c^4)^7$ **38.** $(h^{10})^{20}$

39. $(2x^2)^4$ **40.** $(-3y^3)^2$ **41.** $(-2z^4)^3$ **42.** $(5a^5)^3$ **43.** $(4x^3)^4$

PART B

Simplify.

44. $(4a^3m^2)^2$ **45.** $(3a^2x^3)^2$ **46.** $(2x^2y^3)^2$ **47.** $(2m^3n^4)^3$ **48.** $(5a^2b^3)^3$

49. $(-4a^3m^4)^3$ **50.** $(3x^2y^4)^4$ **51.** $(2xa^2)^3$ **52.** $(-3a^2b^3)^3$ **53.** $(-3xy^2m)^5$

54. $(x^3y^2z^4)^3$ **55.** $(a^2b^4c^3)^5$ **56.** $(x^2y^3z^4)^7$

57. $(3a^3b^2)^3$ **58.** $(2x^6y^4)^3$ **59.** $(-3x^3y^4z^2)^3$

PART C

EXAMPLE   Simplify $(x^3)^{2a} \cdot (x^a)^3$.

$(x^m)^n = x^{m \cdot n}$ ⟶ $x^{3 \cdot 2a} \cdot x^{a \cdot 3}$
$x^{6a} \cdot x^{3a}$

$x^{6a} \cdot x^{3a} = x^{6a+3a}$, or x^{9a} ⟶ x^{9a}

Simplify.

60. $(x^{2a})(x^{2a})$ **61.** $(y^b)(y^{3b})$ **62.** $(2x^3)(3x^a)$

63. $(x^{3a})^2$ **64.** $(y^{5b})^3$ **65.** $(2x^{5a})^a$

Polynomials

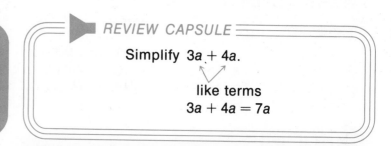

REVIEW CAPSULE

Simplify $3a + 4a$.

like terms

$3a + 4a = 7a$

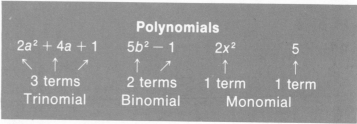

Polynomials

$2a^2 + 4a + 1$	$5b^2 - 1$	$2x^2$	5
3 terms	2 terms	1 term	1 term
Trinomial	Binomial	Monomial	

EXAMPLE 1 Classify each polynomial.

Tri means three; bi means two; mono means one.

$2a^2 + 7a + 9$	$4m^2 - 6$	$12x^2$
3 terms	2 terms	1 term
Trinomial	Binomial	Monomial

EXAMPLE 2 Simplify $9 + 7x^3 + 2x^2 - 5x^2 + 4x^3 - 8$.

Group like terms together. $(7x^3 + 4x^3) + (2x^2 - 5x^2) + (9 - 8)$
$(7x^3 + 4x^3) = (7 + 4)x^3$

$\qquad 11x^3 \qquad -3x^2 \qquad +1$, or $11x^3 - 3x^2 + 1$

EXAMPLE 3 Simplify $8x^3 - 7x^5 + 5x - 4x^2 + 3x^3 - 2x + 6$.
Then write the result in descending order of
exponents.

Group like terms. $\qquad 8x^3 + 3x^3 - 7x^5 + 5x - 2x - 4x^2 + 6$
Combine like terms. $\qquad 11x^3 \quad - 7x^5 \qquad +3x \quad - 4x^2 + 6$

Now write the result in descending order of
exponents.

Arrange terms in order of exponents
with highest exponent first. $\qquad -7x^5 + 11x^3 - 4x^2 + 3x + 6$

EXAMPLE 4 Simplify $7x^3 + 4x^2$.

$7x^3$ and $4x^2$ are not like terms.

$7x^3 + 4x^2$ is not $11x^5$. $\longrightarrow$ **Thus, $7x^3 + 4x^2$ cannot be simplified.**

EXAMPLE 5 Simplify $x^2 - 8 + 5x^4 - 7x + 3x^3 - 2x^4 + 5x^2 + 6x + 3$.

Group like terms. $\longrightarrow$ $\quad 1x^2 + 5x^2 - 8 + 3 + 5x^4 - 2x^4 - 7x + 6x + 3x^3$

Combine like terms. $\longrightarrow$ $\quad\quad 6x^2 \quad\quad -5 \quad\quad +3x^4 \quad\quad -1x \quad +3x^3$

Descending order $\longrightarrow$ $\quad\quad\quad\quad 3x^4 + 3x^3 + 6x^2 - x - 5$

ORAL EXERCISES

Classify each polynomial.

1. $3x^3 - 5x$ 　　　　　**2.** $-4x^2$ 　　　　**3.** $5x^3 - 4x^2 + 7x$ 　　　**4.** 3

Arrange each polynomial in descending order of exponents.

5. $3x^2 - 5x^3 + 7x - 4$ 　　　**6.** $5x - 4x^2 - 3$ 　　　**7.** $4a^2 - 5a^3 + 2a + 1$

8. $-4x^2 - 7x^3 + x^4 + 5x + 1$ 　　　**9.** $5x - 4x^3 + 7x^2 + 2$

10. $6 - 5x^3 + 2x + 3x^2 + x^4$ 　　　**11.** $6x^4 - 3x^2 + 2x^3 - 5 + x$

EXERCISES

PART A

Simplify. Then write the result in descending order of exponents.

1. $3x^2 - 5x + 2x - 8$ 　　　　　　**2.** $5x^2 - 8x + 3x + 4$

3. $5x^2 - 3x + 2 + 4x^2 + 7x + 3$ 　　　**4.** $4 + 8x^2 - 2x + 6x^2 - 4x - 6$

5. $-7x + 2x^2 - 5 + 3x^2 + 8 - 4x$ 　　　**6.** $8x - 2x^2 + 5x - 4 + 5x^2 - 3$

7. $-4 + 3m^2 - 5 - 2m^2$ 　　　　　**8.** $5m^2 - 4 - 7m^2 + 8$

9. $4x - 6x^2 + 5x^3 - 3x^2 + 2x^3 + 5x$ 　　**10.** $4x^3 - 5x + 2x^2 + 7x - 3x^3 + 5x^2$

11. $4m^3 - 5m^3 + 4m^2 - 4m^2 - 3m + 8m$ 　**12.** $m^3 - 9m - 5m^2 + 9m + 4m^2 + 5m^3$

13. $6a^4 - 3a^2 + 2a^4 + 4a^2$ 　　　　**14.** $5a - 3a^4 + 7a + 2a^4$

15. $3 + 6a - 2a^2 - 5a + 4a^2 - 4$ 　　　**16.** $7a - 3 - a^2 + 5a - 4 - 2a^2$

17. $7b^3 - 4b - 2b^2 + 3b + 8$ 　　　　**18.** $4b - 3 - 9b^3 + 5b + 2b^2 - 8$

PART B

Simplify.

19. $1 + 3a^3 - 4a - 2a^2 + 7a^3 - 8a + 4a^2 - 5$ 　　**20.** $6a^2 - 5a - 3 + a^2 - 4a^2 + 3a^3 + 8a + 5$

21. $a^2 + a^4 - 2a^3 - 7a - 2 + 2a^4 - 5a^3 + 8a - 4 + a^2$

22. $7b^2 - 5b^4 + 2b^3 + 2b - 1 - 4b^4 - 3b^3 + 2b^2 - 8b - 2$

23. $1 - 3m^9 - 7m^6 - 19m^9 + 6m^6 - 4$

24. $3b^5 - 6b^7 + b^5 - b^7 - b^4 - 2b^2 + 5b^4$

25. $-3a^2 + 7a - 2a^2 + 4a^3 + 6a - 9 + 8a^3 - 10 + a^4 - 5a^2$

Flow Chart: Ordering Numbers

PROBLEM

Write a flow chart to show how to arrange a given finite set of numbers in order from smallest to largest.

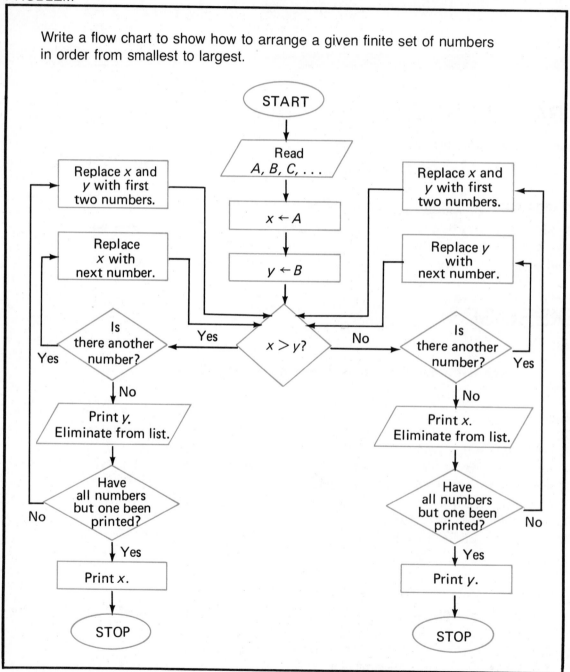

Follow the steps on the flow chart to list the numbers
17, 6, 1, 100 in order from smallest to largest.

Start.
Read 17, 6, 1, 100.
$x = 17$ $y = 6$
$x > y$? Yes.
Is there another number? Yes.
Replace x with the next number.
$x = 1$ $y = 6$
$x > y$? No.
Is there another number? Yes.
Replace y with the next number.
$x = 1$ $y = 100$
$x > y$? No.
Is there another number? No.
Print x.   *Machine prints 1. 1 is removed
$x = 17$ $y = 6$ from list. New list 17, 6, 100.
$x > y$? Yes.
Is there another number? Yes.
Replace x with the next number.
$x = 100$ $y = 6$
$x > y$? Yes.
Is there another number? No.
Print y.   *Machine prints 6. 6 is removed
$x = 17$ $y = 100$ from list. New list 17,100.
$x > y$? No.
Is there another number? No.
Print x.   *Machine prints 17. 17 is removed
Have all the numbers but one   from list.
been printed? Yes.
Print y.   *Machine prints 100.
Stop.

PROJECT

Write the steps in using the flow chart to list each sequence
of numbers from smallest to largest.

1. 8, 6, 10   2. 7, 2, 38, 14   3. −8, 20, 6, −2   4. 59, 26, −3, 18, 3
5. Write a flow chart for listing a sequence of numbers in order from
largest to smallest.

127

Simplifying Polynomials

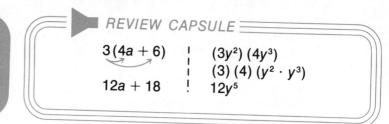

EXAMPLE 1   Multiply $a^2(3a^3 + 2a^2)$.

Distribute a^2.   →
Regroup factors.   →
$x^m \cdot x^n = x^{m+n}$ →

$$a^2(3a^3) + a^2(2a^2)$$
$$3 \cdot a^2 \cdot a^3 + 2 \cdot a^2 \cdot a^2$$
$$3a^5 + 2a^4$$

EXAMPLE 2   Multiply $4m^5(2m^6 - 3m^3 + 4m)$.

m means m^1.   →
Distribute $4m^5$.   →

$$4m^5(2m^6 - 3m^3 + 4m^1)$$
$$4m^5(2m^6) + 4m^5(-3m^3) + 4m^5(4m^1)$$
$$4 \cdot 2 \cdot m^5 \cdot m^6 + 4 \cdot -3 \cdot m^5 \cdot m^3 + 4 \cdot 4 \cdot m^5 \cdot m^1$$
$$8m^{11} - 12m^8 + 16m^6$$

EXAMPLE 3   Simplify $-(p^2 + 2p - 4)$.

$-a = -1 \cdot a$ →

$-1p^2 = -p^2$ →

$$-1(1p^2 + 2p - 4)$$
$$(-1)(1p^2) + (-1)(2p) + (-1)(-4)$$
$$-1p^2 \qquad -2p \qquad +4$$
$$-p^2 - 2p + 4$$

EXAMPLE 4   Simplify $x^3 + 2x^2 - 8x - (-2x^2 + 7x - 5)$.

$a = 1a, -a = -1a$ →

$$1x^3 + 2x^2 - 8x - 1(-2x^2 + 7x - 5)$$

Distribute -1.   →
Group like terms.   →
Combine like terms.   →
$1x^3 = x^3$ →

$$1x^3 + 2x^2 - 8x + 2x^2 - 7x + 5$$
$$1x^3 + 2x^2 + 2x^2 - 8x - 7x + 5$$
$$1x^3 + 4x^2 - 15x + 5$$
$$x^3 + 4x^2 - 15x + 5$$

EXAMPLE 5   Add $(c^4 - 5c + 8) + (c^5 - c^4 + c^3)$.

$$(1c^4 - 5c + 8) + (1c^5 - 1c^4 + 1c^3)$$

Group like terms. ⟶
$$1c^4 - 1c^4 - 5c + 8 + 1c^5 + 1c^3$$

Combine like terms. ⟶
$$0 - 5c + 8 + 1c^5 + 1c^3$$

Descending order of exponents ⟶
$$1c^5 + 1c^3 - 5c + 8$$

$1c^5 = c^5; 1c^3 = c^3$ ⟶
$$c^5 + c^3 - 5c + 8$$

EXAMPLE 6   Simplify $m^2 + 3m + 7 + 2(m^2 - 5m + 7)$

m^2 means $1m^2$. ⟶
$$1m^2 + 3m + 7 + 2(1m^2 - 5m + 7)$$

Distribute 2. ⟶
$$1m^2 + 3m + 7 + 2m^2 - 10m + 14$$
$$1m^2 + 2m^2 + 3m - 10m + 7 + 14$$

Combine like terms. ⟶
$$3m^2 - 7m + 21$$

EXAMPLE 7   Subtract $y^3 - 3y^2$ from $6y^4 - 5y^3 + 7y^2 - 8$.

$$(6y^4 - 5y^3 + 7y^2 - 8) - (y^3 - 3y^2)$$

$-a = -1a; a = 1a$ ⟶
$$(6y^4 - 5y^3 + 7y^2 - 8) - 1(1y^3 - 3y^2)$$

$$6y^4 - 5y^3 + 7y^2 - 8 - 1y^3 + 3y^2$$
$$6y^4 - 5y^3 - 1y^3 + 7y^2 + 3y^2 - 8$$
$$6y^4 - 6y^3 + 10y^2 - 8$$

ORAL EXERCISES

Multiply.

1. $3(2a^2 - 6a - 4)$

2. $5(2a^2 - 4a + 3)$

3. $2(3a^2 - 5a + 6)$

4. $5(4a^3 - 2a^2 + 5a - 2)$

5. $2(3a^3 - 2a^2 + 5a - 2)$

6. $4(4a^3 - 2a^2 + 7a - 3)$

7. $a^2(a^3 + a^2)$

8. $b^3(b^4 + b^2)$

9. $b^5(b^3 + b^2)$

10. $m^2(m^2 + m)$

11. $m^3(m^4 + m)$

12. $a^2(a^2 + a)$

13. $a^4(a^2 + a)$

14. $a^2(a^2 + a + 5)$

15. $a^3(a^2 + a + 1)$

EXERCISES

PART A

Multiply.

1. $f^2(3f^2 - 5f + 4)$

2. $t^2(3t^2 - 5t + 6)$

3. $a(2a^2 - 5a + 4)$

4. $5b(3b^2 - 4b + 3)$

5. $2x^3(3x^2 - 7x)$

6. $5a^3(3a^2 - 7a)$

Simplify.

7. $6b(4b^2 - 5b)$ **8.** $3m(2m^2 - 5m)$ **9.** $5c(4c^3 - 5c^2)$
10. $-(2b^2 - 5b)$ **11.** $-(4x^2 - 5x)$ **12.** $-(3x^2 - 4x + 2)$
13. $-(2x^2 + 5x - 7)$ **14.** $-(-b^2 - 5b)$ **15.** $-(-b^2 + 2b)$
16. $-(-x^2 - x - 2)$ **17.** $-(a^2 - a - 4)$ **18.** $-(-c^3 + c - 5)$
19. $-3a(-3a^2 - 5a + 2)$ **20.** $-5b(-2b^2 - 3b - 4)$ **21.** $-2a^2(2a^2 - 6a - 8)$
22. $-a(2a^2 - a - 3)$ **23.** $-m(-m^2 - m - 5)$ **24.** $-g(-g^2 - 2g + 5)$
25. $x^3 + 5x^2 - 7x - (-3x^2 + 5x - 9)$ **26.** $x^3 + 4x^2 - 5x - (-2x^2 + 3x - 8)$
27. $2x^3 - x^2 - x - 4 - (-x^2 - 2x + 5)$ **28.** $-3c^2 - 5c + 2 - (-2c^2 - 3c - 4)$

Add.

29. $(x^4 - 8x + 7) + (x^5 - x^4 + x^3)$ **30.** $(a^3 - 3a + 5) + (a^4 - a^3 + a^2)$
31. $(a^2 - a - 4) + (2a^2 - a - 3)$ **32.** $(-3b^2 - 5b + 2) + (-2b^2 - 3b - 4)$

Simplify.

33. $x^2 + 3x + 2 + 3(x^2 - 4x + 5)$ **34.** $y^2 - 4y + 3 + 4(y^2 + y - 5)$
35. $2a^2 - 5a - 10 + 2(2a^2 - 3a + 5)$ **36.** $3c^2 - c + 6 + 3(c^2 - 3c - 5)$

37. Subtract $x^3 - 2x^2$ from $5x^4 - x^3 + 2x^2 - 3$.   **38.** Subtract $a^2 - 2a$ from $5a^3 - 7a^2 + 8a - 3$.
39. Subtract $-x^3 - 2x$ from $x^4 + 3x^2 - 5x + 3$.   **40.** Subtract $-c^2 + 5$ from $3c^3 - 2c^2 + c - 5$.

PART B

EXAMPLE   Simplify $a^2b^3(2a^2 - 3ab + b^2)$.

Distribute a^2b^3.   ⟶ $a^2b^3(2a^2) + a^2b^3(-3ab) + a^2b^3(b^2)$

Regroup factors.   ⟶ $2(a^2)(a^2)(b^3) + (-3)(a^2)(a^1)(b^3)(b^1)$
$$+ (a^2)(b^3)(b^2)$$

$x^m \cdot x^n = x^{m+n}$ ⟶ $2(a^4)(b^3) \qquad -3 \qquad (a^3) \qquad (b^4) + 1(a^2)(b^5)$
$$2a^4b^3 - 3a^3b^4 + a^2b^5$$

Simplify.

41. $m^3n^2(2m^2 - 3mn + n^2)$ **42.** $ab(a^2 - 5ab + 7b^2)$
43. $2ab(a^2 - 3ab + 5b^2)$ **44.** $3m^2n^2(m^3 - 3m^2n + mn^2 + n^3)$
45. $-xy^2(2x^2 - xy + y^2)$ **46.** $-pq(p^2 - pq + q^2)$
47. $-2ac(a^3 - a^2c + ac^2 - c^3)$ **48.** $-3x^2y(-x^2 - 2xy - y^2)$

PART C

Simplify.

49. $m^3n^2(2m^2 - 3mn + n^2) + m^3n^2(m^2 - 2mn + 3n^2)$
50. $2ab(a^2 - 3ab + 5b^2) - 3ab(3a^2 - 7ab - 9b^2)$
51. $-xy^2(3x^2 - 2xy + 5y^2) + xy^2(x^2 - xy - y^2)$
52. $-3ab^2(-a^3 - 2a^2b + ab^2 - b^3) - 2ab^2(a^3 + 3a^2b - ab^2 + 2b^3)$

Perfect Numbers

A whole number is perfect if it is the sum of all of its factors less than itself.

Perfect number ⟶ **28**

$$1 + 2 + 4 + 7 + 14 = 28$$

Factors of 28 less than 28

PROJECT

1. Is 18 a perfect number?

2. There is one perfect number less than 28. Can you find it?

3. Is 36 a perfect number?

4. The next perfect number is between 490 and 500. Can you find it?

5. The fourth perfect number is between 8,120 and 8,130. Can you find it?

6. Were any of the first four perfect numbers odd numbers?

Concept of Factoring

▶ *REVIEW CAPSULE*

Simplify $(3a^2b^3)(4a^4b^5)$.

$$(3a^2b^3)(4a^4b^5)$$
$$(3)(4)(a^2)(a^4)(b^3)(b^5)$$
$$12a^{2+4}b^{3+5}$$
$$12a^6b^8$$

Numbers which are multiplied are *factors*.

24 can be factored into $8 \cdot 3$,
or $12 \cdot 2$,
or $2 \cdot 3 \cdot 4$,
or $2 \cdot 2 \cdot 2 \cdot 3$.

In the last case, none of the factors can be factored further except for itself and 1.

The only factors of 3 are 3 and 1.

itself and 1

2 is a prime number.
3 is also a prime number.

Definition of prime number ⟶

A *prime number* is a whole number greater than 1 whose only factors are itself and 1.

EXAMPLE 1   Factor 40 into primes.

Three ways to begin

$$40 = 20 \cdot 2 \qquad 40 = 8 \cdot 5 \qquad 40 = 10 \cdot 4$$

Each gives the same 4 factors. ⟶

$$= 5 \cdot 4 \cdot 2 \qquad = 4 \cdot 2 \cdot 5$$
$$= 5 \cdot 2 \cdot 2 \cdot 2 \qquad = 2 \cdot 2 \cdot 2 \cdot 5 \qquad = 5 \cdot 2 \cdot 2 \cdot 2$$

Each factor is prime. ⟶

Thus, $40 = 5 \cdot 2 \cdot 2 \cdot 2$.

$5 \cdot 2 \cdot 2 \cdot 2$ is the prime factorization of 40.

EXAMPLE 2 Factor 32 into primes.

Begin with any factorization.
16 is NOT prime.
 8 is NOT prime.
 4 is NOT prime.

$$32 = 16 \cdot 2$$
$$= 8 \cdot 2 \cdot 2$$
$$= 4 \cdot 2 \cdot 2 \cdot 2$$
$$= 2 \cdot 2 \cdot 2 \cdot 2 \cdot 2$$

EXAMPLE 3 Find the missing factor.
$$(a^5)(?) = a^8$$

$x^m \cdot x^n = x^{m+n}$ ⟶

$8 = 5 + \boxed{3}$ ⟶

$(a^5)(a^\square)$
$a^{5+\square}$
$\downarrow$
$a^{5+\boxed{3}}$
$(a^5)(a^{\boxed{3}})$

$(a^5)(a^3) = a^{5+3}$, or a^8 ⟶ **Thus,** the missing factor is a^3.

EXAMPLE 4 Find the missing factor.
$$(5a^4)(?) = -20a^7$$

We need a number factor and a
factor $a^\square$. ⟶

$-20 = (5)(-4)$

$a^7 = (a^4)(a^{\boxed{}})$ ⟶

Check by multiplying.

$(5a^4)(-4a^3) = -20a^7$ ⟶ **Thus,** $-4a^3$ is the missing factor.

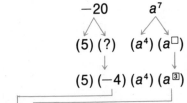

ORAL EXERCISES

Tell whether each is prime.

1. 8	**2.** 19	**3.** 21	**4.** 37
5. 7	**6.** 49	**7.** 15	**8.** 41
9. 52	**10.** 2	**11.** 27	**12.** 31
13. 40	**14.** 5	**15.** 29	**16.** 25

Factor each as the product of two factors.

17. 12	**18.** 60	**19.** 28	**20.** 30
21. 36	**22.** 52	**23.** 42	**24.** 20
25. 18	**26.** 48	**27.** 32	**28.** 44

EXERCISES

Factor into primes.

1. 12	**2.** 24	**3.** 18	**4.** 28
5. 45	**6.** 60	**7.** 26	**8.** 35
9. 50	**10.** 72	**11.** 44	**12.** 30
13. 80	**14.** 42	**15.** 48	**16.** 27

Find the missing factor.

17. $(a^7)(?) = a^{10}$

18. $(a^6)(?) = a^9$

19. $(6m^5)(?) = 36m^8$

20. $(4a^3)(?) = 32a^7$

21. $(-3x^5)(?) = 27x^7$

22. $(-3x^3)(?) = 18x^6$

23. $(?)(5x^5) = 35x^{10}$

24. $(?)(4m^5) = 8m^9$

25. $(?)(3x^3) = -30x^7$

26. $(?)(-20a^8) = 40a^{13}$

27. $(3b^2)(?) = 3b^7$

28. $(?)(5b^9) = 5b^{12}$

29. $(-8b^5)(?) = 16b^6$

30. $(-b^7)(?) = 5b^8$

PART B

EXAMPLE

Find the missing factor.
$$(2a^2b^3)(?) = 8a^7b^9$$

We need a number factor, a factor $a^\square$, and a factor $b^\triangle$. ⟶

$$8 \qquad a^7 \qquad b^9$$

$$(2)\,(?)\,(a^2)\,(a^\square)\,(b^3)\,(b^\triangle)$$

$$\downarrow \qquad \downarrow \qquad \downarrow$$

$$(2)\,(4)\,(a^2)\,(a^5)\,(b^3)\,(b^6)$$

Check by multiplying.
$(2a^2b^3)(4a^5b^6) = 8a^7b^9$ ⟶ **Thus,** $4a^5b^6$ **is the missing factor.**

Find the missing factor.

31. $(3a^2b^3)(?) = 27a^5b^4$

32. $(4a^3m^5)(?) = 24a^7m^9$

33. $(?)(4a^3m^7) = -32a^5m^9$

34. $(3a^2b^5)(?) = 39a^4b^7$

35. $(?)(2a^2b^5) = -2a^3b^6$

36. $(?)(4x^3y^2) = -8x^4y^3$

37. $(?)(3x^3y^4) = -3x^5y^8$

38. $(2ab^2)(?) = -16a^2b^3$

39. $(3x^3y)(?) = 3x^4y$

40. $(8a^3m)(?) = -8a^7m$

PART C

Find the missing factor.

41. $(a^{2m})(?) = a^{5m}$

42. $(x^{3a})(?) = x^{8a}$

43. $(a^{2m+5})(?) = a^{4m+9}$

Factoring Out a Common Monomial

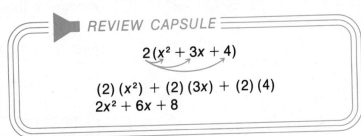

REVIEW CAPSULE

$$2(x^2 + 3x + 4)$$

$$(2)(x^2) + (2)(3x) + (2)(4)$$
$$2x^2 + 6x + 8$$

Use the distributive property in reverse. ⟶

We can rewrite $2m^3 - 6m^2 + 10m - 8$
as $2(m^3 - 3m^2 + 5m - 4)$.

2 is a common monomial factor.

EXAMPLE 1 Factor a common monomial factor from $3b^2 + 9b + 6$.

$$3b^2 + \quad 9b \quad + 6$$

3 divides each term evenly. Use 3 as a factor of each term.

$$3(b^2) + 3(3b) + 3(2)$$

Use the distributive property in reverse. ⟶

$$3(b^2 + 3b + 2)$$

EXAMPLE 2 Factor the greatest common factor from $4x^2 - 8x + 4$.

$$4x^2 - \quad 8x \quad + 4$$

4 is the greatest number that divides each term evenly. Use 4 as a factor of each term.

$$4(x^2) + 4(-2x) + 4(1)$$

Distributive property in reverse ⟶

$$4(x^2 - 2x + 1)$$

4 is the GCF (short for greatest common factor) of $4x^2 - 8x + 4$.

EXAMPLE 3 Find the GCF of $6x^2 + 12$.

Factor 6 and 12 into primes. ⟶

$$(3)(2)(x^2) \quad + \quad (2)(3)(2)$$

one 3, one 2   two 2's, one 3

At most, one 2 and one 3 are common to each term.

Thus, the GCF is $(2)(3)$, or 6.

Example 3 shows a technique for finding the GCF. You need not use that process if you can recognize the GCF immediately.

EXAMPLE 4   Factor the GCF from $20b^2 - 24b + 48$.

Factor into primes. ⟶ $(2)(2)(5)(b^2) - (2)(2)(2)(3)(b) + (2)(2)(2)(2)(3)$

At most, two 2's are common to each term, so the GCF is $(2)(2)$, or 4.

Use 4 as a factor of each term. ⟶
Distributive property in reverse ⟶

$$20b^2 - 24b + 48$$
$$4(5b^2) + 4(-6b) + 4(12)$$
$$4(5b^2 - 6b + 12)$$

EXAMPLE 5   Factor $x^3 + x^2 + x$.

x means x^1. ⟶

$$x^3 \quad + \quad x^2 \quad + \quad x^1$$
$$\uparrow \qquad\quad \uparrow \qquad\quad \uparrow$$

Think. ⟶
three x's   two x's   one x

At most, one x is common to each term, so the GCF is x^1.

Use x^1 as a factor of each term. ⟶
$x^1 = x$

$$x^3 + x^2 + x^1$$
$$x^1(x^2) + x^1(x^1) + x^1(1)$$
$$x^1(x^2 + x^1 + 1), \text{ or } x(x^2 + x + 1)$$

EXAMPLE 6   Factor $2x^4 + 4x^3 + 6x^2$.

First step ⟶ Look for the greatest common whole number factor.

Factor coefficients into primes. ⟶
2 is common to each term. ⟶

$$(2)(x^4) + (2)(2)(x^3) + (2)(3)(x^2)$$

2 is the greatest common whole number factor.

Second step ⟶ Now look for the greatest common variable factor.

$$2x^4 \quad + \quad 4x^3 \quad + \quad 6x^2$$
$$\uparrow \qquad\quad \uparrow \qquad\quad \uparrow$$

Think. ⟶
four x's   three x's   two x's

x^2 is common to each term. ⟶ x^2 is the greatest common variable factor.
$2x^2$ divides each term evenly. ⟶ The GCF of $2x^4 + 4x^3 + 6x^2$ is $2x^2$.
Use $2x^2$ as a factor of each term. ⟶
Distributive property in reverse ⟶

$$2x^2(x^2) + 2x^2(2x^1) + 2x^2(3)$$
$$2x^2(x^2 + 2x + 3)$$

Thus, $2x^4 + 4x^3 + 6x^2 = 2x^2(x^2 + 2x + 3)$.

EXAMPLE 7 Factor $5x^6 - 20x^4 + x^3$.

First step → Look for a common whole number factor.
$$(5)(x^6) - (5)(4)(x^4) + 1(x^3)$$
1 is the common whole number factor. We do not bother to factor out the 1.

Second step → Now look for the greatest common variable factor.
$$5x^6 \quad - \quad 20x^4 \quad + \quad 1x^3$$
$$\uparrow \qquad\qquad \uparrow \qquad\qquad \uparrow$$
six x's   four x's   three x's

Think. →
x^3 is common to each term. → x^3 is the greatest common variable factor.

Use x^3 as a factor of each term. →
Distributive property in reverse →
$$5x^6 - 20x^4 + 1x^3$$
$$x^3(5x^3) + x^3(-20x^1) + x^3(1)$$
$$x^3(5x^3 - 20x^1 + 1), \text{ or } x^3(5x^3 - 20x + 1)$$

SUMMARY **To factor out the greatest common monomial factor:**
First, factor out the greatest common whole number factor other than 1, if any. | **Second, factor out the greatest common variable factor, if any.**

EXERCISES

PART A

Factor.

1. $3x^2 + 27x + 9$
2. $4a^2 + 32a + 20$
3. $6b^2 + 18b + 30$
4. $2m^2 - 10m + 4$
5. $7a^2 - 21a + 49$
6. $m^3 + m^2 + m$
7. $x^5 + x^4 - x^3$
8. $b^4 - 2b^3 + b^2$
9. $2a^3 - a^2 + a$
10. $y^3 - 7y^2 + y$
11. $7a^2 - 28a$
12. $3x^2 - 9x$
13. $4a^3 + 8a^2$
14. $5b^3 - 10b$
15. $6a^2 - 24a$
16. $4a^3 - 16a^2 + 32a$
17. $4a^3 - 12a^2 + 8a$
18. $7b^3 - 14b^2 + 49b$
19. $12x^3 - 6x^2 + 18x$
20. $4m^3 - 24m$
21. $4m^2 - 20$
22. $3a^3 - 5a^2$
23. $4m^3 - 32m^2$
24. $5a^3 - 35a$

PART B

Factor.

25. $7a^5 - 35a^4 + 21a^3$
26. $6a^4 - 12a^3 + 24a^2 + 3a$
27. $3a^2 + 12ab + 36b^2$
28. $39a^3 - 52a^2 + 26a$
29. $18m^4 - 27m^3 - 45m^2 + 36m$
30. $6y^3 - 18y^2 - 12y$

Chapter Five Review

Evaluate for the given values of the variables. [$p.\ 119$]

1. a^3 if $a = -2$

2. $-3x^2$ if $x = -2$

3. $-2a^3$ if $a = -2$

4. $2m^3$ if $m = -4$

5. x^2y^2 if $x = 2,\ y = -3$

6. $-2a^3b$ if $a = -1,\ b = -3$

7. $(-2a)^3$ if $a = -2$

8. $(3m)^2$ if $m = -2$

9. $(x^3y^2)^2$ if $x = -2,\ y = 1$

Simplify. [$p.\ 121$]

10. $(x^3)(x^7)$

11. $(a^7)(a^9)$

12. $(2a^3)(5a^4)$

13. $(3b^2)(5b)$

14. $(-3a^2)(4a^5)$

15. $(-3a^2b)(7a^3b^6)$

16. $(3a^2)^3$

17. $(4b)^2$

18. $(-2m^2n^3)^3$

Classify each polynomial. [$p.\ 124$]

19. $a^2 + 7a$

20. $4x^3$

21. $6x^2 - 4x + 2$

Simplify. Then write the result in descending order of exponents. [$p.\ 124$]

22. $2x^2 + 7x + 3x + 5$

23. $5a^2 - 4a + 2a + 8$

24. $-3 + 5m^2 - 8 - 2m^2$

25. $5b^3 - 3b + b^2 + 8b + 5 + 4b^2 + 2 + 4b^3$

Simplify. [$p.\ 128$]

26. $a^2(a^3 + a^2)$

27. $2b^5(b^3 + b^2 + b)$

28. $a(a^2 - 2a + 3)$

29. $-m(-m^2 - 5m - 2)$

30. $-(-a^2 - a - 1)$

31. $(a^4 - 3a^2 - 5a) - (-3a^3 + 6a - 7)$

32. $x^4 - 3x^2 + 5 + 3(x^5 - x^4 + 2x^3)$

33. $c^2 + 8c + 9 + 2(c^2 - 3c - 5)$

34. $3ab(a^2 - 5ab + 4b^2)$

35. $-3ac^2(a^3 - 2a^2c + ac^2 - c^3)$

Add. [$p.\ 128$]

36. $(x^3 - 2x^2 + 9) + (x^4 - 3x^3 + x^2)$

37. $(a^2 - 5a + 6) + (-4a^2 - a - 1)$

38. Subtract $x^2 - 5x$ from $2x^3 - 5x^2 + 3x - 2$.

39. Subtract $-y^3 - 3y$ from $y^3 + 2y^2 - 5y + 4$.

Factor into primes. [$p.\ 132$]

40. 18

41. 32

42. 28

Find the missing factor. [$p.\ 132$]

43. $(a^2)(?) = a^7$

44. $(x^4)(?) = x^9$

45. $(?)(5a^3) = 5a^4$

46. $(4a)(?) = 20a^2$

47. $(4a^2b^3)(?) = -36a^3b^7$

48. $(-x^5y^2)(?) = x^7y^6$

Factor. [$p.\ 135$]

49. $4a^2 - 8a + 6$

50. $6x - 2$

51. $4x^2 - 7x$

52. $a^3 - 7a^2 + 3a$

53. $4y^3 - 8y^2 + 12y$

54. $5a^4 - 30a^3 + 20a^2 - 15a$

Chapter Five Test

Evaluate for the given values of the variables.

1. $-3a^3$ if $a = -3$ **2.** $-2m^3n^3$ if $m = -3$, $n = -2$ **3.** $(2ab^2)^3$ if $a = -2$, $b = -1$

Simplify.

4. $(3b^2)(7b)$ **5.** $(-3a^2b)(4ab^3)$ **6.** $(3x^2y^3)^2$

Classify each polynomial.

7. $5a^2 + 2a$ **8.** $7a$ **9.** $4a^2 - 6a + 5$

Simplify. Then write the result in descending order of exponents.

10. $4x^2 - 8x + 5x + 7$ **11.** $3a^2 - 7 + 5a^2 + 9$ **12.** $-3 - 2a + 3a^2 - 5a - 7a^2 + 9$

Simplify.

13. $2a^2(4a^3 - 5a^2)$ **14.** $m^3(m^2 + 7m - 5)$ **15.** $-(-e^2 - 2e - 5)$
16. $(a^2 - 5a + 1) - (-a^2 + 2a^2 - a + 1)$ **17.** $4a^3 - 5a^2 + a + 2(a^2 - 3a^2 - a)$
18. $c^2 + 2a + 5 + 3(c^2 - 2a - 4)$ **19.** $-8ac^2(a^3 - 3a^2c + 2ac^2 + c^3)$

Add.

20. $(x^4 - 2x^3 + 3x) + (5x^3 - x + 2)$ **21.** $(c^3 - c^2 - c) + (-2c^3 - c^2 - 3c)$
22. Subtract $x^2 - 3x$ from $4x^3 - 6x^2 + 5x - 1$. **23.** Subtract $-y^3 - 2y$ from $y^3 + 3y^2 - 4y + 2$.

Factor into primes.

24. 12 **25.** 50

Find the missing factor.

26. $(x^4)(?) = x^{10}$ **27.** $(x^5)(?) = x^6$
28. $(4m^2)(?) = 32m^9$ **29.** $(?)(-3a^2) = 18a^5$
30. $(?)(-5a) = 35a^2$ **31.** $(-2a^2b^3)(?) = 8a^3b^7$

Factor.

32. $3a^2 - 18$ **33.** $5a^2 - 10a$
34. $8a^2 - 16a + 40$ **35.** $a^3 - a^2 - 7a$
36. $m^3 - m^2 - m$ **37.** $6x^3 - 12x^2 + 18x$
38. $3a^2 - 7a - 25$ **39.** $4a^4 - 24a^3 + 12a^2 - 28a$

Scientific Notation

Scientific notation is used to write very large numbers.

The distance from the sun to earth is about 1.5×10^8 kilometers.

$$1.5 \times 10^8 = 1.5 \times \underbrace{100,000,000}_{8 \text{ zeros}}$$
$$= \underbrace{150,000,000}_{\text{Standard notation}} \text{ kilometers}$$

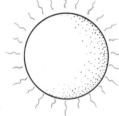

The diameter of the earth is about 13,000 kilometers.

$$13,000 = 13 \times 1,000$$
$$= \underbrace{1.3 \times 10^4}_{\text{Scientific notation}} \text{ kilometers.}$$

PROBLEM

Multiply. Use scientific notation.
$$36,000 \times 25$$
$$3.6 \times 10^4 \times 2.5 \times 10^1 = (3.6 \times 2.5) \times (10^4 \times 10^1)$$
$$= 9.0 \times 10^5, \text{ or } 900,000$$

PROJECT

Write in standard notation.
1. 4×10^2 **2.** 5.8×10^6 **3.** 2.63×10^7

Write in scientific notation.
4. 400,000,000 **5.** 63,000 **6.** 23,200,000,000

Multiply. Use scientific notation.
7. $250 \times 7,000$ **8.** $9,300 \times 30$ **9.** $54,200 \times 8,100$

Multiplying Polynomials

 REVIEW CAPSULE

Simplify $4x(x + 2)$.

$$4x(x + 2) = (4x)(x) + (4x)(2)$$
$$= 4x^2 + 8x$$

EXAMPLE 1   Multiply $(3x + 5)(2x + 4)$.

$$(3x + 5)(2x + 4)$$

Think. ────────────→ $(\boxed{})(2x + 4)$

Distribute $\boxed{}$. ──────→ $(\boxed{})(2x) + (\boxed{})(4)$

$\boxed{}$ is $3x + 5$. ──────→ $(3x + 5)(2x) + (3x + 5)(4)$

Distribute $2x$. Then distribute 4.
Multiply. ────────→ $(3x)(2x) + (5)(2x) + (3x)(4) + (5)(4)$
$$6x^2 + 10x + 12x + 20$$
Combine like terms. ────→ $6x^2 + 22x + 20$

There is a more convenient way to arrange the
work.

Rewrite in vertical form.
$(3x)(2x) = 6x^2$
$(5)(4) = 20$

$$
\begin{array}{lr}
3x & +5 \\
2x & +4 \\
\hline
6x^2 & +20
\end{array}
$$
end terms

Find the middle term by multiplying along the
diagonals and adding.

$$
\begin{array}{lr}
3x & +5 \\
2x & +4 \\
\hline
& +10x
\end{array}
$$

$(2x)(5) = 10x$ ────────────→
$(4)(3x) = 12x$ ────────────→ $6x^2 \quad \begin{array}{c} +12x \\ \hline +22x \end{array} \quad +20$
$+10x + 12x = +22x$ ──────→

Thus, $(3x + 5)(2x + 4) = 6x^2 + 22x + 20$.

EXAMPLE 2　Multiply $(2x - 5)(3x + 4)$.

Rewrite in vertical form.
Find the end terms.
$(3x)(2x) = 6x^2;\ (4)(-5) = -20$ ⟶

$$
\begin{array}{lr}
2x & -5 \\
3x & +4 \\
\hline
6x^2 & -20
\end{array}
$$

More compact form

$$
\begin{array}{lcr}
2x & & -5 \\
3x & & +4 \\
\hline
6x^2 & +8x & -20 \\
& -15x & \\
\hline
& -7x &
\end{array}
$$

Find the middle term.
$(3x)(-5) = -15x$
$(4)(2x) = +8x$
$-15x + 8x = -7x$

$$
\begin{array}{lcr}
2x & & -5 \\
3x & & +4 \\
\hline
& -15x & \\
6x^2 & +8x & -20 \\
\hline
& -7x &
\end{array}
$$

Thus, $(2x - 5)(3x + 4) = 6x^2 - 7x - 20.$

EXAMPLE 3　Multiply $(x + 5)(x - 5)$.

Write x as $1x$.
Find the middle term.
$(1x)(5) = +5x$
$(-5)(1x) = -5x$
$+5x - 5x = 0x$
$0x = 0;\ 1x^2 = x^2$ ⟶
The product of two binomials
may be a binomial.

$$
\begin{array}{lcr}
1x & & +5 \\
1x & & -5 \\
\hline
& +5x & \\
1x^2 & -5x & -25 \\
\hline
& 0x &
\end{array}
$$

$1x^2 + 0 - 25$, or $x^2 - 25$

Thus, $(x + 5)(x - 5) = x^2 - 25.$

EXAMPLE 4　Simplify $(2x - 3)^2$.

$(2x - 3)^2 = (2x - 3)(2x - 3)$
Find the middle term.
$(2x)(-3) = -6x$
$(-3)(2x) = -6x$
$-6x - 6x = -12x$

$$
\begin{array}{lcr}
2x & & -3 \\
2x & & -3 \\
\hline
& -6x & \\
4x^2 & -6x & +9 \\
\hline
& -12x &
\end{array}
$$

Thus, $(2x - 3)^2 = 4x^2 - 12x + 9.$

EXAMPLE 5　Multiply $(4a - b)(a - 2b)$.

Write $-b$ as $-1b$.
Write a as $1a$.
$(1a)(-1b) = (1)(-1)(a)(b)$, or $-1ab$
$(-2b)(4a) = (-2)(4)(a)(b)$, or $-8ab$
$-1ab - 8ab = -9ab$

$$
\begin{array}{lcr}
4a & & -1b \\
1a & & -2b \\
\hline
& -1ab & \\
4a^2 & -8ab & +2b^2 \\
\hline
& -9ab &
\end{array}
$$

Thus, $(4a - b)(a - 2b) = 4a^2 - 9ab + 2b^2.$

EXERCISES

PART A

Multiply.

1. $(3x + 2)(2x + 7)$

2. $(4x + 5)(5x + 3)$

3. $(3m + 5)(2m + 1)$

4. $(2x - 1)(3x + 1)$

5. $(2a - 1)(4a + 7)$

6. $(2b - 5)(3b + 5)$

7. $(m - 5)(m + 5)$

8. $(y - 4)(y + 4)$

9. $(2r - 3)(2r + 3)$

10. $(3x - 1)(x + 2)$

11. $(3a - 2)(a - 1)$

12. $(2m - 6)(2m - 6)$

13. $(2y - 5)(y + 4)$

14. $(3t - 1)(3t + 1)$

15. $(2b - 5)(b + 2)$

16. $(4d - 1)(d + 2)$

17. $(3x + 5)(x - 7)$

18. $(2n - 1)(n + 8)$

19. $(3y - 1)(3y + 1)$

20. $(7a - 1)(2a + 3)$

21. $(6a - 5)(a + 2)$

22. $(3a - 8b)(a - 5b)$

23. $(2y - m)(2y + 9m)$

24. $(3p + q)(2p + 3q)$

Simplify.

25. $(3y - 5)^2$

26. $(4x - 1)^2$

27. $(2x + 3)^2$

28. $(5n + 1)^2$

PART B

EXAMPLE   Multiply $(2x + 3)(3x^2 + 2x - 5)$.

Rewrite in vertical form.

$2x(3x^2 + 2x - 5)$ ⟶

$3(3x^2 + 2x - 5)$ ⟶

Combine like terms. ⟶

$$\begin{array}{r} 3x^2 + 2x - 5 \\ 2x + 3 \\ \hline 6x^3 + 4x^2 - 10x \\ 9x^2 + 6x - 15 \\ \hline 6x^3 + 13x^2 - 4x - 15 \end{array}$$

Multiply.

29. $(3x - 1)(2x^2 + 4x + 3)$

30. $(2x + 7)(4x^2 - 3x + 2)$

31. $(x + 7)(3x^2 - x + 5)$

32. $(x - 5)(x^2 - 7x + 1)$

33. $(3x + 2)(x^3 - 7x^2 + 3x)$

34. $(2x + 3)(x^3 - 2x^2 + x - 3)$

PART C

EXAMPLE   Simplify $(a + b)^2$. Apply the pattern to $(x + 4)^2$.

Think: $(a + b)^2 = (a + b)(a + b)$.

$$\begin{array}{r} a \qquad +b \\ a \qquad +b \\ \hline +1ab \\ a^2 \quad +1ab \qquad +b^2 \\ \hline +2ab \end{array}$$

Pattern for squaring a binomial ⟶ **Thus,** $(a + b)^2 = a^2 + 2ab + b^2$

Replace a with x and b with 4. ⟶ $(x + 4)^2 = x^2 + 2(x)(4) + (4)^2$, or

$$x^2 + 8x + 16.$$

Simplify by using $(a + b)^2 = a^2 + 2ab + b^2$.

35. $(x - 7)^2$

36. $(2x + 3)^2$

37. $(2m - 1)^2$

38. $(3a - 4b)^2$

Rectangle Products

Areas of rectangles and squares can be used to show the product of two binomials.

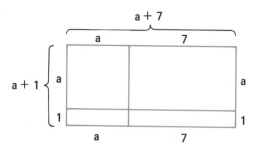

Area = length × width
= $(a + 7)(a + 1)$

But, the area of the rectangle is the sum of the areas of all of its parts.

a	7	a	7
$(a)(a)$ +	$7(a)$ +	$1(a)$ +	$7(1)$
a^2 +	$7a$ +	$1a$ +	7

Thus, $(a + 7)(a + 1) = a^2 + 8a + 7$.

PROJECT Use the rectangle method to multiply the binomials.
1. $(a + 2)(a + 3)$ **2.** $(x + 8)(x + 5)$ **3.** $(x + 2)(x + 5)$

Factoring Trinomials

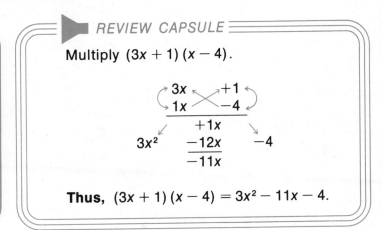

REVIEW CAPSULE

Multiply $(3x + 1)(x - 4)$.

$$3x^2 \quad \begin{array}{c} +1x \\ -12x \\ \hline -11x \end{array} \quad -4$$

Thus, $(3x + 1)(x - 4) = 3x^2 - 11x - 4$.

EXAMPLE 1 Factor $2x^2 + 5x + 3$ into two binomials.

Write a pattern to test factors.

$\left.\begin{array}{c} 2 \\ 1 \end{array}\right\}$ Factors of 2 $\left.\begin{array}{c} 3 \\ 1 \end{array}\right\}$ Factors of 3

$\begin{array}{cc} 2x & \square 3 \\ 1x & \square 1 \end{array}$ → Omit signs for now.

Does choice of factors give correct middle term?

$(1x)(\square 3) = \square 3x$

$(\square 1)(2x) = \square 2x$

$$2x^2 \quad \begin{array}{c} \square 3x \\ \square 2x \\ \hline +5x \end{array} \quad +3$$

Check all sign combinations. ⟶

$$\begin{array}{cccc} +3x & +3x & -3x & -3x \\ +2x & -2x & +2x & -2x \\ \hline +5x & +1x & -1x & -5x \end{array}$$

└─ One sign combination works.

Check by multiplying.

$\left.\begin{array}{c} (1x)(\boxplus 3) = +3x \\ (\boxplus 1)(2x) = +2x \\ +3x + 2x = +5x \end{array}\right\}$

$$2x^2 \quad \begin{array}{c} +3x \\ +2x \\ \hline +5x \end{array} \quad +3$$

The factors are $(2x + 3)$ and $(1x + 1)$. ⟶ **Thus,** $2x^2 + 5x + 3 = (2x + 3)(x + 1)$.

EXAMPLE 2 Factor $6x^2 - 7x + 2$.

$\left.\begin{array}{l}2\\3\end{array}\right\}$ Factors of 6 $\left.\begin{array}{l}2\\1\end{array}\right\}$ Factors of 2

$(3x)(\square 2) = \square 6x$

$(\square 1)(2x) = \square 2x$

No sign combination works.

Try reversing factors of $2\left\{\begin{array}{l}1\\2\end{array}\right.$.

$(3x)(\square 1) = \square 3x$

$(\square 2)(2x) = \square 4x$

One sign combination works.
Check by multiplying.

$\left.\begin{array}{l}(3x)(\boxminus 1) = -3x\\(\boxminus 2)(2x) = -4x\\-3x - 4x = -7x\end{array}\right\}$

Write factors horizontally. $\longrightarrow$

$\begin{array}{l}2x \quad\searrow\quad \square 2\\3x \quad\nearrow\quad \square 1\\\hline 6x^2 \quad \dfrac{\square 6x}{\square 2x} \quad +2\\\qquad \overline{-7x}\end{array}$

$\begin{array}{l}2x \quad\searrow\quad \square 1\\3x \quad\nearrow\quad \square 2\\\hline 6x^2 \quad \dfrac{\square 3x}{\square 4x} \quad +2\\\qquad \overline{-7x}\end{array}$

Check sign combinations.

$+6x$	$+6x$	$-6x$	$-6x$
$+2x$	$-2x$	$+2x$	$-2x$
$+8x$	$+4x$	$-4x$	$-8x$

None gives $-7x$.

Check sign combinations.

$+3x$	$+3x$	$-3x$	$-3x$
$+4x$	$-4x$	$+4x$	$-4x$
$+7x$	$-1x$	$+1x$	$-7x$

One gives $-7x$.

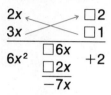
$\begin{array}{l}2x \quad\searrow\quad \boxminus 1\\3x \quad\nearrow\quad \boxminus 2\\\hline 6x^2 \quad \dfrac{-3x}{-4x} \quad +2\\\qquad \overline{-7x}\end{array}$

Thus, $6x^2 - 7x + 2 = (2x - 1)(3x - 2)$.

EXAMPLE 3 Factor $x^2 + x - 20$.

$x^2 = 1x^2,\ x = 1x \longrightarrow$

$\left.\begin{array}{l}1\\1\end{array}\right\}$ Factors of 1 $\left.\begin{array}{l}10\\2\end{array}\right\}$ Factors of 20

$(1x)(\square 10) = \square 10x$

$(\square 2)(1x) = \square 2x$

No sign combination works.

Try $\left.\begin{array}{l}5\\4\end{array}\right\}$ Factors of 20.

One sign combination works.
Check by multiplying.

$\left.\begin{array}{l}(1x)(\boxplus 5) = +5x\\(\boxminus 4)(1x) = -4x\\+5x - 4x = +1x\end{array}\right\}$

The factors are
$(x + 5)$ and $(x - 4)$. $\longrightarrow$

$\begin{array}{l}1x^2 \quad +1x \quad -20\\1x \quad\searrow\quad \square 10\\1x \quad\nearrow\quad \square 2\\\hline 1x^2 \quad \square 10x \quad -20\\\qquad \dfrac{\square 2x}{+1x}\end{array}$

$\begin{array}{l}1x \quad\searrow\quad \square 5\\1x \quad\nearrow\quad \square 4\\\hline 1x^2 \quad \square 5x \quad -20\\\qquad \dfrac{\square 4x}{+1x}\end{array}$

Check sign combinations.

$+10x$	$+10x$	$-10x$	$-10x$
$+2x$	$-2x$	$+2x$	$-2x$
$+12x$	$+8x$	$-8x$	$-12x$

None gives $+1x$.

Check sign combinations.

$+5x$	$+5x$
$+4x$	$-4x$
$+9x$	$+1x$

One gives $+1x$.

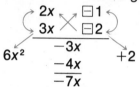
$\begin{array}{l}1x \quad\searrow\quad \boxplus 5\\1x \quad\nearrow\quad \boxminus 4\\\hline 1x^2 \quad +5x \quad -20\\\qquad \dfrac{-4x}{+1x}\end{array}$

Thus, $x^2 + x - 20 = (x + 5)(x - 4)$.

EXAMPLE 4   Factor $2x^2 - 5x - 12$.

$\left.\begin{array}{l}2\\1\end{array}\right\}$ factors of 2 $\left.\begin{array}{l}6\\2\end{array}\right\}$ factors of 12

$(1x)\,(\square 6) = \square 6x$

$(\square 2)\,(2x) = \square 4x$

No sign combination works.

Try $\left.\begin{array}{l}2\\6\end{array}\right\}$ factors of 12.

No sign combination works.

Try $\left.\begin{array}{l}3\\4\end{array}\right\}$ factors of 12.

$(1x)\,(\square 3) = \square 3x$

$(\square 4)\,(2x) = \square 8x$

One sign combination works.

Check by multiplying.

$(1x)\,(\boxplus 3) = +3x$

$(\boxminus 4)\,(2x) = -8x$

$+3x - 8x = -5x$

We can also write $(x - 4)\,(2x + 3)$.

$\begin{array}{ll} 2x \diagdown \square 6 \\ 1x \diagup \square 2 \\ \hline 2x^2 \begin{array}{c}\square 6x\\ \square 4x\end{array} -12 \\ \hline -5x \end{array}$

Check sign combinations.

$+6x$	$+6x$	$-6x$	$-6x$
$+4x$	$-4x$	$+4x$	$-4x$
$+10x$	$+2x$	$-2x$	$-10x$

None gives $-5x$.

$\begin{array}{ll} 2x \diagdown \square 2 \\ 1x \diagup \square 6 \\ \hline 2x^2 \begin{array}{c}\square 2x\\ \square 12x\end{array} -12 \\ \hline -5x \end{array}$

Check sign combinations.

$+2x$	$+2x$	$-2x$	$-2x$
$+12x$	$-12x$	$+12x$	$-12x$
$+14x$	$-10x$	$+10x$	$-14x$

None gives $-5x$.

$\begin{array}{ll} 2x \diagdown \square 3 \\ 1x \diagup \square 4 \\ \hline 2x^2 \begin{array}{c}\square 3x\\ \square 8x\end{array} -12 \\ \hline -5x \end{array}$

Check sign combinations.

$+3x$	$+3x$
$+8x$	$-8x$
$+11x$	$-5x$

One gives $-5x$.

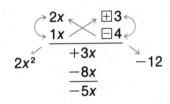

Thus, $2x^2 - 5x - 12 = (2x + 3)\,(x - 4)$.

EXERCISES

PART A

Factor.

1. $2x^2 + 7x + 5$
2. $3x^2 + 10x + 7$
3. $5x^2 + 7x + 2$
4. $8x^2 - 10x + 3$
5. $6x^2 - 17x + 5$
6. $10x^2 - 19x + 7$
7. $x^2 + x - 6$
8. $x^2 + x - 12$
9. $x^2 + x - 30$
10. $2a^2 - 7a - 4$
11. $3x^2 - 10x - 25$
12. $2x^2 - x - 3$
13. $x^2 + 7x + 10$
14. $b^2 + 5b + 6$
15. $a^2 + 4a + 3$
16. $y^2 - 10y + 16$
17. $m^2 - 9m + 20$
18. $d^2 - 11d + 30$

19. $a^2 - a - 20$
20. $y^2 - 2y - 15$
21. $a^2 - 7a - 18$
22. $x^2 + 2x + 1$
23. $b^2 - 6b + 9$
24. $k^2 + 12k + 36$
25. $2a^2 - 7a + 6$
26. $2x^2 + 5x - 3$
27. $2a^2 - 7a - 4$
28. $2m^2 + 9m - 5$
29. $2a^2 + 13a + 15$
30. $3b^2 - 11b + 6$
31. $3x^2 + 10x - 25$
32. $2m^2 + 11m + 15$
33. $2m^2 - 7m + 5$
34. $6a^2 + a - 1$
35. $3y^2 + 7y - 20$
36. $2p^2 - 15p + 25$
37. $2b^2 + 17b + 30$
38. $2x^2 + 5x + 2$
39. $12y^2 + 7y + 1$

PART B

Factor.

40. $2x^2 - 11x - 40$
41. $2x^2 + 23x + 45$
42. $3x^2 + 10x - 48$
43. $2a^2 - 25a + 50$
44. $3a^2 + 8a - 35$
45. $2b^2 - 29b + 60$
46. $3m^2 + 29m + 40$
47. $5x^2 - 42x - 27$
48. $3y^2 - 31y + 56$

PART C

EXAMPLE Factor $6x^2 - 7x - 20$.

$\left.\begin{array}{c}6\\1\end{array}\right\}$ factors of 6 $\left.\begin{array}{c}5\\4\end{array}\right\}$ factors of 20

$$\begin{array}{c}6x \searrow \;\square 5 \\ 1x \;\nearrow\;\square 4 \\ \hline 6x^2 \;\square 5x \;\; -20 \\ \;\;\;\;\square 24x \end{array}$$

Check sign combinations.

$+5x$	$+5x$	$-5x$	$-5x$
$+24x$	$-24x$	$+24x$	$-24x$
$+29x$	$-19x$	$+19x$	$-29x$

None gives $-7x$.

No combination works.

Try some other combinations of factors.

$$\begin{array}{c}1x \searrow \square 5\\6x \nearrow \square 4\end{array} \;\text{or}\; \begin{array}{c}1x \searrow \square 10\\6x \nearrow \square 2\end{array} \;\text{or}\; \begin{array}{c}3x \searrow \square 4\\2x \nearrow \square 5\end{array} \;\text{etc.}$$

Only this one works. $\begin{array}{c}3x \searrow \boxplus 4\\2x \nearrow \boxminus 5\end{array}$

Check by multiplying.

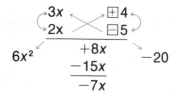

$$\begin{array}{c}3x \;\boxplus 4\\2x \;\boxminus 5\\ \hline 6x^2 \;\; +8x \;\; -20\\ \;\;\;\;-15x\\ \hline \;\;\;\;-7x\end{array}$$

Thus, $6x^2 - 7x - 20 = (3x + 4)(2x - 5)$.

Factor.

49. $15d^2 - 19d + 6$
50. $15y^2 + 17y - 18$
51. $14b^2 - 15b - 9$
52. $4a^2 - 20a + 25$
53. $9a^2 - 12a + 4$
54. $6a^2 - a - 15$
55. $15x^2 - 29x + 12$
56. $16y^2 + 14y - 15$
57. $18a^2 - 9a - 35$

Flow Chart: Solving a Simple Equation

PROBLEM

Write a flow chart to solve an equation of the form $ax + b = c$.

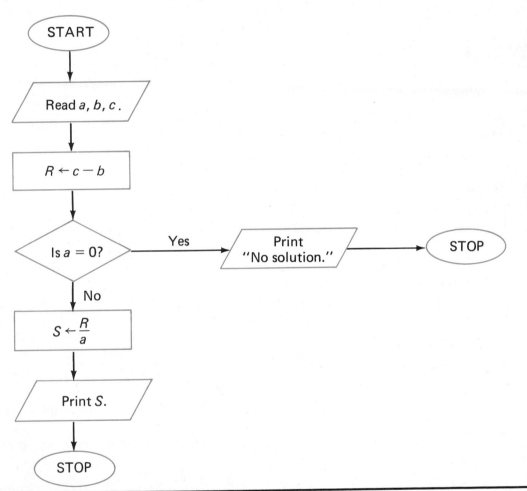

PROJECT

1. Follow the flow chart to solve $2x + 7 = 13$.
2. Write a flow chart to solve an equation of the form $ax + b = cx + d$. Use it to solve $5x + 3 = 3x + 13$.

149

The Difference of Two Squares

▶ REVIEW CAPSULE

Factor $x^2 - 7x + 12$.

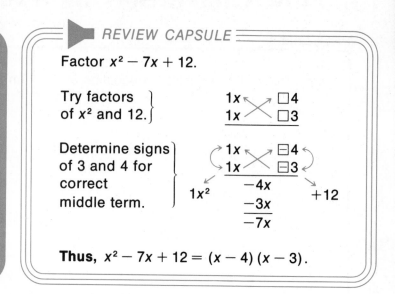

Try factors of x^2 and 12.

Determine signs of 3 and 4 for correct middle term.

Thus, $x^2 - 7x + 12 = (x - 4)(x - 3)$.

EXAMPLE 1 Factor $x^2 - 36$.

Think of $x^2 - 36$ as a disguised trinomial with middle term $0x$. ───────→ Rewrite $x^2 - 36$ as $x^2 + 0x - 36$.

$\left.\begin{array}{c}1\\1\end{array}\right\}$ factors of 1; $\left.\begin{array}{c}9\\4\end{array}\right\}$ factors of 36

$(1x)(\square 9) = \square 9x$
$(\square 4)(1x) = \square 4x$

No sign combination works.

Check sign combinations.

+9x	+9x	−9x	−9x
+4x	−4x	+4x	−4x
+13x	+5x	−5x	−13x

None gives 0x.

Try $\left.\begin{array}{c}6\\6\end{array}\right\}$ factors of 36.

$(1x)(\square 6) = \square 6x$
$(\square 6)(1x) = \square 6x$

One sign combination works.
Check by multiplying.

Check sign combinations.

+6x	+6x
+6x	−6x
+12x	0x

One gives 0x.

$\left.\begin{array}{l}(1x)(\boxplus 6) = +6x\\(\boxminus 6)(1x) = -6x\\+6x - 6x = 0x\end{array}\right\}$

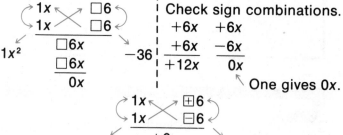

The factors are $(x + 6)$ and $(x - 6)$.

Thus, $x^2 - 36 = (x + 6)(x - 6)$.

$$x^2 - 36$$
$$\downarrow \qquad \downarrow$$
$$= (x)^2 - (6)^2$$
$$\uparrow$$

$x^2 - 36$ is the difference of two squares.

$x^2 = (x)(x)$, or $(x)^2$
$36 = (6)(6)$, or $(6)^2$ ⟶

EXAMPLE 2   Factor $4m^2 - 25$.

Rewrite as a trinomial. ⟶
$$4m^2 + 0m - 25$$

$\left.\begin{matrix} 2 \\ 2 \end{matrix}\right\}$ factors of 4; $\left.\begin{matrix} 5 \\ 5 \end{matrix}\right\}$ factors of 25

$(2m)(\square 5) = \square 10m$
$(\square 5)(2m) = \square 10m$
One sign combination works.

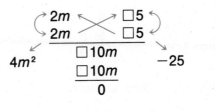

Check sign combinations.

$+10m$	$+10m$
$+10m$	$-10m$
$+20m$	$\nearrow 0$

One gives 0.

Check by multiplying.

$(2m)(\boxplus 5) = {+}10m$
$(\boxminus 5)(2m) = -10m$
$+10m - 10m = 0$

We can also write $(2m - 5)(2m + 5)$.

Thus, $4m^2 - 25 = (2m + 5)(2m - 5)$.

$4m^2 - 25$
$(2m)^2 - (5)^2$
$\,\llcorner$ difference

$4m^2 - 25$ is also the difference of two squares.
$$(2m)^2 - (5)^2$$

Observe a pattern for factoring the difference of two squares.

	$x^2 - 36$		$4m^2 - 25$
Rewrite. ⟶	$(x)^2 - (6)^2$		$(2m)^2 - (5)^2$
Factor. ⟶	$(x - 6)(x + 6)$		$(2m - 5)(2m + 5)$

EXAMPLE 3   Factor $x^2 - 4$.

Rewrite. ⟶
Factor. ⟶
$$(x)^2 - (2)^2$$
$$(x - 2)(x + 2)$$

EXAMPLE 4   Factor $36 - y^2$.

Rewrite. ⟶
Factor. ⟶
$$(6)^2 - (y)^2$$
$$(6 - y)(6 + y)$$

EXAMPLE 5   Factor $144b^2 - 49$.

Rewrite. ————————————————→ $(12b)^2 - (7)^2$
Factor. ————————————————→ $(12b - 7)(12b + 7)$

ORAL EXERCISES

Express each term in the form $(a)^2$.

1. 9   **2.** 64   **3.** 36   **4.** 100   **5.** 16
6. 144   **7.** $16b^2$ **8.** $81x^2$ **9.** $121x^2$ **10.** $49m^2$
11. c^2 **12.** $100x^2$ **13.** $9t^2$ **14.** $25b^2$ **15.** $225k^2$

Tell which are differences of two squares.

16. $x^2 - 16$ **17.** $m^2 + 49$ **18.** $y^2 - 35$
19. $25a^2 - 121$ **20.** $100x^2 - 50$ **21.** $64 - 49t^2$
22. $81k^2 + 225$ **23.** $625 + 10x^2$ **24.** $169 - 13y^2$

EXERCISES

PART A

Factor.

1. $x^2 - 16$ **2.** $m^2 - 49$ **3.** $b^2 - 25$
4. $a^2 - 81$ **5.** $b^2 - 1$ **6.** $m^2 - 100$
7. $m^2 - 64$ **8.** $x^2 - 36$ **9.** $4b^2 - 49$
10. $9a^2 - 25$ **11.** $25a^2 - 36$ **12.** $16x^2 - 25$
13. $49y^2 - 4$ **14.** $16m^2 - 1$ **15.** $25m^2 - 4$
16. $36a^2 - 25$ **17.** $4t^2 - 25$ **18.** $4b^2 - 1$
19. $25 - x^2$ **20.** $64 - y^2$ **21.** $81 - t^2$
22. $36 - a^2$ **23.** $49 - b^2$ **24.** $100 - c^2$
25. $1 - y^2$ **26.** $100 - 49x^2$ **27.** $64 - 81c^2$
28. $1 - 9x^2$ **29.** $16 - 81y^2$ **30.** $64 - 49b^2$

PART B

Factor.

31. $144a^2 - 81$ **32.** $100x^2 - 49$ **33.** $25m^2 - 144$
34. $4m^2 - 169$ **35.** $36x^2 - 25$ **36.** $25 - 144b^2$
37. $169p^2 - 16$ **38.** $x^2 - 196$ **39.** $49 - 225x^2$
40. $121 - 16b^2$ **41.** $16t^2 - 225$ **42.** $100a^2 - 49$
43. $225a^2 - 169$ **44.** $36a^2 - 169$ **45.** $121m^2 - 225$

Combined Types of Factoring

OBJECTIVE

■ To factor polynomials like
$2x^3 - 20x^2 + 18x$

 REVIEW CAPSULE

Factor the GCF from $4x^3 - 12x^2 + 8x$.
$$4(x^3) + 4(-3x^2) + 4(2x)$$
4 is the greatest common whole
number factor.
$$4x^3 \quad - \quad 12x^2 \quad + \quad 8x$$
$$\uparrow \qquad\qquad \uparrow \qquad\qquad \uparrow$$
three x's   two x's   one x
x is the greatest common variable
factor. The GCF is $4x$.
$$4x^3 - 12x^2 + 8x$$
$$4x(x^2) + 4x(-3x) + 4x(2)$$
$$4x(x^2 - 3x + 2)$$

We have factored out the GCF from a polynomial.
We have factored a polynomial into two binomials.
Now, we combine these two types of factoring to
factor a polynomial completely.

EXAMPLE 1   Factor $4x^3 - 12x^2 + 8x$ completely.

Use the steps in the Review to factor out
the GCF.
Factor $x^2 - 3x + 2$ into two binomials.

$(1x)(\square 2) = \square 2x$
$(\square 1)(1x) = \square 1x$

Check by multiplying.

$(1x)(\boxminus 2) = -2x$
$(\boxminus 1)(1x) = -1x$
$-2x - 1x = -3x$

$4x(x^2 - 3x + 2)$

$1x \quad \square 2$
$1x \quad \square 1$
$1x^2 \quad \dfrac{\square 2x}{\square 1x}$
$\qquad -3x$

Check sign combinations.

$+2x$	$+2x$	$-2x$	$-2x$
$+1x$	$-1x$	$+1x$	$-1x$
$+3x$	$+1x$	$-1x$	$-3x$

$+2$ One gives $-3x$.

$1x \quad \boxminus 2$
$1x \quad \boxminus 1$
$1x^2 \quad \dfrac{-2x}{-1x} \qquad +2$
$\qquad -3x$

$$x^2 - 3x + 2 = (x - 2)(x - 1)$$

Put all factors together. ⟶ **Thus,** $4x^3 - 12x^2 + 8x = 4x(x - 2)(x - 1)$.

EXAMPLE 2 Factor $2x^3 - 4x^2 - 48x$ completely.

Find the GCF.
Greatest common whole number factor
is 2.
Greatest common variable factor: x
GCF is $2x$.
Factor out the GCF. ⟶

$$2(x^3) + 2(-2x^2) + 2(-24x)$$
$$\uparrow \qquad\quad \uparrow \qquad\quad \uparrow$$
three x's   two x's   one x
$$2x(x^2) + 2x(-2x) + 2x(-24)$$
$$2x(x^2 - 2x - 24)$$

Factor $x^2 - 2x - 24$ into two binomials.

$1x \searrow \square6$
$1x \times \square4$
$1x^2 \quad \dfrac{\square6x}{\square4x} \quad -24$
$\quad\quad \dfrac{\square4x}{-2x}$

Check sign combinations.

$+6x$	$+6x$	$-6x$
$+4x$	$-4x$	$+4x$
$+10x$	$+2x$	$-2x$

One gives $-2x$.

Check by multiplying.

$(1x)(\boxminus6) = -6x$
$(\boxplus4)(1x) = +4x$
$-6x + 4x = -2x$

$1x \searrow \boxminus6$
$1x \times \boxplus4$
$1x^2 \quad \dfrac{-6x}{+4x} \quad -24$
$\quad\quad \dfrac{+4x}{-2x}$

$x^2 - 2x - 24 = (x - 6)(x + 4)$

Put all factors together. ⟶ **Thus,** $2x^3 - 4x^2 - 48x = 2x(x - 6)(x + 4)$.

EXAMPLE 3 Factor $3x^3 - 3x$ completely.

Find the GCF.
Greatest common whole number factor
is 3.
Greatest common variable factor: x
GCF is $3x$. Factor it out.
$x^2 - 1 = (x)^2 - (1)^2$; factor as the
difference of 2 squares.

$$3(x^3) + 3(-1x)$$
$$\uparrow \qquad\quad \uparrow$$
three x's   one x
$$3x(x^2 - 1)$$
$$3x(x - 1)(x + 1)$$

Put all factors together. ⟶ **Thus,** $3x^3 - 3x = 3x(x - 1)(x + 1)$.

EXAMPLE 4 Factor $x^2 - 6x + 8$ completely.

First look for the GCF.
No common whole number
factor, other than 1
No common variable factor

$$1(x^2) + 2(-3x) + 2(4)$$
$$\uparrow \qquad\quad \uparrow \qquad\quad \uparrow$$
two x's   one x no x's
The GCF is one. Don't bother to factor it out.

Factor $x^2 - 6x + 8$ into two binomials.

$1x \searrow \square4$
$1x \times \square2$
$\dfrac{\square4x}{\square2x}$
$\dfrac{}{\square6x}$

Check sign combinations.

$+4x$	$+4x$	$-4x$	$-4x$
$+2x$	$-2x$	$+2x$	$-2x$
$+6x$	$+2x$	$-2x$	$-6x$

One gives $-6x$.

Check by multiplying. ⟶ **Thus,** $x^2 - 6x + 8 = (x - 4)(x - 2)$.

EXERCISES

Factor completely.

1. $2a^2 - 10a + 8$
2. $2b^2 - 6b + 4$
3. $2a^2 + 4a - 70$
4. $2m^3 - 5m^2 + 3m$
5. $3x^3 + 4x^2 - 4x$
6. $m^3 - 9m$
7. $2x^3 - 2x$
8. $3a^3 - 27a$
9. $8m^3 - 50m$
10. $2x^3 - 14x^2 + 24x$
11. $2m^3 - 20m^2 + 18m$
12. $3x^3 - 24x^2 + 36x$
13. $4a^3 - 12a^2 - 40a$
14. $6x^3 - 28x^2 - 10x$
15. $6b^3 - 3b^2 - 30b$
16. $4a^2 - 24a + 20$
17. $2a^3 + 16a^2 + 30a$
18. $12m^2 + 33m - 9$
19. $2a^2 + 13a - 7$
20. $4y^2 + 7y - 2$
21. $2a^2 + 3a + 1$

Factor completely.

22. $18x^2 - 98$
23. $6x^2 + 9x - 105$
24. $169a - 25a^3$
25. $3y^4 - 7y^3 - 20y^2$
26. $30e^3 - 32e^2 - 14e$
27. $12a^3 - 72a^2 + 33a$
28. $15a^2 - 57a + 54$
29. $9a^3 + 66a^2 - 48a$
30. $18m^3 - 512m$

EXAMPLE　Factor $am + bm + an + bn$.

$$a(m) + b(m) + a(n) + b(n)$$
$$m(a + b) + n(a + b)$$

Treat $(a + b)$ as a single common factor. Factor it out.

$$(a + b)(m + n)$$

Thus, $am + bm + an + bn = (a + b)(m + n)$.

EXAMPLE　Factor $x^2m + x^2 - 4m - 4$.

$$x^2(m) + x^2(1) + (-4)(m) + (-4)(1)$$
$$x^2(m + 1) - 4(m + 1)$$

Factor out $(m + 1)$. $\longrightarrow$

$$(m + 1)(x^2 - 4)$$

Factor $x^2 - 4$. $\longrightarrow$

$$(m + 1)(x - 2)(x + 2)$$

Thus, $x^2m + x^2 - 4m - 4 = (m + 1)(x - 2)(x + 2)$.

Factor.

31. $xm + xn - am - an$
32. $4x + 4y + bx + by$
33. $pr + pt - 2r - 2t$
34. $x^2a + x^2b - 16a - 16b$
35. $p^2y + p^2 - 25y - 25$
36. $16a + 16 - y^2a - y^2$

Factoring Polynomials in Two Variables

OBJECTIVE

■ To factor polynomials like
$2x^3 - 6x^2y + 4xy^2$

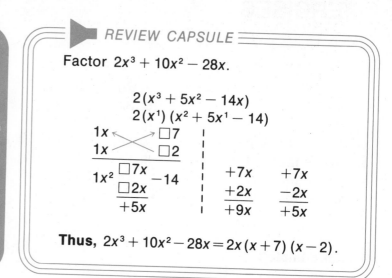

▶ REVIEW CAPSULE

Factor $2x^3 + 10x^2 - 28x$.

$$2(x^3 + 5x^2 - 14x)$$
$$2(x^1)(x^2 + 5x^1 - 14)$$

$1x \diagdown \Box 7$
$1x \diagup \Box 2$

$1x^2$	$\Box 7x$	-14		$+7x$	$+7x$
	$\Box 2x$			$+2x$	$-2x$
	$+5x$			$+9x$	$+5x$

Thus, $2x^3 + 10x^2 - 28x = 2x(x+7)(x-2)$.

EXAMPLE 1 Factor $x^2 + 3xy + 2y^2$ completely.

Check for GCF. ⟶ 1 is the GCF of $x^2 + 3xy + 2y^2$.

$\left.\begin{matrix}1x\\1x\end{matrix}\right\}$ factors of x^2 $\left.\begin{matrix}2y\\1y\end{matrix}\right\}$ factors of $2y^2$

$(1x)(\Box 2y) = \Box 2xy$
$(\Box y)(1x) = \Box 1xy$

$1x \diagdown \Box 2y$ Check sign combinations.
$1x \diagup \Box y$ $+2xy$

$1x^2$ $\Box 2xy$ $+2y^2$ $+1xy$
$\quad\ \Box 1xy$ $+3xy$
$\quad\ +3xy$ ↖ This one works.

Check by multiplying.

$(1x)(\boxplus 2y) = +2xy\ $⎫
$(\boxplus 1y)(1x) = +1xy\ $⎬
$+2xy + 1xy = +3xy\ $⎭

$1x \diagdown \boxplus 2y$
$1x \diagup \boxplus 1y$

$1x^2 \diagup \boxplus 2xy$
$\quad\ \boxplus 1xy \diagdown +2y^2$
$\quad\ +3xy$

Thus, $x^2 + 3xy + 2y^2 = (x + 2y)(x + y)$.

EXAMPLE 2 Factor $5x^2 - 20y^2$ completely.

The GCF is 5. ⟶
$x^2 - 4y^2$
↓   ↓
$(x)^2 - (2y)^2$
difference of two squares

$5(x^2 - 4y^2)$
$5[(x)^2 - (2y)^2]$
$5(x - 2y)(x + 2y)$

Thus, $5x^2 - 20y^2 = 5(x - 2y)(x + 2y)$.

EXAMPLE 3   Factor $2a^2 - 4ab - 70b^2$ completely.

The GCF is 2. ⟶

$$2(a^2 - 2ab - 35b^2)$$

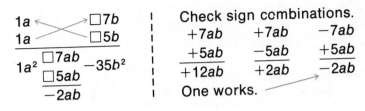

$1a \Big\}a^2 \qquad 7b \Big\}35b^2$
$1a \qquad\qquad 5b$

Check sign combinations.

$+7ab$	$+7ab$	$-7ab$
$+5ab$	$-5ab$	$+5ab$
$+12ab$	$+2ab$	$-2ab$

One works. ⟶

Check by multiplying.

$(1a)(\boxminus 7b) = -7ab$
$(\boxplus 5b)(1a) = +5ab$
$-7ab + 5ab = -2ab$

Thus, $2a^2 - 4ab - 70b^2 = 2(a - 7b)(a + 5b)$.

EXERCISES

PART A

Factor completely.

1. $a^2 + 4ab + 3b^2$
4. $4a^2 - 36b^2$
7. $2m^2 - mb - 10b^2$
10. $a^2 - ab - 42b^2$
13. $2a^2 + 20ab + 42b^2$
16. $2m^2 - 2mn - 40n^2$

2. $x^2 + 5xy + 4y^2$
5. $5x^2 - 45y^2$
8. $2a^2 - 5ab - 3b^2$
11. $a^2 - 3ab + 2b^2$
14. $8x^2 + 24xy + 18y^2$
17. $6x^2 - 26xy - 20y^2$

3. $c^2 + 7cd + 6d^2$
6. $4a^2 - 100b^2$
9. $2a^2 - 9ab - 5b^2$
12. $x^2 - 13xy + 42y^2$
15. $2y^2 + 20yz + 18z^2$
18. $3x^2 - 9xy - 30y^2$

PART B

Factor completely.

19. $a^2b^3 - 25b$
22. $7x^2 + 19xy - 6y^2$
25. $4k^2 - 42kr + 80r^2$

20. $x^3 - 3x^2y + 2xy^2$
23. $6x^2 - 57xy + 105y^2$
26. $12m^2 - 75y^2$

21. $a^3b - ab^3$
24. $2m^2 + 17mn + 30n^2$
27. $3a^2 + 13ab - 30b^2$

PART C

Factor completely.

28. $20m^2 + 60mn + 45n^2$
31. $10x^2 + 21xy + 9y^2$

29. $6a^2 + 5ab - 21b^2$
32. $2a^3b + 11a^2b^2 - 21ab^3$

30. $12x^2 + xy - 6y^2$
33. $6x^3y + 7x^2y^2 - 20xy^3$

Quadratic Equations

REVIEW CAPSULE

Factor $x^2 - 7x + 12$.

$$x^2 - 7x + 12 = (x - 4)(x - 3)$$

EXAMPLE 1   Find the missing factor. Then draw a conclusion.

Multiplying by 0 gives 0. ⟶

$(4)(?) = 0$	$(?)(-7) = 0$	$(0)(?) = 0$
$(4)(0) = 0$	$(0)(-7) = 0$	$(0)(0) = 0$

If a product is 0, then at least one factor must
be 0.

Either factor or both factors must be 0.

If $a \cdot b = 0$, then $a = 0$ or $b = 0$.
If a product is 0, then at least one factor is 0.

EXAMPLE 2   For what values of x will $(2x - 8)(x - 7) = 0$
be true?

If $a \cdot b = 0$, then $a = 0$ or $b = 0$.
Solve each equation for x.

$$2x - 8 = 0 \quad \text{or} \quad x - 7 = 0$$

Divide each side by 2. ⟶

$$\begin{array}{cc} \underline{8\ \ 8} & \underline{7\ \ 7} \\ 2x = 8 & x = 7 \\ x = 4 & \end{array}$$

Check. ⟶

	$(2x-8)$	$(x-7)$	0			$(2x-8)$	$(x-7)$	0
$x=4$	$(2\cdot4-8)$	$(4-7)$	0		$x=7$	$(2\cdot7-8)$	$(7-7)$	0
	$(8-8)$	(-3)				$(14-8)$	(0)	
	(0)	(-3)				(6)	(0)	
		0					0	

$(2x - 8)(x - 7)$ is 0. ⟶

Thus, $(2x - 8)(x - 7) = 0$ if $x = 4$ or $x = 7$.

Each equation contains an x^2 term.

Equations like $2x^2 + 9x - 5 = 0$, $x^2 - 36 = 0$,
and $x^2 - 3x = 0$ are quadratic equations.

EXAMPLE 3   Solve $x^2 - 8x + 12 = 0$.

Factor $x^2 - 8x + 12$:
No GCF.

If $ab = 0$, then $a = 0$ or $b = 0$. ⟶

Solve each equation for x.

$$x^2 - 8x + 12 = 0$$
$$(x - 6)(x - 2) = 0$$
$$x - 6 = 0 \quad \text{or} \quad x - 2 = 0$$
$$\underline{6 \quad 6} \qquad \underline{2 \quad 2}$$
$$x = 6 \qquad\qquad x = 2$$

Check. ⟶

$$\begin{array}{r|l} x^2 - 8x + 12 & 0 \\ \hline x = 6 \quad 6^2 - 8 \cdot 6 + 12 & 0 \\ 36 - 48 + 12 & \\ -12 + 12 & \\ 0 & \end{array}$$

$$\begin{array}{r|l} x^2 - 8x + 12 & 0 \\ \hline x = 2 \quad 2^2 - 8 \cdot 2 + 12 & 0 \\ 4 - 16 + 12 & \\ -12 + 12 & \\ 0 & \end{array}$$

Thus, the solutions are 2 and 6.

The solutions are also called roots.

A quadratic equation may have two solutions.

EXAMPLE 4   Find the solution set of $2x^2 + 5x - 3 = 0$.

Factor $2x^2 + 5x - 3$:
No GCF.
Set each factor $= 0$.
Solve each equation for x.

$$2x^2 + 5x - 3 = 0$$
$$(2x - 1)(x + 3) = 0$$
$$2x - 1 = 0 \quad \text{or} \quad x + 3 = 0$$
$$\underline{1 \quad 1} \qquad \underline{-3 \quad -3}$$
$$2x = 1 \qquad\qquad x = -3$$
$$x = \frac{1}{2}$$

Check on your own. ⟶

The solutions are $\frac{1}{2}$ and -3.

Thus, the solution set is $\left\{\frac{1}{2}, -3\right\}$.

EXAMPLE 5   Solve $x^2 - 7x = 0$.

Look for the GCF.
Factor out x, the GCF. ⟶
Set each factor $= 0$. ⟶
Solve each equation for x.

$$x^2 - 7x = 0$$
$$x(x - 7) = 0$$
$$x = 0 \quad \text{or} \quad x - 7 = 0$$
$$\underline{7 \quad 7}$$
$$x = 7$$

Check on your own. ⟶ **Thus,** the solutions are 0 and 7.

ORAL EXERCISES

For what values of x will each be true?

1. $(2x - 4)(x + 3) = 0$ **2.** $x(x + 5) = 0$ **3.** $5x(x - 7) = 0$

4. $(3x - 1)(2x - 4) = 0$ **5.** $(x - 3)(x - 3) = 0$ **6.** $(x - 5)(x + 5) = 0$

EXERCISES

PART A

Solve.

1. $x^2 - 5x + 6 = 0$ **2.** $x^2 - 7x + 10 = 0$ **3.** $x^2 - 9x + 8 = 0$

4. $x^2 - 6x = 0$ **5.** $x^2 - 36 = 0$ **6.** $x^2 + 8x + 12 = 0$

Find the solution set.

7. $2a^2 + 9a - 5 = 0$ **8.** $3m^2 + 8m - 3 = 0$ **9.** $2p^2 + 5p - 3 = 0$

10. $3x^2 + 14x - 5 = 0$ **11.** $2t^2 + 7t - 15 = 0$ **12.** $2b^2 + 3b - 9 = 0$

13. $3a^2 - 22a + 7 = 0$ **14.** $a^2 - 10a + 16 = 0$ **15.** $2y^2 - 11y + 5 = 0$

16. $2g^2 - 15g - 8 = 0$ **17.** $4a^2 - 25 = 0$ **18.** $x^2 - 64 = 0$

19. $2n^2 - 13n + 15 = 0$ **20.** $m^2 + 17m = 0$ **21.** $3k^2 - 5k = 0$

PART B

Solve.

22. $2x^2 + 13x - 24 = 0$ **23.** $3y^2 + 16y - 35 = 0$ **24.** $5a^2 + 34a - 7 = 0$

25. $2a^2 + 5a - 42 = 0$ **26.** $5a^2 - 22a + 21 = 0$ **27.** $2a^2 + 23a + 56 = 0$

28. $3b^2 - 31b + 36 = 0$ **29.** $a^2 - 20a + 100 = 0$ **30.** $x^2 + 18x + 81 = 0$

PART C

EXAMPLE   Solve $x^3 - 25x = 0$.

Factor out the GCF. ⟶ $x(x^2 - 25) = 0$

$x^2 - 25 = (x)^2 - (5)^2$; factor. ⟶ $x(x - 5)(x + 5) = 0$

If $a \cdot b \cdot c = 0$, then $a = 0$ ⟶ $x = 0$ or $x - 5 = 0$ or $x + 5 = 0$

or $b = 0$ or $c = 0$. $\underline{5 \quad 5}$ $\underline{-5 \quad -5}$

     $x = 5$ $x = -5$

Thus, the solutions are 0, 5, and −5.

Solve.

31. $x^3 - 9x = 0$ **32.** $x^3 - 4x = 0$ **33.** $4b^3 - 16b = 0$

34. $x^3 - 2x^2 = 0$ **35.** $m^3 - 49m = 0$ **36.** $3x^3 - 75x = 0$

Computing Mentally

We can use our ability to multiply binomials to find the square of a two- or three-digit number mentally.

PROBLEM

Square 35.   Think: $(35)^2 = (35)(35) = (30 + 5)(30 + 5)$

$$\begin{array}{ccc} 30 & + & 5 \\ 30 & + & 5 \end{array}$$

$$+150$$

$(3)(3) = 3^2 \longrightarrow$

900	+150	+25
900	+300	+25 = 1,225 ← four-digit number

Let's find the pattern.

$$(35)^2 = 900 + 300 + 25 = 1,200 + 25$$

$100(9 + 3) = 900 + 300 \rightarrow 100(9 + 3) + 25 = 1,225$

$9 = 3^2 \longrightarrow 100(3^2 + 3) + 25 = 1,225$

$\boxed{3^2 + 3}$ $\boxed{25}$

first two digits ——↑   ↑——last two digits

Short Cut for Squaring a Number Ending in 5

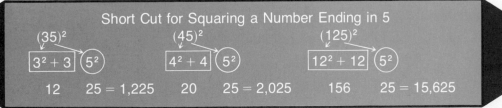

$(35)^2$	$(45)^2$	$(125)^2$
$\boxed{3^2 + 3}$ $\boxed{5^2}$	$\boxed{4^2 + 4}$ $\boxed{5^2}$	$\boxed{12^2 + 12}$ $\boxed{5^2}$
12 25 = 1,225	20 25 = 2,025	156 25 = 15,625

PROJECT Find each mentally.
1. $(75)^2$ **2.** $(65)^2$ **3.** $(95)^2$ **4.** $(135)^2$ **5.** $(205)^2$

Quadratic Equations: Standard Form

<table>
<tr><td>

OBJECTIVE

■ To solve equations like
$$7x = -x^2 - 10$$
by factoring

</td><td>

▶ REVIEW CAPSULE

Solve $2x^2 + 5x - 3 = 0$.
$$(2x - 1)(x + 3) = 0$$
$$2x - 1 = 0 \quad \text{or} \quad x + 3 = 0$$

$$\frac{1 \quad 1}{2x = 1} \qquad \frac{-3 \quad -3}{x = -3}$$

$$x = \frac{1}{2}$$

The solutions are $\frac{1}{2}$ and -3.

</td></tr>
</table>

$2x^2 - 5x + 2 = 0$

↗ positive

$2x^2 - 5x + 2 = 0$

↑ x^2 term   ↗ x^1 term   constant

This quadratic equation is in standard form.

$$2x^2 - 5x + 2 = 0$$

(1) Coefficient of the x^2 term ($2x^2$) is positive.
(2) Polynomial ($2x^2 - 5x + 2$) is equal to 0.
(3) Terms are arranged in descending order of exponents.

EXAMPLE 1   Solve $7x = -x^2 - 10$.

Get coefficient of x^2 term positive.
Add $1x^2$ to each side.
Coefficient of x^2 term is positive.

$$7x = -1x^2 - 10$$
$$\frac{1x^2 \qquad\qquad 1x^2}{1x^2 + 7x = \qquad -10}$$

Get polynomial equal to 0.
Add 10 to each side.
Polynomial is equal to 0.

$$1x^2 + 7x = -10 \qquad \text{Terms arranged}$$
$$\frac{10 \qquad 10}{1x^2 + 7x + 10 = \quad 0} \qquad \text{in descending}$$
$$\qquad\qquad\qquad\qquad \leftarrow \text{order of exponents}$$
$$x^2 + 7x + 10 = \quad 0 \qquad \leftarrow \text{Standard form}$$

Factor. ⟶ $(x + 5)(x + 2) = \quad 0$

Set each factor = 0. ⟶ $x + 5 = \ 0 \quad \text{or} \quad x + 2 = \ 0$

Solve each equation for x.

$$\frac{-5 \quad -5}{x = -5} \qquad \frac{-2 \quad -2}{x = -2}$$

Thus, the solutions are -5 and -2.

EXAMPLE 2   Solve and check $5 - 9x = 2x^2$.

x^2 term is already positive.

Get polynomial equal to 0.

Add $9x$ to each side.

Add -5 to each side.

Polynomial is equal to 0.

Factor. ————————————————————→

Set each factor $= 0$. ————————→

Solve each equation for x.

$$5 - 9x = 2x^2$$
$$\underline{9x \quad 9x}$$
$$5 = 2x^2 + 9x$$
$$\underline{-5 \quad -5}$$
$$0 = 2x^2 + 9x - 5$$
$$0 = (2x - 1)(x + 5)$$

Terms arranged
in descending
← order of exponents

$$2x - 1 = 0 \quad \text{or} \quad x + 5 = 0$$
$$\underline{1 \quad 1} \qquad \underline{-5 \quad -5}$$
$$2x = 1 \qquad\qquad x = -5$$
$$x = \frac{1}{2}$$

Check. ————————————————————→

$5 - 9x$	$2x^2$
$x = \frac{1}{2}$ $\quad 5 - 9\left(\frac{1}{2}\right)$	$2\left(\frac{1}{2}\right)^2$
$5 - \quad 4\frac{1}{2}$	$2\left(\frac{1}{4}\right)$
$\frac{1}{2}$	$\frac{1}{2}$

$5 - 9x$	$2x^2$
$x = -5$ $\quad 5 - 9(-5)$	$2(-5)^2$
$5 + \quad 45$	$2(25)$
50	50

Thus, the solutions are $\frac{1}{2}$ and -5.

EXAMPLE 3   Find the solution set of $-x^2 = 3x$.

Get x^2 term positive.

Add $1x^2$ to each side.

x^2 term is positive.

Polynomial is equal to 0. ————→

Factor out the GCF. ——————→

Set each factor $= 0$. ——————→

Solve each equation for x.

$$-1x^2 = 3x$$
$$\underline{1x^2 \quad 1x^2}$$ Terms arranged in descending
$$0 = 1x^2 + 3x \quad \leftarrow \text{order of exponents}$$
$$0 = x^2 + 3x$$
$$0 = x(x + 3)$$
$$x = 0 \quad \text{or} \quad x + 3 = 0$$
$$\underline{-3 \quad -3}$$
$$x = -3$$

Check. ————————————————————→

$-x^2$	$3x$
$x = 0$ $\quad -(0)^2$	$3(0)$
0	0

$-x^2$	$3x$
$x = -3$ $\quad -(-3)^2$	$3(-3)$
$-1(9)$	-9
-9	

The solutions are 0 and -3.

Thus, the solution set is $\{0, -3\}$.

EXERCISES

PART A

Solve and check.

1. $8x = -x^2 - 15$
4. $18 - 7b = b^2$
7. $-x^2 = 9x$

2. $9x = -x^2 - 20$
5. $12 - 4m = m^2$
8. $-x^2 = 10x$

3. $12m = -m^2 - 32$
6. $6 - 5p = p^2$
9. $-x^2 = 7x$

Find the solution sets.

10. $x^2 + 4x = 5$
13. $13g = -g^2$
16. $2a^2 + 3a = -1$
19. $2x^2 + x = 1$
22. $4n^2 = 1$
25. $2p^2 = -11p + 6$

11. $9m^2 = 4$
14. $2a^2 + a = 10$
17. $5b - 2 = 3b^2$
20. $2a^2 + 7 = 15a$
23. $2x^2 - 21 = 11x$
26. $3x - 20 = -2x^2$

12. $a^2 - 10 = 3a$
15. $b^2 = 49$
18. $n^2 - 7n = 18$
21. $3k^2 = -2k + 1$
24. $3a^2 - 22a = 16$
27. $25 = 4b^2$

PART B

Solve.

28. $12x^2 = 35 - x$
31. $11b - 10 = -6b^2$
34. $4m^2 = 225$
37. $24b = -3b^2$

29. $19a - 6 = 15a^2$
32. $12y^2 + 15 = 29y$
35. $4a + 35 = 4a^2$
38. $17x - 14 = -6x^2$

30. $4m^2 - 42 = 17m$
33. $6x^2 = 35 - 11x$
36. $6b^2 + 13b = 28$
39. $10a^2 - 29a = -10$

PART C

EXAMPLE   Solve $(2x + 3)(x - 5) = x^2 + 9x - 43$.

$$
\begin{array}{rcl}
2x^2 - 7x - 15 &=& x^2 + 9x - 43 \\
-x^2 & & -x^2 \\
\hline
x^2 - 7x - 15 &=& 9x - 43 \\
-9x & & -9x \\
\hline
x^2 - 16x - 15 &=& -43 \\
43 & & 43 \\
\hline
x^2 - 16x + 28 &=& 0 \\
(x - 14)(x - 2) &=& 0 \\
x - 14 = 0 &\text{ or }& x - 2 = 0 \\
x = 14 & & x = 2
\end{array}
$$

Check on your own. ⟶ **Thus,** the solutions are 14 and 2.

Solve.

40. $(3x - 2)(2x + 5) = 5x^2 + 5x - 18$

41. $(x - 3)(x + 3) = 2x^2 - 18$

Consecutive Integers

REVIEW CAPSULE

Even integers have 2 as a factor.
For example: $-4, 0, 28, 40, 90$.

Odd integers do not have 2 as a factor.
For example: $-5, 3, 15, 35, 47$.

EXAMPLE 1   Write the next two consecutive integers.

Add 1 to get the next consecutive
integer.
$(a + 2) + 1 = a + 3$

	Answers
$7, 8, 9, 10, \ldots$	$11, 12$
$-2, -1, 0, 1, 2, \ldots$	$3, 4$
$a, a + 1, a + 2, \ldots$	$a + 3, a + 4$

Example 1 suggests this. ────────▶

$x, x + 1, x + 2, \ldots$ represent consecutive integers
for each integer x.

EXAMPLE 2   Write three consecutive integers, beginning with
the given integer.
-28 7 n

Begin with. ────────────────▶ -28
$-28 + 1 = -27$ ───────────▶ -27
$-28 + 1 + 1 = -26$ ────────▶ -26

-28	7	n
-27	8	$n + 1 \quad = n + 1$
-26	9	$n + 1 + 1 = n + 2$

EXAMPLE 3   Write the next two consecutive even integers.

Add 2 to an even integer to get the next
consecutive even integer.

	Answers
$0, 2, 4, \ldots$	$6, 8$
$-8, -6, -4, \ldots$	$-2, 0$
$b, b + 2, b + 4, \ldots$	$b + 6, b + 8$

Example 3 suggests this. ────────▶

$x, x + 2, x + 4, \ldots$ represent consecutive even
integers, for each even integer x.

EXAMPLE 4   Write three consecutive even integers, beginning with the given even integer.

$$n \qquad\qquad\qquad -8$$

Begin with ⟶

Add 2 to get the next consecutive even integer. }

$$
\begin{array}{ll}
& n & \\
n + 2 & = n + 2 & \\
n + 2 + 2 & = n + 4 &
\end{array}
\;\bigg|\;
\begin{array}{ll}
& -8 \\
-8 + 2 & = -6 \\
-8 + 2 + 2 & = -4
\end{array}
$$

EXAMPLE 5   Write the next two consecutive odd integers.

Add 2 to an odd integer to get the next consecutive odd integer. }

	Answers
$5, 7, 9, \ldots$	$11, 13$
$-9, -7, -5, \ldots$	$-3, -1$
$c, c + 2, c + 4, \ldots$	$c + 6, c + 8$

Example 5 suggests this. ⟶

$x, x + 2, x + 4, \ldots$ represent consecutive odd integers, for each odd integer x.

EXAMPLE 6   Write three consecutive odd integers, beginning with the given odd integer.

$$-9 \qquad\qquad 5 \qquad n$$

Add 2 to get the next consecutive odd integer. }

$$
\begin{array}{ll}
& -9 \\
-9 + 2 & = -7 \\
-7 + 2 & = -5
\end{array}
\;\bigg|\;
\begin{array}{l}
5 \\
7 \\
9
\end{array}
\;\bigg|\;
\begin{array}{ll}
& n \\
n + 2 & = n + 2 \\
n + 2 + 2 & = n + 4
\end{array}
$$

EXAMPLE 7   Write an equation.
The sum of three consecutive integers is 21.

Represent the integers. Add 1 to get the next consecutive integer. }

Sum means add. ⟶

Write the equation. ⟶

$$
\begin{array}{l}
\text{Let} \quad x = \text{first integer} \\
x + 1 = \text{second integer} \\
x + 2 = \text{third integer} \\
\qquad \text{Their sum is 21.} \\
x + (x + 1) + (x + 2) = 21
\end{array}
$$

EXAMPLE 8   Write an equation.
The product of two consecutive odd integers is 15.

Represent the integers. Add 2 to get the next odd integer. }

Product means multiply. ⟶

$$
\begin{array}{l}
\text{Let} \quad x = \text{first odd integer} \\
x + 2 = \text{second odd integer} \\
\qquad x(x + 2) = 15
\end{array}
$$

ORAL EXERCISES

Give three consecutive integers, beginning with the given integer.

1. 7   **2.** 11   **3.** 26   **4.** -2 **5.** -6 **6.** -40 **7.** a

Give four consecutive even integers, beginning with the given integer.

8. 8   **9.** 6   **10.** 38   **11.** -4 **12.** -10 **13.** n **14.** $n+8$

Give five consecutive odd integers beginning with the given integer.

15. 7   **16.** 19   **17.** 53   **18.** -5 **19.** -23 **20.** b **21.** $b+6$

EXERCISES

PART A

Write an equation.

1. The sum of three consecutive integers is 27.

2. The sum of three consecutive integers is 33.

3. The sum of three consecutive integers is -15.

4. The sum of three consecutive integers is -21.

5. The product of two consecutive odd integers is 35.

6. The product of two consecutive odd integers is 99.

7. The product of three consecutive even integers is 48.

8. The product of three consecutive even integers is 192.

9. The sum of four consecutive odd integers is 40.

10. The sum of four consecutive even integers is 36.

PART B

Write an equation.

11. Twice the second of two consecutive integers, increased by the first is 35.

12. Twice the second of two consecutive even integers, decreased by the first is 10.

13. Twice the second of two consecutive odd integers, increased by the first is 19.

14. Three times the second of two consecutive integers, decreased by three times the first is 3.

15. Three times the second of two consecutive even integers, increased by twice the first is 46.

16. Three times the first of two consecutive odd integers, decreased by twice the second is 21.

17. The product of three consecutive integers is the same as 8 times their sum.

18. The product of three consecutive even integers is the same as 4 times their sum.

Consecutive Integer Problems

EXAMPLE 1   Find two consecutive integers whose sum is 67.

Represent the integers. ⎫
Add 1 to get the next integer. ⎬

Sum means add. ────────→

Write an equation. ────────→

Combine like terms. ────────→

Solve for x.

First integer ────────→

Second integer ────────→

Let x = first integer
   $x + 1$ = second integer
Their sum is 67. •

$$x + (x + 1) = 67$$
$$2x + 1 = 67$$
$$2x = 66$$
$$x = 33$$
$$x + 1 = 33 + 1, \text{ or } 34$$

Check: $33 + 34 = 67$.

Thus, the integers are 33 and 34.

EXAMPLE 2   Find two consecutive integers whose product is 20.

Represent the integers.

Product means multiply. ────────→

Write an equation. ────────→

$x(x + 1) = x(x) + x(1)$ ────────→

Get equation in standard form. ⎫
Add -20 to each side. ⎬

Factor. ────────→

Set each factor $= 0$. ────────→

First integer ────────→

Second integer ────────→

There are two pairs of integers.

Let x = first integer
   $x + 1$ = second integer
Their product is 20.

$$x(x + 1) = 20$$
$$x^2 + x = 20$$
$$\underline{ -20 \quad -20}$$
$$x^2 + x - 20 = 0$$
$$(x + 5)(x - 4) = 0$$
$$x + 5 = 0 \quad \text{ or } \quad x - 4 = 0$$
$$x = -5 \quad \text{ or } \quad x = 4$$
$$x + 1 = -5 + 1, \text{ or } -4 \quad \text{ or } \quad x + 1 = 4 + 1, \text{ or } 5$$

Check the first solution in the problem. ────→ -5 and -4 are consecutive integers, since $-5 + 1 = -4$.
Their product is 20, since $(-5)(-4) = 20$.

Check 4 and 5 in the problem. There are two pairs of solutions. ────────→ **Thus,** the integers are -5 and -4, or 4 and 5.

EXAMPLE 3 Find two consecutive integers such that the sum of the first and the square of the second is 19.

Represent the integers algebraically.

Let $x =$ first integer
$x + 1 =$ second integer
Sum of the first and the square of the second is 19.

$(x + 1)^2 = (x + 1)(x + 1)$
$\quad\quad\quad = x^2 + 2x + 1 \longrightarrow$

Combine like terms. $\longrightarrow$

Add -19 to each side. $\longrightarrow$

Factor. $\longrightarrow$

Set each factor $= 0$. $\longrightarrow$

First integer $\longrightarrow$

Second integer $\longrightarrow$

Check both solutions in the problem.

$$x + (x + 1)^2 = 19$$
$$x + x^2 + 2x + 1 = 19$$
$$x^2 + 3x + 1 = 19$$
$$x^2 + 3x - 18 = 0$$
$$(x + 6)(x - 3) = 0$$
$$x + 6 = 0 \quad \text{or} \quad x - 3 = 0$$
$$x = -6 \text{ or} \quad\quad x = 3$$
$$x + 1 = -6 + 1, \text{ or} -5 \text{ or } x + 1 = 3 + 1 = 4$$

Sum of the first and square of the second is 19.

$-6 + (-5)^2$	19	$3 + (4)^2$	19
$-6 + \quad 25$	19	$3 + 16$	19
19		19	

Two pairs of solutions $\longrightarrow$

Thus, the two consecutive integers are -6 and -5, or 3 and 4.

EXAMPLE 4 Find two consecutive odd integers such that the square of the second, decreased by the first is 44.

Represent the integers algebraically.

Let $x =$ first integer
$x + 2 =$ second integer
Square of second, decreased by first is 44.

Write the equation. $\longrightarrow$

$(x + 2)^2$

Add -44 to each side; standard form. $\longrightarrow$

Factor. $\longrightarrow$

Set each factor $= 0$. $\longrightarrow$

First integer $\longrightarrow$

Second integer $\longrightarrow$

There is only one pair of integers.

Check 5 and 7 in the problem.

$$(x + 2)^2 - x = 44$$
$$x^2 + 4x + 4 - x = 44$$
$$x^2 + 3x + 4 = 44$$
$$x^2 + 3x - 40 = 0$$
$$(x - 5)(x + 8) = 0$$
$$x - 5 = 0 \quad\quad \text{or} \quad\quad x + 8 = 0$$
$$x = 5 \quad\quad\quad\quad\quad\quad x = -8$$
$$x + 2 = 5 + 2, \text{ or } 7$$

First integer, x cannot be -8, since -8 is not odd.

Square of second, decreased by first is 44.

$(7)^2 - 5$	44
$49 - 5$	44
44	

There is only one solution. $\longrightarrow$ **Thus,** the two consecutive odd integers are 5 and 7.

EXERCISES

PART A

1. Find two consecutive integers whose sum is 45.

2. Find three consecutive odd integers whose sum is 63.

3. Find five consecutive integers whose sum is 155.

4. Find three consecutive even integers whose sum is 120.

5. Find three consecutive integers such that twice the first added to the last is 23.

6. Find four consecutive odd integers such that twice the second added to the last is 25.

7. Find three consecutive odd integers such that twice the first, decreased by the second is 35.

8. Find three consecutive integers such that three times the second, increased by the last is 81.

9. Find two consecutive integers whose product is 12.

10. Find two consecutive integers whose product is 30.

11. Find two consecutive even integers whose product is 24.

12. Find two consecutive odd integers whose product is 35.

13. Find two consecutive odd integers such that the sum of their squares is 130.

14. Find two consecutive even integers such that the sum of their squares is 52.

15. Find three consecutive integers such that the square of the first, added to the last is 8.

16. Find three consecutive integers such that the square of the first, decreased by the last is 18.

17. Find three consecutive integers such that the square of the first is 18 more than the last.

18. Find three consecutive integers such that the square of the first is equal to the third.

19. Find two consecutive odd integers such that the square of the second, decreased by the first is 14.

20. Find two consecutive even integers such that the square of the second increased by twice the first is 44.

PART B

21. Find four consecutive integers such that 3 times the third, decreased by the second is the last.

22. Find four consecutive even integers such that the sum of the squares of the first and second is 12 more than the last.

23. Find four consecutive integers such that the sum of the squares of the second and third is 61.

24. Find five consecutive integers such that the square of the third, decreased by the square of the second is 3 times the first.

Braking Distance

Braking distance is an important factor in safe driving. Braking distance is the distance traveled by a car from the time the driver applies the brakes until the car actually stops.

$$B \doteq .006s^2$$

Braking distance in meters ← is about → Speed in kilometers per hour

PROBLEM

A car is traveling at a speed of 50 km/h. How far will the car travel after the brakes are applied?

Use the formula. ⟶	$B \doteq .006s^2$
Substitute for s. ⟶	$\doteq .006\,(50)^2$
$(50)^2$ means $(50)(50)$. ⟶	$\doteq .006\,(50)\,(50)$
$(50)(50) = 2,500$ ⟶	$\doteq .006\,(2,500)$
	$\doteq 15.000$

$$\begin{array}{r} 2,500 \\ \times\ .006 \\ \hline 15,000 \end{array}$$

Thus, the car will travel about 15 meters before coming to a complete stop.

PROJECT

1. A car is traveling at a speed of 80 km/h. The driver suddenly applies the brakes. How far will the car travel before coming to a stop?

2. A car is traveling at a speed of 85 km/h. Suddenly the driver spots a stalled car, and hits the brakes. The stalled car is 45 meters away. Will the driver stop in time?

Chapter Six Review

Multiply. [*p. 141*]

1. $(x + 5)(x + 3)$
2. $(x - 7)(x + 9)$
3. $(2x + 3)(x + 5)$
4. $(3x - 1)(x + 6)$
5. $(2b - 3)(b + 4)$
6. $(m - 1)(m + 1)$
7. $(4z - 1)(3z - 2)$
8. $(3x - 5)(x + 5)$
9. $(3x - 1)(5x + 4)$
10. $(x - 5)(x^2 + 7x + 3)$
11. $(2x - 3)(x^2 + 3x - 4)$
12. $(3x - 1)(x^2 + 2x - 4)$

Simplify. [*p. 141*]

13. $(3a - 5)^2$
14. $(4x - 1)^2$
15. $(2x + 3)^2$
16. $(7x + 1)^2$

Factor completely. [*p. 145, 150, 153, 156*]

17. $x^2 - 7x + 12$
18. $p^2 + 7p + 10$
19. $2a^2 + 9a - 5$
20. $x^2 - 5x + 6$
21. $3y^2 + 17y + 10$
22. $3x^2 + 16x - 12$
23. $2m^2 + 3m - 20$
24. $2m^2 + 7m + 6$
25. $2x^2 - 9x + 9$
26. $4a^2 + 2a - 2$
27. $6x^2 - x - 1$
28. $12b^2 + 5b - 2$
29. $a^2 - 4$
30. $x^2 - 36$
31. $4a^2 - 25$
32. $49x^2 - 36y^2$
33. $3x^2 + 21x + 36$
34. $2a^2 - 8a + 6$
35. $2a^2 - 2a - 40$
36. $3b^2 + 6b - 45$
37. $3k^3 + 3k^2 - 90k$
38. $3b^2 - 21b - 90$
39. $6x^3 - 24x^2 + 18x$
40. $b^3 - 49b$
41. $x^2 + 3xy + 2y^2$
42. $a^2 - 9b^2$
43. $a^2 - 3ab - 28b^2$
44. $2p^2 + 13pq + 15q^2$
45. $144x^2 - 169y^2$
46. $4y^2 - 14yb - 30b^2$
47. $3x^2 - 31xy + 56y^2$
48. $yx^2 - 4y^3$
49. $12x^2 - 27$
50. $12x^2 - 60x + 75$

Solve. [*p. 158, 162*]

51. $a^2 - 3a + 2 = 0$
52. $x^2 - 4 = 0$
53. $a^2 - 9a - 36 = 0$
54. $4 = a^2$
55. $24 + p^2 = 10p$
56. $-9r + 14 = -r^2$

Find the solution set. [*p. 158, 162*]

57. $x^2 - 5x = 0$
58. $9m^2 - 49 = 0$
59. $9a - 5 = -2a^2$
60. $2x^2 = 13x - 21$
61. $6x = x^2$
62. $2a^2 = -15a - 28$

Solve these problems. [*p. 165, 168*]

63. Find two consecutive integers whose product is 72.

64. Find two consecutive integers whose sum is 35.

65. Find three consecutive integers such that the square of the first, decreased by 5 times the second is 9.

66. Find three consecutive even integers such that the square of the first, added to the sum of the second and third is 30.

Chapter Six Test

Multiply.

1. $(x + 5)(x + 8)$
2. $(2x - 1)(3x + 4)$
3. $(3x - 2)(3x + 2)$
4. $(2a + 3)(a^2 - 7a + 4)$

Simplify.

5. $(3a - 2)^2$
6. $(4x + 1)^2$

Factor completely.

7. $a^2 - 7a + 10$
8. $x^2 - 2x - 35$
9. $4m^2 + 18m - 36$
10. $p^2 - 49$
11. $2b^3 - 8b^2 - 64b$
12. $16a^3 - 25a$
13. $2x^2 + 5xy - 3y^2$
14. $8b^2 - 8bc - 6c^2$

Solve.

15. $x^2 - 5x + 4 = 0$
16. $a^2 - 4a - 12 = 0$
17. $a^2 - 7a = 0$
18. $m^2 - 10m = -24$
19. $3p + 28 = p^2$
20. $x^2 = 64$

Find the solution set.

21. $m^2 + 14m = 0$
22. $25 = x^2$
23. $-11m - 21 = -2m^2$
24. $2k^2 = -21k - 40$
25. $2b^2 - 9b = 5$
26. $2m^2 - 21 = -m$

Solve these problems.

27. Find two consecutive integers whose sum is 81.
28. Find two consecutive integers whose product is 56.
29. Find two consecutive odd integers such that the square of the second increased by 4 times the first is 37.
30. Find two consecutive even integers such that the square of the first increased by the second is 22.

Mathematics in Music

The distance from middle *C* to the next *C* is one octave.

The frequency of a note is the number of vibrations per second.

Note	Frequency	Note	Frequency
Middle C	264	G	396
D	297	A	440
E	330	B	495
F	352	Higher C	528

From the table, $\dfrac{\text{frequency of higher C}}{\text{frequency of middle C}} = \dfrac{528}{264}$, or $\dfrac{2}{1}$. $\leftarrow$ { All octaves are in this ratio.

Simple frequency ratios indicate pleasing combinations of notes.

$$\frac{E}{C} = \frac{330}{264}, \text{ or } \frac{5}{4}$$
└─pleasing

$$\frac{G}{B} = \frac{396}{495}, \text{ or } \frac{132}{165}$$
└─not pleasing

PROJECT Find as many pleasing combinations of notes as you can.
Try your combinations on a piano, if possible.

Fractions

OBJECTIVES
- To find products of the form $a\left(\dfrac{1}{b}\right)$
- To find reciprocals of fractions
- To find the values of x for which fractions like $\dfrac{x-3}{x+2}$ are undefined

▶ REVIEW CAPSULE

$3(2)$ means $2 + 2 + 2$, or 6
$2(-5)$ means $-5 + (-5)$, or -10
$4(x)$ means $x + x + x + x$, or $4x$
$3(-a)$ means $-a + (-a) + (-a)$, or $-3a$

Fractions on a Number Line

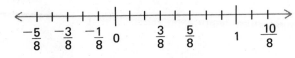

$\dfrac{3}{8}$ ⟵ Numerator
$\dfrac{}{8}$ ⟵ Denominator

EXAMPLE 1 Give the coordinates of points A and B.

Each subdivision is $\dfrac{1}{5}$.

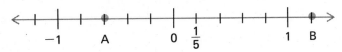

Count from 0.

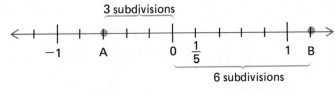

Count $-\dfrac{1}{5}, -\dfrac{2}{5}, -\dfrac{3}{5}$. ⟶

Point A		Point B
3 subdivisions *left* of 0		6 subdivisions *right* of 0
$-\dfrac{3}{5}$		$\dfrac{6}{5}$

EXAMPLE 2 Show that $\dfrac{16}{8} = 2$.

$\dfrac{16}{8}$ means $16 \div 8$, or $8\overline{)16}$.

Check by multiplying. If $\dfrac{a}{b} = c$, then $b \cdot c = a$.

$16 \div 8 = 2$ **Thus,** $\dfrac{16}{8} = 2$.

EXAMPLE 3 Show that $\frac{6}{0}$ is undefined, or meaningless.

If $\frac{a}{b} = c$, then $b \cdot c = a$. ⟶ Is $\frac{6}{0} = 6$? | Is $\frac{6}{0} = 0$?

Check: $0 \cdot 6 = 0$ *not* 6. | Check: $0 \cdot 0 = 0$ *not* 6.

Let $\frac{6}{0} = x$. Then $0 \cdot x = 6$. But $0 \cdot x = 0$ for *every*

number x.

There is no number that can be
multiplied by 0 to get 6. ⟶ **Thus,** $\frac{6}{0}$ is undefined, or meaningless.

Definition of rational number ⟶

A *rational number* is a number which can be

written in the form $\frac{a}{b}$, where a and b are

integers and $b \neq 0$.

$\frac{4}{5}, \frac{-7}{8}, \frac{24}{8}$ are rational numbers.

EXAMPLE 4 Write each in the form $\frac{a}{b}$.

Think. ⟶

5 | $16 \div 4$ | $-2 \div 8$

$5 \div 1$ | |

$\frac{5}{1}$ | $\frac{16}{4}$ | $\frac{-2}{8}$

EXAMPLE 5 Show that $3\left(\frac{1}{6}\right) = \frac{3}{6}$.

$3\left(\frac{1}{6}\right)$ means $\frac{1}{6} + \frac{1}{6} + \frac{1}{6}$.

Mark off sixths on a number line.

Count 3 subdivisions from 0 to $\frac{3}{6}$.

Thus, $3\left(\frac{1}{6}\right) = \frac{3}{6}$.

Example 5 suggests this. ⟶

$$a\left(\frac{1}{b}\right) = \frac{a}{b}, b \neq 0.$$

EXAMPLE 6   Multiply $-2\left(\dfrac{1}{7}\right)$.   Multiply $(x+3)\left(\dfrac{1}{x-5}\right)$.

$a\left(\dfrac{1}{b}\right) = \dfrac{a}{b},\ b \neq 0$ ⟶ $-2\left(\dfrac{1}{7}\right) = \dfrac{-2}{7}$ $(x+3)\left(\dfrac{1}{x-5}\right) = \dfrac{x+3}{x-5}$

EXAMPLE 7   Multiply $4\left(\dfrac{1}{4}\right)$.

$$4\left(\dfrac{1}{4}\right) = \dfrac{4}{4}$$

$\dfrac{4}{4}$ means $4 \div 4$ and $4 \div 4 = 1$.

Thus, $4\left(\dfrac{1}{4}\right) = 1.$

Example 7 suggests this. ⟶

Reciprocals are sometimes called *multiplicative inverses*.

$$a\left(\dfrac{1}{a}\right) = 1.$$

a and $\dfrac{1}{a}$ are *reciprocals* of each other if $a \neq 0$.

EXAMPLE 8   Find the reciprocal of each of the following:
$$6, \dfrac{1}{7}, 0, -8$$

Number	Reciprocal
6	$\dfrac{1}{6}$
$\dfrac{1}{7}$	7
0	No reciprocal
-8	$-\dfrac{1}{8}$

$6\,(?) = 1,\ 6\left(\dfrac{1}{6}\right) = 1$

$\left(\dfrac{1}{7}\right)(?) = 1,\ \left(\dfrac{1}{7}\right)(7) = 1$

$(-8)\,(?) = 1,\ (-8)\left(-\dfrac{1}{8}\right) = 1$

EXAMPLE 9   Find the missing factor or product.

$(?)\left(\dfrac{1}{a}\right) = \dfrac{b}{a}$ $a\,(?) = \dfrac{a}{m}$ $(x-2)\left(\dfrac{1}{x+4}\right) = ?$

$b\left(\dfrac{1}{a}\right) = \dfrac{b}{a}$ $a\left(\dfrac{1}{m}\right) = \dfrac{a}{m}$ $(x-2)\left(\dfrac{1}{x+4}\right) = \dfrac{x-2}{x+4}$

EXERCISES

PART A

Find the missing factor.

1. $4(?) = \dfrac{4}{7}$ **2.** $p(?) = \dfrac{p}{q}$ **3.** $(?)(y) = \dfrac{y}{x}$ **4.** $(?)(-7) = \dfrac{-7}{13}$

5. Give the reciprocal of -3, 0, 1, -1, and $-\dfrac{1}{5}$.

Give the coordinate of each point A.

6.

7.

8.

Write each in the form $\dfrac{a}{b}$.

9. 6 **10.** -3 **11.** $12 \div 3$ **12.** $-8 \div 2$ **13.** $-6 \div 12$

Multiply.

14. $4\left(\dfrac{1}{5}\right)$ **15.** $-5\left(\dfrac{1}{17}\right)$ **16.** $(x+5)\left(\dfrac{1}{x-4}\right)$ **17.** $(a-4)\left(\dfrac{1}{a+2}\right)$

PART B

EXAMPLE For what value of x is $\dfrac{x+2}{2x-4}$ undefined?

$\dfrac{a}{b}$ is undefined for $b = 0$. $\longrightarrow$ $\dfrac{x+2}{2x-4}$ is undefined when $2x - 4 = 0$.

Solve. $2x - 4 = 0$

$2x = 4$

$x = 2$ Thus, $\dfrac{x+2}{2x-4}$ is undefined when $x = 2$.

Find the value(s) of x for which the fraction is undefined.

18. $\dfrac{2x-1}{x-7}$ **19.** $\dfrac{3x+2}{2x-10}$ **20.** $\dfrac{7x+1}{3x-12}$ **21.** $\dfrac{x+5}{x^2-9}$ **22.** $\dfrac{3x+2}{x^2-7x+12}$

PART C

Find the value(s) of x for which the fraction is undefined.

23. $\dfrac{3x-2}{x^3-25x}$ **24.** $\dfrac{x+4}{x^3-7x^2+12x}$ **25.** $\dfrac{2x+5}{x^4-16}$

Zero and Negative Exponents

Consider this pattern.

$$2^5 = 2 \cdot 2 \cdot 2 \cdot 2 \cdot 2 = 32$$

Exponents decrease by 1.

$$2^4 = 2 \cdot 2 \cdot 2 \cdot 2 \quad\quad = 16$$
$$2^3 = 2 \cdot 2 \cdot 2 \quad\quad\quad = 8$$
$$2^2 = 2 \cdot 2 \quad\quad\quad\quad = 4$$
$$2^1 = 2 \quad\quad\quad\quad\quad = 2$$
$$2^0 = \underrightarrow{\quad\quad\quad\quad} = 1$$

Powers are divided by 2.

Thus, $2^0 = 1$.

Continue the pattern for three more entries.

$$2^0 = \underrightarrow{\quad\quad\quad\quad} = 1$$
$$2^{-1} = \frac{1}{2} \quad\quad\quad = \frac{1}{2}$$
$$2^{-2} = \frac{1}{2 \cdot 2} \quad\quad = \frac{1}{4}$$
$$2^{-3} = \frac{1}{2 \cdot 2 \cdot 2} \quad = \frac{1}{8}$$

> For any $a \neq 0$, $a^0 = 1$. For any $a \neq 0$, $a^{-n} = \dfrac{1}{a^n}$.
>
> 0^0 is undefined.

PROJECT   Find the value.

1. 4^0
2. 3^{-2}
3. $(-2)^0$
4. 5^{-3}
5. 6^{-1}
6. $\dfrac{1}{2^{-1}}$
7. $\dfrac{2^0}{3}$
8. $3^{-2} \cdot 5^0$
9. $(2 \cdot 3)^0$
10. $5^{-1} + 2^{-1}$

Multiplying Fractions

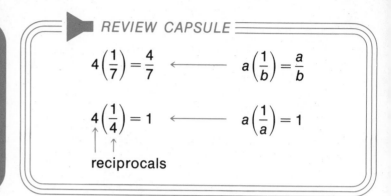

▶ *REVIEW CAPSULE*

$$4\left(\frac{1}{7}\right)=\frac{4}{7} \longleftarrow a\left(\frac{1}{b}\right)=\frac{a}{b}$$

$$4\left(\frac{1}{4}\right)=1 \longleftarrow a\left(\frac{1}{a}\right)=1$$

reciprocals

EXAMPLE 1   Show that $\dfrac{1}{3}\cdot\dfrac{1}{4}=\dfrac{1}{12}$.

A number has exactly one reciprocal.

First show the reciprocal of 12 as $\dfrac{1}{3}\cdot\dfrac{1}{4}$.

$$12\cdot\frac{1}{3}\cdot\frac{1}{4}$$

Factor: $12=3\cdot4$. ⟶

$$3\cdot4\cdot\frac{1}{3}\cdot\frac{1}{4}$$

Regroup. ⟶

$$\left(3\cdot\frac{1}{3}\right)\left(4\cdot\frac{1}{4}\right)$$

$a\cdot\dfrac{1}{a}=1$ ⟶

$$1\cdot1$$
$$1$$

Two numbers whose product is 1 are reciprocals. }

Since $12\cdot\dfrac{1}{3}\cdot\dfrac{1}{4}=1,\ \dfrac{1}{3}\cdot\dfrac{1}{4}$ is the reciprocal of 12.

$12\cdot\dfrac{1}{12}=1$ ⟶ But, $\dfrac{1}{12}$ is also the reciprocal of 12.

Thus, $\dfrac{1}{3}\cdot\dfrac{1}{4}=\dfrac{1}{12}$.

A technique for multiplying fractions like $\dfrac{1}{5}\cdot\dfrac{1}{4}$ ⟶

$$\frac{1}{a}\cdot\frac{1}{b}=\frac{1}{ab},\ a\neq0,\ b\neq0$$

EXAMPLE 2 Multiply $\dfrac{1}{5} \cdot \dfrac{1}{6}$. Multiply $\dfrac{1}{3}\left(-\dfrac{1}{8}\right)$. Multiply $\dfrac{1}{x^2} \cdot \dfrac{1}{x^3}$.

$\dfrac{1}{a} \cdot \dfrac{1}{b} = \dfrac{1}{ab}$ $\longrightarrow$

$\dfrac{1}{5} \cdot \dfrac{1}{6} = \dfrac{1}{5 \cdot 6}$ $\dfrac{1}{3}\left(-\dfrac{1}{8}\right) = -\dfrac{1}{3 \cdot 8}$ $\dfrac{1}{x^2} \cdot \dfrac{1}{x^3} = \dfrac{1}{x^2 \cdot x^3}$

$= \dfrac{1}{30}$ $= -\dfrac{1}{24}$ $= \dfrac{1}{x^5}$

EXAMPLE 3 Multiply $\dfrac{4}{5} \cdot \dfrac{3}{7}$.

$\dfrac{a}{b} = a \cdot \dfrac{1}{b}$ $\longrightarrow$

Multiplication can be done in any order}

$\dfrac{1}{a} \cdot \dfrac{1}{b} = \dfrac{1}{ab}$ $\longrightarrow$

$a \cdot \dfrac{1}{b} = \dfrac{a}{b}$ $\longrightarrow$

$\dfrac{4}{5} \cdot \dfrac{3}{7} = 4 \cdot \dfrac{1}{5} \cdot 3 \cdot \dfrac{1}{7}$

$= (4 \cdot 3)\left(\dfrac{1}{5} \cdot \dfrac{1}{7}\right)$

$= 12 \cdot \dfrac{1}{35}$

$= \dfrac{12}{35}$

Thus, $\dfrac{4}{5} \cdot \dfrac{3}{7} = \dfrac{12}{35}$.

$\dfrac{\text{Product of numerators}}{\text{Product of denominators}}$ $\longrightarrow$

Product of Two Fractions
$$\dfrac{a}{b} \cdot \dfrac{c}{d} = \dfrac{ac}{bd}, \ b \neq 0, \ d \neq 0.$$

EXAMPLE 4 Multiply $5 \cdot \dfrac{3}{7}$.   Multiply $\left(-\dfrac{2}{5}\right)\left(-\dfrac{6}{11}\right)$.

$5 = \dfrac{5}{1}$ $\longrightarrow$

$\dfrac{a}{b} \cdot \dfrac{c}{d} = \dfrac{ac}{bd}$ $\longrightarrow$

$5 \cdot \dfrac{3}{7} = \dfrac{5}{1} \cdot \dfrac{3}{7}$ $\left(-\dfrac{2}{5}\right)\left(-\dfrac{6}{11}\right)$

$= \dfrac{5 \cdot 3}{1 \cdot 7}$ $+\dfrac{12}{55} \longleftarrow (-)\,(-) = +$

$= \dfrac{15}{7}$ or $\dfrac{12}{55}$

EXAMPLE 5 Multiply $\dfrac{7}{9}\left(-\dfrac{2}{3}\right)$.   Multiply $\dfrac{4}{5}\left(\dfrac{2}{3}\right)$.

$(+)\,(-) = -$ $\longrightarrow$

$-\dfrac{7 \cdot 2}{9 \cdot 3} = -\dfrac{14}{27}$ $\dfrac{4 \cdot 2}{5 \cdot 3} = \dfrac{8}{15}$

EXAMPLE 6   Multiply $\dfrac{1}{2} \cdot \dfrac{3}{4} \cdot \dfrac{3}{2}$.

Extend rule for multiplication.

$\dfrac{a}{b} \cdot \dfrac{c}{d} \cdot \dfrac{e}{f} = \dfrac{ace}{bdf}$

$$\dfrac{1}{2} \cdot \dfrac{3}{4} \cdot \dfrac{3}{2} = \dfrac{1 \cdot 3 \cdot 3}{2 \cdot 4 \cdot 2}, \text{ or } \dfrac{9}{16}$$

EXAMPLE 7   Multiply $\dfrac{3a^2}{2b^3} \cdot \dfrac{4a^3}{5b^6}$.

$$\dfrac{3a^2}{2b^3} \cdot \dfrac{4a^3}{5b^6} = \dfrac{3a^2 \cdot 4a^3}{2b^3 \cdot 5b^6}$$

$$= \dfrac{3 \cdot 4 \cdot a^2 \cdot a^3}{2 \cdot 5 \cdot b^3 \cdot b^6}$$

$\left.\begin{array}{l} a^2 \cdot a^3 = a^{2+3}, \text{ or } a^5 \\ b^3 \cdot b^6 = b^{3+6}, \text{ or } b^9 \end{array}\right\}$ ────────→

$$= \dfrac{12a^5}{10b^9}$$

EXAMPLE 8   Multiply $\left(\dfrac{x+1}{x+3}\right)\left(-\dfrac{2x-1}{2x+1}\right)$.

$(-)(+) = -$ ────────────→

$$\left(\dfrac{x+1}{x+3}\right)\left(-\dfrac{2x-1}{2x+1}\right) = -\dfrac{(x+1)(2x-1)}{(x+3)(2x+1)}$$

$$= -\dfrac{2x^2 + x - 1}{2x^2 + 7x + 3}$$

EXAMPLE 9   Multiply $2\left(\dfrac{x-1}{x+3}\right)$.

Rewrite 2 as $\dfrac{2}{1}$. ────────→

$$2\left(\dfrac{x-1}{x+3}\right) = \dfrac{2}{1}\left(\dfrac{x-1}{x+3}\right)$$

$$= \dfrac{2(x-1)}{1(x+3)}$$

$2(x-1) = 2x - 2$ ────────→

$$= \dfrac{2x - 2}{x + 3}$$

EXAMPLE 10   Multiply $(x-1)\left(\dfrac{2x+5}{x-3}\right)$.

$x - 1 = \dfrac{x-1}{1}$ ────────→

$$(x-1)\left(\dfrac{2x+5}{x-3}\right) = \left(\dfrac{x-1}{1}\right)\left(\dfrac{2x+5}{x-3}\right)$$

$$= \dfrac{(x-1)(2x+5)}{1(x-3)}$$

$$= \dfrac{2x^2 + 3x - 5}{x - 3}$$

ORAL EXERCISES
Multiply.

1. $\dfrac{1}{8} \cdot \dfrac{1}{2}$

2. $\dfrac{1}{5} \cdot \dfrac{1}{6}$

3. $\dfrac{1}{m^2} \cdot \dfrac{1}{m^3}$

4. $\dfrac{1}{a^5} \cdot \dfrac{1}{a^3}$

5. $\dfrac{1}{3} \cdot \dfrac{1}{2a}$

6. $5 \cdot \dfrac{1}{2a}$

7. $\dfrac{1}{5} \cdot \dfrac{1}{46}$

8. $\left(-\dfrac{2}{3}\right)\left(-\dfrac{4}{7}\right)$

9. $-\dfrac{3}{5} \cdot \dfrac{1}{2}$

10. $4 \cdot \dfrac{2}{3}$

EXERCISES

PART A
Multiply.

1. $\dfrac{1}{4} \cdot \dfrac{2}{3} \cdot \dfrac{3}{4}$

2. $\dfrac{1}{5} \cdot \dfrac{4}{3} \cdot \dfrac{2}{5}$

3. $\left(\dfrac{2}{3}\right)\left(\dfrac{4}{5}\right)\left(-\dfrac{1}{3}\right)$

4. $\left(\dfrac{2}{5}\right)\left(\dfrac{2}{3}\right)\left(-\dfrac{1}{2}\right)$

5. $\dfrac{2a^2}{3b^3} \cdot \dfrac{5a^3}{6b^6}$

6. $\dfrac{7x^2}{3y^4} \cdot \dfrac{4x^5}{5y^2}$

7. $-\dfrac{5a^2}{3b^5} \cdot \dfrac{4a^3}{3b^4}$

8. $\dfrac{6x^3}{5y^2}\left(-\dfrac{3x^5}{2y^5}\right)$

9. $\dfrac{x^3}{y^7} \cdot \left(-\dfrac{x^2}{y^4}\right)$

10. $\dfrac{a^2}{b^3} \cdot \dfrac{1}{b^4}$

11. $\dfrac{x^2}{y^3} \cdot \dfrac{x^4}{y^2} \cdot \dfrac{x^5}{y}$

12. $\dfrac{a^3}{b^2} \cdot \dfrac{a^2}{b^4} \cdot \dfrac{a}{b^5}$

13. $\dfrac{(x+1)}{(x+2)}\left(-\dfrac{2x-3}{2x+3}\right)$

14. $\left(\dfrac{x+2}{x+1}\right)\left(-\dfrac{3x-1}{3x+1}\right)$

15. $\left(\dfrac{x+3}{x+5}\right)\left(-\dfrac{2x-5}{2x+5}\right)$

16. $3\left(\dfrac{x-1}{x+5}\right)$

17. $5\left(\dfrac{2x-1}{x+4}\right)$

18. $6\left(\dfrac{x+2}{2x-5}\right)$

19. $(x-7)\left(\dfrac{2x+3}{x-4}\right)$

20. $\left(\dfrac{-a-4}{a+3}\right)(2a-1)$

21. $(2a-3)\left(\dfrac{a+5}{3a-7}\right)$

22. $a^3 \cdot \dfrac{a^7}{b^6}$

23. $\left(-\dfrac{x^2}{m^3}\right)(-x^5)$

24. $\left(-\dfrac{a-4}{a+3}\right)\left(-\dfrac{1}{2a-1}\right)$

PART B
Multiply.

25. $\left(\dfrac{a+b}{x-y}\right)\left(\dfrac{a-b}{x+2y}\right)$

26. $\left(\dfrac{2m-n}{m+3n}\right)\left(\dfrac{3m+n}{2m+n}\right)$

27. $\left(\dfrac{3r-t}{r+t}\right)\left(\dfrac{4r+t}{r+2t}\right)$

28. $(x+2y)\left(\dfrac{x-y}{x+y}\right)$

29. $\left(\dfrac{a-2b}{x-y}\right)\left(-\dfrac{a+2b}{x+y}\right)$

30. $\left(\dfrac{2x+3y}{m+n}\right)^2$

31. $\left(-\dfrac{3a+b}{2a+b}\right)^2$

32. $\left(\dfrac{a+b}{2a-3b}\right)(a-b)$

33. $\left(-\dfrac{4a-b}{a+b}\right)\left(\dfrac{a+3b}{2a-b}\right)$

PART C
Multiply.

34. $\left(\dfrac{2x-y}{x+4y}\right)^2$

35. $\left(\dfrac{x-5}{x+5}\right)^2\left(\dfrac{x+2}{x-4}\right)$

36. $\left(\dfrac{3a-b}{a+b}\right)^2\left(\dfrac{2a-b}{a+b}\right)$

Rewriting Fractions in Simplest Form

▶ *REVIEW CAPSULE*

$$\frac{3}{5} \cdot \frac{4}{7} = \frac{3 \cdot 4}{5 \cdot 7}, \text{ or } \frac{12}{35} \longleftarrow \frac{a}{b} \cdot \frac{c}{d} = \frac{ac}{bd}$$

$$\frac{5}{5} = 5 \cdot \frac{1}{5}, \text{ or } 1 \longleftarrow \frac{a}{a} = 1$$

EXAMPLE 1 Write $\frac{6}{15}$ as a product of two fractions.

Factor 6. ⟶
Factor 15. ⟶

$$\frac{6}{15} = \frac{3 \cdot 2}{5 \cdot 3} \qquad \text{or} \qquad \frac{6}{15} = \frac{2 \cdot 3}{5 \cdot 3}$$

$$= \frac{3}{5} \cdot \frac{2}{3} \qquad \qquad\qquad = \frac{2}{5} \cdot \frac{3}{3}$$

We can use the second product to rewrite $\frac{6}{15}$ in a different form.

$\frac{3}{3} = 1$ ⟶

$$\frac{2}{5} \cdot \frac{3}{3} = \frac{2}{5} \cdot 1, \text{ or } \frac{2}{5} \qquad \textbf{Thus, } \frac{6}{15} = \frac{2}{5}.$$

EXAMPLE 2 Write $\frac{20}{30}$ in simplest form.

Factor 20 into primes. ⟶
Factor 30 into primes. ⟶

Rearrange so like factors are over each other. ⟶

$\dfrac{a}{b} \cdot \dfrac{c}{d} \cdot \dfrac{e}{f} = \dfrac{ace}{bdf}$

$\dfrac{2}{2} = 1 \qquad \dfrac{5}{5} = 1$

$$\frac{20}{30} = \frac{2 \cdot 2 \cdot 5}{5 \cdot 3 \cdot 2}$$

$$= \frac{2 \cdot 2 \cdot 5}{3 \cdot 2 \cdot 5}$$

$$= \frac{2}{3} \cdot \frac{2}{2} \cdot \frac{5}{5}$$

$$= \frac{2}{3} \cdot 1 \cdot 1$$

$$= \frac{2}{3}$$

More Compact Form

$$\frac{20}{30} = \frac{2 \cdot 2 \cdot 5}{5 \cdot 3 \cdot 2}$$

$$= \frac{2 \cdot \overset{1}{\cancel{2}} \cdot \overset{1}{\cancel{5}}}{\underset{1}{\cancel{5}} \cdot 3 \cdot \underset{1}{\cancel{2}}} \longleftarrow \frac{2}{2} = \frac{1}{1} \quad \frac{5}{5} = \frac{1}{1}$$

$$= \frac{2 \cdot 1 \cdot 1}{1 \cdot 3 \cdot 1}$$

$$= \frac{2}{3}$$

The GCF of 2 and 3 is 1, so 2 and 3 are relatively prime.

$\dfrac{2}{3}$ is in simplest form, or lowest terms.

EXAMPLE 3 Simplify. (Write in simplest form.)

$$\frac{x^2 - 7x + 12}{2x^2 - 9x + 9}$$

$x^2 - 7x + 12 \quad\mid\quad 2x^2 - 9x - 9$

$$\frac{(x - 3)(x - 4)}{(2x - 3)(x - 3)} \quad\begin{cases}\text{Factor numerator} \\ \text{and denominator.}\end{cases}$$

$\dfrac{x - 3}{x - 3} = \dfrac{1}{1}$

$$\frac{\overset{1}{\cancel{(x - 3)}}(x - 4)}{(2x - 3)\underset{1}{\cancel{(x - 3)}}} \quad\begin{cases}\text{Divide out} \\ \text{common factors.}\end{cases}$$

$1(x - 4) = x - 4$

$(2x - 3)1 = 2x - 3$

$$\frac{x - 4}{2x - 3}$$

EXAMPLE 4 Simplify $\dfrac{a - 4}{2a - 8}$.

$a - 4$ is not factorable.

$2a - 8 = 2(a - 4)$

$$\frac{a - 4}{2a - 8} = \frac{\overset{1}{\cancel{a - 4}}}{2\underset{1}{\cancel{(a - 4)}}} \quad\begin{cases}\text{Factor and divide} \\ \text{out common factors.}\end{cases}$$

The remaining factor 2 is in the denominator.

$$= \frac{1}{2 \cdot 1}, \text{ or } \frac{1}{2}$$

EXAMPLE 5 Show that $\dfrac{x + 3}{x + 4}$ cannot be simplified to $\dfrac{3}{4}$.

Let $x = 2$ in $\dfrac{x + 3}{x + 4}$.

$$\frac{2 + 3}{2 + 4} = \frac{5}{6}$$

But

$$\frac{5}{6} \neq \frac{3}{4}$$

Thus, $\dfrac{x + 3}{x + 4}$ cannot be simplified to $\dfrac{3}{4}$.

$\dfrac{x + 3}{x + 4} \neq \dfrac{3}{4}$

$\dfrac{x + 3}{x + 4}$ is already in simplest form.

EXAMPLE 6 Simplify $-\dfrac{3x^3 - 27x}{2x^2 - 6x}$.

Look for the GCF.

$3x^3 - 27x = 3(x^3 - 9x) = 3 \cdot x(x^2 - 9)$

$2x^2 - 6x = 2(x^2 - 3x) = 2 \cdot x(x - 3)$

$$-\frac{3x^3 - 27x}{2x^2 - 6x} = -\frac{3x(x^2 - 9)}{2x(x - 3)}$$

Factor $x^2 - 9$. Then divide out common factors.

$$= -\frac{3 \cdot \overset{1}{\cancel{x}}\,\overset{1}{\cancel{(x - 3)}}(x + 3)}{2 \cdot \underset{1}{\cancel{x}} \quad \underset{1}{\cancel{(x - 3)}}}$$

$3(x + 3) = 3x + 9$

$$= -\frac{3(x + 3)}{2}, \text{ or } -\frac{3x + 9}{2}$$

EXERCISES

PART A

Simplify.

1. $\dfrac{4}{12}$

2. $\dfrac{8}{16}$

3. $-\dfrac{15}{36}$

4. $-\dfrac{8}{30}$

5. $\dfrac{a^2 - 8a + 15}{2a^2 - 7a + 3}$

6. $\dfrac{m^2 - 3m - 10}{2m^2 - 9m - 5}$

7. $\dfrac{b^2 - 25}{b^2 - 7b + 10}$

8. $-\dfrac{x^2 - 9x + 14}{x^2 - 5x - 14}$

9. $\dfrac{x - 4}{4x - 16}$

10. $\dfrac{a - 8}{a^2 - 8a}$

11. $\dfrac{3b - 15}{b^2 - 7b + 10}$

12. $-\dfrac{x^2 - 5x + 4}{2x - 8}$

13. $\dfrac{4b - 12}{b^2 - 9}$

14. $\dfrac{a^2 - 7a + 12}{2a - 8}$

15. $\dfrac{y^2 + 3y - 28}{y^2 + 7y}$

16. $\dfrac{m^2 + 6m - 16}{m^2 + 8m}$

17. $\dfrac{3x^3 - 12x}{2x^2 - 4x}$

18. $\dfrac{2x^3 - 50x}{3x^2 - 15x}$

19. $\dfrac{b^2 - 7b}{b^2 - 49}$

20. $\dfrac{2x^2 + 3x - 20}{8x - 20}$

21. $\dfrac{3p^2 + 5p - 2}{5p + 10}$

22. $\dfrac{2n^2 + 3n - 2}{n^2 - 4}$

23. $\dfrac{x^2 + 8x + 16}{x^2 - 16}$

24. $\dfrac{a^2 + 2a}{a^2 - 5a - 14}$

PART B

EXAMPLE   Find the quotient $(x^2 + 7x + 12) \div (x + 4)$.

$\dfrac{a}{b}$ means $a \div b$ $\longrightarrow$

Factor. Then divide out common factors.

$(x^2 + 7x + 12) \div (x + 4) = \dfrac{x^2 + 7x + 12}{x + 4}$

$= \dfrac{\overset{1}{\cancel{(x + 4)}} (x + 3)}{\underset{1}{\cancel{x + 4}}}$

$= \dfrac{x + 3}{1}$, or $x + 3$

Thus, the quotient is $x + 3$.

Find the quotient when the first polynomial is divided by the second.

25. $x^2 + x - 12;\ x - 3$

26. $z^2 - 3z - 40;\ z + 5$

27. $2x^2 + 9x - 5;\ 2x - 1$

28. $2a^2 - ab - 3b^2;\ 2a - 3b$

29. $6a^2 - 11a + 3;\ 2a - 3$

30. $10x^2 + 17x - 63;\ 5x - 9$

31. $-11x^2 - 58x - 15;\ x + 5$

32. $-21x^2 - 22x + 63;\ -7x + 9$

PART C

Find the quotient when the first polynomial is divided by the second.

33. $a^4 - 5a^2 + 4;\ a^2 + a - 2$

34. $a^4 - 8a^2 - 9;\ a^2 - 2a - 3$

The Great Airplane Mystery

On an airplane, three passengers got into a conversation with a stewardess. The following facts evolved.

1. The names of the passengers were Miller, Adams, and Baker.

2. The stewardess said that these were the names of the flight crew, which consisted of a pilot, a copilot, and a navigator.

3. Mr. Adams said that he earned $14,000 a year.

4. Mr. Baker said that he lived in Cleveland.

5. The stewardess said that the pilot lived halfway between Cleveland and St. Louis.

6. One of the passengers lived next door to the pilot and received exactly three times as much salary as the navigator.

7. The stewardess said that the copilot often played bridge with Miller, one of the crew members.

8. The pilot had the same name as the passenger who lived in St. Louis.

What is the navigator's name? Prove your answer.

Using The −1 Technique

 REVIEW CAPSULE

Rewrite each polynomial in descending order of exponents.

$-2 + 3x$	$-3x - 2 - x^2$	$-4 + x^2$
↓	↓	↓
$3x - 2$	$-x^2 - 3x - 2$	$x^2 - 4$

EXAMPLE 1 Rewrite $5x - x^2 + 4$ as a polynomial in descending order of exponents and whose first coefficient is positive.

Descending order ⟶ $5x - x^2 + 4$

$-x^2 = -1x^2$ ⟶ $-x^2 + 5x + 4$

Factor out −1. ⟶ $-1x^2 + 5x + 4$

     $-1(x^2 - 5x - 4)$

Convenient Form of a Polynomial
$$5x - x^2 + 4$$
$$-1(\underbrace{1x^2 - 5x - 4})$$

first coefficient positive   descending order

This form is useful when factoring polynomials and simplifying fractions. ⎫

EXAMPLE 2 Simplify $\dfrac{x - 3}{9 - x^2}$.

Descending order ⟶

Convenient form ⟶

Factor $x^2 - 9$. Then divide out common factors. ⎫

$$\frac{x - 3}{9 - x^2} = \frac{x - 3}{-x^2 + 9}$$

$$= \frac{x - 3}{-1(x^2 - 9)}$$

$$= \frac{\overset{1}{\cancel{x - 3}}}{-1(\cancel{x - 3})(x + 3)}$$

$$= \frac{1}{-1(x + 3)}$$

EXAMPLE 3 Show that $-\dfrac{12}{3} = \dfrac{-1(12)}{3} = \dfrac{12}{-1(3)}$.

$$
\begin{array}{c|c|c}
-\dfrac{12}{3} & \dfrac{-1(12)}{3} & \dfrac{12}{-1(3)} \\[2mm]
-(12 \div 3) & \dfrac{-12}{3} & \dfrac{12}{-3} \\[2mm]
-4 & -4 & -4
\end{array}
$$

Same answers ⟶

Thus, $-\dfrac{12}{3} = \dfrac{-1(12)}{3} = \dfrac{12}{-1(3)}$.

Example 3 suggests this. ⟶

$$-\frac{a}{b} = \frac{-1(a)}{b} = \frac{a}{-1(b)}, \; b \neq 0$$

EXAMPLE 4 Rewrite $\dfrac{1}{-1(x+3)}$ in two other ways.

$\dfrac{a}{-1(b)} = -\dfrac{a}{b} = \dfrac{-1(a)}{b}$ ⟶

$$\frac{1}{-1(x+3)} = -\frac{1}{x+3} = \frac{-1(1)}{x+3}$$

Any one of the three is acceptable. Generally, we use the form $-\dfrac{a}{b}$.

EXAMPLE 5 Simplify $\dfrac{-3x^2 - 5x + 2}{2 - 6x}$.

Rewrite denominator in descending order.

$-3x^2 - 5x + 2$ | $-6x + 2$
$= -1(3x^2 + 5x - 2)$ | $= -1(6x - 2)$

2 is the GCF of $6x - 2$: $2(3x - 1)$.

Divide out common factors.

$$\frac{-3x^2 - 5x + 2}{-6x + 2}$$

$$\frac{-1(3x^2 + 5x - 2)}{-1(6x - 2)}$$

$$\frac{-1(3x - 1)(x + 2)}{-1(2)(3x - 1)}$$

$$\frac{\overset{1}{\cancel{-1}}(\overset{1}{\cancel{3x - 1}})(x + 2)}{\underset{1}{\cancel{-1}}(2)(\underset{1}{\cancel{3x - 1}})}$$

$$\frac{x + 2}{2}$$

EXAMPLE 6 Simplify $\dfrac{b^2 - 2b - 15}{30 - b - b^2}$.

$30 - b - b^2 = -b^2 - b + 30$
$\qquad\qquad\quad = -1(b^2 + b - 30)$

Factor. Then divide out common factors.

$\dfrac{a}{-1(b)} = -\dfrac{a}{b}$

$$\dfrac{b^2 - 2b - 15}{-1(b^2 + b - 30)}$$

$$\dfrac{\overset{1}{(b-5)}\,(b + 3)}{-1(b + 6)\,\underset{1}{(b-5)}}$$

$$\dfrac{b + 3}{-1(b + 6)}, \text{ or } -\dfrac{b + 3}{b + 6}$$

EXERCISES

PART A

Simplify.

1. $\dfrac{x - 4}{16 - x^2}$
2. $\dfrac{a + 5}{25 - a^2}$
3. $\dfrac{5 - b}{2b - 10}$
4. $\dfrac{8 - b}{2b - 16}$

5. $\dfrac{-a^2 - 2a + 15}{12 - 4a}$
6. $\dfrac{-m^2 + m + 20}{2m - 10}$
7. $\dfrac{x^2 - 7x + 12}{3 - x}$
8. $\dfrac{p^2 - 2p - 15}{5 - p}$

9. $\dfrac{2m - 8}{4 - m}$
10. $\dfrac{14 - 2x}{x^2 - 49}$
11. $\dfrac{3 - c}{c^2 - 5c + 6}$
12. $\dfrac{6 - 2b}{b^2 - 6b + 9}$

13. $\dfrac{a^2 - 2a - 8}{4 - a}$
14. $\dfrac{16 + 6m - m^2}{m^2 + 5m + 6}$
15. $\dfrac{9 - a^2}{a^2 + 5a - 24}$
16. $\dfrac{c^2 + 8c - 20}{16 - 8c}$

17. $\dfrac{y^2 - y - 42}{14 + 5y - y^2}$
18. $\dfrac{a^2 + 10a + 25}{40 + 3a - a^2}$
19. $\dfrac{x^2 - 8x - 20}{-x^2 + 14x - 40}$
20. $\dfrac{36 - m^2}{2m^2 - 8m - 24}$

PART B

Simplify.

21. $\dfrac{12 + n - n^2}{2n^2 - 18}$
22. $\dfrac{2x^2 - 6x}{24 - 2x - 2x^2}$
23. $\dfrac{-a^2 + b^2}{a^2 + 3ab + 2b^2}$

24. $\dfrac{2x^2 + xy - y^2}{-2x - 2y}$
25. $\dfrac{a^2 - b^2}{-2a^2 - ab + b^2}$
26. $\dfrac{-10 + 22a - 4a^2}{3a^2 - 16a + 5}$

PART C

Simplify.

27. $\dfrac{-a^4 + b^4}{a^3 + ab^2}$
28. $\dfrac{a^6 - a^2b^6}{a^2b^2 - b^5}$
29. $\dfrac{x^4 - 8x^2 + 15}{3x - x^3}$

30. $\dfrac{a^2 - a^3}{a^2 - a}$
31. $\dfrac{-36 + 13b^2 - b^4}{b^2 - 5b + 6}$
32. $\dfrac{5 + 4m - m^2}{m^4 - 26m^2 + 25}$

Fractions with Common Monomial Factors

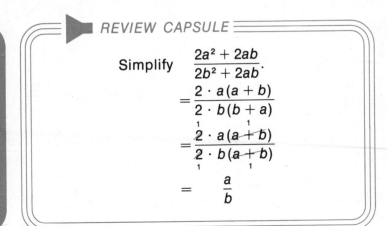

▶ REVIEW CAPSULE

Simplify $\dfrac{2a^2 + 2ab}{2b^2 + 2ab}$.

$$= \frac{2 \cdot a(a + b)}{2 \cdot b(b + a)}$$

$$= \frac{\overset{1}{\cancel{2}} \cdot a \overset{1}{\cancel{(a + b)}}}{\underset{1}{\cancel{2}} \cdot b \underset{1}{\cancel{(a + b)}}}$$

$$= \frac{a}{b}$$

EXAMPLE 1   Simplify $\dfrac{a^3}{a^7}$.

Write numerator and denominator in factored form. Then divide out common factors.

$$\frac{a^3}{a^7} = \frac{\overset{1}{\cancel{a}} \cdot \overset{1}{\cancel{a}} \cdot \overset{1}{\cancel{a}}}{\underset{1}{\cancel{a}} \cdot \underset{1}{\cancel{a}} \cdot \underset{1}{\cancel{a}} \cdot a \cdot a \cdot a \cdot a}$$

$a \cdot a \cdot a \cdot a = a^4$ ⟶

$$= \frac{1}{a^4}$$

EXAMPLE 2   Simplify $\dfrac{x^5}{x^7}$.

Shorten the work by thinking of factored form in your head.

$$\frac{\overset{1}{\cancel{x}} \cdot \overset{1}{\cancel{x}} \cdot \overset{1}{\cancel{x}} \cdot \overset{1}{\cancel{x}} \cdot \overset{1}{\cancel{x}}}{\underset{1}{\cancel{x}} \cdot \underset{1}{\cancel{x}} \cdot \underset{1}{\cancel{x}} \cdot \underset{1}{\cancel{x}} \cdot \underset{1}{\cancel{x}} \cdot x \cdot x}$$

$$\frac{x^5}{x^7} = \frac{\cancel{x^5}}{\underset{x^2}{\cancel{x^7}}}$$

$$= \frac{1}{x^2}$$

EXAMPLE 3   Simplify $\dfrac{b^5}{b^2}$.

b is a factor two times in both numerator and denominator.

$$\frac{\overbrace{b \cdot b} \cdot b \cdot b \cdot b}{\underbrace{b \cdot b}}$$

$$\frac{b^5}{b^2} = \frac{\overset{b^3}{\cancel{b^5}}}{\underset{1}{\cancel{b^2}}}$$

$$= \frac{b^3}{1}, \text{ or } b^3$$

EXAMPLE 4 Simplify $\dfrac{x^7}{x}$.

x is a factor one time in both numerator
and denominator.

$$\dfrac{x^7}{x^1} = \dfrac{\overset{x^6}{\cancel{x^7}}}{\underset{1}{\cancel{x^1}}}$$

$$= \dfrac{x^6}{1}, \text{ or } x^6$$

EXAMPLE 5 Simplify $\dfrac{12a^3b^5}{18ab^7}$.

Factor 12 and 18 into primes. a means a^1.

$\dfrac{a^3}{a^1} = \dfrac{a^2}{1}; \ \dfrac{b^5}{b^7} = \dfrac{1}{b^2}$

$2 \cdot 1 \cdot 1 \cdot a^2 \cdot 1 = 2a^2$
$3 \cdot 1 \cdot 1 \cdot 1 \cdot b^2 = 3b^2$

$$\dfrac{12a^3b^5}{18ab^7} = \dfrac{2 \cdot 2 \cdot 3 \cdot a^3 \cdot b^5}{3 \cdot 3 \cdot 2 \cdot a^1 \cdot b^7}$$

$$= \dfrac{2 \cdot 2 \cdot 3 \cdot \overset{1}{\cancel{a}}^{\overset{a^2}{3}} \cdot \overset{1}{\cancel{b}}^5}{\underset{1}{\cancel{3}} \cdot \underset{1}{\cancel{3}} \cdot \underset{1}{\cancel{2}} \cdot \cancel{a}^1 \cdot \underset{b^2}{\cancel{b}}^7}$$

$$= \dfrac{2a^2}{3b^2}$$

EXAMPLE 6 Simplify $\dfrac{a^3b^4(y^2 + 7y + 10)}{a^6b^2(-5 - y)}$.

Write $-5 - y$ in convenient form.
$-5 - y = -y - 5$
Factor out -1.
$-y - 5 = -1(y + 5)$

Factor $y^2 + 7y + 10$.
Divide out common factors.
$\dfrac{a}{-1(b)} = -\dfrac{a}{b}$

$$\dfrac{a^3b^4(y^2 + 7y + 10)}{a^6b^2(-y - 5)} \leftarrow \text{ Descending order}$$

$$\dfrac{a^3b^4(y^2 + 7y + 10)}{a^6b^2(-1)(y + 5)}$$

$$\dfrac{\overset{1}{\cancel{a}}^3\overset{b^2}{\cancel{b}}^4(y + 2)\,(\cancel{y + 5})^{\,1}}{\underset{a^3}{\cancel{a}}^6b^2(-1)\,(\underset{1}{\cancel{y + 5}})}$$

$$\dfrac{b^2(y + 2)}{-1(a^3)}, \text{ or } -\dfrac{b^2(y + 2)}{a^3}$$

EXAMPLE 7 Simplify $\dfrac{a^2b(3x^2 - 12x + 9)}{ab^2(6x - 18)}$.

Look for common monomial factors.
$3x^2 - 12x + 9 = 3(x^2 - 4x + 3)$
$6x - 18 = 6(x - 3)$

Factor $x^2 - 4x + 3$.
Divide out common factors.

$$\dfrac{a^2b(3)(x^2 - 4x + 3)}{ab^2(6)(x - 3)}$$

$$\dfrac{\overset{a}{\cancel{a}}^2b(3)\,(\cancel{x - 3})^{\,1}(x - 1)^{\,1}}{\underset{1\,b}{\cancel{a}}b^2(6)^{\,2}\,(\underset{1}{\cancel{x - 3}})}$$

$$\dfrac{a(x - 1)}{2b}$$

ORAL EXERCISES

Simplify.

1. $\dfrac{a^4}{a^7}$ **2.** $\dfrac{m^9}{m^3}$ **3.** $\dfrac{a^{10}}{a^{12}}$ **4.** $\dfrac{b^6}{b^5}$ **5.** $\dfrac{b^8}{b^9}$ **6.** $\dfrac{a^2b^3}{a^4b^7}$ **7.** $\dfrac{x^3y^3}{xy^2}$ **8.** $\dfrac{m^4n^6}{m^2n^3}$

EXERCISES

PART A

Simplify.

1. $\dfrac{4m^5n^7}{6m^2n^9}$

2. $\dfrac{10x^6y^4}{15x^3y^8}$

3. $\dfrac{4a^9b^5}{8a^4b^6}$

4. $\dfrac{x^2y^3(a^2+7a+10)}{xy^5(-2-a)}$

5. $\dfrac{m^2n^4(n^2-2n+1)}{m^7n^2(1-n)}$

6. $\dfrac{3a^2b^3(x^2+6x-16)}{9ab^5(2-x)}$

7. $\dfrac{a^8b^5(6x^2-30x+36)}{a^5b^3(3x-9)}$

8. $\dfrac{m^6(4x^2-64)}{m^9(2x-8)}$

9. $\dfrac{x^3(5b^2-20)}{x^4(10b+20)}$

10. $\dfrac{y^4(a+1)}{y^3(a^2+6a+5)}$

11. $\dfrac{k^4(a-8)}{k^5(a^2-4a-32)}$

12. $\dfrac{m^5(y^2-8y-20)}{m^2(y-10)}$

13. $\dfrac{n^4(a^2-4)}{n^5(a^2-3a+2)}$

14. $\dfrac{c^2(y^2-7y+12)}{c^3(2y-8)}$

15. $\dfrac{b^5(x^2-9)}{b^2(x^2-4x+3)}$

16. $\dfrac{a^3b^5(c^2-49)}{a^4b^7(c-7)}$

17. $\dfrac{a^3b^7(2x^2+9x-5)}{a^2b^9(2x^2+7x-15)}$

18. $\dfrac{a^7(3-x)}{a^5(x^2-9)}$

PART B

EXAMPLE   Simplify $\dfrac{a^2b-a^2}{a^5}$.

$$\dfrac{a^2b-a^2}{a^5}=\dfrac{a^2(b-1)}{a^5}$$

$$=\dfrac{\overset{1}{\cancel{a^2}}(b-1)}{\underset{a^3}{\cancel{a^5}}}$$

$$=\dfrac{b-1}{a^3}$$

Simplify.

19. $\dfrac{x^2y-x^2}{x^6}$

20. $\dfrac{a^4}{a^3b-a^3}$

21. $\dfrac{x^7}{x^2b+x^2y}$

22. $\dfrac{a^2(x-3)}{a^4x^2-9a^4}$

23. $\dfrac{b^2x^2-b^2x-2b^2}{b^5(x+1)}$

24. $\dfrac{a^4(5-m)}{a^4m^2-7a^4m+10a^4}$

Simplifying Products of Fractions

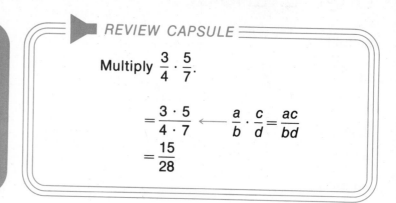

OBJECTIVES
■ To multiply fractions like
$$\frac{x^2 - 3x + 2}{x + 5} \cdot \frac{2x + 10}{x - 2}$$

REVIEW CAPSULE

Multiply $\frac{3}{4} \cdot \frac{5}{7}$.

$$= \frac{3 \cdot 5}{4 \cdot 7} \quad \longleftarrow \quad \frac{a}{b} \cdot \frac{c}{d} = \frac{ac}{bd}$$
$$= \frac{15}{28}$$

EXAMPLE 1   Multiply $\frac{x^2 - 3x + 2}{x + 5} \cdot \frac{2x + 10}{x - 2}$.

$\frac{a}{b} \cdot \frac{c}{d} = \frac{ac}{bd}$

$$\frac{(x^2 - 3x + 2)(2x + 10)}{(x + 5)(x - 2)}$$

Look for common monomial factors.
$2x + 10 = 2(x + 5)$

$$\frac{(x^2 - 3x + 2)(2)(x + 5)}{(x + 5)(x - 2)}$$

$x^2 - 3x + 2 = (x - 2)(x - 1)$

$$\frac{(x - 2)(x - 1)(2)(x + 5)}{(x + 5)(x - 2)}$$

Divide out common factors.

$$\frac{(x \overset{1}{-} 2)(x - 1)(2)(x \overset{1}{+} 5)}{(x + 5)(x - 2)}$$

Multiply remaining factors.

$$\frac{2(x - 1)}{1}$$

$2(x - 1) = 2x - 2$

$$\frac{2x - 2}{1}, \text{ or } 2x - 2$$

EXAMPLE 2   Multiply $(b + 5)\left(\frac{2b + 14}{4b^2 + 12b - 40}\right)$.

Rewrite $(b + 5)$ as $\left(\frac{b + 5}{1}\right)$.

$$\left(\frac{b + 5}{1}\right)\left(\frac{2b + 14}{4b^2 + 12b - 40}\right)$$

$\frac{a}{b} \cdot \frac{c}{d} = \frac{ac}{bd}$

$$\frac{(b + 5)(2b + 14)}{1(4b^2 + 12b - 40)}$$

$2b + 14 = 2(b + 7)$
$4b^2 + 12b - 40 = 4(b^2 + 3b - 10)$

$$\frac{(b + 5)(2)(b + 7)}{1(4)(b^2 + 3b - 10)}$$

$4 = 2 \cdot 2$
$b^2 + 3b - 10 = (b + 5)(b - 2)$
Divide out common factors.

$$\frac{(b \overset{1}{+} 5)(\overset{1}{2})(b + 7)}{1 \cdot \underset{1}{2} \cdot 2(b + 5)(b - 2)}, \text{ or } \frac{b + 7}{2(b - 2)}$$

EXAMPLE 3　Multiply $\dfrac{4x^6b^5}{5} \cdot \dfrac{15}{8x^7b^4}$.

Factor 4, 15, and 8 into primes. Then divide out common factors.

$\dfrac{x^6}{x^7} = \dfrac{1}{x^1} = \dfrac{1}{x} \Big| \dfrac{b^5}{b^4} = \dfrac{b^1}{1} = \dfrac{b}{1}$

$$\dfrac{4x^6b^5 \cdot 15}{5 \cdot 8x^7b^4}$$

$$\dfrac{\overset{1}{2} \cdot \overset{1}{2} \cdot \overset{1}{x^6} \cdot \overset{b^1}{b^5} \cdot 3 \cdot \overset{1}{5}}{\underset{1}{5} \cdot \underset{1}{2} \cdot \underset{1}{2} \cdot 2 \cdot \underset{x^1}{x^7} \cdot \underset{1}{b^4}}$$

$$\dfrac{3b}{2x}$$

EXAMPLE 4　Multiply $\dfrac{y^2 - 3y + 2}{3x^2y^5} \cdot \dfrac{12xy^3}{6 - 6y}$.

$\dfrac{a}{b} \cdot \dfrac{c}{d} = \dfrac{ac}{bd}$ ⟶

Write $6 - 6y$ in convenient form.
$(6 - 6y) = (-6y + 6) = -1(6y - 6)$

Factor.
$6y - 6 = 6(y - 1)$
$12 = 2 \cdot 2 \cdot 3$
$6 = 2 \cdot 3$
$y^2 - 3y + 2 = (y - 2)(y - 1).$

Divide out common factors.
$\dfrac{x}{x^2} = \dfrac{x^1}{x^2} = \dfrac{1}{x}; \dfrac{y^3}{y^5} = \dfrac{1}{y^2}; \dfrac{y-1}{y-1} = 1$

$\dfrac{a}{-1(b)} = -\dfrac{a}{b}$

$$\dfrac{(y^2 - 3y + 2) \cdot 12xy^3}{3x^2y^5(6 - 6y)}$$

$$\dfrac{(y^2 - 3y + 2) \cdot 12 \cdot x \cdot y^3}{3 \cdot x^2 \cdot y^5(-1)(6y - 6)}$$

$$\dfrac{(y^2 - 3y + 2) \cdot 12 \cdot x \cdot y^3}{3 \cdot x^2 \cdot y^5(-1)(6)(y - 1)}$$

$$\dfrac{(y^2 - 3y + 2) \cdot 2 \cdot 2 \cdot 3 \cdot x \cdot y^3}{3 \cdot x^2 \cdot y^5(-1) \cdot 2 \cdot 3(y - 1)}$$

$$\dfrac{(y - 2)(y - 1) \cdot 2 \cdot 2 \cdot 3 \cdot x \cdot y^3}{3 \cdot x^2 \cdot y^5(-1) \cdot 2 \cdot 3(y - 1)}$$

$$\dfrac{(y - 2)(\overset{1}{y - 1}) \cdot \overset{1}{2} \cdot 2 \cdot \overset{1}{3}\overset{1}{x}\overset{1}{y^3}}{\underset{1}{3} \cdot \underset{x^1}{x^2} \cdot \underset{y^2}{y^5}(-1) \cdot \underset{1}{2} \cdot 3(\underset{1}{y - 1})}$$

$$\dfrac{2(y - 2)}{3 \cdot x \cdot y^2(-1)}, \text{ or } -\dfrac{2(y - 2)}{3xy^2}$$

$\begin{cases} 12\,xy^3 = 12 \cdot x \cdot y^3 \\ 3x^2y^5 = 3 \cdot x^2 \cdot y^5 \end{cases}$

ORAL EXERCISES

Give in simplest form.

1. $\dfrac{2x + 5}{x - 2} \cdot \dfrac{x - 2}{3x + 4}$

2. $\dfrac{a - 5}{2x - 3} \cdot \dfrac{2x - 3}{7}$

3. $(b + 3)\left(\dfrac{x}{b + 3}\right)$

4. $\dfrac{a^3}{a^7} \cdot \dfrac{x - 2}{x + 5}$

5. $\dfrac{b^3}{2x - 5} \cdot \dfrac{3x + 2}{b^7}$

6. $\dfrac{3x + 4}{m^4} \cdot \dfrac{m^6}{2x + 5}$

7. $\dfrac{-1(x - 3)}{5} \cdot \dfrac{4}{x - 3}$

8. $\dfrac{c - 3}{a^3} \cdot \dfrac{a^5}{c - 3}$

9. $\dfrac{a - 5}{x^7} \cdot \dfrac{x^5}{a - 5}$

10. $\dfrac{2x - 3}{15} \cdot \dfrac{10}{3x + 2}$

11. $\left(\dfrac{2a - 5}{4a + 3}\right)(4a + 3)$

12. $\dfrac{x^7}{y^9} \cdot \dfrac{y^4}{x^5}$

EXERCISES

PART A

Multiply.

1. $\dfrac{x^2 - 7x + 10}{x + 7} \cdot \dfrac{3x + 21}{x - 5}$

2. $\dfrac{a - 10}{a - 3} \cdot \dfrac{a^2 - 8a + 15}{3a - 30}$

3. $\dfrac{3n + 18}{n^2 - 2n - 8} \cdot \dfrac{n - 4}{n + 6}$

4. $(x - 4)\left(\dfrac{3x - 3}{x^2 - 5x + 4}\right)$

5. $\left(\dfrac{2b + 8}{4b^2 - 16b - 48}\right)(b - 6)$

6. $(m - 4)\left(\dfrac{6m + 30}{3m^2 - 48}\right)$

7. $\dfrac{3x^6b^5}{7} \cdot \dfrac{14}{15x^7b^3}$

8. $\dfrac{9}{5m^3n^8} \cdot \dfrac{10m^5n^4}{27}$

9. $\dfrac{5x^9y^5}{6} \cdot \dfrac{18}{25x^7y^6}$

10. $\dfrac{a^2 - 8a + 15}{7x^4y} \cdot \dfrac{10x^2y^4}{15 - 5a}$

11. $\dfrac{x^2 - 36}{2a^3b^5} \cdot \dfrac{9a^4b}{18 - 3x}$

12. $\dfrac{14 - 7x}{28x^3y^6} \cdot \dfrac{5x^2y^8}{x^2 - 4x + 4}$

13. $\dfrac{b^2 - 7b + 12}{b^2 - 7b + 10} \cdot \dfrac{4b - 20}{2b - 6}$

14. $\dfrac{x^2 - 2x - 15}{x - 6} \cdot \dfrac{3x - 18}{x^2 + 10x + 21}$

15. $\dfrac{b^2 - b - 20}{b^2 - 49} \cdot \dfrac{2b + 14}{2b + 8}$

16. $\dfrac{m^2 - m - 6}{m^2 + 6m + 8} \cdot \dfrac{m + 4}{3m - 9}$

17. $\dfrac{a - 2}{a - 5} \cdot \dfrac{a^2 - 25}{2a - 4}$

18. $\dfrac{6a - 9}{a - 1} \cdot \dfrac{a^2 - 1}{2a - 3}$

19. $\dfrac{7x^3y^4}{2a^2 + 5a + 3} \cdot \dfrac{4a + 4}{21x^2y^7}$

20. $\dfrac{4x^2 - 25}{x^2 + 10x + 16} \cdot \dfrac{6x + 12}{4x - 10}$

21. $\dfrac{2a^2 + 5a + 2}{a + 5} \cdot \dfrac{3a + 15}{2a^2 + 7a + 3}$

22. $\dfrac{6a^2 + 15a + 6}{6a + 30} \cdot \dfrac{6a + 30}{6a^2 + 21a + 9}$

23. $\dfrac{12x^2 - 75}{2x^2 + 20x + 32} \cdot \dfrac{24x + 48}{12x - 30}$

PART B

Multiply.

24. $\dfrac{5 - x}{x^2 - x - 20} \cdot \dfrac{x^2 + 8x + 16}{x^2 + 7x + 12}$

25. $\dfrac{c^2 - 5c - 6}{c^2 + 3c} \cdot \dfrac{4c + 12}{12 - 2c}$

26. $\dfrac{2n^2 - 13n - 7}{n} \cdot \dfrac{6n}{21 - 3n}$

27. $\dfrac{2a^2 - 4a - 16}{a^2 - a - 12} \cdot \dfrac{a^2 + a - 6}{a^2 - 6a + 8}$

28. $\dfrac{a^2 - 5a + 6}{a^2 - 7a + 10} \cdot \dfrac{5 + 4a - a^2}{a^2 - 2a - 3}$

29. $\dfrac{c + d}{c} \cdot \dfrac{c^2}{c^2 + 2cd + d^2}$

30. $\dfrac{35 - 2x - x^2}{x^3 - 9x} \cdot \dfrac{x^2 + 3x}{x + 7}$

31. $\dfrac{x^2 + 5xy + 6y^2}{a^5b^2} \cdot \dfrac{4a^3b}{2x + 6y}$

32. $\dfrac{4m^2 - n^2}{2m^2 + 3m - 35} \cdot \dfrac{m + 5}{n - 2m}$

33. $\dfrac{a^2 - 7ab - 18b^2}{-a + 9b} \cdot \dfrac{3a + 9b}{a^2 - 4b^2}$

34. $\dfrac{2c^2 - 10cd + 12d^2}{3c^2 - 21cd + 30d^2} \cdot \dfrac{15c^2 + 12cd - 3d^2}{4c^2 - 8cd - 12d^2}$

PART C

Multiply.

35. $\dfrac{10 + m - 2m^2}{4m^2 - 1} \cdot \dfrac{2m^2 - 3m + 1}{2m^2 - 7m + 5}$

36. $\dfrac{10 - 16a - 8a^2}{2a^2 - 3a - 20} \cdot \dfrac{3a^2 - 12a}{12a^2 - 6a}$

37. $\dfrac{m^4 - 50m^2 + 49}{m^2 + 6m - 7} \cdot \dfrac{2}{28 - 4m}$

38. $\dfrac{x^6 - y^6}{x^6 - 3x^3y^3 - 4y^6} \cdot \dfrac{4x^3 - 16y^3}{4x^3 - 4y^3}$

Puzzlers

PUZZLE 1.

Fill in the missing numbers for
this multiplication problem.

```
1.      * * 3
          2 * *
        ———————
        * 1 * 7
        * * *
      * 1 4 *
      ———————————
      * * * * * *
```

PUZZLE 2.

Division puzzlers are even harder.
Fill in the numbers.

```
2.              1 * *
        2 1 5 | * * * * * *
              * * *
              ———————
              * * * *
              * 5 * *
              ———————
                * 4 *
                * * *
                ———————
```

```
3.            . * 8 *
        2 * | * * 8 *
              * 8
              ———————
              * * *
              * * 8
              ———————
              * * *
              * * *
              ———————
```

Dividing Fractions

REVIEW CAPSULE

$$\frac{2}{3} \div \frac{5}{7} = \frac{2}{3} \cdot \frac{7}{5}$$

$$= \frac{2 \cdot 7}{3 \cdot 5}, \text{ or } \frac{14}{15}$$

$$\frac{a}{b} \div \frac{c}{d} = \frac{a}{b} \cdot \frac{d}{c}, \; b \neq 0, \; c \neq 0, \; d \neq 0.$$

EXAMPLE 1 Divide $\dfrac{x^2 - 7x + 12}{x^2 - 25} \div \dfrac{2x - 8}{x - 5}$.

$\dfrac{a}{b} \div \dfrac{c}{d} = \dfrac{a}{b} \cdot \dfrac{d}{c}$ ──────────→

$\dfrac{a}{b} \cdot \dfrac{d}{c} = \dfrac{ad}{bc}$ ──────────→

$$\frac{x^2 - 7x + 12}{x^2 - 25} \cdot \frac{x - 5}{2x - 8}$$

Look for common monomial factors.
$2x - 8 = 2(x - 4)$

$$\frac{(x^2 - 7x + 12)(x - 5)}{(x^2 - 25)(2x - 8)}$$

$$\frac{(x^2 - 7x + 12)(x - 5)}{(x^2 - 25)(2)(x - 4)}$$

Factor $x^2 - 7x + 12$ and $x^2 - 25$.
Then divide out common factors.

$$\frac{(x - 3)\,\overset{1}{\cancel{(x - 4)}}\,\overset{1}{\cancel{(x - 5)}}}{\underset{1}{\cancel{(x - 5)}}(x + 5)(2)\underset{1}{\cancel{(x - 4)}}}$$

$$\frac{x - 3}{2(x + 5)}$$

EXAMPLE 2 Divide $\dfrac{k^2 - 7k - 18}{k^5} \div \dfrac{2k^2 - 18k}{6k^3}$.

$\dfrac{a}{b} \div \dfrac{c}{d} = \dfrac{a}{b} \cdot \dfrac{d}{c}$ ──────────→

$\dfrac{a}{b} \cdot \dfrac{d}{c} = \dfrac{ad}{bc}$ ──────────→

$$\frac{k^2 - 7k - 18}{k^5} \cdot \frac{6k^3}{2k^2 - 18k}$$

$$\frac{(k^2 - 7k - 18)(6k^3)}{k^5(2k^2 - 18k)}$$

$k^2 - 7k - 18 = (k - 9)(k + 2)$,
$6 = 2 \cdot 3$, $2k^2 - 18k = 2 \cdot k(k - 9)$
Divide out common factors.

$$\frac{\overset{1}{\cancel{(k - 9)}}(k + 2) \cdot \overset{1}{\cancel{2}} \cdot 3 \cdot \overset{1}{\cancel{k^3}}}{\underset{k^2}{\cancel{k^5}} \cdot \underset{1}{\cancel{2}} \cdot k\underset{1}{\cancel{(k - 9)}}}$$

$$\frac{3(k + 2)}{k^3}$$

EXAMPLE 3 Divide $\dfrac{3a^2b^3}{6a - 2a^2} \div \dfrac{ab^4}{4a - 12}$.

$\dfrac{a}{b} \div \dfrac{c}{d} = \dfrac{a}{b} \cdot \dfrac{d}{c}$ ───────────►

$\dfrac{a}{b} \cdot \dfrac{d}{c} = \dfrac{ad}{bc}$ ───────────►

$\dfrac{3a^2b^3}{6a - 2a^2} \cdot \dfrac{4a - 12}{ab^4}$

$\dfrac{3a^2b^3(4a - 12)}{(6a - 2a^2)ab^4}$

$6a - 2a^2 = -2a^2 + 6a = -1(2a^2 - 6a)$ ───────►

Look for common monomial factors.
$4a - 12 = 4(a - 3)$; $2a^2 - 6a = 2a(a - 3)$

$\dfrac{3 \cdot a^2 \cdot b^3(4a - 12)}{-1(2a^2 - 6a)ab^4}$

$\dfrac{3 \cdot a^2 \cdot b^3 \cdot 4(a - 3)}{-1 \cdot 2 \cdot a(a - 3)ab^4}$

Factor 4 into primes. Multiplication can
be done in any order. Divide out
common factors.

$\dfrac{3 \cdot \overset{1}{\cancel{a^2}} \cdot \overset{1}{\cancel{b^3}} \cdot \overset{1}{\cancel{2}} \cdot 2\overset{1}{\cancel{(a - 3)}}}{-1 \cdot \underset{1}{\cancel{2}} \cdot \underset{1}{\cancel{a}} \cdot \underset{1}{\cancel{a}} \cdot \underset{b}{\cancel{b^4}}\underset{1}{\cancel{(a - 3)}}}$

$\dfrac{a}{-1(b)} = -\dfrac{a}{b}$

$\dfrac{6}{-1(b)}$, or $-\dfrac{6}{b}$

EXERCISES

PART A

Divide.

1. $\dfrac{x^2 - 6x + 8}{x^2 - 36} \div \dfrac{3x - 12}{x - 6}$

2. $\dfrac{4a - 28}{6} \div \dfrac{a^2 - 49}{3a - 21}$

3. $\dfrac{a^2 - 25}{a + 1} \div \dfrac{2a + 10}{4a + 4}$

4. $\dfrac{k^2 - 6k - 16}{k^7} \div \dfrac{2k^2 - 16k}{8k^5}$

5. $\dfrac{5a^4}{a^2 - 5a - 14} \div \dfrac{9a^7}{3a^2 - 21a}$

6. $\dfrac{x^2 - 5x + 4}{5x^8} \div \dfrac{3x^2 - 12x}{6x^3}$

7. $\dfrac{7a^3b^5}{9a - 3a^2} \div \dfrac{a^8b}{5a - 15}$

8. $\dfrac{16 - 2x}{xy^4} \div \dfrac{x^2 - 8x}{7x^3y^2}$

9. $\dfrac{25 - m^2}{mn^5} \div \dfrac{3m^2 - 15m}{18m^3n^4}$

10. $\dfrac{m^2 - 4m + 3}{m^2 - 1} \div \dfrac{2m - 6}{m^2 + 2m + 1}$

11. $\dfrac{5b^2 - 20}{b^2 - 5b + 6} \div \dfrac{6b + 12}{3b - 6}$

12. $\dfrac{m}{m^2 + 6m + 9} \div \dfrac{1}{m + 3}$

13. $\dfrac{x^2 - 3x + 2}{x^2 - 1} \div \dfrac{2 - x}{x - 1}$

14. $\dfrac{y}{5 - y} \div \dfrac{y^3}{2y - 10}$

15. $\dfrac{3 - m}{m - 6} \div \dfrac{m^2 + 2m - 15}{m^2 - m - 30}$

16. $\dfrac{4a^3b^2}{3a^2 + 5a} \div \dfrac{6a^5b^7}{3a^2 + 17a + 20}$

17. $\dfrac{8x^7y^5}{5x^2 - 10x} \div \dfrac{4x^8y^4}{5x^2 + 15x - 50}$

PART B

Divide.

18. $\dfrac{4m^2 + 8m + 3}{6m^3 + 3m^2} \div \dfrac{4m^2 - 9}{2m^2 + m}$

19. $\dfrac{m^3 - m}{4m^2} \div \dfrac{2 - 2m}{m^8}$

20. $\dfrac{b^2 + 3b - 4}{b^2 + 6b + 8} \div \dfrac{b^2 + 4b + 3}{b^2 + 3b + 2}$

21. $\dfrac{a^2 + 3a - 10}{a^2 + 9a + 20} \div \dfrac{a^2 + 2a - 8}{a^2 + 7a + 12}$

Chapter Seven Review

Give the coordinate of point A. $[p.\ 175]$

1.    **2.**

Find the missing factor. $[p.\ 175]$

4. $(7)\,(?) = \dfrac{7}{12}$

5. $(a - 3)\,(?) = \dfrac{a - 3}{a + 7}$

6. $(?)\left(\dfrac{1}{3m + 2}\right) = \dfrac{m}{3m + 2}$

7. Find the reciprocal of 4, 0, -5, and $-\frac{1}{3}$.

Find the value(s) of x for which the fraction is undefined. $[p.\ 175]$

8. $\dfrac{7}{x - 5}$

9. $\dfrac{3x + 5}{2x - 8}$

10. $\dfrac{7x - 8}{x^2 - 10x + 24}$

Multiply. $[p.\ 180]$

11. $\dfrac{4}{9} \cdot \dfrac{5}{7}$ **12.** $\left(\dfrac{3a^2}{5b^2}\right)\!\left(\dfrac{2a^3}{7b^7}\right)$ **13.** $(x - 3)\left(\dfrac{x + 5}{2x - 3}\right)$ **14.** $\left(-\dfrac{a - 2b}{a + b}\right)\!\left(\dfrac{a + 2b}{a + 3b}\right)$

Simplify. $[p.\ 184]$

15. $\dfrac{8}{20}$ **16.** $\dfrac{3a - 15}{4a - 20}$ **17.** $\dfrac{b^2 - b}{2b - 2}$ **18.** $\dfrac{12p^2 + 26p - 10}{3p^2 + 11p - 4}$

Find the quotient when the first polynomial is divided by the second. $[p.\ 184]$

19. $x^2 - 8x + 12;\ x - 6$ **20.** $z^2 - 3z - 10;\ z - 5$

Simplify. $[p.\ 188,\ 191]$

21. $\dfrac{3m - 12}{4 - m}$ **22.** $\dfrac{16 - y^2}{y^2 - 8y + 16}$ **23.** $\dfrac{10 + a - 3a^2}{a^2 + 5a - 14}$

24. $\dfrac{8a^5 b^9}{20a^7 b^6}$ **25.** $\dfrac{x^3 b - x^3}{x^4}$ **26.** $\dfrac{6x^2 y^7 (a^2 - 3a - 40)}{14xy^8 (16 + 6a - a^2)}$

Multiply or divide as indicated. $[p.\ 194,\ 198]$

27. $\dfrac{x^2 - 9x + 14}{x + 8} \cdot \dfrac{5x + 40}{x - 7}$

28. $(x - 3)\left(\dfrac{3x + 7}{x^2 + 3x - 28}\right)$

29. $\dfrac{7x^9 y^8}{5} \cdot \dfrac{15}{21x^6 y^9}$

30. $\dfrac{a^2 - 10a + 21}{x^7 y^2} \cdot \dfrac{6x^3 y^4}{21 - 3a}$

31. $\dfrac{a^2 - 13a + 36}{a^2 - 49} \div \dfrac{5a - 20}{a - 7}$

32. $\dfrac{k^2 - 12k + 27}{k^8} \div \dfrac{2k^2 - 18k}{14k^5}$

33. $\dfrac{3a^4 b^6}{20a - 5a^2} \div \dfrac{a^9 b}{7a - 28}$

34. $\dfrac{x^3 - 49x}{6x^3} \div \dfrac{21 - 3x}{12x^7}$

Chapter Seven Test

Give the coordinate of point A.

1.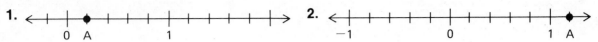

2.

Find the missing factor.

3. $(x - 2)(?) = \dfrac{x - 2}{3x + 1}$

4. $(?)\left(\dfrac{1}{5x - 1}\right) = \dfrac{2x - 9}{5x - 1}$

5. Find the reciprocal of $3, -7, 0,$ and $-\dfrac{1}{9}$.

Find the value(s) of m for which the fraction is undefined.

6. $\dfrac{3}{2m - 8}$

7. $\dfrac{2m - 3}{m^2 - 7m + 12}$

Multiply.

8. $\dfrac{5}{7} \cdot \dfrac{3}{2}$

9. $\left(\dfrac{4m^3}{7b^6}\right)\left(\dfrac{3m^9}{5b^4}\right)$

10. $\left(\dfrac{m - 4}{2m - 7}\right)(m + 3)$

Simplify.

11. $\dfrac{12}{20}$

12. $\dfrac{5p - 35}{4p - 28}$

13. $\dfrac{6p^2 + 20p - 50}{3p^2 + 13p - 10}$

14. $\dfrac{9 - y^2}{y^2 - 10y + 21}$

15. $\dfrac{y^3 - y^3a}{y^7}$

16. $\dfrac{4x^3y^3(t^2 - 13t + 42)}{12xy^7(28 + 3t - t^2)}$

Find the quotient when the first polynomial is divided by the second.

17. $a^2 + 7a + 10; a + 5$

18. $m^2 - 6m - 16; m - 8$

Multiply or divide as indicated.

19. $\dfrac{m^2 - 8m + 12}{m + 9} \cdot \dfrac{5m + 45}{m - 6}$

20. $(x - 8)\left(\dfrac{2x + 5}{x^2 - 2x - 48}\right)$

21. $\dfrac{a^2 - 7a - 8}{x^8y^9} \cdot \dfrac{15x^7y^5}{24 - 3a}$

22. $\dfrac{a^2 + 4a - 12}{4 - 2a} \div \dfrac{a^2 + 8a + 12}{2}$

23. $\dfrac{a^2 - 3ab + 2b^2}{a^2 - ab} \div \dfrac{2b - a}{a^3}$

24. $\dfrac{x^3 - 36x}{14x^4} \div \dfrac{30 - 5x}{12x^6}$

COMBINING FRACTIONS

Mathematics in the Trades

Several trades, such as the three pictured here, involve computing areas by first making accurate measurements.

Painters must measure walls in order to calculate the amount of paint needed to cover a room.

Tile setters must calculate the number of tiles that are needed in order to cover the floor.

Carpet layers must measure and cut precisely in order to cover the required area.

Adding Fractions: Same Denominator

 REVIEW CAPSULE

$$3\left(\frac{1}{7}\right) = \frac{3}{7}$$
$$2\left(\frac{1}{5}\right) = \frac{2}{5}$$
$$\left.\right\} \quad a\left(\frac{1}{b}\right) = \frac{a}{b}$$

EXAMPLE 1 Add $\frac{3}{7} + \frac{2}{7}$. | Add $\frac{4}{x} + \frac{5}{x}$.

$\frac{a}{b} = a\left(\frac{1}{b}\right)$ ⟶

$$\frac{3}{7} + \frac{2}{7} = 3\left(\frac{1}{7}\right) + 2\left(\frac{1}{7}\right)$$

Use the distributive property.
$ac + bc = (a + b)c$

$$= (3 + 2)\left(\frac{1}{7}\right)$$

$$= 5\left(\frac{1}{7}\right)$$

$a\left(\frac{1}{b}\right) = \frac{a}{b}$ ⟶

$$= \frac{5}{7}$$

$$\frac{4}{x} + \frac{5}{x} = 4\left(\frac{1}{x}\right) + 5\left(\frac{1}{x}\right)$$

$$= (4 + 5)\left(\frac{1}{x}\right)$$

$$= 9\left(\frac{1}{x}\right)$$

$$= \frac{9}{x}$$

Example 1 suggests this. ⟶

$$\frac{a}{b} + \frac{c}{b} = \frac{a + c}{b},\ b \neq 0.$$

EXAMPLE 2 Add $\frac{5}{18} + \frac{1}{18}$. | Add $\frac{7}{3m} + \frac{2}{3m}$.

$\frac{a}{b} + \frac{c}{b} = \frac{a + c}{b}$ ⟶

$$\frac{5}{18} + \frac{1}{18} = \frac{5 + 1}{18}$$

$$= \frac{6}{18}$$

Factor into primes.
Divide out common factors.

$$= \frac{\overset{1}{\cancel{3}} \cdot \overset{1}{\cancel{2}}}{\underset{1}{\cancel{3}} \cdot 3 \cdot \underset{1}{\cancel{2}}}$$

Simplest form ⟶

$$= \frac{1}{3}$$

$$\frac{7}{3m} + \frac{2}{3m} = \frac{7 + 2}{3m}$$

$$= \frac{9}{3m}$$

$$= \frac{\overset{1}{\cancel{3}} \cdot 3}{\underset{1}{\cancel{3}} \cdot m}$$

$$= \frac{3}{m}$$

EXAMPLE 3   Add $\dfrac{2y}{y-4}+\dfrac{3y}{y-4}$.

$\dfrac{a}{b}+\dfrac{c}{b}=\dfrac{a+c}{b}$ ──────────→ $\qquad\qquad \dfrac{2y}{y-4}+\dfrac{3y}{y-4}=\dfrac{2y+3y}{y-4}$

Combine like terms. ──────────→ $\qquad\qquad\qquad\qquad\quad =\dfrac{5y}{y-4}$
The result is in simplest form.

EXAMPLE 4   Add $\dfrac{x^2}{2x+14}+\dfrac{-49}{2x+14}$.

$\dfrac{a}{b}+\dfrac{c}{b}=\dfrac{a+c}{b}$ ──────────→ $\qquad\qquad \dfrac{x^2}{2x+14}+\dfrac{-49}{2x+14}=\dfrac{x^2-49}{2x+14}$

Factor. $x^2-49=(x+7)(x-7)$ ──────→ $\qquad\qquad\qquad\qquad =\dfrac{\overset{1}{(x+7)}(x-7)}{2\underset{1}{(x+7)}}$
$\qquad\quad 2x+14=2(x+7)$ ──────→

Simplest form ──────────────→ $\qquad\qquad\qquad\qquad =\dfrac{x-7}{2}$

EXAMPLE 5   Add $\dfrac{-3}{x^2-7x+12}+\dfrac{x}{x^2-7x+12}+\dfrac{-1}{x^2-7x+12}$.

$\dfrac{a}{b}+\dfrac{c}{b}+\dfrac{d}{b}=\dfrac{a+c+d}{b}$ ──────→ $\qquad\qquad\qquad \dfrac{-3+x-1}{x^2-7x+12}$

$\qquad\qquad\qquad\qquad\qquad\qquad\qquad\qquad\qquad\quad \dfrac{x-4}{x^2-7x+12}$

Factor the denominator. $\Big\}$ ──────→ $\qquad\qquad\qquad \dfrac{\overset{1}{x-4}}{\underset{1}{(x-4)}(x-3)}$
Divide out common factors.

Simplest form ──────────────→ $\qquad\qquad\qquad\qquad \dfrac{1}{x-3}$

ORAL EXERCISES

Add.

1. $\dfrac{3}{5}+\dfrac{1}{5}$ **2.** $\dfrac{5}{9}+\dfrac{3}{9}$ **3.** $\dfrac{3}{13}+\dfrac{7}{13}$ **4.** $\dfrac{5}{14}+\dfrac{4}{14}$

5. $\dfrac{3}{m}+\dfrac{2}{m}$ **6.** $\dfrac{3}{a}+\dfrac{-7}{a}$ **7.** $\dfrac{x}{5}+\dfrac{3}{5}+\dfrac{2x}{5}$ **8.** $\dfrac{7m}{2}+\dfrac{5}{2}+\dfrac{-9m}{2}$

EXERCISES

PART A

Add.

1. $\dfrac{5}{9} + \dfrac{1}{9}$

2. $\dfrac{3}{18} + \dfrac{6}{18}$

3. $\dfrac{4}{7a} + \dfrac{3}{7a}$

4. $\dfrac{3}{10x} + \dfrac{5}{10x}$

5. $\dfrac{5y}{y-3} + \dfrac{2y}{y-3}$

6. $\dfrac{7x}{x-6} + \dfrac{6x}{x-6}$

7. $\dfrac{3m}{m+7} + \dfrac{14m}{m+7}$

8. $\dfrac{x^2}{3x-18} + \dfrac{-36}{3x-18}$

9. $\dfrac{a}{6a-18} + \dfrac{-3}{6a-18}$

10. $\dfrac{a}{7a+28} + \dfrac{4}{7a+28}$

11. $\dfrac{6}{m^2+m-30} + \dfrac{m}{m^2+m-30}$

12. $\dfrac{-15}{x^2-36} + \dfrac{x}{x^2-36} + \dfrac{9}{x^2-36}$

13. $\dfrac{-10}{a^2+7a} + \dfrac{a+17}{a^2+7a}$

14. $\dfrac{a}{a^2-a-20} + \dfrac{-5}{a^2-a-20}$

15. $\dfrac{2a}{2a^2-5a-3} + \dfrac{1}{2a^2-5a-3}$

16. $\dfrac{x}{x^2-5x} + \dfrac{-5}{x^2-5x}$

PART B

Add.

17. $\dfrac{3}{26} + \dfrac{5}{26} + \dfrac{5}{26}$

18. $\dfrac{2}{21} + \dfrac{7}{21} + \dfrac{5}{21}$

19. $\dfrac{3a}{28} + \dfrac{5b}{28} + \dfrac{9a}{28} + \dfrac{3b}{28}$

20. $\dfrac{5a}{32} + \dfrac{3b}{32} + \dfrac{7a}{32} + \dfrac{7b}{32}$

21. $\dfrac{2x}{2x^2+13x+15} + \dfrac{3}{2x^2+13x+15}$

22. $\dfrac{3a}{6a^2+a-12} + \dfrac{-4}{6a^2+a-12}$

23. $\dfrac{2a^2}{6a^2-5a-25} + \dfrac{a-15}{6a^2-5a-25}$

24. $\dfrac{4b}{6b^2+11b-35} + \dfrac{-15}{6b^2+11b-35} + \dfrac{3b^2}{6b^2+11b-35}$

PART C

Add.

25. $\dfrac{a^3}{a^2+a} + \dfrac{4a^2}{a^2+a} + \dfrac{3a}{a^2+a}$

26. $\dfrac{4b^3+14b^2}{8b^2-12b} + \dfrac{-30b}{8b^2-12b}$

27. $\dfrac{8x^2-15y^2}{2x-5y} + \dfrac{-14xy}{2x-5y}$

28. $\dfrac{2x^2}{3x+6y} + \dfrac{7xy}{3x+6y} + \dfrac{6y^2}{3x+6y}$

Age Problems

OBJECTIVE

■ To solve problems about ages

REVIEW CAPSULE

	Now	3 Years from Now	5 Years Ago
Pat's age	13	$13 + 3$, or 16	$13 - 5$, or 8
Lee's age	x	$x + 3$	$x - 5$
Ray's age	$4y$	$4y + 3$	$4y - 5$

EXAMPLE 1 Geri's age now is $x + 2$. Write algebraic expressions for Geri's age 3 years from now and 5 years ago.

$$\text{Geri's age now} = x + 2$$

Add 3 to the age now. $\longrightarrow$ Geri's age 3 years from now $= (x + 2) + 3$, or $x + 5$

Subtract 5 from the age now. $\longrightarrow$ Geri's age 5 years ago $= (x + 2) - 5$, or $x - 3$

Thus, $x + 5$ represents Geri's age 3 years from now and $x - 3$ represents Geri's age 5 years ago.

EXAMPLE 2 Amy is 4 years older than Mario. Write an algebraic expression for each of their ages 6 years from now.

Represent their ages now algebraically. $\longrightarrow$ Let $x =$ Mario's age now

$x + 4 =$ Amy's age now

Make a chart. $\longrightarrow$

	Now	6 Years from Now
Mario's age	x	$x + 6$
Amy's age	$x + 4$	$(x + 4) + 6$, or $x + 10$

Thus, $x + 6$ represents Mario's age 6 years from now and $x + 10$ represents Amy's age 6 years from now.

EXAMPLE 3 Dave is 5 years older than Grace. Write an algebraic expression for each of their ages 7 years ago.

Represent their ages now algebraically. $\longrightarrow$ Let $x =$ Grace's age now

$x + 5 =$ Dave's age now

Make a chart. $\longrightarrow$

	Now	7 Years Ago
Grace	x	$x - 7$
Dave	$x + 5$	$(x + 5) - 7$, or $x - 2$

Thus, $x - 7$ represents Grace's age 7 years ago and $x - 2$ represents Dave's age 7 years ago.

EXAMPLE 4 Fumiko is 3 years older than Omari. The sum of their ages is 25. Find their ages.

Represent the ages algebraically. ──────→ Let x = Omari's age
$x + 3$ = Fumiko's age

Write an equation. ──────────────→
Substitute. ───────────────────→
Solve the equation.

$$\text{Sum of their ages} = 25$$
$$x + (x + 3) = 25$$
$$2x + 3 = 25$$
$$2x = 22$$

Omari's age ─────────────────→ $x = 11$
Fumiko's age ────────────────→ $x + 3 = 14$

Thus, Omari is 11 and Fumiko is 14.

EXAMPLE 5 Ralph is 3 times as old as Peg. In 6 years Ralph will be only twice as old as Peg will be then. Find their ages now.

Represent the ages algebraically. ──────→ Let x = Peg's age now
$3x$ = Ralph's age now

Make a chart. ──────────────────→

	Now	6 Years from Now
Peg's age	x	$x + 6$
Ralph's age	$3x$	$3x + 6$

Write an equation. ──────────────→

$$\left(\begin{array}{c}\text{Ralph's age} \\ \text{in 6 yr}\end{array}\right) = \text{twice} \left(\begin{array}{c}\text{Peg's age} \\ \text{in 6 yr}\end{array}\right)$$

Substitute. ───────────────────→
Solve the equation.

$$3x + 6 = 2 \cdot (x + 6)$$
$$3x + 6 = 2x + 12$$
$$x = 6$$
$$3x = 3(6), \text{ or } 18$$

Check.

Ralph's age is 3 times Peg's age.

18	3(6)
	18

Ralph's age in 6 yr is twice Peg's age in 6 yr.

18 + 6	2(6 + 6)
24	2(12)
	24

Thus, Peg is 6 and Ralph is 18.

EXAMPLE 6   Mrs. Schrader is 36 and her son is 9. In how many years will Mrs. Schrader be exactly twice as old as her son?

Represent the number of years algebraically.

Let x = number of years until Mrs. Schrader is exactly twice as old as her son

Make a chart. ———————→

	Now	x Years from Now
Mrs. Schrader's age	36	$36 + x$
Son's age	9	$9 + x$

Write an equation. ———————→

$$\left(\begin{matrix} \text{Mrs. Schrader's age} \\ \text{in } x \text{ yr} \end{matrix}\right) = \text{twice} \left(\begin{matrix} \text{Son's age} \\ \text{in } x \text{ yr} \end{matrix}\right)$$

Substitute. ———————→
Solve the equation.

$$36 + x = 2 \cdot (9 + x)$$
$$36 + x = 18 + 2x$$
$$36 = 18 + x$$
$$18 = x$$

Thus, in 18 years Mrs. Schrader will be exactly twice as old as her son.

EXAMPLE 7   Rhoda is 8 years younger than Irving. Two years ago, Irving was 3 times as old as Rhoda was then. Find their ages now.

Represent the ages algebraically. ———→

Let x = Irving's age now
$x - 8$ = Rhoda's age now

Make a chart. ———————→

	Now	2 Years Ago
Irving's age	x	$x - 2$
Rhoda's age	$x - 8$	$(x - 8) - 2$, or $x - 10$

Write an equation. ———————→

$$\left(\begin{matrix} \text{Irving's age} \\ \text{2 yr ago} \end{matrix}\right) = 3 \text{ times} \left(\begin{matrix} \text{Rhoda's age} \\ \text{2 yr ago} \end{matrix}\right)$$

Substitute. ———————→
Solve the equation.

$$x - 2 = 3 \cdot (x - 10)$$
$$x - 2 = 3x - 30$$
$$-2x - 2 = -30$$
$$-2x = -28$$

Irving's age ———————→
Rhoda's age ———————→

$$x = 14$$
$$x - 8 = 14 - 8, \text{ or } 6$$

Thus, Rhoda is 6 and Irving is 14.

EXERCISES

1. Tom is 7 years older than Joe. The sum of their ages is 37. Find their ages.

2. Beth is twice as old as Donna. The sum of their ages is 54. Find their ages.

3. Dorothy is 4 times as old as Louis. In 6 years Dorothy will be twice as old as Louis will be then. Find their ages now.

4. Steve is 16 years older than Denise. In 3 years he will be exactly 3 times as old as Denise will be then. Find their ages now.

5. Sylvia is 16 years younger than Martin. In 5 years Martin will be twice as old as Sylvia will be then. Find their ages now.

6. Andrew is 40 years younger than Sarah. In 10 years Sarah will be 3 times as old as Andrew will be then. Find their ages now.

7. Mrs. Wang is 29 and her daughter is 7. In how many years will Mrs. Wang be exactly 3 times as old as as her daughter?

8. Mr. Kickingbird is 39 and his son is 11. In how many years will Mr. Kickingbird be exactly 3 times as old as his son?

9. Debbie is 20 and Rita is 13. How many years ago was Debbie exactly twice as old as Rita?

10. John is 29 and Dianna is 18. How many years ago was John exactly twice as old as Dianna?

11. Pedro is twice as old as Mona. Four years ago, Pedro was 4 times as old as Mona was then. Find their ages now.

12. Lee is 7 years older than Phil. Eleven years ago, Lee was twice as old as Phil was then. Find their ages now.

13. Ruby is 37 and Eva is 21. How many years ago was Ruby exactly 3 times as old as Eva?

14. Ms. Ford is 75 and Ms. Garcia is 50. How many years ago was Ms. Ford exactly twice as old as Ms. Garcia?

15. Marge is 16 and her grandfather is 60. In how many years will Marge's grandfather be 3 times as old as she?

16. Sue and Jeff are twins. Their brother, Harry is 5 years older. The sum of their ages is 23. Find their ages.

Adding: Different Denominators

OBJECTIVE
■ To add fractions like
$$\frac{2b-3}{6b} + \frac{4b+1}{2b}$$

REVIEW CAPSULE

$$\frac{2a}{5} + \frac{7a}{5} = \frac{2a+7a}{5}$$

same denominator $= \frac{9a}{5}$

To add fractions with the same
denominator, add the numerators.

EXAMPLE 1 Show that $\frac{2}{5} = \frac{2 \cdot 3}{5 \cdot 3}$.

$$
\begin{array}{c|c}
\dfrac{2}{5} & \dfrac{2 \cdot 3}{5 \cdot 3} \\[2ex]
\dfrac{2}{5} & \dfrac{2}{5} \cdot \dfrac{3}{3} \\[2ex]
& \dfrac{2}{5} \cdot 1 \\[2ex]
& \dfrac{2}{5}
\end{array}
$$

$\frac{3}{3} = 1$

Thus, $\frac{2}{5} = \frac{2 \cdot 3}{5 \cdot 3}$.

Example 1 suggests this. ⟶

$\frac{a}{b} = \frac{a \cdot c}{b \cdot c}$, $c \neq 0$.

Multiplying both numerator and denominator of
a fraction by the same number does not
change its value.

EXAMPLE 2 Add $\frac{5}{6} + \frac{1}{3}$.

Denominators are not the same. Factor
6 into primes, $6 = 2 \cdot 3$.

Multiply both numerator and
denominator of $\frac{1}{3}$ by 2.

$\frac{5}{6} + \frac{2}{6} = \frac{5+2}{6}$, or $\frac{7}{6}$ ⟶

$$\frac{5}{2 \cdot 3} + \frac{1}{3} \longleftarrow \begin{cases} \text{This denominator needs the} \\ \text{factor 2 to be like } 2 \cdot 3. \end{cases}$$

$$\frac{5}{2 \cdot 3} + \frac{1 \cdot 2}{3 \cdot 2} = \frac{5}{6} + \frac{2}{6}$$

Thus, $\frac{5}{6} + \frac{1}{3} = \frac{7}{6}$.

In Example 2, $3 \cdot 2$ is the *least common denominator* (LCD).

EXAMPLE 3   Add $\dfrac{7}{12} + \dfrac{2}{3} + \dfrac{1}{6}$.

First find the LCD.

$$\frac{7}{2 \cdot 2 \cdot 3} + \frac{2}{3} + \frac{1}{3 \cdot 2}$$

Factor the denominators. ⟶

The only factors present are 2 and 3. To have a common denominator, we must have exactly the same factors in each denominator.

$$\underset{\substack{\uparrow \quad \uparrow \\ \text{two 2's, one 3}}}{2 \cdot 2 \cdot 3} \qquad \underset{\substack{\uparrow \\ \text{one 3}}}{3} \qquad \underset{\substack{\nearrow \quad \nwarrow \\ \text{one 3, one 2}}}{3 \cdot 2}$$

$$\text{LCD} = \underset{\substack{\text{two 2's, one 3}}}{2 \cdot 2 \cdot 3}$$

In each denominator, there are at most two 2's and one 3.

$$\underset{\substack{\text{has two 2's,} \\ \text{one 3}}}{\frac{7}{2 \cdot 2 \cdot 3}} + \underset{\substack{\text{needs} \\ \text{two 2's}}}{\frac{2}{3}} + \underset{\substack{\text{needs} \\ \text{one 2}}}{\frac{1}{3 \cdot 2}}$$

In each fraction, multiply by the missing factors.

$$\frac{7}{2 \cdot 2 \cdot 3} + \frac{2 \cdot 2 \cdot 2}{3 \cdot 2 \cdot 2} + \frac{1 \cdot 2}{3 \cdot 2 \cdot 2}$$

$$\frac{7}{12} + \frac{8}{12} + \frac{2}{12}$$

The denominators are the same. ⟶
Add the numerators. ⟶

$$\frac{7 + 8 + 2}{12}$$

$$\frac{17}{12}$$

EXAMPLE 4   Add $\dfrac{5a}{6} + \dfrac{a}{3}$.

Denominators are not the same. Factor 6.

$$\frac{5a}{2 \cdot 3} + \frac{a}{3} \longleftarrow \quad \left\{ \begin{array}{l} \text{This denominator needs the factor} \\ \text{2 to be like 6.} \end{array} \right.$$

Rewrite each fraction with the LCD, $2 \cdot 3$.

$$\frac{5a}{2 \cdot 3} + \frac{a \cdot 2}{3 \cdot 2}$$

The denominators are the same. Add the numerators.

$$\frac{5a}{6} + \frac{2a}{6}$$

$$\frac{7a}{6}$$

EXAMPLE 5   Add $\dfrac{7a}{18} + \dfrac{5a}{6} + \dfrac{7}{2}$.

Find the LCD.
Factor the denominators. }

$$\dfrac{7a}{3 \cdot 3 \cdot 2} + \dfrac{5a}{3 \cdot 2} + \dfrac{7}{2}$$
$$\text{LCD} = 3 \cdot 3 \cdot 2 \longleftarrow \left\{ \begin{array}{l} \text{At most two 3's, one 2} \\ \text{in any denominator} \end{array} \right.$$

In each fraction, multiply
by the missing factors. }

$$\dfrac{7a}{3 \cdot 3 \cdot 2} + \dfrac{5a \cdot 3}{3 \cdot 2 \cdot 3} + \dfrac{7 \cdot 3 \cdot 3}{2 \cdot 3 \cdot 3}$$
needed one 3   needed two 3's

$5a \cdot 3 = 5 \cdot 3 \cdot a$, or $15a$

$$\dfrac{7a}{18} + \dfrac{15a}{18} + \dfrac{63}{18}$$

Combine numerators. $\longrightarrow$

$$\dfrac{7a + 15a + 63}{18}$$

$7a + 15a = 22a$ $\longrightarrow$

$$\dfrac{22a + 63}{18}$$

EXAMPLE 6   Add $\dfrac{2b + 3}{8b} + \dfrac{3b + 5}{2b}$.

Find the LCD.
Factor the denominators. }

$$\dfrac{2b + 3}{2 \cdot 2 \cdot 2 \cdot b} + \dfrac{3b + 5}{2 \cdot b}$$
$$\text{LCD} = 2 \cdot 2 \cdot 2 \cdot b \longleftarrow \left\{ \begin{array}{l} \text{At most three 2's, one } b \\ \text{in any denominator} \end{array} \right.$$

In each fraction, multiply
by the missing factors. }

$$\dfrac{2b + 3}{2 \cdot 2 \cdot 2 \cdot b} + \dfrac{(3b + 5) \cdot 2 \cdot 2}{2 \cdot b \cdot 2 \cdot 2} \longleftarrow \text{needed two 2's}$$

$$\dfrac{2b + 3}{8b} + \dfrac{(3b + 5)4}{8b}$$

$(3b + 5)4 = 12b + 20$ $\longrightarrow$

$$\dfrac{2b + 3}{8b} + \dfrac{12b + 20}{8b}$$

Combine numerators. $\longrightarrow$

$$\dfrac{14b + 23}{8b}$$

EXAMPLE 7   Add $\dfrac{2x - 3}{6x} + \dfrac{4x - 1}{2x}$.

Rewrite each fraction with
the LCD: $2 \cdot 3 \cdot x$. }

$$\dfrac{2x - 3}{2 \cdot 3 \cdot x} + \dfrac{(4x - 1) \cdot 3}{2 \cdot x \cdot 3}$$

$(4x - 1) \cdot 3 = 12x - 3$ $\longrightarrow$

$$\dfrac{2x - 3}{6x} + \dfrac{12x - 3}{6x}$$

Combine numerators. $\longrightarrow$

$$\dfrac{14x - 6}{6x}$$

Factor: $14x - 6 = 2(7x - 3)$.
Then divide out common factors. }

$$\dfrac{\overset{1}{2}(7x - 3)}{\underset{3}{6x}} = \dfrac{7x - 3}{3x}$$

ORAL EXERCISES

Find the LCD.

1. $\dfrac{2}{3} + \dfrac{5}{3 \cdot 2}$

2. $\dfrac{3}{5} + \dfrac{7}{5 \cdot 2}$

3. $\dfrac{7a}{3} + \dfrac{5a}{3 \cdot 2} + \dfrac{7a}{3 \cdot 3 \cdot 2}$

4. $\dfrac{3m}{2} + \dfrac{5m}{7 \cdot 2} + \dfrac{3m}{2 \cdot 7 \cdot 2}$

5. $\dfrac{3}{5 \cdot 2 \cdot 2} + \dfrac{3a}{2 \cdot 2 \cdot 2} + \dfrac{1}{2 \cdot 5}$

6. $\dfrac{3a}{2 \cdot 5 \cdot 7} + \dfrac{2a}{5 \cdot 5} + \dfrac{11a}{7 \cdot 2}$

7. $\dfrac{3k + 1}{2 \cdot 3 \cdot 3} + \dfrac{3k - 4}{3 \cdot 3 \cdot 3} + \dfrac{2k - 6}{2 \cdot 2}$

8. $\dfrac{7b + 5}{8a} + \dfrac{3b + 2}{4a}$

9. $\dfrac{2m + 1}{3m} + \dfrac{3m + 2}{27m}$

EXERCISES

PART A

Add.

1. $\dfrac{2}{3} + \dfrac{5}{6}$

2. $\dfrac{1}{8} + \dfrac{3}{4}$

3. $\dfrac{4}{5} + \dfrac{7}{10}$

4. $\dfrac{2}{3} + \dfrac{1}{2} + \dfrac{5}{6}$

5. $\dfrac{2b}{7} + \dfrac{3b}{14}$

6. $\dfrac{7m}{9} + \dfrac{2m}{3}$

7. $\dfrac{3a}{8} + \dfrac{5a}{2}$

8. $\dfrac{7k}{15} + \dfrac{3k}{5}$

9. $\dfrac{5a}{12} + \dfrac{3a}{2} + \dfrac{5}{6}$

10. $\dfrac{5m}{3} + \dfrac{3}{2} + \dfrac{5m}{18}$

11. $\dfrac{3m}{28} + \dfrac{5m}{7} + \dfrac{3}{4}$

12. $\dfrac{3b - 1}{6b} + \dfrac{4b + 1}{2b}$

13. $\dfrac{2m - 3}{5m} + \dfrac{4m - 1}{15m}$

14. $\dfrac{m - 1}{8m} + \dfrac{3m - 1}{4m}$

15. $\dfrac{7a + 5}{12a} + \dfrac{2a + 1}{3a}$

16. $\dfrac{3m - 2}{10m} + \dfrac{m + 6}{5m}$

17. $\dfrac{2b - 3}{6b} + \dfrac{4b + 1}{2b}$

PART B

Add.

18. $\dfrac{2a - 5}{6} + \dfrac{1}{3} + \dfrac{5a + 2}{2}$

19. $\dfrac{4x - 1}{3} + \dfrac{2x}{15} + \dfrac{3x - 2}{5}$

20. $\dfrac{t + 1}{2} + \dfrac{3t - 5}{14} + \dfrac{4t - 3}{21}$

21. $\dfrac{4a + 1}{3a} + \dfrac{5}{6a} + \dfrac{7a - 3}{2a}$

PART C

Add.

22. $\dfrac{2m^2 - 5m + 3}{2m} + \dfrac{3m - 1}{7m} + \dfrac{m^2}{4m}$

23. $\dfrac{2a^2 - a - 3}{3a} + \dfrac{5a + 4}{5a} + \dfrac{a^2 - 9}{10a}$

Adding: Polynomial Denominators

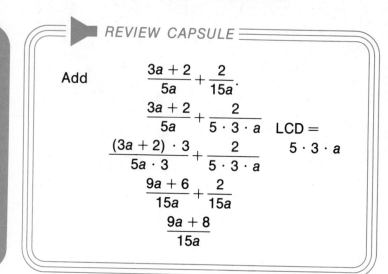

▶ *REVIEW CAPSULE*

Add $\dfrac{3a + 2}{5a} + \dfrac{2}{15a}$.

$$\frac{3a + 2}{5a} + \frac{2}{5 \cdot 3 \cdot a} \qquad \text{LCD} =$$

$$\frac{(3a + 2) \cdot 3}{5a \cdot 3} + \frac{2}{5 \cdot 3 \cdot a} \qquad 5 \cdot 3 \cdot a$$

$$\frac{9a + 6}{15a} + \frac{2}{15a}$$

$$\frac{9a + 8}{15a}$$

EXAMPLE 1   Add $\dfrac{3}{x - 3} + \dfrac{2}{x^2 - 9} + \dfrac{5}{x + 3}$

Factor $x^2 - 9$. ⟶

$$\frac{3}{x - 3} + \frac{2}{(x + 3)(x - 3)} + \frac{5}{x + 3}$$

$$\text{LCD} = (x + 3)(x - 3)$$

$$\frac{3(x + 3)}{(x - 3)(x + 3)} + \frac{2}{(x + 3)(x - 3)} + \frac{5(x - 3)}{(x + 3)(x - 3)}$$

↑ needed $(x + 3)$ ↗ needed $(x - 3)$

$3(x + 3) = 3x + 9$ ⎱
$5(x - 3) = 5x - 15$ ⎰

$$\frac{3x + 9}{(x - 3)(x + 3)} + \frac{2}{(x + 3)(x - 3)} + \frac{5x - 15}{(x + 3)(x - 3)}$$

$\dfrac{a}{b} + \dfrac{c}{b} + \dfrac{d}{b} = \dfrac{a + c + d}{b}$ ⟶

$$\frac{3x + 9 + 2 + 5x - 15}{(x + 3)(x - 3)}$$

Combine like terms. ⟶

$$\frac{8x - 4}{(x + 3)(x - 3)}$$

Factor the numerator. See if the fraction can be simplified.

$$\frac{4(2x - 1)}{(x + 3)(x - 3)}$$

There are no common factors other ⟶ than 1.

Thus, the sum is $\dfrac{4(2x - 1)}{(x + 3)(x - 3)}$ in simplest form.

EXAMPLE 2 Add $\dfrac{8x + 15}{x^2 + 5x} + \dfrac{x}{x + 5}$.

$x^2 + 5x = x(x + 5)$ $\longrightarrow$
LCD $= x(x + 5)$

$$\frac{8x + 15}{x(x + 5)} + \frac{x}{x + 5}$$
needs x

$$\frac{8x + 15}{x(x + 5)} + \frac{x \cdot x}{(x + 5) \cdot x}$$

$x \cdot x = x^2$ $\longrightarrow$

$$\frac{8x + 15}{x(x + 5)} + \frac{x^2}{(x + 5)x}$$

Combine numerators.
Write in descending order. $\Big\}$

$$\frac{x^2 + 8x + 15}{x(x + 5)}$$

Factor the numerator.
$x^2 + 8x + 15 = (x + 5)(x + 3)$ $\Big\}$

$$\frac{(x + 5)(x + 3)}{x(x + 5)}$$

Divide out common factors. $\longrightarrow$

$$\frac{\overset{1}{\cancel{(x + 5)}}(x + 3)}{x\underset{1}{\cancel{(x + 5)}}}$$

Thus, the sum is $\dfrac{x + 3}{x}$ in simplest form.

EXAMPLE 3 Add $\dfrac{2}{x^2 - 12x + 27} + \dfrac{3}{x - 3} + \dfrac{5}{x - 9}$.

$x^2 - 12x + 27 = (x - 9)(x - 3)$ $\longrightarrow$
LCD $= (x - 9)(x - 3)$

$$\frac{2}{(x - 9)(x - 3)} + \frac{3}{x - 3} + \frac{5}{x - 9}$$
needs $(x - 9)$ $\nearrow$ $\nwarrow$ needs $(x - 3)$

$$\frac{2}{(x - 9)(x - 3)} + \frac{3(x - 9)}{(x - 3)(x - 9)} + \frac{5(x - 3)}{(x - 9)(x - 3)}$$

$3(x - 9) = 3x - 27$ $\Big\}$
$5(x - 3) = 5x - 15$

$$\frac{2}{(x - 9)(x - 3)} + \frac{3x - 27}{(x - 3)(x - 9)} + \frac{5x - 15}{(x - 9)(x - 3)}$$

Combine numerators. $\longrightarrow$

$$\frac{2 + 3x - 27 + 5x - 15}{(x - 9)(x - 3)}$$

Combine like terms. $\longrightarrow$

$$\frac{8x - 40}{(x - 9)(x - 3)}$$

Factor. See if the fraction can be
simplified.

$$\frac{8(x - 5)}{(x - 9)(x - 3)}$$

There are no common factors $\longrightarrow$ **Thus,** the sum is $\dfrac{8(x - 5)}{(x - 9)(x - 3)}$ in simplest form.
other than 1.

EXERCISES

PART A

Add.

1. $\dfrac{7}{a-4} + \dfrac{3}{a^2-16} + \dfrac{2}{a+4}$

2. $\dfrac{5}{b+5} + \dfrac{2}{b^2-25} + \dfrac{4}{b-5}$

3. $\dfrac{9x+14}{x^2+7x} + \dfrac{x}{x+7}$

4. $\dfrac{a}{a-5} + \dfrac{-3a-10}{a^2-5a}$

5. $\dfrac{7}{x^2+5x} + \dfrac{3}{x}$

6. $\dfrac{4}{m} + \dfrac{3}{m^2-4m}$

7. $\dfrac{2}{x-3} + \dfrac{5}{x^2-9}$

8. $\dfrac{7}{m-4} + \dfrac{2}{m^2-m-12}$

9. $\dfrac{5}{x^2-6x-16} + \dfrac{3}{x-8}$

10. $\dfrac{7}{m-7} + \dfrac{3}{m^2-2m-35}$

11. $\dfrac{5}{a+1} + \dfrac{2}{a^2-1} + \dfrac{4}{a-1}$

12. $\dfrac{2}{a-5} + \dfrac{3}{a^2-7a+10} + \dfrac{4}{a-2}$

13. $\dfrac{2}{a+3} + \dfrac{4}{2a^2+a-15} + \dfrac{6}{2a-5}$

14. $\dfrac{4}{k^2-k-20} + \dfrac{2}{k-5} + \dfrac{3}{k+4}$

PART B

EXAMPLE   Add $\dfrac{x+1}{x^2-5x+6} + \dfrac{x+4}{x-3}$.

LCD $= (x-3)(x-2)$.
Second fraction needs $(x-2)$. ⟶

$\dfrac{x+1}{(x-3)(x-2)} + \dfrac{x+4}{x-3}$

$\dfrac{x+1}{(x-3)(x-2)} + \dfrac{(x+4)(x-2)}{(x-3)(x-2)}$

$\dfrac{x+1}{(x-3)(x-2)} + \dfrac{x^2+2x-8}{(x-3)(x-2)}$

$\dfrac{x^2+3x-7}{(x-3)(x-2)}$

$\begin{array}{c} x \quad + \quad 4 \\ x \quad - \quad 2 \\ \hline x^2 + 2x - 8 \end{array}$

Add.

15. $\dfrac{4k-3}{k^2-5k+6} + \dfrac{k+1}{k-3}$

16. $\dfrac{2a+1}{a^2+3a+2} + \dfrac{a-4}{a+2}$

17. $\dfrac{4m-1}{2m^2+5m} + \dfrac{m-2}{m}$

Operations

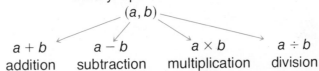

Binary Operations on
(a, b)

$a + b$	$a - b$	$a \times b$	$a \div b$
addition	subtraction	multiplication	division

> A *binary operation* is a rule which assigns one element to an ordered pair (a, b).

$(a, b) \longrightarrow a + b + 2$ is a binary operation.

Read: maps into.

$(2, 5) \longrightarrow 2 + 5 + 2$
$\qquad = 9$

$(3, 1) \longrightarrow 3 + 1 + 2$
$\qquad = 6$

PROBLEM

Does the operation $(a, b) \longrightarrow a + b + 2$ on $(4, 5)$ give the same number as on $(5, 4)$?

$(4, 5) \longrightarrow 4 + 5 + 2$
$\qquad = 11$

$(5, 4) \longrightarrow 5 + 4 + 2$
$\qquad = 11$

Yes

Since $a + b = b + a$ for all a and b,
the operation $(a, b) \longrightarrow a + b + 2$ is commutative.

PROJECT

Find the values of $(3, 2)$ and $(1, 4)$ for the following operations.

1. $(a, b) \longrightarrow ab + 3$ **2.** $(a, b) \longrightarrow 2a + 3b$ **3.** $(a, b) \longrightarrow (a + b)^2$
4. Do you think that $(a, b) \longrightarrow a + b + 2$ is associative?
5. For the operations described in 1–3, which might be commutative? associative?

More on Adding Fractions

  REVIEW CAPSULE

Find the LCD.

$$\frac{5x+1}{2} + \frac{2x+1}{9} + \frac{2x+9}{8}$$

$$\frac{5x+1}{2} + \frac{2x+1}{3 \cdot 3} + \frac{2x+9}{2 \cdot 2 \cdot 2}$$

The LCD is $2 \cdot 2 \cdot 2 \cdot 3 \cdot 3$.

EXAMPLE 1 Add $4 + \dfrac{5}{3m}$.

Rewrite 4 as $\dfrac{4}{1}$. $3m$ means $3 \cdot m$. $\longrightarrow$

LCD $= 3 \cdot m$

$$\frac{4}{1} + \frac{5}{3 \cdot m}$$
needs $3 \cdot m$

Multiply by the needed missing factors. $\longrightarrow$

$4 \cdot 3 \cdot m = 12m$ $\longrightarrow$
$1 \cdot 3 \cdot m = 3m$ $\longrightarrow$

$$\frac{4 \cdot 3 \cdot m}{1 \cdot 3 \cdot m} + \frac{5}{3 \cdot m}$$

$$\frac{12m}{3m} + \frac{5}{3m}$$

There are no common factors. $\longrightarrow$ **Thus,** the sum is $\dfrac{12m + 5}{3m}$ in simplest form.

EXAMPLE 2 Add $\dfrac{9}{y+4} + \dfrac{6}{y-4}$.

$\left.\begin{array}{l} y+4 \\ y-4 \end{array}\right\}$ cannot be factored. $\longrightarrow$

In each fraction, multiply by the $\Big\}$
missing factors.

$\left.\begin{array}{l} 9(y-4) = 9y - 36 \\ 6(y+4) = 6y + 24 \end{array}\right\}$

$\dfrac{a}{b} + \dfrac{c}{b} = \dfrac{a+c}{b}$ $\longrightarrow$

Factor $15y - 12$. See if the fraction
can be simplified.

$$\text{LCD} = (y+4)(y-4)$$

$$\frac{9(y-4)}{(y+4)(y-4)} + \frac{6(y+4)}{(y-4)(y+4)}$$

$$\frac{9y-36}{(y+4)(y-4)} + \frac{6y+24}{(y-4)(y+4)}$$

$$\frac{15y-12}{(y+4)(y-4)}$$

$$\frac{3(5y-4)}{(y+4)(y-4)}$$

There are no common factors, so the $\Big\}$
fraction cannot be simplified.

Thus, the sum is $\dfrac{3(5y-4)}{(y+4)(y-4)}$ in simplest form.

EXAMPLE 3   Add $\dfrac{6}{5x^2} + \dfrac{-7}{3x} + \dfrac{2}{15x^3}$.

Find the LCD.
Factor the denominators.
At most one 3, one 5, three x's in
any denominator

$$\dfrac{6}{5 \cdot x \cdot x} + \dfrac{-7}{3 \cdot x} + \dfrac{2}{3 \cdot 5 \cdot x \cdot x \cdot x}$$
$$\text{LCD} = 3 \cdot 5 \cdot x \cdot x \cdot x, \text{ or } 15x^3$$

In each fraction, multiply by the
missing factors.

$$\dfrac{6 \cdot 3 \cdot x}{5 \cdot x \cdot x \cdot 3 \cdot x} + \dfrac{-7 \cdot 5 \cdot x \cdot x}{3 \cdot x \cdot 5 \cdot x \cdot x} + \dfrac{2}{3 \cdot 5 \cdot x \cdot x \cdot x}$$

$6 \cdot 3 \cdot x = 18x, -7 \cdot 5 \cdot x \cdot x = -35x^2 \longrightarrow$

$$\dfrac{18x}{15x^3} \quad + \quad \dfrac{-35x^2}{15x^3} \quad + \quad \dfrac{2}{15x^3}$$

Combine numerators.
Write in descending order. }

$$\dfrac{-35x^2 + 18x + 2}{15x^3}$$

EXAMPLE 4   Add $\dfrac{2}{3y} + \dfrac{7 - 4y}{6y^3} + \dfrac{3 + 2y}{4y^2}$.

Find the LCD.
Factor the denominators.
At most two 2's, one 3, three y's in
any denominator.

$$\dfrac{2}{3 \cdot y} + \dfrac{7 - 4y}{2 \cdot 3 \cdot y \cdot y \cdot y} + \dfrac{3 + 2y}{2 \cdot 2 \cdot y \cdot y}$$
$$\text{LCD} = 2 \cdot 2 \cdot 3 \cdot y \cdot y \cdot y, \text{ or } 12y^3$$

In each fraction, multiply by the
missing factors.

$$\dfrac{2 \cdot 2 \cdot 2 \cdot y \cdot y}{3 \cdot y \cdot 2 \cdot 2 \cdot y \cdot y} + \dfrac{(7 - 4y) \cdot 2}{2 \cdot 3 \cdot y \cdot y \cdot y \cdot 2} + \dfrac{(3 + 2y) \cdot 3 \cdot y}{2 \cdot 2 \cdot y \cdot y \cdot 3 \cdot y}$$

$(7 - 4y)2 = 14 - 8y$
$(3 + 2y)3y = 9y + 6y^2$

$$\dfrac{8y^2}{12y^3} \quad + \quad \dfrac{14 - 8y}{12y^3} \quad + \quad \dfrac{9y + 6y^2}{12y^3}$$

$\dfrac{a}{b} + \dfrac{c}{b} + \dfrac{d}{b} = \dfrac{a + c + d}{b} \longrightarrow$

$$\dfrac{8y^2 + 14 - 8y + 9y + 6y^2}{12y^3}$$

Combine like terms. $\longrightarrow$

$$\dfrac{14y^2 + y + 14}{12y^3}$$

ORAL EXERCISES

Find the LCD.

1. $\dfrac{3}{y^2} + \dfrac{7}{y} + \dfrac{8}{y^3}$

2. $\dfrac{7}{a^2} + \dfrac{2}{a^3} + \dfrac{4}{a}$

3. $\dfrac{3}{p^2} + \dfrac{4}{p} + \dfrac{2}{p^5}$

EXERCISES

PART A

Add.

1. $\dfrac{3}{m} + 2$

2. $8 + \dfrac{3}{7b}$

3. $3 + \dfrac{2}{m}$

4. $\dfrac{7}{a-1}+\dfrac{4}{a+2}$

5. $\dfrac{4}{x+2}+\dfrac{3}{x-4}$

6. $\dfrac{2}{3a-1}+\dfrac{4}{2a+5}$

7. $\dfrac{5}{a-3}+\dfrac{7}{2a+5}$

8. $\dfrac{3}{b-7}+\dfrac{-2}{2b+3}$

9. $\dfrac{8}{x^2}+\dfrac{7}{x}+\dfrac{3}{x^3}$

10. $\dfrac{7}{15y}+\dfrac{-3}{5y^3}+\dfrac{2}{3y^2}$

11. $\dfrac{3}{2a^2}+\dfrac{5}{3a^3}+\dfrac{7}{6a}$

12. $\dfrac{5}{x}+\dfrac{3}{x^2}+\dfrac{2}{x^3}$

13. $\dfrac{3}{m}+\dfrac{2}{m^2}+5$

14. $6k+\dfrac{5}{3k}$

15. $\dfrac{3}{a^2}+\dfrac{2}{a}+1$

16. $\dfrac{7}{2a}+\dfrac{2-a}{3a^2}+\dfrac{3+5a}{6a^3}$

17. $\dfrac{2}{5b}+\dfrac{4-3b}{3b^2}+\dfrac{2b-3}{b^3}$

18. $\dfrac{7-x}{2x^2}+\dfrac{3+2x}{10x^3}+\dfrac{2-5x}{5x}$

19. $\dfrac{2a+5}{4a}+\dfrac{a-1}{6a^3}+\dfrac{3-a}{3a^2}$

PART B

EXAMPLE   Add $x+3+\dfrac{7}{x-2}$.

$$\dfrac{x+3}{1}+\dfrac{7}{x-2}$$

$$\dfrac{(x+3)(x-2)}{1\cdot(x-2)}+\dfrac{7}{x-2}$$

LCD $= 1\cdot(x-2)$, or $x-2$.
$(x+3)(x-2)=x^2+x-6$ ⟶

$$\dfrac{x^2+x-6}{x-2}+\dfrac{7}{x-2}$$

Combine numerators.

$$\dfrac{x^2+x+1}{x-2}$$

Add.

20. $a-2+\dfrac{4}{a+5}$

21. $2m-1+\dfrac{3}{m+5}$

22. $\dfrac{5}{3a+1}+a-4$

23. $2x-1+\dfrac{x-7}{2x-1}$

24. $\dfrac{a-5}{2a+3}+a-2$

25. $x-5+\dfrac{7}{3x+2}$

PART C
Add.

26. $\dfrac{7}{x-3}+\dfrac{x+4}{x-5}+\dfrac{x}{x+2}$

27. $x^2+3x+1+\dfrac{4}{x-5}$

Subtracting Fractions

▶ REVIEW CAPSULE

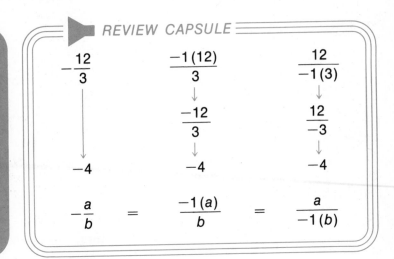

$$-\frac{12}{3} \qquad \frac{-1(12)}{3} \qquad \frac{12}{-1(3)}$$

$$\downarrow \qquad\qquad \downarrow \qquad\qquad \downarrow$$

$$\qquad\qquad \frac{-12}{3} \qquad \frac{12}{-3}$$

$$\downarrow \qquad\qquad \downarrow \qquad\qquad \downarrow$$

$$-4 \qquad\qquad -4 \qquad\qquad -4$$

$$-\frac{a}{b} \;=\; \frac{-1(a)}{b} \;=\; \frac{a}{-1(b)}$$

EXAMPLE 1 Rewrite $-\dfrac{2x-3}{x+5}$.

$-\dfrac{a}{b}=\dfrac{-1(a)}{b}$ ⟶

$-1(2x-3)=-1(2x)+(-1)(-3)$

$$-\frac{2x-3}{x+5}=\frac{-1(2x-3)}{x+5}$$
$$=\frac{-2x+3}{x+5}$$

EXAMPLE 2 Simplify $\dfrac{x}{x^2-4x+3}-\dfrac{2}{x-3}$.

Rewrite as addition.
$$-\frac{2}{x-3}=\frac{-1(2)}{x-3}$$

Factor: $x^2-4x+3=(x-3)(x-1)$.
LCD $=(x-3)(x-1)$

$-2(x-1)=-2x+2$ ⟶

$\dfrac{a}{b}+\dfrac{c}{b}=\dfrac{a+c}{b}$ ⟶

$x-2x=1x-2x=-1x$, or $-x$

$$\frac{x}{x^2-4x+3}+\frac{-1(2)}{x-3}$$

$$\frac{x}{(x-3)(x-1)}+\frac{-2}{x-3}$$
needs $(x-1)$

$$\frac{x}{(x-3)(x-1)}+\frac{-2(x-1)}{(x-3)(x-1)}$$

$$\frac{x}{(x-3)(x-1)}+\frac{-2x+2}{(x-3)(x-1)}$$

$$\frac{x-2x+2}{(x-3)(x-1)}$$

$$\frac{-x+2}{(x-3)(x-1)}$$

EXAMPLE 3 Simplify $3 - \dfrac{3x-1}{2x}$.

Rewrite as addition.

$-\dfrac{3x-1}{2x} = \dfrac{-1(3x-1)}{2x}$ ⟶ $\dfrac{3}{1} + \dfrac{-1(3x-1)}{2x}$

$-1(3x-1) = -3x + 1$ ⟶ $\dfrac{3}{1} + \dfrac{-3x+1}{2x}$

LCD $= 2 \cdot x$, or $2x$ $\searrow$ needs $2 \cdot x$

                  $\dfrac{3 \cdot 2 \cdot x}{1 \cdot 2 \cdot x} + \dfrac{-3x+1}{2 \cdot x}$

$3 \cdot 2 \cdot x = 6x$ ⟶ $\dfrac{6x}{2x} + \dfrac{-3x+1}{2x}$

$1 \cdot 2 \cdot x = 2x$ ⟶

$\dfrac{a}{b} + \dfrac{c}{b} = \dfrac{a+c}{b}$ ⟶ $\dfrac{6x - 3x + 1}{2x}$

Thus, the result is $\dfrac{3x+1}{2x}$.

EXAMPLE 4 Simplify $\dfrac{x^2+2}{x^2-5x+4} - \dfrac{x-2}{x-1}$.

Rewrite as addition.

                $\dfrac{x^2+2}{x^2-5x+4} + \dfrac{-1(x-2)}{x-1}$

$-1(x-2) = -1x + 2$ ⟶ $\dfrac{x^2+2}{x^2-5x+4} + \dfrac{-1x+2}{x-1}$

Find the LCD.
$x^2 - 5x + 4 = (x-4)(x-1)$
LCD $= (x-4)(x-1)$ $\dfrac{x^2+2}{(x-4)(x-1)} + \dfrac{-1x+2}{x-1}$

                          $\searrow$ needs $x - 4$

$\overset{-1x \quad + \quad 2}{\underset{1x \quad - \quad 4}{\times}}$

$-1x^2 + 6x - 8$ ⟶ $\dfrac{x^2+2}{(x-4)(x-1)} + \dfrac{(-1x+2)(x-4)}{(x-1)(x-4)}$

                 $\dfrac{x^2+2}{(x-4)(x-1)} + \dfrac{-1x^2+6x-8}{(x-1)(x-4)}$

$\dfrac{a}{b} + \dfrac{c}{b} = \dfrac{a+c}{b}$ ⟶ $\dfrac{x^2+2-1x^2+6x-8}{(x-4)(x-1)}$

Combine like terms. ⟶ $\dfrac{6x-6}{(x-4)(x-1)}$

Factor the numerator:
$6x - 6 = 6(x-1)$.
Divide out common factors. $\dfrac{6(\overset{1}{\cancel{x-1}})}{(x-4)(\underset{1}{\cancel{x-1}})}$

                      $\dfrac{6}{x-4}$

Thus, the result is $\dfrac{6}{x-4}$.

EXERCISES

PART A

Rewrite.

1. $-\dfrac{2}{a+5}$

2. $-\dfrac{2a+5}{a^2-9}$

3. $-\dfrac{x^2-3x}{x^2+5x+1}$

Simplify.

4. $\dfrac{5}{x^2-4}-\dfrac{2}{x-2}$

5. $\dfrac{7}{a^2-7a+10}-\dfrac{3}{a-5}$

6. $\dfrac{4}{b^2+4b+3}-\dfrac{3}{b+3}$

7. $5-\dfrac{3}{2x}$

8. $8-\dfrac{7}{5x}$

9. $4-\dfrac{2a+3}{a-2}$

10. $\dfrac{5}{x-7}-\dfrac{x+3}{x^2-49}$

11. $\dfrac{3}{x-2}-\dfrac{2x-3}{x^2-6x+8}$

12. $\dfrac{2}{b-4}-\dfrac{b+5}{b^2-3b-4}$

13. $\dfrac{5}{3b-1}-\dfrac{4}{2b+7}$

14. $\dfrac{3}{5x-2}-\dfrac{2}{3x+4}$

15. $\dfrac{3}{8y^2}-\dfrac{5}{12y^3}$

PART B

Simplify.

16. $\dfrac{m^2-8}{m^2-8m+12}-\dfrac{m+1}{m-6}$

17. $\dfrac{a^2-22}{a^2-9a+20}-\dfrac{a-2}{a-5}$

18. $\dfrac{m^2-5}{m^2-5m}-\dfrac{m+3}{m}$

19. $\dfrac{5}{a+3}-\dfrac{2a+1}{a+2}$

20. $\dfrac{2a-3}{a^2-4}-\dfrac{a+1}{a-2}$

21. $\dfrac{3a^2}{2a^2-7a-15}-\dfrac{2a-5}{2a+3}$

22. $\dfrac{y+3}{y-6}-\dfrac{y+1}{y^2-4y-12}$

23. $\dfrac{2a+1}{a}-\dfrac{3a+1}{a^2-5a}$

24. $\dfrac{4}{y-4}-\dfrac{2y-1}{y-2}$

PART C

Simplify.

25. $\dfrac{a-2}{a+4}-\dfrac{a-3}{2a-5}$

26. $\dfrac{x-5}{2x-5}-\dfrac{2x+1}{x-7}$

27. $\dfrac{3}{2y^2-5y-12}-\dfrac{y+1}{2y+3}+\dfrac{y-5}{y-4}$

28. $\dfrac{2m^2-5}{4m^3-9m}-\dfrac{3}{2m-3}+\dfrac{2m-1}{2m^2+3m}$

Simplifying Fractions: −1 Technique

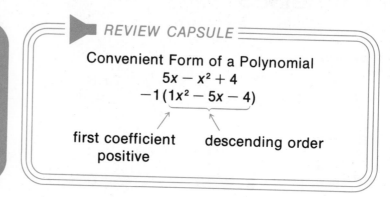

▶ REVIEW CAPSULE

Convenient Form of a Polynomial

$$5x - x^2 + 4$$
$$-1(1x^2 - 5x - 4)$$

first coefficient positive   descending order

EXAMPLE 1   Simplify $\dfrac{4x}{x^2 - 4} + \dfrac{2}{2-x}$.

Get $2 - x$ in convenient form.
Arrange in descending order.
$$\frac{4x}{x^2 - 4} + \frac{2}{-x + 2}$$

Factor out -1: $-x + 2 = -1(x - 2)$.
$2 - x$ is now in convenient form.
$$\frac{4x}{x^2 - 4} + \frac{2}{-1(x - 2)}$$

$\dfrac{a}{-1(b)} = \dfrac{-1(a)}{b}$ ⟶
$$\frac{4x}{x^2 - 4} + \frac{-1(2)}{x - 2}$$

$$\frac{4x}{x^2 - 4} + \frac{-2}{x - 2}$$

Find the LCD.
Factor: $x^2 - 4 = (x - 2)(x + 2)$.
LCD $= (x - 2)(x + 2)$
$$\frac{4x}{(x - 2)(x + 2)} + \frac{-2}{x - 2}$$

↖ needs $x + 2$

$$\frac{4x}{(x - 2)(x + 2)} + \frac{-2(x + 2)}{(x - 2)(x + 2)}$$

Use the distributive property. ⟶
$-2(x + 2) = -2x - 4$
$$\frac{4x}{(x - 2)(x + 2)} + \frac{-2x - 4}{(x - 2)(x + 2)}$$

$\dfrac{a}{b} + \dfrac{c}{b} = \dfrac{a + c}{b}$ ⟶
$$\frac{4x - 2x - 4}{(x - 2)(x + 2)}$$

Combine like terms. ⟶
$$\frac{2x - 4}{(x - 2)(x + 2)}$$

Factor: $2x - 4 = 2(x - 2)$.
Divide out common factors.
$$\frac{2(\overset{1}{\cancel{x - 2}})}{(\underset{1}{\cancel{x - 2}})(x + 2)}$$

The result is in simplest form. ⟶
$$\frac{2}{x + 2}$$

EXAMPLE 2 Simplify $\dfrac{3}{m-1} + \dfrac{3m+2}{m-m^2} + \dfrac{3}{m}$.

Get $m - m^2$ in convenient form. $\Big\}$
$m - m^2 = -m^2 + m = -1(m^2 - m)$

$\dfrac{3m+2}{-1(m^2-m)} = \dfrac{-1(3m+2)}{m^2-m} = \dfrac{-3m-2}{m^2-m} \longrightarrow$

Factor: $m^2 - m = m(m-1)$ $\longrightarrow$

LCD $= m(m-1)$ $\longrightarrow$
$3(m-1) = 3m - 3$ $\longrightarrow$

$\dfrac{a}{b} + \dfrac{c}{b} = \dfrac{a+c}{b}$ $\longrightarrow$

The result is in simplest form. $\longrightarrow$

$\dfrac{3}{m-1} + \dfrac{3m+2}{-1(m^2-m)} + \dfrac{3}{m}$

$\dfrac{3}{m-1} + \dfrac{-3m-2}{m^2-m} + \dfrac{3}{m}$

$\dfrac{3}{m-1} + \dfrac{-3m-2}{m(m-1)} + \dfrac{3}{m}$

$\dfrac{3 \cdot m}{(m-1) \cdot m} + \dfrac{-3m-2}{m(m-1)} + \dfrac{3(m-1)}{m(m-1)}$

$\dfrac{3m}{(m-1)m} + \dfrac{-3m-2}{m(m-1)} + \dfrac{3m-3}{m(m-1)}$

$\dfrac{3m-3m-2+3m-3}{m(m-1)}$

$\dfrac{3m-5}{m(m-1)}$

EXAMPLE 3 Simplify $\dfrac{-6}{x^2-7x+12} - \dfrac{x+2}{4-x}$.

Rewrite as addition:
$-\dfrac{x+2}{4-x} = \dfrac{-1(x+2)}{4-x}$

$4 - x = -x + 4 = -1(x-4)$ $\longrightarrow$

$\dfrac{\cancel{-1}(x+2)}{\cancel{-1}(x-4)} = \dfrac{x+2}{x-4}$ $\longrightarrow$

LCD $= (x-3)(x-4)$

$\begin{array}{c} x + 2 \\ x - 3 \end{array}$ (cross multiply)
$\dfrac{}{x^2-x-6}$ $\longrightarrow$

Combine numerators. $\Big\}$
Write in descending order.

Factor: $x^2 - x - 12 = (x-4)(x+3)$
Divide out common factors.

$\dfrac{-6}{x^2-7x+12} + \dfrac{-1(x+2)}{4-x}$

$\dfrac{-6}{x^2-7x+12} + \dfrac{-1(x+2)}{-1(x-4)}$

$\dfrac{-6}{x^2-7x+12} + \dfrac{x+2}{x-4}$

$\dfrac{-6}{(x-3)(x-4)} + \dfrac{x+2}{x-4}$ needs $(x-3)$

$\dfrac{-6}{(x-3)(x-4)} + \dfrac{(x+2)(x-3)}{(x-4)(x-3)}$

$\dfrac{-6}{(x-3)(x-4)} + \dfrac{x^2-x-6}{(x-4)(x-3)}$

$\dfrac{x^2-x-12}{(x-3)(x-4)}$

$\dfrac{(\overset{1}{\cancel{x-4}})(x+3)}{(x-3)(\underset{1}{\cancel{x-4}})}$

$\dfrac{x+3}{x-3}$

EXERCISES

PART A

Simplify.

1. $\dfrac{6x}{x^2 - 49} + \dfrac{3}{7 - x}$

2. $\dfrac{8x}{x^2 - 25} + \dfrac{4}{5 - x}$

3. $\dfrac{7b - 9}{b^2 - 3b + 2} + \dfrac{5}{2 - b}$

4. $\dfrac{3a + 6}{4a - 8} + \dfrac{3}{2 - a}$

5. $\dfrac{3b - 1}{b^2 - b - 2} + \dfrac{4}{2 - b}$

6. $\dfrac{3a - 5}{7a - 21} + \dfrac{2a - 5}{3 - a}$

7. $\dfrac{2a}{a^2 - 6a + 8} - \dfrac{a}{2 - a}$

8. $\dfrac{-5x}{x^2 - 9x + 14} - \dfrac{x}{7 - x}$

9. $\dfrac{-7a}{a^2 - 3a - 10} - \dfrac{a}{5 - a}$

10. $\dfrac{-2a}{a^2 - 12a + 35} - \dfrac{a}{7 - a}$

11. $\dfrac{7}{m - 1} + \dfrac{4m - 6}{m - m^2} + \dfrac{5}{m}$

12. $\dfrac{5}{a - 4} + \dfrac{2a - 1}{4a - a^2} + \dfrac{7}{a}$

13. $\dfrac{k + 2}{k^2 - 8k + 12} + \dfrac{k}{6 - k}$

14. $\dfrac{2}{a + 2} - \dfrac{3}{8 - a} + \dfrac{2a}{a^2 - 6a - 16}$

15. $\dfrac{-2m}{m^2 - 12m + 35} - \dfrac{m}{7 - m}$

16. $\dfrac{x^2 + 3x + 15}{x^2 + 5x - 24} + \dfrac{-2}{3 - x} + \dfrac{5}{x + 8}$

PART B

Simplify.

17. $\dfrac{2m}{m^2 - 7m + 10} + \dfrac{2m - 1}{5 - m}$

18. $\dfrac{3a + 1}{a^2 - 25} - \dfrac{2a + 1}{5 - a}$

19. $\dfrac{2n - 1}{n + 3} - \dfrac{4n^2}{9 - n^2} + \dfrac{2}{n - 3}$

20. $\dfrac{2m + 1}{4 - m} - \dfrac{3m^2}{m^2 - 16} + \dfrac{7}{m + 4}$

PART C

Simplify.

21. $\dfrac{7}{a^2 - b^2} - \dfrac{2}{b - a} + \dfrac{a + 3b}{a + b}$

22. $\dfrac{7}{a^2 - 2ab} - \dfrac{3a - 2b}{4b^2 - a^2}$

23. $\dfrac{b - c}{b + c} - \dfrac{3bc}{c^2 - b^2}$

24. $\dfrac{4b}{b + 1} - \dfrac{2 + b}{1 - b} - \dfrac{4}{1 - b^2}$

Groups

An operation on a set forms a group if
- the set is closed under the operation
- the operation is associative
- there is an identity element
- every element has an inverse

TEST CASE

Let the integers be the set and addition the operation.

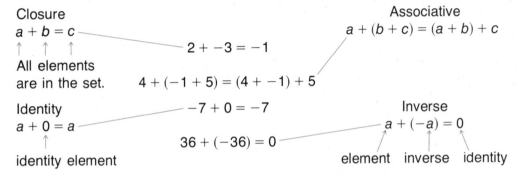

Closure
$a + b = c$
↑   ↑   ↑
All elements
are in the set.

$2 + -3 = -1$

$4 + (-1 + 5) = (4 + -1) + 5$

Associative
$a + (b + c) = (a + b) + c$

Identity
$a + 0 = a$
↑
identity element

$-7 + 0 = -7$

$36 + (-36) = 0$

Inverse
$a + (-a) = 0$
↑   ↑   ↑
element inverse identity

We have not proved that the integers form a group under addition, but we can think of no case where the four conditions do not hold.

Note: For multiplication, the zero element does not have to have an inverse to form a group.

A group is a *commutative group* if the operation is commutative.

Which do you think form groups? commutative groups?

PROJECT

1. The odd numbers under addition
2. The even numbers under addition
3. The odd numbers under multiplication
4. The even numbers under multiplication

Chapter Eight Review

Add. $[p.\,203, 210, 214]$

1. $\dfrac{2}{15} + \dfrac{1}{15} + \dfrac{7}{15}$

2. $\dfrac{3a}{6a^2 - a - 15} + \dfrac{-5}{6a^2 - a - 15}$

3. $\dfrac{3}{8} + \dfrac{1}{4}$

4. $\dfrac{1}{3} + \dfrac{1}{2} + \dfrac{5}{6}$

5. $\dfrac{5m}{6} + \dfrac{3m}{2}$

6. $\dfrac{3m}{7} + \dfrac{1}{2} + \dfrac{3m}{14}$

7. $\dfrac{2b + 3}{3b} + \dfrac{2b + 9}{6b}$

8. $\dfrac{3x - 1}{2} + \dfrac{3x}{14} + \dfrac{2x - 5}{7}$

9. $\dfrac{8x + 12}{x^2 + 2x} + \dfrac{x}{x + 2}$

10. $\dfrac{5}{a - 3} + \dfrac{4}{a^2 - 9}$

11. $\dfrac{3}{a - 6} + \dfrac{4}{a^2 - 2a - 24} + \dfrac{2}{a + 4}$

12. $\dfrac{-3x + 6}{x^2 - 7x + 10} + \dfrac{x + 3}{x - 5}$

Simplify. $[p.\,218, 221, 224]$

13. $7 + \dfrac{4}{5m}$

14. $\dfrac{7}{y + 3} + \dfrac{4}{y - 3}$

15. $\dfrac{5}{2x^2} + \dfrac{-3}{7x} + \dfrac{3}{14x^3}$

16. $\dfrac{4}{3y} + \dfrac{6 - 3y}{2y^3} + \dfrac{5 + 2y}{9y^2}$

17. $x + 5 + \dfrac{4}{x - 3}$

18. $x + \dfrac{2}{x - 5}$

19. $\dfrac{x}{x^2 - 7x + 12} - \dfrac{5}{x - 4}$

20. $5 - \dfrac{2x - 7}{3x}$

21. $\dfrac{x^2 - 1}{x^2 - 7x + 10} - \dfrac{x - 3}{x - 2}$

22. $\dfrac{7}{x - 2} - \dfrac{x + 3}{x^2 - 4}$

23. $\dfrac{10x}{x^2 - 9} + \dfrac{5}{3 - x}$

24. $\dfrac{7}{x - 1} + \dfrac{5x + 3}{x - x^2} + \dfrac{4}{x}$

25. $\dfrac{6m}{m^2 - 12m + 27} - \dfrac{m}{3 - m}$

26. $\dfrac{3m}{m^2 - 8m + 12} + \dfrac{2m - 1}{6 - m}$

Chapter Eight Test

Add.

1. $\dfrac{1}{18} + \dfrac{7}{18} + \dfrac{5}{18}$

2. $\dfrac{3m}{5} + \dfrac{1}{3} + \dfrac{2m}{15}$

3. $\dfrac{4a + 2}{5a} + \dfrac{7a + 11}{10a}$

4. $\dfrac{2x - 1}{3} + \dfrac{5x}{21} + \dfrac{2x + 5}{7}$

5. $\dfrac{10x + 21}{x^2 + 3x} + \dfrac{x}{x + 3}$

6. $\dfrac{7}{a - 6} + \dfrac{4}{a^2 - 36}$

7. $\dfrac{4}{a - 5} + \dfrac{2}{a^2 - 3a - 10} + \dfrac{3}{a + 2}$

8. $\dfrac{-14m - 6}{m^2 - 7m - 18} + \dfrac{m + 3}{m - 9}$

Simplify.

9. $6 + \dfrac{7}{3m}$

10. $\dfrac{4}{y + 2} + \dfrac{3}{y - 6}$

11. $\dfrac{5}{3x^2} + \dfrac{-4}{7x} + \dfrac{2}{21x^3}$

12. $\dfrac{7}{5a} + \dfrac{3 - 2a}{2a^3} + \dfrac{4 + 3a}{20a^2}$

13. $x - 4 + \dfrac{2}{x + 3}$

14. $\dfrac{x}{x^2 - 11x + 28} - \dfrac{6}{x - 7}$

15. $7 - \dfrac{3x - 2}{2x}$

16. $\dfrac{y^2 - 22}{y^2 - 9y + 20} - \dfrac{y - 2}{y - 5}$

17. $\dfrac{8x}{x^2 - 64} + \dfrac{4}{8 - x}$

18. $\dfrac{5}{m - 1} + \dfrac{4m + 2}{m - m^2} + \dfrac{6}{m}$

19. $\dfrac{4a}{a^2 - 12a + 32} - \dfrac{a}{4 - a}$

20. $\dfrac{8x}{x^2 - 10x + 9} + \dfrac{3x - 2}{9 - x}$

9 ALGEBRA IN A PLANE

The Great Swami

A	B	C	D	E	F
1	2	3	6	9	18
4	5	4	7	10	19
7	8	5	8	11	20
10	11	12	15	12	21
13	14	13	16	13	22
16	17	14	17	14	23
19	20	21	24	15	24
22	23	22	25	16	25
25	26	23	26	17	26

PROJECT

Have a friend tell the letter of each column that contains his or her age. The sum of the first numbers in each column will give the age. For example, if your friend answers column B, C, and E, then your friend's age is 2 + 3 + 9, or 14.

Absolute Value

 REVIEW CAPSULE

Points A and B are graphed on a number line.

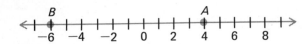

Point A is 4 units from the origin.
Point B is 6 units from the origin.

EXAMPLE 1   Find the distance between city A and city D.

$$80 + 100 + 150 = 330$$

Thus, the distance from A to D is 330 km,
and the distance from D to A is 330 km.

EXAMPLE 2   Find the points on a number line
whose distance is 4 units from the origin.

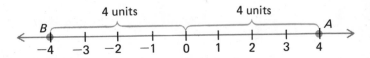

Points A and B are each 4 units from the origin.

Absolute values can be found by measuring distances on a number line.

We say that
$$\left.\begin{array}{l}\text{the absolute value of } 4 \\ \text{the absolute value of } -4\end{array}\right\} \text{ is } 4.$$

An absolute value is associated
with each number.

Number ⟶

Absolute value ⟶   3   5   0

EXAMPLE 3 Find the absolute value of 13 and of −13.

Say. ⟶ | The absolute value of 13 is 13. | The absolute value of −13 is 13.
Write. ⟶ | $|13| = 13$ | $|-13| = 13$

Definition of absolute value ⟶

$13 > 0 \quad |13| = 13$
$-13 < 0 \quad |-13| = -(-13) \text{ or } 13$

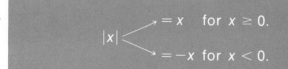

$$|x| \begin{cases} = x & \text{for } x \geq 0. \\ = -x & \text{for } x < 0. \end{cases}$$

EXAMPLE 4 Find $|7|$.   Find $|0|$.   Find $|-3|$.

Read $|7|$ as "absolute value of 7."

$|7| = 7 \quad |0| = 0 \quad |-3| = 3$

EXAMPLE 5 Find $|-8 + 4|$.   Find $|-7 + 9|$.

Simplify the expression inside the absolute value symbol first.

$$|-8 + 4| = |-4| \qquad |-7 + 9| = |2|$$
$$= 4 \qquad\qquad = 2$$

EXAMPLE 6 Find $|3x - 2|$ if $x = -4$.

Substitute −4 for x. ⟶
$3(-4) = -12$ ⟶

$$|3(-4) - 2|$$
$$|-12 - 2|$$
$$|-14|$$

Absolute value of −14 is 14. ⟶
$$14$$

EXAMPLE 7 Solve $|a| = 6$.

6 units   6 units

We must find numbers with absolute value 6.
$$|a| = 6$$

$$a = -6 \text{ or } a = 6$$

Both −6 and 6 are 6 units from the origin; so $|-6| = 6$ and $|6| = 6$. ⟶ **Thus,** the solutions are 6 and −6.

ORAL EXERCISES

Give the absolute value.

1. $|6|$ 2. $|-5|$ 3. $|-19|$ 4. $|9|$
5. $|-8 + 2|$ 6. $|4 - 3|$ 7. $|7 - 9|$ 8. $|3 - 4 - 1|$

EXERCISES

PART A

Find each.

1. $|x - 5|$ if $x = 2$
4. $|4x - 2|$ if $x = 5$
7. $|4 - 3a|$ if $a = -2$
10. $|5a - 3|$ if $a = -7$

2. $|a - 7|$ if $a = -4$
5. $|6k - 3|$ if $k = -2$
8. $|2 - m|$ if $m = 3$
11. $|6 - 4b|$ if $b = -3$

3. $|m - 5|$ if $m = -1$
6. $|3y - 6|$ if $y = 1$
9. $|5 - 4m|$ if $m = 3$
12. $|5 - 3t|$ if $t = -3$

Solve.

13. $|a| = 4$
14. $|m| = 1$
15. $|p| = 2$
16. $|r| = 3$

PART B

Find each.

17. $\left|\dfrac{3a}{2} - \dfrac{3}{5}\right|$ if $a = -2$

18. $\left|\dfrac{2m - 1}{3} + \dfrac{m}{2}\right|$ if $m = -3$

19. $\left|\dfrac{5}{a^2 - 4} + \dfrac{3}{a - 2}\right|$ if $a = -1$

20. $\left|\dfrac{1}{2} - \dfrac{3x}{x^2 - 3x + 1}\right|$ if $x = 0$

PART C

EXAMPLE   Graph the solution set of $|x| < 3$ on a number line.

The solution set contains all numbers which are less than 3 units from the origin.

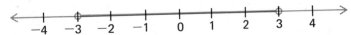

−3 and 3 are not solutions. The solutions are the numbers between −3 and 3. ⟶ The solution set is $\{x \mid -3 < x < 3\}$.

EXAMPLE   Graph the solution set of $|x| > 3$.

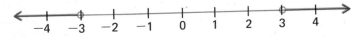

Numbers which are more than 3 units from the origin are solutions. ⟶ The solution set is $\{x \mid x < -3 \text{ or } x > 3\}$.

Find and graph the solution set.

21. $|x| < 2$
24. $|x| > 0$

22. $|x| \leq 4$
25. $|x| \geq 2$

23. $|x| < 1$
26. $|x| > 5$

Equations with Absolute Value

▶ *REVIEW CAPSULE*

Solve $|x| = 4$.

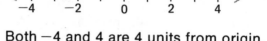

$x = -4$ or $x = 4$

Both -4 and 4 are 4 units from origin.
Thus, -4 and 4 are the solutions.

EXAMPLE 1 Solve $|3x - 3| = 6$.

$|6| = 6$ or $|-6| = 6$

$3x - 3$ can be -6 or 6. ⟶

Add 3 to each side.
Divide each side by 3.

Think of $3x - 3$ as some number a.

$$|3x - 3| = 6$$
$$\downarrow$$
$$|a| = 6$$

$$a = -6 \text{ or } a = 6$$

So, $\quad 3x - 3 = -6 \qquad 3x - 3 = 6$
$$3x = -3 \qquad\qquad 3x = 9$$
$$x = -1 \qquad\qquad x = 3$$

Check. ⟶

$$\begin{array}{c|c}
|3x - 3| & 6 \\
\text{Let } x = -1 \quad |3(-1) - 3| & 6 \\
|-3 - 3| & \\
|-6| & \\
6 &
\end{array} \quad
\begin{array}{c|c}
|3x - 3| & 6 \\
\text{Let } x = 3 \quad |3(3) - 3| & 6 \\
|9 - 3| & \\
|6| & \\
6 &
\end{array}$$

Thus, the solutions are -1 and 3.

EXAMPLE 2 Solve $|x + 2| = 7$.

$x + 2$ can be -7 or 7. ⟶

$$x + 2 = -7 \text{ or } x + 2 = 7$$
$$x = -9 \qquad\qquad x = 5$$

Thus, the solutions are -9 and 5.

EXAMPLE 3 Find the solution set of $|2 - 3x| = 10$.

$$|2 - 3x| = 10$$

Write two equations. $\longrightarrow$

Add -2 to each side. $\longrightarrow$

$$2 - 3x = -10 \text{ or } 2 - 3x = 10$$
$$\underline{-2 \qquad\quad -2} \qquad \underline{-2 \qquad\quad -2}$$
$$-3x = -12 \qquad\qquad -3x = 8$$

Divide each side by -3. $\longrightarrow$

$$x = 4 \qquad\qquad\quad x = -\frac{8}{3}$$

Thus, the solution set is $\{-\frac{8}{3}, 4\}$.

EXERCISES

PART A

Solve and check.

1. $|x - 3| = 4$

2. $|4 - x| = 7$

3. $|2m - 2| = 4$

4. $|2x - 5| = 7$

5. $|2m + 1| = 5$

6. $|3x| = 12$

Find the solution set.

7. $|2x - 6| = 4$

8. $|4 - 3x| = 7$

9. $|a + 4| = 7$

10. $|3 - 7k| = 5$

11. $|3x - 5| = 7$

12. $|5 - p| = 19$

13. $|2m - 14| = 1$

14. $|7y - 13| = 2$

15. $|2b - 7| = 5$

PART B

EXAMPLE Solve $3|x - 5| + 4 = 7$.

$$3|x - 5| + 4 = 7$$

Add -4 to each side. $\longrightarrow$

$$3|x - 5| = 3$$

Divide each side by 3.

$$|x - 5| = 1$$

$$x - 5 = -1 \text{ or } x - 5 = 1$$

Add 5 to each side.

$$x = 4 \qquad\qquad x = 6$$

Thus, the solutions are 4 and 6.

Solve.

16. $2|a - 3| + 7 = 13$

17. $3|2x - 7| - 4 = 17$

18. $6 - |2x - 5| = 1$

PART C

Solve.

19. $|3x - 2| = |6 - x|$

20. $|x - 5| - |2x + 3| = -18$

Directed Distance on a Number Line

No direction is indicated. ──────────→

$$\underbrace{\text{50 kilometers}}_{\uparrow}$$
distance

Distance and direction
↓ ↓
50 km   right

$$\underbrace{\text{50 kilometers to the right}}_{\uparrow}$$
directed distance

EXAMPLE 1 Find the directed distance *from A to B*.

The coordinate of A is 6.
The coordinate of B is 8.

Start at *A*. Move 2 units to the *right* to *B*.

$\vec{d}(AB)$ means directed distance *from A to B.* ──────────→ **Thus, $\vec{d}(AB) = +2$.**

Example 1 suggests this. ──────────→ A directed distance to the right is positive.

EXAMPLE 2 Find $\vec{d}(QP)$.

$\vec{d}(QP)$ means directed distance *from Q to P.* ──────────→

left   distance
-3

Start at *Q*. Move 3 units to the *left* to *P*.

Thus, $\vec{d}(QP) = -3$.

Example 2 suggests this. ──────────→ A directed distance to the left is negative.

We now look for a formula to find directed distances.

EXAMPLE 3 Find $\vec{d}(RS)$.

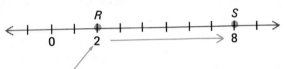

Start at R. Move 6 units to the *right* to S.

Directed distance to the right is positive. ⟶ **Thus,** $\vec{d}(RS) = +6$.

Notice that
$$\vec{d}(RS) = \text{coordinate of } S - \text{coordinate of } R$$
$$\qquad\qquad\quad 8 \qquad\qquad - \qquad\quad 2$$

$8 - 2 = 6$

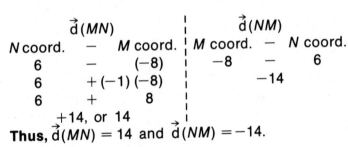

Directed distance from P to Q

$\vec{d}(PQ) = \text{coordinate of } Q - \text{coordinate of } P$

Example 3 suggests this. ⟶

EXAMPLE 4 Find $\vec{d}(MN)$ and $\vec{d}(NM)$.

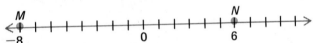

$\vec{d}(MN)$
N coord. $- M$ coord. | $\vec{d}(NM)$
M coord. $- N$ coord.

$a - b$ means $a + (-1)(b)$. ⟶
$\vec{d}(MN)$ is to the right.
$\vec{d}(NM)$ is to the left.

$\vec{d}(MN)$		$\vec{d}(NM)$	
N coord.	$- \quad M$ coord.	M coord.	$- \quad N$ coord.
6	$- \quad (-8)$	-8	$- \quad 6$
6	$+ (-1)(-8)$	-14	
6	$+ \quad 8$		

$+14$, or 14

Thus, $\vec{d}(MN) = 14$ and $\vec{d}(NM) = -14$.

$+14 = -(-14)$ ⟶ Observe that $\vec{d}(MN) = -\vec{d}(NM)$.

EXAMPLE 5 Find $\vec{d}(PQ)$.

coordinate of P: -3
coordinate of Q: -5

$\vec{d}(PQ)$
Q coord. $- P$ coord.

$a - b$ means $a + (-1)(b)$. ⟶

$$\begin{aligned}
\vec{d}(PQ) &= Q \text{ coord.} & - & \quad P \text{ coord.} \\
&= -5 & - & \quad (-3) \\
&= -5 & + & (-1)(-3) \\
&= -5 & & +3 \\
&= -2
\end{aligned}$$

ORAL EXERCISES

Tell whether the directed distance is positive or negative.

1. $\vec{d}(CE)$
2. $\vec{d}(BA)$
3. $\vec{d}(JB)$
4. $\vec{d}(FE)$
5. $\vec{d}(FC)$
6. $\vec{d}(AD)$
7. $\vec{d}(IG)$
8. $\vec{d}(HF)$
9. $\vec{d}(AE)$
10. $\vec{d}(FJ)$
11. $\vec{d}(DB)$
12. $\vec{d}(EJ)$

Use the number line above to find each directed distance.

13. $\vec{d}(CE)$
14. $\vec{d}(BA)$
15. $\vec{d}(JB)$
16. $\vec{d}(FE)$
17. $\vec{d}(FC)$
18. $\vec{d}(AD)$
19. $\vec{d}(IG)$
20. $\vec{d}(HF)$

EXERCISES

PART A

Find $\vec{d}(PQ)$.

1. coordinate of P: 4
   coordinate of Q: 8

2. coordinate of P: −8
   coordinate of Q: −4

3. coordinate of P: −6
   coordinate of Q: 4

4. coordinate of P: −8
   coordinate of Q: 10

5. coordinate of P: −2
   coordinate of Q: 4

6. coordinate of P: 7
   coordinate of Q: 18

7. coordinate of P: −16
   coordinate of Q: 2

8. coordinate of P: −8
   coordinate of Q: −3

9. coordinate of P: −18
   coordinate of Q: −14

PART B

Find $\vec{d}(AB)$.

10. coordinate of A: $-3\frac{1}{2}$

   coordinate of B: $4\frac{1}{4}$

11. coordinate of A: $-\frac{1}{3}$

   coordinate of B: $\frac{1}{2}$

12. coordinate of A: $-\frac{2}{3}$

   coordinate of B: $\frac{5}{9}$

PART C

Find each. Use the number line at the top of the page.

13. $\vec{d}(AB) + \vec{d}(BC)$
14. $\vec{d}(BD) + \vec{d}(DC)$
15. $\vec{d}(GF) + \vec{d}(GH)$

Fun for Philatelists

A philatelist (fi·lat′e·list) is a stamp collector. The two stamps illustrated are from a group of ten stamps issued by Nicaragua in 1971. The series gives the ten equations that changed the face of the earth. Each represents a major turning point in mathematics or science. On the back of each stamp is a brief history of the equation.

$$1 + 1 = 2$$

$$A^2 + B^2 = C^2$$

By counting on his fingers, an ancient man worked out the elementary equation, $1 + 1 = 2$. This equation brought an end to inexact tallying. It is the basis of our system of counting.

This geometric theorem, named after Pythagoras, compares the squares of the lengths of sides of a right triangle.

 PROJECT

1. If anyone you know is a stamp collector, see if he or she has these stamps. Prepare a report on the history of the equations.

2. Prepare a display on other stamps which pertain to mathematics. Consult stamp collections, magazines, newspapers, and reference sources in the library.

Designed and printed by Thos De La Rue & Co. Ltd. Each stamp is 48 × 32 mm in sheets of 50 stamps. Reprinted by permission of Oficina de Control de Especies, Postales y Filatella, Managua, Nicaragua.

Locating Points in a Plane

OBJECTIVES
- To give the ordered pair for a point in a plane
- To identify the quadrant in which a given point lies

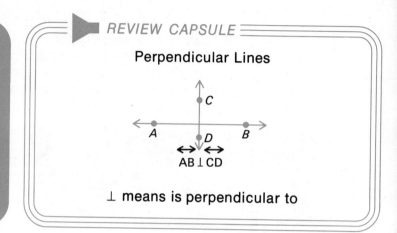

▶ REVIEW CAPSULE

Perpendicular Lines

AB ⊥ CD

⊥ means is perpendicular to

A plane is a flat surface.

Points are located in a plane by using two perpendicular number lines.

EXAMPLE 1   Describe the location of point *P*.

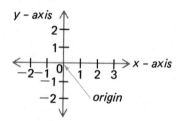

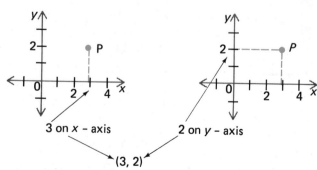

3 on *x* – axis   2 on *y* – axis

(3, 2)

The position of *P* is described by an ordered pair.

x-coordinate   *y*-coordinate

(3,   2)

The *x*-coordinate is always first.

EXAMPLE 2   Give the ordered pair for *P, Q, R,* and *S.*

For *P*: Read 4 on *x*-axis. ⎤
       Read 2 on *y*-axis. ⎦
For *Q*: Read −3 on *x*-axis. ⎤
       Read −2 on *y*-axis. ⎦

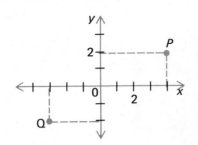

Point *S* is the origin. The coordinates are (0, 0).

$P(4, 2)$ $Q(-3, -2)$ $R(-3, 2)$ $S(0, 0)$

EXERCISES

PART A

Give the ordered pair for each point.

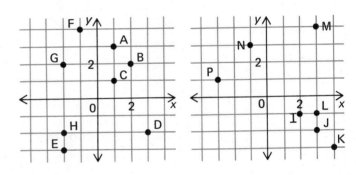

1. *A*	**2.** *B*
3. *C*	**4.** *D*
5. *E*	**6.** *F*
7. *G*	**8.** *H*
9. *I*	**10.** *J*
11. *K*	**12.** *L*
13. *M*	**14.** *N*
15. *P*	

PART B

Each point except the origin is located in one of the quadrants or on one of the axes. The origin is on both axes.

The axes divide the plane into four quadrants.

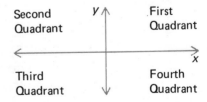

Second Quadrant   First Quadrant

Third Quadrant   Fourth Quadrant

Give the quadrant in which each point lies.

16. $(-1, -5)$ **17.** $(6, 10)$ **18.** $(2, -8)$

19. $(-7, -3)$ **20.** $(1, -8)$ **21.** $(-6, 5)$

22. Describe the coordinates of all points in the second quadrant.

Plotting Points in a Plane

OBJECTIVE

■ To plot points in a plane

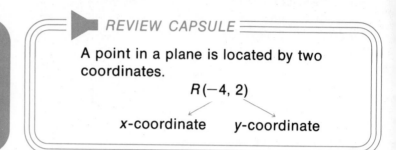

REVIEW CAPSULE

A point in a plane is located by two coordinates.

$$R(-4, 2)$$

x-coordinate   y-coordinate

EXAMPLE 1   Plot the point (2, 3).

Draw and mark axes on graph paper.

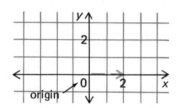 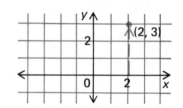

Start at the origin. ———————————→

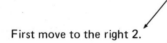

(2, 3)

First move to the right 2.   Then move up 3.

EXAMPLE 2   Plot the point (−4, 2).

Start at the origin.

(−4, 2)

Move left 4.   Move up 2.

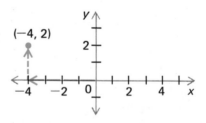

Examples 1 and 2 show that the signs of the coordinates tell in which directions to move from the origin.

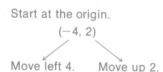

(x   ,   y)

right or left   up or down

+   −   +   −

(2, 3)	(−4, 2)	(−1, −3)	(4, −3)
(+, +)	(−, +)	(−, −)	(+, −)
↓ ↓	↓ ↓	↓ ↓	↓ ↓
right up	left up	left down	right down

EXAMPLE 3　**Plot the points.**
$A(-2,-1), B(-1,3), C(3,-3), D(-2,-4)$

Draw and mark axes on graph paper.

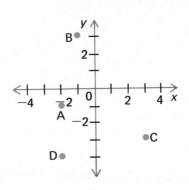

$A(-2,-1)$

left 2　　down 1

$B(-1,3)$

left 1　up 3

EXAMPLE 4　**Plot $(-4,0)$.**　　　　**Plot $(0,-2)$.**

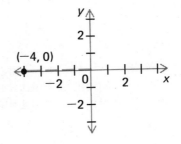

Begin at the origin.　　Begin at the origin.
　$(-4,　0)$　　　　　　$(0,　　-2)$

left 4　neither up　　neither right　　down 2
　　　nor down　　nor left

$(-4,0)$ lies on the x-axis.
$(0,-2)$ lies on the y-axis.

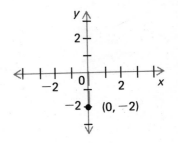

Any point on the
x-axis has
y-coordinate 0.

Any point on the
y-axis has
x-coordinate 0.

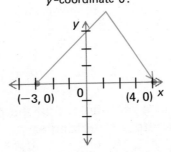

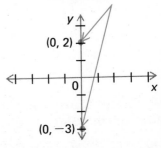

ORAL EXERCISES

Tell in which directions to move in order to plot each point.

1. $A(3, 4)$ **2.** $B(2, -5)$ **3.** $C(-3, 7)$ **4.** $D(-2, -5)$ **5.** $E(-8, 2)$
6. $M(0, 2)$ **7.** $N(4, 0)$ **8.** $P(-5, 0)$ **9.** $Q(0, -4)$ **10.** $R(-1, -3)$

EXERCISES

PART A

Plot each point.

1. $A(2, 3)$ **2.** $B(-4, 1)$ **3.** $C(-3, -1)$ **4.** $D(2, -3)$ **5.** $E(3, 0)$
6. $F(0, 0)$ **7.** $G(-3, 0)$ **8.** $H(0, -4)$ **9.** $I(0, -7)$ **10.** $J(-5, 2)$
11. $K(4, -1)$ **12.** $L(-5, 1)$ **13.** $M(0, 3)$ **14.** $N(6, 0)$ **15.** $P(-8, 0)$

PART B

Plot each point.

16. $Q(3\frac{1}{2}, 4\frac{1}{2})$ **17.** $R(-2\frac{1}{2}, 4\frac{1}{2})$ **18.** $S(4.5, -3.5)$ **19.** $T(-1\frac{1}{4}, 0)$

PART C

EXAMPLE A, B, and C are 3 vertices of a rectangle. Plot the points. Find the coordinates of the fourth point, D, to complete the rectangle.

$$A(2, 1), B(6, 1), C(6, 4)$$

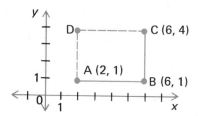

D has the same x-coord. as A and the same y-coord. as C. ⟶ **Thus, $D(2, 4)$ is the fourth point.**

A, B, and C are 3 vertices of a rectangle. Plot the points. Find the coordinates of the fourth point, D, to complete the rectangle.

20. $A(2, 3)$, $B(7, 3)$, $C(7, 5)$ **21.** $A(-4, 2)$, $B(7, 2)$, $C(7, 8)$

Pascal's Triangle

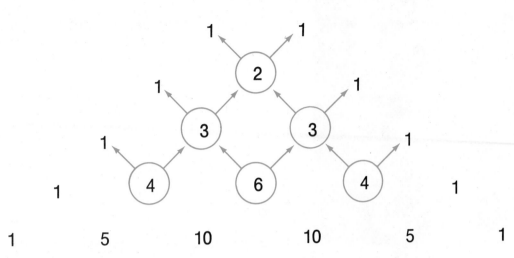

Pascal's triangle is an arrangement of numbers. Each number is the sum of the two numbers just above it. Each row begins and ends with 1.

This list shows the powers of $(a + b)$.

$(a + b)^0 =$ 1

$(a + b)^1 =$ $1a + 1b$

$(a + b)^2 =$ $1a^2 + 2ab + 1b^2$

$(a + b)^3 =$ $1a^3 + 3a^2b + 3ab^2 + 1b^3$

$(a + b)^4 =$ $1a^4 + 4a^3b + 6a^2b^2 + 4ab^3 + 1b^4$

$(a + b)^5 =$ $1a^5 + 5a^4b + 10a^3b^2 + 10a^2b^3 + 5ab^4 + 1b^5$

Do you see Pascal's triangle?

PROJECT

1. What do the numerals of Pascal's triangle represent?

2. Write the next two rows of Pascal's triangle.

3. Write the expansions for $(a + b)^6$ and $(a + b)^7$.

Lines Parallel to the Axes

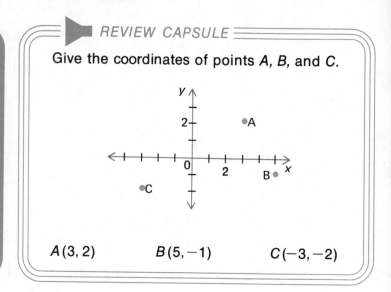

▶ REVIEW CAPSULE

Give the coordinates of points A, B, and C.

$A(3, 2)$ $B(5, -1)$ $C(-3, -2)$

EXAMPLE 1 The line containing A, B, and C is horizontal. The line containing D, E, and F is vertical. Give the coordinates for each point A, B, C, D, E, F.

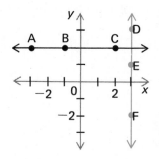

$A(-3, 2)$, $B(-1, 2)$, $C(2, 2)$

same y-coordinate

$D(3, 3)$, $E(3, 1)$, $F(3, -2)$

same x-coordinate

Example 1 suggests this. ————→

Every point on a horizontal line has the same y-coordinate.

Every point on a vertical line has the same x-coordinate.

EXAMPLE 2   Determine to which axis the line joining
$M(-3, 5)$ and $N(7, 5)$ is parallel.

$$M(-3, 5) \quad\quad N(7, 5)$$

same y-coordinate

$\overleftrightarrow{MN}$ is a horizontal line.

Thus, $\overleftrightarrow{MN}$ is parallel to the x-axis.

EXAMPLE 3   Determine to which axis the line joining
$R(2, -5)$ and $S(2, 3)$ is parallel.

$$R(2, -5) \quad\quad S(2, 3)$$

same x-coordinate

$\overleftrightarrow{RS}$ is a vertical line.

Thus, $\overleftrightarrow{RS}$ is parallel to the y-axis.

EXERCISES

PART A

**Determine, without sketching, to which axis the line joining M and N is parallel.
Then sketch to check.**

1. $M(3, 7)$, $N(-2, 7)$ **2.** $M(-2, 4)$, $N(-2, -1)$ **3.** $M(3, -5)$, $N(4, -5)$
4. $M(-2, 4)$, $N(-2, -4)$ **5.** $M(-3, 3)$, $N(-3, 2)$ **6.** $M(-5, -3)$, $N(-1, -3)$
7. $M(-6, -2)$, $N(6, -2)$ **8.** $M(5, 1)$, $N(5, -8)$ **9.** $M(-7, 3)$, $N(-7, -3)$

PART B

For what value of b will the line joining P and Q be parallel to the indicated axis?

10. $P(-4, 3)$, $Q(b, 1)$; y-axis   **11.** $P(-5, 2)$, $Q(7, b)$; x-axis
12. $P(5, 12)$, $Q(-4, 3b)$; x-axis   **13.** $P(8, 5)$, $Q(2b, 4)$; y-axis
14. $P(3b - 1, 5)$, $Q(8, 4)$; y-axis   **15.** $P(-6, 2b + 1)$, $Q(2, 7)$; x-axis

PART C

**For what value of b will the line joining P and Q be parallel
to the indicated axis?**

16. $P(4b + 6, 7)$, $Q(3 + 4b, 5)$; y-axis   **17.** $P(8, b^2 - 7b)$, $Q(7, -12)$; x-axis

Directed Distances

OBJECTIVE
■ To find directed distances on lines parallel to one of the axes

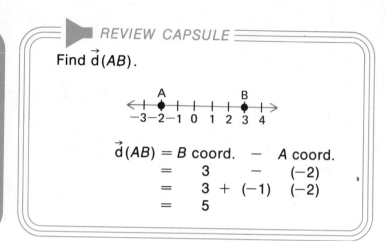

REVIEW CAPSULE

Find $\vec{d}(AB)$.

$$\vec{d}(AB) = B \text{ coord.} \quad - \quad A \text{ coord.}$$
$$= \quad 3 \quad - \quad (-2)$$
$$= \quad 3 + (-1) \quad (-2)$$
$$= \quad 5$$

EXAMPLE 1   Find $\vec{d}(PQ)$.

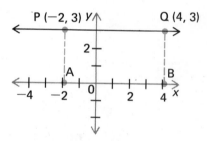

Use points directly below P and Q on the x-axis.

A and B are points on a number line. ⟶

$$\vec{d}(AB) = B \text{ coord.} \quad - \quad A \text{ coord.}$$
$$= \quad 4 \quad - \quad (-2)$$
$$= \quad 4 \quad + (-1)(-2)$$
$$= \quad 4 \quad + \quad 2 \quad \text{or } 6.$$

$a - b = a + (-1)b.$ ⟶
A and B are directly below P and Q.

But, $\vec{d}(PQ) = \vec{d}(AB)$.
Thus, $\vec{d}(PQ) = 6$.

$P(-2, 3) \qquad Q(4, 3)$
$\vec{d}(PQ) = 4 - (-2)$

$\vec{d}(PQ)$ is determined only by the x-coordinates of P and Q.

Example 1 suggests this. ⟶

If $\overleftrightarrow{PQ}$ is a horizontal line,
$\vec{d}(PQ) = (x\text{-coord. of } Q) - (x\text{-coord. of } P)$.

EXAMPLE 2   Find $\vec{d}(ST)$ for $S(2,5)$ and $T(-7,5)$.

Both y-coord. are the same.
$S(2,5), T(-7,5)$

$\overleftrightarrow{ST}$ is a horizontal line.
So, $\vec{d}(ST)$ = (x-coord. of T) − (x-coord. of S)
$\qquad = \qquad -7 \qquad - \qquad 2$
$\qquad = \qquad -9$

Thus, $\vec{d}(ST) = -9$.

EXAMPLE 3   Find $\vec{d}(RS)$.

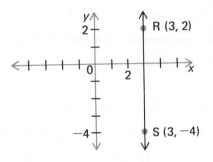

$\overleftrightarrow{RS}$ is a vertical line, since the
x-coordinates of R and S are the same.
$R(3,2), S(3,-4)$

Find points directly across from R and S on the
y-axis.

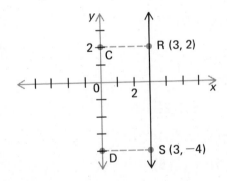

C and D are points on a number line. ⟶

$\vec{d}(RS)$ is determined only by the
y-coord. of R and S.

$\vec{d}(CD) = D$ coord. − C coord.
$\qquad = \quad -4 \quad - \quad 2$
$\qquad = \quad -6$
But, $\vec{d}(RS) = \vec{d}(CD)$.
Thus, $\vec{d}(RS) = -6$.

Example 3 suggests this. ⟶

If $\overleftrightarrow{PQ}$ is a vertical line,
$\qquad \vec{d}(PQ)$ = (y-coord. of Q) − (y-coord. of P).

EXAMPLE 4   Find $\vec{d}(GH)$ for $G(-3,-4)$ and $H(-3,7)$.

Both *x*-coord. are the same.
$G(-3,-4)$, $H(-3,7)$

$\overleftrightarrow{GH}$ is a vertical line.
So, $\vec{d}(GH) = $ (*y*-coord. of *H*) $-$ (*y*-coord. of *G*)
$$7 \qquad - \qquad (-4)$$
$$= 7 + (-1)(-4)$$
$$= 11$$
Thus, $\vec{d}(GH) = 11$.

EXERCISES

PART A

Find $\vec{d}(MN)$.

1. $M(2,-7)$, $N(-5,-7)$

2. $M(1,4)$, $N(1,-3)$

3. $M(2,-6)$, $N(3,-6)$

4. $M(-1,5)$, $N(-1,-3)$

5. $M(6,-4)$, $N(-2,-4)$

6. $M(-8,-2)$, $N(-8,-5)$

7. $M(-2,-3)$, $N(-5,-3)$

8. $M(0,-4)$, $N(3,-4)$

9. $M(1,2)$, $N(1,-9)$

10. $M(0,-8)$, $N(-3,-8)$

11. $M(-3,0)$, $N(-3,8)$

12. $M(4,0)$, $N(4,-3)$

13. $M(4,0)$, $N(4,-6)$

14. $M(-3,-3)$, $N(5,-3)$

15. $M(-4,6)$, $N(-4,-17)$

16. $M(-5,3)$, $N(42,3)$

17. $M(0,-15)$, $N(0,14)$

18. $M(-17,0)$, $N(6,0)$

PART B

Find $\vec{d}(PQ)$.

19. $P(3\frac{1}{2},-5)$, $Q(2\frac{1}{4},-5)$

20. $P(\frac{5}{6},4)$, $Q(-\frac{2}{3},4)$

21. $P(6,-\frac{4}{3})$, $Q(6,\frac{5}{6})$

22. $P(3\frac{1}{8},-\frac{3}{4})$, $Q(3\frac{1}{8},\frac{5}{12})$

23. $P(-\frac{4}{5},5)$, $Q(\frac{7}{15},5)$

24. $P(3.8,2)$, $Q(-1.7,2)$

25. $P(-4,1.6)$, $Q(-3.2,1.6)$

26. $P(7,-5.3)$, $Q(7,4.9)$

27. $P(1\frac{1}{8},4)$, $Q(-1\frac{3}{4},4)$

28. $P(-\frac{4}{9},5)$, $Q(\frac{1}{27},5)$

PART C

Express $\vec{d}(RT)$ in terms of variables.

29. $R(3a,2b)$, $T(-5a,2b)$

30. $R(2m,5n)$, $T(2m,-7n)$

31. $R(3m,-2k)$, $T(3m,-5k)$

32. $R(2a-3,b)$, $T(-4a+3,b)$

33. $R(\frac{3m}{2},5)$, $T(\frac{2m}{3},5)$

34. $R(-4,\frac{5}{m^2})$, $T(-4,\frac{3}{m^2})$

Slopes of Line Segments

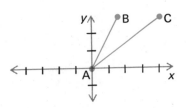
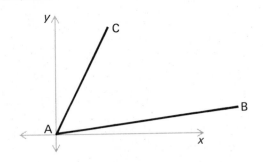

$\overline{AC}$ and $\overline{AB}$ are not parallel to either axis.

If the *x*-axis represents level ground and $\overline{AB}$ and $\overline{AC}$ represent paths up a hill, $\overline{AC}$ would be more difficult to climb than $\overline{AB}$.

Think of slope of a hill.

We say that $\overline{AC}$ has greater *slope* than $\overline{AB}$.

EXAMPLE 1   Find $\dfrac{\vec{d}(AE)}{\vec{d}(EB)}$.

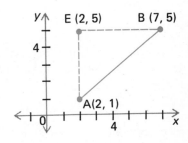

$\vec{d}(AE)$ measures the vertical, or rise. ⟶ $\vec{d}(AE) = 5 - 1$
$\qquad\qquad\qquad\qquad\qquad\qquad\qquad\quad = 4$

$\vec{d}(EB)$ measures the horizontal, or run. ⟶ $\vec{d}(EB) = 7 - 2$
$\qquad\qquad\qquad\qquad\qquad\qquad\qquad\quad = 5$

$\dfrac{\text{Vertical directed distance}}{\text{Horizontal directed distance}}$ ⟶ **Thus,** $\dfrac{\vec{d}(AE)}{\vec{d}(EB)} = \dfrac{4}{5}$.

$\text{Slope} = \dfrac{\text{rise}}{\text{run}}$. ⟶ We say that the slope of $\overline{AB}$ is $\frac{4}{5}$.

EXAMPLE 2 Find the slopes of $\overline{AB}$ and $\overline{AC}$. Compare the slopes.

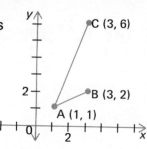

Draw the graph of each line segment separately.

Form a right triangle.———————→

Slope $=\dfrac{\text{rise}}{\text{run}}$.——————————→

Vertical directed distance————————→
Horizontal directed distance ———————→

Slope of $\overline{AB}=\dfrac{\vec{d}(AD)}{\vec{d}(DB)}$

$=\dfrac{2-1}{3-1}$, or $\dfrac{1}{2}$

Slope of $\overline{AC}=\dfrac{\vec{d}(AE)}{\vec{d}(EC)}$

$=\dfrac{6-1}{3-1}$, or $\dfrac{5}{2}$

Thus, the slope of $\overline{AC}$ is greater than the slope of $\overline{AB}$.

EXAMPLE 3 Find the slope of the line segment joining $A(2, 1)$ and $B(5, 3)$.

Draw a diagram.

Build a right triangle by drawing a vertical line segment through A and a horizontal line segment through B.

Slope $=\dfrac{\text{rise}}{\text{run}}$.——————————→

Slope of $\overline{AB}=\dfrac{\vec{d}(AC)}{\vec{d}(CB)}$

$=\dfrac{3-1}{5-2}$, or $\dfrac{2}{3}$

Thus, the slope of $\overline{AB}$ is $\frac{2}{3}$.

In Example 3, for $A(2, 1)$ and $B(5, 3)$ we found:

$$\text{Slope of } \overline{AB} = \cfrac{\overset{\substack{y\text{-coord.} \\ \text{of } B}}{3} \quad - \quad \overset{\substack{y\text{-coord.} \\ \text{of } A}}{1}}{\underset{\substack{x\text{-coord.} \\ \text{of } B}}{5} \quad - \quad \underset{\substack{x\text{-coord.} \\ \text{of } A}}{2}}$$

Difference of y-coordinates
Difference of x-coordinates

We can find the slope of a segment directly from the coordinates of its endpoints.

$$\text{Slope} = \frac{\text{difference of the } y\text{-coordinates}}{\text{difference of the } x\text{-coordinates}}.$$

EXAMPLE 4   Find the slope of $\overline{AB}$ for $A(6, 3)$, $B(-1, -4)$.

First way

Difference of y-coordinates
Difference of x-coordinates
$A(6, 3)$, $B(-1, -4)$

$$\text{Slope} = \frac{y\text{-coord. of } B - y\text{-coord. of } A}{x\text{-coord. of } B - x\text{-coord. of } A}$$

$$= \frac{-4 - 3}{-1 - 6}$$

$$= \frac{-7}{-7}$$

$$= 1$$

Second way

Difference of y-coordinates
Difference of x-coordinates
$A(6, 3)$, $B(-1, -4)$

$$\text{Slope} = \frac{y\text{-coord. of } A - y\text{-coord. of } B}{x\text{-coord. of } A - x\text{-coord. of } B}$$

$$= \frac{3 - (-4)}{6 - (-1)}$$

$$= \frac{3 + (-1)(-4)}{6 + (-1)(-1)}$$

$$= \frac{3 + 4}{6 + 1}$$

$$= \frac{7}{7}, \text{ or } 1$$

Both ways give the same slope. $\longrightarrow$ **Thus,** the slope of $\overline{AB}$ is 1.

EXAMPLE 5 Find the slope of $\overline{CD}$ for $C(8, 2)$ and $D(-2, 6)$.

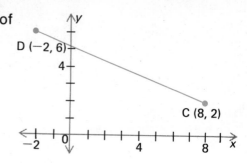

Also, $\dfrac{2-6}{8-(-2)} = \dfrac{-4}{10}$.

The slope of a line segment can be negative. ────────────→

Slope of $\overline{CD} = \dfrac{6-2}{-2-8}$, or $\dfrac{4}{-10}$.

Thus, the slope of $\overline{CD}$ is $-\frac{4}{10}$, or $-\frac{2}{5}$.

EXAMPLE 6 Find the slope of $\overline{AB}$ for $A(3, 5)$ and $B(6, 5)$.

$\overline{AB}$ is a horizontal line segment.

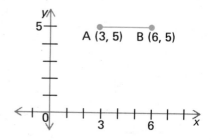

Also, $\dfrac{5-5}{3-6} = \dfrac{0}{-3} = 0$.

The slope of a line segment can be zero. ────────────→

Slope of $\overline{AB} = \dfrac{5-5}{6-3}$, or $\dfrac{0}{3}$.

Thus, the slope of $\overline{AB}$ is 0.

EXERCISES

PART A

Find the slope of $\overline{AB}$.

1. $A(0, 0)$, $B(4, 3)$ **2.** $A(3, 5)$, $B(7, 6)$ **3.** $A(2, 5)$, $B(5, 7)$
4. $A(-3, -4)$, $B(8, 2)$ **5.** $A(-4, -1)$, $B(6, 2)$ **6.** $A(5, 3)$, $B(1, 8)$
7. $A(-8, 3)$, $B(7, -1)$ **8.** $A(-1, 1)$, $B(7, 4)$ **9.** $A(0, 4)$, $B(7, 4)$

PART B

Express the slope of $\overline{AB}$ in terms of variables.

10. $A(2b, 5k)$, $B(4b, 8k)$ **11.** $A(3i, 5t)$, $B(-4i, 7t)$
12. $A(2c, -4d)$, $B(-5c, 7d)$ **13.** $A(-3b, 5k)$, $B(b, k)$

Slope of Lines

REVIEW CAPSULE

Find the slope of $\overline{PQ}$ for $P(-4, -2)$ and $Q(7, 6)$.

$$\frac{y\text{-coord. of } Q - y\text{-coord. of } P}{x\text{-coord. of } Q - x\text{-coord. of } P}$$

$$\frac{6 \quad - \quad (-2)}{7 \quad - \quad (-4)}$$

$$\frac{6 + (-1)(-2)}{7 + (-1)(-4)}, \text{ or } \frac{8}{11}$$

EXAMPLE 1 A, B, C, and D are points on the same line. Find the slopes of $\overline{AB}$ and $\overline{CD}$.

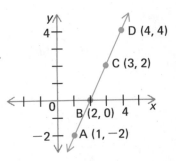

$A(1, -2)$, $B(2, 0)$; $C(3, 2)$, $D(4, 4)$

The slope of both segments is the same.

Slope of $\overline{AB} = \dfrac{0 - (-2)}{2 - 1}$

$= \dfrac{2}{1}$, or 2

Slope of $\overline{CD} = \dfrac{4 - 2}{4 - 3}$

$= \dfrac{2}{1}$, or 2

We say that the slope of $\overleftrightarrow{AB}$ is 2.

Use any two points on the line to find the slope.

The slope of a line is the slope of any line segment on the line.

EXAMPLE 2   Find the slope of $\overleftrightarrow{PQ}$ for $P(4, 1)$ and $Q(1, 3)$.

diff. of y-coords.
diff. of x-coords.

Slope of $\overleftrightarrow{PQ} = \dfrac{3 - 1}{1 - 4}$

$= \dfrac{2}{-3}$, or $-\dfrac{2}{3}$

EXAMPLE 3   Find the slope of $\overleftrightarrow{AB}$.

$\overleftrightarrow{AB}$ is a horizontal line.

$$\text{Slope of } \overleftrightarrow{AB} = \frac{2-2}{4-(-1)}$$
$$= \frac{0}{5}, \text{ or } 0$$

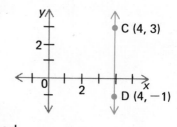

EXAMPLE 4   Find the slope of $\overleftrightarrow{CD}$.

$$\text{Slope of } \overleftrightarrow{CD} = \frac{3-(-1)}{4-4}$$

A fraction cannot have 0 in the denominator.

$$= \frac{4}{0}$$

$\llcorner$ undefined

Thus, the slope of the vertical line $\overleftrightarrow{CD}$ is undefined.

Examples 3 and 4 suggest this. ———→

> The slope of a horizontal line is zero.
> The slope of a vertical line is undefined.

See Examples 1–4. ——————————→   **The slope of a line determines its slant.**

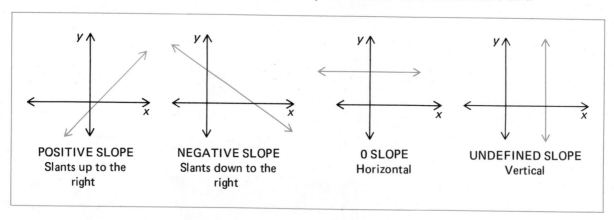

POSITIVE SLOPE
Slants up to the
right

NEGATIVE SLOPE
Slants down to the
right

0 SLOPE
Horizontal

UNDEFINED SLOPE
Vertical

EXAMPLE 5   Find the slope of $\overleftrightarrow{CD}$ for $C(-2, -4)$ and $D(5, 8)$. Then describe the slant of $\overleftrightarrow{CD}$.

Difference of y-coordinates
Difference of x-coordinates

$$\text{Slope of } \overleftrightarrow{CD} = \frac{8-(-4)}{5-(-2)} = \frac{12}{7}.$$

The slope of $\overleftrightarrow{CD}$ is positive. ——→   **Thus,** the slope of $\overleftrightarrow{CD}$ is $\frac{12}{7}$.
$\overleftrightarrow{CD}$ slants up to the right.

EXAMPLE 6 $\overleftrightarrow{PQ}$ is parallel to $\overleftrightarrow{AB}$.
Find the slope of each.

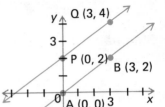

Slope of $\overleftrightarrow{AB}$ Slope of $\overleftrightarrow{PQ}$

Difference of y-coordinates $\longrightarrow$
Difference of x-coordinates $\longrightarrow$

$$\dfrac{2-0}{3-0} \quad \bigm| \quad \dfrac{4-2}{3-0}$$

$$\dfrac{2}{3} \quad \bigm| \quad \dfrac{2}{3}$$

Thus, the slope of each line is $\frac{2}{3}$.

Example 6 suggests this. $\longrightarrow$ Parallel lines have the same slope.

ORAL EXERCISES

Describe the slant of the line whose slope is given.

1. $\dfrac{2}{3}$ **2.** $-\dfrac{4}{5}$ **3.** $\dfrac{0}{4}$ **4.** $\dfrac{5}{0}$ **5.** $-\dfrac{1}{2}$

EXERCISES

PART A

Find the slope of $\overleftrightarrow{PQ}$ and describe its slant.

1. $P(3,4)$, $Q(3,7)$ **2.** $P(3,2)$, $Q(-2,5)$ **3.** $P(2,5)$, $Q(3,5)$
4. $P(-5,-3)$, $Q(7,-4)$ **5.** $P(0,0)$, $Q(-8,-5)$ **6.** $P(-6,5)$, $Q(7,5)$
7. $P(-3,-4)$, $Q(-3,6)$ **8.** $P(-6,1)$, $Q(7,5)$ **9.** $P(1,-2)$, $Q(-5,-2)$

Determine whether $\overleftrightarrow{PQ}$ is parallel to $\overleftrightarrow{RS}$.

10. $P(2,5)$, $Q(3,7)$ **11.** $P(3,7)$, $Q(6,9)$ **12.** $P(1,3)$, $Q(2,5)$
    $R(2,7)$, $S(0,5)$ $R(3,1)$, $Q(9,5)$ $R(0,1)$, $S(2,11)$

PART B

Determine whether A, B, and C lie on the same line. [Hint: Check if the slope of $\overline{AB}$ = the slope of $\overline{BC}$.]

13. $A(1,1)$, $B(-3,-7)$, $C(5,9)$ **14.** $A(0,3)$, $B(-2,5)$, $C(1,0)$
15. $A(2,-3)$, $B(-2,-7)$, $C(0,-3)$ **16.** $A(4,3)$, $B(-6,-2)$, $C(8,5)$
17. $A(0,0)$, $B(1,-3)$, $C(-2,4)$ **18.** $A(3,-3)$, $B(-1,2)$, $C(6,-2)$
19. $A(10,5)$, $B(-5,-1)$, $C(0,1)$ **20.** $A(2,1)$, $B(-4,-8)$, $C(6,7)$

Chapter Nine Review

Find each. [p. 231]

1. $|-6|$

2. $|-7+5|$

3. $|3a - 2|$ if $a = -4$

4. $|\frac{2a}{3} - \frac{1}{5}|$ if $a = -2$

Solve. [p. 231, 234]

5. $|x| = 7$

6. $|5 - 2x| = 1$

7. $|3x - 5| = 2$

8. $2|x - 4| + 3 = 9$

Find $\vec{d}(MN)$. [p. 236]

9. coordinate of M: -5
coordinate of N: 4

10. coordinate of M: 6
coordinate of N: -3

11. coordinate of M: $\frac{5}{6}$
coordinate of N: $-\frac{2}{3}$

Give the ordered pair for each point. [p. 240]

12. A **17.** F
13. B **18.** G
14. C **19.** H
15. D **20.** I
16. E **21.** J

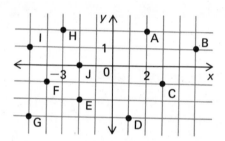

Give the quadrant in which each point lies. Then plot the point. [p. 240, 242]

22. $A(3, 5)$

23. $B(-3, 2)$

24. $C(-5, 0)$

25. $D(0, 3)$

[p. 246]

Determine, without sketching, to which axis the line joining P and Q is parallel.

26. $P(3, 5)$, $Q(-7, 5)$

27. $P(4, 8)$, $Q(4, -8)$

28. $P(a, b)$, $Q(c, b)$

[p. 246]

For what value of b will the line joining P and Q be parallel to the indicated axis?

29. $P(-5, 2)$, $Q(b, 1)$; y-axis

30. $P(6, 3b + 1)$, $Q(2, 4)$; x-axis

Find $\vec{d}(MN)$. [p. 248]

31. $M(-4, 3)$, $N(7, 3)$

32. $M(2, -6)$, $N(2, 8)$

33. $M(-1, -5)$, $N(4, -5)$

Find the slope of $\overleftrightarrow{PQ}$. Then describe its slant. [p. 251, 255]

34. $P(1, 5)$, $Q(2, 9)$

35. $P(4, 3)$, $Q(7, 3)$

36. $P(2, 5)$, $Q(5, -2)$

37. $P(3, 4)$, $Q(3, 1)$

Determine whether $\overleftrightarrow{PQ}$ is parallel to $\overleftrightarrow{RS}$. [p. 255]

38. $P(1, -5)$, $Q(4, 1)$
$R(6, 13)$, $S(-4, -7)$

39. $P(5, 2)$, $Q(-5, -4)$
$R(10, 7)$, $S(-15, -8)$

40. $P(3, 1)$, $Q(-6, -2)$
$R(9, 5)$, $S(6, 2)$

Chapter Nine Test

Find each.

1. $|-4|$
2. $|2 - 8|$
3. $|3a - 5|$ if $a = -4$
4. $|\frac{3a}{5} - \frac{1}{2}|$ if $a = -2$

Solve.

5. $|x| = 6$
6. $|3x - 4| = 7$
7. $3|x - 2| + 5 = 14$

Find $\vec{d}(MN)$.

8. coordinate of M: -6
coordinate of N: 1

9. coordinate of M: $\frac{1}{8}$
coordinate of N: $-\frac{3}{4}$

Give the ordered pair for each point.

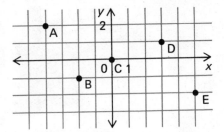

10. A
11. B
12. C
13. D
14. E

Give the quadrant in which each point lies. Then plot each point.

15. $A(5, 2)$
16. $B(-3, -6)$
17. $C(0, -4)$

Determine, without sketching, to which axis the line joining P and Q is parallel.

18. $P(-2, 4)$, $Q(8, 4)$
19. $P(-3, -4)$, $Q(-3, 2)$

For what value of b will the line joining P and Q be parallel to the indicated axis?

20. $P(-6, 3)$, $Q(b, 4)$; y-axis
21. $P(5, 6)$, $Q(12, 2b + 1)$; x-axis

Find $\vec{d}(MN)$.

22. $M(-5, 3)$, $N(7, 3)$
23. $M(5, 2\frac{1}{2})$, $N(5, 3\frac{3}{4})$

Find the slope of $\overleftrightarrow{PQ}$. Then describe its slant.

24. $P(2, 3)$, $Q(7, 9)$
26. $P(5, 1)$, $Q(7, 1)$
25. $P(-4, 2)$, $Q(3, 2)$
27. $P(3, 4)$, $Q(3, 8)$

Determine whether $\overleftrightarrow{PQ}$ is parallel to $\overleftrightarrow{RS}$.

28. $P(6, 3)$, $Q(-3, -3)$
$R(0, 4)$, $S(3, 6)$

29. $P(0, 0)$, $Q(-6, -15)$
$R(2, 6)$, $S(4, 9)$

Mathematics in Construction

Construction workers must make careful plans in the form of cost budgets, time schedules, and blueprints (scale drawing of project). Pictured above is a foreman preparing a time schedule.

Find the perimeter of the room shown on the scale drawing.

Scale: 1 cm → 5 m

Ratio and Proportion

REVIEW CAPSULE

Solve
$$5(x - 5) = 21$$
$$5x - 25 = 21 \quad \leftarrow \text{Distributive property}$$
$$5x = 46 \quad \leftarrow \text{Add 25 to each side.}$$
$$x = \frac{46}{5}, \text{ or } 9\frac{1}{5}$$

EXAMPLE 1   John can paint a house in 4 days. He works 3 days. Write a fraction which compares the number of days actually worked with the number of days needed to do the entire job.

$\frac{3}{4}$ is a *ratio*.

$$\frac{\text{Number of days worked}}{\text{Number of days to do entire job}} = \frac{3}{4}$$

Numbers being compared should represent the same units. In Example 1, 3 and 4 represent days.

The comparison of two numbers by division is a *ratio*.

Two ways to write the ratio 3 to 4

$$\frac{3}{4} \qquad 3:4$$

EXAMPLE 2   Write the ratio 5 to 7 in two ways.

Compare 5 to 7. ⟶ $\frac{5}{7}$, or 5:7

EXAMPLE 3   Write an equation.

The ratio is the same as the ratio

3 to 4		a to 16
↓	↓	↓
$\frac{3}{4}$	$=$	$\frac{a}{16}$
or 3:4	$=$	a:16

The ratios are equal.
The equation is a proportion.

A *proportion* is an equation which states that two ratios are equal.

$$\frac{a}{b} = \frac{c}{d} \qquad \text{or} \qquad a:b = c:d$$

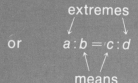

a and *d* are *extremes*.
b and *c* are *means*.

EXAMPLE 4 Identify the extremes and means.

$$\frac{7}{10} = \frac{14}{20}$$

$7:10 = 14:20$

means

extremes

Extremes are 7 and 20. Means are 10 and 14.

EXAMPLE 5 Solve the proportion $\frac{3}{4} = \frac{x}{16}$.

Multiply each side by the product of the denominators: $4 \cdot 16 = 64$.

$$\overset{16}{64} \cdot \frac{3}{\underset{1}{4}} = \frac{x}{\underset{1}{16}} \cdot \overset{4}{64}$$

$$3 \cdot 16 = 4 \cdot x$$
$$48 = 4x$$
$$12 = x$$

$\frac{3}{4} = \frac{12}{16}.$ ⟶ **Thus,** the solution is 12.

Example 4 suggests this. ⟶

$\left.\begin{array}{c}\frac{3}{4} = \frac{12}{16} \\ 3 \cdot 16 = 4 \cdot 12\end{array}\right\}$

In a proportion $\quad \frac{a}{b} = \frac{c}{d}$,

$$ad = bc$$

product of extremes = product of means

EXAMPLE 6 Solve the proportion $\frac{x}{3} = \frac{2}{5}$.

$\frac{a}{b} = \frac{c}{d}$ ⟶

$a \cdot d = b \cdot c$ ⟶

$$\frac{x}{3} = \frac{2}{5}$$
$$x \cdot 5 = 3 \cdot 2$$
$$5x = 6$$

Thus, $x = \frac{6}{5}$ and the solution is $\frac{6}{5}$, or $1\frac{1}{5}$.

EXAMPLE 7 Solve $\dfrac{x-5}{7}=\dfrac{3}{5}$.

Use
prod. of extremes = prod. of means.
$5(x-5)=5 \cdot x + 5 \cdot -5$, or $5x-25$

$$5(x-5)=7 \cdot 3$$
$$5x - 25 = 21$$
$$5x = 46$$

Divide each side by 5.

Thus, $x=\dfrac{46}{5}$ and the solution is $\dfrac{46}{5}$, or $9\dfrac{1}{5}$.

EXAMPLE 8 If one out of five people use Cavity Toothpaste, how many people can be expected to use this brand in a city of 30,000 population?

Let $t=$ number of people using Cavity

Write a proportion by setting the ratios equal.

$$\dfrac{t}{30,000}=\dfrac{\text{Cavity users}}{\text{total population}}$$

1 out of $5 = \dfrac{1}{5}$ ⟶

But, $\dfrac{1}{5}=\dfrac{\text{Cavity users}}{\text{total population}}$

$$\dfrac{t}{30,000}=\dfrac{1}{5}$$

$t \cdot 5 = 30,000 \cdot 1$ ⟶
$$5t = 30,000$$
$$t = 6,000$$

Thus, 6,000 people use Cavity Toothpaste.

EXAMPLE 9 Solve $\dfrac{m}{3}=\dfrac{2}{m+5}$.

Prod. of extremes = prod. of means.
$m(m+5)=m^2+5m$ ⟶
Add -6 to each side. ⟶
Factor. ⟶
Set each factor equal to 0. ⟶
$m=-6$ or $m=1$ ⟶

$$m(m+5)=3 \cdot 2$$
$$m^2+5m=6$$
$$m^2+5m-6=0$$
$$(m+6)(m-1)=0$$
$$m+6=0 \quad \text{or} \quad m-1=0$$

Thus, the solutions are -6 and 1.

ORAL EXERCISES

Identify the means and extremes of each proportion.

1. $\dfrac{3}{5}=\dfrac{6}{10}$

2. $7:14=21:42$

3. $\dfrac{a}{b}=\dfrac{m}{n}$

4. $\dfrac{3}{5}=\dfrac{x}{4}$

5. $2:5=7:5a$

6. $\dfrac{5}{9}=\dfrac{2m}{3}$

7. $\dfrac{3m}{2b}=\dfrac{7x}{5y}$

8. $x:b=2y:t$

EXERCISES

Solve.

1. $\dfrac{5}{3} = \dfrac{a}{2}$

2. $\dfrac{3}{10} = \dfrac{x}{4}$

3. $\dfrac{7}{14} = \dfrac{m}{21}$

4. $\dfrac{2}{m} = \dfrac{3}{7}$

5. $\dfrac{3}{x} = \dfrac{7}{x+5}$

6. $\dfrac{m+4}{2} = \dfrac{m-3}{5}$

7. $\dfrac{a+3}{5} = \dfrac{14}{10}$

8. $\dfrac{x-2}{3} = \dfrac{2x+7}{5}$

9. $\dfrac{5}{2m+5} = \dfrac{2}{4m-1}$

10. In Centerville, 3 out of 5 people belong to a union. How many union members can we find if the population is 70,000?

11. Pat's batting average is .385 (385 : 1,000). How many hits should Pat get in 6,000 times at bat?

12. One out of 4 people earns less than $2,000 per year. How many people in a city of 40,000 earn less than $2,000 per year?

13. Four out of 5 freshmen study algebra. How many study algebra in a freshman class of 400?

Solve.

14. $\dfrac{4}{x} = \dfrac{x}{9}$

15. $\dfrac{a}{2} = \dfrac{32}{a}$

16. $\dfrac{x}{2} = \dfrac{2}{x+3}$

17. $\dfrac{y-4}{1} = \dfrac{2}{y-3}$

PART B

EXAMPLE Find two numbers in the ratio 2:3 whose sum is 15.

$\dfrac{2x}{3x} = \dfrac{\overset{1}{\cancel{2x}}}{\underset{1}{\cancel{3x}}} = \dfrac{2}{3}$ $\longrightarrow$

Let $2x =$ one of the numbers
$3x =$ the other number
$$2x + 3x = 15$$
$$5x = 15$$
$$x = 3$$

Check: $\dfrac{6}{9} = \dfrac{2}{3}$ and $6 + 9 = 15.$

Thus, first number, $2x$, is $2 \cdot 3$, or 6
and second number, $3x$, is $3 \cdot 3$, or 9.

18. Find two numbers whose ratio is 3:5 and whose sum is 24.

19. Find two numbers whose ratio is 3:8 and whose sum is 33.

PART C

20. Find three numbers whose ratio is 2:3:5 and whose sum is 30.

21. Find two numbers whose ratio is 7:3 and whose difference is 28.

Equation of a Line

OBJECTIVES
- To write an equation of a line given two points on it
- To show that a point lies on a line if an equation of the line is given

Find the slope of $\overleftrightarrow{PQ}$.
$$P(3,4),\ Q(7,9)$$

$$\text{Slope of } \overleftrightarrow{PQ} = \frac{9-4}{7-3}$$

$$= \frac{5}{4}$$

Given two points, only one line can be drawn through them.

The line through the points $R(-2,-7)$ and $S(3,8)$ is shown. $G(x,y)$ represents any other point on the same line.

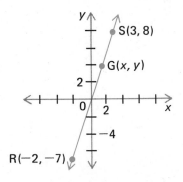

(x, y) represents the coordinates of a general point (G) on the line.

$\overleftrightarrow{RS}$, $\overleftrightarrow{RG}$, and $\overleftrightarrow{SG}$ are different names for the same line. The slope of the line is the slope of any segment on it.

EXAMPLE 1 Write an equation of the line through $R(-2,-7)$ and $S(3,8)$.

$$\text{Slope} = \frac{\text{diff. of } y\text{-coordinates}}{\text{diff. of } x\text{-coordinates}}$$

$$\text{Slope of } \overline{RS} = \frac{8-(-7)}{3-(-2)} = \frac{8+7}{3+2} = \frac{15}{5} = \frac{3}{1}.$$

We could have found slope of $\overline{GR}$ instead.

$$\text{Slope of } \overline{SG} = \frac{y-8}{x-3}.$$

R, S, and G are on the same line. ⟶ But, slope of $\overline{SG} =$ slope of $\overline{RS}$.

Set the two slopes equal. ⟶ **Thus,** $\dfrac{y-8}{x-3} = \dfrac{3}{1}$ is an equation of the line.

EXAMPLE 2   Solve the equation $\dfrac{y-8}{x-3}=\dfrac{3}{1}$ for y (from Example 1).

The equation is a proportion.

$$\dfrac{y-8}{x-3}=\dfrac{3}{1}$$

Prod. of extremes = prod. of means. $\longrightarrow$ $1(y-8)=3(x-3)$

$3(x-3)=3x-9$ $\longrightarrow$ $y-8=3x-9$

Add 8 to each side. $\longrightarrow$ $y=3x-1$

An equation of the line in Example 1 is $y=3x-1$. It describes every point on the line.

EXAMPLE 3   Show that the point $P(-5,-16)$ lies on the line $\overleftrightarrow{RS}$ in Example 1.

To show that a point is on a line, we show that its coordinates satisfy an equation of the line.

Substitute in the equation.

Let $\begin{aligned}x &=-5 \\ y &=-16\end{aligned}\Big\}$

y	$3x-1$
-16	$3(-5)-1$
	$-15-1$
	-16

Thus, $P(-5,-16)$ lies on $\overleftrightarrow{RS}$.

EXAMPLE 4   Write an equation for $\overleftrightarrow{PQ}$ given $P(-1,4)$ and $Q(2,-5)$.

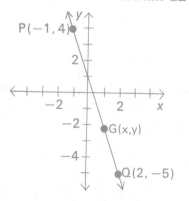

Let $G(x,y)$ represent any point on the line.

$$\text{Slope of } \overline{PG} = \text{Slope of } \overline{QP}$$

$$\dfrac{y-4}{x-(-1)} = \dfrac{4-(-5)}{-1-2}$$

$$\dfrac{y-4}{x+1} = \dfrac{9}{-3}$$

Solve the proportion.

$-3(y-4)=-3y+12$ $\longrightarrow$ $-3(y-4)=9(x+1)$

$-3y+12=9x+9$

$\underline{-12-12}$

$-3y=9x-3$

$y=\dfrac{9x-3}{-3}$

Divide each side by -3. $\longrightarrow$

$\dfrac{9x-3}{-3}=\dfrac{9}{-3}x+\dfrac{-3}{-3}$ $\longrightarrow$ $y=-3x+1$

Thus, an equation of $\overleftrightarrow{PQ}$ is $y=-3x+1$.

EXAMPLE 5   Show that $R(5,-14)$ is on $\overleftrightarrow{PQ}$ of Example 4.

See if the coordinates of R
satisfy an equation of $\overleftrightarrow{PQ}$.

Let $\left.\begin{array}{l} x=5 \\ y=-14 \end{array}\right\}$

y	$-3x+1$
-14	$-3(5)+1$
	$-15+1$
	-14

Thus, $R(5,-14)$ is on $\overleftrightarrow{PQ}$.

ORAL EXERCISES

Give an expression for the slope of $\overleftrightarrow{PG}$.

1. $P(1,3)$, $G(x,y)$

2. $P(4,3)$, $G(x,y)$

3. $P(-3,1)$, $G(x,y)$

4. $P(-3,-5)$, $G(x,y)$

5. $P(1,-2)$, $G(x,y)$

6. $P(-1,-1)$, $G(x,y)$

EXERCISES

PART A

Write an equation for $\overleftrightarrow{PQ}$.

1. $P(1,1)$, $Q(2,3)$

2. $P(1,5)$, $Q(3,11)$

3. $P(3,1)$, $Q(4,3)$

4. $P(2,-1)$, $Q(5,2)$

5. $P(-1,3)$, $Q(1,5)$

6. $P(-2,-6)$, $Q(5,8)$

7. $P(-2,-10)$, $Q(1,2)$

8. $P(-1,15)$, $Q(2,6)$

9. $P(-1,0)$, $Q(3,-8)$

10. $P(-3,8)$, $Q(2,-7)$

11. $P(1,7)$, $Q(-2,-2)$

12. $P(-3,-13)$, $Q(4,1)$

13. $P(0,4)$, $Q(2,-2)$

14. $P(0,1)$, $Q(2,-9)$

15. $P(4,0)$, $Q(3,-2)$

Show that P lies on the line with the given equation.

16. $P(-1,-1)$ $y=2x+1$

17. $P(-3,1)$ $y=-2x-5$

18. $P(-3,-1)$ $y=-x-4$

PART B

Write an equation for $\overleftrightarrow{PQ}$. Show that R lies on $\overleftrightarrow{PQ}$.

19. $P(1,4)$, $Q(2,8)$, $R(3,12)$

20. $P(0,4)$, $Q(2,-2)$, $R(3,-5)$

21. $P(0,-5)$, $Q(2,1)$, $R(3,4)$

22. $P(-1,5)$, $Q(1,1)$, $R(3,-3)$

PART C

Write an equation of the line through the given point and having the given slope.

23. $P(-2,1)$; slope 2

24. $P(0,5)$; slope -3

25. $P(0,0)$; slope 1

26. $P(1,6)$; slope 0

More Difficult Equations

 REVIEW CAPSULE

Write an equation of the line through $P(2, 7)$ and $Q(4, 13)$.

Let $G(x, y)$ represent any point on the line.

Slope of $\overline{QG}$ = Slope of $\overline{PQ}$

$$\frac{y - 13}{x - 4} = \frac{13 - 7}{4 - 2}$$

$$\frac{y - 13}{x - 4} = \frac{6}{2}$$

$$2(y - 13) = 6(x - 4)$$

$$2y - 26 = 6x - 24$$

$$y = 3x + 1$$

EXAMPLE 1 Write an equation for $\overleftrightarrow{AB}$ given $A(1, -1)$ and $B(7, 3)$.

$G(x, y)$ represents any point on the line. ⟶

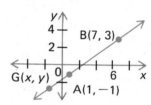

Slope of $\overline{BG}$ = Slope of $\overline{AB}$

$$\frac{y - 3}{x - 7} = \frac{3 - (-1)}{7 - 1}$$

$3 - (-1) = 3 + (-1)(-1) = 3 + 1$

$$\frac{y - 3}{x - 7} = \frac{4}{6}$$

Prod. of extremes = prod. of means. ⟶

Use the distributive property. ⟶

Add 18 to each side. ⟶

$$6(y - 3) = 4(x - 7)$$

$$6y - 18 = 4x - 28$$

$$6y = 4x - 10$$

Divide each side by 6. ⟶

$$y = \frac{4x - 10}{6}$$

$$y = \frac{4}{6}x - \frac{10}{6}$$

Rewrite each fraction in simplest form. ⟶

$$y = \frac{2}{3}x - \frac{5}{3}$$

EXAMPLE 2 Write an equation for $\overleftrightarrow{AB}$ given $A(3, 3)$ and $B(0, 5)$.

Let $G(x, y)$ represent any point on the line.
Slope of $\overline{AG}$ = Slope of $\overline{AB}$

Find the slope of each segment. ———→
$$\frac{y - 3}{x - 3} = \frac{5 - 3}{0 - 3}$$

$$\frac{y - 3}{x - 3} = \frac{2}{-3}$$

Prod. of means = prod. of extremes ———→
$$-3(y - 3) = 2(x - 3)$$
$$-3y + 9 = 2x - 6$$

Add -9 to each side. ———→
$$-3y = 2x - 15$$

Divide each side by -3. ———→
$$y = \frac{2x - 15}{-3}$$

$\dfrac{2x - 15}{-3} = \dfrac{2}{-3}x + \dfrac{-15}{-3}$ ———→
$$y = -\frac{2}{3}x + 5$$

EXAMPLE 3 $C(6, y)$ lies on $\overleftrightarrow{AB}$ of Example 2. Find y.

Use the equation of $\overleftrightarrow{AB}$.
$$y = -\frac{2}{3}x + 5$$

$C(6, y)$

↑
x

Let $x = 6$ in the equation. ———→
$$y = -\frac{2}{3}(6) + 5$$

$\left.\begin{array}{l} -\dfrac{2}{3}(6) = \dfrac{-2}{3} \cdot \dfrac{6}{1} \\[2mm] \quad = \dfrac{-2 \cdot \overset{1}{\cancel{3}} \cdot 2}{\underset{1}{\cancel{3}} \cdot 1} = -4 \end{array}\right\}$

$$y = -4 + 5$$
$$y = 1$$

The point $C(6, 1)$ lies on $\overleftrightarrow{AB}$.

Check by drawing the line joining
$A(3, 3)$ and $B(0, 5)$.

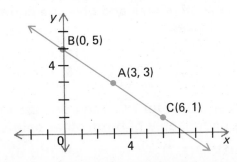

ORAL EXERCISES
Rename each.

1. $\dfrac{3x - 5}{2}$

2. $\dfrac{-2x + 5}{7}$

3. $\dfrac{4x - 8}{5}$

4. $\dfrac{-3x + 5}{2}$

EXERCISES

PART A

Write an equation for $\overleftrightarrow{PQ}$.

1. $P(1, 2)$, $Q(3, 5)$ **2.** $P(3, 5)$, $Q(8, 7)$ **3.** $P(2, 5)$, $Q(6, 6)$
4. $P(0, 5)$, $Q(4, 6)$ **5.** $P(3, 3)$, $Q(-2, 5)$ **6.** $P(-2, -3)$, $Q(-7, -5)$
7. $P(-2, 0)$, $Q(3, 4)$ **8.** $P(0, 8)$, $Q(3, 0)$ **9.** $P(-2, 0)$, $Q(0, 5)$

Write an equation for $\overleftrightarrow{AB}$. Then use the equation to find the y-coordinate of point C on $\overleftrightarrow{AB}$.

10. $A(0, 2)$, $B(-4, -1)$, $C(4, y)$ **11.** $A(-3, -5)$, $B(3, -1)$, $C(6, y)$
12. $A(0, 1)$, $B(-3, -1)$, $C(-6, y)$ **13.** $A(2, 5)$, $B(6, 11)$, $C(-2, y)$

PART B

EXAMPLE   An equation of $\overleftrightarrow{MN}$ is $y = 3x - 2$. Write a table of values and give the coordinates of three points on the line.

Choose any three numbers for x.
Use numbers that will make the
arithmetic easy.

x	$3x - 2$	y
1	$3(1) - 2$	1
0	$3(0) - 2$	-2
-1	$3(-1) - 2$	-5

Thus, $(1, 1)$, $(0, -2)$, and $(-1, -5)$ are three points on $\overleftrightarrow{MN}$.

Write a table of values and give the coordinates of three points on the line whose equation is given.

14. $y = x + 1$ **15.** $y = 2x - 3$ **16.** $y = -3x + 4$
17. $y = \frac{1}{2}x - 2$ **18.** $y = \frac{2}{3}x + 3$ **19.** $y = -\frac{1}{4}x - 1$

Write an equation for $\overleftrightarrow{PQ}$. Then use the equation to set up a table of values and give the coordinates of three other points on the line.

20. $P(0, 1)$, $Q(2, 7)$ **21.** $P(6, 8)$, $Q(12, 11)$ **22.** $P(-9, -11)$, $Q(15, 5)$
23. $P(0, -6)$, $Q(10, -1)$ **24.** $P(-16, 10)$, $Q(0, 6)$ **25.** $P(0, 1)$, $Q(12, 9)$

PART C

Find the value of b so that the given point lies on the line.

26. $y = bx - 3$; $(3, -1)$ **27.** $y = bx + 1$; $(4, -1)$
28. $y = bx + 4$; $(10, 8)$ **29.** $y = bx - \frac{1}{2}$; $(12, -2)$

Ratio and Proportion Applied to Travel

In recent years we have become concerned with two problems in travel: the rising costs of fuel and the increasing shortage of fuel. These problems have caused the automobile industry to produce cars that will average more kilometers per liter of gas.

PROBLEM

Anita's car averages 15 km/L. How many liters of gas will she need for a 500-km trip? How much will the gas cost if gas sells at $.20/L?

Let n = number of liters of gas needed

Write the ratio: total km to total L.

$$\frac{500}{n} = \frac{\text{number of km}}{\text{number of liters of gas}}$$

Write 15 km/L as a ratio. ⟶

$$\frac{15}{1} = \frac{\text{number of km}}{\text{number of liters of gas}}$$

Set the ratios equal. ⟶

$$\frac{500}{n} = \frac{15}{1}$$

If $\frac{a}{b} = \frac{c}{d}$, then $ad = bc$. ⟶ $15n = 500$

Divide each side by 15. ⟶ $n = 33\frac{1}{3}$

For practicality, round off to the next whole number. She needs 34L of gas.

Find the cost. ⟶ Cost = (.20) (34) = 6.80

Thus, the trip will cost $6.80.

 PROJECT

1. A sales representative's car averages 12 km/L. How much will the gas for a 1,000-km trip cost if gas sells at $.25/L?

2. An insurance agent travels 70,000 km in a year. The car averages 10 km/L. Find the agent's yearly gas expense if gas sells at $.22/L.

$y = mx + b$

  REVIEW CAPSULE

Write an equation of the line passing through points $P(5, 6)$ and $Q(10, 4)$.

Let $G(x, y)$ represent any point on the line.
Slope of $\overline{QG}$ = Slope of $\overline{PQ}$

$$\frac{y - 4}{x - 10} = \frac{4 - 6}{10 - 5}$$

$$\frac{y - 4}{x - 10} = \frac{-2}{5}$$

$$5y - 20 = -2x + 20$$

$$5y = -2x + 40$$

$$y = -\frac{2}{5}x + 8$$

Notice this pattern from the Review Capsule.

$$\text{Slope of } \overleftrightarrow{PQ} = -\frac{2}{5}$$

$$\text{Equation of } \overleftrightarrow{PQ} \text{ is } y = -\frac{2}{5}x + 8.$$

The slope is the coefficient of x.

EXAMPLE 1   Give the slope of each line.

The slope is the coefficient of x.

$$y = \frac{4}{7}x - 3$$

Slope is $\frac{4}{7}$.

$$y = -\frac{3}{5}x + 8$$

Slope is $-\frac{3}{5}$.

Graphing $\overleftrightarrow{PQ}$ reveals another pattern.

The x-coordinate of any point on the y-axis is 0.

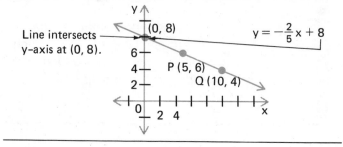

Line intersects y-axis at (0, 8).

$y = -\frac{2}{5}x + 8$

The *y*-coordinate of the point of intersection of a line with the *y*-axis is the *y*-intercept.

EXAMPLE 2   Find the *y*-intercept.

$$y = \frac{4}{7}x - 3 \qquad\qquad y = -\frac{3}{5}x + 8$$

$$y = \frac{4}{7}x - 3$$

$$y = \frac{4}{7}(0) - 3$$

$$y = -3$$

$$y = -\frac{3}{5}x + 8$$

$$y = -\frac{3}{5}(0) + 8$$

$$y = 8$$

Let *x* = 0 to find *y*.

Examples 1 and 2 suggest this.

If $y = mx + b$ is an equation of a line, then
slope is *m*   and   *y*-intercept is *b*.

EXAMPLE 3   Give the slope and the *y*-intercept.

$$y = \frac{4}{5}x - 12$$

The line crosses the *y*-axis at $(0, -12)$.

Slope is $\frac{4}{5}$.   *y*-intercept is -12.

EXAMPLE 4   Write an equation for the line whose slope is *m* and whose *y*-intercept is *b*.

b is the *y*-intercept, *x* = 0.

The slope of a line is the slope of any segment on it.

$P(0, b)$ is a point on the line.
Let $G(x, y)$ represent any point on the line.
Slope of $\overline{PG} = m$

$$\frac{y - b}{x - 0} = \frac{m}{1}$$

Prod. of extremes = prod. of means.

Get *y* alone on one side. }
Add *b* to each side. }

$$1(y - b) = mx$$
$$y - b = mx$$
$$y = mx + b$$

A line with slope *m* and *y*-intercept *b* has equation $y = mx + b$.

EXAMPLE 5 Write an equation for the line whose slope is −5 and whose y-intercept is −3.

m is the slope.
b is the y-intercept.

$$m = -5 \quad b = -3$$
$$y = mx + b$$

Thus, $y = -5x - 3$ is the equation.

EXAMPLE 6 Graph $y = \frac{2}{3}x + 1$.

The y-intercept is 1. ───────────⟶ Plot $P(0, 1)$.

Use the slope to locate another point Q.

Slope $= \dfrac{2}{3}$ ⟵ up 2
⟵ right 3

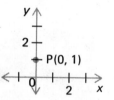

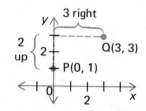

Connect P and Q.

Graph of $y = \frac{2}{3}x + 1$ ───────────⟶

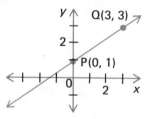

Read: the set of points (x, y) such ──⟶ The graph shows $\left\{(x, y) \mid y = \frac{2}{3}x + 1\right\}$.
that $y = \frac{2}{3}x + 1$.

Each point on a line satisfies its equation.
See the graph. ───────────⟶ For example, $(-3, -1)$ is on $\overleftrightarrow{PQ}$,

y	$\frac{2}{3}x + 1$
−1	$\frac{2}{3}(-3) + 1$
	$-2 + 1$
	-1

Plot (0, 1), (3, 3), and (−3, −1)
to check that all three points are on
the same line.

since $(-3, -1)$ satisfies the equation.

EXAMPLE 7   Graph $\left\{(x,y) \mid y = -\dfrac{2}{5}x + 3\right\}$.

Rewrite $-\dfrac{2}{5}$ as $\dfrac{-2}{5}$. ⟶

$$y = \dfrac{-2}{5}x + 3$$

slope   y-intercept

The y-intercept is 3. ⟶   Plot $(0, 3)$.
Then use the slope.   Draw $\overleftrightarrow{PQ}$.

Slope $= \dfrac{-2}{5}$ ⟵ down 2
                         ⟵ right 5

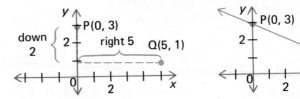
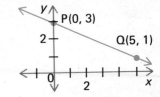

EXERCISES

PART A

Give the slope and y-intercept.

1. $y = \frac{1}{2}x - 7$ **2.** $y = \frac{2}{3}x + 4$ **3.** $y = -\frac{4}{5}x + 7$ **4.** $y = 2x$

Write an equation for the line.

5. slope $= 2$
   y-intercept $= 4$

6. slope $= -3$
   y-intercept $= -5$

7. slope $= 5$
   y-intercept $= 0$

Graph.

8. $y = \frac{2}{3}x + 1$ **9.** $y = -\frac{3}{4}x + 2$ **10.** $y = -\frac{2}{5}x - 4$
11. $y = 3x + 1$ (Hint: Write the slope as $\frac{3}{1}$.) **12.** $y = 4x - 3$
13. $y = -2x + 4$ **14.** $y = -3x - 1$ **15.** $y = -4x + 5$
16. $\{(x,y) \mid y = \frac{2}{3}x + 6\}$ **17.** $\{(x,y) \mid y = -\frac{5}{3}x + 2\}$ **18.** $\{(x,y) \mid y = \frac{3}{4}x - 2\}$

PART B

Graph.

19. $y = 2x$ (Hint: Crosses y-axis at $(0, 0)$.) **20.** $y = 3x$ **21.** $y = -3x$

PART C

Graph. [Hint: Parallel lines have the same slope.]

22. The line with y-intercept 3
and parallel to $y = \frac{2}{3}x + 5$.

23. The line with y-intercept -2
and parallel to $y = -\frac{4}{5}x + 8$.

$y = mx + b$ **275**

Graphing A Line

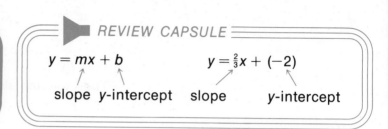

REVIEW CAPSULE

$y = mx + b$ $y = \frac{2}{3}x + (-2)$

slope y-intercept   slope   y-intercept

EXAMPLE 1   Give the slope and y-intercept of $3x - 2y = 10$.

Put the equation in $y = mx + b$ form.

Get y alone on one side.
Add $-3x$ to each side.
Divide each side by -2.

$\dfrac{-3x + 10}{-2} = \dfrac{-3}{-2}x + \dfrac{10}{-2}$ ─────────→

Solve for y.

$$3x - 2y = \qquad 10$$
$$\underline{-3x \qquad\qquad -3x}$$
$$-2y = -3x + 10$$
$$y = \dfrac{-3x + 10}{-2}$$

$$y = \dfrac{3}{2}x - 5$$

Thus, the slope is $\frac{3}{2}$ and the y-intercept is -5.

EXAMPLE 2   Graph $\{(x, y) \mid -y - x = 2\}$.

$$-1y - 1x = \qquad 2$$
$$\underline{\qquad + 1x \quad +1x}$$
$$-1y \qquad = +1x + 2$$
$$1y \qquad = -1x - 2$$
$$y \qquad = -\dfrac{1}{1}x - 2$$

Slope is $-\frac{1}{1}$; y-intercept is -2.

Plot $(0, -2)$.
Then use the slope.   Draw $\overleftrightarrow{PQ}$.

$\text{Slope} = \dfrac{-1}{1} \begin{array}{l} \leftarrow \text{down 1} \\ \leftarrow \text{right 1} \end{array}$

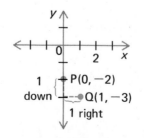

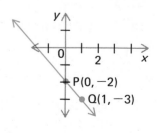

EXAMPLE 3 Graph $x + 3y = 0$.

Solve for y.
Add $-1x$ to each side.
Divide each side by 3.

$$1x + 3y = 0$$
$$3y = -1x$$
$$y = \tfrac{-1}{3}x, \text{ or } y = \tfrac{-1}{3}x + 0$$

Slope is $\tfrac{-1}{3}$. y-intercept is 0.

Since the y-intercept is 0, the line passes through the origin. $\longrightarrow$ Plot $(0, 0)$.
Then use the slope.

Draw $\overleftrightarrow{PQ}$.

$$\text{Slope} = \frac{-1}{3} \quad \begin{array}{l} \longleftarrow \text{ down 1} \\ \longleftarrow \text{ right 3} \end{array}$$

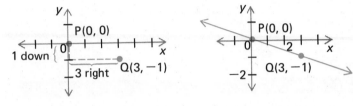

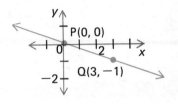

EXAMPLE 4 Graph $\{(x, y) \mid y = -2\}$.

Rewrite: $0x = 0 \cdot x = 0$ $\longrightarrow$

$$y = 0x - 2$$
$$y = \frac{0}{1}x - 2$$

Slope is $\tfrac{0}{1}$ y-intercept is -2.

Plot $(0, -2)$.
Then use the slope.

Draw $\overleftrightarrow{PQ}$.

$$\text{Slope} = \frac{0}{1} \quad \begin{array}{l} \longleftarrow \text{ neither up nor down} \\ \longleftarrow \text{ right 1} \end{array}$$

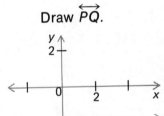

A horizontal line has 0 slope. $\longrightarrow$ $\overleftrightarrow{PQ}$ is a horizontal line.

$y = -2$ represents a horizontal line.
$P(0, -2)$ $Q(1, -2)$

Same y-coordinate

Instead of the method shown in Example 4, we can graph a horizontal line like this.

First plot the y-intercept.
Then plot any other point with the same y-coordinate and draw the line through these points.

EXAMPLE 5   Graph $3y - 9 = 0$.

Solve for y.
Add 9 to each side.
Divide each side by 3.

$$3y - 9 = 0$$
$$3y = 9$$
$$y = 3, \text{ or } y = 0x + 3$$

The y-intercept is 3. ⟶ Plot $P(0, 3)$.

Then, use any other point with y-coordinate 3 like $Q(4, 3)$.

Draw the horizontal line. ⟶

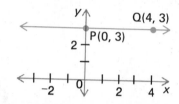

EXERCISES

PART A

Graph.

1. $3x - 2y = 3$
4. $y - 1 = x$

2. $4y + 3x = 8$
5. $y = 6$

3. $5y + 2x = -10$
6. $2y + 6 = 0$

Graph.

7. $\{(x, y) \mid 3y - 2x = 12\}$
10. $\{(x, y) \mid y = 4\}$

8. $\{(x, y) \mid y - 2x = 0\}$
11. $\{(x, y) \mid 2y - 5x = 10\}$

9. $\{(x, y) \mid 4x + 2y = 8\}$
12. $\{(x, y) \mid x + y = 2\}$

PART B

EXAMPLE   Graph $y = 2x - 1$. Use a table of values.

Choose any 3 numbers for x.
Find the y-coordinates.
Plot the 3 points.
Draw the line.

x	$2x - 1$	y
1	$2(1) - 1$	1
0	$2(0) - 1$	-1
-1	$2(-1) - 1$	-3

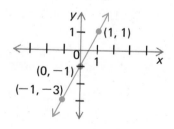

Graph. Use a table of values.

13. $y = x + 3$
16. $2x + y = 1$

14. $y = -3x + 1$
17. $2x - 3y = 4$

15. $y = -2x$
18. $6x - y = 1$

Vertical Lines

▶ REVIEW CAPSULE

Find the slope of $\overleftrightarrow{PQ}$ for $P(3, 2)$, $Q(3, -1)$.

$$\text{Slope of } \overleftrightarrow{PQ} = \frac{2 - (-1)}{3 - 3}$$

$$= \frac{3}{0} \leftarrow \begin{array}{l}\text{Division by 0}\\ \text{is undefined.}\end{array}$$

Thus, the slope of $\overleftrightarrow{PQ}$ is undefined.

EXAMPLE 1 Graph $\overleftrightarrow{PQ}$ for $P(3, 2)$, $Q(3, -1)$. Identify the slope and the y-intercept.

See the Review Capsule. ⟶ The slope of $\overleftrightarrow{PQ}$ is undefined.

It does not cross the y-axis. ⟶ $\overleftrightarrow{PQ}$ has no y-intercept.
It is parallel to the y-axis.

$\overleftrightarrow{PQ}$ in Example 1 is a vertical line.
A vertical line does not have an equation of the form.

$$y = mx + b.$$

A vertical line (other than the y-axis) has no y-intercept.

undefined slope ⟶ ⟵ no y-intercept

EXAMPLE 2 Write an equation for $\overleftrightarrow{PQ}$ in Example 1.

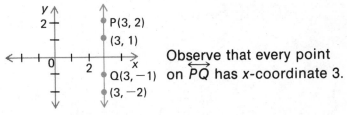

$\overleftrightarrow{PQ}$ is parallel to the y-axis and 3 units to the right of the y-axis.

Observe that every point on $\overleftrightarrow{PQ}$ has x-coordinate 3.

$\overleftrightarrow{PQ}$ is the set of all points (x, y) such that $x = 3$.
$$\{(x, y) \mid x = 3\}$$

y is not mentioned in the equation. It can be any number. But x is always 3. ⟶ **Thus,** an equation is $x = 3$.

EXAMPLE 3   Graph $\{(x, y) \mid x = -6\}$.

y is not mentioned in $x = -6$. ⟶ The graph is a vertical line.

y is any number. x is -6. ⟶ The line is the set of all points with x-coordinate -6.

Use any two points with x-coordinate -6 to graph.
For example, $P(-6, 0)$ and $Q(-6, 2)$.

Draw a line through the points P and Q.

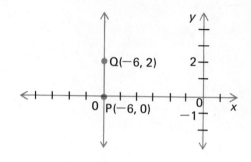

EXAMPLE 4   Graph $x = 5$.

y is not mentioned in $x = 5$.
The graph is a vertical line.

The line will be the set of all points whose x-coordinate is 5.

y can be any number.
x is always 5.

Use any two points with x-coordinate 5 like $P(5, 2)$ and $Q(5, -1)$ to draw the graph.

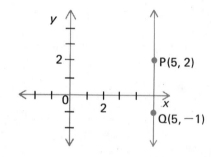

EXERCISES

PART A

Graph.

1. $x = -2$
2. $x = 1$
3. $x = -3$
4. $x = 9$
5. $\{(x, y) \mid x = 3\}$
6. $\{(x, y) \mid x = -4\}$
7. $\{(x, y) \mid x = 7\}$
8. $\{(x, y) \mid 8 = x\}$

PART B

Graph. (Hint: Solve for x.)

9. $\{(x, y) \mid 3x - 9 = 0\}$
10. $\{(x, y) \mid 8 + 2x = 0\}$
11. $\{(x, y) \mid 6 - x = 0\}$

Graphing Inequalities in Two Variables

REVIEW CAPSULE

Inequalities in one variable can be graphed on a number line.

$$-2x + 4 \leq 10$$

Add -4 to each side. ⟶ $-2x \leq 6$
Divide each side by -2.
Reverse the order. ⟶ $x \geq -3$

Graph. ⟶

EXAMPLE 1   Graph $y < 2$ on a plane.

First graph $y = 2$ with a dashed line.

Graph of $y = 2$ is a horizontal line. The
y-coordinate of every point is 2.

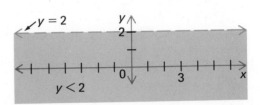

The y-coordinate of every point below
the line is less than 2. ⟶   The graph of $y < 2$ is *below* the line. The shaded
region is the graph of $y < 2$.

EXAMPLE 2   Graph $y > 2$ on a plane.

First graph $y = 2$ with a dashed line.

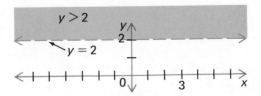

The y-coordinate of every point above
the line is greater than 2.

The graph of $y > 2$ is the shaded region *above*
the line.

EXAMPLE 3 Graph $y = 2x - 1$ with a dashed line. Show that $(-2, 1)$ satisfies the inequality $y > 2x - 1$. Show that $(3, -4)$ satisfies the inequality $y < 2x - 1$.

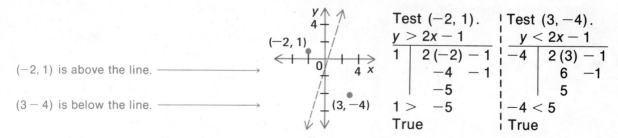

$(-2, 1)$ is above the line. ⟶

$(3 - 4)$ is below the line. ⟶

Test $(-2, 1)$.

$$y > 2x - 1$$

1	$2(-2) - 1$
	$-4 \quad - 1$
	-5
$1 >$	-5

True

Test $(3, -4)$.

$$y < 2x - 1$$

-4	$2(3) - 1$
	$6 \quad -1$
	5
$-4 < 5$	

True

Example 3 suggests this. ⟶

The graph of $y = mx + b$ is a line.
The graph of $y > mx + b$ is the region *above* the line.
The graph of $y < mx + b$ is the region *below* the line.

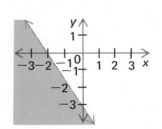

EXAMPLE 4 Graph $-3x - 2y > 6$.

Solve for y.
Add $3x$ to each side. ⟶
Divide each side by -2.⎫
Reverse the order. ⎭

$$-3x - 2y > 6$$
$$-2y > 3x + 6$$
$$y < \frac{3x + 6}{-2}$$
$$y < -\frac{3}{2}x - 3$$

Graph $y = -\frac{3}{2}x - 3$ with a dashed line.

$$y = -\frac{3}{2}x - 3$$

slope $-\frac{3}{2}$ y-intercept -3

To graph $y < -\frac{3}{2}x - 3$, shade the region

below the line. ⟶

Thus, the graph of $-3x - 2y > 6$ is the shaded region *below* the line.

EXAMPLE 5   Graph $\{(x, y) \mid y \ge 3x - 1\}$

Graph $y = 3x - 1$.

Slope $\dfrac{3}{1}$ y-intercept -1

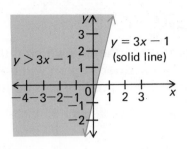

$\ge$ means is greater than or equal to. The graph must include the line $y = 3x - 1$. Draw a solid line.

Thus, the graph of $\{(x, y) \mid y \ge 3x - 1\}$ is the *line* and the shaded region *above* the line.

EXAMPLE 6   Graph $\{(x, y) \mid x > 3\}$. Then graph $\{(x, y) \mid x < 3\}$.

First graph $x = 3$ with a dashed line.

Graph of $x = 3$ is a vertical line. The x-coordinate of every point is 3.

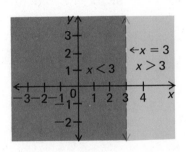

The x-coordinate of every point to the *right* of the line is *greater* than 3.

The x-coordinate of every point to the *left* of the line is less than 3.

The graph of $\{(x, y) \mid x > 3\}$ is the shaded portion to the *right* of the line.
The graph of $\{(x, y) \mid x < 3\}$ is the shaded portion to the *left* of the line.

Example 6 suggests this. ⟶

The graph of $x = a$ is a vertical line.
The graph of $x > a$ is the region to the right of the line.
The graph of $x < a$ is the region to the left of the line.

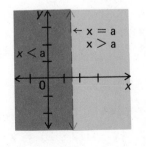

ORAL EXERCISES

Give the equation of the line which must be graphed in order to graph each inequality. Tell whether the shaded region will be above, below, to the left, or to the right of the line. Tell whether the line will be included in the graph.

1. $y \leq 3x + 2$ 2. $y > x + 5$ 3. $y \leq 4$ 4. $y < x + 3$ 5. $y \geq 2x - 1$ 6. $x \geq 5$
7. $x < 2$ 8. $y > 7$ 9. $y \leq 4x + 1$ 10. $y > x$ 11. $x \leq 3$ 12. $y < 3$

EXERCISES

PART A

Solve for y.

1. $x + y < 3$ 2. $x - y > 8$ 3. $x + 3 > -y$ 4. $2x - y \leq 4$
5. $3x + 2y > 0$ 6. $4x + y \geq 6$ 7. $-3x + y < 4$ 8. $3y < x$

Graph each inequality.

 9. $y > 3$ 10. $x < -1$ 11. $y \leq -4$ 12. $\{(x, y) \mid x \geq 2\}$
13. $y < 3x$ 14. $y > 2x$ 15. $y \leq x$ 16. $\{(x, y) \mid y \geq -2x\}$
17. $y \leq x + 5$ 18. $y \geq 2x - 3$ 19. $y < -x - 3$ 20. $\{(x, y) \mid y > 3x - 4\}$
21. $y \leq 2x + 1$ 22. $y \geq 3x - 2$ 23. $x < 0$ 24. $\{(x, y) \mid y \geq 0\}$
25. $y < \frac{2}{3}x + 1$ 26. $y \geq \frac{3}{5}x - 2$ 27. $y \leq \frac{1}{2}x + 1$ 28. $\{(x, y) \mid y > \frac{2}{3}x - 2\}$

Graph each inequality. Then determine which of the given points belong to the graph.

29. $y > 1$; (3, 1), (3, 7)   30. $x \leq 4$; (-5, 3), (7, 3)
31. $y > x - 6$; (3, -3), (3, 8)   32. $y \geq x - 6$; (8, 2), (8, 1)
33. $y \leq 3x + 1$; (3, 11), (3, 0)   34. $y < 3x - 4$; (3, 5), (3, 2)

PART B

Graph each inequality.

35. $2y < 8$ 36. $-3x \leq 9$ 37. $3x \geq 2y$ 38. $\{(x, y) \mid -4y \geq 8\}$
39. $3x - 2y \leq 6$ 40. $2x - 3y \geq 9$ 41. $4x - 3y \geq 6$ 42. $\{(x, y) \mid 2x - 5y \geq 10\}$
43. $3x - 5y \leq 15$ 44. $3x \leq 4y + 12$ 45. $8x + 4y > 2$ 46. $\{(x, y) \mid 6x - 3y < 9\}$

PART C

Graph each.

47. $4x - 3(y - 2) \leq y - (6 - x)$ 48. $3x - (6 - 2y) > x - (4 - y)$
49. $6 < y \leq 9$ 50. $8 \leq x < 10$

Diophantus

HERE YOU SEE THE TOMB CONTAINING
THE REMAINS OF DIOPHANTUS. ONE SIXTH
OF HIS LIFE GOD GRANTED HIM YOUTH. AFTER
A TWELFTH MORE HIS CHEEKS WERE BEARDED.
AFTER AN ADDITIONAL SEVENTH HE KINDLED
THE LIGHT OF MARRIAGE AND IN THE FIFTH
YEAR HE FATHERED A SON. ALAS THE
UNFORTUNATE SON'S LIFE SPAN WAS ONLY
HALF THAT OF HIS FATHER WHO CONSOLED
HIS GRIEF IN THE REMAINING FOUR YEARS
OF HIS LIFE. BY THIS DEVICE OF NUMBERS
TELL THE EXTENT OF HIS LIFE...

According to legend the above is the inscription on Diophantus' tomb. He was a Greek mathematician who lived in Alexandria in the 3rd century A.D. Diophantus is thought to be one of the originators of algebra. He was probably the first to use symbols for unknowns and operations. He also developed analytical approaches to solve problems. Diophantus was dedicated to algebra, as his epitaph indicates.

PROJECT Can you find how old Diophantus was when he died?

Chapter Ten Review

Identify the means and extremes. Solve. $[p.\ 261]$

1. $\dfrac{x}{6} = \dfrac{4}{3}$ **2.** $\dfrac{2}{5} = \dfrac{x}{10}$ **3.** $\dfrac{x+2}{4} = \dfrac{x-5}{3}$ **4.** $\dfrac{3}{2x-1} = \dfrac{4}{x+4}$

5. $\dfrac{2x+1}{5} = \dfrac{x}{4}$ **6.** $\dfrac{3x+1}{2} = \dfrac{4x-3}{5}$ **7.** $\dfrac{x}{9} = \dfrac{1}{x}$ **8.** $\dfrac{x+5}{4} = \dfrac{-1}{x}$

Solve. $[p.\ 261]$

9. Two out of 9 people use Gum Tooth-brushes. How many use this brand in a town of 27,000 people?

10. Lee's batting average is .675. How many hits should Lee score in 5,000 times at bat?

Write an equation for $\overleftrightarrow{PQ}$. $[p.\ 265,\ 268]$

11. $P(3, 1)$, $Q(5, 5)$ **12.** $P(0, 1)$, $Q(2, 7)$ **13.** $P(1, 4)$, $Q(3, 0)$

14. $P(1, 1)$, $Q(5, 3)$ **15.** $P(-2, 3)$, $Q(1, 4)$ **16.** $P(-3, -2)$, $Q(1, 1)$

Write an equation for $\overleftrightarrow{PQ}$. Show that R lies on $\overleftrightarrow{PQ}$. $[p.\ 265]$

17. $P(2, 4)$, $Q(3, 6)$, $R(4, 8)$ **18.** $P(1, 2)$, $Q(2, 5)$, $R(3, 8)$

Write an equation for the line. $[p.\ 272]$

19. slope $= \dfrac{2}{3}$

y-intercept $= -5$

20. slope $= -\dfrac{3}{7}$

y-intercept $= 6$

21. slope $= 3$

y-intercept $= -1$

Give the slope and y-intercept. Graph the line. $[p.\ 272,\ 276]$

22. $y = \dfrac{2}{3}x - 4$ **23.** $y = -\dfrac{4}{5}x + 2$ **24.** $y = -2x$

25. $\{(x, y) \mid y = 2x + 1\}$ **26.** $\{(x, y) \mid x - 3y = 6\}$ **27.** $\{(x, y) \mid y = -6\}$

Graph. Use a table of values. $[p.\ 276]$

28. $y = 2x - 1$ **29.** $y = x + 4$ **30.** $2x - 3y = 15$

Graph. $[p.\ 279,\ 281]$

31. $x = 3$ **32.** $x = -4$ **33.** $\{(x, y) \mid 2x + 4 = 0\}$

34. $\{(x, y) \mid y < x + 5\}$ **35.** $\{(x, y) \mid 3x - 2y > 8\}$ **36.** $\{(x, y) \mid x \geq 2\}$

Chapter Ten Test

Identify the means and extremes. Solve.

1. $\dfrac{x}{14} = \dfrac{1}{7}$

2. $\dfrac{2x+1}{3} = \dfrac{x-4}{5}$

3. $\dfrac{x+2}{6} = \dfrac{-2}{x-5}$

Solve.

4. Two out of 5 people shave with Dull Blades. How many use this brand in a town of 20,000?

5. Pat's batting average is .125. How many hits should Pat expect in 2,000 times at bat?

Write an equation for $\overleftrightarrow{PQ}$.

6. $P(4, 9)$, $Q(6, 13)$
8. $P(2, 3)$, $Q(5, 1)$

7. $P(0, 1)$, $Q(2, -3)$
9. $P(0, 2)$, $Q(5, 0)$

Write an equation for $\overleftrightarrow{PQ}$. Show that R lies on $\overleftrightarrow{PQ}$.

10. $P(3, 4)$, $Q(5, 5)$, $R(7, 6)$

11. $P(0, 3)$, $Q(2, 10)$, $R(4, 17)$

Write an equation for the line.

12. slope $= \dfrac{3}{4}$
y-intercept $= -7$

13. slope $= 2$
y-intercept $= 3$

Give the slope and y-intercept. Graph the line.

14. $y = \dfrac{2}{3}x - 4$

15. $y = -\dfrac{4}{5}x + 2$

16. $y = 8$

17. $x + y = 5$

18. $\{(x, y) \mid y = 3x + 2)\}$

19. $\{(x, y) \mid 2x - 3y = 6\}$

Graph. Use a table of values.

20. $y = 2x - 7$

21. $x - 2y = -16$

Graph.

22. $x = -2$

23. $\{(x, y) \mid x = 3\}$

24. $\{(x, y) \mid 5x + 20 = 0\}$

25. $\{(x, y) \mid y > x + 2\}$

26. $\{(x, y) \mid 4x - 3y \le 15\}$

27. $\{(x, y) \mid x < 3\}$

Linear Programming

The shaded region of the graph below is called a polygonal region. It represents the intersection of the solution of the system of inequalities listed below.

$$x \geq 0$$
$$y \geq 0$$
$$x \leq 4$$
$$x + y \leq 8$$

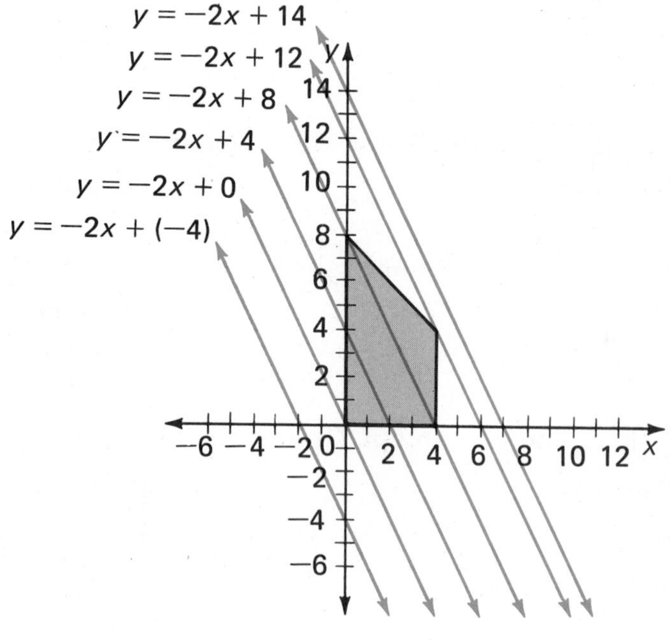

$$y = -2x + 14$$
$$y = -2x + 12$$
$$y = -2x + 8$$
$$y = -2x + 4$$
$$y = -2x + 0$$
$$y = -2x + (-4)$$

The lines are the graphs of
$y = -2x + k$ for
$k = \{-4, 0, 4, 8, 12, 14\}$.

The graphs of inequalities and equations as shown above are useful in solving problems in industry. This technique is called linear programming. The graph tells us the maximum (12) and minimum (0) values of k that the equation may use and still have a solution in the polygonal region.

PROJECT

Graph $y = -x + k$ for $k = \{-6, -3, 0, 3, 6, 9, 12\}$ and $x \geq -3$, $y \geq 0$, $x \leq 2$, $y \leq x + 5$.
Find the maximum and minimum values of k in the polygonal region.

Systems of Equations: Graphing

REVIEW CAPSULE

The intersection of two sets is the set of all elements common to both sets.

$$\{3, 4, 5, 6\} \cap \{2, 4, 5, 8\} = \{4, 5\}$$

The graph of $\{(x, y) \mid y = 3x + 2\}$ is the line whose equation is $y = 3x + 2$.

EXAMPLE 1 Graph $\{(x, y) \mid y = 3x - 9\}$ and $\{(x, y) \mid y = -4x + 5\}$ on the same set of axes.

Use the slope-intercept method to graph each line:

$$y = 3x - 9$$

slope $\dfrac{3}{1}$ y-intercept -9

$$y = -4x + 5$$

slope $\dfrac{-4}{1}$ y-intercept 5

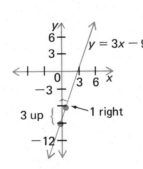

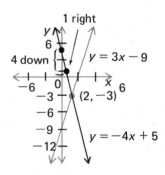

From the graph, $(2, -3)$ is a point common to both lines.

EXAMPLE 2 Find $\{(x, y) \mid y = 3x - 9\} \cap \{(x, y) \mid y = -4x + 5\}$.

Each set of points is graphed in Example 1.
$(2, -3)$ is in both sets.

Intersection is the set of points in common. ——————————→ **Thus,** $\{(2, -3)\}$ is the intersection of the two sets.

The two equations in Example 1 form a *system* of equations. ——————→

A System of Equations
$$y = 3x - 9$$
$$y = -4x + 5$$
$(2, -3)$ is a solution of the system.

$(2, -3)$ satisfies both equations. ——————→

EXAMPLE 3   Verify that $(2, -3)$ satisfies both $y = 3x - 9$ and $y = -4x + 5$ in Example 1.

$(2, -3)$ (x, y)
Let $x = 2$ and $y = -3$.

y	$3x - 9$
-3	$3(2) - 9$
	$6 - 9$
	-3

y	$-4x + 5$
-3	$-4(2) + 5$
	$-8 + 5$
	-3

Thus, $(2, -3)$ satisfies both equations.

EXAMPLE 4   Solve the system by graphing.
$$3x - 2y = 4$$
$$y = -2x + 5$$

Put $3x - 2y = 4$ in $y = mx + b$ form; solve for y.

Add $-3x$ to each side.

Divide each side by -2.

$$3x - 2y = 4$$
$$-2y = -3x + 4$$
$$y = \frac{3}{2}x - 2$$

slope   y-intercept

$y = -2x + 5$ is already in $y = mx + b$ form.

$$y = -2x + 5$$

$$y = \frac{-2}{1}x + 5$$
   slope

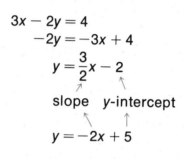

2 down
1 right
2 right
3 up

$(2, 1)$

$y = \frac{3}{2}x - 2$

$y = -2x + 5$

From the graph, find the solution.
The two lines intersect at $(2, 1)$. $\longrightarrow$ $(2, 1)$ is a solution of the system.

Check by letting $x = 2$ and $y = 1$ in each $\longrightarrow$ **Thus,** $(2, 1)$ is a solution of both $3x - 2y = 4$
equation.   and $y = -2x + 5$.

SUMMARY   To solve a system of equations by graphing:

Graph each equation on the same set of axes.

Then read the coordinates of the point of intersection from the graph.

EXERCISES

Find the intersection. Verify that its coordinates satisfy both equations.

1. $\{(x, y) \mid y = -2x + 1\} \cap \{(x, y) \mid y = \frac{1}{2}x - 4\}$
2. $\{(x, y) \mid y = \frac{1}{2}x + 6\} \cap \{(x, y) \mid y = -2x + 11\}$
3. $\{(x, y) \mid y = -2x + 4\} \cap \{(x, y) \mid y = 3x + 4\}$
4. $\{(x, y) \mid y = 3x - 6\} \cap \{(x, y) \mid y = -\frac{2}{3}x + 5\}$
5. $\{(x, y) \mid y = x + 4\} \cap \{(x, y) \mid y = -\frac{3}{2}x + 9\}$
6. $\{(x, y) \mid 3x - 2y = 4\} \cap \{(x, y) \mid 3x + 2y = 8\}$

Solve each system by graphing.

7. $y = 2x + 1$
   $y = -\frac{3}{2}x + 8$

8. $3x - 2y = 6$
   $x - y = 2$

9. $y = 2x$
   $x + y = 9$

10. $x = 3y + 6$
   $x + 3y = 6$

PART B

EXAMPLE   Find $\{(x, y) \mid y = 3x + 5\} \cap \{(x, y) \mid y = 3x - 2\}$.

The lines are parallel. They never intersect.

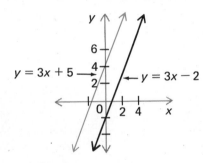

The lines have no points in common.

$y = 3x + 5$ $y = 3x - 2$

$$\{(x, y) \mid y = 3x + 5\} \cap \{(x, y) \mid y = 3x - 2\} = \phi$$

We call this an *inconsistent system.*
A *consistent system* is one which has a solution.

Determine whether each system is consistent or inconsistent.

11. $3x - 2y = 14$
   $6x - 4y = 8$

12. $x + y = 8$
   $x - y = 10$

13. $y = 3x - 2$
   $y - 3x = 4$

14. $y = 4$
   $y = -2$

PART C

For what value of *m* will the system be inconsistent?

15. $3x - 2y = 8$
   $mx - 2y = 10$

16. $5x + 2y = 4$
   $mx + 4y = 8$

17. $mx - 4y = 10$
   $5x - 2y = 4$

18. $mx + 4y = 8$
   $2x + 8y = 16$

Systems of Inequalities: Graphing

<table>
<tr><td>

OBJECTIVE

■ To solve a system of
inequalities by graphing

</td><td>

▶ REVIEW CAPSULE

Graph $y > 3x + 2$.

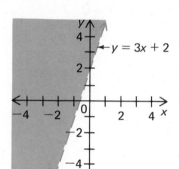

Graph $y = 3x + 2$
with a dashed line.
Then shade the
region above the
line.

Thus, the graph of
$y > 3x + 2$ is
the shaded region
above the line.

</td></tr>
</table>

EXAMPLE 1   Find $\{(x, y) \mid y \leq 3\} \cap \{(x, y) \mid x < 4\}$ by graphing.

Graph $y \leq 3$. | Graph $x < 4$ on the same set of axes.

Graph $y = 3$ with a solid line.
The y-coord. is always 3.
Shade the region below the line.

Graph $x = 4$ with a dashed line.
The x-coord. is always 4.
Shade the region to the left of
the line.
The two shadings overlap each other.

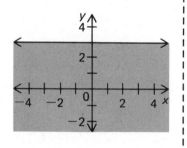   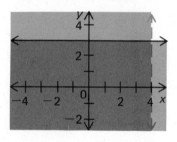

The double shaded region contains all points
common to both sets.

Thus, $\{(x, y) \mid y \leq 3\} \cap \{(x, y) \mid x < 4\}$ is the
double shaded region.

EXAMPLE 2   Verify that $(1, 2)$ satisfies both $y \leq 3$ and $x < 4$.

Test $(1, 2)$.

y	3
2	3

$2 \leq 3$

x	r
1	4

$1 < 4$

$2 \leq 3$ is true and $1 < 4$ is true.

Thus, $(1, 2)$ satisfies both $y \leq 3$ and $x < 4$.

EXAMPLE 3   Solve the system by graphing.

$$3x - 2y < 2$$
$$y < -\frac{3}{5}x - 2$$

Solve $3x - 2y < 2$ for y.

Add $-3x$ to each side. ⎯⎯⎯⎯⎯⎯⎯⎯⟶

Divide each side by -2. Reverse
the order from $<$ to $>$.

$$3x - 2y < 2$$
$$-2y < -3x + 2$$
$$y > \frac{3}{2}x - 1$$

Graph $y = \frac{3}{2}x - 1$ with a dashed line.

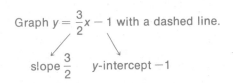

slope $\frac{3}{2}$ y-intercept -1

Shade the region above the line.

Graph $y = -\frac{3}{5}x - 2$ with a dashed line.

Shade the region below the line.

Graph $y > \frac{3}{2}x - 1$.

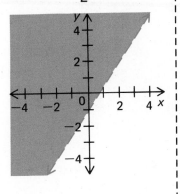

Graph $y < -\frac{3}{5}x - 2$
on the same set of
axes.

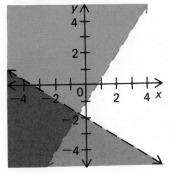

The double shaded region contains all points
common to both inequalities.

Thus, the solution of the system is the double
shaded region.

EXERCISES

Find the intersection. Pick a point in each intersection and check algebraically.

1. $\{(x, y) | x < 4\} \cap \{(x, y) | y \geq -2\}$

2. $\{(x, y) | y > x + 4\} \cap (x, y) | y < -2x - 5\}$

Solve each system by graphing.

3. $y \geq 2$
$x < -5$

4. $x < 4$
$y \geq -5$

5. $y > x + 5$
$x \leq 2$

6. $2x - y \leq 8$
$y < 6$

7. $y < x$
$y \geq \frac{2}{3}x - 5$

8. $y \leq 3x - 2$
$y > x + 4$

9. $y > 2x - 3$
$x - 3y < 9$

10. $3x - 2y \leq 8$
$x - y > 4$

Systems of Equations: Substitution

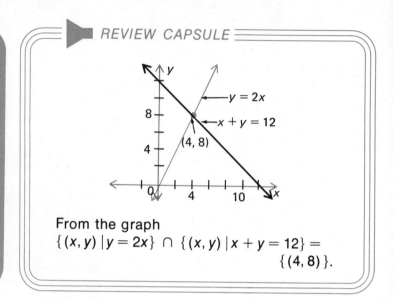

▶ REVIEW CAPSULE

From the graph
$$\{(x, y) \,|\, y = 2x\} \cap \{(x, y) \,|\, x + y = 12\} = \{(4, 8)\}.$$

EXAMPLE 1   Solve the system algebraically.
$$y = 2x$$
$$x + y = 12$$

We·want values of x and y that satisfy both equations. y must be the same in both equations.

$$y = 2x$$

$$x + y = 12$$
$$\downarrow$$

$\left\{ \begin{array}{l} \text{Substitute for } y \text{ to get an} \\ \text{equation with one variable.} \end{array} \right.$

Replace y by 2x in x + y = 12. ⟶
Solve the equation for x.

$$x + 2x = 12$$
$$3x = 12$$
$$x = 4$$

To find y, let $x = 4$ in either equation.

Replace x by 4 in one of the equations. ⟶
Solve for y.

$y = 2x$	or	$x + y = 12$
$y = 2(4)$		$4 + y = 12$
$y = 8$		$y = 8$

So, $x = 4$ and $y = 8$.

Check. ⟶
Let x = 4 and y = 8 in each equation. ⟶

y	$2x$
8	$2(4)$
	8

$x + y$	12
$4 + 8$	12
12	

Thus, $(4, 8)$ is a solution of the system.

EXAMPLE 2   Solve.

$$3x + 2y = 13$$
$$2x - y\ = 4$$

Choose a variable whose coefficient is 1 or -1. ────────────→ First solve $2x - y = 4$ for y.

$-y = -1y$ ────────────→

Add $-2x$ to each side. ────────────→

Divide each side by -1. $\dfrac{-2}{-1} = 2;$

$\dfrac{+4}{-1} = -4$

$$2x - 1y = 4$$
$$-1y = -2x + 4$$
$$y = \frac{-2x + 4}{-1}, \text{ or } \frac{-2}{-1}x + \frac{4}{-1}$$
$$y = 2x - 4$$

The other equation ────────────→

$$3x + 2y = 13$$

Replace y by $2x - 4$. ────────────→

$2(2x - 4) = 4x - 8$ ────────────→

Combine like terms. ────────────→

Add 8 to each side. ────────────→

$$3x + 2(2x - 4) = 13$$
$$3x + 4x - 8 = 13$$
$$7x - 8 = 13$$
$$\underline{\quad 8 \quad\quad 8}$$
$$7x = 21$$

Divide each side by 7. ────────────→

$$x = 3$$

Any of the equations could be used. $y = 2x - 4$ is easiest to use, since it is already solved for y.

To find y, let $x = 3$ in $y = 2x - 4$.

$$y = 2x - 4$$
$$y = 2 \cdot 3 - 4$$
$$y = 6 - 4$$
$$y = 2$$

So, $x = 3$ and $y = 2$.

Check by letting $x = 3$ and $y = 2$ in both equations. ────────────→

Thus, $(3, 2)$ is a solution of the system.

$2x - y = 4$, or
$2x - 1y = 4$
coefficient is -1

The method of substitution is easy to use when one equation contains a variable with a coefficient of 1 or -1.

SUMMARY   **To solve a system of equations by substitution:**

Solve one equation for one of its variables.

Then substitute for that variable in the other equation.

ORAL EXERCISES

Identify the variable for which it is easier to solve.

1. $2x - y = 7$
$3x + 7y = 8$

2. $3x - 4y = 6$
$x + 2y = 8$

3. $x + 3y = 9$
$2x - 5y = 6$

4. $3x - 7y = 1$
$2x - y = 4$

EXERCISES

PART A

Solve.

1. $y = 2x$
$x + y = 9$

2. $x + y = 6$
$y = x - 4$

3. $y = 2x - 5$
$x - y = 2$

4. $x + y = 7$
$y = x + 1$

5. $3x - 2y = 9$
$x + 2y = 3$

6. $2x - 3y = 8$
$x + y = 4$

7. $x - 3y = 2$
$3x - 2y = 6$

8. $x - 2y = 6$
$x + 2y = 2$

PART B

Solve.

9. $x - y = 6$
$x + y = 5$

10. $x + y = 8$
$2x - y = -6$

11. $y = 2x$
$2x + y = 10$

12. $x + y = 1$
$y = x$

PART C

EXAMPLE Solve by substitution.

$$3y = 5 - 2x$$
$$4x + 3y = 11$$

Replace $3y$ by $5 - 2x$. ⟶
Combine like terms. ⟶

$$4x + 3y = 11$$
$$4x + (5 - 2x) = 11$$
$$2x + 5 = 11$$
$$x = 3$$

Use $3y = 5 - 2x$ and find y. ⟶
Let $x = 3$. ⟶

$$3y = 5 - 2x$$
$$3y = 5 - 2 \cdot 3$$
$$y = -\tfrac{1}{3}$$

Thus, $(3, -\tfrac{1}{3})$ is a solution.

Solve.

13. $5y = x - 1$
$2x = 5y$

14. $4x = 2y - 5$
$2y - 5 + 3x = 14$

15. $2x - 5y = 2$
$5y = 3x + 1$

16. $7y = 3x - 2$
$2x + 7y = 13$

Systems of Equations: $\begin{aligned} ax + by &= c \\ dx - by &= e \end{aligned}$

OBJECTIVE

■ To solve a system of equations like
$$5x + 2y = 12$$
$$3x - 2y = 4$$
by addition

REVIEW CAPSULE

The addition property for equations

$3 + 1 = 4$	$x - 5 = 3x$	$3x = 12$
$5 + 2 = 7$	$-x = -x$	$2x = 18$
$8 + 3 = 11$	$-5 = 2x$	$5x = 30$

EXAMPLE 1 Add the equations.
$$5x + 2y = 12$$
$$3x - 2y = 4$$
Solve the resulting equation.

$$\begin{aligned} 5x + 2y &= 12 \quad \longleftarrow \text{ first equation (1)} \\ 3x - 2y &= 4 \quad \longleftarrow \text{ second equation (2)} \\ \overline{8x + 0} &= 16 \quad \longleftarrow \text{ third, or resulting equation (3)} \\ x &= 2 \end{aligned}$$

$\left. \begin{aligned} +2y \\ -2y \end{aligned} \right\}$ opposites

Equation with only one variable

Divide each side by 2. ⟶

EXAMPLE 2 Let $x = 2$ in $5x + 2y = 12$ in Example 1. Solve for the corresponding value of y.

$$\begin{aligned} 5x + 2y &= 12 \\ 5 \cdot 2 + 2y &= 12 \\ 10 + 2y &= 12 \\ 2y &= 2 \\ y &= 1 \end{aligned}$$

Replace x with 2. ⟶

$\left. \begin{aligned} \text{Solve for } y. \\ \text{Add } -10 \text{ to each side.} \\ \text{Divide each side by 2.} \end{aligned} \right\}$

Show that $(2, 1)$ is a solution of the system.
$$5x + 2y = 12$$
$$3x - 2y = 4$$

Check in both equations.
Let $x = 2$ and $y = 1$. ⟶

$5x + 2y$	12	$3x - 2y$	4
$5 \cdot 2 + 2 \cdot 1$	12	$3 \cdot 2 - 2 \cdot 1$	4
$10 + 2$		$6 - 2$	
12		4	

Thus, $(2, 1)$ is a solution of the system.

EXAMPLE 3   Solve.

$$4x - 3y = 6$$
$$2x + 3y = 12$$

Get an equation with one variable.
Add the two equations.
An equation with only one variable
Solve $6x = 18$ for x. ⟶

$$
\begin{array}{ll}
4x - 3y = 6 & (1) \\
2x + 3y = 12 & (2) \\
\hline
6x = 18 & (3) \\
x = 3 &
\end{array}
$$

To find y, let $x = 3$ in either equation (1) or (2).

Replace x with 3. ⟶
Solve for y.
Add -12 to each side.
Divide each side by -3.

$$
\begin{array}{c|c}
4x - 3y = 6 & 2x + 3y = 12 \\
4 \cdot 3 - 3y = 6 & 2 \cdot 3 + 3y = 12 \\
12 - 3y = 6 & 6 + 3y = 12 \\
-3y = -6 & 3y = 6 \\
y = 2 & y = 2
\end{array}
$$

So, $x = 3$ and $y = 2$.

Check in both equations. ⟶   **Thus,** $(3, 2)$ is a solution of the system.

$-3y$ ⟍
$3y$ ⟋ opposites

A system of equations like
$$4x - 3y = 6$$
$$2x + 3y = 12$$
can be solved by addition.

EXAMPLE 4   Solve by addition.

$$x + 3y = -7$$
$$-x - 7y = 19$$

x ⟍
$-x$ ⟋ opposites

Equation with only one variable y

$$
\begin{array}{ll}
x + 3y = -7 & (1) \\
-x - 7y = 19 & (2) \\
\hline
-4y = 12 & (3) \\
y = -3 &
\end{array}
$$

To find x, let $y = -3$ in either equation (1) or (2).

Replace y with -3. ⟶
Add 9 to each side. ⟶

$$
\begin{array}{ll}
x + 3y = -7 & (1) \\
x + 3(-3) = -7 & \\
x - 9 = -7 & \\
x = 2 &
\end{array}
$$

So, $x = 2$ and $y = -3$.

Check in both equations. ⟶   **Thus,** $(2, -3)$ is a solution of the system.

EXERCISES

Solve.

1. $x + y = 8$
$x - y = 4$

2. $-2x + y = 6$
$2x + 3y = 10$

3. $3x - 2y = 2$
$5x + 2y = 14$

4. $-7x + y = 1$
$7x + 3y = 3$

5. $3x - y = 5$
$2x + y = 5$

6. $2x - 3y = 3$
$x + 3y = 3$

7. $5x - 2y = 6$
$x + 2y = 6$

8. $-2x + 5y = -3$
$2x + 3y = 11$

PART B

EXAMPLE   Solve.

$$4x - 3y = 14 \quad (1)$$
$$5x = -3y + 31 \quad (2)$$

The variables are not on one side in
$5x = -3y + 31$.
Add 3y to each side. The variables are now
on one side. $\longrightarrow$

The addition method works best if both variables
are on one side in each equation.

$$5x = -3y + 31 \quad (2)$$
$$5x + 3y = 31 \quad (2)$$
$$\underline{4x - 3y = 14 \quad (1)}$$
$$9x \qquad = 45 \quad (3)$$
$$x = 5$$

Add the two equations. $\longrightarrow$

To find y, let $x = 5$ in either equation (1) or (2).

$$5x = -3y + 31 \quad (2)$$
$$5 \cdot 5 = -3y + 31$$
$$25 = -3y + 31$$

Substitute 5 for x. $\longrightarrow$

Add −31 to each side. $\longrightarrow$

$$-6 = -3y$$
$$2 = y$$

So, $x = 5$ and $y = 2$.

Check (5, 2) in both equations. $\longrightarrow$ **Thus,** (5, 2) is a solution of the system.

Solve.

9. $5x + 8y = 31$
$4y = 5x - 7$

10. $x - 4y = 5$
$2x = -4y - 2$

11. $2x = -9y + 24$
$-9y + 4x = -6$

12. $3x + 2y = 13$
$5x = 2y + 11$

PART C

Solve.

13. $2x - (4 - y) = 8$
$5x - y = 9$

14. $.05x - .23y = -.13$
$-.05x + .46y = .36$

15. $\frac{2}{3}x - \frac{1}{5}y = 8$
$\frac{1}{3}x + \frac{1}{5}y = 7$

Systems of Equations: $\begin{aligned}ax + by &= c\\ dx + ey &= f\end{aligned}$

OBJECTIVE

■ To solve systems like
$$3x + 2y = 13$$
$$2x + 5y = 16$$
by addition

 REVIEW CAPSULE

Transform $3x + 2y = 8$ into another equation by multiplying each side by 2.

$$2(3x + 2y) = 2 \cdot 8$$
$$6x + 4y = 16$$

Both $3x + 2y = 8$ and $6x + 4y = 16$ have the same solutions.

EXAMPLE 1   Solve by addition.
$$3x + 2y = 13 \quad (1)$$
$$2x + 5y = 16 \quad (2)$$

Adding (1) and (2) does not give an equation in one variable.

$$3x + 2y = 13 \quad (1)$$
$$\underline{2x + 5y = 16} \quad (2)$$
$$5x + 7y = 29 \quad (3)$$

Transform each equation so that adding them gives an equation in one variable.

Multiply each side by 5. $\longrightarrow$

Multiply each side by -2. $\longrightarrow$

$+10y \leftarrow$ opposites
$-10y \leftarrow$

An equation in one variable $\longrightarrow$

$$5(3x + 2y) = 5 \cdot 13$$
$$-2(2x + 5y) = -2 \cdot 16$$
$$15x + 10y = 65$$
$$\underline{-4x - 10y = -32}$$
$$11x \qquad = 33$$
$$x = 3$$

To find y, let $x = 3$ in either equation (1) or (2).

Replace x with 3. $\longrightarrow$
Solve for y.
Add -9 to each side.
Divide each side by 2.

$$3x + 2y = 13 \quad (1)$$
$$3 \cdot 3 + 2y = 13$$
$$9 + 2y = 13$$
$$2y = 4$$
$$y = 2$$

So, $x = 3$ and $y = 2$.

Check (3, 2) in both equations. $\longrightarrow$ **Thus,** (3, 2) is a solution of the system.

EXAMPLE 2   Solve.

$$3x - 2y = 6 \quad (1)$$
$$5x + 7y = 41 \quad (2)$$

↙ Two ways ↘

Make the coefficients of y opposites.	Make the coefficients of x opposites.
$7(3x - 2y) = 7 \cdot 6$	$5(3x - 2y) = 5 \cdot 6$
$2(5x + 7y) = 2 \cdot 41$	$-3(5x + 7y) = -3 \cdot 41$

$-14y$ ↖ opposites ↗ $+15x$
$+14y$ ↙   ↘ $-15x$

$21x - 14y = 42$	$15x - 10y = 30$
$\underline{10x + 14y = 82}$	$\underline{-15x - 21y = -123}$
$31x \qquad\;\; = 124$	$-31y = -93$
$x = 4$	$y = 3$

We can solve for the other variable by using either equation.

To find y, let $x = 4$ in either (1) or (2).	To find x, let $y = 3$ in either (1) or (2).
$5x + 7y = 41 \quad (2)$	$3x - 2y = 6 \quad (1)$
$5 \cdot 4 + 7y = 41$	$3x - 2 \cdot 3 = 6$
$20 + 7y = 41$	$3x - 6 = 6$
$7y = 21$	$3x = 12$
$y = 3$	$x = 4$

Both ways give the same solution. ⟶ **Thus,** $(4, 3)$ is a solution of the system.

EXAMPLE 3   Solve.

$$x + y = -2 \quad (1)$$
$$x - 2y = 7 \quad (2)$$

Make the coefficients of x opposites.
Multiply each side of equation (1) by -1.
Leave equation (2) alone.

$$-1(x + y) = -1(-2)$$
$$-1x - 1y = 2$$

$-1x$ ↖ opposites
$+1x$ ↙

$$-1x - 1y = 2$$
$$\underline{1x - 2y = 7}$$
$$-3y = 9$$

Divide each side by -3. ⟶
$$y = -3$$

To find x, let $y = -3$ in either equation (1) or (2).
$$x + y = -2 \quad (1)$$
$$x + (-3) = -2$$
Replace y by -3. ⟶
$$x - 3 = -2$$
$$x = 1$$

Check $(1, -3)$ in both equations. ⟶ **Thus,** $(1, -3)$ is a solution of the system.

ORAL EXERCISES

Select a multiplier for each equation so that addition leads to an equation in one variable.

1. $3x + 2y = 8$
$2x + 5y = 9$

2. $5x - 2y = 3$
$2x + 7y = 9$

3. $2x + 2y = 8$
$5x - 3y = 4$

4. $5x - 3y = 2$
$4x + 2y = 6$

5. $5x + 4y = 29$
$3x - 2y = 13$

6. $3x - 5y = 1$
$2x + 10y = 14$

7. $7x + 2y = 9$
$3x + 8y = 11$

8. $4x - 7y = 5$
$2x + 8y = 14$

9. $8x - 6y = 10$
$4x - 5y = 3$

10. $-12x + y = 14$
$-7x + y = -11$

11. $11x - 3y = 16$
$4x + 2y = 12$

12. $7x + 5y = 31$
$-14x + 6y = -30$

13. $x + y = 4$
$2x + y = 2$

14. $x - 7y = 4$
$x + 7y = 16$

15. $6x - 2y = -7$
$13x - 2y = 0$

16. $5x - y = 13$
$x - y = -1$

EXERCISES

PART A

Solve each system in Exercises 1–16 above.

PART B

EXAMPLE Solve.

$$3x - 2y = 6$$
$$5x = -7y + 41$$

Add 7y to each side to get both variables on one side. $\longrightarrow$

$$5x = -7y + 41$$
$$5x + 7y = 41$$

Solve as in Example 2.

$$3x - 2y = 6$$
$$5x + 7y = 41$$

Thus, $(4, 3)$ is a solution of the system.

Solve.

17. $3x - 2y = 5$
$2x = 5y - 4$

18. $2x - 5y = 1$
$3x = 4y - 2$

19. $3x = -7y + 2$
$2x + 5y = 4$

20. $3y = -2x + 7$
$4x + 3y = 1$

PART C

Solve.

21. $8x - 3(y - x) = 2x + 19$
$y - (2y - x) = 7x - 13$

22. $\frac{1}{2}x - y = 3\frac{1}{2}$
$x + 2y = 3$

23. $\frac{4}{5}x - y = \frac{4}{5}$
$\frac{9}{5}x + 4y = \frac{4}{5}$

Mathematics in Pharmacy

As drugs are manufactured, their quality is constantly checked. Results of such tests are known immediately through the use of computer-video systems as shown above. Other aspects of a pharmacist's job are the development of new drugs and the careful preparation of doctors' prescriptions.

PROJECT   A prescription for 120 cm³ of cough syrup called for 7% alcohol. Find the amount of alcohol in the prescription.

Dry Mixtures: Representing Costs

OBJECTIVE
■ To represent the total cost of a mixture of two brands

 REVIEW CAPSULE

Find the cost in cents of 5 kg of gumdrops at $1.25 per kg.

$1.25 = 125$ cents $5(125) = 625$ cents

$$\begin{pmatrix} \text{number} \\ \text{of kg} \end{pmatrix}\begin{pmatrix} \text{cost in cents} \\ \text{of 1 kg} \end{pmatrix} = \begin{pmatrix} \text{cost} \\ \text{in cents} \end{pmatrix}$$

EXAMPLE 1

Cheese costs 89¢ per kg. Find the cost in cents of 4 kg. Find the cost in cents of x kg.

$$\begin{pmatrix} \text{number} \\ \text{of kg} \end{pmatrix}\begin{pmatrix} \text{cost in cents} \\ \text{of 1 kg} \end{pmatrix} = \begin{pmatrix} \text{cost} \\ \text{in cents} \end{pmatrix}$$

$4 \cdot 89 = 356$ cents $x \cdot 89 = 89x$ cents

EXAMPLE 2

Find the cost in cents of a mixture of 3 kg of coffee at $3.25 per kg and 5 kg of coffee at $2.95 per kg.

Use $\begin{pmatrix} \text{number} \\ \text{of kg} \end{pmatrix}\begin{pmatrix} \text{cost in cents} \\ \text{of 1 kg} \end{pmatrix}$ twice. ⟶

$3(325) + 5(295) = 975 + 1{,}475$, or $2{,}450$
Thus, the cost of the mixture is 2,450 cents.

EXAMPLE 3

Find the cost in cents of a mixture of x kg of candy at $1.35 per kg and y kg of candy at $.85 per kg.

Use $\begin{pmatrix} \text{number} \\ \text{of kg} \end{pmatrix}\begin{pmatrix} \text{cost in cents} \\ \text{of 1 kg} \end{pmatrix}$ twice. ⟶

$x(135) + y(85)$
Thus, the cost of the mixture is $(135x + 85y)$ cents.

EXAMPLE 4

Complete the chart.

	Number of kg	Cost per kg	Cost in Cents
Brand A	x	$1.45	?
Brand B	y	$1.95	?
Total cost in cents			

$1.45 = 145$ cents
$1.95 = 195$ cents

	Number of kg	Cost per kg	Cost in Cents
Brand A	x	$1.45	145x
Brand B	y	$1.95	195y
Total cost in cents			145x + 195y

EXAMPLE 5

Three kg of candy at $1.70 per kg are to be mixed with 5 kg of candy at $1.10 per kg to form an 8-kg box. Find the cost of the 8-kg box.

Use a chart to display the information.
Then use

$$\binom{\text{number}}{\text{of kg}} \binom{\text{cost in cents}}{\text{of 1 kg}} = \binom{\text{cost}}{\text{in cents}}.$$

	Number of kg	Cost per kg	Cost in Cents
1st Brand	3	170	$3 \cdot 170 = 510$
2nd Brand	5	110	$5 \cdot 110 = 550$
		Total cost in cents	1,060

1,060 cents = $10.60

Thus, $10.60 is the cost of the 8-kg box.

EXAMPLE 6

x kg of candy at $.75 per kg are to be mixed with y kg of candy at $.95 per kg. Find the number of kg in the mixture and the total cost.

Use a chart to display the information.
Then use

$$\binom{\text{number}}{\text{of kg}} \binom{\text{cost in cents}}{\text{of 1 kg}} = \binom{\text{cost}}{\text{in cents}}.$$

	Number of kg	Cost per kg	Cost in Cents
1st Brand	x	75	$x \cdot 75 = 75x$
2nd Brand	y	95	$y \cdot 95 = 95y$
		Total cost in cents	$75x + 95y$

Thus, $(x + y)$ kg cost $(75x + 95y)$ cents.

ORAL EXERCISES

Give the cost in cents.

1. 5 kg at 45¢ per kg

2. 6 kg at $2.00 per kg

3. x kg at 85¢ per kg

EXERCISES

PART A

Find the number of kilograms and the total cost in cents of the combined mixture.

1. 5 kg at $.90 per kg
6 kg at $1.35 per kg

2. 7 kg at $.85 per kg
9 kg at $1.35 per kg

3. x kg at $1.58 per kg
y kg at $2.10 per kg

4. x kg at $2.15 per kg
y kg at $3.35 per kg

5. x kg at $.04 per kg
y kg at $.78 per kg

6. x kg at $1.41 per kg
y kg at $2.10 per kg

PART B

Find the number of kilograms and the total cost in cents of the combined mixture.

7. x kg at $1.35 per kg
y kg at m¢ per kg

8. x kg at $1.40 per kg
$(y + 3)$ kg at $.75 per kg

9. x kg at p¢ per kg
y kg at q¢ per kg

Solving Dry Mixture Problems

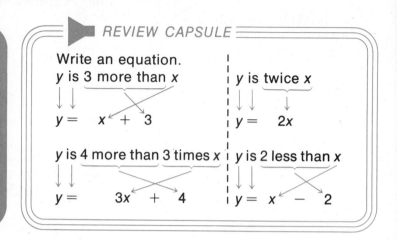

EXAMPLE 1

One brand of candy costs $1.70 per kg. Another costs $1.50 per kg. The two brands are to be mixed to form a 5-kg gift box that will cost $8.10. How many kg of each should be included?

Use a chart to display the information. Then use

$\left(\begin{matrix}\text{number} \\ \text{of kg}\end{matrix}\right)\left(\begin{matrix}\text{cost in cents} \\ \text{of 1 kg}\end{matrix}\right) = \left(\begin{matrix}\text{cost} \\ \text{in cents}\end{matrix}\right).$

	Number of kg	Cost per kg	Cost in Cents
1st Brand	x	170	$x \cdot 170 = 170x$
2nd Brand	y	150	$y \cdot 150 = 150y$
		Total cost in cents	$170x + 150y$

The total number of kilograms is 5. Write an equation. The total cost is 810 cents. Write an equation.

total kg: $x + y = 5$
cost in cents: $170x + 150y = 810$

Solve the system by substitution.
Solve for x in $x + y = 5$.

Replace x by $-y + 5$. ⟶

Distribute the 170. ⟶

Add -850 to each side. ⟶

$x = -y + 5$ (1)   { The two equations
$170x + 150y = 810$ (2)   { form a system.

$170(-y + 5) + 150y = 810$
$-170y + 850 + 150y = 810$
$-20y + 850 = 810$
$-20y = -40$
$y = 2$

To find x, let $y = 2$ in equation (1).

$x = -y + 5$
$x = -2 + 5$
$x = 3$

Thus, 3 kg at $1.70 per kg and 2 kg at $1.50 per kg should be included in the mixture.

EXAMPLE 2

Juan wants to make up packs of $.25 comic books mixed with $.15 comic books to sell at $2.45 per pack. The number of $.15 books is 3 more than the number of $.25 books. Write a system of equations which can be used to find the number of each type in a pack.

Use a chart to display the information.
Then use
$\left(\begin{matrix}\text{no. of} \\ \text{books}\end{matrix}\right)\left(\begin{matrix}\text{cost in cents} \\ \text{of 1 book}\end{matrix}\right) = \left(\begin{matrix}\text{cost} \\ \text{in cents}\end{matrix}\right).$

No. of Books	Cost per Book	Cost in Cents
x	25	$x \cdot 25 = 25x$
y	15	$y \cdot 15 = 15y$
Total cost in cents		$25x + 15y$

No. of 15¢ books is 3 more than no. of 25¢ books.

$$y = x + 3$$

Total cost is 245 cents.

$$25x + 15y = 245$$

Write an equation. →
$2.45 = 245 cents →

Write an equation. →
The two equations form a system.
Solve the system on your own.

Thus, a system which can be used is $y = x + 3$
$25x + 15y = 245.$

EXAMPLE 3

A wholesaler wants to mix pencils costing $.05 each with those costing $.04 each. She wants to make a single pack of pencils that will cost $1.04. How many of each type should be in the pack if the number at $.04 is twice the number at $.05?

Use a chart to display the information.
Then use
$\left(\begin{matrix}\text{no. of} \\ \text{pencils}\end{matrix}\right)\left(\begin{matrix}\text{cost in cents} \\ \text{of 1 pencil}\end{matrix}\right) = \left(\begin{matrix}\text{cost} \\ \text{in cents}\end{matrix}\right).$

No. of Pencils	Cost per Pencil	Cost in Cents
x	5	$x (5) = 5x$
y	4	$y (4) = 4y$
Total cost in cents		$5x + 4y$

No. of 4¢ pencils is twice no. of 5¢ pencils.

$$y = 2 \cdot x$$

Total cost is 104 cents.

$$5x + 4y = 104$$

Write an equation. →
$1.04 = 104 cents →

Write an equation. →
Solve the system by substitution.
Replace y by 2x.
$5x + 8x = 104$
$13x = 104$
$x = 8$

$y = 2x \quad (1)$
$5x + 4y = 104 \quad (2)$ {The two equations form a system.
$5x + 4 (2x) = 104$
$5x + 8x = 104$
$x = 8$

To find y, let $x = 8$ in equation (1).
$$y = 2x = 2 \cdot 8, \text{ or } 16$$
Thus, no. of $.04 pencils is 16; no. of $.05 pencils is 8.

EXAMPLE 4   Show the check for Example 3.

No. of $.04 pencils: 16 ⎫
No. of $.05 pencils: 8 ⎭

No. of $.04 pencils is twice no. of $.05 pencils.

16	2(8)
	16

$$\left(\begin{matrix}\text{No. of}\\\text{pencils}\end{matrix}\right)\left(\begin{matrix}\text{Cost in cents}\\\text{of 1 pencil}\end{matrix}\right)=\left(\begin{matrix}\text{cost}\\\text{in cents}\end{matrix}\right).$$

Cost of 4¢ pencils + cost of 5¢ pencils is 104¢.

16 (4)	+	8 (5)	104
64	+	40	
	104		

EXERCISES

PART A

Write a system of equations which can be used to solve the problem.

1. Ike wants to mix candy costing $.90 per kg with candy costing $1.30 per kg. He wants to make a 7-kg box that will cost $7.50. How many kg of each should he use?

2. Gina wants to mix candy costing $2.60 per kg with candy costing $2.90 per kg. She wants to make a 5-kg box that will cost $13.30. How many kg of each should she use?

3. Lois wants to mix pencils costing $.05 each with pencils costing $.15 each. The mixture will cost $1.30. The number of $.15 pencils is 2 more than the number of $.05 pencils. How many of each type should be included in the package?

4. Two varieties of cards are to be mixed. The assortment will cost $3.65. One kind costs $.45 each, the other $.25 each. The number of $.45 cards is 1 more than 3 times the number of $.25 cards. How many of each kind should be included?

5. Assorted creams cost $2.30 per kg. Caramels cost $1.70 per kg. The number of kg of creams is 2 less than the number of kg of caramels. How many kg of each type should be mixed to make a box that will cost $7.40?

6. A $6.00 box of nuts contains two varieties. One type costs $1.40 per kg and the other $1.80 per kg. The number of kg at $1.40 per kg is 3 times the number of kg at $1.80 per kg. Find the number of kg of each.

Solve.

7. Jan sold a 9-kg box of candy that contained two varieties. One sold at $.50 per kg and the other at $.70 per kg. The mixture sold at $5.30. How many kg of each type were included?

8. Two brands of candy were mixed in a 10-kg gift box. One cost $3.00 per kg and the other $2.70 per kg. The gift box cost $29.10. How many kg of each were included?

9. Mr. Lead wants to mix pencils costing $.15 each with pencils costing $.35 each. The mixture will cost $3.45. The number of $.35 pencils is 7 more than the number of $.15 pencils. How many of each type should be included in the package?

10. Cashews cost $2.50 per kg. Pecans cost $2.70 per kg. The number of kg of cashews is one less than the number of kg of pecans. How many kg of each should be mixed to make a box to sell at $28.70?

11. A $20.80 gift box of candy contains two varieties. One type costs $1.60 per kg and the other costs $1.80 per kg. The number of kg at $1.80 per kg is twice the number of kg at $1.60 per kg. Find the number of kg of each.

12. Two types of gift-wrap paper are to be mixed. The assortment will cost $2.90. One type sells at $.25 per sheet, the other at $.30 per sheet. The number of sheets of $.30 paper is 2 more than 3 times the number of sheets of $.25 paper. How many of each type should be included?

PART B

13. Ribbons costing $.20 each are to be mixed with ribbons costing $.15 each. The mixture will cost $1.20. The number of $.20 ribbons is $\frac{3}{4}$ the number of $.15 ribbons. Find the number of each type in the box.

14. Party decorations costing $.20 each are to be mixed with decorations costing $.30 each. The assortment will cost $4.30. The number at $.30 each is 5 more than $\frac{1}{2}$ the number at $.20 each. Find the number of each type.

15. Meg wants to sell a box of candy which contains two varieties for $14.40. The number of kg at $1.60 per kg is 1 less than $\frac{3}{4}$ the number of kg at $.80 per kg. Find the number of kg of each kind.

16. A $1.60 assortment of pads contains $.20 pads and $.15 pads. The number of $.20 pads is 2 less than $\frac{1}{2}$ the number of $.15 pads. Find the number of each type of pad.

PART C

17. Ms. Garcia wants to sell a box of candy which contains two varieties for $9.60. One variety sells at $1.20 per kg, the other at $1.80 per kg. The total weight is 3 kg more than twice the weight of the $1.80 type. How many kg of each type are included in the box?

18. Mr. Weiss wants to sell a box of candy which contains two varieties for $6.70. One variety sells at $1.50 per kg, the other at $1.30 per kg. The total weight is 5 times the weight of the $1.50 variety. How many kg of each type are included in the box?

Solving Number Relation Problems

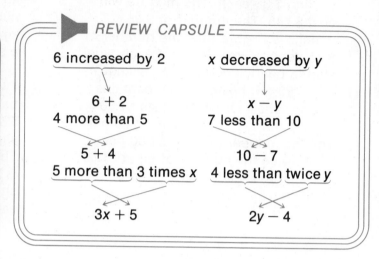

REVIEW CAPSULE

6 increased by 2

$6 + 2$

4 more than 5

$5 + 4$

5 more than 3 times x

$3x + 5$

x decreased by y

$x - y$

7 less than 10

$10 - 7$

4 less than twice y

$2y - 4$

EXAMPLE 1 The sum of two numbers is 42. One number is 5 times the other number. Find the numbers.

Let x = one number
y = other number
The sum of the numbers is 42.

Write an equation.
Sum means add.

$x + y$ $= 42$
One number is 5 times the other number.

Write another equation.

$x = 5 \cdot y$
$x + y = 42$ (1)   The two equations
$x = 5y$ (2)   form a system.
$5y + y = 42$
$6y = 42$
$y = 7$

Solve the system by substitution.
Replace x by $5y$ in equation (1).

Use either equation to find x.
Equation (2) is already solved for x.

To find x, let $y = 7$ in equation (2).
$x = 5y$
$x = 5 \cdot 7$
$x = 35$

Check.

Sum is 42.	One is 5 times the other.
$7 + 35 \mid 42$	$35 \mid 5 \cdot 7$
$42 \mid$	$\mid 35$

Thus, the two numbers are 35 and 7.

EXAMPLE 2   One number is 5 times another number. Their
difference is 8. Find the numbers.

The problem tells us that one number is
larger than the other. ————————→   Let x = larger number
y = smaller number
One number is 5 times another number.

The larger is 5 times the smaller. ————→

$$x = 5 \cdot y$$

Their difference is 8.

Larger $-$ smaller $= 8.$

$$x \quad - \quad y \quad = 8$$
$$x = 5y \qquad (1)$$

The two equations form a system.

Replace x by $5y$ in equation (2). ————→

$$x - y = 8 \quad (2)$$
$$5y - y = 8$$
$$4y = 8$$
$$y = 2$$

To find x, let $y = 2$ in equation (1).
$$x = 5y$$
$$x = 5 \cdot 2$$
$$x = 10$$

Thus, the two numbers are 2 and 10.

EXAMPLE 3   The sum of two numbers is 50. One number is 5 less
than 4 times the other number. Find the numbers.

Let x = one number
y = other number
Their sum is 50.

$$x + y = 50$$

One number is 5 less than 4 times the other.

$$x \quad = \quad 4y \quad - \quad 5$$
$$x + y = 50 \quad (1)$$
$$x = 4y - 5 \quad (2)$$

Replace x by $4y - 5$ in equation (1). ————→

$$4y - 5 + y = 50$$
$$5y - 5 = 50$$
$$5y = 55$$
$$y = 11$$

To find x, let $y = 11$ in (2).
$$x = 4y - 5$$
$$x = 4(11) - 5$$
$$x = 44 - 5, \text{ or } 39$$

Thus, the two numbers are 39 and 11.

EXAMPLE 4   One number is 3 less than another number. If twice the smaller number is increased by the larger number, the result is 18. Find the numbers.

The problem tells us that one number is smaller than the other. ————————→ Let x = smaller number

y = larger number

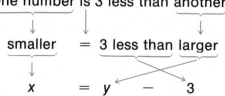

One number is 3 less than another.

smaller   =   3 less than larger

x = y — 3

Twice smaller increased by larger is 18.

$2x$ + y = 18

$x = y - 3$ (1)

Solve by substitution. Replace x by $y - 3$ in equation (2). ————————→

$2x + y = 18$ (2)

$2(y - 3) + 1y = 2y - 6 + 1y = 3y - 6$ ————→

$2(y - 3) + y = 18$

$3y - 6 = 18$

$3y = 24$

$y = 8$

To find x, let $y = 8$ in equation (1).

$x = y - 3$

$x = 8 - 3$

$x = 5$

Check. ————————————————→ Smaller is 3 less than larger.

5	8 − 3
	5

Twice smaller increased by larger is 18.

2 · 5	+	8	18
10	+	8	
	18		

Thus, the two numbers are 5 and 8.

EXERCISES

PART A

Find the numbers.

1. The sum of two numbers is 50. One number is 4 times the other.

2. One number is 3 more than twice another. Their sum is 24.

3. The sum of two numbers is 18. Their difference is 6.

4. The sum of two numbers is 72. One number is 8 more than the other.

5. One number is 9 more than another. If the larger is increased by 7, the result is 5 times the smaller.

6. One number is 3 less than another. If the larger is decreased by twice the smaller, the result is −7.

7. The sum of two numbers is 22. One number is 2 more than three times the other.

8. One number is 9 less than twice another. The sum of the numbers is 12.

9. One number is 4 more than another. If twice the smaller is added to the larger, the result is 28.

10. One number is 2 less than another. If twice the larger is decreased by 3 times the smaller, the result is −10.

PART B

EXAMPLE The length of a rectangle is 5 meters more than the width. The perimeter is 38 meters. Find the length and width.

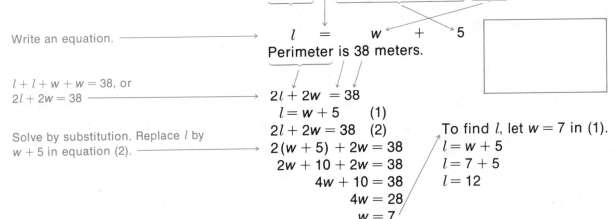

Length is 5 meters more than width.

Write an equation. ⟶ $l = w + 5$

Perimeter is 38 meters.

$l + l + w + w = 38$, or
$2l + 2w = 38$ ⟶ $2l + 2w = 38$

$l = w + 5$ (1)
$2l + 2w = 38$ (2)

Solve by substitution. Replace l by $w + 5$ in equation (2). ⟶
$2(w + 5) + 2w = 38$
$2w + 10 + 2w = 38$
$4w + 10 = 38$
$4w = 28$
$w = 7$

To find l, let $w = 7$ in (1).
$l = w + 5$
$l = 7 + 5$
$l = 12$

Thus, the length is 12 meters and the width is 7 meters.

Solve.

11. The length of a rectangle is twice the width. The perimeter is 42 meters. Find the length and width.

12. The perimeter of a rectangle is 68 meters. The length is 2 meters less than 3 times the width. Find the length and width.

13. The length of a rectangle is 8 kilometers more than 6 times the width. Find the length and width if the perimeter is 156 kilometers.

14. A rectangle is 4 times as long as it is wide. Find the length and width if the perimeter is 50 centimeters.

Chapter Eleven Review

Find the intersection. Verify that its coordinates satisfy both equations. [$p.289$]

1. $\{(x, y) \mid x + y = 8\} \cap \{(x, y) \mid x - y = 2\}$
2. $\{(x, y) \mid y = 3x\} \cap \{(x, y) \mid x + y = 8\}$
3. $\{(x, y) \mid 3x - 2y = 4\} \cap \{(x, y) \mid y = x\}$
4. $\{(x, y) \mid y = 3x + 2\} \cap \{(x, y) \mid y + x = 10\}$

Determine whether each system is consistent or inconsistent. [$p.289$]

5. $x + y = 4$
   $x + y = 6$

6. $2x - y = 5$
   $x + y = 4$

7. $x - y = 2$
   $3x + 3y = 4$

8. $3y = 2x - 15$
   $2x - 3y = -2$

Solve by addition. [$p.297, 300$]

9. $x + y = 4$
   $x - y = 2$

10. $x - 5y = 6$
   $-x = y + 6$

11. $2x + 5y = 5$
   $3x + 3y = 12$

12. $3x = 4y + 5$
   $2x + 2y = 8$

Solve by substitution. [$p.294$]

13. $y = 2x$
   $x + y = 9$

14. $x - y = 8$
   $x + y = 12$

15. $x - 5y = 6$
   $x + y = 6$

16. $x + y = 1$
   $x - y = 4$

Use a system of equations to solve each of the following problems. [$p.306, 310$]

17. Nan wants to sell a 5-kg box of candy containing two varieties. One sells at $1.50 per kg, the other at $1.90 per kg. The mixture is to cost $8.30. How many kg of each are included in the mixture?

18. Pedro wants to mix candy selling at $2.20 per kg with another selling at $2.40 per kg. He wants to make an $11.60 gift box. The number of kg at $2.20 per kg is 1 less than the number of kg at $2.40 per kg. Find the number of kg of each.

19. Two varieties of gift-wrap paper are to be mixed. The assortment will cost $2.00. One sells at $.40 per sheet, the other at $.30 per sheet. The number of sheets at $.30 per sheet is twice the number of sheets at $.40 per sheet. How many of each type should be included?

20. Diane wants to sell a box of two varieties of birthday cards for $5.80. The number of $.30 cards is 6 more than $\dfrac{1}{2}$ the number of $.35 cards. Find the number of cards of each type.

21. The sum of two numbers is 40. One number is 8 more than the other. Find the numbers.

22. The sum of two numbers is 24. Their difference is 8. Find the numbers.

23. One number is 3 more than twice another. If the larger is increased by the smaller, the result is 18. Find the numbers.

24. The perimeter of a rectangle is 36. The length is 6 more than twice the width. Find the length and width.

Chapter Eleven Test

Find the intersection. Verify that its coordinates satisfy both equations.

1. $\{(x, y) \,|\, x + y = 4\} \cap \{(x, y) \,|\, x - y = 6\}$
2. $\{(x, y) \,|\, y = 3x\} \cap \{(x, y) \,|\, 3x + y = 6\}$

Determine whether each system is consistent or inconsistent.

3. $x + y = 7$
   $x + y = 5$

4. $3x - y = 4$
   $x + y = 4$

5. $2x = y + 3$
   $2x - y = 6$

Solve by substitution.

6. $y = 3x$
   $x + y = 8$

7. $x - y = 8$
   $x + y = 4$

8. $2x + y = 3$
   $y = 2x + 1$

Solve by addition.

9. $2x + y = 4$
   $x - y = 8$

10. $2x - 3y = 1$
    $3x - 5y = 1$

11. $2x = 7y + 1$
    $5x + 3y = 23$

Use a system of equations to solve each of the following problems.

12. Ed wants to sell a 7-kg box of candy containing two varieties. One sells at $1.30 per kg, the other at $1.70 per kg. The mixture is to cost $10.30. How many kg of each are included in the mixture?

13. Tanya wants to mix candy selling at $2.80 per kg with another selling at $2.40 per kg. She wants to make a $26.40 gift box. The number of kg at $2.80 per kg is 2 more than the number of kg at $2.40 per kg. Find the number of kg of each.

14. The sum of two numbers is 60. One number is 20 less than the other. Find the numbers.

15. One number is 5 less than twice another. Their sum is 16. Find the numbers.

16. One number is 7 more than 3 times another. If the larger is decreased by twice the smaller, the result is 9. Find the numbers.

17. The perimeter of a rectangle is 28. The width is 2 less than the length. Find the length and the width of the rectangle.

12 FUNCTIONS

Galileo and Free Fall

Galileo Galilei, the renowned Italian astronomer and physicist, made a remarkable discovery in 1585. He timed an object as it fell from a given height, discovering the "free fall" equation.

$$d = 4.9t^2$$

distance of the fall in meters

elapsed time in seconds after the start of the fall

According to legend, Galileo dropped small cannon balls from the colonnades of the Leaning Tower of Pisa, timing their fall.
Even though the cannon balls were of different sizes and weights, they all took the same number of seconds to hit the ground.

PROJECT

1. Stand on a chair and drop a book and a pencil at the same time. What do you notice?
2. Drop a pencil and a large piece of paper. What do you notice? Crumble the paper into a ball and drop it at the same time with a pencil. What do you notice?
3. Using Galileo's formula, compute how long it will take an object to fall 122.5 meters.

Relations and Functions

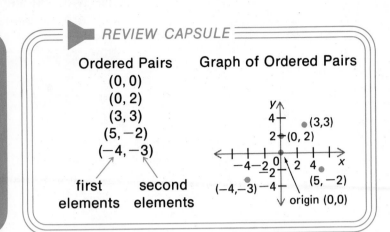

▶ REVIEW CAPSULE

Ordered Pairs
(0, 0)
(0, 2)
(3, 3)
(5, −2)
(−4, −3)

first elements   second elements

Graph of Ordered Pairs

Set C is a relation. ─────────────→ $C = \{(-1, 3),\ (2, 4),\ (0, -2),\ (-1, -5)\}$.

Definition of relation ─────────────→ A *relation* is a set of ordered pairs.

List −1 only once. ─────────────→ Domain of relation $C = \{-1, 2, 0\}$.
Range of relation $C = \{3, 4, -2, -5\}$.

Definition of domain and range ─────────────→ The set of all first elements of the ordered pairs in a relation is the *domain*. The set of all second elements is the *range*.

EXAMPLE 1 Graph $A = \{(5, 0),\ (-3, 4),\ (-3, -1),\ (-2, 4)\}$.
Then give the domain and the range of relation A.

Graph of relation A ─────────────→

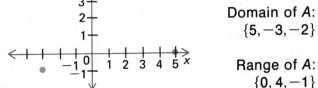

In the domain, list −3 only once.

Domain of A:
$\{5, -3, -2\}$

In the range, list 4 only once.

Range of A:
$\{0, 4, -1\}$

Set S is a function. ————————→ $S = \{(4, 8), (2, -1), (-6, 7), (5, 7)\}$.

A function is a special kind of a relation.

No two first elements
are the same.

Second elements
may be the same.

Definition of function ————————→

A *function* is a relation in which no two
ordered pairs have the same first element.

EXAMPLE 2   Graph
$B = \{(0, -3), (3, 1), (4, -3), (-3, -5), (-6, 6)\}$.
Give the domain and the range of relation B. Is B
a function?

Graph of relation B ————————→

$\{(0, -3), (3, 1), (4, -3), (-3, -5), (-6, 6)\}$

No two first elements are the same in a
function.

Domain of B:
$\{0, 3, 4, -3, -6\}$

Range of B:
$\{-3, 1, -5, 6\}$

B is a function.

EXAMPLE 3   List the ordered pairs in relation C graphed below.
Give the domain and the range of C. Is C a
function?

Graph of relation C ————————→

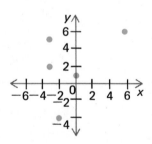

Ordered pairs in relation C ————————→ $C = \{(-3, 2), (-3, 5), (-2, -4), (0, 1), (6, 6)\}$.
Domain of $C = \{-3, -2, 0, 6\}$.
Range of $C = \{2, 5, -4, 1, 6\}$.

Both $(-3, 2)$ and $(-3, 5)$ are in C. ————————→ -3 is the first element in two of the ordered pairs
in C.

Two first elements are the same.   **Thus, C is not a function.**

EXERCISES

List the ordered pairs in each relation graphed below. Give the domain and the range of the relation. Is the relation a function?

1.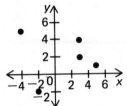

2.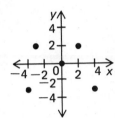

3.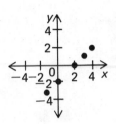

Graph each relation. Give the domain and the range. Is the relation a function?

4. $\{(0, 1), (-1, 1), (3, -2), (-4, 4)\}$

5. $\{(3, 2), (4, 2), (-1, 2), (0, 2)\}$

6. $\{(2, -2), (2, -3), (2, -1), (2, 0)\}$

7. $\{(3, 0), (-3, 0), (0, 3), (0, -3)\}$

8. $\{(-1, 1), (-2, 2), (0, 0), (1, -1), (2, -2)\}$

9. $\{(-1, -1), (-2, -2), (0, 0), (1, 1), (2, 2)\}$

10. $\{(3, 0), (-1, 2), (2, 4), (3, -4), (0, -2)\}$

PART B

EXAMPLE

$A = \{(1, 3), (2, 0), (-1, 3)\}$

The inverse of relation A is relation B. ⟶

The first and second elements of the ordered pairs in A are interchanged to form B.

$B = \{(3, 1), (0, 2), (3, -1)\}$

B is the inverse of A. Also, A is the inverse of B. Is A a function? Is B a function?

A is a function. B is not a function.

Give the inverse of each relation. Is the relation a function? Is its inverse a function?

11. $\{(-2, 4), (-1, 1), (0, 4)\}$

12. $\{(2, 3), (1, -2), (2, -4), (3, 0)\}$

13. $\{(-1, 1), (-2, 1), (0, 1), (1, 1), (2, 1)\}$

PART C

For what value of k will each relation not be a function?

14. $\{(-12, 4), (k^2 - 7k, 5)\}$

15. $\{(\frac{k}{4}, 7), (\frac{9}{k}, -3)\}$

Types of Functions

REVIEW CAPSULE

Graph of Relation A

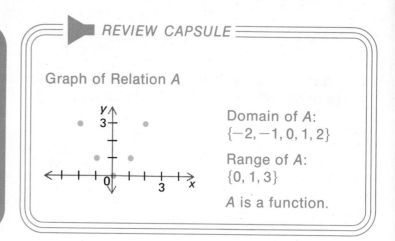

Domain of A:
$\{-2, -1, 0, 1, 2\}$

Range of A:
$\{0, 1, 3\}$

A is a function.

EXAMPLE 1   Is the following the graph of a function?

The dashed vertical line crosses the graph in two points:

$(4, 2)$ and $(4, -2)$.

same first element

Two ordered pairs have the same first element. ———————

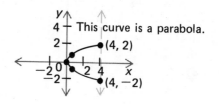

This curve is a parabola.

$(4, 2)$

$(4, -2)$

Thus, the graph is not the graph of a function.

Vertical Line Test

A *relation* is a function if no vertical line crosses its graph in more than one point.

EXAMPLE 2   Is $\{(x, y) \mid y = 2x + 1\}$ a function?

Use the slope-intercept method to graph $y = 2x + 1$.

Slope $\frac{2}{1}$ y-intercept 1

No vertical line will cross the graph in more than one point.

No two ordered pairs have the same first element. ———————

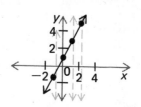

Thus, $\{(x, y) \mid y = 2x + 1\}$ is a function.

Definition of linear function ───────→ | A *linear function* is a function whose graph is a line or a subset of a line which is neither vertical nor horizontal.

EXAMPLE 3   Is $\{(x, y) \mid y = -3\}$ a function? If so, is it a linear function?

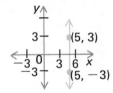

Plot $(0, -3)$, since the y-intercept is -3.
Then plot any other point with y-coord.
-3 like $(5, -3)$.
Draw the horizontal line.
No two ordered pairs have the same first element. ───────→ **Thus,** $\{(x, y) \mid y = -3\}$ is a function.
Its graph is a horizontal line. ───────→ $\{(x, y \mid y = -3\}$ is not a linear function.

Definition of constant function ───────→ | A *constant function* is a function whose graph is a horizontal line or a subset of a horizontal line.
Example 3 shows a constant function.

EXAMPLE 4   Is $\{(x, y) \mid x = 5\}$ a function? If so, is it a linear function or a constant function?

y is not mentioned in $x = 5$. The graph is a vertical line. Use any two points with x-coordinate 5 like $(5, 3)$ and $(5, -3)$.

The graph is a vertical line. ───────→ **Thus,** $\{(x, y) \mid x = 5\}$ is not a function.

ORAL EXERCISES

Which relations are functions? Which functions are linear functions? Which functions are constant functions?

1. 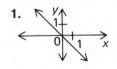   2. 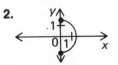   3. 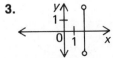   4. 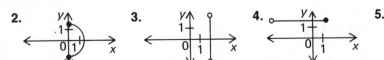   5.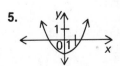

EXERCISES

PART A

Graph each relation. Which relations are functions? Which functions are linear functions? Which functions are constant functions?

1. $\{(x, y \mid y = 3x\}$
2. $\{(x, y) \mid y = -2x\}$
3. $\{(x, y) \mid y = x\}$
4. $\{(x, y) \mid y = 5\}$
5. $\{(x, y) \mid x = -4\}$
6. $\{(x, y) \mid -2 = y\}$
7. $\{(x, y) \mid 3 = x\}$
8. $\{(x, y) \mid y = x + 1\}$
9. $\{(x, y) \mid y = 2x - 3\}$
10. $\{(x, y) \mid x = 4y\}$
11. $\{(x, y) \mid x = 3y - 1\}$
12. $\{(x, y) \mid x = 0\}$
13. $\{(x, y) \mid y = 0\}$
14. $\{(x, y) \mid y = -2x - 4\}$
15. $\{(x, y) \mid y = 3x - 2\}$
16. $\{(x, y) \mid 2x + y = 3\}$
17. $\{(x, y) \mid x + 2y = -1\}$
18. $\{(x, y) \mid y = -x\}$
19. $\{(x, y) \mid x + y = 4\}$
20. $\{(x, y) \mid x - y = -6\}$
21. $\{(x, y) \mid x = 4\}$
22. $\{(x, y) \mid y = -3\}$
23. $\{(x, y) \mid 2x + 4y = -1\}$
24. $\{(x, y) \mid 3x = y - 1\}$
25. $\{(x, y) \mid 3y = 4 + x\}$
26. $\{(x, y) \mid x + 1 = 0\}$
27. $\{(x, y) \mid 3 + y = 0\}$
28. $\{(x, y) \mid 2x = y - 1\}$
29. $\{(x, y) \mid -3x + y = 5\}$
30. $\{(x, y) \mid -y - x = -4\}$

PART B

EXAMPLE Graph $\{(x, y) \mid y = -x^2\}$. Is the relation a function?

Find some ordered pairs.
Choose any numbers for x.
Find the y-coordinates.
Draw a smooth curve through the points.

The curve is a parabola.

x	$-x^2$	y
0	$-(0)^2$	0
1	$-(1)^2$	-1
-1	$-(-1)^2$	-1
2	$-(2)^2$	-4
-2	$-(-2)^2$	-4
3	$-(3)^2$	-9
-3	$-(-3)^2$	-9

No vertical line will cross the graph in more than one point. ⟶ **Thus,** $\{(x, y) \mid y = -x^2\}$ is a function.

Graph each relation. Which relations are functions?

31. $\{(x, y) \mid y = x^2\}$
32. $\{(x, y) \mid y = x^2 + 1\}$
33. $\{(x, y) \mid y = x^2 - 3\}$
34. $\{(x, y) \mid y = 2x^2\}$
35. $\{(x, y) \mid y = -3x^2\}$
36. $\{(x, y) \mid 4x^2 = -2y\}$
37. $\{(x, y) \mid x = y^2\}$
38. $\{(x, y) \mid x = -1y^2\}$
39. $\{(x, y) \mid x = 3y^2\}$
40. $\{(x, y) \mid 2y^2 = -1x\}$
41. $\{(x, y) \mid x = y^2 + 2\}$
42. $\{(x, y) \mid x = y^2 - 1\}$

PART C

Graph each relation. Which relations are functions?

43. $\{(x, y) \mid y = x^3\}$
44. $\{(x, y) \mid y = x^3 + 2\}$
45. $\{(x, y) \mid y = 3x^3\}$
46. $\{(x, y) \mid y = -1x^3\}$
47. $\{(x, y) \mid x = y^4\}$
48. $\{(x, y) \mid y = -1x^4\}$

f(x) Notation

 REVIEW CAPSULE

Small letters are used to name functions.

$$f = \{(0, 1), (-4, 3), (2, -3)\}$$

Domain of *f*: $\{0, -4, 2\}$.
Range of f: $\{1, 3, -3\}$.

EXAMPLE 1 In the function above, what value of *y* is paired with each of these values of $x: 0, -4, 2$?

Examine each ordered pair:
$(0, 1), (-4, 3), (2, -3)$.

When *x* is 0, *y* is 1.
When *x* is -4, *y* is 3.
When *x* is 2, *y* is -3.

Definition of value of *f* at *x* ⟶
Read $f(x) = y$ as the value of *f* at *x* is *y*, or as *f* at *x* is *y*.

If (x, y) is an ordered pair in function *f*, then the value of *f* at *x* is *y*.
$$f(x) = y$$

For (0, 1)   For (−4, 3)   For (2, −3)
$f(0) = 1$ $f(-4) = 3$ $f(2) = -3$

For function *f* above,
$f(0) = 1$ $f(-4) = 3$ $f(2) = -3$.
f at 0 is 1.   *f* at −4 is 3.   *f* at 2 is −3.

EXAMPLE 2 $f = \{(x, y) \,|\, y = 2x - 1\}$. Find $f(2), f(-1),$ and $f(20)$.

Find $f(2)$.   Find $f(-1)$.   Find $f(20)$.

Substitute 2, −1, and 20 for *x*.

$f(x) = 2x - 1$ $f(x) = 2x - 1$ $f(x) = 2x - 1$
$f(2) = 2 \cdot 2 - 1$ $f(-1) = 2(-1) - 1$ $f(20) = 2 \cdot 20 - 1$
   $= 4 - 1$ $= -2 - 1$ $= 40 - 1$
   $= 3$ $= -3$ $= 39$

f at 2 is 3.   *f* at −1 is −3.   *f* at 20 is 39.

EXAMPLE 3 $h(x) = x^2 - 2$, and the domain of h is $\{-1, 0, 1\}$.
Determine the range of h.

Substitute -1, 0, and 1 for x.

Find $h(-1)$.	Find $h(0)$.	Find $h(1)$.
$h(x) = x^2 - 2$	$h(x) = x^2 - 2$	$h(x) = x^2 - 2$
$h(-1) = (-1)^2 - 2$	$h(0) = 0^2 - 2$	$h(1) = 1^2 - 2$
$= 1 - 2$	$= 0 - 2$	$= 1 - 2$
$= -1$	$= -2$	$= -1$

List -1 only once. $\longrightarrow$ **Thus,** the range of h is $\{-1, -2\}$.

EXERCISES

PART A

$f = \{(x, y) \mid y = 3x - 2\}$. **Find each.**

1. $f(0)$ **2.** $f(4)$ **3.** $f(-2)$ **4.** $f(15)$ **5.** $f(-22)$

$g = \{(x, y) \mid y = -4x + 7\}$. **Find each.**

6. $g(-1)$ **7.** $g(5)$ **8.** $g(13)$ **9.** $g(-7)$ **10.** $g(30)$

$h(x) = x^2 - 5$. **Find each.**

11. $h(0)$ **12.** $h(-4)$ **13.** $h(4)$ **14.** $h(15)$ **15.** $h(-20)$

D **is the domain of each function. Determine the range.**

16. $f(x) = 4x - 3$ $D = \{0, 1, 2\}$
18. $g(x) = -2x - 9$ $D = \{2, 4, 6\}$
20. $f(x) = x^2 + 1$ $D = \{-3, 0, 9\}$
22. $k(x) = x^2 + x - 1$ $D = \{2, 1, 0\}$

17. $h(x) = 6x + 2$ $D = \{-3, 1, 4\}$
19. $r(x) = -7x + 4$ $D = \{-2, -4, -6\}$
21. $g(x) = 2x^2 + 3$ $D = \{-8, -7, -6\}$
23. $r(x) = 2x^2 - 3x - 2$ $D = \{1, 3, 6\}$

PART B

D **is the domain of each function. Determine the range.**

24. $f(x) = 2x - 8$ $D = \{\frac{1}{2}, \frac{1}{4}, \frac{1}{3}\}$
26. $f(x) = (x + 1)^2$ $D = \{0, 2, 4\}$
28. $r(x) = (x^2 - 2)^2$ $D = \{-2, 0, 2\}$

25. $g(x) = -3x + 7$ $D = \{.5, .6, .7\}$
27. $k(x) = (2x - 3)^2$ $D = \{-1, -2, -3\}$
29. $j(x) = x^2 - 5$ $D = \{-\frac{1}{2}, \frac{1}{2}, \frac{1}{4}\}$

PART C

$f(x) = 4x - 5$ and $g(x) = x^2 + 3$. **Find each.**

30. $f(2) + g(2)$ **31.** $g(6) - f(6)$ **32.** $f(7) - g(-3)$ **33.** $g(-8) + f(-2)$
34. $g[f(1)]$ **35.** $g[f(-2)]$ **36.** $f[g(4)]$ **37.** $f[g(-6)]$

The Greatest Integer Function

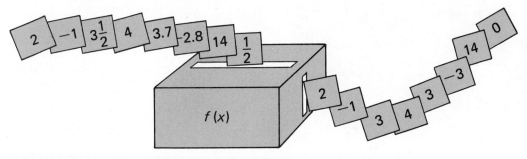

PROBLEM

Can you see a pattern here?

x	$f(x)$
$35\dfrac{3}{4}$	35
21	21
3.2	3
$\dfrac{1}{3}$	0
0	0
$-2\dfrac{1}{4}$	-3
-7	-7

$$\left.\begin{array}{l} 13 \\ 13.1 \\ 13\dfrac{1}{2} \\ 13.23 \\ 13\dfrac{2}{7} \\ 13.99 \end{array}\right\} \longrightarrow 13$$

In each case, $f(x)$ is the nearest integer to x which is less than or equal to x. This is called the *greatest integer function* and is written $[x]$.

For any number n, $[n]$ is the greatest integer less than or equal to n.

$$[2.3] = 2 \qquad \left[34\dfrac{1}{2}\right] = 34 \qquad \left[-\dfrac{1}{4}\right] = -1$$

PROJECT   Draw the graph of the greatest integer function.

Digit Problems

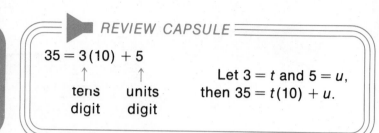

REVIEW CAPSULE

$$35 = 3(10) + 5$$

   ↑   ↑

tens   units
digit   digit

Let $3 = t$ and $5 = u$,
then $35 = t(10) + u$.

The Review Capsule suggests this. ———→

> If t is the tens digit and u is the units digit of a two-digit number, then $10t + u$ is the number.

EXAMPLE 1 $10t + u$ represents a two-digit number. Express the sum of the digits in algebraic terms.

$10t + u$ is the number.

Let $t =$ tens digit
   $u =$ units digit

Thus, the sum of the digits is $t + u$.

EXAMPLE 2 $10t + u$ represents a two-digit number. Express 13 less than the number in algebraic terms.

13 less than the number

$$(10t + u) - 13$$

Thus, the expression is $(10t + u) - 13$.

EXAMPLE 3   Reverse the digits of 65.

$$65 = 6(10) + 5$$
$$56 = 5(10) + 6$$

Thus, 56 is the result of reversing the digits of 65.

EXAMPLE 4   Reverse the digits of $10t + u$.

$$10t + u$$
$$10u + t$$

Thus, $10u + t$ is the result of reversing the digits of $10t + u$.

EXAMPLE 5   The sum of the digits of a two-digit number is 10. If the digits of the number are reversed, the new number is 18 less than the original number. Find the original number.

Represent the digits algebraically. ⟶ Let $t =$ tens digit of the original number
$u =$ units digit of the original number
$10t + u =$ the original number
$10u + t =$ the number with its digits reversed

Write two equations.
First equation ⟶

Sum of the digits is 10.
$$t + u = 10$$

Second equation ⟶
Simplify.

New number is 18 less than original.
$$10u + t = (10t + u) - 18$$
$$-9t + 9u = -18$$
$$9t - 9u = 18$$

Solve the system. (Use substitution.)
$$t + u = 10$$
$$9t - 9u = 18$$

First solve $t + u = 10$ for t.

Subtract u from each side. ⟶
$$t = 10 - u.$$

Replace t with $10 - u$. ⟶
Solve the equation.

$$9(10 - u) - 9u = 18$$
$$90 - 9u - 9u = 18$$
$$90 - 18u = 18$$

Add -90 to each side. ⟶
Divide each side by -18. ⟶
$$-18u = -72$$
$$u = 4$$

Find t. Substitute for u in one of
the equations. ⟶
$$t + u = 10$$
$$t + 4 = 10$$
$$t = 6$$

$10t + u = 10(6) + 4$ ⟶ **Thus,** the original number is 64.

EXAMPLE 6   Three times the tens digit of a two-digit number, increased by the units digit, is 21. If the digits are reversed, the new number is 9 more than the original number. Find the original number.

Represent the digits algebraically. ⟶ Let t = tens digit of the original number
u = units digit of the original number
$10t + u$ = the original number
$10u + t$ = the number with its digits reversed

Write two equations.
First equation ⟶

3 times tens digit, increased by units digit, is 21.

$$3t \qquad + \qquad u \qquad = 21$$

Second equation ⟶
Simplify.

New number is 9 more than original number.
$$10u + t = (10t + u) + 9$$
$$9u - 9t = 9$$

Solve the system.
$$3t + u = 21 \qquad (1)$$
$$9u - 9t = 9 \qquad (2)$$

Divide each side of (2) by -1. ⟶
$$-u + t = -1 \qquad (3)$$

Rearrange the variables in (3). ⟶
$$t - u = -1$$

Add equations (1) and (3).
$$3t + u = 21$$
$$\underline{t - u = -1}$$
$$4t = 20$$

Divide each side by 4. ⟶
$$t = 5$$

Find u.
Substitute for t in (1). ⟶
$$3t + u = 21 \qquad (1)$$
$$3(5) + u = 21$$
$$15 + u = 21$$
$$u = 21 - 15$$
$$u = 6$$

Thus, the original number is 56.

EXERCISES

1. The sum of the digits of a two-digit number is 15. If the digits are reversed, the new number is 27 less than the original number. Find the original number.

2. The sum of the digits of a two-digit number is 6. If the digits are reversed, the new number is 18 more than the original number. Find the original number.

3. The tens digit of a two-digit number is twice the units digit. If the digits are reversed, the new number is 36 less than the original number. Find the original number.

4. The units digit of a two-digit number is twice the tens digit. If the digits are reversed, the new number is 18 more than the original number. Find the original number.

5. The tens digit of a two-digit number is 3 times the units digit. If the digits are reversed, the new number is 54 less than the original number. Find the original number.

6. The units digit of a two-digit number is 3 times the tens digit. If the digits are reversed, the new number is 36 more than the original number. Find the original number.

7. The sum of the digits of a two-digit number is 11. If the digits are reversed, the new number is 7 more than twice the original number. Find the original number.

8. The sum of the digits of a two-digit number is 6. If the digits are reversed, the new number is 9 less than 4 times the original number. Find the original number.

9. The sum of the digits of a two-digit number is 13. If the digits are reversed, the new number is 4 less than twice the original number. Find the original number.

10. The sum of the digits of a two-digit number is 8. If the digits are reversed, the new number is 3 more than 4 times the original number. Find the original number.

11. The units digit of a two-digit number is 1 more than 3 times the tens digit. If the digits are reversed, the new number is 9 less than 3 times the original number. Find the new number.

12. The tens digit of a two-digit number is 7. If the digits are reversed, the new number is 9 less than the original number. Find the new number.

Direct Variation

OBJECTIVES

- To determine if a relation is a direct variation
- To find the constant of proportionality in a direct variation
- To solve direct variation problems

REVIEW CAPSULE

Formula for the perimeter of an equilateral triangle:

$$p = 3s$$

If $s = 2$, then
$p = 3 \cdot 2 = 6$.

If $s = 5$, then
$p = 3 \cdot 5 = 15$.

EXAMPLE 1

The table shows ordered pairs, $(2, 6)$, $(4, 12)$, $(5, 15)$, etc.

Find the ratio $\dfrac{p}{s}$ for each pair of numbers in the table below.

s	p
2	6
4	12
5	15
6	18
10	30

$\dfrac{p}{s} = \dfrac{6}{2} = 3$

$\dfrac{p}{s} = \dfrac{12}{4} = 3$

$\dfrac{p}{s} = \dfrac{15}{5} = 3$

Thus, the ratio $\dfrac{p}{s} = 3$ in all cases.

$\{(s, p)\,|\,p = 3s\}$ is a function.

The formula $\dfrac{p}{s} = 3$ describes a direct variation.

Definition of direct variation ⟶

A *direct variation* is a function in which the ratio y to x is always the same.

Table of values for graph of $y = 3x$

x	y
2	6
1	3
−1	−3
−2	−6

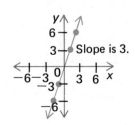

Slope is 3.

3 is the constant of variation.

For a direct variation,
$$\frac{y}{x} = k,$$
or $y = kx$, where k is a constant.
y varies directly as x
or
y is directly proportional to x.

k is the constant of variation, or constant of proportionality. ⟶

We say. ⟶

EXAMPLE 2   From the table, determine if y varies directly as x. If so, find the constant of proportionality.

x	y
2	-10
3	-15
-1	5
-4	20

See if $\frac{y}{x} = k$, a constant.

$$\frac{-10}{2} = -5 \qquad \frac{-15}{3} = -5$$

$$\frac{5}{-1} = -5 \qquad \frac{20}{-4} = -5$$

$\frac{y}{x} = -5$ for all pairs (x, y).

$\frac{y}{x} = k$, where $k = -5$. ⟶ **Thus,** y varies directly as x. The constant of proportionality is -5.

EXAMPLE 3 y varies directly as x, and $y = 32$ when $x = 4$. Find y when $x = 9$.

(x_1, y_1)

x-sub-one, y-sub-one

Let (x_1, y_1) and (x_2, y_2) be any two ordered pairs that satisfy $y = kx$.

$\frac{y}{x} = k$ for all (x, y). ⟶

$$\frac{y_1}{x_1} = k \qquad \frac{y_2}{x_2} = k$$

Therefore,
$$\frac{y_1}{x_1} = \frac{y_2}{x_2}$$

Let $(x_1, y_1) = (4, 32)$ and
$(x_2, y_2) = (9, y_2)$.
Solve the proportion.

$$\frac{32}{4} = \frac{y_2}{9}$$

$$4 \cdot y_2 = 32 \cdot 9$$

$$4y_2 = 288$$

Divide each side by 4. ⟶
$$\frac{4y_2}{4} = \frac{288}{4}$$

$$y_2 = 72$$

Thus, $y = 72$ when $x = 9$.

EXAMPLE 4 On a map, 50 km are represented by 3 cm. How many km are represented by 2 cm?

The relationship between cm and km describes a direct variation.

$\dfrac{cm_1}{km_1} = \dfrac{cm_2}{km_2}$ —————————→
Use prod. of means = prod.⎫
of extremes.   ⎬ —————————→
                        ⎭

Let x = no. of km represented by 2 cm

$$\frac{3}{50} = \frac{2}{x}$$
$$3(x) = 50(2)$$
$$3x = 100$$
$$x = \frac{100}{3}, \text{ or } 33\frac{1}{3}$$

Thus, 2 cm represents $33\frac{1}{3}$ km.

EXAMPLE 5 The cost of a certain metal varies directly as its weight. If 6 g cost $9, find the cost of 15 g.

Cost varies directly as weight.

$\dfrac{c_1}{g_1} = \dfrac{c_2}{g_2} \quad \Big| \quad \dfrac{9}{6} = \dfrac{x}{15}$ ⎫
                                              ⎬
Prod. of extremes = prod. of means ⎭

Let x = cost of 15 g

$$\frac{9}{6} = \frac{x}{15}$$
$$9(15) = 6(x)$$
$$135 = 6x$$
$$\frac{135}{6} = x$$

Divide each side by 6. —————————→

$$6 \overline{)135.00} \quad \overset{22.50}{}$$

Thus, the cost of 15 g is $22.50.

EXERCISES

PART A

Which tables express direct variations? For each direct variation, give the constant of proportionality.

1.

x	y
1	6
2	12
3	18
4	24

2.

x	y
1	2
3	4
5	6
7	8

3.

x	y
−2	8
−1	4
1	−4
2	−8

4.

x	y
5	20
10	15
15	10
20	5

5.

x	y
−1	2
−2	4
−3	6
−4	8

y varies directly as x.

6. y is 24 when x is 3. Find y when x is 4.

7. y is −12 when x is −6. Find y when x is 7.

8. y is 3 when x is 21. Find y when x is 35.

9. y is −4 when x is 36. Find x when y is 6.

PART B

10. On a map, 40 km are represented by 7 cm. How many km are represented by 14 cm?

11. On a map, 250 km are represented by 4 cm. How many km are represented by 7 cm?

12. The cost of a certain metal varies directly as its weight. If 5 kg cost $15, find the cost of 8 kg.

13. The cost of gold varies directly as its weight. If 3 g cost $125, find the cost of 5 g.

14. At a given time and place, the height of an object varies directly as the length of the shadow it casts. A building casts a 170-m shadow while a 6-m flagpole casts a 10-m shadow. How tall is the building?

15. In a recipe, the amount of flour varies directly as the amount of sugar. Three cups of flour are used for every 2 cups of sugar. How much sugar is used with 15 cups of flour?

16. The ratio of an object's weight on Earth to its weight on Mars is $5:2$. A rock weighs 60 kg on Earth. How much would it weigh on Mars?

17. On a blueprint, a 5-m hallway is represented by 3 cm. Find the dimensions of a room represented by a rectangle 8 cm by 10 cm.

PART C

EXAMPLE y varies directly as the square of x.
$y = 25$ when $x = 3$. Find y when $x = 2$.

$$\frac{25}{3^2} = \frac{y}{2^2}$$

$$\frac{25}{9} = \frac{y}{4}$$

$$100 = 9y$$

$$\frac{100}{9} = y \qquad \textbf{Thus, } y = \frac{100}{9}.$$

18. y varies directly as the square of x. $y = 36$ when $x = 2$. Find y when $x = 10$.

19. y varies directly as the square of x. $y = 15$ when $x = 4$. Find y when $x = 6$.

20. The distance needed to stop a car varies directly as the square of its speed. It requires 190 m to stop a car at 75 km per hour. What distance is needed to stop a car at 90 km per hour? $\left[\text{Hint: } \dfrac{190}{75^2} = \dfrac{x}{90^2}\right]$

21. The distance which a freely falling body falls varies directly as the square of the time it falls. A brick falls 22 m in 2 seconds. How far will it fall in 10 seconds?

Inverse Variation

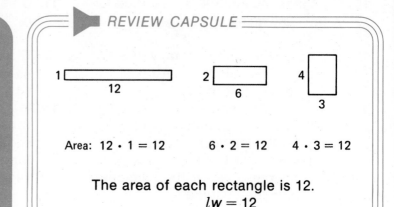

REVIEW CAPSULE

Area: $12 \cdot 1 = 12$ $6 \cdot 2 = 12$ $4 \cdot 3 = 12$

The area of each rectangle is 12.
$$lw = 12$$

EXAMPLE 1

Find the product lw for each pair of numbers in the table below.

l	w	
12	1	⟵ $12 \cdot 1 = 12$
6	2	⟵ $6 \cdot 2 = 12$
4	3	⟵ $4 \cdot 3 = 12$
24	$\frac{1}{2}$	⟵ $24 \cdot \frac{1}{2} = 12$

The table shows ordered pairs, (12, 1), (6, 2), (4, 3), etc.

Thus, the product $lw = 12$ in all cases.

$\{(l, w) \mid lw = 12\}$ is a function.

The formula $lw = 12$ describes an inverse variation.

Definition of inverse function ⟶

An *inverse variation* is a function in which the product xy is always the same.

Table of values for graph of $xy = 12$

x	y
12	1
6	2
4	3
−1	−12
−2	−6
−3	−4
−6	−2
−12	−1

Other ordered pairs are (3, 4), (2, 6), (1, 12).

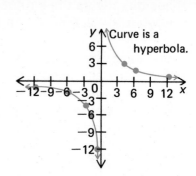

Curve is a hyperbola.

k is the constant of variation.

Also, $y = k \cdot \dfrac{1}{x}$.

We say.

For an inverse variation,
$$xy = k,$$
or $\quad y = \dfrac{k}{x},$ where *k* is a constant.

y varies inversely as *x*
or
y is inversely proportional to *x*.

EXAMPLE 2

From the table, determine if *y* varies inversely as *x*. If so, find the constant of variation.

x	y
2	9
6	3
−1	−18
−9	−2

See if $x \cdot y = k$, a constant.
$$2 \cdot 9 = 18$$
$$6 \cdot 3 = 18$$
$$-1\,(-18) = 18$$
$$-9\,(-2) = 18$$

$x \cdot y = 18$ for all pairs (x, y).

$x \cdot y = k$, where $k = 18$. ⟶ **Thus,** *y* varies inversely as *x*. The constant of variation is 18.

EXAMPLE 3

y varies inversely as *x*, and $y = 5$ *when* $x = 12$. Find *x* when $y = -4$.

Let $x \cdot y = k$ be the inverse variation.
Let (x_1, y_1) and (x_2, y_2) be any two ordered pairs that satisfy $x \cdot y = k$.

$x \cdot y = k$, for all (x, y). ⟶ $\qquad x_1 \cdot y_1 = k \qquad\qquad x_2 \cdot y_2 = k$

Let $(x_1, y_1) = (12, 5)$ and
$\quad (x_2, y_2) = (x_2, -4)$. ⟶

Therefore,
$$x_1 \cdot y_1 = x_2 \cdot y_2$$
$$12 \cdot 5 = x_2\,(-4)$$
$$60 = -4x_2$$

Divide each side by −4. ⟶
$$\frac{60}{-4} = \frac{-4x_2}{-4}$$
$$-15 = x_2$$

Thus, $x = -15$ when $y = -4$.

ORAL EXERCISES

Which formulas describe inverse variations? For each inverse variation, give the constant of variation.

1. $r \cdot t = 60$ **2.** $c = 3.14d$ **3.** $x \cdot y = -8$ **4.** $36 = b \cdot h$ **5.** $x \cdot y = 1$

6. $\dfrac{20}{y} = x$ **7.** $r = \dfrac{s}{-6}$ **8.** $\dfrac{-22}{b} = a$ **9.** $\dfrac{p}{4} = s$ **10.** $\dfrac{1}{5} \cdot y = x$

EXERCISES

PART A

Which tables express inverse variations? For each inverse variation, give the constant of variation.

1.

x	y
3	6
−2	−9
36	$\frac{1}{2}$
−18	−1

2.

x	y
1	1
−1	−1
0	0
2	2

3.

x	y
3	6
6	12
−3	−6
−6	−12

4.

x	y
5	20
−10	−10
−4	−25
$\frac{1}{2}$	200

5.

x	y
$\frac{1}{2}$	−2
−1	1
−$\frac{3}{4}$	$\frac{4}{3}$
1	−1

y varies inversely as x.

6. y is 24 when x is 8. Find y when x is 4.
7. y is 30 when x is 2. Find y when x is 15.
8. y is −7 when x is 8. Find y when x is 4.

PART B

EXAMPLE   Jane weighs 70 kg and is sitting 160 cm from the fulcrum of a seesaw. John weighs 56 kg. How far from the fulcrum must he sit to balance the seesaw?

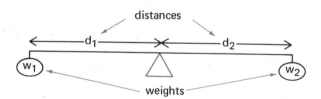

Law of the Lever

	Jane	John
weight	w_1	w_2
distance	d_1	d_2

The lever is in balance if $w_1 \cdot d_1 = w_2 \cdot d_2$.

$$70 \cdot 160 = 56 \cdot d_2$$
$$11{,}200 = 56 \cdot d_2$$
$$200 = d_2$$

Thus, John must sit 200 cm from the fulcrum.

9. Laurie weighs 60 kg and is sitting 165 cm from the fulcrum of a seesaw. Bill weighs 55 kg. How far from the fulcrum must Bill sit to balance the seesaw?

10. Jack is sitting 170 cm from the fulcrum of a seesaw. Mary weighs 65 kg and is sitting 210 cm from the fulcrum. How heavy is Jack if the seesaw is in balance?

11. The dimensions of a rectangle are 6 meters and 18 meters. Find the width of another rectangle with the same area and a length of 12 meters.

12. The volume of a gas is 60 cubic meters under 6 kg of pressure. What is its volume at the same temperature under 9 kg of pressure?

13. A trip takes 5 hours at 50 km per hour. How long does it take at 60 km per hour?

14. It takes 8 women 6 hours to do a job. How long will it take 12 women working at the same rate?

15. What amount invested at 6% yields the same yearly income as $1,000 invested at $4\frac{1}{2}$%?

16. At what rate does $15,000 yield the same annual income as $12,000 invested at 5%?

17. The base of a triangle is 16 centimeters and the altitude is 9 centimeters. Find the base of a triangle of equal area whose altitude is 6 centimeters.

18. Nancy weighs 72 kg and Bob weighs 60 kg. Nancy is sitting 2 m from the fulcrum of a seesaw. How far from Nancy should Bob sit to balance the seesaw?

19. Sophia has enough money to buy 3 meters of fabric priced at $6.40 per meter. How many meters of fabric priced at $3.60 per meter can she buy with the same amount of money?

20. The current through a circuit is 25 amperes when the resistance is 16 ohms. What is the current when the resistance is increased to 20 ohms?

PART C

21. Tina and Wilt are sitting 4 meters apart on a seesaw. Tina weighs 65 kg, and Wilt weighs 80 kg. How far from the fulcrum must Tina be sitting if the seesaw is in balance?

22. Ruiz drove a round trip between cities A and B in $7\frac{1}{2}$ hours. From A to B he averaged 60 km/hr, and from B back to A he averaged 65 km/hr. How far apart are A and B?

23. Cylinders A and B have the same volume. Their altitudes vary inversely as the squares of the radii of the bases. The altitude of cylinder A is 8 m, and the radius of its base is 6 m. Find the altitude of cylinder B if the radius of its base is 4 m.

24. The weight of a body at or above the Earth's surface varies inversely as the square of the body's distance from the Earth's center. What does a 220-kg object weigh when it is 370 km above the Earth's surface? (Use 6,500 km as the Earth's radius.)

Chapter Twelve Review

List the ordered pairs in each relation graphed below. Give the domain and the range. Is the relation a function? [p. 317]

1.

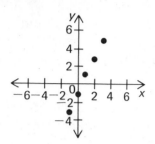

2.

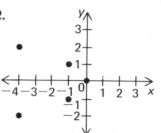

3.

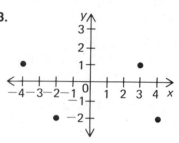

Graph each relation. Give the domain and range. Is the relation a function? [p. 317]

4. $\{(-1,-1), (-2,-2), (0,0), (-1,1), (-2,2)\}$
5. $\{(-2,1), (-1,1), (0,1), (1,1), (2,1)\}$

Graph each relation. Which relations are functions? Which functions are linear functions? Which functions are constant functions? [p. 320]

6. $\{(x,y) \mid y = 2x\}$ **7.** $\{(x,y) \mid x = 4\}$ **8.** $\{(x,y) \mid y = x + 2\}$
9. $\{(x,y) \mid y - 3x = -1\}$ **10.** $\{(x,y) \mid y = -1\}$ **11.** $\{(x,y) \mid y = 2x^2 + 1\}$

$f = \{(x,y) \mid y = x^2 + 3\}$. **Find each.** [p. 323]

12. $f(0)$ **13.** $f(3)$ **14.** $f(-2)$ **15.** $f(6)$ **16.** $f(-12)$

D is the domain of each function. Determine the range. [p. 323]

17. $f(x) = 3x - 2$ $D = \{0, 1, -1\}$ **18.** $g(x) = -x^2 + 3$ $D = \{-3, -2, -1\}$

Which tables express direct variations? Which express inverse variations? For each variation give the constant of variation. [p. 330, 334]

19.

x	y
-3	-9
-1	-3
1	3
2	6

20.

x	y
2	3
-1	-6
-3	-2
12	$\frac{1}{2}$

21.

x	y
-1	-3
0	-1
1	1
2	3

22.

x	y
-2	4
5	-10
-3	6
4	-8

23.

x	y
2	-6
-3	-4
-1	12
4	3

24. y varies directly as x, and $y = -4$ when x is 12. Find y when x is -18.

25. y varies inversely as x, and y is 5 when x is 4. Find x when y is -2.

26. The cost of a metal varies directly as its weight. If 3 kg cost \$10, what is the cost of 24 kg?

27. Sheila weighs 50 kg and is sitting 180 cm from the fulcrum of a seesaw. Joan weighs 60 kg. How far from the fulcrum must Joan sit to balance the seesaw?

Chapter Twelve Test

List the ordered pairs in each relation graphed below. Give the domain and the range. Is the relation a function?

1.

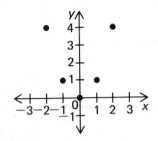

2.

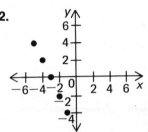

3.

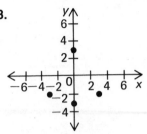

Graph each relation. Which relations are functions? Which functions are linear functions? Which functions are constant functions?

4. $\{(x, y) \mid x = -2\}$

5. $\{(x, y) \mid y = 3\}$

6. $\{(x, y) \mid y = x^2 + 1\}$

$f = \{(x, y) \mid y = 2x - 3\}$. **Find each.**

7. $f(3)$

8. $f(0)$

9. $f(-10)$

D is the domain of each function. Find the range.

10. $f(x) = 2x^2 - 1 \quad D = \{-1, 0, 1\}$

11. $h(x) = -3x + 4 \quad D = \{-2, 0, 2\}$

Which tables express direct variations? Which express inverse variations? For each variation, give the constant of variation.

12.

x	y
-1	4
0	3
1	2
2	1

13.

x	y
8	-8
-2	32
-4	16
-8	8

14.

x	y
2	-6
1	-3
-1	3
-2	6

15. y varies directly as x, and y is 24 when x is 6. Find y when x is -8.

16. y varies inversely as x, and y is 8 when x is -4. Find x when y is -2.

17. The cost of a metal varies directly as its weight. If 7 g cost $20, what is the cost of 35 g?

18. Moira weighs 45 kg and is sitting 2 m from the fulcrum of a seesaw. Juan weighs 50 kg. How far from the fulcrum must Juan sit to balance the seesaw?

FRACTIONAL EQUATIONS

Mathematics and Electricians

The electrician and his assistant are upgrading the existing wiring in this house from 60 amps to 150 amps.

An electrician must apply some basic algebraic and scientific formulas. One of these is Ohm's law.

$$V = IR \quad \text{or} \quad E = IR$$

voltage   current   resistance

If $R = 100$ *ohms* $(100\,\Omega)$ and $I = 20$ amps, the voltage V is $(100)(20)$, or $2{,}000\ v$.

PROJECT Suppose the voltage is $400v$. What will happen to I (the current) as the resistance (value of R) is steadily increased?

Solving Fractional Equations

Two equations which have the same solution are equivalent equations.

We can use the equation properties to transform an equation into another equation which has the same solution.

$a = b$	$a = b$	$a = b$
$a + c = b + c$	$ac = bc$	$\dfrac{a}{c} = \dfrac{b}{c}$
Add the same number to each side.	Multiply each side by the same number.	Divide each side by the same number.

EXAMPLE 1 Rewrite $\dfrac{x}{2} + \dfrac{2}{3} = \dfrac{x}{6}$ as an equation with no fractions.

Find the LCD by factoring the denominators. ⟶

$$\frac{x}{2} + \frac{2}{3} = \frac{x}{3 \cdot 2} \quad \text{The LCD is } 3 \cdot 2.$$

Multiply each side by the LCD, $3 \cdot 2$. ⟶

$$3 \cdot 2\left(\frac{x}{2} + \frac{2}{3}\right) = 3 \cdot 2 \cdot \frac{x}{3 \cdot 2}$$

Use the distributive property. ⟶

$$3 \cdot 2 \cdot \frac{x}{2} + 3 \cdot 2 \cdot \frac{2}{3} = 3 \cdot 2 \cdot \frac{x}{3 \cdot 2}$$

Do multiplications. ⟶

$$3 \cdot \overset{1}{\cancel{2}} \cdot \frac{x}{\cancel{2}} + \overset{1}{\cancel{3}} \cdot 2 \cdot \frac{2}{\underset{1}{\cancel{3}}} = \overset{1}{\cancel{3}} \cdot \overset{1}{\cancel{2}} \cdot \frac{x}{\underset{1}{\cancel{3}} \cdot \underset{1}{\cancel{2}}}$$

This equation has no fractions. It is a simpler equation to solve. ⟶

$$3x \quad + \quad 4 \quad = x$$

EXAMPLE 2   Solve $3x + 4 = x$, the resulting equation in Example 1. Then show that the solution also satisfies the original fractional equation $\dfrac{x}{2} + \dfrac{2}{3} = \dfrac{x}{6}$.

$x = 1x$ $\longrightarrow$

Add $-3x$ to each side. $\longrightarrow$

$$
\begin{aligned}
3x + 4 &= 1x \\
-3x & -3x \\
\hline
4 &= -2x
\end{aligned}
$$

Divide each side by -2. $\longrightarrow$

$$-2 = x$$

Check -2 in $\dfrac{x}{2} + \dfrac{2}{3} = \dfrac{x}{6}$.

Replace x by -2. $\longrightarrow$

$$
\begin{array}{c|c}
\dfrac{x}{2} + \dfrac{2}{3} & \dfrac{x}{6} \\[2mm]
\hline
\dfrac{-2}{2} + \dfrac{2}{3} & \dfrac{-2}{6} \\[2mm]
\dfrac{-1}{1} + \dfrac{2}{3} & -\dfrac{1}{3} \\[2mm]
-\dfrac{1}{3} &
\end{array}
$$

$\left. \begin{aligned} \dfrac{-1}{1} + \dfrac{2}{3} &= \dfrac{-3}{3} + \dfrac{2}{3} \\ &= -\dfrac{1}{3} \end{aligned} \right\}$

Thus, -2 is the solution of $\dfrac{x}{2} + \dfrac{2}{3} = \dfrac{x}{6}$.

To solve a fractional equation:
First, find the LCD for all fractions.
Next, multiply each side by the LCD.
Then, solve the resulting equation.

EXAMPLE 3   Find the solution set of $\dfrac{3a}{5} + \dfrac{3}{2} = \dfrac{7a}{10}$.

Find the LCD by factoring the denominators. $\longrightarrow$

$$\frac{3a}{5} + \frac{3}{2} = \frac{7a}{5 \cdot 2} \qquad \text{The LCD is } 5 \cdot 2.$$

Multiply each side by the LCD, $5 \cdot 2$. $\longrightarrow$

$$5 \cdot 2\left(\frac{3a}{5} + \frac{3}{2}\right) = 5 \cdot 2 \cdot \frac{7a}{5 \cdot 2}$$

Distribute the $5 \cdot 2$: $5 \cdot 2\left(\dfrac{3a}{5} + \dfrac{3}{2}\right)$ $\longrightarrow$

$$5 \cdot 2 \cdot \frac{3a}{5} + 5 \cdot 2 \cdot \frac{3}{2} = 5 \cdot 2 \cdot \frac{7a}{5 \cdot 2}$$

Do multiplications. $\longrightarrow$

$$\overset{1}{5} \cdot 2 \cdot \frac{3a}{\underset{1}{5}} + 5 \cdot \overset{1}{2} \cdot \frac{3}{\underset{1}{2}} = \overset{1}{5} \cdot \overset{1}{2} \cdot \frac{7a}{\underset{1}{5} \cdot \underset{1}{2}}$$

$2 \cdot 3a = 6a;\ 5 \cdot 3 = 15$ $\longrightarrow$

$$6a + 15 = 7a$$

Add $-6a$ to each side. $\longrightarrow$

$$15 = a$$

Check on your own. $\longrightarrow$ **Thus,** the solution set is $\{15\}$.

EXAMPLE 4 Solve $\dfrac{3a}{4} - \dfrac{2a-1}{2} = \dfrac{a-7}{6}$.

$-\dfrac{2a-1}{2} = \dfrac{-1(2a-1)}{2}$ $\longrightarrow$

$\qquad\qquad\qquad\qquad\qquad\qquad\quad \dfrac{3a}{4} + \dfrac{-1(2a-1)}{2} = \dfrac{a-7}{6}$

$-1(2a-1) = -2a+1$ $\longrightarrow$ The LCD is

Factor the denominators. $\longrightarrow$ $3 \cdot 2 \cdot 2$.

$\qquad\qquad\qquad\qquad\qquad\qquad\quad \dfrac{3a}{2\cdot 2} + \dfrac{-2a+1}{2} = \dfrac{a-7}{2\cdot 3}$

Multiply each side by the LCD. $\longrightarrow$

$$3\cdot 2\cdot 2\left(\dfrac{3a}{2\cdot 2} + \dfrac{-2a+1}{2}\right) = 3\cdot 2\cdot 2\cdot \dfrac{a-7}{2\cdot 3}$$

Use the distributive property. $\longrightarrow$ $3\cdot 2\cdot 2\cdot \dfrac{3a}{2\cdot 2} + 3\cdot 2\cdot 2\cdot \dfrac{-2a+1}{2} = 3\cdot 2\cdot 2\cdot \dfrac{a-7}{2\cdot 3}$

$$3\cdot \overset{1}{2}\cdot \overset{1}{2}\cdot \dfrac{3a}{\underset{1}{2}\cdot \underset{1}{2}} + 3\cdot 2\cdot \overset{1}{2}\cdot \dfrac{-2a+1}{\underset{1}{2}} = \overset{1}{3}\cdot \overset{1}{2}\cdot 2\cdot \dfrac{a-7}{\underset{1}{2}\cdot \underset{1}{3}}$$

Simplify. $\longrightarrow$

$6(-2a+1) = -12a+6$ $\Big\}$

$2(a-7) = 2a-14$

Add $3a$ to each side. $\longrightarrow$

Add 14 to each side. $\longrightarrow$

Check by letting $a = 4$ in the original
equation. $\longrightarrow$

$$3\cdot 3a + 6(-2a+1) = 2(a-7)$$
$$9a \qquad -12a+6 = 2a-14$$
$$-3a+6 = 2a-14$$
$$6 = 5a-14$$
$$20 = 5a$$
$$4 = a$$

Thus, the solution is 4.

EXAMPLE 5 Solve $\dfrac{4}{5} + \dfrac{3}{a} = 2$.

$2 = \dfrac{2}{1}$; the denominators are already
factored. $\longrightarrow$

$$\dfrac{4}{5} + \dfrac{3}{a} = \dfrac{2}{1} \qquad\qquad \text{The LCD is } 5\cdot a.$$

Multiply each side by the LCD, $5\cdot a$. $\longrightarrow$

$$5\cdot a\left(\dfrac{4}{5} + \dfrac{3}{a}\right) = 5\cdot a\cdot \dfrac{2}{1}$$

Distributive property: $5\cdot a\left(\dfrac{4}{5} + \dfrac{3}{a}\right)$ $\longrightarrow$ $5\cdot a\cdot \dfrac{4}{5} + 5\cdot a\cdot \dfrac{3}{a} = 5\cdot a\cdot \dfrac{2}{1}$

$$\overset{1}{5}\cdot a\cdot \dfrac{4}{\underset{1}{5}} + 5\cdot \overset{1}{a}\cdot \dfrac{3}{\underset{1}{a}} = 5\cdot a\cdot 2$$

$a\cdot 4 = 4\cdot a = 4a$;
$5\cdot a\cdot 2 = 5\cdot 2\cdot a = 10a$ $\longrightarrow$

Add $-4a$ to each side. $\longrightarrow$

Divide each side by 6. $\longrightarrow$

$$4a+15 = 10a$$
$$15 = 6a$$
$$\dfrac{15}{6} = a$$

$\dfrac{15}{6} = \dfrac{5}{2}$ $\longrightarrow$ **Thus,** the solution is $\dfrac{5}{2}$, or $2\dfrac{1}{2}$.

EXAMPLE 6 Solve the proportion $\dfrac{3x-1}{2}=\dfrac{5x+1}{4}$.

	First Method	Second Method

In a proportion, $\dfrac{a}{b}=\dfrac{c}{d}$, $a\cdot d=b\cdot c$;

prod. of extremes = prod. of means. $\longrightarrow$

or

In the second method multiply each side by the LCD.

First Method

$$\frac{3x-1}{2}=\frac{5x+1}{4}$$

$$4(3x-1)=2(5x+1)$$

$$\begin{array}{rl} 12x-4= & 10x+2 \\ -10x & -10x \\ \hline 2x-4= & 2 \\ 4 & 4 \\ \hline 2x= & 6 \\ x= & 3 \end{array}$$

Second Method

$$\frac{3x-1}{2}=\frac{5x+1}{2\cdot 2}$$

$$2\cdot 2\cdot \frac{3x-1}{\overset{}{2}}=\overset{1}{2}\cdot \overset{1}{2}\cdot \frac{5x+1}{\underset{1\;1}{2\cdot 2}}$$

$$\begin{array}{rl} 2(3x-1)= & 5x+1 \\ 6x-2= & 5x+1 \\ -5x & -5x \\ \hline x-2= & 1 \\ x= & 3 \end{array}$$

Both methods give the same solution.

One way $\longrightarrow$
Second way $\longrightarrow$

A proportion can be solved in two ways:
Product of the extremes = product of the means.
Multiply each side of the equation by the LCD.

EXERCISES

PART A

Solve.

1. $\dfrac{2a-3}{6}=\dfrac{2a}{3}+\dfrac{1}{2}$

2. $\dfrac{3a}{5}+\dfrac{3}{2}=\dfrac{7a}{10}$

3. $\dfrac{3m}{2}+\dfrac{5}{4}=\dfrac{5m}{2}$

4. $\dfrac{5}{4x}+\dfrac{1}{x}=3$

5. $\dfrac{3}{5b}+\dfrac{7}{2b}=1$

6. $\dfrac{1}{m}+\dfrac{2}{3}=1$

7. $\dfrac{3r+4}{12}-\dfrac{5}{3}=\dfrac{2r-1}{2}$

8. $\dfrac{2x-3}{7}-\dfrac{x}{2}=\dfrac{x+3}{14}$

9. $\dfrac{a}{4}-\dfrac{a}{3}=7$

Find the solution set.

10. $\dfrac{3a+2}{6}=\dfrac{2a+2}{3}$

11. $\dfrac{2m-5}{3}=\dfrac{m+1}{2}$

12. $\dfrac{2a-3}{5}=\dfrac{3a+1}{7}$

PART B

Find the solution set.

13. $\dfrac{2}{3}(x-2)+\dfrac{x+3}{2}=\dfrac{5x+3}{6}$

14. $\dfrac{3}{5}(a-3)+\dfrac{a+1}{15}=\dfrac{1}{3}$

15. $\dfrac{2}{3}b-\dfrac{5}{6}(3-b)=\dfrac{2b-5}{3}$

16. $\dfrac{3m}{5}+\dfrac{1-2m}{3}=\dfrac{m+1}{15}$

Percent of a Number

PROBLEM 1.

45% of freshmen study algebra. How many freshmen in a class of 400 study algebra?

Let t = number of freshmen taking algebra

Write a proportion. $\longrightarrow$ $\dfrac{t}{400} = \dfrac{\text{number of algebra students}}{\text{total number of freshmen}}$

45% means $\dfrac{45}{100}$ or $\dfrac{.45}{1}$ $\longrightarrow$ $\dfrac{.45}{1} = \dfrac{\text{number of algebra students}}{\text{total number of freshmen}}$

Set the ratios equal. $\longrightarrow$ $\dfrac{t}{400} = \dfrac{.45}{1}$

If $\dfrac{a}{b} = \dfrac{c}{d}$, then $ad = bc$. $\longrightarrow$ $t(1) = .45(400)$

$$\begin{array}{r} 400 \\ \underline{.45} \\ 20\ 00 \\ \underline{160\ 0} \\ 180.00 \end{array}$$

To find 45% of 400, write 45% as a decimal, then multiply.

Thus, 180 students study algebra.

PROBLEM 2.

A $256.24 television is advertised at a 23% discount. How much is saved?

23% of 256.24
means .23(256.24).

$$\begin{array}{r} 256.24 \\ \underline{.23} \\ 76872 \\ 51248 \\ \hline 58.9352 \end{array} \longleftarrow \text{Move decimal point 4 places.}$$

Sometimes with discounts, merchants round to the next lower penny.

Thus, the savings are $58.94.

 PROJECT

1. Find 32% of 78.   2. Find 43% of $6,598.   3. Find 62% of 19.
4. Find the savings when buying a $243.65 washer at a 27% discount.
5. Find the savings when buying a $49.95 radio at a 6% discount.
   [Hint: 6%=.06.]

More Fractional Equations

▶ *REVIEW CAPSULE*

Solve
$$4a - 6 = a^2 - 3a + 6$$
$$\underline{-4a \qquad\qquad -4a}$$
$$-6 = a^2 - 7a + 6$$
$$0 = a^2 - 7a + 12$$
$$0 = (a-4)(a-3)$$

$$a - 4 = 0 \text{ or } a - 3 = 0$$
$$a = 4 \qquad\qquad a = 3$$

EXAMPLE 1   Solve $\dfrac{3x}{x^2 - 5x + 4} = \dfrac{2}{x-4} + \dfrac{3}{x-1}$.

Factor $x^2 - 5x + 4$; LCD is $(x-4)(x-1)$. → $\dfrac{3x}{(x-4)(x-1)} = \dfrac{2}{x-4} + \dfrac{3}{x-1}$

Multiply each side by the LCD, $(x-4)(x-1)$. $(x-4)(x-1) \cdot \dfrac{3x}{(x-4)(x-1)} =$

$$(x-4)(x-1)\left(\frac{2}{x-4} + \frac{3}{x-1}\right)$$

$$(x-4)(x-1) \cdot \frac{3x}{(x-4)(x-1)} =$$

$(x-4)(x-1)\left(\dfrac{2}{x-4} + \dfrac{3}{x-1}\right)$ ⟶ $(x-4)(x-1) \cdot \dfrac{2}{x-4} + (x-4)(x-1) \cdot \dfrac{3}{x-1}$.

Do multiplications. ⟶ $(\overset{1}{x-4})(\overset{1}{x-1}) \cdot \dfrac{3x}{\underset{1}{(x-4)}\underset{1}{(x-1)}} =$

$$(\overset{1}{x-4})(x-1) \cdot \frac{2}{\underset{1}{x-4}} + (x-4)(\overset{1}{x-1}) \cdot \frac{3}{\underset{1}{x-1}}$$

$(x-1)2 = 2x - 2$;

$(x-4)3 = 3x - 12$ ⟶ $3x = (x-1)2 + (x-4)3$

Combine like terms. ⟶ $3x = 2x - 2 + 3x - 12$

Add $-5x$ to each side. ⟶ $3x = 5x - 14$

Divide each side by -2. ⟶ $-2x = -14$

$$x = 7$$

Thus, the solution is 7.

EXAMPLE 2 Show that 7 is the solution of

$$\frac{3x}{x^2 - 5x + 4} = \frac{2}{x - 4} + \frac{3}{x - 1}.$$

$\dfrac{3x}{x^2 - 5x + 4}$	$\dfrac{2}{x - 4} + \dfrac{3}{x - 1}$
$\dfrac{3 \cdot 7}{7^2 - 5 \cdot 7 + 4}$	$\dfrac{2}{7 - 4} + \dfrac{3}{7 - 1}$
$\dfrac{21}{18}$	$\dfrac{2}{3} + \dfrac{3}{6}$
$\dfrac{7}{6}$	$\dfrac{4}{6} + \dfrac{3}{6},$ or $\dfrac{7}{6}$

Replace x by 7.

$7^2 - 5 \cdot 7 + 4 = 49 - 35 + 4 = 18$ ⟶

$\dfrac{21}{18} = \dfrac{7}{6}; \dfrac{2}{3} = \dfrac{4}{6}$ ————————

Thus, 7 is the solution of $\dfrac{3x}{x^2 - 5x + 4} = \dfrac{2}{x - 4} + \dfrac{3}{x - 1}.$

EXAMPLE 3 Find the solution set of $\dfrac{7}{m^2 - 5m} + \dfrac{3}{5 - m} = \dfrac{4}{m}.$

Put $5 - m$ in convenient form.
$5 - m = -1m + 5 = -1(m - 5)$ ⟶

$\dfrac{7}{m^2 - 5m} + \dfrac{3}{-1(m - 5)} = \dfrac{4}{m}$

↖ descending order

$\dfrac{3}{-1(m - 5)} = \dfrac{-1 \cdot 3}{m - 5} = \dfrac{-3}{m - 5}$ ⟶

$\dfrac{7}{m^2 - 5m} + \dfrac{-3}{m - 5} = \dfrac{4}{m}$

Factor $m^2 - 5m$; LCD is $m(m - 5)$. ⟶
Multiply each side by the LCD, $m(m - 5)$. }

$\dfrac{7}{m(m - 5)} + \dfrac{-3}{m - 5} = \dfrac{4}{m}$

$m(m - 5)\left[\dfrac{7}{m(m - 5)} + \dfrac{-3}{m - 5}\right] = m(m - 5) \cdot \dfrac{4}{m}$

Distribute $m(m - 5)$. Do multiplications.

$\overset{1}{m}(\overset{1}{m - 5}) \cdot \dfrac{7}{\underset{1}{m}(\underset{1}{m - 5})} + m(\overset{1}{m - 5}) \cdot \dfrac{-3}{\underset{1}{m - 5}} =$

$\overset{1}{m}(m - 5) \cdot \dfrac{4}{\underset{1}{m}}$

$m(-3) = -3m;$
$(m - 5)4 = 4m - 20$ ⟶
Add $3m$ to each side. ⟶

Add 20 to each side. ⟶

Divide each side by 7. ⟶

$$7 + m(-3) = (m - 5)4$$
$$7 \quad -3m = 4m - 20$$
$$\underline{ \quad 3m \qquad 3m}$$
$$7 = 7m - 20$$
$$\underline{20 \qquad\qquad 20}$$
$$27 = 7m$$
$$\dfrac{27}{7} = m$$

Thus, the solution set is $\{\tfrac{27}{7}\}$.

EXAMPLE 4   Solve $\dfrac{6}{a+2} + \dfrac{3}{a^2-4} = \dfrac{2a-7}{a-2}$.

Factor $a^2 - 4$; LCD is $(a-2)(a+2)$. $\longrightarrow$ $\dfrac{6}{a+2} + \dfrac{3}{(a-2)(a+2)} = \dfrac{2a-7}{a-2}$

Multiply each side by the LCD, $(a-2)(a+2)$.

$$(a-2)(a+2)\left[\dfrac{6}{a+2} + \dfrac{3}{(a-2)(a+2)}\right] =$$

$$(a-2)(a+2)\cdot\dfrac{2a-7}{a-2}$$

Distribute $(a-2)(a+2)$. $\longrightarrow$ $(a-2)(a+2)\cdot\dfrac{6}{a+2} + (a-2)(a+2)\,\cdot$

$$\dfrac{3}{(a-2)(a+2)} = (a-2)(a+2)\cdot\dfrac{2a-7}{a-2}$$

$$(a-2)\overset{1}{(a+2)}\cdot\dfrac{6}{\underset{1}{a+2}} + \overset{1}{(a-2)}\overset{1}{(a+2)}\,\cdot$$

$$\dfrac{3}{\underset{1}{(a-2)}\,\underset{1}{(a+2)}} = \overset{1}{(a-2)}(a+2)\cdot\dfrac{2a-7}{\underset{1}{a-2}}$$

$$(a-2)6 + 3 = (a+2)(2a-7)$$
$$6a - 12 + 3 = (a+2)(2a-7)$$
$$6a - 9 = 2a^2 - 3a - 14$$

$(a-2)6 = 6a - 12$

$\begin{array}{c} a \qquad +\ 2 \\ 2a \qquad -\ 7 \\ \hline 2a^2 \quad -3a \quad -14 \end{array}$

Put the quadratic equation in standard form.
$$6a - 9 = 2a^2 - 3a - 14$$

Coefficient of a^2 term is positive. Get polynomial $= 0$. Add $-6a$, then 9 to each side.

$$-9 = 2a^2 - 9a - 14 \qquad \text{Terms are arranged in}$$
$$0 = 2a^2 - 9a - 5 \longleftarrow \text{descending order.}$$

Factor. $\longrightarrow$

$$0 = (2a+1)(a-5)$$

Set each factor $= 0$. $\longrightarrow$ $2a + 1 = 0$ or $a - 5 = 0$

Solve each equation for a. $\longrightarrow$

$$2a = -1 \qquad\qquad\qquad a = 5$$
$$a = -\tfrac{1}{2}$$

Thus, the solutions are $-\tfrac{1}{2}$ and 5.

EXERCISES

PART A

Solve.

1. $\dfrac{3}{x^2-4} + \dfrac{5}{x-2} = \dfrac{7}{x+2}$

2. $\dfrac{8}{x^2-7x+12} = \dfrac{5}{x-3} + \dfrac{2}{x-4}$

3. $\dfrac{9}{a^2 - 5a} + \dfrac{3}{a - 5} = \dfrac{2}{a}$

4. $\dfrac{4}{x - 5} = \dfrac{2x - 30}{x^2 - 25} + \dfrac{4}{x + 5}$

5. $\dfrac{5}{n^2 - 3n} - \dfrac{3}{n - 3} = \dfrac{2}{n}$

6. $\dfrac{2}{b^2 - 5b - 14} = \dfrac{3}{b - 7} - \dfrac{4}{b + 2}$

Find the solution set.

7. $\dfrac{4}{y + 5} - \dfrac{2}{y - 8} = \dfrac{3}{y^2 - 3y - 40}$

8. $\dfrac{7}{a^2 - 5a} - \dfrac{2}{a - 5} = \dfrac{4}{a}$

9. $\dfrac{8}{4 - x} + \dfrac{2x + 3}{x^2 - 2x - 8} = \dfrac{7}{x + 2}$

10. $\dfrac{7}{m^2 - 3m} - \dfrac{4}{m} = \dfrac{5}{3 - m}$

11. $\dfrac{4}{a + 3} + \dfrac{2}{3 - a} = \dfrac{4}{a^2 - 9}$

12. $\dfrac{2x + 3}{x^2 - 5x + 6} = \dfrac{2}{x - 2} - \dfrac{5}{x - 3}$

13. $\dfrac{-7}{b^2 - 9b + 20} = \dfrac{b}{b - 4} + \dfrac{1}{b - 5}$

14. $\dfrac{x + 3}{x + 5} + \dfrac{2}{x - 9} = \dfrac{-20}{x^2 - 4x - 45}$

PART B

EXAMPLE Solve $\dfrac{x + 1}{x - 3} = \dfrac{3}{x} + \dfrac{12}{x^2 - 3x}$.

Multiply each side by the LCD, $x(x - 3)$. ──────→

$x(x - 3) \cdot \dfrac{x + 1}{x - 3} = x(x - 3) \cdot \dfrac{3}{x} + x(x - 3) \cdot \dfrac{12}{x(x - 3)}$

$x\overset{\frown}{(x + 1)} = x^2 + x;$
$(x - 3)3 = 3x - 9$ ──────→
Write the equation in standard form.

$x(x + 1) = (x - 3)3 + 12$
$x^2 + x = 3x - 9 + 12$
$x^2 - 2x - 3 = 0$
$(x - 3)(x + 1) = 0$
$x - 3 = 0$ or $x + 1 = 0$
$x = 3$ $x = -1$

If we replace x with 3 in the original equation $\dfrac{x + 1}{x - 3} = \dfrac{3 + 1}{3 - 3}$, or $\dfrac{4}{0}$ which is undefined.

The fraction $\dfrac{x + 1}{x - 3}$ is undefined when $x = 3$.
So, 3 cannot be a solution.

Thus, the solution is -1.

In the example, 3 is an extraneous solution.

An *extraneous solution* of an equation is an apparent solution that does not check.

Solve and check for extraneous solutions.

15. $\dfrac{4}{y^2 - 8y + 12} = \dfrac{y}{y - 2} + \dfrac{1}{y - 6}$

16. $\dfrac{2}{a + 2} - \dfrac{a}{a - 2} = \dfrac{-13}{a^2 - 4}$

17. $x - \dfrac{5x}{x - 2} = \dfrac{-10}{x - 2}$

18. $\dfrac{x^2 + 7x}{x - 2} = 4 + \dfrac{36}{2x - 4}$

Representing Amounts of Work

<table>
<tr><td>

OBJECTIVE

■ To express the amount of work done on a job as a fraction

</td><td>

▶ *REVIEW CAPSULE*

Fractions are used to compare parts of an object with the whole.

What part of the diagram is shaded?

Four of the 5 squares are shaded.

Thus, $\frac{4}{5}$ of the diagram is shaded.

</td></tr>
</table>

EXAMPLE 1 Sheila can mow a lawn in 3 hours. What part of the lawn can she mow in 1 hour?

Lawn

3 hours   1 hour
                 3 hours

In 1 hour, she can mow $\frac{1}{3}$ of the lawn.

EXAMPLE 2 Pedro can paint a house in 5 days. What part will he paint in 1 day? in 3 days? in 4 days? in x days?

He will have finished in

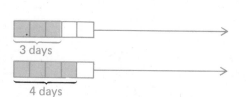

1 day		$\frac{1}{5}$ of the job.
3 days	$3 \cdot \frac{1}{5} = \frac{3}{5}$	of the job.
4 days	$4 \cdot \frac{1}{5} = \frac{4}{5}$	of the job.
x days	$x \cdot \frac{1}{5} = \frac{x}{5}$	of the job.

Example 2 shows this. ———————→

Number of hours to do the job	Part of job done in 1 hour	Part of job done in h hours
x	$\dfrac{1}{x}$	$h\left(\dfrac{1}{x}\right) = \dfrac{h}{x}$

EXAMPLE 3 Emma can mow a lawn in 8 hours. If John helps her they can finish in 5 hours. What part of the job will Emma do?

$a\left(\dfrac{1}{b}\right) = \dfrac{a}{b}$

Emma will do
in 1 hour $\Big\}$ $\dfrac{1}{8}$ of the job.   in 5 hours $\Big\}$ $5 \cdot \dfrac{1}{8}$, or $\dfrac{5}{8}$ of the job.

EXAMPLE 4 Morris can build a fence in 5 days. Helen can build the same fence in x days. If they work together, they can finish in 3 days. What part of the fence is built by each if they work together?

Morris completes
in 1 day $\Big\}$ $\dfrac{1}{5}$ of the work.   in 3 days $\Big\}$ $3 \cdot \dfrac{1}{5}$, or $\dfrac{3}{5}$ of the work.

Helen completes
in 1 day $\Big\}$ $\dfrac{1}{x}$ of the work.   in 3 days $\Big\}$ $3 \cdot \dfrac{1}{x}$, or $\dfrac{3}{x}$ work.

Thus, in 3 days, Morris does $\dfrac{3}{5}$ of the work and

Helen does $\dfrac{3}{x}$ of the work.

EXAMPLE 5 Robert and Sandra sewed costumes for a school play. Working together, they completed a costume in 5 hours. By himself, Robert could sew the costume in 9 hours. Working together, what part of the job did Sandra complete?

Robert completes
in 1 hour $\Big\}$ $\dfrac{1}{9}$ of the job.   in 5 hours $\Big\}$ $5\left(\dfrac{1}{9}\right)$, or $\dfrac{5}{9}$

$\dfrac{5}{9} + \dfrac{4}{9} = 1$ ————————→ **Thus,** Sandra completed $\dfrac{4}{9}$ of the job.

1 means the whole job.

ORAL EXERCISES

What fractional part of the work is completed by each?

		Hours for Entire Job	Hours Worked
1.	Joel	5	1
2.	Peg	4	3
3.	Mary	7	5

		Hours for Entire Job	Hours Worked
4.	José	7	2
5.	Linda	5a	4
6.	Jeff	$3x + 1$	3

EXERCISES

PART A

What fractional part of the job is completed by each when they work together?

1. It takes Jake 5 hours and Bill x hours to do a job. Working together, they finish in 3 hours.

2. It takes Janet m hours and Paula 8 hours to wallpaper a room. Working together, they finish the job in 5 hours.

3. It takes Maria x hours and Todd $2x$ hours to do a job. Working together, they finish in 12 hours.

4. It takes Rudy $3x + 1$ hours and Jane $2x + 4$ hours to repair a radio. Working together, they complete the job in 6 hours.

5. It takes Lester $2m$ hours and Jim $m + 1$ hours to put up a shed. Working together, they finish in 14 hours.

6. It takes Shirley $2x + 3$ days and Ruth x days to paint a kitchen. Working together, they finish the work in 2 days.

7. It takes Mark $3m + 1$ days and Stuart $m - 4$ days to plant a field. Working together, they finish in 3 days.

8. It takes Joyce $a - 2$ hours and Lee $3a + 4$ hours to wax a floor. Working together, they complete the work in 3 hours.

9. It takes Helene and Joan 5 days to complete a job if they work together. Joan can do it alone in 7 days.

10. Working together, it takes Mark and Tina 10 hours to clean a house. Mark can clean it in 30 hours.

PART B

What fractional part of the job is completed by each when they work together?

11. It takes Eleanor 5 hours and Ted twice as long to do a job. Working together, they complete the job in x hours.

12. It takes Martha 4 days and Chris 3 days longer than Martha to do a job. Working together, they finish in x days.

13. It takes Donald x hours and Merv 3 times as long to do a job. Working together, they finish in 5 hours.

14. It takes Hank x hours to do a job. It takes Sylvia 1 hour longer to do the job. Working together, they finish in 6 hours.

Work Problems

 REVIEW CAPSULE

John can paint a house in 5 days.

Part of Job Done in 1 Day	Number of Days Worked	Part of Job Completed
$\dfrac{1}{5}$	x	$x \cdot \dfrac{1}{5} = \dfrac{x}{5}$

EXAMPLE 1 It takes Jack 5 hours and Joan 10 hours to paint a shed. How long will it take them to do the job if they work together?

Let x = hours worked together. ⟶

	Part of Job Done in 1 Hour	Number Hours Working Together	Part of Job Completed
Jack	$\dfrac{1}{5}$	x	$x \cdot \dfrac{1}{5} = \dfrac{x}{5}$
Joan	$\dfrac{1}{10}$	x	$x \cdot \dfrac{1}{10} = \dfrac{x}{10}$

The sum of the fractional parts of a job is 1 whole job. ⟶

$$\underbrace{\text{Part Jack did}} + \underbrace{\text{part Joan did}} = \underbrace{\text{whole job.}}$$

$$\frac{x}{5} \qquad + \qquad \frac{x}{10} \qquad = \qquad 1$$

$$\frac{x}{5} + \frac{x}{5 \cdot 2} = 1$$

Factor 10; LCD is $5 \cdot 2$. ⟶

Multiply each side by $5 \cdot 2$. ⟶

$$5 \cdot 2\left(\frac{x}{5} + \frac{x}{5 \cdot 2}\right) = 5 \cdot 2 \cdot \frac{1}{1}$$

Distribute $5 \cdot 2$; do multiplications.

$$\overset{1}{5} \cdot 2 \cdot \frac{x}{\underset{1}{5}} + \overset{1}{5} \cdot \overset{1}{2} \cdot \frac{x}{\underset{1}{5} \cdot \underset{1}{2}} = 5 \cdot 2 \cdot 1$$

$$2x + 1x = 10$$
$$3x = 10$$
$$x = \frac{10}{3}$$

Thus, it takes $3\frac{1}{3}$ hours if they work together.

EXAMPLE 2 Mike can build a fence in twice the time it would take Henry. Working together, they can build the fence in 7 hours. How long would it take each?

	Part of Job Done in 1 Hour	Number Hours Working Together	Part of Job Completed
Henry	$\dfrac{1}{x}$	7	$7 \cdot \dfrac{1}{x} = \dfrac{7}{x}$
Mike	$\dfrac{1}{2x}$	7	$7 \cdot \dfrac{1}{2x} = \dfrac{7}{2x}$

Let x = hours for Henry alone. ────→

$2x$ = hours for Mike alone. ────→

Part Henry did + part Mike did = 1.

$$\frac{7}{x} + \frac{7}{2x} = 1$$

Multiply each side by the LCD, $2 \cdot x$.

$$2 \cdot x \left(\frac{7}{x} + \frac{7}{2 \cdot x} \right) = 2 \cdot x \cdot \frac{1}{1}$$

Distribute $2 \cdot x$; do multiplications.

$$2 \cdot \overset{1}{\cancel{x}} \cdot \frac{7}{\underset{1}{\cancel{x}}} + 2 \cdot \overset{1}{\cancel{x}} \cdot \frac{7}{2 \cdot \underset{1}{\cancel{x}}} = 2 \cdot x \cdot 1$$

$$14 + 7 = 2x$$
$$21 = 2x$$
$$10\tfrac{1}{2} = x$$

Hours for Mike alone ────────→
Hours for Henry alone ────────→

Thus, it would take Henry $10\tfrac{1}{2}$ hours and Mike 21 hours.

EXAMPLE 3 Working together, Pat and Pam can paint a house in 14 hours. If it takes Pam 30 hours alone, how long would it take Pat alone?

	Part of Job Done in 1 Hour	Number Hours Working Together	Part of Job Completed
Pam	$\dfrac{1}{30}$	14	$14 \cdot \dfrac{1}{30} = \dfrac{14}{30}$
Pat	$\dfrac{1}{x}$	14	$14 \cdot \dfrac{1}{x} = \dfrac{14}{x}$

Let x = hours for Pat alone. ────→

Part Pam did + part Pat did = 1.

$$\frac{14}{30} + \frac{14}{x} = 1$$

Multiply each side by the LCD, $30 \cdot x$.

$$30 \cdot x \left(\frac{14}{30} + \frac{14}{x} \right) = 30 \cdot x \cdot \frac{1}{1}$$

Distribute $30 \cdot x$; do multiplications.

$$\overset{1}{\cancel{30}} \cdot x \cdot \frac{14}{\underset{1}{\cancel{30}}} + 30 \cdot \overset{1}{\cancel{x}} \cdot \frac{14}{\underset{1}{\cancel{x}}} = 30 \cdot x \cdot 1$$

$$14x + 420 = 30x$$
$$420 = 16x$$
$$26\tfrac{1}{4} = x$$

Add $-14x$ to each side. ────→
$\dfrac{420}{16} = \dfrac{105}{4}$, or $26\tfrac{1}{4}$ ────→

Thus, it would take Pat $26\tfrac{1}{4}$ hours.

EXERCISES

PART A

1. Fay can prepare surgical equipment in 3 hours. Another nurse, Carlo, can do it in 4 hours. How long will it take if they work together?

2. A mason can put up a tile wall in 6 days. A helper can do it alone in 8 days. How long will it take them if they work together?

3. Together, Stanley and Elsie can mow a lawn in 3 hours. It would take Elsie 5 hours to do it alone. How long would it take Stanley?

4. Together, Pat and Pam can prepare a turkey dinner in 6 hours. It would take Pam 8 hours by herself. How long would it take Pat?

5. George can address envelopes in 4 hours. If Flora helps him, they can complete the job in 1 hour. How long would it take Flora alone?

6. Noah can deliver papers in twice the time it would take Jake. How long would it take each if they can do the job together in 3 hours?

7. Working together, Josephine and Lois can clean a house in 6 hours. It takes Lois 3 times longer than Josephine to do it alone. How long would it take each girl alone?

8. Working together, two carpenters can build a house in 5 months. It takes one of them twice as long as the other to do it alone. How long would it take each alone?

PART B

9. To do a job alone, it would take Rose 4 hours, Bill 3 hours, and Marc 5 hours. How long would it take if they all work together?

10. To do a job alone, it would take Jane 3 hours, Mary 5 hours, and Jerry 6 hours. How long would it take if they all work together?

11. Eva can mow a lawn in 4 hours. It would take Bob 3 hours. How long would it take Ted if, working together, all three can do the job in 1 hour?

12. Martha can build a desk in 3 weeks. It would take Joe 5 weeks. How long would it take Kim if, working together, all three can do the job in 1 week?

13. Mary can make a suit in 5 hours. It would take Jane twice as long as Jerome. How long would it take Jane if, working together, all three can do it in 2 hours?

14. Bill can repair a transmission in 8 hours. It would take Henry 3 times as long as Clara. How long would it take Clara if, working together, all three can do it in 4 hours?

Applying Percent

PROBLEM 1.

8 is what % of 14?

Let x = the %

8 is what % of 14?

x% of 14 means $x \cdot 14$.

$8 = x \cdot 14$

$8 = 14x$

$\dfrac{8}{14} = x$

$.57 = x$

$$\begin{array}{r} .57 \\ 14\overline{)8.00} \\ \underline{70} \\ 100 \\ \underline{98} \\ 2 \end{array}$$

.57 means 57%.   Thus, 8 is 57% of 14.

PROBLEM 2.

A basketball team won 5 games and lost 3 games. What % of the games played did the team win?

Let x = % of games won

What % of games played are games won?

5 wins + 3 losses = 8 games

$x \cdot 8 = 5$

$8x = 5$

$x = \dfrac{5}{8}$ or .63

.63 means 63%.   Thus, the team won 63% of their games.

PROJECT

1. 6 is what % of 30?   **2.** 14 is what % of 42?

3. A team won 7 games and lost 5. What % of the games are wins?

4. A class has 20 girls and 15 boys. What % of the class are boys?

PROBLEM 3.

60% of what number is 300?

$$\begin{aligned} \text{Let } n &= \text{number} \end{aligned}$$

60% of what number is 300?

$$60\% \text{ of } n = 300$$

60% of n = .60(n) ⎫
        = .60n ⎬

Multiply each side by 100. ⟶

Divide each side by 60. ⟶

$$\begin{aligned}.60n &= 300 \\ 100(.60n) &= 100(300) \\ 60n &= 30000 \\ n &= 500 \end{aligned}$$

Thus, 60% of 500 is 300.

PROBLEM 4.

A store manager lists the selling price of a television at $156. If the profit is 30% of the cost, find the cost.

Let x = cost

Profit is 30% of cost ⎫
      30% of x ⎬

30% of x: .30(x)

cost + profit = selling price

$$\begin{aligned} x + 30\% \text{ of } x &= 156 \\ x + .30(x) &= 156 \\ 1x + .30x &= 156 \end{aligned}$$

Multiply each side by 100. ⟶

$$\begin{aligned} 100(1x + .30x) &= 100(156) \\ 100x + 30x &= 15600 \\ 130x &= 15600 \end{aligned}$$

Divide each side by 130. ⟶

$$x = 120$$

$$\dfrac{120}{130\overline{)15600}}$$

Thus, the cost of the T.V. is $120.

PROJECT

5. 40% of what number is 20?

6. 60% of what number is 24?

7. A merchant sells a camera for $250. Find the cost if the profit is 25% of the cost.

8. A couch is sold for $550. Find the cost if the profit is 40% of the cost.

Equations with Decimals

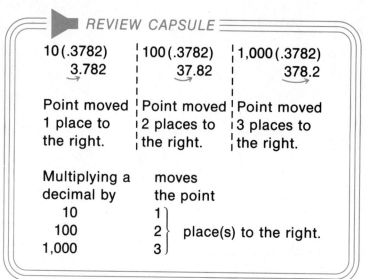

REVIEW CAPSULE

| 10(.3782) | 100(.3782) | 1,000(.3782) |
| 3.782 | 37.82 | 378.2 |

Point moved 1 place to the right. | Point moved 2 places to the right. | Point moved 3 places to the right.

Multiplying a decimal by 10, 100, 1,000 moves the point 1, 2, 3 place(s) to the right.

EXAMPLE 1

Rewrite $.3x + .45 = .984$ as an equation which has only whole numbers.

First rewrite all decimals as fractions.

$$\frac{3}{10}x + \frac{45}{100} = \frac{984}{1,000} \leftarrow \text{LCD is 1,000.}$$

Multiply each side by 1,000. →

$$1,000\left(\frac{3}{10}x + \frac{45}{100}\right) = 1,000\left(\frac{984}{1,000}\right)$$

$.3 = \frac{3}{10}$; $.45 = \frac{45}{100}$; $.984 = \frac{984}{1,000}$

Distribute 1,000; do multiplications. →

$$\overset{100}{1,000}\left(\frac{3}{10}x\right) + \overset{10}{1,000}\left(\frac{45}{100}\right) = \overset{1}{1,000}\left(\frac{984}{1,000}\right)$$

$$300x + 450 = 984$$

Equation with only whole numbers

$.3 \quad .45 \quad .984$
$\downarrow \quad \downarrow \quad \downarrow \quad$ LCD = 1,000
$\frac{3}{10} \quad \frac{45}{100} \quad \frac{984}{1,000}$

$1,000(.3) = 300.$ $1,000(.45) = 450.$
$1,000(.984) = 984.$

Here is a more convenient technique.

$$.3x + .45 = .984$$

$$1,000(.3x + .45) = 1,000(.984)$$
$$1,000(.3x) + 1,000(.45) = 1,000(.984)$$
$$300x + 450 = 984$$

Notice that this is the same equation as the resulting equation in Example 1.

For the equation,

$$.3x \quad + \quad .45 \quad = \quad .984$$

one digit   two digits   three digits
past point   past point   past point

the LCD is 1,000.

three zeros

The greatest number of digits past any decimal point is three. LCD = 1,000.

EXAMPLE 2   Give the LCD for each equation.
$$.03x - .004 = .72x + 1.8 \qquad .2x + .04 = 5x - .36$$

$$.03x - .004 = .72x + 1.8 \mid .2x + .04 = 5(x) - .36$$

Number of digits past decimal point

two   three   two   one | one   two   none   two

LCD is 1,000. | LCD is 100.

EXAMPLE 3   Solve $.5x - 1.2 = 6.4$.

The greatest number of digits past any decimal point is one. LCD = 10.

To multiply by 10, move the decimal point one place to the right. ———⟶

Add 12 to each side. ———⟶

Divide each side by 5. ———⟶

$$10(.5x - 1.2) = 10(6.4)$$
$$10(.5x) - 10(1.2) = 10(6.4)$$
$$5x \quad - \quad 12 \quad = 64$$
$$5x = 76$$
$$x = \frac{76}{5}, \text{ or } 15\frac{1}{5}$$

$\frac{1}{5} = 1 \div 5 = .2$ ———⟶ **Thus,** the solution is $15\frac{1}{5}$, or 15.2.

EXAMPLE 4   Solve $.15x - 7.2 = 8.5$.

$$.15x - 7.2 = 8.5$$

two   one   one

The greatest number of digits past any decimal point is two. LCD = 100.

Multiply each side by 100. ———⟶

To multiply by 100, move the decimal point two places to the right. ———⟶

Add 720 to each side. ———⟶

Divide each side by 15. ———⟶

$$100(.15x - 7.2) = 100(8.5)$$
$$100(.15x) - 100(7.2) = 100(8.5)$$
$$15x \quad - \quad 720 \quad = 850$$
$$15x = 1,570$$
$$x = \frac{1,570}{15}, \text{ or } 104\frac{2}{3}$$

Thus, the solution is $104\frac{2}{3}$.

EXERCISES

Solve. Answers may be written in fraction or decimal form.

1. $.03x = .2$
4. $.1x - 2.4 = 1.17$
7. $.18x - 24 = .1x + .6$
10. $.012x - 4 = .112x + 1$

2. $.016 = .32x$
5. $.007 = .7x - .21$
8. $5 - .03x = .7x - .11$
11. $.7x - 1 = .6x + .002$

3. $.004x - 7.1 = .12$
6. $2.1x = .72 + 1.8x$
9. $.7x - .2 = .13x - 80$
12. $.5 - .08x = .004x + .2$

PART B

EXAMPLE Solve $.02(4 - .3x) = .15x + 3.2$.

Distribute .02. ————————————→

$.02(.3) = \dfrac{2}{100}\left(\dfrac{3}{10}\right) = \dfrac{6}{1,000} = .006$

$$.02(4) - .02(.3x) = .15x + 3.2$$
$$\underbrace{.08}_{\uparrow} - \underbrace{.006x}_{\uparrow} = \underbrace{.15x}_{\uparrow} + \underbrace{3.2}_{\uparrow}$$
$$\text{two} \qquad \text{three} \qquad \text{two} \qquad \text{one}$$

Multiply each side by the LCD, 1,000. ——→

$$1,000(.08 - .006x) = 1,000(.15x + 3.2)$$
$$1,000(.08) - 1,000(.006x) = 1,000(.15x) + 1,000(3.2)$$
$$80 \quad - \quad 6x \quad = \quad 150x \quad + \quad 3,200$$
$$-156x = 3,120$$
$$x = \frac{3,120}{-156}, \text{ or } -20$$

Thus, the solution is -20.

Solve. Answers may be written in fraction or decimal form.

13. $.03(4 - .2x) = .17x - 1.2$
15. $.3x + 2.91 = 5 - .2(3 - .01x)$
17. $.04(.2 - .1x) = 7.12 + .02x$

14. $.01(5 - .2x) = .75 + .198x$
16. $47.582 - .01(.2 + 3x) = 7.9x$
18. $.1(2 - 7x) = 7.1 - 3x$

PART C

Solve. Answers may be written in fraction or decimal form.

19. $.3x - .02[.7 - .1(5 - .04x)] = .006$
20. $7 - .04[6x - (2 - .01x)] = .005$

Rational Numbers

▶ *REVIEW CAPSULE*

Write $\frac{7}{8}$ as a decimal.

```
    .875
8)7.000
    64
    ──
    60
    56
    ──
    40
    40
    ──
     0
```

$\frac{7}{8} = .875$

↑
terminating decimal

Write $\frac{5}{6}$ as a decimal.

```
    .833 . . .
6)5.000
   48
   ──
   20
   18
   ──
   20
   18
   ──
    2
```

←The bar means 3 repeats.

$\frac{5}{6} = .83\overline{3}$

↑
repeating decimal

Definition of rational number ──────→

A *rational number* is a number which can be written in the form $\frac{a}{b}$, where a and b are integers and $b \neq 0$.

EXAMPLE 1 Show that the integers -16, 0, 1, and 23 are rational numbers.

Write each as $\frac{a}{b}$, where a is the integer itself and b is 1.

$$-16 = \frac{-16}{1} \quad\Big|\quad 0 = \frac{0}{1} \quad\Big|\quad 1 = \frac{1}{1} \quad\Big|\quad 23 = \frac{23}{1}$$

Thus, -16, 0, 1, and 23 are rational numbers.

Every integer is a rational number.

EXAMPLE 2 Show that $\frac{2}{3}$, $\frac{5}{2}$, and $-\frac{9}{16}$ are rational numbers.

$-\frac{9}{16} = \frac{-9}{16}$

$$\frac{2}{3} \quad\Big|\quad \frac{5}{2} \quad\Big|\quad \frac{-9}{16}$$

All are in the form $\frac{a}{b}$, where a and b are integers.

Thus, $\frac{2}{3}$, $\frac{5}{2}$, and $-\frac{9}{16}$ are rational numbers.

EXAMPLE 3   Show that these decimals are rational numbers.

.7	−.06	2.591
↓	↓	↓

Write each as $\frac{a}{b}$, where b is 10, 100, and 1,000. ⟶ $\frac{7}{10}$ | $\frac{-6}{100}$ | $\frac{2,591}{1,000}$

Thus, .7, −.06, and 2.591 are rational numbers.

Every terminating decimal is a rational number.

EXAMPLE 4   Show that $.3\overline{3}$ is a rational number.

The bar means 3 repeats.
$.3\overline{3} = .3333\ldots$ ⟶ Let $n = .333\overline{3}$ (1)

Multiply each side by 10; the decimal point moves one place. ⟶

$$10n = 3.333\overline{3} \quad (2)$$

Multiply each side of equation (1) by −1. Add equations (2) and (3). ⟶

$$-\ 1n = -\ .333\overline{3} \quad (3)$$
$$\overline{9n = 3.0000}$$

or

$$9n = 3$$

Divide each side by 9. ⟶

$$n = \frac{3}{9}, \text{ or } \frac{1}{3}$$

$\frac{3}{9} = \frac{1}{3}$ ↙ integer ⟶ **Thus,** $.3\overline{3}$ is the rational number $\frac{1}{3}$.

EXAMPLE 5   Show that $.94\overline{4}$ is a rational number.

Let $n = .944\overline{4}$ (1)

Multiply each side by 10; the decimal point moves one place. ⟶

$$10n = 9.444\overline{4} \quad (2)$$

Multiply each side of equation (1) by −1. Add equations (2) and (3). ⟶

$$-\ 1n = -\ .944\overline{4} \quad (3)$$
$$\overline{9n = 8.5000}$$

or

$$9n = 8.5$$

Divide each side by 9. ⟶

$$n = \frac{8.5}{9}$$

$\frac{8.5}{9} = \frac{8.5(10)}{9(10)} = \frac{85}{90}$ ↙ integer ⟶

$$n = \frac{85}{90}, \text{ or } \frac{17}{18}$$

Check. $18\overline{)17.000}$ .94$\overline{4}$ ⟶ **Thus,** $.94\overline{4}$ is the rational number $\frac{17}{18}$.

Every repeating decimal is a rational number.

EXAMPLE 6 Show that $2.6\overline{6}$ is a rational number.

Let $n = 2.666\overline{6}$ (1)

Multiply each side by 10; the decimal point moves one place. $\longrightarrow$

Multiply each side of equation (1) by -1.

Add equations (2) and (3). $\longrightarrow$

$$
\begin{array}{rl}
10n = & 26.666\overline{6} \ \ (2) \\
-\ \ 1n = -& 2.666\overline{6} \ \ (3) \\
\hline
9n = & 24.0000
\end{array}
$$

or $9n = 24$

Divide each side by 9. $\longrightarrow$

$n = \dfrac{24}{9}$, or $\dfrac{8}{3}$

Thus, $2.6\overline{6}$ is the rational number $\dfrac{8}{3}$.

EXERCISES

PART A

Show that each is a rational number.

1. -1 **2.** 32 **3.** -16 **4.** 0 **5.** $-\dfrac{24}{36}$ **6.** .00706 **7.** -3.64

8. $.7\overline{7}$ **9.** $.4\overline{4}$ **10.** $.62\overline{2}$ **11.** $.75\overline{5}$ **12.** $1.2\overline{2}$ **13.** $3.5\overline{5}$ **14.** $.48\overline{8}$

PART B

EXAMPLE Show that $1.7\overline{878}$ is a rational number.

Let $n = 1.787878$ (1)

Multiply each side by 100; the decimal point moves two places. $\longrightarrow$

Multiply each side of equation (1) by -1. Add equations (2) and (3). $\longrightarrow$

$$
\begin{array}{rl}
100n = & 178.787878 \ \ (2) \\
-\ \ 1n = -& 1.787878 \ \ (3) \\
\hline
99n = & 177
\end{array}
$$

Divide each side by 99. $\longrightarrow$

$n = \dfrac{177}{99}$, or $\dfrac{59}{33}$

Thus, $1.7\overline{878}$ is the rational number $\dfrac{59}{33}$.

Show that each is a rational number.

15. $.16\overline{16}$ **16.** $.24\overline{24}$ **17.** $.83\overline{83}$ **18.** $.75\overline{75}$ **19.** $.98\overline{98}$

PART C

Show that each is a rational number.

20. $5.781234\overline{234}$ **21.** $3.06789\overline{789}$ **22.** $214.5681428\overline{142}$

Investment and Loan Problems

OBJECTIVE

■ To solve problems about investments and loans using the formula $i = prt$

 REVIEW CAPSULE

John invested $400 at 6% for 1 year. How much interest did he earn?

$i = ?$	$i = prt$
$p = \$400$	$= 400\,(.06)\,(1)$
$r = 6\%$	$= 24.$ ⌐—Change the
$t = 1$ yr	percent to a decimal.

Thus, he earned $24 interest.

i	$=$	p	$\times$	r	$\times$	t
↓		↓		↓		↓
Interest: Money paid to use money invested or loaned		Principal Money invested or loaned		Rate Percent paid per year to use money invested or loaned		Time Years money is invested or loaned

Interest formula

EXAMPLE 1 Marita borrowed x dollars at $7\frac{1}{2}\%$ interest for 1 year. Write an algebraic expression for the amount of interest she paid.

Use the formula. ———————→
Substitute; $7\frac{1}{2}\% = .075$. ———————→

$$i = prt$$
$$= x\,(.075)\,(1)$$
$$= .075x$$

Thus, $.075x$ represents the interest Marita paid.

EXAMPLE 2 The Lees invested $1,000 for 1 year. They earned $60 interest. What was the rate of return?

Use the formula. ———————→
Substitute. ———————→

$$i = prt$$
$$60 = 1,000\,(x)\,(1)$$
$$\frac{60}{1,000} = x$$

$\dfrac{60}{1,000} = \dfrac{6}{100} = .06$, or 6%. ———————→ **Thus,** the rate of return was 6%.

EXAMPLE 3   Ellen invested one sum of money at $5\frac{1}{2}$% and another sum at 6%. She invested $300 more at the 6% rate than at the $5\frac{1}{2}$% rate. If her total interest for 1 year was $133, find the amount she invested at each rate.

Represent the amounts invested algebraically.

Let x = amount (in dollars) invested at $5\frac{1}{2}$%
$x + 300$ = amount (in dollars) invested at 6%

Make a chart. ───────────→

Principal	Rate	Time	Interest ($i = prt$)
x	.055	1 yr	.055x
$x + 300$	.06	1 yr	.06$(x + 300)$

Write an equation. ───────→ (Interest at $5\frac{1}{2}$%) + (Interest at 6%) = (Total interest)
Substitute. ───────────→ $.055x + .06(x + 300) = 133$
$.055x + .06x + 18 = 133$
Multiply each side by 1,000. ──→ $55x + 60x + 18,000 = 133,000$
$115x = 115,000$
Amount invested at $5\frac{1}{2}$% ──────→ $x = 1,000$
$x + 300 = 1,000 + 300,$
Amount invested at 6% ────────→ or 1,300

Thus, Ellen invested $1,000 at $5\frac{1}{2}$% and $1,300 at 6%.

EXAMPLE 4   Irving borrowed $1,900, part from a bank at an interest rate of 8% and the rest from his father at 5%. At the end of 6 months, he owed $64 in interest. How much did he borrow from each?

Represent the amounts borrowed algebraically.

Let x = amount (in dollars) borrowed at 8%
$1,900 - x$ = amount (in dollars) borrowed at 5%

Make a chart. ───────────→
6 months = .5 yr

Principal	Rate	Time	Interest ($i = prt$)
x	.08	.5 yr	.04x
$1,900 - x$	.05	.5 yr	.025$(1,900 - x)$

Write an equation. ───────→ (Interest at 8%) + (Interest at 5%) = (Total interest)
Substitute. ───────────→ $.04x + .025(1,900 - x) = 64$
$.04x + 47.5 - .025x = 64$
Multiply each side by 1,000. ──→ $40x + 47,500 - 25x = 64,000$
$15x = 16,500$
Amount borrowed at 8% ───────→ $x = 1,100$
Amount borrowed at 5% ───────→ $1,900 - x = 1,900 - 1,100,$
or 800

Thus, he borrowed $1,100 at 8% and $800 at 5%.

EXAMPLE 5

Alba invested one-half of her money at $5\frac{3}{4}$% and one-fourth of her money at $5\frac{1}{2}$%. If her total interest at the end of 1 year was $136, find her original sum of money.

Represent the amounts invested algebraically.

Let $x =$ amount of original sum of money
$\frac{1}{2}x =$ amount (in dollars) invested at $5\frac{3}{4}$%
$\frac{1}{4}x =$ amount (in dollars) invested at $5\frac{1}{2}$%

Make a chart. ──────────→

$5\frac{3}{4}$% = 5.75% = .0575

$5\frac{1}{2}$% = 5.5% = .055

Principal	Rate	Time	Interest ($i = prt$)
$\frac{1}{2}x$	.0575	1 yr	$\frac{.0575}{2}x$
$\frac{1}{4}x$	.055	1 yr	$\frac{.055}{4}x$

Write an equation. ──────────→ (Interest at $5\frac{3}{4}$%) + (Interest at $5\frac{1}{2}$%) = (Total interest)

Substitute. ──────────→ $\frac{.0575}{2}x + \frac{.055}{4}x = 136$

Multiply each side by 4. ──────→ $.115x + .055x = 544$

Multiply each side by 1,000. ──────→
$115x + 55x = 544,000$
$170x = 544,000$
$x = 3,200$

Thus, Alba's original sum of money was $3,200.

EXAMPLE 6

Harry had $600. He invested part of it at 6% and the rest at 5%. At the end of 1 year, his total return on these investments was $34. How much did he invest at each rate?

Represent the amounts invested algebraically.

Let $x =$ amount (in dollars) invested at 6%
$600 - x =$ amount (in dollars) invested at 5%

Make a chart. ──────────→

Principal	Rate	Time	Interest ($i = prt$)
x	.06	1 yr	$.06x$
$600 - x$	.05	1 yr	$.05(600 - x)$

Write an equation. ──────────→ (Interest at 6%) + (Interest at 5%) = (Total interest)

Substitute. ──────────→ $.06x + .05(600 - x) = 34$
$.06x + 30 - .05x = 34$

Multiply each side by 100. ──────→ $6x + 3,000 - 5x = 3,400$
$1x = 400$
$x = 400$
$600 - x = 600 - 400,$
or 200

Thus, he invested $400 at 6% and $200 at 5%.

EXERCISES

1. Bill borrowed $5,000 at $7\frac{1}{2}$% interest for 1 year. How much interest did he pay at the end of 1 year?

2. Ms. Diaz invested $5,000 for 1 year. She earned $300 interest. What was the rate of return?

3. Liz invested $1,800, part at 5% and the rest at 6%. If her total interest at the end of 1 year was $96, find the amount she invested at each rate.

4. Mr. Susan had $2,500. He invested part of it at $5\frac{3}{4}$% and the rest at 5%. At the end of 3 years, his total return was $420. How much did he invest at each rate?

5. Tony borrowed some money from friends. He borrowed part of it at 4% and the rest at 6%. The amount borrowed at 6% was twice the amount borrowed at 4%. If the total interest after 1 year was $96, how much did he borrow at each rate?

6. Doris borrowed some money from friends. She borrowed part of it at 8% and the rest at 5%. The amount borrowed at 5% was $1,200 more than the amount borrowed at 8%. If the total interest after $\frac{1}{2}$ year was $160, find the amount of each loan.

7. Melba had $1,300. She invested part of it at 5% and the rest at 6%. At the end of 2 years, her total return was $146. How much did she invest at each rate?

8. Rodney invested $800, part of it at 4% and the rest at 5%. At the end of 3 years, his total return was $111. How much did he invest at each rate?

9. The Kickingbirds invested $10,000, part at 5% and the rest at $4\frac{1}{2}$%. At the end of 6 years, their total return was $2,880. How much did they invest at each rate?

10. The Yoshidas invested $5,000, part at 6% and the rest at $6\frac{1}{2}$%. At the end of 4 years, their total return was $1,245. How much did they invest at each rate?

11. Ann invested one-half of her money at $5\frac{1}{2}$% and one-fourth at 6%. At the end of 2 years, she had earned $595 in interest. What was the original sum of money?

12. Bob invested one-third of his money at 6% and three-fifths at $6\frac{1}{2}$%. At the end of 3 years, he had earned $531 in interest. What was the original sum of money?

Complex Fractions

▶ *REVIEW CAPSULE*

Simplify $6a^2\left(\dfrac{3}{a}+\dfrac{5}{2}\right)$.

$$6a^2 \cdot \frac{3}{a} + 6a^2 \cdot \frac{5}{2}$$

$$3 \cdot 2 \cdot \overset{1}{\cancel{a}} \cdot a \cdot \frac{3}{\underset{1}{\cancel{a}}} + 3 \cdot \overset{1}{\cancel{2}} \cdot a \cdot a \cdot \frac{5}{\underset{1}{\cancel{2}}}$$

$$18a + 15a^2$$

or $\qquad 15a^2 + 18a$

Complex Fractions

$$\frac{\dfrac{1}{2}\Big\}\text{numerator}}{6\ \ \text{denominator}} \qquad\qquad \frac{\dfrac{2}{3}\Big\}\text{numerator}}{\dfrac{1}{5}\Big\}\text{denominator}}$$

$$\frac{x+3\ \ \text{numerator}}{\dfrac{2}{x}\Big\}\ \ \text{denominator}}$$

Definition of complex fraction $\longrightarrow$ | A *complex fraction* is one whose numerator or denominator or both contain a fraction.

EXAMPLE 1

Simplify $\dfrac{\dfrac{2}{3}}{\dfrac{1}{5}}$.

The LCD of $\dfrac{2}{3}$ and $\dfrac{1}{5}$ is $3 \cdot 5$.

Multiply both numerator and denominator

by $3 \cdot 5$; $\dfrac{a}{b} = \dfrac{a \cdot c}{b \cdot c}$

$$\frac{3 \cdot 5 \cdot \dfrac{2}{3}}{3 \cdot 5 \cdot \dfrac{1}{5}} = \frac{\overset{1}{\cancel{3}} \cdot 5 \cdot \dfrac{2}{\underset{1}{\cancel{3}}}}{3 \cdot \overset{1}{\cancel{5}} \cdot \dfrac{1}{\underset{1}{\cancel{5}}}}$$

$$= \frac{10}{3}$$

EXAMPLE 2 Simplify $\dfrac{3a + \dfrac{2}{3}}{\dfrac{a}{2} + \dfrac{5}{6}}$.

$3a = \dfrac{3a}{1}$ ⟶

$\dfrac{\dfrac{3a}{1} + \dfrac{2}{3}}{\dfrac{a}{2} + \dfrac{5}{3 \cdot 2}}$

Factor the denominators. ⟶

The LCD of $\dfrac{3a}{1}, \dfrac{2}{3}, \dfrac{a}{2}, \dfrac{5}{3 \cdot 2}$ is $3 \cdot 2$.

Multiply both numerator and denominator by $3 \cdot 2$.

$\dfrac{3 \cdot 2\left(\dfrac{3a}{1} + \dfrac{2}{3}\right)}{3 \cdot 2\left(\dfrac{a}{2} + \dfrac{5}{3 \cdot 2}\right)}$

Distribute $3 \cdot 2$. Divide out common factors in each product.

$\dfrac{3 \cdot 2 \cdot \dfrac{3a}{1} + \overset{1}{3} \cdot 2 \cdot \dfrac{2}{\underset{1}{3}}}{3 \cdot \overset{1}{2} \cdot \dfrac{a}{\underset{1}{2}} + \overset{1}{3} \cdot \overset{1}{2} \cdot \dfrac{5}{\underset{1}{3} \cdot \underset{1}{2}}}$

Multiply remaining factors in each product.

$\dfrac{18a + 4}{3a + 5}$

EXAMPLE 3 Simplify $\dfrac{\dfrac{3}{a} - \dfrac{5}{2}}{\dfrac{7}{3} + \dfrac{4}{a^2}}$.

$\dfrac{3}{a} - \dfrac{5}{2} = \dfrac{3}{a} + \dfrac{-1 \cdot 5}{2} = \dfrac{3}{a} + \dfrac{-5}{2}$ ⟶

$\dfrac{\dfrac{3}{a} + \dfrac{-5}{2}}{\dfrac{7}{3} + \dfrac{4}{a \cdot a}}$

Factor the denominators. ⟶

The LCD of $\dfrac{3}{a}, \dfrac{-5}{2}, \dfrac{7}{3}, \dfrac{4}{a \cdot a}$ is $3 \cdot 2 \cdot a \cdot a$.

Multiply both numerator and denominator by the LCD.

$\dfrac{3 \cdot 2 \cdot a \cdot a\left(\dfrac{3}{a} + \dfrac{-5}{2}\right)}{3 \cdot 2 \cdot a \cdot a\left(\dfrac{7}{3} + \dfrac{4}{a \cdot a}\right)}$

Distribute $3 \cdot 2 \cdot a \cdot a$. Divide out common factors in each product.

$\dfrac{3 \cdot 2 \cdot \overset{1}{a} \cdot a \cdot \dfrac{3}{\underset{1}{a}} + 3 \cdot \overset{1}{2} \cdot a \cdot a \cdot \dfrac{-5}{\underset{1}{2}}}{\overset{1}{3} \cdot 2 \cdot a \cdot a \cdot \dfrac{7}{\underset{1}{3}} + 3 \cdot 2 \cdot \overset{1}{a} \cdot \overset{1}{a} \cdot \dfrac{4}{\underset{1}{a} \cdot \underset{1}{a}}}$

Multiply remaining factors in each product.

$\dfrac{18a - 15a^2}{14a^2 + 24}$, or $\dfrac{-15a^2 + 18a}{14a^2 + 24}$

EXERCISES

Simplify.

1. $\dfrac{\dfrac{2}{5}}{\dfrac{1}{7}}$

2. $\dfrac{\dfrac{1}{2}}{\dfrac{3}{5}}$

3. $\dfrac{\dfrac{2}{5} + \dfrac{1}{10}}{\dfrac{1}{2} + \dfrac{3}{5}}$

4. $\dfrac{\dfrac{2}{3} + \dfrac{1}{2}}{\dfrac{1}{6} + \dfrac{1}{2}}$

5. $\dfrac{3a + \dfrac{1}{2}}{\dfrac{a}{5} + \dfrac{3}{10}}$

6. $\dfrac{\dfrac{3a}{2} + 1}{\dfrac{a}{4} + \dfrac{1}{2}}$

7. $\dfrac{4a + \dfrac{1}{3}}{2a + \dfrac{1}{3}}$

8. $\dfrac{\dfrac{3b}{5} + \dfrac{2}{3}}{\dfrac{b}{15} + \dfrac{3}{5}}$

9. $\dfrac{\dfrac{4}{a} - \dfrac{3}{5}}{\dfrac{3}{2} + \dfrac{7}{a^2}}$

10. $\dfrac{\dfrac{3}{5} - \dfrac{4}{b}}{\dfrac{2}{b^2} + \dfrac{3}{2}}$

11. $\dfrac{\dfrac{3}{a^2} - \dfrac{5}{a}}{\dfrac{2}{a} + \dfrac{1}{a^2}}$

12. $\dfrac{\dfrac{4}{b^2} + \dfrac{3}{b}}{\dfrac{2}{b} + \dfrac{5}{3b^2}}$

EXAMPLE

Simplify $\dfrac{1 - \dfrac{5}{m} + \dfrac{4}{m^2}}{1 - \dfrac{16}{m^2}}$.

$$\dfrac{m^2\left(1 - \dfrac{5}{m} + \dfrac{4}{m^2}\right)}{m^2\left(1 - \dfrac{16}{m^2}\right)} = \dfrac{m^2 + m^2 \cdot \dfrac{-5}{m} + m^2 \cdot \dfrac{4}{m^2}}{m^2 + m^2 \cdot \dfrac{-16}{m^2}}$$

$$= \dfrac{m^2 - 5m + 4}{m^2 - 16}$$

$$= \dfrac{(m - 4)(m - 1)}{(m - 4)(m + 4)}, \text{ or } \dfrac{m - 1}{m + 4}$$

Simplify.

13. $\dfrac{1 + \dfrac{3}{x} + \dfrac{2}{x^2}}{\dfrac{1}{x} + \dfrac{2}{x^2}}$

14. $\dfrac{1 - \dfrac{9}{x} + \dfrac{14}{x^2}}{\dfrac{1}{x} - \dfrac{7}{x^2}}$

15. $\dfrac{\dfrac{1}{m} + \dfrac{2}{m^2}}{1 - \dfrac{6}{m} - \dfrac{16}{m^2}}$

More Complex Fractions

OBJECTIVE

■ To simplify fractions like

$$\frac{x - 2 + \dfrac{3}{x + 3}}{\dfrac{x^2 - 9}{x^2 - x - 6}}$$

▶ REVIEW CAPSULE

Simplify $\dfrac{\dfrac{c}{2} + \dfrac{3}{5}}{\dfrac{c}{10} + \dfrac{1}{2}}$.

$$\frac{5 \cdot 2\left(\dfrac{c}{2} + \dfrac{3}{5}\right)}{5 \cdot 2\left(\dfrac{c}{5 \cdot 2} + \dfrac{1}{2}\right)}$$

$$\frac{5 \cdot \overset{1}{\cancel{2}} \cdot \dfrac{c}{\cancel{2}_1} + \cancel{5} \cdot 2 \cdot \dfrac{3}{\cancel{5}_1}}{\cancel{5} \cdot \cancel{2} \cdot \dfrac{c}{\cancel{5 \cdot 2}} + 5 \cdot \cancel{2} \cdot \dfrac{1}{\cancel{2}}} = \frac{5c + 6}{c + 5}$$

EXAMPLE 1

Simplify $\dfrac{\dfrac{5}{m - 3} + \dfrac{7}{m + 2}}{\dfrac{7}{m^2 - m - 6} + \dfrac{1}{m - 3}}$.

$m^2 - m - 6 = (m - 3)(m + 2)$;
LCD $= (m - 3)(m + 2)$. $\longrightarrow$

$$\frac{\dfrac{5}{m - 3} + \dfrac{7}{m + 2}}{\dfrac{7}{(m - 3)(m + 2)} + \dfrac{1}{m - 3}}$$

Multiply both numerator and denominator
by the LCD, $(m - 3)(m + 2)$. $\Big\}$

$$\frac{(m - 3)(m + 2)\left(\dfrac{5}{m - 3} + \dfrac{7}{m + 2}\right)}{(m - 3)(m + 2)\left[\dfrac{7}{(m - 3)(m + 2)} + \dfrac{1}{m - 3}\right]}$$

Use the distributive property. Divide out
common factors in each product. $\Big\}$

$$\frac{(\overset{1}{\cancel{m - 3}})(m + 2) \cdot \dfrac{5}{\cancel{m - 3}_1} + (m - 3)(\overset{1}{\cancel{m + 2}}) \cdot \dfrac{7}{\cancel{m + 2}_1}}{(\cancel{m - 3})(\cancel{m + 2}) \cdot \dfrac{7}{\cancel{(m - 3)(m + 2)}} + (\overset{1}{\cancel{m - 3}})(m + 2) \cdot \dfrac{1}{\cancel{m - 3}_1}}$$

Multiply remaining factors in each
product. Combine like terms. $\Big\}$

$$\frac{5m + 10 + 7m - 21}{7 + m + 2} = \frac{12m - 11}{m + 9}$$

EXAMPLE 2

Simplify $\dfrac{\dfrac{2}{a} + \dfrac{-16}{a^2 + 6a}}{\dfrac{4}{a+6} - \dfrac{1}{a}}$.

Factor: $a^2 + 6a = a(a+6)$.

$\dfrac{4}{a+6} - \dfrac{1}{a} = \dfrac{4}{a+6} + \dfrac{-1 \cdot 1}{a}$

$\quad = \dfrac{4}{a+6} + \dfrac{-1}{a}$

$$\dfrac{\dfrac{2}{a} + \dfrac{-16}{a(a+6)}}{\dfrac{4}{a+6} + \dfrac{-1}{a}} \quad \leftarrow \text{LCD is } a(a+6).$$

Multiply both numerator and denominator by the LCD, $a(a+6)$.

$$\dfrac{a(a+6)\left[\dfrac{2}{a} + \dfrac{-16}{a(a+6)}\right]}{a(a+6)\left(\dfrac{4}{a+6} + \dfrac{-1}{a}\right)}$$

Use the distributive property. Divide out common factors in each product.

$$\dfrac{\cancel{a}(a+6) \cdot \dfrac{2}{\cancel{a}_1} + \cancel{a}\cancel{(a+6)} \cdot \dfrac{-16}{_1\cancel{a}\cancel{(a+6)}_1}}{a\cancel{(a+6)} \cdot \dfrac{4}{\cancel{a+6}_1} + \cancel{a}(a+6) \cdot \dfrac{-1}{\cancel{a}_1}}$$

Multiply remaining factors in each product. Combine like terms.

$\dfrac{2a + 12 - 16}{4a - 1a - 6}$, or $\dfrac{2a - 4}{3a - 6}$

Factor numerator and denominator. Then write in simplest form.

$\dfrac{2\cancel{(a-2)}^1}{3\cancel{(a-2)}_1} = \dfrac{2}{3}$

EXAMPLE 3

Simplify $\dfrac{b + 8 + \dfrac{5}{b-3}}{1 + \dfrac{-1}{b-3}}$.

$b - 3$ cannot be factored. Multiply both numerator and denominator by the LCD, $b - 3$.

$$\dfrac{(b-3)\left(\dfrac{b+8}{1} + \dfrac{5}{b-3}\right)}{(b-3)\left(1 + \dfrac{-1}{b-3}\right)}$$

Use the distributive property. Divide out common factors in each product.

$$\dfrac{(b-3)(b+8) + \cancel{(b-3)}^1 \cdot \dfrac{5}{\cancel{b-3}_1}}{b-3 + \cancel{(b-3)}^1 \cdot \dfrac{-1}{\cancel{b-3}_1}}$$

$$\dfrac{b^2 + 5b - 24 + 5}{b - 3 - 1}$$

Combine like terms. ⟶

$\dfrac{b^2 + 5b - 19}{b - 4}$

EXERCISES

Simplify.

1. $$\dfrac{\dfrac{3}{a^2 - 7a + 10} + \dfrac{2}{a - 5}}{\dfrac{4}{a - 5} + \dfrac{2}{a - 2}}$$

2. $$\dfrac{\dfrac{5}{x^2 - 9} + \dfrac{2}{x - 3}}{\dfrac{3}{x - 3} + \dfrac{2}{x + 3}}$$

3. $$\dfrac{\dfrac{7}{x^2 - 7x + 12} + \dfrac{3}{x - 4}}{\dfrac{2}{x - 4} + \dfrac{7}{x - 3}}$$

4. $$\dfrac{\dfrac{3}{m} + \dfrac{-12}{m^2 + 2m}}{\dfrac{2}{m + 2} - \dfrac{1}{m}}$$

5. $$\dfrac{\dfrac{2}{x} + \dfrac{-10}{x^2 + 7x}}{\dfrac{5}{x + 7} + \dfrac{2}{x}}$$

6. $$\dfrac{\dfrac{6}{x} + \dfrac{-24}{x^2 + 3x}}{\dfrac{4}{x + 3} - \dfrac{1}{x}}$$

7. $$\dfrac{a + 6 + \dfrac{4}{a - 2}}{1 + \dfrac{-2}{a - 2}}$$

8. $$\dfrac{m + 2 + \dfrac{3}{m - 5}}{\dfrac{4}{m - 5} + 1}$$

9. $$\dfrac{\dfrac{2}{x - 4} + x - 2}{1 + \dfrac{1}{x - 4}}$$

10. $$\dfrac{\dfrac{4}{m + 5} + \dfrac{-20}{m^2 + 5m}}{\dfrac{2}{m + 5} - \dfrac{1}{m}}$$

11. $$\dfrac{5 + \dfrac{7}{x - 3}}{4 + \dfrac{3}{x - 3}}$$

12. $$\dfrac{\dfrac{6b}{3b - 1} + \dfrac{1}{2}}{\dfrac{5}{2} + \dfrac{4}{3b - 1}}$$

13. $$\dfrac{\dfrac{4}{x^2 - 6x - 16} - \dfrac{3}{x - 8}}{\dfrac{5}{x - 8} + \dfrac{2}{x + 2}}$$

14. $$\dfrac{\dfrac{4}{a - 2} + \dfrac{2}{2a + 1}}{\dfrac{5a}{2a^2 - 3a - 2}}$$

15. $$\dfrac{\dfrac{3x}{x^2 - 9}}{\dfrac{6}{x - 3} + \dfrac{6}{x + 3}}$$

Simplify.

16. $$\dfrac{\dfrac{x + 1}{x} - \dfrac{5}{x + 2}}{\dfrac{x + 1}{x^2 + 2x} + \dfrac{3}{x + 2}}$$

17. $$\dfrac{\dfrac{1}{x + 3} + \dfrac{1}{x - 7}}{\dfrac{2x^2 + x - 10}{x^2 - 4x - 21}}$$

18. $$\dfrac{\dfrac{x + 1}{x + 2} + \dfrac{x + 7}{x - 5}}{\dfrac{5}{x^2 - 3x - 10}}$$

Simplify.

19. $$\dfrac{\dfrac{a}{b} + 2 + \dfrac{b}{a}}{\dfrac{a^2 - b^2}{ab}}$$

20. $$\dfrac{\dfrac{x}{y} - 6 + \dfrac{7y}{6}}{\dfrac{x^2 - 49y^2}{xy}}$$

21. $$\dfrac{\dfrac{x - y}{x - 2y} + \dfrac{x + 7y}{x + 5y}}{\dfrac{3x}{x^2 + 3xy - 10y^2}}$$

Formulas

 REVIEW CAPSULE

Solve for y. Then find y if $x = 3$.

$$2x + 3y = 10$$
$$\underline{-2x \qquad -2x}$$
$$3y = 10 - 2x$$
$$y = \frac{10 - 2x}{3}$$

If $x = 3$, then
$$y = \frac{10 - 2(3)}{3}$$
$$= \frac{10 - 6}{3}, \text{ or } \frac{4}{3}.$$

EXAMPLE 1 Solve $ax = b$ for x.

Divide each side by a. ⟶
Similar to $3x = 17$
$$x = \frac{17}{3}$$

$$ax = b$$
$$\frac{ax}{a} = \frac{b}{a}$$
$$x = \frac{b}{a}$$

EXAMPLE 2 The formula for perimeter of a rectangle is
$p = l + w + l + w$, or
$p = 2l + 2w$.
Solve $p = 2l + 2w$ for l.
Then find l if $p = 46$ cm and $w = 9$ cm.

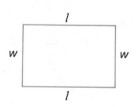

Get $2l$ alone on one side.
Add $-2w$ to each side.
l is alone on one side.
Divide each side by 2.
Formula is solved for l.

$$p = 2l + 2w$$
$$\underline{-2w \qquad\qquad -2w}$$
$$p - 2w = 2l$$
$$\frac{p - 2w}{2} = l, \text{ or } l = \frac{p - 2w}{2}$$

Now, find l if $p = 46$ and $w = 9$.

Replace p with 46, w with 9. ⟶

$$l = \frac{p - 2w}{2}$$
$$= \frac{46 - 2(9)}{2}$$
$$= \frac{46 - 18}{2}, \text{ or } 14 \text{ cm}$$

EXAMPLE 3   Solve $pkt - m = 5m$ for k.

Get pkt alone on one side.
Add m to each side.

Rewrite pkt as $(pt)k$, since we can multiply in any order. $\longrightarrow$

Divide each side by pt. $\longrightarrow$

$$pkt - m = 5m$$
$$\underline{m \qquad m}$$
$$pkt = 6m$$
$$(pt)k = 6m$$
$$\frac{(pt)k}{pt} = \frac{6m}{pt}$$
$$k = \frac{6m}{pt}$$

EXAMPLE 4   Solve $R = \dfrac{5}{3}t + 40$ for t. Then find t if $R = 70$.

$$\frac{R}{1} = \frac{5}{3}t + \frac{40}{1} \qquad \longleftarrow \text{ } LCD \text{ is } 3.$$

Multiply each side by 3. $\longrightarrow$

$$3 \cdot \frac{R}{1} = 3\left(\frac{5}{3}t + \frac{40}{1}\right)$$

Use the distributive property.
Divide out common factors.

$$3R = \overset{1}{3} \cdot \frac{5}{\underset{1}{3}}t + 3 \cdot 40$$

Get $5t$ alone on one side.
Add -120 to each side.

$$3R = 5t + 120$$
$$\underline{-120 \qquad\qquad -120}$$
$$3R - 120 = 5t$$

Divide each side by 5. $\longrightarrow$

$$\frac{3R - 120}{5} = t, \text{ or } t = \frac{3R - 120}{5}$$

Now find t if $R = 70$.

$$\left.\begin{array}{l}\dfrac{3(70) - 120}{5} = \dfrac{210 - 120}{5} \\[2mm] \qquad\qquad = 18\end{array}\right\}$$

$$t = \frac{3R - 120}{5}$$
$$= \frac{3(70) - 120}{5}$$
$$= 18$$

EXAMPLE 5   Solve $ax = c - bx$ for x.

Get all the x terms on one side.
Add bx to each side.

Factor out the common monomial, x. $\longrightarrow$

Divide each side by $(a + b)$, since x is multiplied by $(a + b)$.

$$ax = c - bx$$
$$\underline{bx \qquad\qquad bx}$$
$$ax + bx = c$$
$$x(a + b) = c$$
$$\frac{x(a + b)}{a + b} = \frac{c}{a + b}$$
$$x = \frac{c}{a + b}$$

EXERCISES

PART A

Solve for x.

1. $ax = 2$
2. $rx = 5$
3. $3x = 3a$
4. $bc = 2x$
5. $x + 3a = 0$
6. $2c + x = a$
7. $x - 4a = 0$
8. $5 = x - 3c$
9. $2x - c = d$
10. $bx - 7 = 3c$
11. $4a + 2x = 3b$
12. $7x + 2a = 6h$
13. $8 - 2x = kx$
14. $ax = 4 - cx$
15. $3ax = ax + b$
16. $mx = px - t$
17. $\dfrac{x}{3} = \dfrac{b}{2} + \dfrac{c}{6}$
18. $\dfrac{m}{5} + \dfrac{p}{3} = \dfrac{x}{15}$
19. $\dfrac{x}{2a} = \dfrac{b}{c}$
20. $\dfrac{x}{b} - c = a$

Solve each formula for the variable indicated. Then evaluate.

21. Solve $p = 4s$ for s. Then find s if $p = 28$.
22. Solve $A = pti$ for i. Then find i if $p = 180$, $A = 270$, and $t = \frac{1}{2}$.
23. Solve $p = 2s + b$ for s. Then find s if $p = 52$ and $b = 14$.
24. Solve $l = a + 15d$ for d. Then find d if $l = 125$ and $a = 35$.
25. Solve $C = 2\pi r$ for r. Then find r if $C = 12.56$ m and $\pi \doteq 3.14$.
26. Solve $i = prt$ for r. Then find r if $i = 30$, $p = 200$, and $t = 4$.
27. Solve $V = lwh$ for h. Then find h if $V = 48$ cm^3, $l = 2$ cm, and $w = 6$ cm.
28. Solve $C = \frac{1}{3}fd^2$ for f. Then find f if $C = 20$ and $d = 2$.

PART B

Solve for x.

29. $5a + 2bx = 3c$
30. $6x - 6a = 2x + 10a$
31. $ax - c = 2d + 3c$
32. $3b - 3c = 2bx - 3c$
33. $2 - 2bx = -4b + 3bx$
34. $7a + 3x = 6a + 4x$
35. $a^2 - ax + 4 = 2x - 4a$
36. $4x - ax = 16 - a^2$
37. $ax + bx = a^2 + 2ab + b^2$

PART C

Solve each formula for the variable indicated. Then evaluate.

38. Solve $P = \dfrac{2}{3}(m - 16)$ for m. Then find m if $p = 8$.
39. Solve $V = \dfrac{1}{3}\pi r^2 h$ for h. Then find h if $V = 157$ km^3, $\pi \doteq 3.14$, and $r = 5$ km.
40. Solve $T = \pi r(r + l)$ for l. Then find l if $T = 942$, $r = 10$, and $\pi \doteq 3.14$.
41. Solve $A = p + prt$ for p. Then find p if $A = 134.40$, $r = .06$, and $t = 2$.
42. Solve $T = 2\pi r(r + h)$ for h. Then find h if $T = 301.44$, $r = 4$, and $\pi \doteq 3.14$.
43. Solve $A = \dfrac{b + c + a}{3}$ for a. Then find a if $A = 34$, $b = 39$, and $c = 32$.

Parallel Series Circuits

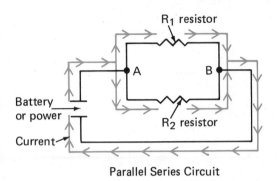

R₁ resistor

A   B

Battery or power

Current

Parallel Series Circuit

When you turn the power on, voltage from the battery forces current to flow. Current flows to A, then splits, part flowing through R_1 and part through R_2. The two branches join up again at B forming a single current flowing back to the battery. Resistors control the flow of current, that is, the greater the resistance, the less current.

A volume control on a radio is a resistor. Turning down the sound cuts or resists the flow of current.

Total resistance of two resistors in a parallel circuit

$$R = \cfrac{1}{\cfrac{1}{R_1} + \cfrac{1}{R_2}}$$

Resistance is measured in ohms: Ω.

PROBLEM

Two resistors in a parallel series circuit have resistances of $20\,\Omega$ and $30\,\Omega$. Find the total resistance.

Use $R = \cfrac{1}{\cfrac{1}{R_1} + \cfrac{1}{R_2}}$ where $R_1 = 20$ and $R_2 = 30$.

$$\cfrac{1}{\cfrac{1}{20} + \cfrac{1}{30}} \longleftarrow \text{A complex fraction}$$

$$\cfrac{60\,(1)}{60\left(\cfrac{1}{20} + \cfrac{1}{30}\right)}$$

LCD is 60.

Distribute 60. $\longrightarrow$

$$\cfrac{60\,(1)}{\overset{3}{\cancel{60}}\left(\cfrac{1}{\underset{1}{\cancel{20}}}\right) + \overset{2}{\cancel{60}}\left(\cfrac{1}{\underset{1}{\cancel{30}}}\right)}, \text{ or } \cfrac{60}{3 + 2}$$

Simplify. $\dfrac{60}{3 + 2} = \dfrac{60}{5} = 12.$ $\longrightarrow$ Thus, the total resistance is $12\,\Omega$.

PROJECT   Find the total resistance in a parallel circuit with these resistances.
1. $5\,\Omega$, $10\,\Omega$ **2.** $25\,\Omega$, $75\,\Omega$ **3.** $200\,\Omega$, $150\,\Omega$ **4.** $4\,\Omega$, $8\,\Omega$, $6\,\Omega$

Chapter Thirteen Review

Solve and check for extraneous solutions. [*p. 341, 346*]

1. $\dfrac{2a-3}{6} = \dfrac{4a}{3} + \dfrac{1}{2}$

2. $\dfrac{3}{5} + \dfrac{6}{x} = 1$

3. $\dfrac{2}{3}(x-4) + \dfrac{x+5}{2} = \dfrac{2x-1}{3}$

4. $\dfrac{7}{y+3} + \dfrac{4}{y-7} = \dfrac{2}{y^2 - 4y - 21}$

5. $\dfrac{x}{x-7} + \dfrac{3}{x} = \dfrac{-23}{x^2 - 7x}$

6. $\dfrac{2}{b+2} + \dfrac{13}{b^2 - 4} = \dfrac{b}{b-2}$

[*p. 350, 353*]

7. Working together, Mona and Martin can mow a lawn in 5 hours. It would take Mona 9 hours to do it alone. How long would it take Martin?

8. George can repair a radio in 5 hours. If Tina helps him, they can complete the job in 2 hours. How long would it take Tina to do it alone?

9. Working together, two women can build a house in 7 months. It would take one of them 3 times as long as the other to do it alone. How long would it take each alone?

10. By herself, Jane can build a table in 2 weeks. It would take Juan 5 weeks. How long would it take Irv if, working together, all three can complete the job in 1 week?

Solve. [*p. 358*]

11. $.03x = 7$

12. $.6x + 3 = .21x + 18$

13. $.01(2 - .5x) = .48 - .003x$

Show that each is a rational number. [*p. 361*]

14. -18

15. 0

16. $7\frac{1}{2}$

17. $4.6\overline{6}$

18. $.32\overline{2}$

19. $.18\overline{18}$

Simplify. [*p. 368, 371*]

20. $\dfrac{\dfrac{3}{5} + \dfrac{1}{2}}{\dfrac{3}{10} + \dfrac{2}{5}}$

21. $\dfrac{\dfrac{3}{b^2} + \dfrac{5}{b}}{\dfrac{2}{b} + \dfrac{7}{3b^2}}$

22. $\dfrac{1 - \dfrac{2}{x} - \dfrac{15}{x^2}}{\dfrac{1}{x} - \dfrac{5}{x^2}}$

23. $\dfrac{\dfrac{6}{a-3} + \dfrac{4}{a}}{\dfrac{7}{a^2 - 3a}}$

24. $\dfrac{\dfrac{3}{a-4} + \dfrac{5}{2a+3}}{\dfrac{4a}{2a^2 - 5a - 12}}$

25. $\dfrac{x - 5 + \dfrac{3}{x-2}}{\dfrac{3}{x-2} + 2}$

Solve for x. [*p. 374*]

26. $bx - 8 = 3m$

27. $5a + mx = tr$

28. $8 - 5x = kx$

29. $6a + 5x = 4a + 3x$

Solve each formula for the variable indicated. Then evaluate. [*p. 374*]

30. Solve $a = mpq$ for p. Then find p if $a = 32$, $m = 2$, and $q = 7$.

31. Solve $k = \frac{1}{4}fd^2$ for f. Then find f if $k = 7$ and $d = 2$.

Chapter Thirteen Test

Solve and check for extraneous solutions.

1. $\dfrac{3a-4}{15} = \dfrac{2a}{5} + \dfrac{1}{3}$

2. $\dfrac{2}{3} + \dfrac{6}{x} = 2$

3. $\dfrac{4}{y-8} - \dfrac{3}{y+2} = \dfrac{4}{y^2-6y-16}$

4. $\dfrac{2}{7}(x-2) + \dfrac{x+4}{7} = \dfrac{x+15}{14}$

5. Working together, Janice and Jack can mow a lawn in 4 hours. It would take Janice 7 hours to do it alone. How long would it take Jack?

6. Rodney can repair a T.V. set in 9 hours. If Lisa helps him, they can complete the job in 4 hours. How long would it take Lisa to do it alone?

7. Working together, two men can build a shed in 15 hours. It would take one of them 4 times as long as the other to do it alone. How long would it take each alone?

8. By herself, Joan can build a desk in 4 weeks. It would take José 5 weeks. How long would it take Sue if, working together, all three can complete the job in 2 weeks?

Solve.

9. $.05x = 4$

10. $.5x + 2 = .32x + 12$

11. $.01(3 - .4x) = .23 - .002x$

Show that each is a rational number.

12. -14

13. $8\frac{1}{3}$

14. $.4\overline{4}$

15. $.12\overline{12}$

Simplify.

16. $\dfrac{\dfrac{4}{7} + \dfrac{1}{3}}{\dfrac{2}{3} + \dfrac{5}{21}}$

17. $\dfrac{\dfrac{7}{a-2} + \dfrac{5}{a}}{\dfrac{3}{a^2-2a}}$

18. $\dfrac{1 - \dfrac{5}{m} - \dfrac{14}{m^2}}{\dfrac{1}{m} - \dfrac{7}{m^2}}$

19. $\dfrac{x - 2 + \dfrac{5}{x+3}}{\dfrac{7}{x+3} + 5}$

Solve for x.

20. $mx - 4 = 2a$

21. $7 + 2x = tx$

22. $5x - 4b = 3x + 8b$

Solve each formula for the variable indicated. Then evaluate.

23. Solve $m = abd$ for b. Then find b if $m = 28$, $a = 2$, and $d = 7$.

24. Solve $l = \frac{1}{5}mp^2$ for m. Then find m if $p = 2$ and $l = 20$.

The Normal Curve

64 students were categorized according to their height. The results are given below.

Height	Number of Students
Under 152 cm	1
155 cm to under 160 cm	6
160 cm to under 165 cm	15
165 cm to under 170 cm	20
170 cm to under 175 cm	15
175 cm to under 180 cm	6
180 cm or over	1
	Total 64 students

The graph below, which is composed of rectangles, is called a histogram. It represents the data from the table.

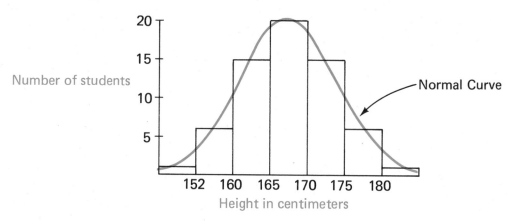

The smooth curve drawn through the graph is shaped like a bell. It is called the *normal curve*.

The Apex Lighting Company took a survey of 10,000, 150-watt light bulbs to determine the number of hours each bulb would burn. The results are given below.

MORTALITY RATE OF 150-WATT LIGHT BULBS

Number of Hours Burned	Number of Bulbs
100-299.9	3
300-499.9	321
500-699.9	1,108
700-899.9	2,193
900-1,099.9	2,745
1,100-1,299.9	2,196
1,300-1,499.9	1,113
1,500-1,699.9	319
1,700-1,899.9	2
	Total 10,000 bulbs

These results fit the normal curve.

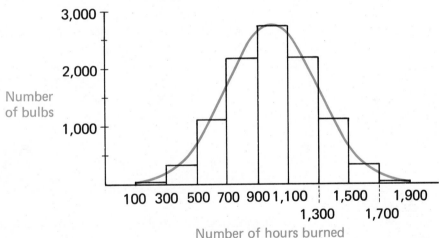

PROJECT   Survey each. Then see if the results fit the normal curve.

1. The batting averages of a large group of baseball players

2. The weights of thousands of apples

381

The Set of Real Numbers

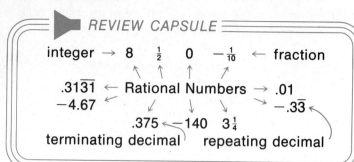

REVIEW CAPSULE

integer → 8 $\frac{1}{2}$ 0 $-\frac{1}{10}$ ← fraction

.31$\overline{31}$ ← Rational Numbers → .01

−4.67

.375 ← −140 $3\frac{1}{4}$ −.3$\overline{3}$

terminating decimal   repeating decimal

EXAMPLE 1   If possible, write these decimals with a bar.
.311311311311. . .
.313113111311113111113. . .

This decimal repeats. ————→   .311311311311. . . = .311$\overline{311}$

.313113111311113111113. . . cannot be written with a bar since no group of digits continues to repeat.

These cannot be written with a bar.

Decimal approximation for π ————→

Nonrepeating decimals cannot be written in the form $\frac{a}{b}$, where a and b are integers and $b \neq 0$.

These are nonrepeating decimals.
.57557555755557. . .
−7.40414243444546. . .
3.14159265358979. . .
43.00600660066600666600. . .

Nonrepeating decimals are *irrational* numbers.

repeating decimal   nonrepeating decimal
↓   ↓
.399939993999. . .   .3939939993. . .
↓   ↓
rational number   irrational number

EXAMPLE 2   Which are rational and which are irrational numbers?

Answers

Terminating decimal ————→   −4.287   Rational
Nonrepeating decimal ————→   6.161161116. . .   Irrational
Repeating decimal ————→   37.237$\overline{237}$ Rational

{rationals} ∪ {irrationals} = {reals}.

The set of *real* numbers contains all the rational and all the irrational numbers.

EXERCISES

PART A

Which are rational and which are irrational numbers?

1. .424242. . .   **2.** .424424442. . .   **3.** −.5639   **4.** .68$\overline{68}$

5. −.31323334. . .   **6.** .3083$\overline{83}$ **7.** .123123123. . .   **8.** −.00009

9. π **10.** 7.1234$\overline{1234}$ **11.** $\frac{34}{3,434}$ **12.** 0

13. −2.101101110. . .   **14.** −.1121231234. . .   **15.** 456,456   **16.** 3.1416

17. −.438438   **18.** $\frac{22}{7}$ **19.** −.682$\overline{682}$ **20.** .20212223. . .

PART B

21. Make up five real numbers that are rational.

22. Make up decimal numerals for five real numbers that are irrational.

23. Name five real numbers that are integers.

24. Is every integer a real number? Why or why not?

25. A number called *e* is used in higher mathematics. $e \doteq 2.71828$. . . . At no time does a group of digits repeat, no matter how far the decimal is carried out. Is *e* rational or irrational?

26. Start with a decimal point. Flip a coin. If heads comes up, write 1. If tails comes up, write 2. Imagine doing this indefinitely. Does the numeral you are constructing name a rational or an irrational number?

27. Start with a decimal point. Toss a die. Record the number shown on the die. Imagine that this continues forever. Does the numeral you are constructing name a rational or an irrational number?

28. Start with a decimal point. Toss two dice. Record the number that is the sum of the numbers shown on the dice. Imagine that this continues forever. Does the numeral you are constructing name a rational or an irrational number?

PART C

True or false?

29. {rationals} ∩ {irrationals} = {reals}

30. {integers} ⊆ {reals}

31. {rationals} ∩ {irrationals} = ϕ

32. {reals} = {rationals}

33. {reals} ∩ {rationals} = {rationals}

34. {rationals} ∪ {reals} = {reals}

Square Roots

 REVIEW CAPSULE

$(2)(2) = 4$
$(-2)(-2) = 4$

$(15)(15) = 225$
$(-15)(-15) = 225$

$(3.1)(3.1) = 9.61$
$(-3.1)(-3.1) = 9.61$

$\left(\dfrac{3}{4}\right)\left(\dfrac{3}{4}\right) = \dfrac{9}{16}$

$\left(-\dfrac{3}{4}\right)\left(-\dfrac{3}{4}\right) = \dfrac{9}{16}$

Definition of square root ——————→ | If $x \cdot x = n$, then x is a square root of n.

Every positive real number has two square roots, one positive and one negative.

2 is a square root of 4, since $(2)(2) = 4$.
Also, -2 is a square root of 4, since $(-2)(-2) = 4$.

Number	Positive Square Root	Negative Square Root
4	2	-2
9.61	3.1	-3.1
$\dfrac{9}{16}$	$\dfrac{3}{4}$	$-\dfrac{3}{4}$

Definition of principal square root——————→ | The positive square root of a number is called the *principal* square root. It is indicated by the symbol $\sqrt{}$.

The principal square root of 4 is 2.

$\sqrt{4} = 2$ $\sqrt{9.61} = 3.1$ $\sqrt{225} = 15$ $\sqrt{\dfrac{9}{16}} = \dfrac{3}{4}$

EXAMPLE 1   Are $\sqrt{16}$ and $\sqrt{33}$ whole numbers?

$(5)(5) = 25$ and $(6)(6) = 36$; so, $\sqrt{33}$ is not 5 or 6. ——————→

$\sqrt{16}$ is the whole number 4, since $(4)(4) = 16$.
$\sqrt{33}$ is not a whole number.

Definition of a perfect square ──────→ | A *perfect square* is a number whose principal square root is a whole number.

16 is a perfect square.

The table on page 476 gives 3-decimal place values for square roots of whole numbers from 1 to 100.

$\doteq$ means is approximately equal to.

$\sqrt{33} \doteq 5.745$ $(5.745)(5.745) = 33.005025 \doteq 33$
$\sqrt{65} \doteq 8.062$ $(8.062)(8.062) = 64.995844 \doteq 65$

EXAMPLE 2   The area of a square is 86 square cm. Find the length of a side, to the nearest tenth of a cm.

Formula for area of a square ──────→ $s^2 = A$
Substitute 86 for A. ──────────────→ $s^2 = 86$
                                      $s = \sqrt{86}$
From the table, $\sqrt{86} \doteq 9.274$. ──────→ $s \doteq 9.274$
Round to the nearest tenth. ──────→ $s \doteq 9.3$

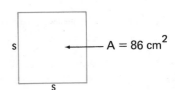

s — $A = 86$ cm^2

Thus, the length of a side is 9.3 cm, to the nearest tenth.

EXAMPLE 3   The area of a rectangle is 48 square meters. The length is 4 times the width. Find the length and the width, to the nearest tenth of a meter.

Let x = width in meters
$4x$ = length in meters

Formula for area of a rectangle ──────→ $l \cdot w = A$
Substitute $4x$, x, and 48. ──────→ $(4x)(x) = 48$
                                       $4x^2 = 48$
Divide each side by 4. ──────────────→ $x^2 = 12$
                                       $x = \sqrt{12}$
From the table, $\sqrt{12} \doteq 3.464$. $x \doteq 3.464$
Round to the nearest tenth. ──────→ $x \doteq 3.5$
Find the length, $4x$. ──────────────→ $4x \doteq 4(3.464)$
Multiply 3.464 by 4. ──────────────→ $4x \doteq 13.856$
Round to the nearest tenth. ──────→ $4x \doteq 13.9$

x $A = 48$ m^2 $4x$

Thus, the length is 13.9 m and the width is 3.5 m, to the nearest tenth.

ORAL EXERCISES

Tell which are perfect squares. Then give the principal square root of each number. Approximate to the nearest tenth for nonperfect squares. Use the table on page 476.

1. 25	**2.** 6	**3.** 100	**4.** 26	**5.** 36
6. 38	**7.** 42	**8.** 49	**9.** 11	**10.** 59
11. 1	**12.** 67	**13.** 12	**14.** 64	**15.** 8
16. 74	**17.** 39	**18.** 78	**19.** 9	**20.** 92

EXERCISES

PART A

Give answers to the nearest tenth.

1.
s │ $A = 37$ m^2
s

Find s.

2.
s │ $A = 62$ cm^2
s

Find s.

3.
$A = 110$ m^2 │ x
$2x$

Find x and $2x$.

4.
s │ $A = 94$ cm^2
s

Find s.

5.
x │ $A = 90$ m^2
$3x$

Find x and $3x$.

6.
$A = 255$ cm^2 │ x
$5x$

Find x and $5x$.

7.
s │ $A = 28$ cm^2
s

Find s.

8.
$A = 102$ m^2 │ $3x$
$2x$

Find $2x$ and $3x$.

9. The length of a rectangle is 5 times the width. The area is 220 m². Find the length and the width.

10. The area of a rectangle is 166 cm². The length is twice the width. Find the length and the width.

PART B

Give answers to the nearest tenth.

11. Find r.
(Hint: $A = \pi r^2$.)
Use 3.14 for π.

$A \doteq 25.12$ cm^2

12. Find $3x$ and $2x$.
(Hint: $A = \frac{1}{2}bh$.)

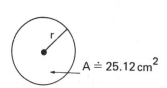

$2x$
$b = 3x$
h
$A = 222$ m^2

The Galton Board

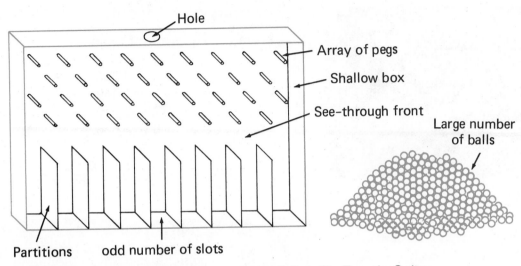

Hole

Array of pegs

Shallow box

See-through front

Large number of balls

Partitions

odd number of slots

The board was invented by a British mathematician, Sir Francis Galton (1822-1911).

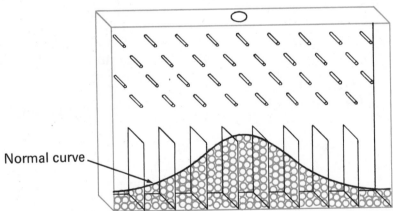

Normal curve

If the balls are poured into the hole, they will form a model of the normal curve.

PROJECT Build a model of the Galton board.
(Suggested materials: wood, plastic, heavy cardboard)

Approximating Square Roots

 REVIEW CAPSULE

From the square root table:
$$\sqrt{4} = 2$$
$$\sqrt{5} \doteq 2.236$$
$$\sqrt{6} \doteq 2.449$$
$$\sqrt{7} \doteq 2.646$$
$$\sqrt{8} \doteq 2.828$$
$$\sqrt{9} = 3$$

The decimal for $\sqrt{5}$ is nonrepeating. $\sqrt{5}$ is an irrational number. ⟶

If the square root of a whole number is not a whole number, then it is an irrational number.

EXAMPLE 1   Approximate $\sqrt{34}$ to the nearest tenth.

Step 1 ⟶ Guess the square root.

$5 \times 5 = 25$ and $6 \times 6 = 36$ ⟶ $\sqrt{34}$ is between 5 and 6. GUESS: 5.5.

Step 2 ⟶ Divide the guess into the number. Carry to hundredths. Do not round.

Divide 5.5 into 34. Carry to two decimal places.

```
      6.18
5.5)34.000
    33 0
     1 00
       55
      450
      440
```

$\sqrt{34}$ is between 5.5 and 6.18.

$$5.5 < \sqrt{34} < 6.18$$

Step 3 ⟶ Average the divisor and the quotient. Round to the nearest tenth.

To average 5.5 and 6.18, add them and divide by 2. Then round to the nearest tenth.

```
  5.5
 +6.18
 11.68
```

```
     5.84 ≐ 5.8
2)11.68
  10
   1 6
   1 6
      8
      8
```

5.8 is the average.

If they were the same, we would be finished. However, we must continue.

Check to see if the average is the same as the previous divisor: $5.8 \neq 5.5$.

Step 4

Divide 5.8 into 34. ──────────────→

Divide the average into the number. Carry to hundredths. Do not round.

$$
\begin{array}{r}
5.86 \\
5.8\,\overline{)34.000} \\
29\ 0 \\
\hline
5\ 00 \\
4\ 64 \\
\hline
360 \\
348 \\
\hline
\end{array}
$$

If they were not the same, we would have to repeat Step 3.

$5.8 < \sqrt{34} < 5.86$

The divisor and the quotient are the same in the tenths place: 5.8 5.86

Thus, $\sqrt{34} = 5.8$ to the nearest tenth.

This method of approximating square roots is called the divide and average method.

> To approximate a square root to the nearest tenth:
> *Step 1* Guess the square root.
> *Step 2* Divide the guess into the number. Carry to hundredths. Do not round.
> *Step 3* Average the divisor and quotient. Round to the nearest tenth.
> *Step 4* Divide the average into the number. Carry to hundredths. Do not round.
> Repeat Steps 3 and 4 until the average is the same as the divisor in Step 3 or until the divisor and quotient agree in the tenths place in Step 4.

EXAMPLE 2 Approximate $\sqrt{86}$ to the nearest tenth.

Step 1
$9 \times 9 = 81$ and $10 \times 10 = 100$
$9 < \sqrt{86} < 10$ ──────────→ GUESS: 9.5

Guess the square root.

Step 2

Divide 9.5 into 86. Carry to two decimal places.

Divide the guess into the number. Carry to hundredths. Do not round.

$$
\begin{array}{r}
9.05 \\
9.5\,\overline{)86.000} \\
85\ 5 \\
\hline
500 \\
475 \\
\hline
\end{array}
$$

$\sqrt{86}$ is between 9.05 and 9.5.

$9.05 < \sqrt{86} < 9.5$

Step 3	Average the divisor and quotient. Round to the nearest tenth.

Add and divide by 2. Then round to the nearest tenth.

$$\begin{array}{r} 9.5 \\ +9.05 \\ \hline 18.55 \end{array}$$

$$\begin{array}{r} 9.27 \doteq 9.3 \\ 2\overline{)18.55} \\ \underline{18} \\ 5 \\ \underline{4} \\ 15 \end{array}$$

9.3 is the average.

9.3 ≠ 9.5. We must continue.

Step 4

Divide the average into the number. Carry to hundredths. Do not round.

Divide 9.3 into 86. Carry to two decimal places.

$$\begin{array}{r} 9.24 \\ 9.3\overline{)86.000} \\ \underline{83\ 7} \\ 2\ 30 \\ \underline{1\ 86} \\ 440 \\ \underline{372} \end{array}$$

$\sqrt{86}$ is between 9.24 and 9.3.

$9.24 < \sqrt{86} < 9.3$

9.3 ⌐ 9.27 We must continue. ⟶ Divisor and quotient do not agree in the tenths place. Average divisor and quotient. Round to the nearest tenth.

Repeat Step 3.

Add and divide by 2. Then round to the nearest tenth.

$$\begin{array}{r} 9.3 \\ +9.24 \\ \hline 18.54 \end{array}$$

$$\begin{array}{r} 9.27 \doteq 9.3 \\ 2\overline{)18.54} \\ \underline{18} \\ 5 \\ \underline{4} \\ 14 \end{array}$$

9.3 is the average.

Average equals previous quotient.

Thus, $\sqrt{86} = 9.3$ to the nearest tenth.

EXERCISES

PART A

Approximate to the nearest tenth. Use the divide and average method.

1. $\sqrt{26}$ 2. $\sqrt{1}$ 3. $\sqrt{48}$ 4. $\sqrt{25}$ 5. $\sqrt{89}$ 6. $\sqrt{62}$ 7. $\sqrt{18}$
8. $\sqrt{49}$ 9. $\sqrt{52}$ 10. $\sqrt{7}$ 11. $\sqrt{12}$ 12. $\sqrt{36}$ 13. $\sqrt{37}$ 14. $\sqrt{78}$
15. $\sqrt{32}$ 16. $\sqrt{90}$ 17. $\sqrt{67}$ 18. $\sqrt{58}$ 19. $\sqrt{70}$ 20. $\sqrt{100}$ 21. $\sqrt{82}$

PART B

Approximate to the nearest tenth. Use the divide and average method.

22. $\sqrt{243}$ 23. $\sqrt{116}$ 24. $\sqrt{255}$ 25. $\sqrt{200}$ 26. $\sqrt{378}$

Simplifying Radicals

▶ REVIEW CAPSULE

Factor 48 into primes.
$$48 = (2)(24)$$
$$= (2)(2)(12)$$
$$= (2)(2)(2)(6)$$
$$= (2)(2)(2)(2)(3)$$

Thus, $48 = (2)(2)(2)(2)(3)$.

EXAMPLE 1 Simplify $\sqrt{9} \cdot \sqrt{4}$. Then simplify $\sqrt{9 \cdot 4}$. What conclusion can you draw?

Results are the same. ⟶

$\sqrt{9} \cdot \sqrt{4}$		$\sqrt{9 \cdot 4}$
$3 \cdot 2$		$\sqrt{36}$
6		6

Thus, $\sqrt{9} \cdot \sqrt{4} = \sqrt{9 \cdot 4}$.

Example 1 suggests this. ⟶
a is nonnegative if $a \geq 0$.

$$\sqrt{a} \cdot \sqrt{b} = \sqrt{a \cdot b} \text{ and } \sqrt{a \cdot b} = \sqrt{a} \cdot \sqrt{b}, \text{ for all nonnegative numbers } a \text{ and } b.$$

EXAMPLE 2 Simplify $\sqrt{5} \cdot \sqrt{11}$.

$\sqrt{a} \cdot \sqrt{b} = \sqrt{a \cdot b}$ ⟶ $\sqrt{5} \cdot \sqrt{11} = \sqrt{5 \cdot 11} = \sqrt{55}$

Thus, $\sqrt{5} \cdot \sqrt{11} = \sqrt{55}$.

EXAMPLE 3 Simplify $\sqrt{5} \cdot \sqrt{5}$.　　Simplify $\sqrt{8} \cdot \sqrt{8}$.

Multiply first. ⟶
Then simplify. ⟶

$\sqrt{5} \cdot \sqrt{5} = \sqrt{5 \cdot 5}$		$\sqrt{8} \cdot \sqrt{8} = \sqrt{8 \cdot 8}$
$= \sqrt{25}$		$= \sqrt{64}$
$= 5$		$= 8$

Thus, $\sqrt{5} \cdot \sqrt{5} = 5$ and $\sqrt{8} \cdot \sqrt{8} = 8$.

Example 3 suggests this. ⟶ | $\sqrt{x} \cdot \sqrt{x} = x$, for each nonnegative number x.

EXAMPLE 4 Simplify $\sqrt{36 \cdot 81}$.

$\sqrt{a \cdot b} = \sqrt{a} \cdot \sqrt{b}$ ⟶

$$\sqrt{36 \cdot 81} = \sqrt{36} \cdot \sqrt{81}$$
$$= 6 \cdot 9$$
$$= 54$$

Thus, $\sqrt{36 \cdot 81} = 54$.

EXAMPLE 5 Simplify $\sqrt{72}$.

| One way
Factor into primes. | Another way
Find greatest
perfect square
factor. |

Group pairs of the same factors. }
$\sqrt{a \cdot b} = \sqrt{a} \cdot \sqrt{b}$

$$\sqrt{72} = \sqrt{3 \cdot 3 \cdot 2 \cdot 2 \cdot 2}$$
$$= \underbrace{\sqrt{3} \cdot \sqrt{3}} \cdot \underbrace{\sqrt{2} \cdot \sqrt{2}} \cdot \sqrt{2}$$

$\sqrt{x} \cdot \sqrt{x} = x$ ⟶
$$= \quad 3 \quad \cdot \quad 2 \quad \cdot \sqrt{2}$$
$$= 6\sqrt{2}$$
Thus, $\sqrt{72} = 6\sqrt{2}$.

$$\sqrt{72} = \sqrt{36 \cdot 2}$$
$$= \sqrt{36} \cdot \sqrt{2}$$
$$= \underbrace{6\sqrt{2}}$$

Simplest radical
form

$\sqrt{72}$ is a *radical*. $\sqrt{}$ is the *radical sign*.
72 is the *radicand*. A radical is *simplified* when
the radicand does not have a perfect square
factor.

EXAMPLE 6 Simplify $\sqrt{90}$.

| One way
Factor into primes. | Another way
Find greatest
perfect square
factor. |

Factor 90 into primes. ⟶
Group like factors.

$$\sqrt{90} = \sqrt{2 \cdot 3 \cdot 5 \cdot 3}$$
$$= \underbrace{\sqrt{3} \cdot \sqrt{3}} \cdot \sqrt{2} \cdot \sqrt{5}$$

$\sqrt{a} \cdot \sqrt{a} = a$ ⟶
$$= \quad 3 \quad \cdot \underbrace{\sqrt{2} \cdot \sqrt{5}}$$

$\sqrt{a} \cdot \sqrt{b} = \sqrt{ab}$ ⟶
$$= \quad 3 \quad \sqrt{10}$$
Thus, $\sqrt{90} = 3\sqrt{10}$.

$$\sqrt{90} = \sqrt{9 \cdot 10}$$
$$= \sqrt{9} \cdot \sqrt{10}$$
$$= \underbrace{3\sqrt{10}}$$

Simplest radical
form

EXAMPLE 7

Simplify $-5\sqrt{147}$. Then approximate to the nearest tenth.

147 = 49 · 3. 49 is the greatest perfect square factor of 147. ⟶

$$
\begin{aligned}
-5\sqrt{147} &= -5\sqrt{49 \cdot 3} \\
&= -5\sqrt{49} \cdot \sqrt{3} \\
&= -5 \cdot 7 \cdot \sqrt{3} \\
&= -35\sqrt{3} \\
&\doteq -35(1.732) \\
&\doteq -60.620 \\
&\doteq -60.6
\end{aligned}
$$

Simplest radical form ⟶

From the table, $\sqrt{3} \doteq 1.732$. ⟶

Round to the nearest tenth. ⟶

Thus, $-5\sqrt{147} = -35\sqrt{3} \doteq -60.6$.

EXERCISES

PART A

Simplify.

1. $\sqrt{2} \cdot \sqrt{5}$ 2. $\sqrt{3} \cdot \sqrt{7}$ 3. $\sqrt{5} \cdot \sqrt{6}$ 4. $\sqrt{3} \cdot \sqrt{11}$ 5. $\sqrt{7} \cdot \sqrt{2}$

Simplify.

6. $\sqrt{9 \cdot 25}$ 7. $\sqrt{64 \cdot 16}$ 8. $\sqrt{81 \cdot 4}$ 9. $\sqrt{49 \cdot 25}$ 10. $\sqrt{100 \cdot 121}$

11. $\sqrt{12}$ 12. $\sqrt{80}$ 13. $\sqrt{27}$ 14. $\sqrt{50}$ 15. $\sqrt{98}$

16. $\sqrt{28}$ 17. $-2\sqrt{60}$ 18. $4\sqrt{40}$ 19. $2\sqrt{32}$ 20. $3\sqrt{45}$

PART B

Simplify. Then approximate to the nearest tenth.

21. $\sqrt{75}$ 22. $2\sqrt{144}$ 23. $-3\sqrt{20}$ 24. $2\sqrt{54}$ 25. $3\sqrt{180}$ 26. $4\sqrt{160}$

PART C

EXAMPLE   Simplify $\sqrt{675}$.

$$
\begin{aligned}
\sqrt{675} &= \sqrt{3 \cdot 3 \cdot 3 \cdot 5 \cdot 5} \\
&= \sqrt{3} \cdot \sqrt{3} \cdot \sqrt{5} \cdot \sqrt{5} \cdot \sqrt{3} \\
&= \quad 3 \quad \cdot \quad 5 \quad \cdot \sqrt{3}, \text{ or } 15\sqrt{3}
\end{aligned}
$$

Simplify.

27. $-\sqrt{1,372}$ 28. $5\sqrt{1,014}$ 29. $-2\sqrt{1,805}$ 30. $-17\sqrt{972}$ 31. $6\sqrt{3,179}$

Even Exponents

▶ REVIEW CAPSULE

$$a^2 \cdot a^2 = a^{2+2} = a^4$$
$$x^5 \cdot x^5 = x^{5+5} = x^{10}$$

Also,
$$y^8 = y^{4+4} = y^4 \cdot y^4$$
$$z^6 = z^{3+3} = z^3 \cdot z^3$$

EXAMPLE 1   Simplify $\sqrt{a^6b^2}$.

$\sqrt{x \cdot y} = \sqrt{x} \cdot \sqrt{y}$ ⟶

a^6 and b^2 are perfect squares. ⟶

$\sqrt{x} \cdot \sqrt{x} = x$ ⟶

$$\sqrt{a^6b^2} = \sqrt{a^6} \cdot \sqrt{b^2}$$
$$= \sqrt{a^3 \cdot a^3} \cdot \sqrt{b^1 \cdot b^1}$$
$$= \sqrt{a^3} \cdot \sqrt{a^3} \cdot \sqrt{b} \cdot \sqrt{b}$$
$$= a^3b$$

EXAMPLE 2   Simplify $-\sqrt{49x^{10}y^4z^{18}}$.

x^{10} is a perfect square;
$\sqrt{x^{10}} = \sqrt{x^5} \cdot \sqrt{x^5} = x^5.$

$$-\sqrt{49} \cdot \sqrt{x^{10}} \cdot \sqrt{y^4} \cdot \sqrt{z^{18}} = -7x^5y^2z^9$$

EXAMPLE 3   Try to express $\sqrt{-64}$ as a real number.

Neither product is -64. ⟶

8 and -8 are not the same. ⟶

No real number squared is -64. ⟶

$$(8)(8) = 64 \text{ and } (-8)(-8) = 64$$
$$(8)(-8) = -64$$

It seems that $\sqrt{-64}$ is not a real number.

> The square root of a negative number is not a real number.

EXAMPLE 4   Simplify $\sqrt{-81}$ and $-\sqrt{81}$ if possible.

$\sqrt{-81}$ is not a real number.
$-\sqrt{81} = -9$

We will assume that variables under a radical sign represent only positive numbers or zero.

ORAL EXERCISES

Simplify, if possible.

1. $\sqrt{1}$
2. $\sqrt{-1}$
3. $-\sqrt{1}$
4. $-\sqrt{-1}$
5. $\sqrt{25}$
6. $-\sqrt{36}$
7. $\sqrt{-100}$
8. $\sqrt{49}$
9. $-\sqrt{-25}$
10. $\sqrt{-16}$
11. $-\sqrt{9}$
12. $\sqrt{121}$

EXERCISES

PART A

Simplify.

1. $\sqrt{x^8 y^4}$
2. $-\sqrt{a^6 b^{10}}$
3. $\sqrt{c^2 d^8}$
4. $\sqrt{25x^2}$
5. $-\sqrt{9y^4}$
6. $\sqrt{49a^{10}}$
7. $-\sqrt{81a^2 b^6}$
8. $\sqrt{64x^4 y^8}$
9. $-\sqrt{4c^{10} d^2}$
10. $-\sqrt{16x^8 y^{12}}$
11. $\sqrt{9a^6 b^8}$
12. $\sqrt{100x^4 y^{14}}$
13. $\sqrt{a^4 b^6 c^8}$
14. $\sqrt{x^2 y^6 z^{10}}$
15. $-\sqrt{c^4 d^2 e^{12}}$
16. $-\sqrt{4x^2 y^8 z^2}$
17. $\sqrt{9a^6 b^8 c^2}$
18. $-\sqrt{49x^4 y^8 z^2}$
19. $\sqrt{64a^4 b^{12} c^2}$
20. $-\sqrt{81x^8 y^{12} z^4}$
21. $\sqrt{36c^8 d^{10} e^{12}}$
22. $-\sqrt{100x^2 y^{12} z^{10}}$
23. $\sqrt{25a^{12} b^{10} c^4}$
24. $-\sqrt{16c^2 d^6 e^{14}}$
25. $\sqrt{121c^8 d^6 e^2}$
26. $-\sqrt{169x^8 y^2 z^{10}}$
27. $\sqrt{144a^8 b^2 c^{16}}$

PART B

EXAMPLE Simplify $\sqrt{12x^4 y^{16} z^2}$.

$$\sqrt{12} = \sqrt{2 \cdot 2 \cdot 3} = \sqrt{2} \cdot \sqrt{2} \cdot \sqrt{3}$$
$$= 2\sqrt{3}$$

$$\sqrt{12x^4 y^{16} z^2} = \sqrt{12} \cdot \sqrt{x^4} \cdot \sqrt{y^{16}} \cdot \sqrt{z^2}$$
$$= 2\sqrt{3}\, x^2 y^8 z$$

Simplify.

28. $\sqrt{20x^2 y^8}$
29. $-\sqrt{27a^4 b^{10}}$
30. $-\sqrt{28c^8 d^2}$
31. $-\sqrt{32a^6 b^{12}}$
32. $\sqrt{50x^2 y^6}$
33. $-\sqrt{48a^{10} b^{12}}$
34. $\sqrt{200x^4 y^2 z^6}$
35. $\sqrt{45a^{12} b^{14} c^2}$
36. $\sqrt{75c^8 d^2 e^{12}}$
37. $-\sqrt{98a^4 b^8 c^{16}}$
38. $\sqrt{128x^4 y^{10} z^8}$
39. $-\sqrt{243x^8 y^2 z^{18}}$

PART C

Simplify.

40. $\sqrt{.04x^2 y^8}$
41. $-\sqrt{1.69a^2 b^8 c^{20}}$
42. $\sqrt{.000016x^4 y^2 z^{18}}$
43. $\sqrt{\dfrac{1}{25} x^{10} y^2 z^{12}}$
44. $\sqrt{\dfrac{4}{49} x^8 y^{12} z^{24}}$
45. $-\sqrt{\dfrac{81}{16} a^2 b^{36} c^{100}}$

Odd Exponents

REVIEW CAPSULE

$$x^6 \cdot x = x^6 \cdot x^1 = x^{6+1} = x^7$$
$$a^{10} \cdot a = a^{10} \cdot a^1 = a^{10+1} = a^{11}$$

Also, $y^9 = y^{8+1} = y^8 \cdot y^1 = y^8 \cdot y$
$$z^5 = z^{4+1} = z^4 \cdot z^1 = z^4 \cdot z$$

EXAMPLE 1 Simplify $\sqrt{x^5}$.

x^4 is a perfect square. $\longrightarrow$

$\sqrt{x^4} = \sqrt{x^2 \cdot x^2} = x^2 \longrightarrow$

$$\sqrt{x^5} = \sqrt{x^4 \cdot x^1}$$
$$= \sqrt{x^4} \cdot \sqrt{x^1}$$
$$= x^2 \sqrt{x}$$

EXAMPLE 2 Simplify $\sqrt{a^3b^7}$.

a^2 and b^6 are perfect squares. $\longrightarrow$
Group perfect squares together. $\longrightarrow$
$\sqrt{a^2b^6} = \sqrt{a^2} \cdot \sqrt{b^6} = ab^3 \longrightarrow$

$$\sqrt{a^3b^7} = \sqrt{a^2 \cdot a^1 \cdot b^6 \cdot b^1}$$
$$= \sqrt{a^2 \cdot b^6} \cdot \sqrt{ab}$$
$$= ab^3 \sqrt{ab}$$

EXAMPLE 3 Simplify $\sqrt{40xy^9}$.

The greatest perfect square factor of $40xy^9$ is $4y^8$.

$\sqrt{4y^8} = \sqrt{4} \cdot \sqrt{y^8} = 2y^4 \longrightarrow$

$$\sqrt{40xy^9} = \sqrt{4 \cdot 10 \cdot x \cdot y^8 \cdot y^1}$$
$$= \sqrt{4y^8} \cdot \sqrt{10xy}$$
$$= 2y^4 \sqrt{10xy}$$

EXAMPLE 4 Simplify $-4x^2y \sqrt{45x^3y^4}$.

The greatest perfect square factor of $45x^3y^4$ is $9x^2y^4$.

$\sqrt{9x^2y^4} = \sqrt{9} \sqrt{x^2} \sqrt{y^4} = 3xy^2 \longrightarrow$

$x^2 \cdot x^1 = x^3; y^1 \cdot y^2 = y^3 \longrightarrow$

$$-4x^2y \sqrt{45x^3y^4} = -4x^2y \sqrt{9 \cdot 5 \cdot x^2 \cdot x^1 \cdot y^4}$$
$$= -4x^2y \sqrt{9x^2y^4} \cdot \sqrt{5x}$$
$$= -4x^2y(3xy^2) \sqrt{5x}$$
$$= -12x^3y^3 \sqrt{5x}$$

Read: the cube root of 8 equals 2. $\longrightarrow$

$\sqrt[3]{8} = 2$, since $2 \cdot 2 \cdot 2 = 8$. $[2^3 = 8]$

$\sqrt[3]{-64} = -4$, since $(-4)(-4)(-4) = -64$.

$[(-4)^3 = -64]$

EXAMPLE 5 Simplify $\sqrt[3]{24x^3y^7}$

$$= \sqrt[3]{2 \cdot 2 \cdot 2 \cdot 3 \cdot x^1 \cdot x^1 \cdot x^1 \cdot y^2 \cdot y^2 \cdot y^2 \cdot y^1}$$

$$= \sqrt[3]{2 \cdot 2 \cdot 2 \cdot x^1 \cdot x^1 \cdot x^1 \cdot y^2 \cdot y^2 \cdot y^2}\ \sqrt[3]{3y^1}$$

Read: $2xy^2$ times the cube root of $3y$. ⟶ $= 2xy^2\sqrt[3]{3y}$

EXERCISES

PART A

Simplify.

1. $\sqrt{x^3}$ 2. $-\sqrt{a^7}$ 3. $\sqrt{9x^5}$ 4. $\sqrt{25c}$

5. $\sqrt{8x^5}$ 6. $\sqrt{18a^9}$ 7. $\sqrt{7x^3}$ 8. $-\sqrt{5x^{11}}$

9. $\sqrt{x^4y^7}$ 10. $\sqrt{a^2b^5}$ 11. $-\sqrt{c^6d^3}$ 12. $\sqrt{m^8n}$

13. $\sqrt{x^5y^7}$ 14. $\sqrt{a^9b^3}$ 15. $\sqrt{c^3d}$ 16. $\sqrt{mn^7}$

17. $\sqrt{a^5b^8}$ 18. $-\sqrt{4cd^2}$ 19. $\sqrt{5x^3y^4}$ 20. $\sqrt{99m^3b^8}$

21. $\sqrt{36x^2y}$ 22. $-\sqrt{16m^8n^7}$ 23. $\sqrt{6x^6y^9}$ 24. $\sqrt{20a^4b^3}$

25. $\sqrt{19x^5y^9}$ 26. $\sqrt{40xy^3}$ 27. $-\sqrt{50m^3n^4}$ 28. $\sqrt{72ab^6}$

29. $4\sqrt{44xy^2z^6}$ 30. $-7\sqrt{90a^3b^6c^7}$ 31. $6\sqrt{28a^4bc^{12}}$

32. $x\sqrt{x^3yz^8}$ 33. $-cd\sqrt{c^4d^5e^6}$ 34. $-a^2bc\sqrt{a^3b^8c^9}$

35. $-3y\sqrt{x^3y^5z}$ 36. $4xz\sqrt{x^4y^7z^2}$ 37. $-5c^2d\sqrt{b^7c^3d^6}$

38. $4a^2b\sqrt{75a^6b^7}$ 39. $-12xy^3\sqrt{32x^2y^5}$ 40. $8e^3f^2\sqrt{128ef^2g^3}$

PART B

Simplify.

41. $\sqrt[3]{x^3y^9}$ 42. $\sqrt[3]{a^6b^{12}}$ 43. $-\sqrt[3]{c^3d^{12}}$

44. $\sqrt[3]{-x^6y^9}$ 45. $\sqrt[3]{8a^3b^9}$ 46. $\sqrt[3]{-27x^6y^3}$

47. $-\sqrt[3]{64a^4b^6}$ 48. $\sqrt[3]{-125x^7y^9}$ 49. $-\sqrt[3]{40a^2b^8}$

50. $\sqrt[3]{-56ab^6c^{10}}$ 51. $-\sqrt[3]{-192x^7yz^{12}}$ 52. $-\sqrt[3]{32x^9y^{10}z^{11}}$

PART C

Read:

The fourth root of 81 equals 3. ⟶ $\sqrt[4]{81} = 3$, since $3 \cdot 3 \cdot 3 \cdot 3 = 81$. $[3^4 = 81]$

The fifth root of 32 equals 2. ⟶ $\sqrt[5]{32} = 2$, since $2 \cdot 2 \cdot 2 \cdot 2 \cdot 2 = 32$. $[2^5 = 32]$

Simplify.

53. $\sqrt[4]{x^4y^{12}}$ 54. $\sqrt[5]{a^5b^{10}}$ 55. $-\sqrt[4]{16x^8y^4}$

56. $\sqrt[6]{64x^6y^{12}}$ 57. $\sqrt[5]{243x^6y^{10}}$ 58. $-\sqrt[4]{81a^3b^5}$

59. $\sqrt[5]{-96a^2b^7c^3}$ 60. $\sqrt[4]{80x^3y^7z^{12}}$ 61. $-2a\sqrt[5]{160c^5d^6e^7}$

62. $-3a^3b\sqrt[4]{162a^6bc^9}$ 63. $6xy^2\sqrt[3]{54x^2yz^8}$ 64. $-7c^2d^3\sqrt[4]{12c^9d^{21}e}$

Flow Chart: Finding Square Roots

This is a flow chart of a process used in computers to find square roots.

Find $\sqrt{x}$

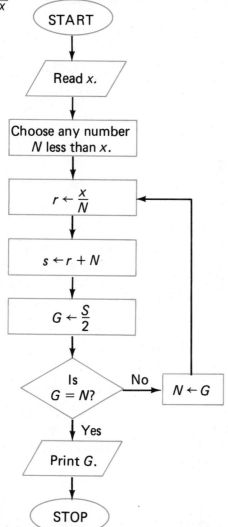

Find $\sqrt{3}$ to two decimal places.

Read 3.

- Choose 1.5 (1.5 < 3).
  Divide. $\dfrac{3}{1.5} = 2$
  Add. $2 + 1.5 = 3.5$
  Divide. $\dfrac{3.5}{2} = 1.75$
  Is 1.75 = 1.5? No

- Choose 1.75. (1.75 < 3)
  Divide. $\dfrac{3}{1.75} = 1.71$
  Add. $1.71 + 1.75 = 3.46$
  Divide. $\dfrac{3.46}{2} = 1.73$
  Is 1.73 = 1.75? No

- Choose 1.73 (1.73 < 3)
  Divide. $\dfrac{3}{1.73} = 1.73$
  Add. $1.73 + 1.73 = 3.46$
  Divide. $\dfrac{3.46}{2} = 1.73$
  Is 1.73 = 1.73? Yes
  Print 1.73.

  Thus, $\sqrt{3} = 1.73$.

PROJECT Carry all calculations to 2 decimal places. Use the flow chart.
1. $\sqrt{5}$ **2.** $\sqrt{7}$

The Pythagorean Theorem

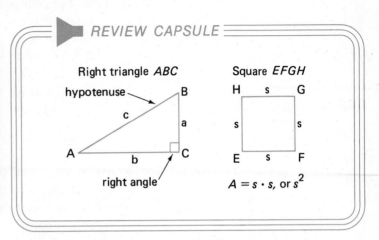

REVIEW CAPSULE

Right triangle *ABC*

Square *EFGH*

$A = s \cdot s$, or s^2

EXAMPLE 1   Examine right triangle *ABC* and the three squares shown. Find the area of each square. See what you can discover.

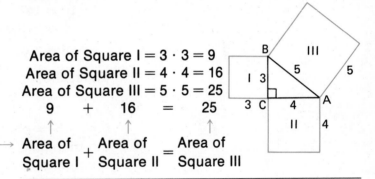

Area of Square I $= 3 \cdot 3 = 9$
Area of Square II $= 4 \cdot 4 = 16$
Area of Square III $= 5 \cdot 5 = 25$
  9   +   16   =   25

This is true for all right triangles. ──→

$$\underset{\text{Square I}}{\text{Area of}} + \underset{\text{Square II}}{\text{Area of}} = \underset{\text{Square III}}{\text{Area of}}$$

Pythagoras, a Greek philosopher and mathematician, discovered the relationship above in 500 B.C.

c is the length of the hypotenuse. *a* and *b* are the lengths of the other two sides.

If $\triangle ABC$ is a right triangle, then $a^2 + b^2 = c^2$.

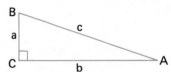

Pythagorean theorem ──────→

A *theorem* is a property which can be proved.

In any right triangle, the square of the length of the hypotenuse equals the sum of the squares of the lengths of the other two sides.

EXAMPLE 2   If the lengths of two sides of a right triangle are 5 meters and 12 meters, find the length of the hypotenuse.

Pythagorean theorem ——————→ $a^2 + b^2 = c^2$

Substitute 5 for a, 12 for b. ——————→ $5^2 + 12^2 = c^2$

$25 + 144 = c^2$

$169 = c^2$

$\sqrt{169} = c$

$13 \cdot 13 = 169$ ——————————→ $13 = c$

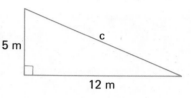

Thus, the length of the hypotenuse is 13 meters.

EXAMPLE 3   The length of the hypotenuse of a right triangle is 14 cm, and the length of one side is 7 cm. Find the length of the other side, in simplest radical form.

Pythagorean theorem ——————→ $a^2 + b^2 = c^2$

Substitute 7 for b, 14 for c. ——————→ $a^2 + 7^2 = 14^2$

$a^2 + 49 = 196$

Add -49 to each side. ——————→ $a^2 = 147$

$a = \sqrt{147}$

$\sqrt{147} = \sqrt{7 \cdot 7 \cdot 3} = 7\sqrt{3}$ ——————→ $a = 7\sqrt{3}$

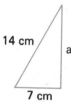

Thus, the length of the other side is $7\sqrt{3}$ cm.

If $a^2 + b^2 = c^2$, then the triangle is a right triangle with c the hypotenuse.

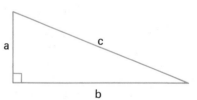

Converse of the Pythagorean theorem ——→

To form a converse of a statement, reverse the if and the then parts.

If the sum of the squares of the lengths of two sides of a triangle equals the square of the length of the third side, then the triangle is a right triangle.

EXAMPLE 4   If the lengths of the sides of a triangle are 7, 24, and 25, is the triangle a right triangle?

See if $7^2 + 24^2 = 25^2$. ——————→ $7^2 = 49 \quad 24^2 = 576 \quad 25^2 = 625 \quad 49 + 576 = 625$

Thus, the triangle is a right triangle.

EXERCISES

PART A

Tell whether each triangle described is a right triangle. The lengths of the three sides are given.

1. 4, 5, 6   **2.** 6, 8, 10   **3.** 3, 5, 7   **4.** 12, 16, 20
5. 12, 14, 16   **6.** 9, 40, 41   **7.** 1, 3, $\sqrt{11}$ **8.** $\sqrt{2}$, $\sqrt{3}$, $\sqrt{5}$

For each right triangle, find the missing length. Give answers in simplest radical form.

9. $a = 8$, $b = 6$ **10.** $a = 12$, $b = 16$ **11.** $a = 9$, $c = 15$
12. $a = 2$, $b = 6$ **13.** $b = 4$, $c = 8$ **14.** $b = 1$, $c = 3$
15. $a = 14$, $c = 50$ **16.** $b = 4$, $c = 4\sqrt{5}$ **17.** $a = 2\sqrt{2}$, $b = 2\sqrt{3}$

PART B

EXAMPLE   A rectangular field is 50 m wide by 100 m long. How long is a diagonal path connecting two opposite corners? Give the answer to the nearest tenth of a meter.

$a^2 + b^2 = c^2$ ⟶

$$50^2 + 100^2 = c^2$$
$$2,500 + 10,000 = c^2$$
$$12,500 = c^2$$
$$\sqrt{12,500} = c$$

$\sqrt{12,500} = \sqrt{2,500} \cdot \sqrt{5} = 50\sqrt{5}$ ⟶

$$50\sqrt{5} = c$$
$$50(2.236) = c$$
$$111.800 = c$$

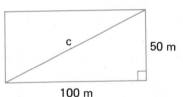

Round to the nearest tenth. ⟶ **Thus,** the diagonal path is approx. 111.8 meters long.

Give answers to the nearest tenth.

18. Paul walked 8 km north and 3 km west. How far was he from his starting point?

19. A 4-m ramp covers 3 m of ground. How high does it rise?

20. A T.V. screen is 15 cm by 12 cm. What is its diagonal length?

21. A 6-m ladder is 2 m from the base of a building. At what height does it touch the building?

PART C

22. Find the length of the side of a square if the length of the diagonal is 4 cm.

23. Find the length of the side of a square if the length of the diagonal is 6 m.

THE PYTHAGOREAN THEOREM   **401**

Combining Radicals

 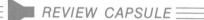
$\sqrt{2}$ in each ⟶ $5\sqrt{2}$ and $2\sqrt{2}$ are *like radicals*.

EXAMPLE 1   Simplify $5\sqrt{2} + 2\sqrt{2}$.

Distributive Property ⟶ $5\sqrt{2} + 2\sqrt{2} = (5 + 2)\sqrt{2} = 7\sqrt{2}$

Illustration of $5\sqrt{2} + 2\sqrt{2} = 7\sqrt{2}$ ⟶

| $\sqrt{2}$ | $\sqrt{2}$ | $\sqrt{2}$ | $\sqrt{2}$ | $\sqrt{2}$ | $\sqrt{2}$ | $\sqrt{2}$ |

$5\sqrt{2}$ $\qquad$ $2\sqrt{2}$

$7\sqrt{2}$

EXAMPLE 2   Simplify $5\sqrt{7} - 9\sqrt{13} + 6\sqrt{7}$.

Rearrange the terms. ⟶ $5\sqrt{7} - 9\sqrt{13} + 6\sqrt{7} = 5\sqrt{7} + 6\sqrt{7} - 9\sqrt{13}$

$\qquad\qquad\qquad\qquad\qquad = (5 + 6)\sqrt{7} - 9\sqrt{13}$

$11\sqrt{7}$ and $-9\sqrt{13}$ are unlike radicals. ⟶ $= 11\sqrt{7} - 9\sqrt{13}$

EXAMPLE 3   Simplify $\sqrt{75} - \sqrt{27} + \sqrt{12}$.

Simplify each radical. ⟶ $\sqrt{75} - \sqrt{27} + \sqrt{12}$

$\qquad\qquad\qquad\qquad = \sqrt{25 \cdot 3} - \sqrt{9 \cdot 3} + \sqrt{4 \cdot 3}$

$\qquad\qquad\qquad\qquad = \sqrt{25} \cdot \sqrt{3} - \sqrt{9} \cdot \sqrt{3} + \sqrt{4} \cdot \sqrt{3}$

$\sqrt{3}$ is common to each term. ⟶ $= 5\sqrt{3} - 3\sqrt{3} + 2\sqrt{3}$

Distributive property ⟶ $= (5 - 3 + 2)\sqrt{3}$

$\qquad\qquad\qquad\qquad = 4\sqrt{3}$

EXAMPLE 4   Simplify $2\sqrt{cd} - 5\sqrt{cd} + 9\sqrt{cd}$.

Distributive property ⟶ $2\sqrt{cd} - 5\sqrt{cd} + 9\sqrt{cd} = (2 - 5 + 9)\sqrt{cd}$

$\qquad\qquad\qquad\qquad\qquad\qquad = 6\sqrt{cd}$

EXAMPLE 5 Simplify $\sqrt{ab^3} + \sqrt{9ab^3} - 5b\sqrt{16ab}$.

$$\sqrt{ab^3} + \sqrt{9ab^3} - 5b\sqrt{16ab}$$
$$= \sqrt{b^2 \cdot ab} + \sqrt{9b^2 \cdot ab} - 5b\sqrt{16 \cdot ab}$$
$$= b\sqrt{ab} + 3b\sqrt{ab} - 5b(4)\sqrt{ab}$$

$\sqrt{ab}$ is common to each term. ⟶ $= b\sqrt{ab} + 3b\sqrt{ab} - 20b\sqrt{ab}$

Distributive Property ⟶ $= (b + 3b - 20b)\sqrt{ab} = -16b\sqrt{ab}$

EXERCISES

PART A

Simplify.

1. $2\sqrt{5} + 7\sqrt{5}$
2. $5\sqrt{3} - 2\sqrt{3}$
3. $7\sqrt{6} + 8\sqrt{6}$
4. $9\sqrt{2} - 8\sqrt{2}$
5. $4\sqrt{10} + 2\sqrt{10} - 5\sqrt{10}$
6. $6\sqrt{7} - 10\sqrt{7} - 4\sqrt{7}$
7. $5\sqrt{6} - 3\sqrt{6} + 6\sqrt{3}$
8. $4\sqrt{3} - 8\sqrt{2} - 7\sqrt{2}$
9. $4\sqrt{5} - 6\sqrt{7} + 8\sqrt{5}$
10. $6\sqrt{5} - \sqrt{11} + 5\sqrt{11} - 10\sqrt{5}$
11. $\sqrt{5} + 3\sqrt{2} - 6\sqrt{2} + 7\sqrt{5}$
12. $8\sqrt{7} - 7\sqrt{3} + 6\sqrt{7} + 9\sqrt{3}$
13. $3\sqrt{8} + \sqrt{2}$
14. $4\sqrt{3} + \sqrt{12}$
15. $2\sqrt{24} - 3\sqrt{54}$
16. $6\sqrt{27} - 3\sqrt{48}$
17. $3\sqrt{44} - 7\sqrt{11} + \sqrt{99}$
18. $-\sqrt{32} + 5\sqrt{18} - 7\sqrt{98}$
19. $\sqrt{a} + 8\sqrt{a}$
20. $6\sqrt{x} + 7\sqrt{x} - \sqrt{x}$
21. $4\sqrt{mn} - 2\sqrt{mn} + 5\sqrt{mn}$
22. $3\sqrt{xy} - \sqrt{xy} + 8\sqrt{xy} + \sqrt{xy}$
23. $\sqrt{xy} + \sqrt{4xy} - 2\sqrt{9xy}$
24. $-6\sqrt{9c} + 8\sqrt{16c} - 4c\sqrt{4c}$
25. $5x\sqrt{3z} + x\sqrt{5z} - x\sqrt{3z} - 2x\sqrt{5z}$
26. $2\sqrt{xy} - 5\sqrt{4xy} - \sqrt{25xy}$
27. $3\sqrt{a^3b^3} + 2b\sqrt{4a^3b} - 7a\sqrt{16ab^3}$
28. $c\sqrt{cd^3} + cd\sqrt{cd} + d\sqrt{c^3d}$

PART B

Simplify.

29. $\sqrt{27x} - \sqrt{48x} + \sqrt{75x}$
30. $2\sqrt{24y} - 5\sqrt{54y} + 7\sqrt{96y}$
31. $\sqrt{33a} + \sqrt{11a} - \sqrt{77a}$
32. $2\sqrt{98z} + \sqrt{18z} - 5\sqrt{32z}$
33. $2\sqrt{10x} + \sqrt{40x} - 5\sqrt{90x}$
34. $\sqrt{3xy} + \sqrt{27xy} - \sqrt{12xy}$
35. $2x\sqrt{5xy^2} + 3\sqrt{20x^3y^2}$
36. $7\sqrt{8a^2b^3} - 4b\sqrt{50a^2b}$

PART C

Simplify.

37. $\sqrt{.04xy^2} + y\sqrt{.16x}$
38. $3\sqrt{.25a^3b} + 4a\sqrt{.0001ab}$
39. $6x\sqrt{.0036xy^2} - 2yx\sqrt{.0049x}$
40. $2x\sqrt{.01xy^2} - 5\sqrt{.0025x^3y^2}$
41. $-2b\sqrt{.0004a^3b} + 6a\sqrt{.36ab^3}$
42. $7xy\sqrt{.64xy} - 8y\sqrt{.0081x^3y}$

Products of Radicals

OBJECTIVE

■ To multiply expressions containing radicals

▶ REVIEW CAPSULE

$$\sqrt{3} \cdot \sqrt{3} = 3 \qquad \sqrt{5} \cdot \sqrt{2} = \sqrt{10}$$
$$\sqrt{8} \cdot \sqrt{8} = 8 \qquad \sqrt{3} \cdot \sqrt{7} = \sqrt{21}$$
$$\downarrow \qquad \downarrow \qquad \qquad \downarrow$$
$$\sqrt{x} \cdot \sqrt{x} = x \qquad \sqrt{a} \cdot \sqrt{b} = \sqrt{ab}$$

EXAMPLE 1   Multiply $6\sqrt{5} \cdot 4\sqrt{3}$.

Rearrange factors. ──────────────→

$6 \cdot 4 = 24$; $\sqrt{5} \cdot \sqrt{3} = \sqrt{5 \cdot 3}$ ──────→

$\sqrt{5 \cdot 3} = \sqrt{15}$

$$6\sqrt{5} \cdot 4\sqrt{3} = 6 \cdot 4 \cdot \sqrt{5} \cdot \sqrt{3}$$
$$= 24 \cdot \sqrt{5 \cdot 3}$$
$$= 24\sqrt{15}$$

EXAMPLE 2   Multiply $-7\sqrt{6x} \cdot 2\sqrt{3x}$.

$$-7\sqrt{6x} \cdot 2\sqrt{3x} = -7 \cdot 2 \cdot \sqrt{6x} \cdot \sqrt{3x}$$
$$= -14\sqrt{6x \cdot 3x}$$
$$= -14\sqrt{2 \cdot 3x \cdot 3x}$$

$\sqrt{3x \cdot 3x} = 3x$ ──────────────→

$-14 \cdot 3 = -42$ ──────────────→

$$= -14 \cdot 3x \cdot \sqrt{2}$$
$$= -42x\sqrt{2}$$

EXAMPLE 3   Multiply $\sqrt{3}(\sqrt{5} + 4\sqrt{3})$.

Distribute the $\sqrt{3}$. ──────────────→

$\sqrt{3} \cdot 4\sqrt{3} = 4\sqrt{3} \cdot \sqrt{3}$ ──────────→

$\sqrt{3 \cdot 5} = \sqrt{15}$; $\sqrt{3} \cdot \sqrt{3} = 3$ ──────→

$$\sqrt{3}(\sqrt{5} + 4\sqrt{3}) = \sqrt{3} \cdot \sqrt{5} + \sqrt{3} \cdot 4\sqrt{3}$$
$$= \sqrt{3 \cdot 5} + 4\sqrt{3} \cdot \sqrt{3}$$
$$= \sqrt{15} + 4 \cdot 3$$
$$= \sqrt{15} + 12$$

EXAMPLE 4   Multiply $-6\sqrt{2}(\sqrt{10} - 7\sqrt{8})$.

Distribute the $-6\sqrt{2}$. ──────────────→

$\sqrt{a} \cdot \sqrt{b} = \sqrt{ab}$ ──────────────→

4 and 16 are perfect squares. ──────────→

$\sqrt{4} = 2$; $\sqrt{16} = 4$ ──────────────→

$$-6\sqrt{2}(\sqrt{10} - 7\sqrt{8})$$
$$= (-6\sqrt{2})(\sqrt{10}) + (-6\sqrt{2})(-7\sqrt{8})$$
$$= -6\sqrt{20} + 42\sqrt{16}$$
$$= -6\sqrt{4 \cdot 5} + 42\sqrt{16}$$
$$= -6 \cdot 2\sqrt{5} + 42 \cdot 4$$
$$= -12\sqrt{5} + 168$$

EXAMPLE 5 Multiply $(2 \sqrt{6} + \sqrt{5})(8 \sqrt{6} - \sqrt{5})$.

Write vertically.
Multiply like two binomials.

$8 \sqrt{6}(+ \sqrt{5}) = +8 \cdot \sqrt{6} \cdot \sqrt{5} = +8 \sqrt{30}$ ⟶
$-\sqrt{5}(2 \sqrt{6}) = -2 \cdot \sqrt{5} \cdot \sqrt{6} = -2 \sqrt{30}$ ⟶

$$\begin{array}{c} 2\sqrt{6} \quad\quad +\sqrt{5} \\ 8\sqrt{6} \quad\quad -\sqrt{5} \end{array}$$

$$2 \cdot 8 \cdot \sqrt{6} \cdot \sqrt{6} \quad \begin{array}{c} +8\sqrt{30} \\ -2\sqrt{30} \end{array} \quad -\sqrt{5} \cdot \sqrt{5}$$

$+8 \sqrt{30} - 2 \sqrt{30} = +6 \sqrt{30}$ ⟶

$$16 \quad\cdot\quad 6 \quad\quad +6\sqrt{30} \quad\quad - \quad 5$$
$$96 \quad\quad\quad +6\sqrt{30} \quad\quad - \quad 5$$

$96 - 5 = 91$ ⟶

$$91 + 6 \sqrt{30}$$

EXAMPLE 6 Multiply $(7 \sqrt{2} - 3 \sqrt{10})(7 \sqrt{2} + 3 \sqrt{10})$.

$$\begin{array}{c} 7\sqrt{2} \quad\quad -3\sqrt{10} \\ 7\sqrt{2} \quad\quad +3\sqrt{10} \end{array}$$

$7 \sqrt{2}(-3 \sqrt{10}) = 7(-3) \sqrt{2} \cdot \sqrt{10} = -21 \sqrt{20}$
$+3 \sqrt{10}(7 \sqrt{2}) = +3 \cdot 7 \cdot \sqrt{10} \cdot \sqrt{2} = +21 \sqrt{20}$

$$7 \cdot 7 \cdot \sqrt{2} \cdot \sqrt{2} \quad \begin{array}{c} -21\sqrt{20} \\ +21\sqrt{20} \end{array} \quad -3 \cdot 3 \cdot \sqrt{10} \cdot \sqrt{10}$$

$-21 \sqrt{20} + 21 \sqrt{20} = 0$ ⟶

$$49 \quad\cdot\quad 2 \quad\quad + \quad 0 \quad\quad - \quad 9 \quad\cdot\quad 10$$
$$98 \quad\quad\quad\quad\quad\quad\quad\quad - \quad 90$$

$$8$$

EXAMPLE 7 Multiply $(2 \sqrt{3} + \sqrt{5})^2$.

$(a + b)^2$ means $(a + b)(a + b)$.

$$\begin{array}{c} 2\sqrt{3} \quad\quad +\sqrt{5} \\ 2\sqrt{3} \quad\quad +\sqrt{5} \end{array}$$

$$2 \cdot 2 \cdot \sqrt{3} \cdot \sqrt{3} \quad \begin{array}{c} +2\sqrt{15} \\ +2\sqrt{15} \end{array} \quad + \sqrt{5} \cdot \sqrt{5}$$

$2 \sqrt{15} + 2 \sqrt{15} = 4 \sqrt{15}$

$$4 \quad\cdot\quad 3 \quad\quad +4\sqrt{15} \quad\quad + \quad 5$$
$$12 \quad\quad\quad +4 \cdot \sqrt{15} \quad\quad + \quad 5$$
$$17 \quad\quad\quad +4\sqrt{15}$$

ORAL EXERCISES

Multiply.

1. $\sqrt{7} \cdot \sqrt{7}$

2. $(\sqrt{8})^2$

3. $(-\sqrt{5})^2$

4. $2 \sqrt{3} \cdot 2 \sqrt{3}$

5. $(4 \sqrt{6})^2$

6. $(-5 \sqrt{2})^2$

7. $3 \sqrt{5} \cdot 4 \sqrt{5}$

8. $-8 \sqrt{2} \cdot 3 \sqrt{2}$

9. $-2 \sqrt{3} \cdot 2 \sqrt{3}$

10. $2 \cdot 4 \sqrt{7}$

11. $5 \cdot (-6 \sqrt{2})$

12. $4 \sqrt{10} \cdot 6 \sqrt{3}$

EXERCISES

Multiply.

1. $5\sqrt{6} \cdot 4\sqrt{2}$
2. $3\sqrt{7} \cdot 2\sqrt{5}$
3. $4\sqrt{10} \cdot 6\sqrt{3}$
4. $2\sqrt{7} \cdot 3\sqrt{14}$
5. $5\sqrt{3} \cdot 3\sqrt{10}$
6. $-8\sqrt{2} \cdot 4\sqrt{6}$
7. $2\sqrt{x} \cdot \sqrt{x}$
8. $5\sqrt{c} \cdot 3\sqrt{c}$
9. $(-\sqrt{y})^2$
10. $3\sqrt{2x} \cdot \sqrt{2x}$
11. $-4\sqrt{3y} \cdot 6\sqrt{3y}$
12. $8\sqrt{2x} \cdot 5\sqrt{6x}$

Multiply.

13. $\sqrt{2}(\sqrt{18} - 3\sqrt{2})$
14. $4\sqrt{2}(\sqrt{5} - 2\sqrt{2})$
15. $-5\sqrt{6}(2\sqrt{2} + 4\sqrt{3})$
16. $2\sqrt{5}(2\sqrt{2} + 8\sqrt{10})$
17. $(2\sqrt{3} - \sqrt{2})(3\sqrt{3} + \sqrt{2})$
18. $(\sqrt{5} - \sqrt{3})(2\sqrt{5} + 4\sqrt{3})$
19. $(6\sqrt{3} - 2\sqrt{2})(3\sqrt{3} + 5\sqrt{2})$
20. $(4\sqrt{7} - 2\sqrt{3})(3\sqrt{7} + 2\sqrt{3})$
21. $(\sqrt{5} + \sqrt{3})(\sqrt{5} - \sqrt{3})$
22. $(\sqrt{7} + \sqrt{2})(\sqrt{7} - \sqrt{2})$
23. $(3\sqrt{2} + 4\sqrt{3})(3\sqrt{2} - 4\sqrt{3})$
24. $(2\sqrt{5} - 3\sqrt{6})(2\sqrt{5} + 3\sqrt{6})$
25. $(2\sqrt{3} + \sqrt{7})^2$
26. $(3\sqrt{2} - \sqrt{5})^2$
27. $(\sqrt{6} - 2\sqrt{5})^2$
28. $(2\sqrt{5} + 3\sqrt{2})^2$

EXAMPLE   Multiply $(2\sqrt{3} + \sqrt{6})^2$.

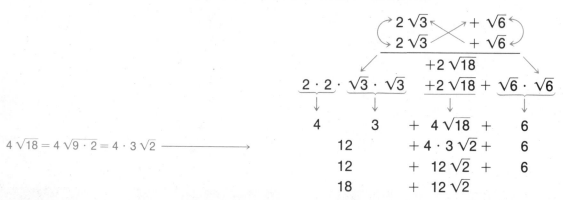

$$4\sqrt{18} = 4\sqrt{9 \cdot 2} = 4 \cdot 3\sqrt{2}$$

Multiply.

29. $(3\sqrt{6} + 2\sqrt{2})^2$
30. $(5\sqrt{3} - 4\sqrt{8})^2$
31. $(6\sqrt{14} - 3\sqrt{2})^2$
32. $(2\sqrt{8} - 3\sqrt{2})^2$
33. $(4\sqrt{5} - 2\sqrt{10})^2$
34. $(5\sqrt{6} + 3\sqrt{3})^2$

Multiply.

35. $(\sqrt{3} + \sqrt{2} - \sqrt{5})^2$
36. $(\sqrt{3} + \sqrt{2})(\sqrt{3} + \sqrt{6} + \sqrt{2})$
37. $\sqrt[3]{2}(\sqrt[3]{4} + \sqrt[3]{32})$

Points for Irrational Numbers

PROBLEM 1.

Find a point corresponding to $\sqrt{2}$ on a number line.

Construct a right triangle
with each leg 1 unit in length.
Use the Pythagorean theorem
to find the length of the
hypotenuse.

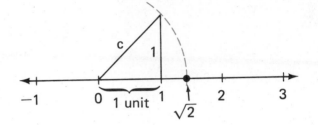

$$c^2 = 1^2 + 1^2$$
$$c^2 = 1 + 1$$
$$c^2 = 2$$
So, $c = \sqrt{2}$

Thus, the hypotenuse is $\sqrt{2}$ units long. Mark off a segment the
length of the hypotenuse on the number line. The endpoint is $\sqrt{2}$.

PROBLEM 2.

Find a point corresponding to $\sqrt{3}$ on a number line.

Construct a right triangle
with legs 1 and $\sqrt{2}$ units long.
Again, use the Pythagorean
theorem.

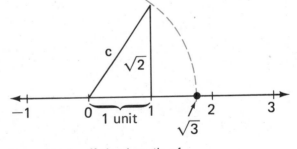

$$c^2 = 1^2 + (\sqrt{2})^2$$
$$c^2 = 1 + 2$$
$$c^2 = 3$$
So, $c = \sqrt{3}$

Thus, the hypotenuse is $\sqrt{3}$ units long. Mark off the length of
the hypotenuse on the number line. The endpoint is $\sqrt{3}$.

PROJECT Find the points corresponding to $\sqrt{5}$ and $\sqrt{6}$ on a number line.

Rationalizing Denominators

REVIEW CAPSULE

$$\frac{\sqrt{4}}{\sqrt{25}} = \frac{2}{5} \qquad\qquad \frac{\sqrt{49}}{\sqrt{16}} = \frac{7}{4}$$

$$\sqrt{\frac{4}{25}} = \sqrt{\frac{2}{5} \cdot \frac{2}{5}} = \frac{2}{5} \qquad \sqrt{\frac{49}{16}} = \sqrt{\frac{7}{4} \cdot \frac{7}{4}} = \frac{7}{4}$$

Thus, $\dfrac{\sqrt{4}}{\sqrt{25}} = \sqrt{\dfrac{4}{25}}$. | Thus, $\dfrac{\sqrt{49}}{\sqrt{16}} = \sqrt{\dfrac{49}{16}}$.

The examples in the Review suggest this rule.

$$\frac{\sqrt{a}}{\sqrt{b}} = \sqrt{\frac{a}{b}}, \text{ for all positive numbers } a \text{ and } b.$$

EXAMPLE 1   Simplify $\dfrac{\sqrt{15}}{\sqrt{3}}$.   Simplify $\dfrac{\sqrt{32x^3}}{\sqrt{8x}}$.

$$\frac{\sqrt{a}}{\sqrt{b}} = \sqrt{\frac{a}{b}}$$

$$\frac{\sqrt{15}}{\sqrt{3}} = \sqrt{\frac{15}{3}} \qquad\qquad \frac{\sqrt{32x^3}}{\sqrt{8x}} = \sqrt{\frac{32x^3}{8x}}$$
$$= \sqrt{5} \qquad\qquad\qquad = \sqrt{4x^2}$$
$$\qquad\qquad\qquad\qquad = 2x$$

EXAMPLE 2   Rewrite $\dfrac{5}{\sqrt{7}}$ with no radical in the denominator.

$\dfrac{\sqrt{7}}{\sqrt{7}} = 1$; multiply by $\dfrac{\sqrt{7}}{\sqrt{7}}$.

$\sqrt{7} \cdot \sqrt{7} = 7$
There is no radical in the denominator.

$$\frac{5}{\sqrt{7}} = \frac{5}{\sqrt{7}} \cdot \frac{\sqrt{7}}{\sqrt{7}}$$
$$= \frac{5\sqrt{7}}{7}$$

Definition of rationalize

> To *rationalize* the denominator of a fraction means to rewrite the fraction with no radical in the denominator.

EXAMPLE 3 Rationalize the denominator of $\dfrac{3}{\sqrt{12}}$.

First Method	Second Method
$\dfrac{3}{\sqrt{12}} \cdot \dfrac{\sqrt{12}}{\sqrt{12}} = \dfrac{3\sqrt{12}}{12}$	$\dfrac{3}{\sqrt{12}} \cdot \dfrac{\sqrt{3}}{\sqrt{3}} = \dfrac{3\sqrt{3}}{\sqrt{36}}$
$= \dfrac{3 \cdot 2\sqrt{3}}{12}$	$= \dfrac{3\sqrt{3}}{6}$
$= \dfrac{6\sqrt{3}}{12}$	$= \dfrac{\overset{1}{\cancel{3}}\sqrt{3}}{\underset{2}{\cancel{6}}}$
$= \dfrac{\sqrt{3}}{2}$	$= \dfrac{\sqrt{3}}{2}$

$\sqrt{12} = \sqrt{4 \cdot 3} = 2\sqrt{3}$ ⟶

Second Method: Multiply by the smallest square root needed to make a perfect square in the denominator.

$\dfrac{6\sqrt{3}}{12} = \dfrac{\overset{1}{\cancel{2}} \cdot \overset{1}{\cancel{3}} \cdot \sqrt{3}}{\underset{1}{\cancel{2}} \cdot 2 \cdot \underset{1}{\cancel{3}}} = \dfrac{\sqrt{3}}{2}$

Both methods give the same result.

Thus, $\dfrac{3}{\sqrt{12}} = \dfrac{\sqrt{3}}{2}$.

EXAMPLE 4 Rationalize the denominator of $\dfrac{3}{\sqrt{x^3}}$.

$x^3 \cdot x^1 = x^4$, a perfect square.

$$\dfrac{3}{\sqrt{x^3}} \cdot \dfrac{\sqrt{x^1}}{\sqrt{x^1}} = \dfrac{3\sqrt{x^1}}{\sqrt{x^4}}$$

$$= \dfrac{3\sqrt{x}}{x^2}$$

EXAMPLE 5 Rationalize the denominator of $\dfrac{3ab}{\sqrt{a^4 b}}$.

$a^4 b^1 \cdot b^1 = a^4 b^2$, a perfect square.

$a^4 b^1 \cdot b^1 = a^4 b^2$ ⟶

$\sqrt{a^4 b^2} = a^2 b^1$

$$\dfrac{3ab}{\sqrt{a^4 b^1}} = \dfrac{3ab}{\sqrt{a^4 b^1}} \cdot \dfrac{\sqrt{b^1}}{\sqrt{b^1}}$$

$$= \dfrac{3ab\sqrt{b}}{\sqrt{a^4 b^2}}$$

$$= \dfrac{3ab\sqrt{b}}{a^2 b^1} = \dfrac{3 \cdot \overset{1}{\cancel{a}} \cdot \overset{1}{\cancel{b}} \cdot \sqrt{b}}{\underset{a^1}{a^2} \cdot \underset{1}{\cancel{b^1}}}$$

Thus, $\dfrac{3ab}{\sqrt{a^4 b}} = \dfrac{3\sqrt{b}}{a}$.

EXAMPLE 6 Rationalize the denominator of $\dfrac{8y^2}{\sqrt{12y}}$.

Multiply by $\dfrac{\sqrt{3y}}{\sqrt{3y}}$. Then 36 and y^2 are perfect squares.

$\sqrt{36y^2} = 6y$ ⟶

$$\dfrac{8y^2}{\sqrt{12y}} = \dfrac{8y^2}{\sqrt{12y}} \cdot \dfrac{\sqrt{3y}}{\sqrt{3y}}$$

$$= \dfrac{8y^2\sqrt{3y}}{\sqrt{36y^2}} = \dfrac{8y^2\sqrt{3y}}{6y} = \dfrac{\overset{4}{\cancel{8}}y^{\overset{y}{\cancel{2}}}\sqrt{3y}}{\underset{3\ 1}{\cancel{6}\cancel{y}}} = \dfrac{4y\sqrt{3y}}{3}$$

EXERCISES

PART A

Rationalize the denominator.

1. $\dfrac{1}{\sqrt{2}}$ 2. $\dfrac{5}{\sqrt{3}}$ 3. $\dfrac{5}{\sqrt{5}}$ 4. $\dfrac{28}{\sqrt{7}}$ 5. $\dfrac{6}{\sqrt{3}}$

6. $\dfrac{3}{\sqrt{18}}$ 7. $\dfrac{6}{\sqrt{12}}$ 8. $\dfrac{4}{\sqrt{20}}$ 9. $\dfrac{5}{\sqrt{10}}$ 10. $\dfrac{8}{\sqrt{50}}$

11. $\dfrac{4}{\sqrt{x^5}}$ 12. $\dfrac{3}{\sqrt{x^7}}$ 13. $\dfrac{2}{\sqrt{m^3}}$ 14. $\dfrac{5}{\sqrt{m^9}}$ 15. $\dfrac{6}{\sqrt{x}}$

16. $\dfrac{4}{\sqrt{12a^3}}$ 17. $\dfrac{6}{\sqrt{8a^5}}$ 18. $\dfrac{4}{\sqrt{18b^3}}$ 19. $\dfrac{3x}{\sqrt{6x^3}}$ 20. $\dfrac{27a}{\sqrt{3a^5}}$

PART B

Rationalize the denominator.

21. $\dfrac{5xy}{\sqrt{x}}$ 22. $\dfrac{12ab}{\sqrt{a^2 b}}$ 23. $\dfrac{3x}{\sqrt{x^2 y}}$ 24. $\dfrac{5c^3 d}{\sqrt{cd}}$ 25. $\dfrac{12x^3 y^3}{\sqrt{xy}}$

26. $\dfrac{6x^2 y}{\sqrt{xy^2}}$ 27. $\dfrac{6y^2}{\sqrt{18y}}$ 28. $\dfrac{4m^3}{\sqrt{8m^7}}$ 29. $\dfrac{2a^3}{\sqrt{20a^5}}$ 30. $\dfrac{3x^5}{\sqrt{6x^3}}$

PART C

EXAMPLE Rationalize the denominator of $\dfrac{7}{5 - \sqrt{3}}$.

Multiply by 1: $\dfrac{5 + \sqrt{3}}{5 + \sqrt{3}}$

$5 + \sqrt{3}$ is the conjugate of $5 - \sqrt{3}$. ⟶

$$\begin{array}{rcl} & 5 & - \sqrt{3} \\ & 5 & + \sqrt{3} \\ \hline 25 & -5\sqrt{3} & -3 \\ & +5\sqrt{3} & \\ \hline 25 & +0 & -3 = 22 \end{array}$$

$$\dfrac{7}{5 - \sqrt{3}} = \dfrac{7}{5 - \sqrt{3}} \cdot \dfrac{5 + \sqrt{3}}{5 + \sqrt{3}}$$

$$= \dfrac{7(5 + \sqrt{3})}{(5 - \sqrt{3})(5 + \sqrt{3})}$$

$$= \dfrac{35 + 7\sqrt{3}}{22}$$

Thus, $\dfrac{7}{5 - \sqrt{3}} = \dfrac{35 + 7\sqrt{3}}{22}$.

Rationalize the denominator of each.

31. $\dfrac{5}{3 - \sqrt{3}}$ 32. $\dfrac{-2}{3 + \sqrt{2}}$ 33. $\dfrac{\sqrt{3}}{\sqrt{10} - 2}$ 34. $\dfrac{5}{2\sqrt{5} + 1}$ 35. $\dfrac{-3}{\sqrt{7} - 2}$

Fractional Radicands

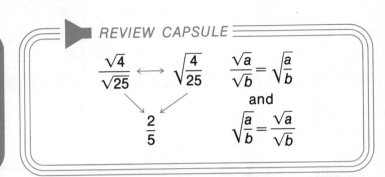

REVIEW CAPSULE

$$\frac{\sqrt{4}}{\sqrt{25}} \longleftrightarrow \sqrt{\frac{4}{25}} \qquad \frac{\sqrt{a}}{\sqrt{b}} = \sqrt{\frac{a}{b}}$$

$$\frac{2}{5} \qquad\qquad \text{and}$$

$$\sqrt{\frac{a}{b}} = \frac{\sqrt{a}}{\sqrt{b}}$$

$\sqrt{10}$ ← radical
10 ← radicand

To simplify $\sqrt{\dfrac{3}{4}}$, rewrite it so that the radicand is not a fraction.

EXAMPLE 1 Simplify $\sqrt{\dfrac{3}{4}}$.

The radicand is 3; 3 is not a fraction. ───→

$$\frac{\sqrt{3}}{\sqrt{4}} = \frac{\sqrt{3}}{2}$$

EXAMPLE 2 Simplify $\sqrt{\dfrac{24}{25}}$.

$\sqrt{24} = \sqrt{4 \cdot 6} = 2\sqrt{6}$ ───────────→

$$\frac{\sqrt{24}}{\sqrt{25}} = \frac{2\sqrt{6}}{5}$$

EXAMPLE 3 Simplify $\sqrt{\dfrac{5}{8}}$.

Multiply by $\dfrac{\sqrt{2}}{\sqrt{2}}$, since $8 \cdot 2 = 16$, and
16 is a perfect square.

$$\frac{\sqrt{5}}{\sqrt{8}} = \frac{\sqrt{5}}{\sqrt{8}} \cdot \frac{\sqrt{2}}{\sqrt{2}}$$

$$= \frac{\sqrt{10}}{\sqrt{16}} = \frac{\sqrt{10}}{4}$$

EXAMPLE 4 Simplify $\sqrt{\dfrac{3}{2y^3}}$.

Rationalize the denominator of $\dfrac{\sqrt{3}}{\sqrt{2y^3}}$. ───→

$$\frac{\sqrt{3}}{\sqrt{2y^3}} = \frac{\sqrt{3}}{\sqrt{2y^3}} \cdot \frac{\sqrt{2y}}{\sqrt{2y}}$$

$$= \frac{\sqrt{6y}}{\sqrt{4y^4}} = \frac{\sqrt{6y}}{2y^2}$$

EXAMPLE 5 Simplify $\sqrt{\dfrac{14x}{24x^2}}$.

$$\dfrac{14x}{24x^2} = \dfrac{\overset{1}{\cancel{2}} \cdot 7 \cdot \overset{1}{\cancel{x}}}{\underset{1}{\cancel{2}} \cdot 12 \cdot \underset{1}{\cancel{x}} \cdot x} = \dfrac{7}{12x} \longrightarrow \sqrt{\dfrac{7}{12x}} = \dfrac{\sqrt{7}}{\sqrt{12x}} = \dfrac{\sqrt{7}}{\sqrt{12x}} \cdot \dfrac{\sqrt{3x}}{\sqrt{3x}} = \dfrac{\sqrt{21x}}{\sqrt{36x^2}} = \dfrac{\sqrt{21x}}{6x}$$

EXERCISES

PART A

Simplify.

1. $\sqrt{\dfrac{9}{16}}$ 2. $\sqrt{\dfrac{25}{49}}$ 3. $\sqrt{\dfrac{100}{81}}$ 4. $\sqrt{\dfrac{64}{36}}$ 5. $\sqrt{\dfrac{121}{25}}$

6. $\sqrt{\dfrac{7}{4}}$ 7. $\sqrt{\dfrac{54}{25}}$ 8. $\sqrt{\dfrac{31}{49}}$ 9. $\sqrt{\dfrac{67}{81}}$ 10. $\sqrt{\dfrac{27}{16}}$

11. $\sqrt{\dfrac{3}{8}}$ 12. $\sqrt{\dfrac{4}{27}}$ 13. $\sqrt{\dfrac{5}{12}}$ 14. $\sqrt{\dfrac{7}{20}}$ 15. $\sqrt{\dfrac{11}{40}}$

16. $\sqrt{\dfrac{5}{y}}$ 17. $\sqrt{\dfrac{16}{x^3}}$ 18. $\sqrt{\dfrac{7}{3z^2}}$ 19. $\sqrt{\dfrac{6}{5y^3}}$ 20. $\sqrt{\dfrac{27}{xy^3}}$

21. $\sqrt{\dfrac{54x}{y^5}}$ 22. $\sqrt{\dfrac{60}{x^2y^3}}$ 23. $\sqrt{\dfrac{x}{2x^4}}$ 24. $\sqrt{\dfrac{12z^2}{3yz}}$ 25. $\sqrt{\dfrac{5xz}{15x^3z^2}}$

26. $\sqrt{\dfrac{3y}{18y^4}}$ 27. $\sqrt{\dfrac{22y}{14y^3}}$ 28. $\sqrt{\dfrac{24a^2b^3}{6ab}}$ 29. $\sqrt{\dfrac{56y^4z}{4yz^2}}$ 30. $\sqrt{\dfrac{64a^2b^2}{20ab^3}}$

PART B

EXAMPLE   Simplify $\sqrt{\dfrac{3y + 2}{y}}$.

$$\dfrac{\sqrt{3y + 2}}{\sqrt{y}} = \dfrac{\sqrt{3y + 2}}{\sqrt{y}} \cdot \dfrac{\sqrt{y}}{\sqrt{y}} = \dfrac{\sqrt{(3y + 2)y}}{\sqrt{y^2}} = \dfrac{\sqrt{3y^2 + 2y}}{y}$$

Simplify.

31. $\sqrt{\dfrac{2x + 3}{2}}$ 32. $\sqrt{\dfrac{5z - 3}{3}}$ 33. $\sqrt{\dfrac{4x + 7}{7}}$ 34. $\sqrt{\dfrac{5x + 5}{2}}$

35. $\sqrt{\dfrac{3 - 5z}{5}}$ 36. $\sqrt{\dfrac{4x^2 - 7}{2}}$ 37. $\sqrt{\dfrac{2z^2 + 3}{3}}$ 38. $\sqrt{\dfrac{6y^2 - y}{2}}$

PART C

Simplify.

39. $\sqrt{\dfrac{y + 6}{y} + \dfrac{9}{y^2}}$ 40. $\sqrt{1 + \dfrac{10}{x} + \dfrac{25}{x^2}}$

Mathematics in Banking

Pictured above are two bank managers studying a manual on interest rates.

PROJECT A checkbook showed a balance of $155 at the beginning of a month. During the month deposits of $50, $125, and $200 were made and checks were written for $15, $25.50, $48.75, $100, $10, $35, $40, and $200. When the bank sent its monthly statement, the balance was $340.75. Only the first four checks had cleared the bank.

1. Find the checkbook balance by adding the deposits to the original balance and deducting only the checks that have cleared the bank.

2. Does the checkbook balance agree with the bank balance?

Chapter Fourteen Review

Which are rational and which are irrational numbers? $[p.\ 382]$

1. .131131113. . .   **2.** .13$\overline{13}$ **3.** .468   **4.** $2\frac{7}{8}$
5. π **6.** $-\sqrt{81}$ **7.** $\sqrt{21}$ **8.** -3.6

Give answers to the nearest tenth. Use the table on page 476. $[p.\ 384]$

9.

$$s \begin{array}{|c|} \hline A = 46 \\ cm^2 \\ \hline \end{array}$$
s

Find s.

10.

$$x \begin{array}{|c|} \hline A = 159\ m^2 \\ \hline \end{array}$$
3x

Find x and 3x.

11. The length of a rectangle is twice the width. The area is 70 square cm. Find the length and the width.

Which are irrational numbers? For each irrational number, approximate the square root to the nearest tenth. Use the divide and average method. $[p.\ 388]$

12. $\sqrt{81}$ **13.** $\sqrt{74}$ **14.** $\sqrt{41}$ **15.** $\sqrt{16}$ **16.** $\sqrt{15}$ **17.** $\sqrt{62}$

Simplify. $[p.\ 391,\ 394,\ 396]$

18. $\sqrt{49} \cdot \sqrt{9}$ **19.** $\sqrt{16 \cdot 81}$ **20.** $-\sqrt{48}$ **21.** $\sqrt{64a^4 b^{10}}$ **22.** $-\sqrt{49x^8 y^2 z^{10}}$
23. $\sqrt{144c^2 d^4 e^{10}}$ **24.** $\sqrt{xy^3}$ **25.** $-2x^2 y \sqrt{27x^7 y^9}$ **26.** $\sqrt[3]{27x^6 y^{11}}$ **27.** $-\sqrt[3]{-64x^4 y^5 z^6}$

Tell whether each triangle described is a right triangle. The lengths of the three sides are given. $[p.\ 399]$

28. 5, 12, 13   **29.** 4, 5, 6   **30.** 15, 20, 25   **31.** 1, 5, $\sqrt{26}$

For each right triangle, find the missing length. Give answers in simplest radical form. $[p.\ 399]$

32. $a = 15,\ b = 8$ **33.** $b = 6,\ c = 3\sqrt{5}$ **34.** $a = 7,\ c = 9$

Simplify. $[p.\ 402]$

35. $4\sqrt{5} - 8\sqrt{5} + 3\sqrt{5}$ **36.** $5x\sqrt{4y} + 7x\sqrt{y} - 3\sqrt{16x^2 y}$

Multiply. $[p.\ 404]$

37. $5\sqrt{x}(3\sqrt{x} - 2)$ **38.** $(2\sqrt{2} - 3\sqrt{3})^2$ **39.** $(\sqrt{3} - \sqrt{5})(\sqrt{3} + \sqrt{5})$

Rationalize the denominator. $[p.\ 408]$

40. $\dfrac{1}{\sqrt{3}}$ **41.** $\dfrac{12}{\sqrt{18}}$ **42.** $\dfrac{3x}{\sqrt{12x^3}}$ **43.** $\dfrac{24xy^4}{\sqrt{8xy^3}}$

Simplify. $[p.\ 411]$

44. $\dfrac{\sqrt{98}}{\sqrt{2}}$ **45.** $\dfrac{\sqrt{75x^3 y}}{\sqrt{3xy}}$ **46.** $\sqrt{\dfrac{56a^2 b^2}{4ab^3}}$ **47.** $\sqrt{\dfrac{4x + 2}{3}}$

Chapter Fourteen Test

Which are rational and which are irrational numbers?

1. .001

2. $\sqrt{64}$

3. $.123\overline{123}$

4. $.123122312223\ldots$

5. -2.37

6. π

7. $-\sqrt{52}$

8. $-6\frac{5}{8}$

Give answers to the nearest tenth. Use the table on page 476.

9.

Find s.

10.

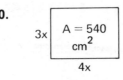

Find 3x and 4x.

11. The length of a rectangle is 3 times the width. The area is 216 square cm. Find the length and the width.

Which are irrational numbers? For each irrational number, approximate the square root to the nearest tenth. Use the divide and average method.

12. $\sqrt{10}$

13. $\sqrt{49}$

14. $\sqrt{52}$

15. $\sqrt{100}$

Simplify.

16. $\sqrt{5} \cdot \sqrt{13}$

17. $\sqrt{100 \cdot 16}$

18. $-\sqrt{80}$

19. $\sqrt{49a^4 b^2}$

20. $-\sqrt{81x^6 y^2 z^{12}}$

21. $\sqrt{15cd^2}$

22. $-5x^2 y \sqrt{54xy^3}$

23. $-\sqrt[3]{-27x^9 y^{13}}$

Tell whether each triangle described is a right triangle. The lengths of the three sides are given.

24. 8, 6, 10

25. 7, 8, 9

26. 4, 4 $\sqrt{3}$, 8

For each right triangle, find the missing length. Give answers in simplest radical form.

27. $a = 2, b = 4$

28. $a = 12, c = 13$

29. $b = 6, c = 6\sqrt{2}$

Simplify.

30. $2\sqrt{3} - 9\sqrt{3} + 6\sqrt{3}$

31. $2x\sqrt{16y} + 5x\sqrt{y} - 7\sqrt{25x^2 y}$

Multiply.

32. $(1 - \sqrt{2})^2$

33. $(\sqrt{5} + \sqrt{7})(\sqrt{5} - \sqrt{7})$

34. $3\sqrt{x}(2\sqrt{x} - 5)$

Rationalize the denominator.

35. $\dfrac{7}{\sqrt{3}}$

36. $\dfrac{4}{\sqrt{8}}$

37. $\dfrac{15x^2}{\sqrt{5x}}$

38. $\dfrac{15cd^3}{\sqrt{3cd}}$

Simplify.

39. $\dfrac{\sqrt{48}}{\sqrt{3}}$

40. $\dfrac{\sqrt{54xy^5}}{\sqrt{2xy^2}}$

41. $\sqrt{\dfrac{34xy^3}{4x^2 y}}$

42. $\sqrt{\dfrac{3x - 5}{7}}$

Pythagorean Triples

PYTHAGOREANS

This is the symbol of the Order of the Pythagoreans, a society of ancient Greek mathematicians.

A Pythagorean triple is a group of positive integers a, b, and c which make the sentence $a^2 + b^2 = c^2$ true. 3, 4, 5 is a *Pythagorean triple* because $3^2 + 4^2 = 5^2$.

PROJECT

1. Verify that each is a Pythagorean triple.

3	4	5
5	12	13
7	24	25
9	40	41
11	60	61
•	•	•
•	•	•
•	•	•

2. All of the triples above start with an odd number. Can you see a pattern in the formation?

3. List the next three triples which fit the pattern.

Radical Equations

OBJECTIVES

■ To solve radical equations like $x + 4 = \sqrt{2x + 8}$

■ To solve word problems which result in radical equations

▶ REVIEW CAPSULE

	Equation	Solution set
Square each side of $x = 5$. →	$x = 5$ $x^2 = 5^2$, or $x^2 = 25$	$\{5\}$ $\{5, -5\}$
Square each side of $x = 7$. →	$x = 7$ $x^2 = 7^2$, or $x^2 = 49$	$\{7\}$ $\{7, -7\}$

The equations in the Review Capsule suggest this property. ⟶

The solution of the equation $x = a$ is a solution of the equation $x^2 = a^2$. But, a solution of $x^2 = a^2$ may not be a solution of $x = a$.

$\sqrt{x} = 6$ is a radical equation since the variable is in the radicand.

EXAMPLE 1 Find the solution set of $\sqrt{x} = 6$.

Square each side of $\sqrt{x} = 6$. ⟶
$(\sqrt{x})^2 = \sqrt{x} \cdot \sqrt{x} = x$ ⟶

$$\sqrt{x} = 6$$
$$(\sqrt{x})^2 = 6^2$$
$$x = 36$$

Check.

$\sqrt{x}$	6
$\sqrt{36}$	6
6	

Thus, the solution set is $\{36\}$.

EXAMPLE 2 Find the solution set of $\sqrt{2x - 5} + 8 = 7$.

Add -8 to each side. Now the radical is by itself. ⟶

Square each side. ⟶
$(\sqrt{2x - 5})^2 = \sqrt{2x - 5} \cdot \sqrt{2x - 5} = 2x - 5 →$

Add 5 to each side. ⟶
Divide each side by 2. ⟶

$$\sqrt{2x - 5} + 8 = 7$$
$$\sqrt{2x - 5} = -1$$
$$(\sqrt{2x - 5})^2 = (-1)^2$$
$$2x - 5 = 1$$
$$2x = 6$$
$$x = 3$$

Check.

$\sqrt{2x - 5} + 8$	7
$\sqrt{2(3) - 5} + 8$	7
$\sqrt{6 - 5} + 8$	
$\sqrt{1} + 8$	
$1 + 8$	
9	

3 doesn't check. $9 \neq 7$.
ϕ is the empty set. ⟶ **Thus,** the solution set is ϕ.

EXAMPLE 3   Solve $\sqrt{2y} = 4\sqrt{5}$.

$$\sqrt{2y} = 4\sqrt{5}$$

Square each side. $\longrightarrow$
$$(\sqrt{2y})^2 = (4\sqrt{5})^2$$
$(4\sqrt{5})^2 = (4\sqrt{5})(4\sqrt{5}) = 16 \cdot 5 = 80 \longrightarrow$
$$2y = 80$$
Divide each side by 2. $\longrightarrow$
$$y = 40$$

Check.

$\sqrt{2y}$	$4\sqrt{5}$
$\sqrt{2 \cdot 40}$	$4\sqrt{5}$
$\sqrt{80}$	
$4\sqrt{5}$	

40 checks. $\longrightarrow$ **Thus,** the solution is 40.

EXAMPLE 4   Solve $x - 2 = \sqrt{19 - 6x}$.

$$x - 2 = \sqrt{19 - 6x}$$

Square each side. $\longrightarrow$
$$(x-2)^2 = (\sqrt{19 - 6x})^2$$
$(x-2)^2 = (x-2)(x-2) \longrightarrow$
$$x^2 - 4x + 4 = 19 - 6x$$
Add -19 and $6x$ to each side. $\longrightarrow$
$$x^2 + 2x - 15 = 0$$
Factor. $\longrightarrow$
$$(x-3)(x+5) = 0$$
$$x - 3 = 0 \text{ or } x + 5 = 0$$
$$x = 3 \text{ or } \quad x = -5$$

Check 3.

$x - 2$	$\sqrt{19 - 6x}$
$3 - 2$	$\sqrt{19 - 6(3)}$
1	$\sqrt{19 - 18}$
	$\sqrt{1}$
	1

Check -5.

$x - 2$	$\sqrt{19 - 6x}$
$-5 - 2$	$\sqrt{19 - 6(-5)}$
-7	$\sqrt{19 + 30}$
	$\sqrt{49}$
	7

$$-7 \neq 7$$

-5 doesn't check. $\longrightarrow$ **Thus,** the solution is 3.

EXAMPLE 5   If 4 is added to 3 times a number, the square root is 5. Find the number.

Let $x =$ the number.

Write an equation. $\longrightarrow$
$$\sqrt{3x + 4} = 5$$
Square each side. $\longrightarrow$
$$(\sqrt{3x + 4})^2 = 5^2$$
$$3x + 4 = 25$$
$$3x = 21$$
$$x = 7$$

Check 7 in the original problem; add 4 to 3 times 7. $\longrightarrow$
$$3(7) + 4 = 21 + 4$$
$$= 25$$

7 checks. $\longrightarrow$ Is $\sqrt{25} = 5$? Yes.

Thus, the number is 7.

EXERCISES

PART A

Find the solution set.

1. $\sqrt{y} = 3$ **2.** $\sqrt{x} = 8$ **3.** $\sqrt{5x} = 10$ **4.** $\sqrt{2y} = 24$

5. $\sqrt{4x} = \frac{1}{2}$ **6.** $\sqrt{3y} = \frac{1}{6}$ **7.** $\sqrt{18y} = 6$ **8.** $\sqrt{3x} = 3$

Solve.

9. $\sqrt{x} + 1 = 2$ **10.** $\sqrt{z} + 3 = 7$

11. $\sqrt{6x} + 5 = 2$ **12.** $\sqrt{2x} + 4 = 10$

13. $\sqrt{3x + 2} = 9$ **14.** $\sqrt{y + 2} = 4$

15. $\sqrt{2x - 1} = \sqrt{x + 3}$ **16.** $\sqrt{x - 3} = \sqrt{2x + 7}$

17. $\sqrt{x + 3} + 4 = 0$ **18.** $\sqrt{x - 5} - 8 = 0$

19. $\sqrt{x} = 2\sqrt{3}$ **20.** $2\sqrt{x} = \sqrt{48}$

PART B

Solve.

21. $\sqrt{3x + 10} = x + 4$ **22.** $\sqrt{x^2 - 9} = -4$

23. $x + 1 = \sqrt{17 - 4x}$ **24.** $\sqrt{2x - 20} = x - 1$

25. The square root of a number, decreased by 2, equals 3. Find the number.

26. Twice the square root of a number is equal to 20. Find the number.

27. A number is multiplied by 2 and 5 is added to the product. The square root of the result is equal to 3. Find the number.

28. A number is increased by 6. The square root of the sum is multiplied by 3, resulting in 12. Find the number.

PART C

EXAMPLE   Solve $\sqrt{x} + 2 = \sqrt{x + 20}$.

Square each side. ⟶ $(\sqrt{x} + 2)^2 = (\sqrt{x + 20})^2$

$x + 4\sqrt{x} + 4 = x + 20$

Add $-x$ and -4 to each side. ⟶ $4\sqrt{x} = 16$

Divide each side by 4. ⟶ $\sqrt{x} = 4$

Square each side. ⟶ $x = 16$

Check.

$\sqrt{x} + 2$	$\sqrt{x + 20}$
$\sqrt{16} + 2$	$\sqrt{16 + 20}$
$4 + 2$	$\sqrt{36}$
6	6

Thus, the solution is 16.

Solve.

29. $\sqrt{x} - 5 = -\sqrt{x + 15}$ **30.** $\sqrt{x} + 3 = \sqrt{x - 9}$ **31.** $\sqrt{x} = \sqrt{x + 77} - 7$
         [Hint: First add 7 to each side.]

The Solution Set of $x^2 = a$

▶ REVIEW CAPSULE

$$(\sqrt{25})^2 = \sqrt{25} \cdot \sqrt{25} = 5 \cdot 5 = 25$$
$$(-\sqrt{25})^2 = (-\sqrt{25})(-\sqrt{25}) = (-5)(-5)$$
$$= 25$$

$$(\sqrt{17})^2 = \sqrt{17} \cdot \sqrt{17} = 17$$
$$(-\sqrt{17})^2 = (-\sqrt{17})(-\sqrt{17}) = 17$$

$$\left.\begin{array}{l} (\sqrt{a})^2 = \sqrt{a} \cdot \sqrt{a} = a \\ (-\sqrt{a})^2 = (-\sqrt{a})(-\sqrt{a}) = a \end{array}\right\} \begin{array}{l}\text{for each} \\ a \geq 0.\end{array}$$

EXAMPLE 1 Find the solution set of $x^2 = 25$.

$$x^2 = 25$$

For $x = 5$ or $x = -5$, we could write
$$x = \pm 5.$$
└ read: plus or minus

$$x = \sqrt{25} \quad \text{or} \quad x = -\sqrt{25}$$
$$x = 5 \quad \text{or} \quad x = -5$$

$(5)^2 = 25$ and $(-5)^2 = 25.$ ──────────→ **Thus,** the solution set is $\{5, -5\}$.

EXAMPLE 2 Solve $x^2 = 17$.

$$x^2 = 17$$

$$x = \sqrt{17} \quad \text{or} \quad x = -\sqrt{17}$$

$(\sqrt{17})^2 = 17$ and $(-\sqrt{17})^2 = 17.$ ──────→ **Thus,** the solutions are $\sqrt{17}$ and $-\sqrt{17}$.

Examples 1 and 2 suggest this. ────────→ If $x^2 = a$, then $x = \sqrt{a}$ or $x = -\sqrt{a}$, for each $a \geq 0$.

EXAMPLE 3 Find the solution set of $y^2 = 12$.

$$y^2 = 12$$

If $x^2 = a$, then $x = \sqrt{a}$ or $x = -\sqrt{a}$. ──────→
$\sqrt{12} = \sqrt{4 \cdot 3} = 2\sqrt{3}$ ──────────→
$$y = \sqrt{12} \quad \text{or} \quad y = -\sqrt{12}$$
$$y = 2\sqrt{3} \quad \text{or} \quad y = -2\sqrt{3}$$

Thus, the solution set is $\{2\sqrt{3}, -2\sqrt{3}\}$.

EXAMPLE 4   Solve $(y + 4)^2 = 49$.

$$(y + 4)^2 = 49$$

If $x^2 = a$, then $x = \sqrt{a}$ or $x = -\sqrt{a}$. $\longrightarrow$

$y + 4 = \sqrt{49}$	or	$y = 4 = -\sqrt{49}$

Solve each equation.

$y + 4 = 7$ $y + 4 = -7$

Add -4 to each side. $\longrightarrow$

$y = 3$ or $y = -11$

Check 3 and -11 in $(y + 4)^2 = 49$. $\longrightarrow$ **Thus,** the solutions are 3 and -11.

EXAMPLE 5   Find the solution set of $(x - 3)^2 = 100$.

$$(x - 3)^2 = 100$$

$x - 3 = \sqrt{100}$ or $x - 3 = -\sqrt{100}$

Solve each equation. $x - 3 = 10$ $x - 3 = -10$

Add 3 to each side. $\longrightarrow$ $x = 13$ or $x = -7$

Check 13 and -7 in $(x - 3)^2 = 100$. $\longrightarrow$ **Thus,** the solution set is $\{13, -7\}$.

EXAMPLE 6   Solve $3x^2 = 7$.

$$3x^2 = 7$$

Divide each side by 3. $\longrightarrow$

$$\frac{3x^2}{3} = \frac{7}{3}$$

$$x^2 = \frac{7}{3}$$

$$x = \sqrt{\frac{7}{3}} \quad \text{or} \quad x = -\sqrt{\frac{7}{3}}$$

$\sqrt{\dfrac{7}{3}} = \dfrac{\sqrt{7}}{\sqrt{3}} \cdot \dfrac{\sqrt{3}}{\sqrt{3}} = \dfrac{\sqrt{21}}{3}$ $\longrightarrow$

$$x = \frac{\sqrt{21}}{3} \quad \text{or} \quad x = -\frac{\sqrt{21}}{3}$$

Check $\dfrac{\sqrt{21}}{3}$ and $-\dfrac{\sqrt{21}}{3}$ in $3x^2 = 7$. $\longrightarrow$ **Thus,** the solutions are $\dfrac{\sqrt{21}}{3}$ and $-\dfrac{\sqrt{21}}{3}$.

EXERCISES

PART A

Find the solution set.

1. $x^2 = 1$ $\left[\begin{array}{l}\text{Hint: What} \\ \text{number squared} \\ \text{equals } -16?\end{array}\right.$
2. $x^2 = 36$
3. $x^2 = 4$
4. $x^2 = -16$ $\longleftarrow$
5. $x^2 = 49$
6. $x^2 = 0$
7. $x^2 = 9$
8. $x^2 = -36$
9. $x^2 = 64$
10. $x^2 = 100$
11. $x^2 = -100$
12. $x^2 = 144$
13. $x^2 = 15$
14. $x^2 = 11$
15. $x^2 = 13$

16. $x^2 = 28$
19. $y^2 = 18$

17. $x^2 = 24$
20. $m^2 = 44$

18. $x^2 = 32$
21. $x^2 = -24$

Solve.

22. $(x - 7)^2 = 9$
25. $3x^2 = 5$
28. $4a^2 = 64$

23. $(x + 5)^2 = 16$
26. $2x^2 = 7$
29. $2x^2 = 50$

24. $(x - 8)^2 = 1$
27. $5x^2 = 13$
30. $3x^2 = 36$

PART B

EXAMPLE   Solve $(x - 4)^2 = 8$.

$$(x - 4)^2 = 8$$
$$x - 4 = +\sqrt{8} \quad \text{or} \quad x - 4 = -\sqrt{8}$$

Add 4 to each side.

$$\underline{4\quad4} \qquad \underline{4\quad4}$$
$$x = 4 + \sqrt{8} \quad \text{or} \quad x = 4 - \sqrt{8}$$

$\sqrt{8} = \sqrt{4 \cdot 2} = 2\sqrt{2}$ ⟶

$$x = 4 + 2\sqrt{2} \quad \text{or} \quad x = 4 - 2\sqrt{2}$$

Thus, the solutions are $4 + 2\sqrt{2}$ and $4 - 2\sqrt{2}$.

Solve.

31. $(x + 3)^2 = 8$
34. $(x + 1)^2 = 12$

32. $(x - 4)^2 = 32$
35. $(x - 7)^2 = 24$

33. $(x + 6)^2 = 28$
36. $(x - 3)^2 = 40$

PART C

EXAMPLE   Find the solution set of $3(2x - 3)^2 + 8 = 44$.

$$3(2x - 3)^2 + 8 = 44$$

Add -8 to each side. ⟶
$$3(2x - 3)^2 = 36$$

Divide each side by 3. ⟶
$$(2x - 3)^2 = 12$$
$$2x - 3 = +\sqrt{12} \quad \text{or} \quad 2x - 3 = -\sqrt{12}$$

Add 3 to each side. ⟶
$$2x = 3 + \sqrt{12} \quad \text{or} \quad 2x = 3 - \sqrt{12}$$

$\sqrt{12} = \sqrt{4 \cdot 3} = 2\sqrt{3}$ ⟶
$$2x = 3 + 2\sqrt{3} \quad \text{or} \quad 2x = 3 - 2\sqrt{3}$$

Divide each side by 2. ⟶
$$x = \frac{3 + 2\sqrt{3}}{2} \quad \text{or} \quad x = \frac{3 - 2\sqrt{3}}{2}$$

Thus, the solution set is $\left\{ \dfrac{3 + 2\sqrt{3}}{2}, \dfrac{3 - 2\sqrt{3}}{2} \right\}$.

Find the solution set of each.

37. $4(2x - 5)^2 + 6 = 54$

38. $3(2x + 3)^2 - 7 = 29$

39. $5(4x - 2)^2 - 6 = 94$

Completing the Square

 REVIEW CAPSULE

Perfect Square Trinomials
$$(x + 3)^2 = x^2 \underbrace{+ 6x}_{2(3)} \underbrace{+ 9}_{3^2}$$

$$(x - 5)^2 = x^2 \underbrace{- 10x}_{2(-5)} \underbrace{+ 25}_{(-5)^2}$$

The Review Capsule suggests this. ⟶ $(a + b)^2 = a^2 \underbrace{+ 2ba}_{2(b)} \underbrace{+ b^2}_{b^2}$

twice b ⟶ $2(b)$ b^2 ⟵ b squared

EXAMPLE 1   What number do we add to $x^2 + 14x$ to make a perfect square trinomial?

$$x^2 \underbrace{+ 14x}_{2(7)}$$

$14 = 2(7)$ ⟶

$7^2 = 49$ ⟶ Add 49: $x^2 + 14x + 49$

Check by squaring $(x + 7)$. ⟶ $(x + 7)^2 = x^2 + 14x + 49$, a perfect square trinomial.

EXAMPLE 2   What number do we add to $x^2 - 20x$ to make a perfect square trinomial?

$$x^2 \underbrace{- 20x}_{2(-10)}$$

$-20 = 2(-10)$ ⟶

$(-10)^2 = 100$ ⟶ Add 100: $x^2 - 20x + 100$

$(x - 10)^2 = x^2 - 20x + 100$, a perfect square trinomial.

In Example 3, we show a method called *completing the square* for finding the solution set of a quadratic equation.

EXAMPLE 3 Find the solution set of $x^2 - 6x = 27$ by completing the square.

$-6 = 2(-3)$ and $(-3)^2 = 9.$
Add 9 to each side.

$x^2 - 6x + 9$:

$x^2 - 6x + 9 = (x - 3)^2$

Add 3 to each side. $\longrightarrow$

$$x^2 - 6x + \underline{\quad} = 27 + \underline{\quad}$$
$$x^2 - 6x + 9 = 27 + 9$$
$$(x - 3)^2 = 36$$

$$x - 3 = +\sqrt{36} \text{ or } x - 3 = -\sqrt{36}$$
$$x - 3 = +6 \qquad\qquad x - 3 = -6$$
$$\underline{\quad 3 \quad 3 \quad} \qquad\qquad \underline{\quad 3 \quad 3 \quad}$$
$$x = 9 \qquad\qquad\qquad x = -3$$

Thus, the solution set is $\{9, -3\}$.

EXAMPLE 4 Find the solution set of $x^2 + 16x + 55 = 0$ by completing the square.

To get $x^2 + 16x$ by itself on the left, add -55 to each side.

Complete the square. $\longrightarrow$

$16 = 2(8)$ and $8^2 = 64$. Add 64 to each side.

$x^2 + 16x + 64$:

$x^2 + 16x + 64 = (x + 8)^2$

Add -8 to each side. $\longrightarrow$

$$x^2 + 16x + 55 = 0$$
$$\underline{\qquad\quad -55 \qquad -55}$$
$$x^2 + 16x = -55$$
$$x^2 + 16x + \underline{\quad} = -55 + \underline{\quad}$$
$$x^2 + 16x + 64 = -55 + 64$$
$$x^2 + 16x + 64 = 9$$
$$(x + 8)^2 = 9$$

$$x + 8 = +\sqrt{9} \text{ or } x + 8 = -\sqrt{9}$$
$$x + 8 = +3 \qquad\qquad x + 8 = -3$$
$$x = -5 \qquad\qquad\quad x = -11$$

Check -5 and -11 in $x^2 + 16x + 55 = 0$. $\longrightarrow$ **Thus,** the solution set is $\{-5, -11\}$.

EXAMPLE 5 Find the solution set of $x^2 + 10x - 4 = 0$ by completing the square.

Add 4 to each side. $\longmapsto\longrightarrow$
Complete the square. $\longrightarrow$
$10 = 2(5)$ and $5^2 = 25.$ $\longrightarrow$
$x^2 + 10x + 25 = (x + 5)^2$ $\longrightarrow$

Add -5 to each side. $\longrightarrow$

We may show the solution set as
$\{-5 \pm \sqrt{29}\}$.

$$x^2 + 10x - 4 = 0$$
$$x^2 + 10x = 4$$
$$x^2 + 10x + \underline{\quad} = 4 + \underline{\quad}$$
$$x^2 + 10x + 25 = 4 + 25$$
$$(x + 5)^2 = 29$$
$$x + 5 = +\sqrt{29} \text{ or } x + 5 = -\sqrt{29}$$
$$x = -5 + \sqrt{29} \text{ or } x = -5 - \sqrt{29}$$

Thus, the solution set is $\{-5 + \sqrt{29}, -5 - \sqrt{29}\}$.

ORAL EXERCISES

What number should be added to each expression to make a perfect square trinomial?

1. $x^2 + 2x$ **2.** $x^2 - 6x$ **3.** $x^2 + 10x$ **4.** $x^2 - 4x$

5. $x^2 + 16x$ **6.** $x^2 - 8x$ **7.** $x^2 - 12x$ **8.** $x^2 + 18x$

EXERCISES

PART A

Find the solution set by completing the square.

1. $x^2 + 10x = -16$ **2.** $x^2 + 2x = 3$ **3.** $x^2 + 16x = -15$

4. $x^2 + 2x = 8$ **5.** $x^2 - 8x = -5$ **6.** $x^2 - 6x = 27$

7. $x^2 + 10x + 15 = 0$ **8.** $x^2 + 12x - 13 = 0$ **9.** $x^2 - 4x - 21 = 0$

10. $x^2 + 8x + 3 = 0$ **11.** $x^2 - 4x + 4 = 0$ **12.** $x^2 + 6x - 7 = 0$

13. $x^2 + 4x - 77 = 0$ **14.** $x^2 + 6x - 3 = 0$ **15.** $x^2 - 16x + 28 = 0$

16. $x^2 - 2x - 48 = 0$ **17.** $x^2 - 18x + 72 = 0$ **18.** $x^2 + 16x + 60 = 0$

19. $x^2 - 10x - 39 = 0$ **20.** $x^2 + 4x - 3 = 0$ **21.** $x^2 + 20x + 51 = 0$

22. $x^2 + 2x - 5 = 0$ **23.** $x^2 - 16x + 60 = 0$ **24.** $x^2 + 18x + 77 = 0$

25. $x^2 - 20x - 21 = 0$ **26.** $x^2 - 24x + 80 = 0$ **27.** $x^2 + 30x + 155 = 0$

PART B

EXAMPLE   Find the solution set of $x^2 + 3x - 40 = 0$ by completing the square.

$\left(\dfrac{1}{2}\right)(3) = \dfrac{3}{2}; \quad \left(\dfrac{3}{2}\right)^2 = \dfrac{9}{4}$

$$x^2 + 3x - 40 = 0$$
$$x^2 + 3x \qquad = 40$$

Add $\dfrac{9}{4}$ to each side. $\longrightarrow$
$$x^2 + 3x + \dfrac{9}{4} = 40 + \dfrac{9}{4}$$

$40 + \dfrac{9}{4} = \dfrac{169}{4}$ $\longrightarrow$
$$\left(x + \dfrac{3}{2}\right)^2 = \dfrac{169}{4}$$

$$x + \dfrac{3}{2} = \sqrt{\dfrac{169}{4}} \quad \text{or} \quad x + \dfrac{3}{2} = -\sqrt{\dfrac{169}{4}}$$

$$x + \dfrac{3}{2} = \dfrac{13}{2} \qquad\qquad x + \dfrac{3}{2} = -\dfrac{13}{2}$$

Add $-\dfrac{3}{2}$ to each side. $\longrightarrow$
$$x = \dfrac{13}{2} - \dfrac{3}{2} \qquad\qquad x = -\dfrac{13}{2} - \dfrac{3}{2}$$

$$x = \dfrac{10}{2} \qquad\qquad\qquad x = -\dfrac{16}{2}$$

Check 5 and -8 in
$x^2 + 3x - 40 = 0$. $\longrightarrow$
$$x = 5 \qquad \text{or} \qquad x = -8$$

Thus, the solution set is $\{5, -8\}$.

Find the solution set by completing the square.

28. $x^2 - 3x = 10$ **29.** $x^2 + 9x = -8$ **30.** $x^2 - 7x = -6$
31. $x^2 + 5x = 50$ **32.** $x^2 - 3x = 4$ **33.** $x^2 - x = 6$
34. $x^2 - 11x + 28 = 0$ **35.** $x^2 + x - 30 = 0$ **36.** $x^2 + 5x + 6 = 0$
37. $x^2 + x - 12 = 0$ **38.** $x^2 - 9x - 10 = 0$ **39.** $x^2 - 5x - 14 = 0$
40. $x^2 + 15x + 36 = 0$ **41.** $x^2 - 17x + 30 = 0$ **42.** $x^2 - 3x + 2 = 0$
43. $x^2 + x - 56 = 0$ **44.** $x^2 - 7x - 8 = 0$ **45.** $x^2 + 11 + 28 = 0$
46. $x^2 - 13x + 36 = 0$ **47.** $x^2 - 19x + 84 = 0$ **48.** $x^2 - 15x + 54 = 0$
49. $x^2 - 21x + 38 = 0$ **50.** $x^2 + 17x + 72 = 0$ **51.** $x^2 + 15x - 34 = 0$
52. $x^2 + 23x + 60 = 0$ **53.** $x^2 - 25x + 100 = 0$ **54.** $x^2 - 21x - 46 = 0$

PART C

EXAMPLE   Find the solution set of $x^2 + 7x - 2 = 0$ by completing the square.

$$x^2 + 7x - 2 = 0$$
$$x^2 + 7x \quad = 2$$

$\left(\frac{1}{2}\right)(7) = \frac{7}{2}; \quad \left(\frac{7}{2}\right)^2 = \frac{49}{4}$ ⟶ $x^2 + 7x + \dfrac{49}{4} = 2 + \dfrac{49}{4}$

Add $\dfrac{49}{4}$ to each side.

$$\left(x + \frac{7}{2}\right)^2 = \frac{57}{4}$$

$$x + \frac{7}{2} = \sqrt{\frac{57}{4}} \qquad \text{or} \quad x + \frac{7}{2} = -\sqrt{\frac{57}{4}}$$

$\sqrt{\dfrac{57}{4}} = \dfrac{\sqrt{57}}{\sqrt{4}} = \dfrac{\sqrt{57}}{2}$ ⟶ $x + \dfrac{7}{2} = \dfrac{\sqrt{57}}{2} \qquad\qquad x + \dfrac{7}{2} = -\dfrac{\sqrt{57}}{2}$

Add $-\dfrac{7}{2}$ to each side. ⟶ $x = -\dfrac{7}{2} + \dfrac{\sqrt{57}}{2} \qquad\qquad x = -\dfrac{7}{2} - \dfrac{\sqrt{57}}{2}$

$$x = \frac{-7 + \sqrt{57}}{2} \quad \text{or} \qquad x = \frac{-7 - \sqrt{57}}{2}$$

We may show the solution set as $\left\{\dfrac{-7 \pm \sqrt{57}}{2}\right\}$.

Thus, the solution set is $\left\{\dfrac{-7 + \sqrt{57}}{2}, \dfrac{-7 - \sqrt{57}}{2}\right\}$.

Find the solution set by completing the square.

55. $x^2 + 7x + 3 = 0$ **56.** $x^2 + 11x + 20 = 0$ **57.** $x^2 + 5x + 1 = 0$
58. $x^2 - 3x - 5 = 0$ **59.** $x^2 + 5x - 1 = 0$ **60.** $x^2 - 7x - 2 = 0$
61. $x^2 - x - 3 = 0$ **62.** $x^2 + 2x + 2 = 0$ **63.** $x^2 + 7x + 4 = 0$
64. $x^2 + 3x - 1 = 0$ **65.** $x^2 - x + 1 = 0$ **66.** $x^2 - 9x + 3 = 0$

The Quadratic Formula

OBJECTIVES

■ To determine a, b, and c in a quadratic equation $ax^2 + bx + c = 0$
■ To solve a quadratic equation with integer solutions by using the quadratic formula

REVIEW CAPSULE

Determine a, b, and c in $x^2 - 5x + 2 = 0$.

Standard form: $ax^2 + bx + c = 0$
$\quad\quad\quad\quad\quad\quad\uparrow\quad\quad\quad\uparrow\quad\quad\uparrow$
$\quad\quad\quad\quad (1)x^2 + (-5)x + 2 = 0$

Thus, $a = 1$, $b = -5$, and $c = 2$.

EXAMPLE 1　Find the solution set of $2x^2 + 3x - 1 = 0$ by completing the square.

$$2x^2 + 3x - 1 = 0$$

Add 1 to each side. ⟶ $\quad 2x^2 + 3x = 1$

Divide each side by 2. ⟶ $\quad \dfrac{2x^2 + 3x}{2} = \dfrac{1}{2}$

$\left(\dfrac{1}{2}\right)\left(\dfrac{3}{2}\right) = \dfrac{3}{4}; \left(\dfrac{3}{4}\right)^2 = \dfrac{9}{16};$ $\quad x^2 + \dfrac{3}{2}x = \dfrac{1}{2}$

Add $\dfrac{9}{16}$ to each side. ⟶ $\quad x^2 + \dfrac{3}{2}x + \dfrac{9}{16} = \dfrac{1}{2} + \dfrac{9}{16}$

$$\left(x + \dfrac{3}{4}\right)^2 = \dfrac{17}{16}$$

Solve each equation.

$\quad x + \dfrac{3}{4} = \sqrt{\dfrac{17}{16}} \quad$ or $\quad x + \dfrac{3}{4} = -\sqrt{\dfrac{17}{16}}$

$\sqrt{\dfrac{17}{16}} = \dfrac{\sqrt{17}}{\sqrt{16}} = \dfrac{\sqrt{17}}{4}$ ⟶ $\quad x + \dfrac{3}{4} = \dfrac{\sqrt{17}}{4} \quad\quad\quad x + \dfrac{3}{4} = -\dfrac{\sqrt{17}}{4}$

Add $-\dfrac{3}{4}$ to each side. ⟶ $\quad x = -\dfrac{3}{4} + \dfrac{\sqrt{17}}{4} \quad\quad x = -\dfrac{3}{4} - \dfrac{\sqrt{17}}{4}$

4 is the common denominator. $\quad x = \dfrac{-3 + \sqrt{17}}{4} \quad$ or $\quad x = \dfrac{-3 - \sqrt{17}}{4}$

We may write the solution set as

$\left\{\dfrac{-3 \pm \sqrt{17}}{4}\right\}.$ ⟶ **Thus,** the solution set is $\left\{\dfrac{-3 + \sqrt{17}}{4}, \dfrac{-3 - \sqrt{17}}{4}\right\}.$

We now use this process to derive a formula for solving a quadratic equation.

EXAMPLE 2 Solve $ax^2 + bx + c = 0$, $(a > 0)$ by completing the square.

$$ax^2 + bx + c = 0$$

Add $-c$ to each side. $\longrightarrow$
$$ax^2 + bx = -c$$

Divide each side by a. $\longrightarrow$
$$\frac{ax^2 + bx}{a} = \frac{-c}{a}$$

$\left(\dfrac{1}{2}\right)\left(\dfrac{b}{a}\right) = \dfrac{b}{2a}; \left(\dfrac{b}{2a}\right)^2 = \dfrac{b^2}{4a^2};$
$$x^2 + \frac{b}{a}x = \frac{-c}{a}$$

Add $\dfrac{b^2}{4a^2}$ to each side. $\longrightarrow$
$$x^2 + \frac{b}{a}x + \frac{b^2}{4a^2} = \frac{-c}{a} + \frac{b^2}{4a^2}$$

$4a^2$ is a common denominator on the right. $\longrightarrow$
$$\left(x + \frac{b}{2a}\right)^2 = \frac{-4ac + b^2}{4a^2}$$

$$\left(x + \frac{b}{2a}\right)^2 = \frac{b^2 - 4ac}{4a^2}$$

$$x + \frac{b}{2a} \qquad \text{or} \qquad x + \frac{b}{2a}$$

$$= \sqrt{\frac{b^2 - 4ac}{4a^2}} \qquad\qquad = -\sqrt{\frac{b^2 - 4ac}{4a^2}}$$

Add $-\dfrac{b}{2a}$ to each side; $\sqrt{4a^2} = 2a$. $\longrightarrow$
$$x = -\frac{b}{2a} + \frac{\sqrt{b^2 - 4ac}}{2a} \qquad x = -\frac{b}{2a} - \frac{\sqrt{b^2 - 4ac}}{2a}$$

$2a$ is a common denominator. $\longrightarrow$
$$x = \frac{-b + \sqrt{b^2 - 4ac}}{2a} \qquad \text{or} \qquad x = \frac{-b - \sqrt{b^2 - 4ac}}{2a}$$

$\pm$ means $+$ or $-$. $\longrightarrow$ **Thus,** $x = \dfrac{-b \pm \sqrt{b^2 - 4ac}}{2a}$.

A similar proof can be shown for $a < 0$.

Example 2 gives this formula. $\longrightarrow$

The Quadratic Formula

The solutions of a quadratic equation of the form
$$ax^2 + bx + c = 0$$
may be found by the formula
$$x = \frac{-b \pm \sqrt{b^2 - 4ac}}{2a}$$

EXAMPLE 3 Rewrite $5x = 6x^2 - 7$ in standard form. Then determine a, b, and c.

$$5x = 6x^2 - 7$$

Add $-5x$ to each side. $\longrightarrow$
$$0 = 6x^2 - 7 - 5x$$

Rearrange in descending order. $\longrightarrow$
$$0 = 6x^2 - 5x - 7$$

Standard form $\longrightarrow$
$$0 = ax^2 + bx + c$$

$$a = 6, \ b = -5, \text{ and } c = -7.$$

EXAMPLE 4   Solve $x^2 - 9x + 14 = 0$ by using the quadratic formula.

Determine a, b, and c. $\longrightarrow$ $a = 1$, $b = -9$, $c = 14$

Quadratic formula $\longrightarrow$ $x = \dfrac{-b \pm \sqrt{b^2 - 4ac}}{2a}$

Substitute for a, b, and c. $\longrightarrow$ $x = \dfrac{-(-9) \pm \sqrt{(-9)^2 - 4(1)(14)}}{2(1)}$

$-(-9) = 9$ $\longrightarrow$ $x = \dfrac{9 \pm \sqrt{81 - 56}}{2}$

$x = \dfrac{9 \pm \sqrt{25}}{2}$

$x = \dfrac{9 \pm 5}{2}$

$\pm$ means $+$ or $-$. $\longrightarrow$ $x = \dfrac{9 + 5}{2}$ or $x = \dfrac{9 - 5}{2}$

$x = \dfrac{14}{2}$ or $x = \dfrac{4}{2}$ $\longrightarrow$ $x = 7$ or $x = 2$

Check 7 and 2 in $x^2 - 9x + 14 = 0$. $\longrightarrow$ **Thus,** the solutions are 7 and 2.

EXERCISES

PART A

Rewrite each equation in standard form. Then determine a, b, and c.

1. $2x^2 + 6x + 5 = 0$
2. $4x^2 + 3x + 2 = 0$
3. $2x^2 - 4x - 8 = 0$
4. $2x^2 - 4x = 0$
5. $x^2 + 2x = 0$
6. $3x^2 + 7 = 0$
7. $x^2 - 5 = 0$
8. $x^2 = 6x - 3$
9. $3x^2 - 6x = 2$
10. $x^2 = 4$
11. $5x^2 = 3x$
12. $2 + 6x = 4x^2$

Solve by using the quadratic formula.

13. $x^2 + 4x + 3 = 0$
14. $x^2 - 5x + 6 = 0$
15. $x^2 - 2x + 1 = 0$
16. $x^2 + 3x - 10 = 0$
17. $x^2 - 4x - 21 = 0$
18. $x^2 - 2x - 24 = 0$
19. $x^2 + 3x - 40 = 0$
20. $x^2 - 12x - 13 = 0$
21. $x^2 - 8x + 16 = 0$

PART B

Find the solution set by using the quadratic formula.

22. $x^2 = 6 - x$
23. $x^2 - 11 = -10x$
24. $-12x = 45 - x^2$
25. $-30 = x - x^2$
26. $x^2 = -2x + 3$
27. $5x = -x^2 - 4$
28. $9x - x^2 = 8$
29. $16 = 4x^2$
30. $-3x = x^2 + 2$
31. $6x^2 = 12 + 6x$
32. $3x^2 = -9x$
33. $-36 = 16x - x^2$

Wet Mixture Problems

 REVIEW CAPSULE

A 30-liter solution is made up of iodine and alcohol. The solution is 20% iodine. How many liters of iodine are in the solution?

$$\begin{pmatrix} \text{Number} \\ \text{of liters} \\ \text{of iodine} \end{pmatrix} = \begin{pmatrix} \text{Percent} \\ \text{iodine} \end{pmatrix} \cdot \begin{pmatrix} \text{Total number} \\ \text{of liters} \\ \text{in solution} \end{pmatrix}$$

Liters of iodine = .20 · 30

— Decimal is used

= 6.00   for percent.

Thus, there are 6 liters (L) of iodine in the solution.

EXAMPLE 1   A solution of 60 liters contains a mixture of alcohol and water. If 30% of the solution is alcohol, how many liters are water?

Total liters, 60 is 100%. ⟶ If 30% is alcohol, 100% − 30%, or 70%, is water.

Liters of water = Percent water · Total liters
= .70(60)
= 42.00

Thus, there are 42 liters of water in the solution.

EXAMPLE 2   A chemist had 20 liters of a 65% salt solution. X liters of water were added to reduce it to a 45% salt solution. Write an algebraic solution for the number of liters of water in the 45% salt solution.

L in new solution = original total + water added
=   20   +   x

Percent water = 100% − Percent salt
= 100% − 45% = 55%

Liters of water = Percent water · Total liters
= .55(20 + x)

Thus, there are .55(20 + x) liters of water.

EXAMPLE 3

How many liters of water must be added to 32 liters of a 25% sulfuric acid solution to reduce it to a 20% acid solution?

Represent the amount needed algebraically.

Let x = number of liters of water to be added

Make a chart. ————————————→
Total L in new solution:
original total, 32
+
water added, x

	Total L	L of Acid	L of Water
25% solution	32	.25(32)	.75(32)
20% solution	32 + x	.20(32 + x)	.80(32 + x)

Only water is added. The amounts of acid are the same in both solutions.

Write an equation. ————————————→

Substitute. ————————————→

$$\left(\begin{matrix}\text{Acid in 25\%} \\ \text{solution}\end{matrix}\right) = \left(\begin{matrix}\text{Acid in 20\%} \\ \text{solution}\end{matrix}\right)$$
$$.25(32) = .20(32 + x)$$
$$8 = 6.4 + .2x$$

Multiply each side by 10.

$$80 = 64 + 2x$$
$$16 = 2x$$
$$8 = x$$

Thus, 8 liters of water must be added.

EXAMPLE 4

A solution is made of an antiseptic and distilled water. How many deciliters of antiseptic must be added to 80 deciliters of a 5% antiseptic solution to make it a 24% solution?

Represent the amount needed algebraically.

Let x = number of deciliters (dL) of antiseptic to be added

Make a chart. ————————————→
Total dL in new solution:
original total, 80
+
Antiseptic added, x

	Total dL	dL of Antiseptic	dL of Water
5% solution	80	.05(80)	.95(80)
24% solution	80 + x	.24(80 + x)	.76(80 + x)

Write an equation. ————————————→
Only antiseptic is added.

Substitute. ————————————→

$$\left(\begin{matrix}\text{Water in} \\ \text{5\% solution}\end{matrix}\right) = \left(\begin{matrix}\text{Water in} \\ \text{24\% solution}\end{matrix}\right)$$
$$.95(80) = .76(80 + x)$$
$$76 = 60.8 + .76x$$

Multiply each side by 100.

$$7,600 = 6,080 + 76x$$
$$1,520 = 76x$$
$$20 = x$$

Thus, 20 dL of antiseptic must be added.

EXAMPLE 5　How many liters of antifreeze must be added to 20 liters of a 15% antifreeze solution (antifreeze and water), to make a 40% antifreeze solution?

Represent the amount needed algebraically.

Let x = number of liters of antifreeze to be added

Make a chart. ————→

	Total L	L of Antifreeze	L of Water
15% solution	20	.15(20)	.85(20)
40% solution	20 + x	.40(20 + x)	.60(20 + x)

Write an equation.
Since only antifreeze is added, amount of water in each stays the same.

Multiply each side by 100.

$$\left(\begin{array}{c}\text{L of water in}\\\text{15\% solution}\end{array}\right) = \left(\begin{array}{c}\text{L of water in}\\\text{40\% solution}\end{array}\right)$$
$$.85(20) = .60(20 + x)$$
$$17.00 = 12.00 + .60x$$
$$1{,}700 = 1{,}200 + 60x$$
$$500 = 60x$$
$$8\tfrac{1}{3} = x$$

Thus, $8\tfrac{1}{3}$ L of antifreeze must be added.

EXAMPLE 6　A chemist has one solution that is 20% alcohol and a more concentrated solution that is 85% alcohol. How much of the more concentrated solution must be added to 8 dL of the original solution to obtain a solution that is 45% alcohol?

Represent the amount needed algebraically.

Let x = number of dL of 85% solution to be added

Make a chart. ————→
Total dL in new solution:
original total, 8
        +
added concentrate, x

	Total dL	dL of Alcohol
20% solution	8	.20(8)
85% solution	x	.85(x)
45% solution	8 + x	.45(8 + x)

Write an equation. ————→

Substitute. ————→

Multiply each side by 100.

$$\left(\begin{array}{c}\text{Alcohol in}\\\text{20\% solution}\end{array}\right) + \left(\begin{array}{c}\text{Alcohol in}\\\text{85\% solution}\end{array}\right) = \left(\begin{array}{c}\text{Alcohol in}\\\text{45\% solution}\end{array}\right)$$

.20(8)	+	.85(x)	= .45(8 + x)
1.6	+	.85x	= 3.6 + .45x
160	+	85x	= 360 + 45x
		40x	= 200
		x	= 5

Thus, 5 dL of the 85% solution must be added.

EXERCISES

1. How many liters of water must be added to 9 liters of a 40% solution of hydrochloric acid to make it a 30% acid solution?

2. A nurse has 4 liters of a mixture that is 20% medicine. How much more medicine must be added to make it a 36% mixture?

3. Dr. Rivers has 3 liters of a 60% salt solution. How many liters of water must be added to obtain a 20% solution?

4. A pharmacist has 100 deciliters of a 10% peroxide in water solution. How much peroxide must be added to obtain a 20% solution?

5. A farmer has 200 liters of milk that tests 9.2% butterfat. How many liters of skimmed milk (without butterfat) must be added to obtain milk that tests 6.4% butterfat?

6. A chemist has a solution of alcohol and water. How many cubic centimeters (cm^3) of alcohol must be added to 60 cm^3 of a 28% solution to make it a 46% solution?

7. How many liters of water must a chemist add to 24 liters of a sulfuric acid solution that is 30% acid to obtain a solution that is 10% acid?

8. A pharmacist has 3 deciliters of cough medicine that is 10% water. For children, it must be 40% water. How much water must be added?

9. How many liters of water must be added to 26 liters of a 15% antifreeze solution to dilute it to a 12% solution?

10. A solution of 40 milliliters is 50% acid. How many milliliters of water must be added to dilute it to a 20% acid solution?

11. A solution of 4 deciliters is 20% iodine. How many deciliters of a 50% iodine solution must be added in order to obtain a 30% iodine solution?

12. How many cubic centimeters of a solution that is 65% alcohol must be added to 50 cm^3 of a 25% alcohol solution to make a 40% solution?

13. Dr. Green has one solution that is 40% salt and another solution that is 65% salt. How much of the 65% solution must be added to 5 deciliters of the original solution to obtain a solution that is 55% salt?

14. A chemist wants to add a 15% acid solution to 30 deciliters of a 70% acid solution to reduce it to a 45% acid solution. How much of the 15% solution must be added?

Applying the Quadratic Formula

OBJECTIVE

■ To find solution sets of quadratic equations with rational, irrational, and no solutions by using the quadratic formula

 REVIEW CAPSULE

Quadratic

Equation	*Standard Form*	*a*	*b*	*c*
$x^2 - 7x + 2 = 0$	same	1	−7	2
$5x^2 = 3x$	$5x^2 - 3x + 0 = 0$	5	−3	0
$-x - 8 = -x^2$	$x^2 - x - 8 = 0$	1	−1	−8

Quadratic Formula

$$x = \frac{-b \pm \sqrt{b^2 - 4ac}}{2a}$$

EXAMPLE 1 Find the solution set of $2x^2 + x = 6$ by using the quadratic formula.

Add −6 to each side to get standard form. ————————→

$$2x^2 + x = 6$$
$$2x^2 + 1x - 6 = 0$$

Determine *a*, *b*, and *c*. ————————→

$$a = 2 \qquad b = 1 \qquad c = -6$$

Quadratic formula ————————→

$$x = \frac{-b \pm \sqrt{b^2 - 4ac}}{2a}$$

Substitute for *a*, *b*, and *c*. ————→

$$x = \frac{-1 \pm \sqrt{1^2 - 4(2)(-6)}}{2(2)}$$

$-4(2)(-6) = 48$ ————————→

$$x = \frac{-1 \pm \sqrt{1 + 48}}{4}$$

$$x = \frac{-1 \pm \sqrt{49}}{4}$$

$$x = \frac{-1 \pm 7}{4}$$

$$x = \frac{-1 + 7}{4} \quad \text{or} \quad x = \frac{-1 - 7}{4}$$

$$x = \frac{6}{4} \quad \text{or} \quad x = \frac{-8}{4}$$

$$x = \frac{3}{2} \quad \text{or} \quad x = -2$$

Rational solutions ————————→ **Thus,** the solution set is $\left\{\frac{3}{2}, -2\right\}$.

EXAMPLE 2 Find the solution set of $3x^2 + x - 1 = 0$ by using the quadratic formula.

$$x = \frac{-b \pm \sqrt{b^2 - 4ac}}{2a}$$

$3x^2 + 1x - 1 = 0$
$a = 3, b = 1, c = -1$

$$x = \frac{-1 \pm \sqrt{1^2 - 4(3)(-1)}}{2(3)}$$

$$x = \frac{-1 \pm \sqrt{1 + 12}}{6}$$

Irrational solutions ⟶

$$x = \frac{-1 \pm \sqrt{13}}{6}$$

Thus, the solution set is $\left\{\dfrac{-1 \pm \sqrt{13}}{6}\right\}$.

EXAMPLE 3 Find the solution set of $3x^2 - x + 1 = 0$ by using the quadratic formula.

$$x = \frac{-b \pm \sqrt{b^2 - 4ac}}{2a}$$

$3x^2 - 1x + 1 = 0$
$a = 3, b = -1, c = 1.$

$$x = \frac{-(-1) \pm \sqrt{(-1)^2 - 4(3)(1)}}{2(3)}$$

$$x = \frac{1 \pm \sqrt{1 - 12}}{6}$$

$\sqrt{-11}$ is not a real number. ⟶

$$x = \frac{1 \pm \sqrt{-11}}{6}$$

No real solutions ⟶ **Thus,** the solution set is ϕ.

EXAMPLE 4 Find the solution set of $x^2 - 2x - 1 = 0$ by using the quadratic formula.

$$x = \frac{-b \pm \sqrt{b^2 - 4ac}}{2a}$$

$1x^2 - 2x - 1 = 0$
$a = 1, b = -2, c = -1.$

$$x = \frac{-(-2) \pm \sqrt{(-2)^2 - 4(1)(-1)}}{2(1)}$$

$$x = \frac{2 \pm \sqrt{4 + 4}}{2}$$

$$x = \frac{2 \pm \sqrt{8}}{2}$$

$\sqrt{8} = \sqrt{4 \cdot 2} = 2\sqrt{2}$ ⟶

$$x = \frac{2 \pm 2\sqrt{2}}{2}$$

Factor numerator and denominator. ⎫
Simplify. ⎭

$$x = \frac{\overset{1}{\cancel{2}}(1 \pm \sqrt{2})}{\cancel{2}_1}$$

$$x = 1 \pm \sqrt{2}$$

Irrational solutions ⟶ **Thus,** the solution set is $\{1 \pm \sqrt{2}\}$.

EXERCISES

PART A

Find the solution set by using the quadratic formula.

1. $2x^2 + 5x - 3 = 0$
2. $3x^2 - 7x + 2 = 0$
3. $6x^2 - x - 2 = 0$
4. $2x^2 - 7x + 3 = 0$
5. $2x^2 - 11x + 12 = 0$
6. $8x^2 - 22x + 15 = 0$
7. $3x^2 + 5x - 2 = 0$
8. $2x^2 - 3x - 9 = 0$
9. $9x^2 - 60x + 100 = 0$
10. $x^2 - 5x - 2 = 0$
11. $x^2 - 7x + 3 = 0$
12. $x^2 - 7x - 3 = 0$
13. $2x^2 + 4x + 3 = 0$
14. $x^2 + x - 1 = 0$
15. $x^2 + 5x - 3 = 0$
16. $x^2 + x - 5 = 0$
17. $3x^2 - 7x + 9 = 0$
18. $x^2 - 3x + 1 = 0$
19. $5x^2 - 3x + 2 = 0$
20. $x^2 - 6x - 2 = 0$
21. $x^2 - 4x - 10 = 0$
22. $x^2 - 10x = -5$
23. $x^2 = 8x - 3$
24. $x^2 + 2x + 7 = 0$
25. $2x^2 - 12 = -5x$
26. $15x = 9x^2 + 4$
27. $x^2 + 1 = -4x$
28. $x^2 + 8 = 3x$
29. $x^2 = 7x - 11$
30. $2x^2 + 9 = 9x$

PART B

EXAMPLE   Find the solution set of $\dfrac{1}{2}x^2 - \dfrac{3}{2}x + \dfrac{5}{6} = 0$.

Multiply by the LCD, 6. ⟶ $6\left(\dfrac{1}{2}x^2 - \dfrac{3}{2}x + \dfrac{5}{6}\right) = 6\,(0)$

$$3x^2 - 9x + 5 = 0$$

$$x = \frac{-(-9) \pm \sqrt{(-9)^2 - 4\,(3)\,(5)}}{2\,(3)}$$

$$x = \frac{9 \pm \sqrt{21}}{6}$$

Thus, the solution set is $\left\{\dfrac{9 + \sqrt{21}}{6}, \dfrac{9 - \sqrt{21}}{6}\right\}$.

Find the solution set.

31. $x^2 + \dfrac{3}{2}x - \dfrac{5}{2} = 0$
32. $x^2 - \dfrac{7}{4}x + \dfrac{3}{4} = 0$
33. $x^2 - \dfrac{3}{2}x + \dfrac{9}{16} = 0$

34. $x^2 + \dfrac{5}{2}x + 1 = 0$
35. $x^2 - \dfrac{4}{5}x - 1 = 0$
36. $\dfrac{1}{2}x^2 + \dfrac{1}{2}x - 2 = 0$

PART C

Find the solution set. Use the quadratic formula.

37. $x^2 - (2\sqrt{2})x - 2 = 0$
38. $(\sqrt{3})x^2 - 2x - 2\sqrt{3} = 0$
39. $\dfrac{x+6}{2} = \dfrac{2}{x}$

Area Problems

 REVIEW CAPSULE

$$A = lw$$

w

l

Find the area of a rectangle whose length is 7 m and whose width is 3 m.

$$A = lw$$
$$= 7 \cdot 3, \text{ or 21 square meters or 21 m}^2$$

EXAMPLE 1 The length of a rectangle is 3 cm more than the width. The area is 70 square cm. Find the length and the width.

Represent length and width algebraically; draw a rough sketch. ——————→

Let x = width in cm
$x + 3$ = length in cm

x

x + 3

Formula for area ——————————→
Substitute for A, l, and w. ——————→
$(x + 3)x = x \cdot x + 3 \cdot x = x^2 + 3x$ ——→

Add -70 to each side to get standard form. ——————————————————→

$$A = lw$$
$$70 = (x + 3)x$$
$$70 = x^2 + 3x$$
$$\underline{-70 = \qquad\qquad -70}$$
$$0 = x^2 + 3x - 70$$

Two ways to solve $x^2 + 3x - 70$

Factor   Quadratic formula

$$0 = (x + 10)(x - 7)$$ $$x = \frac{-b \pm \sqrt{b^2 - 4ac}}{2a}$$
$$x + 10 = 0 \quad \text{or} \quad x - 7 = 0$$
$$x = -10 \quad \text{or} \quad x = 7$$ $$x = \frac{-3 \pm \sqrt{9 + 280}}{2}$$

$a = 1$, $b = 3$, $c = 70$.

$$x = \frac{-3 \pm \sqrt{289}}{2}$$

-10 is an extraneous solution. ——————→

Reject -10, since a rectangle cannot have a negative number as its width.

$$x = \frac{-3 \pm 17}{2}$$

$\dfrac{-3 \pm 17}{2}$ means $\dfrac{-3 + 17}{2}$ or $\dfrac{-3 - 17}{2}$

Width, x is 7.
Length, $x + 3$ is 10.

$$x = \tfrac{14}{2} \quad \text{or} \quad x = \tfrac{-20}{2}$$
$$x = 7 \quad \text{or} \quad x = -10$$

Check: $A = lw$
$\qquad = 10 \cdot 7 = 70.$ ——————————————→

Thus, the length is 10 cm and the width is 7 cm.

EXAMPLE 2   The length of a rectangle is twice the width. The area is 50 m². Find the length and the width.

Represent length and width algebraically; draw a rough sketch. ————→

Let $x =$ width in m
  $2x =$ length in m
  $A = lw$

Substitute for A, l, and w. ————→ $50 = 2x(x)$
$50 = 2x^2$

Divide each side by 2. ————→ $25 = x^2$

If $x^2 = a$, then $x = \sqrt{a}$ or $x = -\sqrt{a}$. ————→ $x = \sqrt{25}$ or $x = -\sqrt{25}$
$x = 5$ or $x = -5$ ← Extraneous solution
Width, x is 5.
Length, $2x$ is 10.

Check: $A = lw$
  $= 10 \cdot 5 = 50.$ ————→ **Thus,** the length is 10 m and the width is 5 m.

EXAMPLE 3   The length of a rectangle is 8 cm more than the width. The area is 50 cm². Find the length and the width.

Represent length and width algebraically; draw a rough sketch. ————→

Let $x =$ width in cm
$x + 8 =$ length in cm
  $A = lw$

Substitute for A, l, and w. ————→ $50 = (x + 8)x$

Distribute x. ————→ $50 = x^2 + 8x$

Add -50 to each side. ————→ $0 = x^2 + 8x - 50$

$$x = \frac{-b \pm \sqrt{b^2 - 4ac}}{2a}$$

Replace a with 1, b with 8, and c with -50.

$$x = \frac{-8 \pm \sqrt{(8)^2 - 4(1)(-50)}}{2(1)}$$

$(8)^2 = 64. \ -4(1)(-50) = 200;$
$64 + 200 = 264$ $\Big\}$

$$x = \frac{-8 \pm \sqrt{264}}{2}$$

$$x = \frac{-8 \pm \sqrt{4(66)}}{2}$$

$$x = \frac{-8 \pm 2\sqrt{66}}{2}$$

Divide numerator and denominator by the common factor, 2. ————→ $x = -4 \pm \sqrt{66}$

From the table, $\sqrt{66} \doteq 8.12.$ ————→ $x = -4 + \sqrt{66} \doteq -4 + 8.12 = 4.12 \doteq 4.1$, or

Extraneous solution. ————→ $x = -4 - \sqrt{66} \doteq -4 - 8.12 = -12.12$
Width, x is 4.1.
Length, $x + 8$ is 12.1.

Check: $(12.1)(4.1) = 49.61$, which is 50 to the nearest whole number. ————→ **Thus,** the length is 12.1 cm and the width is 4.1 cm, to the nearest tenth.

ORAL EXERCISES

Give the area of each rectangle in terms of x.

1. $l = 7x; w = 2x$
2. $l = x + 1; w = x$
3. $l = 3x; w = x + 5$
4. $l = x + 3; w = x - 3$
5. $l = 2x + 5; w = 2x - 5$
6. $l = 3x + 2; w = 2x - 3$

EXERCISES

PART A

Find the length and the width of each rectangle.

1. The length is 3 m more than the width. The area is 40 m².

2. The length is 5 cm less than 3 times the width. The area is 50 cm².

3. The length is twice the width. The area is 32 m².

4. The length is 3 times the width. The area is 27 m².

5. The length is 3 cm more than twice the width. The area is 44 cm².

6. The length is 2 m more than twice the width. The area is 60 m².

7. The length is 3 cm less than twice the width. The area is 20 cm².

8. The length is 1 m less than twice the width. The area is 28 m².

9. The length is 6 cm more than the width. The area is 20 cm².

10. The length is 15 m more than the width. The area is 50 m².

11. The width is 2 m less than the length. The area is 44 m².

12. The width is 4 km less than the length. The area is 6 km².

PART B

Find the length and the width of each rectangle.

13. The length is 4 cm less than twice the width. The area is 96 cm².

14. The length is 5 m less than 3 times the width. The area is 152 m².

15. The length is 3 km greater than twice the width. The area is 90 km².

16. The length is 1 cm less than twice the width. The area is 91 cm².

17. The length is 2 km more than 4 times the width. The area is 72 km².

18. The length is twice the width. The area is 128 cm².

19. The width is 5 m less than the length. The area is 25 m².

20. The width is 3 km less than twice the length. The area is 4 km².

PART C

Find the length and the width of each rectangle.

21. The perimeter is 24. The area is 35.

22. The perimeter is 44. The area is 120.

Zeller's Congruence

ON WHAT DAY OF THE WEEK
DID JULY 4, 1776 FALL?

Almanacs have perpetual calendars to answer this question. A mathematical
formula can also be used.

Zeller's Congruence

$$f = \left\{ [2.6m - 0.2] + k + D + \left[\frac{D}{4}\right] + \left[\frac{C}{4}\right] - 2C \right\} \bmod 7$$

m = month code number $\qquad$ C = first two digits of year
k = date of month $\qquad$ D = last two digits of year
f = day of week code number

Chart 1: Code Number for Month

Month	Code Number (m)
January	11*
February	12*
March	1
April	2
May	3
June	4
July	5
August	6
September	7
October	8
November	9
December	10

Chart 2: Code Number for Day

Day of Week	Code Number (f)
Sunday	0
Monday	1
Tuesday	2
Wednesday	3
Thursday	4
Friday	5
Saturday	6

*Use the last two digits
of the preceding year.

On what day of the week did July 4, 1776 fall? Use Zeller's congruence.

JULY	4	17	76
↓	↓	↓	↓
$m = 5$	$k = 4$	$C = 17$	$D = 76$
(See Chart 1.)			

$$[2.6m - 0.2] + k + D + \left[\frac{D}{4}\right] + \left[\frac{C}{4}\right] - 2C$$

$$[2.6(5) - 0.2] + 4 + 76 + \left[\frac{76}{4}\right] + \left[\frac{17}{4}\right] - 2 \cdot 17$$

$$[13.0 - 0.2] + 4 + 76 + \left[\frac{76}{4}\right] + \left[\frac{17}{4}\right] - 34$$

[ ] means the greatest integer less than or equal to the number. →

$$[12.8] \quad + 4 + 76 + \left[\frac{76}{4}\right] + \left[\frac{17}{4}\right] - 34$$

$$12 \qquad + 4 + 76 + \quad 19 \quad + \quad 4 \quad - 34$$

$$81$$

$$\begin{array}{r} 11 \\ 7{\overline{)81}} \\ 77 \\ \hline 4 \end{array} \to \text{remainder}$$

The { } mod 7 around the formula means that we must find the remainder from dividing 81 by 7.

Now, use Chart 2. July 4, 1776 fell on a Thursday.

PROJECT

1. Check to see if Zeller's congruence works for today's date.

2. Use Zeller's congruence to find out on what day of the week you were born. Consult an almanac to check your answer.

3. Use Zeller's congruence to find out on what day of the week October 31, 2001 will fall. Consult an almanac to check your answer.

Chapter Fifteen Review

Find the solution set. $[p.\ 417,\ 420]$

1. $\sqrt{3x} = 15$
2. $\sqrt{y} + 5 = 11$
3. $\sqrt{4x - 5} = -2$
4. $4\sqrt{3x} = \sqrt{96}$
5. $\sqrt{x^2 - 4} = -8$
6. $\sqrt{19 + 3x} = x + 3$
7. $x^2 = 100$
8. $x^2 = -49$
9. $x^2 - 36 = 0$
10. $(x - 4)^2 = 64$
11. $(x + 8)^2 = 144$
12. $(x - 3)^2 = 8$

What number should be added to each expression to make a perfect square trinomial?

13. $x^2 + 8x$
14. $x^2 - 14x$
15. $x^2 - 2x$ $\quad[p.\ 423]$
16. $x^2 + 20x$
17. $x^2 + 5x$
18. $x^2 - 15x$

Find the solution set by completing the square. $[p.\ 423]$

19. $x^2 - 12x - 13 = 0$
20. $x^2 + 2x - 3 = 0$
21. $x^2 - 14x + 45 = 0$
22. $x^2 + 8x - 48 = 0$
23. $x^2 - 4x - 21 = 0$
24. $x^2 - 10x + 24 = 0$
25. $x^2 + 6x + 8 = 0$
26. $x^2 - 20x + 51 = 0$
27. $x^2 + 16x + 60 = 0$

Rewrite each quadratic equation in standard form. Then determine a, b, and c.

28. $3x^2 - 5x + 4 = 0$
29. $x^2 - x + 6 = 0$
30. $3x^2 + 6x = 0$ $\quad[p.\ 427]$
31. $x^2 - 7 = 0$
32. $4x^2 = 3x$
33. $7 = 5x^2 - 4$
34. $-4x + 3x^2 = 8$
35. $1 - 2x = -7x^2$
36. $\dfrac{x^2}{2} + 4x = \dfrac{1}{6}$

Find the solution set by using the quadratic formula. $[p.\ 434]$

37. $x^2 - 6x + 8 = 0$
38. $x^2 + 2x - 15 = 0$
39. $x^2 - 7x + 12 = 0$
40. $x^2 - 5x - 6 = 0$
41. $x^2 + 7x + 10 = 0$
42. $x^2 - 10x - 11 = 0$
43. $x^2 + 4x - 21 = 0$
44. $x^2 - 15x + 50 = 0$
45. $2x - 3 = -x^2$
46. $x^2 - 10x = -24$
47. $x^2 = 7x$
48. $x^2 = 3x + 54$
49. $3x^2 + 5x - 2 = 0$
50. $4x^2 - 10x - 24 = 0$
51. $4x^2 + 8x - 5 = 0$
52. $x^2 + 3x + 10 = 0$
53. $3x^2 + 2x - 4 = 0$
54. $x^2 + 6x - 1 = 0$
55. $x^2 - 7x + 11 = 0$
56. $2x^2 - x + 7 = 0$
57. $2x^2 - 4x - 7 = 0$
58. $x^2 = 1 - x$
59. $-5x + 1 = -2x^2$
60. $3 + 2x^2 = -5x$

61. $x^2 - \dfrac{5}{3}x - 2 = 0$
62. $x^2 - \dfrac{2}{7}x = \dfrac{1}{7}$

Solve each problem. $[p.\ 437]$

63. The length of a rectangle is 3 m less than twice the width. The area is 20 m². Find the length and the width.

64. The length of a rectangle is 5 times the width. The area is 80 m². Find the length and the width.

Chapter Fifteen Test

Find the solution set.

1. $\sqrt{7x - 3} = 5$

2. $\sqrt{3y} + 8 = 2$

3. $x - 2 = \sqrt{x + 10}$

4. $x^2 = 36$

5. $x^2 - 100 = 0$

6. $(x + 5)^2 = 12$

What number should be added to each expression to make a perfect square trinomial?

7. $x^2 + 10x$

8. $x^2 - 4x$

9. $x^2 - 18x$

10. $x^2 + 7x$

Find the solution set by completing the square.

11. $x^2 + 4x + 3 = 0$

12. $x^2 - 10x - 39 = 0$

13. $x^2 + 6x - 16 = 0$

14. $x^2 - 18x - 19 = 0$

Rewrite each quadratic equation in standard form. Then determine *a*, *b*, and *c*.

15. $2x^2 - 5x + 4 = 0$

16. $x^2 = x + 8$

17. $-3x = 7 - 2x^2$

18. $\dfrac{x^2}{3} = 6x + \dfrac{1}{9}$

Find the solution set by using the quadratic formula.

19. $x^2 + 9x + 18 = 0$

20. $x^2 + x - 30 = 0$

21. $x^2 + 7x - 2 = 0$

22. $6x^2 - 7x + 2 = 0$

23. $2x^2 - x - 3 = 0$

24. $3x^2 - 2x = 4$

25. $7x^2 + 15 = 2x$

26. $6x^2 + 3x + 5 = 0$

27. $x^2 - \dfrac{2}{3}x - 1 = 0$

28. $x^2 + \dfrac{7}{4}x + \dfrac{3}{4} = 0$

Solve each problem.

29. The length of a rectangle is 5 meters less than twice the width. The area is 12 m². Find the length and the width.

30. The length of a rectangle is 3 times the width. The area is 12 km². Find the length and the width.

Approximating Cube Roots

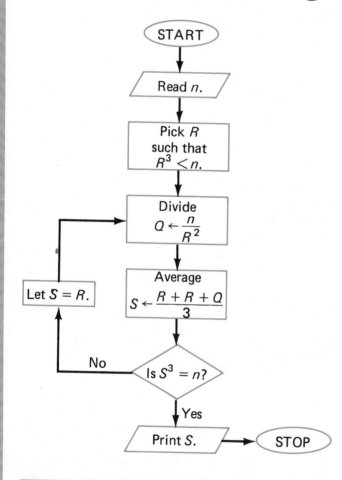

$n = 100$

Let $R = 4$. $(4)^3 < 100$

Divide by $(4)^2$, or 16.

$$\begin{array}{r} 6.2 = 6.3 \leftarrow \text{divide to} \\ 16\overline{)100.0} \qquad \text{one decimal} \\ 96 \qquad\qquad \text{place} \\ \overline{40} \\ 32 \\ \overline{8} \end{array}$$

Average. $\dfrac{4 + 4 + 6.3}{3} = \dfrac{14.3}{3}$ or 4.8

Is $(4.8)^3 = 100$? No

Divide by $(4.8)^2 = 23.04$

$$\begin{array}{r} 4.34 \qquad \leftarrow \text{divide to} \\ 23.04\overline{)100.00{\wedge}00} \qquad \text{two decimal} \\ 92\ 16 \qquad\qquad \text{places} \\ \overline{7\ 84\ 0} \\ 6\ 91\ 2 \\ \overline{92\ 80} \\ 92\ 16 \\ \hline \end{array}$$

Average. $\dfrac{4.8 + 4.8 + 4.34}{3} = \dfrac{13.94}{3}$

$$= 4.65$$

$4.65^3 = 100.5$

Thus, $\sqrt[3]{100} = 4.7$ correct to one decimal place.

PROJECT Approximate $\sqrt[3]{n}$ to one decimal place.

1. 89   **2.** 21   **3.** 180   **4.** 300

Angles and Triangles

▶ *REVIEW CAPSULE*

Protractor

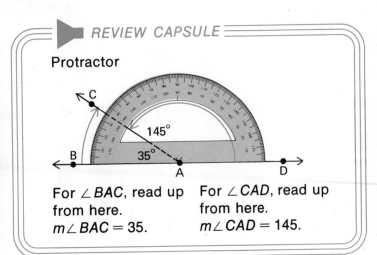

For ∠BAC, read up from here.
$m\angle BAC = 35.$

For ∠CAD, read up from here.
$m\angle CAD = 145.$

Pairs of complementary angles ──→

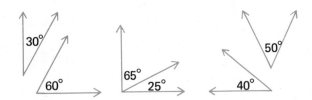

Definition of complementary angles ──→

Complementary angles are two angles the sum of whose measures is 90°. Each is the *complement* of the other.

EXAMPLE 1   An angle is 12° greater in measure than its complement. Find the measure of the angle and its complement.

Let x = degree measure of the complement
$x + 12$ = degree measure of the angle

Write an equation: The sum of the degree measures is 90. ──→
$$x + (x + 12) = 90$$
$$2x + 12 = 90$$
$$2x = 78$$
$$x = 39$$
$$x + 12 = 51$$

Measure of complement ──→
Measure of angle ──→
Check: 39 + 51 = 90. ──→

Thus, the angle measures 51° and its complement measures 39°.

EXAMPLE 2   Try this experiment. Cut a triangle out of paper. Tear off the three corners and fit them together, as shown below.

This is true for every triangle. ———————→ The three angles form a straight line, or 180°.

This can be proved in a geometry course. ————————————→

> The sum of the measures of the three angles of a triangle is 180°.

EXAMPLE 3   The second angle of a triangle measures twice the first. The third angle measures 8 degrees more than the first. Find the measures of the three angles.

Let x = degree measure of first angle
$2x$ = degree measure of second angle
$x + 8$ = degree measure of third angle

Sum of the measures of the three angles of a triangle is 180°. ————————→ $x + 2x + (x + 8) = 180$

$$4x + 8 = 180$$

Add -8 to each side. ————————→ $4x = 172$
Measure of first angle ————————→ $x = 43$
Measure of second angle ————————→ $2x = 86$
Measure of third angle ————————→ $x + 8 = 51$

Thus, the angles measure 43°, 86°, and 51°.

EXAMPLE 4   In right triangle ABC, $m\angle C = 90$, and $m\angle A = 32$. Find $m\angle B$.

Sum of the measures of the angles of a triangle is 180°. ————————→ $m\angle A + m\angle B + m\angle C = 180$
Let $x = m\angle B$. ————————→ $32 + x + 90 = 180$
$32 + 90 = 122$ ————————→ $122 + x = 180$
Add -122 to each side. ————————→ $x = 58$

Thus, $m\angle B = 58$.

In Example 4,
$m\angle A + m\angle B = 32 + 58 = 90.$ ————————→

An acute angle has a measure of less than 90°.

> $m\angle A + m\angle B = 90$
> *The acute angles of a right triangle are complementary.*

ORAL EXERCISES

Find the measure of the complement of the angle whose measure is given.

1. 20°　　　**2.** 35°　　　**3.** 15°　　　**4.** 60°　　　**5.** 85°　　　**6.** $x°$

In right triangle ABC, $m \angle C = 90$. Find $m \angle A$ for the given $m \angle B$.

7. 30°　　　**8.** 45°　　　**9.** 75°　　　**10.** 2°　　　**11.** 82°　　　**12.** $y°$

EXERCISES

PART A

1. An angle measures 24° less than its complement. Find the measure of the angle and its complement.

2. All three angles of an equilateral triangle have the same measure. What is the measure of each?

3. An angle measures 15° more than twice its complement. Find the measure of each angle.

4. The measures of the angles of a triangle are in the ratio 1:2:3. Find the measures.

5. The acute angles of a right triangle have the same measure. Find the measure of the acute angles.

6. One of two complementary angles measures 20° more than 4 times the other. Find the measures of the two angles.

7. Two angles of a triangle have the same measure. The third angle measures 20° more than 8 times the first, or second. Find the measures of the two acute angles.

8. The degree-measures of the angles of a triangle are consecutive even integers. Find the measures of the three angles.

9. One acute angle of a right triangle measures 30° more than 3 times the other acute angle. Find the measures of the two acute angles.

10. One of two complementary angles has $\frac{2}{3}$ the degree-measure of the other. Find the measures of the two angles.

PART B

11. One angle of a triangle measures 5° less than the second. The third angle measures 20° more than the complement of the second angle. Find the measures of the three angles.

12. One angle of a triangle measures 6° more than the second. The third angle measures 4° less than 3 times the sum of the measures of the first two angles. Find the measures of the three angles.

Similar Triangles

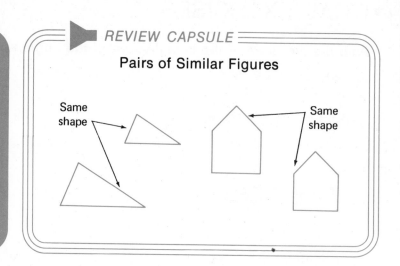

REVIEW CAPSULE

Pairs of Similar Figures

Same shape
Same shape

Read. ─────────────────────→

Write. ─────────────────────→

$\triangle ABC \sim \triangle DEF$

$m\angle A = m\angle D$, $m\angle B = m\angle E$, $m\angle C = m\angle F$. The angles of each triangle are congruent, equal in measure, in the order given. $\cong$ means is congruent to.

In $\triangle ABC$, $\overline{BC}$ is opposite $\angle A$.
In $\triangle DEF$, $\overline{EF}$ is opposite $\angle D$.

$\triangle ABC$ is similar to $\triangle DEF$.
$\triangle ABC \sim \triangle DEF$

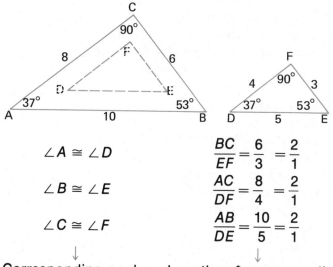

$\angle A \cong \angle D$

$\angle B \cong \angle E$

$\angle C \cong \angle F$

↓
Corresponding angles are congruent.

$\dfrac{BC}{EF} = \dfrac{6}{3} = \dfrac{2}{1}$

$\dfrac{AC}{DF} = \dfrac{8}{4} = \dfrac{2}{1}$

$\dfrac{AB}{DE} = \dfrac{10}{5} = \dfrac{2}{1}$

↓
Lengths of corresponding sides have the same ratio.

Corresponding sides are opposite corresponding angles in similar triangles. }

Definition of similar triangles ─────→
First condition ─────────────────→
Second condition ────────────────→

Two triangles are similar if the corresponding angles are congruent and the lengths of the corresponding sides have the same ratio.

EXAMPLE 1 $\triangle ABC \sim \triangle DEF$. **Find x and y.**

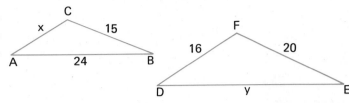

$\overline{AB}$ corresponds to $\overline{DE}$.

$\overline{BC}$ corresponds to $\overline{EF}$.

$\overline{AC}$ corresponds to $\overline{DF}$.

Lengths of corresponding sides have the same ratio. Write and solve these proportions.

$$\frac{x}{16} = \frac{15}{20} \qquad\qquad \frac{y}{24} = \frac{20}{15}$$

Simplify $\frac{15}{20}$ to $\frac{3}{4}$.

$$\frac{x}{16} = \frac{3}{4} \qquad\qquad \frac{y}{24} = \frac{4}{3}$$

$$4x = 3 \cdot 16 \qquad\qquad 3y = 4 \cdot 24$$

$$4x = 48 \qquad\qquad\quad 3y = 96$$

$$x = 12 \qquad\qquad\quad y = 32$$

Thus, x is 12 and y is 32.

EXAMPLE 2 $\triangle ABC \sim \triangle DEF$. $AC = 9$, $BC = 10$, and $DF = 6$.
Find *EF*.

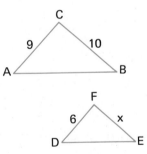

$\triangle ABC \sim \triangle DEF$
$\overline{AB}$ corresponds to $\overline{DE}$.
$\overline{BC}$ corresponds to $\overline{EF}$.
$\overline{AC}$ corresponds to $\overline{DF}$.

Let $x = EF$ $\dfrac{x}{10} = \dfrac{6}{9}$

$$\frac{x}{10} = \frac{2}{3}$$

$$3x = 2 \cdot 10$$

$$3x = 20$$

$$x = 6\tfrac{2}{3}$$

Thus, EF is $6\tfrac{2}{3}$.

EXAMPLE 3 A boy 2 m tall casts a shadow 8 m long. How tall is a nearby flagpole if its shadow is 50 m long?

Two similar triangles are formed.

Let $x =$ height of flagpole

$$\frac{x}{2} = \frac{50}{8}$$

$$\frac{x}{2} = \frac{25}{4}$$

$$4x = 50$$

$$x = 12\tfrac{1}{2}$$

Thus, the flagpole is $12\tfrac{1}{2}$ m tall.

EXERCISES

PART A

In Exercises 1–8, △ABC ~ △DEF. Find the indicated measures.

1.

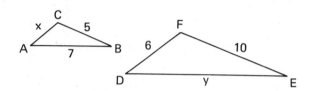

2.

3. $AB = 12$, $AC = 13$, $BC = 5$ and $DE = 8$. Find DF and EF.

5. $AB = 7$, $AC = 9$, $BC = 12$, and $DF = 15$. Find DE and EF.

7. $AB = 12$, $AC = 10$, $DE = 18$, and $FE = 20$. Find CB and DF.

9. A vertical meterstick casts a 4-m shadow while a flagpole casts a 24-m shadow. How tall is the flagpole?

4. $DE = 15$, $EF = 6$. $AB = 10$, $AC = 9$. Find BC and DF.

6. $AC = 5$, $CB = 8$, $DF = 15$, and $DE = 18$. Find AB and FE.

8. $DE = 16$, $FE = 14$, $DF = 11$, and $AB = 24$. Find CB and AC.

10. A tree 2 m tall casts a shadow 4 m long while a tower casts a shadow 90 m long. How tall is the tower?

PART B

11. A 10-m ladder touches the side of a building at a height of 8 m. At what height would a 12-m ladder touch the building if it makes the same angle with the ground?

12. △VRS ~ △UTS. Find the width of the river.

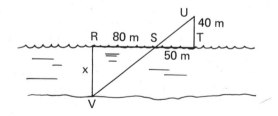

13. Jim walked 8 meters up a ramp and was 3 meters above the ground. If he walked 12 meters farther up the ramp, how far above the ground would he be?

14. Mary was standing 12 m from the base of a 10-m tree. She could spot the top of a 500-m building just beyond the top of the tree. How far was she from the base of the building?

Trigonometric Ratios

<table>
<tr><td>

OBJECTIVES

■ To identify the sides of a right triangle with respect to one of its acute angles

■ To compute the tangent, sine, and cosine of an acute angle of a triangle

</td><td>

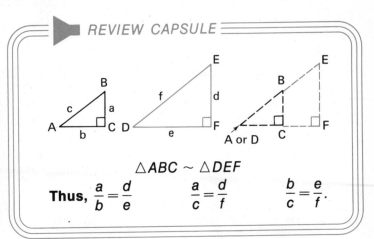

$$\triangle ABC \sim \triangle DEF$$

Thus, $\dfrac{a}{b} = \dfrac{d}{e}$ $\qquad$ $\dfrac{a}{c} = \dfrac{d}{f}$ $\qquad$ $\dfrac{b}{c} = \dfrac{e}{f}$.

</td></tr>
</table>

From the Greek language ⟶ **Trigonometry** means *triangle measurement.* We will work with right triangles.

Words associated with right triangles.

hypotenuse $\qquad$ B $\quad$ leg opposite ∠ A

leg adjacent to ∠ A

All right triangles with a given $m \angle A$ are similar: The ratios, $\dfrac{a}{b}, \dfrac{a}{c}$, and $\dfrac{b}{c}$ are the same for each $m \angle A$.

Ratio	Abbreviation
tangent of $m \angle A =$ $\dfrac{\text{measure of opposite leg}}{\text{measure of adjacent leg}}$	$\tan A = \dfrac{a}{b}$
sine of $m \angle A =$ $\dfrac{\text{measure of opposite leg}}{\text{measure of hypotenuse}}$	$\sin A = \dfrac{a}{c}$
cosine of $m \angle A =$ $\dfrac{\text{measure of adjacent leg}}{\text{measure of hypotenuse}}$	$\cos A = \dfrac{b}{c}$

EXAMPLE 1 $\quad$ For $\triangle ABC$, find $\tan A$, $\sin A$, and $\cos A$.

$\tan = \dfrac{\text{opp.}}{\text{adj.}};$ opp. means opposite. adj. means adjacent.

$\sin = \dfrac{\text{opp.}}{\text{hyp.}};$ hyp. means hypotenuse.

$\cos = \dfrac{\text{adj.}}{\text{hyp.}}$

$\tan A = \dfrac{3}{4}$, or .75

$\sin A = \dfrac{3}{5}$, or .6

$\cos A = \dfrac{4}{5}$, or .8

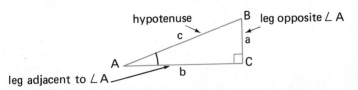

EXAMPLE 2 For △ABC, find tan B, sin B, and cos B, to three decimal places.

$\overline{AC}$ is opposite ∠B. $\overline{BC}$ is adjacent to ∠B.

$$\tan = \frac{\text{opp.}}{\text{adj.}} \longrightarrow \tan B = \frac{12}{5} = 2.400$$

$$\sin = \frac{\text{opp.}}{\text{hyp.}} \longrightarrow \sin B = \frac{12}{13} = .923$$

$$\cos = \frac{\text{adj.}}{\text{hyp.}} \longrightarrow \cos B = \frac{5}{13} = .385$$

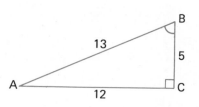

EXAMPLE 3 Use △ABC to find tan 60°, sin 60°, and cos 60°, to three decimal places.

These ratios will be the same for all 30°–60° right triangles.

$$\tan 60° = \frac{\sqrt{3}}{1} \doteq \frac{1.732}{1} = 1.732$$

$$\sin 60° = \frac{\sqrt{3}}{2} \doteq \frac{1.732}{2} = .866$$

$$\cos 60° = \frac{1}{2} \quad = .500$$

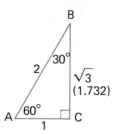

EXAMPLE 4 Use the figure in Example 3 to find tan 30°, sin 30°, cos 30° to three decimal places.

First rationalize the denominator. $\longrightarrow$

$$\tan 30° = \frac{1}{\sqrt{3}} = \frac{1}{\sqrt{3}} \cdot \frac{\sqrt{3}}{\sqrt{3}} = \frac{\sqrt{3}}{3} \doteq \frac{1.732}{3} \doteq .577$$

$$\sin 30° = \frac{1}{2} \quad = .500$$

$$\cos 30° = \frac{\sqrt{3}}{2} \doteq \frac{1.732}{2} = .866$$

ORAL EXERCISES

Refer to the figure at the right.

1. Name the leg adjacent to ∠P.
2. Name the leg opposite ∠Q.
3. Name the hypotenuse.
4. Name the leg opposite ∠P.
5. Name the leg adjacent to ∠Q.
6. What is sin P?
7. What is cos Q?
9. What is cos P?

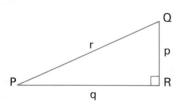

8. What is tan Q?
10. What is sin Q?

EXERCISES

PART A

Find tan A, sin A, cos A, tan B, sin B, and cos B to three decimal places.

1.

2.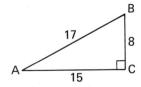

3.

4.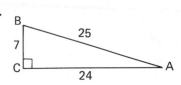

5.

6.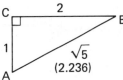

Find the value of each, to three decimal places. Use the figure at the right.

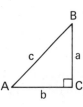

7. tan 45°   **8.** sin 45°   **9.** cos 45°

PART B

Show that each statement is true. Use the figure at the right.

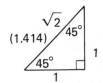

10. sin A = cos B

11. sin B = cos A

12. tan $A = \dfrac{1}{\tan B}$

13. $(\sin A)^2 + (\cos A)^2 = 1$ (Hint: Use the Pythagorean theorem.)

PART C

Find tan A, sin A, cos A, tan B, sin B, and cos B, to three decimal places.

14.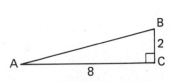

15.

16.

17. Show that the sine of an angle is equal to the cosine of its complement.

18. Explain why the sine of an angle is between 0 and 1.

Graphing in Space

We add a z-axis perpendicular to both the x- and y-axes in order to plot points in space.

The points are described by ordered triples (x, y, z).

To plot point
$E(-5, -2, 4)$

x-coordinate / z-coordinate
y-coordinate

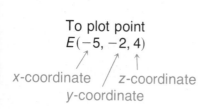

First plot the point
$B(-5, -2)$ in the
xy-plane, then move
the point to the 4
position on the z-axis.

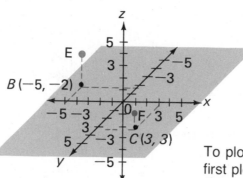

The z-axis is
perpendicular to
the xy-plane.

To plot point $F(3, 3, -1)$,
first plot the point $C(3, 3)$
on the xy-plane then
move the point to the -1
position on the z-axis.

Plot $(-5, -1)$ in xy-plane
then move point to 2
position on z-axis.

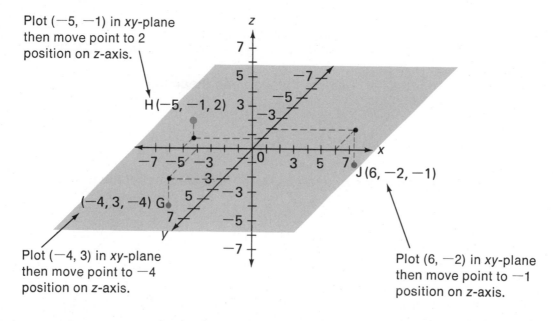

Plot $(-4, 3)$ in xy-plane
then move point to -4
position on z-axis.

Plot $(6, -2)$ in xy-plane
then move point to -1
position on z-axis.

What does the graph of the equation $z = 4$ look like?

Graph $\{(x, y, z) \mid z = 4\}$.

the set of all   such $z = 4$
ordered triples   that

All points in space which have z-coordinate 4 lie in a plane parallel to the xy-plane and 4 units above it.

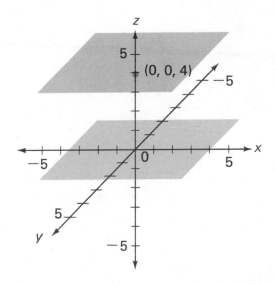

Similarly, the graph of $\{(x, y, z) \mid y = -2\}$ is a plane parallel to the xz-plane and perpendicular to the xy-plane.

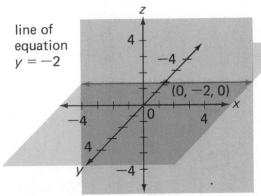

line of equation $y = -2$

PROJECT   What do you think the graph of $\{(x, y, z) \mid x = -3\}$ looks like? Draw a three-dimensional system and graph $x = -3$.

Tables of Trigonometric Ratios

OBJECTIVES
■ To find sin A, cos A, and tan A, given m ∠ A, by using a table
■ To find m ∠ A, given sin A, cos A, or tan A, by using a table

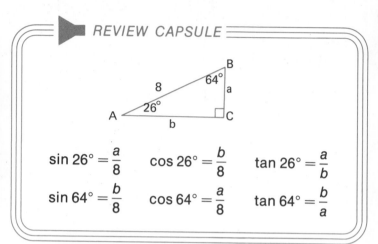

▶ REVIEW CAPSULE

$$\sin 26° = \frac{a}{8} \qquad \cos 26° = \frac{b}{8} \qquad \tan 26° = \frac{a}{b}$$

$$\sin 64° = \frac{b}{8} \qquad \cos 64° = \frac{a}{8} \qquad \tan 64° = \frac{b}{a}$$

The table gives decimal approximations. ⟶ The table on page 477 gives the values of sine, cosine, and tangent for angles from 0° to 90°.

Angle Measure	Sin	Cos	Tan	Angle Measure	Sin	Cos	Tan
10°	.1736	.9848	.1763	56°	.8290	.5592	1.483
11°	.1908	.9816	.1944	57°	.8387	.5446	1.540
12°	.2079	.9781	.2126	58°	.8480	.5299	1.600
13°	.2250	.9744	.2309	59°	.8572	.5150	1.664
14°	.2419	.9703	.2493	60°	.8660	.5000	1.732
15°	.2588	.9659	.2679	61°	.8746	.4848	1.804
16°	.2756	.9613	.2867	62°	.8829	.4695	1.881
17°	.2924	.9563	.3057	63°	.8910	.4540	1.963

Part of the table ⟶

EXAMPLE 1 Use the table to find sin 61°, cos 61°, and tan 61°.

Find 61° in the angle column. ⟶ sin 61° = .8746   cos 61° = .4848   tan 61° = 1.804

EXAMPLE 2 Find m ∠ A if tan A = .3249.

Find .3249 in the tan column. ⟶
$$\tan 18° = .3249$$
Thus, m ∠ A = 18.

EXAMPLE 3 Find m ∠ B to the nearest degree, if cos B = .5392.

Find the closest value to .5392 in the cos column. ⟶
$$\cos 57° = .5446$$
Thus, m ∠ B = 57, to the nearest degree.

ORAL EXERCISES

Use the table on page 477 to find each value.

1. sin 5° **2.** tan 21° **3.** cos 78° **4.** tan 36° **5.** sin 59°
6. cos 48° **7.** cos 8° **8.** tan 12° **9.** sin 86° **10.** tan 53°

Use the table on page 477 to find $m \angle A$.

11. sin A = .2250 **12.** tan A = 1.428 **13.** sin A = .6428
14. cos A = .9998 **15.** tan A = 28.64 **16.** cos A = .7193

EXERCISES

PART A

Use the table on page 477 to find each value.

1. sin 74° **2.** cos 81° **3.** sin 26° **4.** cos 30° **5.** tan 89°
6. cos 18° **7.** tan 65° **8.** sin 42° **9.** sin 15° **10.** cos 61°

Find $m \angle B$, to the nearest degree. Use the table on page 477.

11. tan B = .1398 **12.** cos B = .7452 **13.** sin B = .3915
14. cos B = .9281 **15.** tan B = .6637 **16.** cos B = .5099
17. sin B = .7583 **18.** tan B = 1.396 **19.** sin B = .9725
20. tan B = 1.126 **21.** cos B = .1186 **22.** sin B = .0716

PART B

True or false? Use the figure at the right.

23. $\tan A = \dfrac{b}{a}$ **24.** $\sin B = \dfrac{b}{c}$ **25.** $\cos A = \dfrac{b}{c}$

26. tan A = tan B **27.** sin A = cos B **28.** $\tan A = \dfrac{1}{\tan A}$

29. sin B = cos B **30.** $a^2 + b^2 = c^2$ **31.** $a + b = c$
32. $\angle A$ and $\angle B$ are complementary. **33.** $\angle A$ and $\angle B$ are acute.
34. If $m \angle A > m \angle B$, then sin A > sin B. **35.** If $m \angle A > m \angle B$, then cos A > cos B.
36. If tan A < tan B, then $m \angle A > m \angle B$. **37.** $(\sin A)^2 + (\cos A)^2 = 1$
38. sin 45° = cos 45° **39.** $(\cos A)^2 = 1 - (\sin A)^2$

PART C

Suppose $m \angle A$ increases from 0° to 90°.

40. What happens to sin A? Why? **41.** What happens to cos A? Why? **42.** What happens to tan A? Why?

Solving Right Triangles

OBJECTIVE
■ To solve right triangles by using sine, cosine, and tangent (find the lengths of missing sides, to the nearest tenth, and the measures of missing angles, to the nearest degree)

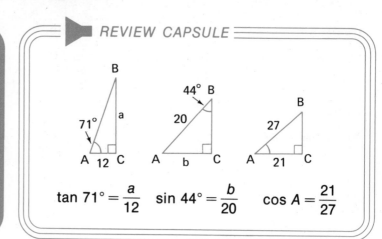

▶ REVIEW CAPSULE

$$\tan 71° = \frac{a}{12} \qquad \sin 44° = \frac{b}{20} \qquad \cos A = \frac{21}{27}$$

EXAMPLE 1 If $m\angle A = 65$ and $c = 15$, find a, to the nearest tenth.

Sketch the figure. Use sin A, since we are dealing with a and c. Substitute 65° for A, 15 for c. ⟶

$$\sin A = \frac{a}{c}$$

$$\sin 65° = \frac{a}{15}$$

Use the table to get sin 65°. ⟶

$$.9063 = \frac{a}{15}$$

Multiply each side by 15. ⟶

$$(.9063)(15) = a$$
$$13.5945 \quad = a$$

Round to the nearest tenth. ⟶

$$13.6 \doteq a$$

Thus, a is 13.6, to the nearest tenth.

EXAMPLE 2 If $m\angle B = 51$ and $a = 10$, find c, to the nearest tenth.

$$\cos B = \frac{a}{c}$$

Substitute 51° for B, 10 for a. ⟶

$$\cos 51° = \frac{10}{c}$$

Use the table. ⟶

$$.6293 = \frac{10}{c}$$

Multiply each side by c. ⟶

$$.6293c = 10$$

Divide each side by .6293. ⟶

$$c = \frac{10}{.6293}$$

$$c \doteq 15.9$$

Thus c is 15.9, to the nearest tenth.

EXAMPLE 3   If $m\angle A = 27$ and $a = 18$, find b, to the nearest tenth.

Sketch the figure. ————————→

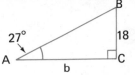

First way

$$\tan A = \frac{a}{b}$$

We can use tan A or tan B. ————————→

$$\tan 27° = \frac{18}{b}$$

$$\tan A = \frac{18}{b}$$

$$.5095 = \frac{18}{b}$$

$$\tan B = \frac{b}{18}$$

$$.5095b = 18$$

$$b = \frac{18}{.5095}$$

Note: In the second way, we multiply rather than divide.

$$b \doteq 35.3$$

Second way

$$m\angle B = 90 - 27 = 63$$

$$\tan B = \frac{b}{a}$$

$$\tan 63° = \frac{b}{18}$$

$$1.963 = \frac{b}{18}$$

$$(1.963)(18) = b$$

$$35.334 = b$$

$$35.3 \doteq b$$

Thus, b is 35.3, to the nearest tenth.

EXAMPLE 4   If $a = 16$ and $b = 10$, find $m\angle A$, to the nearest degree.

$$\tan A = \frac{a}{b}$$

Substitute 16 for a, 10 for b. ————————→

$$\tan A = \frac{16}{10}$$

$$\tan A = 1.600$$

Use the tan column: tan 58° = 1.600. ————→ $m\angle A \doteq 58$

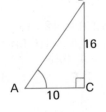

Thus, $m\angle A$ is 58, to the nearest degree.

EXAMPLE 5   If $a = 12$ and $c = 18$, find $m\angle B$, to the nearest degree.

Note: An alternate way is to use sin A.

$$\cos B = \frac{a}{c}$$

Substitute 12 for a, 18 for c. ————————→

$$\cos B = \frac{12}{18}$$

$$\cos B = \frac{2}{3}$$

$$\cos B = .6667$$

Use the cos column: cos 48° = .6691. ————→ $m\angle B \doteq 48$

Thus, $m\angle B$ is 48, to the nearest degree.

EXERCISES

PART A

Find the indicated measure (side, to the nearest tenth or angle, to the nearest degree).

1.
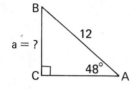

2.
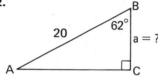

3.
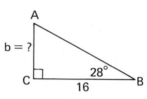

4.
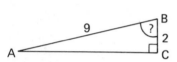

5.
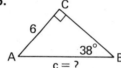

6.
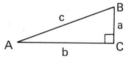

Find the indicated measure (side to the nearest tenth or angle to the nearest degree). Use the figure at the right.

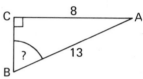

7. If $c = 7$ and $m\angle A = 42$, find a.

8. If $b = 8$ and $c = 13$, find $m\angle B$.

9. If $b = 18$ and $m\angle A = 10$, find c.

10. If $b = 28$ and $m\angle B = 82$, find a.

11. If $a = 2$ and $c = 4$, find $m\angle A$.

12. If $b = 16$ and $c = 20$, find $m\angle A$.

13. If $b = 18$ and $m\angle B = 35$, find a.

14. If $c = 30$ and $m\angle A = 27$, find a.

PART B

Find all the missing measures (sides to the nearest tenth or angles to the nearest degree).

15.
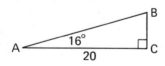

16.

17.

18.
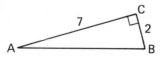

19.
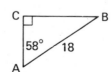

20.

Applications of Trigonometry

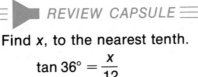

REVIEW CAPSULE

Find x, to the nearest tenth.

$$\tan 36° = \frac{x}{12}$$

$$.7265 = \frac{x}{12}$$

$$(.7265)(12) = x$$

$$8.7180 = x$$

$$8.7 \doteq x$$

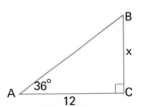

EXAMPLE 1 Find the height of the tree, to the nearest tenth of a meter.

Let x = height of tree in meters.

$\tan = \dfrac{\text{opp.}}{\text{adj.}}$ ————————→

Use tan column. ————————→

Multiply each side by 25. ————————→

$$\tan 42° = \frac{x}{25}$$

$$.9004 = \frac{x}{25}$$

$$(.9004)(25) = x$$

$$22.5100 = x$$

$$22.5 \doteq x$$

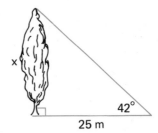

Thus, the tree is 22.5 meters tall, to the nearest tenth.

EXAMPLE 2 Find the distance across the lake from P to Q, to the nearest tenth of a meter.

Let x = PQ in meters.

$\cos = \dfrac{\text{adj.}}{\text{hyp.}}$ ————————→

Use cos column. ————————→

Multiply each side by x. ————————→

Divide each side by .3746. ————————→

$$\cos 68° = \frac{36}{x}$$

$$.3746 = \frac{36}{x}$$

$$.3746x = 36$$

$$x = \frac{36}{.3746}$$

$$x \doteq 96.1$$

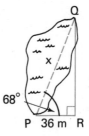

Thus, the distance from P to Q is 96.1 meters, to the nearest tenth.

An angle of elevation is the angle between the horizontal and the line of sight.
An angle of depression is the angle between the horizontal and the line of sight.
Angle of depression = angle of elevation

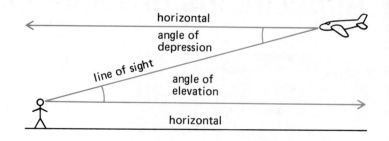

EXAMPLE 3   A power-line tower casts a 160-m shadow when the angle of elevation of the sun measures 20°. How high is the tower?

$\tan = \dfrac{\text{opp.}}{\text{adj.}}$ ⟶

Use tan column. ⟶

$$\tan 20° = \frac{x}{160}$$

$$.3640 = \frac{x}{160}$$

$$(.3640)(160) = x$$
$$58.2400 = x$$

Round to the nearest tenth. ⟶

$$58.2 \doteq x$$

Thus, the power-line tower is about 58.2 m high.

EXAMPLE 4   A lighthouse is 55 meters high. The angle of depression from the top of the lighthouse to a boat out at sea is 72°. How far from the base of the lighthouse is the boat?

Angle of depression = angle of elevation

Let x = distance between boat and lighthouse in meters; $\tan = \dfrac{\text{opp.}}{\text{adj.}}$ ⟶

$$\tan 72° = \frac{55}{x}$$

Use the tan column. ⟶

$$3.077 = \frac{55}{x}$$

$$3.077x = 55$$

$$x = \frac{55}{3.077}$$

Divide and round to the nearest tenth. ⟶

$$x \doteq 17.9$$

Thus, the boat is about 17.9 meters from the lighthouse.

462   APPLICATIONS OF TRIGONOMETRY

EXERCISES

Find x, to the nearest tenth.

1.

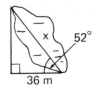

36 m

52°

x

2.

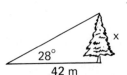

28°

42 m

x

3.

80 km

54°

x

4.

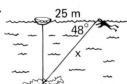

25 m

48°

x

5.

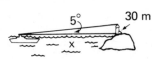

5°

30 m

x

6.

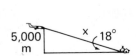

5,000 m

x

18°

7.

x

32°

55 m

8.

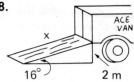

ACE VAN

x

16°

2 m

Give answers to the nearest tenth or to the nearest degree.

9. The angle of elevation from a ship to the top of a 50-m lighthouse on the coast measures 13°. How far from the coast is the ship?

10. A kite is flying at the end of a 200-m string (straight). The string makes an angle of 68° with the ground. How high above the ground is the kite?

11. A tree casts a 60-m shadow when the angle of elevation of the sun measures 58°. How tall is the tree?

12. A ramp is 400 m long. It rises a vertical distance of 32 m. Find the measure of its angle of elevation.

13. Each step of a stairway rises 15 cm for a tread width of 24 cm. What angle does the stairway make with the floor?

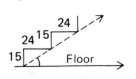

24

24 15

15

Floor

14. A 30-m ladder makes an angle of 55° with the ground as it leans against a building. At what height does it touch the building?

15. A plane is flying at an altitude of 10,000 m. The angle of elevation from an object on the ground to the plane measures 28°. How far is the object from the plane?

16. A cliff is 150 m above the sea. From the cliff the angle of depression of a boat in the sea measures 8°. How far is the boat from the base of the cliff?

17. The leg opposite the 20° angle in a right triangle measures 6 km. Find the area of the triangle. [Hint:
$A = \frac{1}{2}bh$.]

18. A 12-m diagonal of a rectangle makes an angle of 56° with a side of the rectangle. Find the dimensions of the rectangle.

Chapter Sixteen Review

In each case, △ABC ~ △DEF. Find x and y. $[p.448]$

1.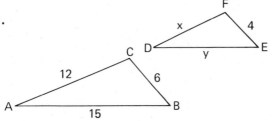

2.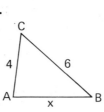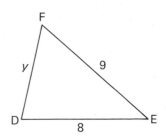

For △ABC, find the following, to three decimal places, or to the nearest degree. Use the table on page 477. $[p.451, 456]$

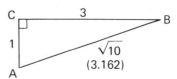

3. tan A

4. cos B

5. sin A

6. sin B

7. m ∠ A

8. m ∠ B

Find the indicated measure (side to the nearest tenth or angle to the nearest degree). Use the figure at the right. $[p.458]$

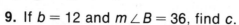

9. If b = 12 and m ∠ B = 36, find c.

11. If c = 8 and m ∠ A = 59, find a.

10. If a = 20 and m ∠ B = 16, find b.

12. If b = 6 and c = 10, find m ∠ A.

Find x, to the nearest tenth.

13.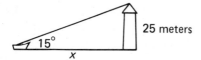

14.

15. Two angles of a triangle have the same measure. The third angle measures 4° more than the sum of the first two. Find the measures of the three angles. $[p.445]$

16. One acute angle of a right triangle measures 10° more than 4 times the other. Find the measures of the two acute angles. $[p.445]$

17. An angle measures 15° less than twice its complement. Find the measure of the angle and its complement. $[p.445]$

18. A pole 2 m tall casts a shadow 10 m long while a tree casts a shadow 13 m long. How tall is the tree? $[p.448]$

19. The angle of elevation from point A to the top of a building measures 38°. Point A is 40 meters from the base of the building. How tall is the building? $[p.461]$

20. A ramp is to be constructed so that it rises 6 m and makes an angle of 12° with the ground. How long should the ramp be? $[p.461]$

Chapter Sixteen Test

In each case, △ABC ~ △DEF. Find x and y.

1.

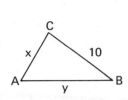

2.

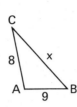

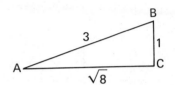

For △ABC, find the following, to three decimal places, or to the nearest degree. Use the table on page 477.

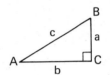

3. cos A **4.** cos B
5. sin A **6** tan B
7. m∠A **8.** m∠B

Find the indicated measure (side to the nearest tenth or angle to the nearest degree). Use the figure at the right.

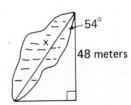

9. If c = 16 and m∠A = 38, find a.
11. If a = 15 and m∠B = 47, find b.

10. If b = 22 and m∠A = 71, find c.
12. If a = 17 and c = 22, find m∠B.

Find x, to the nearest tenth.

13.

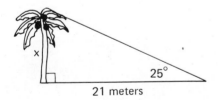

21 meters

14.

54°
x
48 meters

15. The complement of an angle measures 14° less than 3 times the measure of the angle. Find the measure of the angle and its complement.

16. One angle of a triangle measures 5° more than the second. The third angle measures 25° less than twice the measure of the second. Find the measures of the three angles.

17. A 7-m flagpole casts a shadow 25 m long while a tree casts a shadow 40 m long. How tall is the tree?

18. A building casts a 200-m shadow when the angle of elevation of the sun measures 55°. How tall is the building?

Distance Formula

Find the distance between A (3, 2) and B (7, 5).

Plot the points.

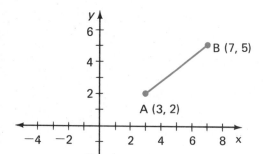

Draw a right triangle.

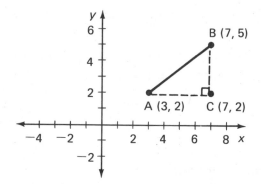

Use the Pythagorean theorem.

$$(AB)^2 = (AC)^2 + (BC)^2$$

$$(AB)^2 = 4^2 + 3^2$$
$$AB = \sqrt{16 + 9}$$
$$AB = \sqrt{25}$$
$$AB = 5$$

Distance Formula

The distance between points A and B is
$$d = \sqrt{(x\text{-coord. } B - x\text{-coord. } A)^2 + (y\text{-coord. } B - y\text{-coord. } A)^2}.$$

PROJECT

Use the distance formula to show that the triangles with these given vertices are isosceles.

1. $A(1,0)$ $B(5,0)$ $C(3,4)$ **2.** $A(2,3)$ $B(5,7)$ $C(1,4)$

GLOSSARY

The explanations given in this glossary are intended to be brief descriptions of the terms listed. They are not necessarily definitions.

Absolute value   The absolute value of a positive number or zero is the number itself. The absolute value of a negative number is the opposite of the number. We read $|x|$ as the absolute value of x.
Examples $|-3| = 3$, $|2| = 2$, $|0| = 0$

Acute   An angle is an acute angle if its measure is less than $90°$.
Example $m\angle A = 72$; $\angle A$ is an acute angle.

Addition property for equations   We can add the same number to each side of an equation. If $a = b$ is true, then $a + c = b + c$ is also true, for all numbers a, b, and c.

Addition property for inequalities   We can add the same number to each side of a true inequality, and the result is another true inequality of the same order. If $a < b$, then $a + c < b + c$.

Additive identity   Zero is the additive identity since adding zero to a number gives the same number.

Additive inverse   The additive inverse of a number is the opposite of the number. -6 is the additive inverse of 6. 8 is the additive inverse of -8. 0 is its own additive inverse.

Adjacent side   In a triangle, a side is adjacent to an angle if it is contained in the angle.

Angle   An angle is a figure formed by two rays with a common endpoint.

Area of a rectangle   The area of a rectangle is given by the formula $A = l \cdot w$, where l is the length and w is the width.

Associative property of addition   When adding, we can change the grouping of the addends. $(a + b) + c = a + (b + c)$, for all numbers a, b, and c.

Associative property of multiplication   When multiplying, we can change the grouping of the factors. $(a \cdot b) \cdot c = a \cdot (b \cdot c)$, for all numbers a, b, and c.

Base   In 3^4, the 3 is the base. $3^4 = 3 \cdot 3 \cdot 3 \cdot 3$. The base is used 4 times as a factor.

Binomial   A binomial is a polynomial with two terms.

Coefficient   A coefficient is the multiplier of a variable. In $6a - 3b + 8$, 6 is the coefficient of a, and -3 is the coefficient of b.

Combine   To combine like terms in an expression such as $5y - 9y$, we use the distributive property.
$$5y - 9y = (5 - 9)y$$
$$= -4y$$

Commutative property of addition   When adding, we can change the order of the addends. $a + b = b + a$, for all numbers a and b.

Commutative property of multiplication   When multiplying, we can change the order of the factors. $a \cdot b = b \cdot a$, for all numbers a and b.

Complement   If the sum of the measures of two angles is 90°, then each angle is the complement of the other.

Complementary angles   Two angles are complementary if the sum of their measures is 90°.

Completing the square   Completing the square is a method for finding the solution set of a quadratic equation.

Complex fraction   A complex fraction is one whose numerator or denominator or both contain a fraction. $\frac{\frac{3}{4}}{\frac{1}{3}}$ is a complex fraction.

Consecutive even integers   Consecutive even integers have a factor of 2 and follow each other from smallest to largest. 6, 8, and 10 are consecutive even integers.

Consecutive integers   Consecutive integers follow each other from smallest to largest.
Examples   4, 5, 6; −23, −22, −21, −20

Consecutive odd integers   Consecutive odd integers do not have a factor of 2, and they follow each other from smallest to largest. 7, 9, and 11 are consecutive odd integers.

Constant function   A constant function is a function whose graph is a horizontal line or a subset of a horizontal line.

Constant of variation   For a direct variation $\frac{y}{x} = k$, k is the constant of variation, or constant of proportionality. For an inverse variation $xy = k$, k is the constant of variation.

Convenient form   A polynomial is in convenient form if its terms are in descending order of exponents, and the coefficient of the first term is positive. $6x - 2x^2 + 3$ is in convenient form when it is expressed as $-1(2x^2 - 6x - 3)$.

Converse   The converse of an if–then statement is formed by reversing the if and the then parts.

Converse of the pythagorean theorem   If the sum of the squares of the lengths of two sides of a triangle equals the square of the length of the third side, then the triangle is a right triangle. In a triangle, if $a^2 + b^2 = c^2$, then the triangle is a right triangle.

Coordinate(s) of a point   On a number line, the coordinate of a point is the number which corresponds to the point. In a coordinate plane, the coordinates of a point make up the ordered pair which corresponds to the point.

Coordinate plane   Two perpendicular number lines in a plane make up a coordinate plane, or a coordinate system. Each point in a coordinate plane corresponds to an ordered pair of numbers, and vice versa.

Correspond   A number corresponds to a point on a number line, and vice versa. An ordered pair corresponds to a point in a coordinate plane, and vice versa. "Corresponds to" means "is associated with."

Pythagorean theorem　In any right triangle, the square of the length of the hypotenuse equals the sum of the squares of the lengths of the other two sides. If $\triangle ABC$ is a right triangle, then $a^2 + b^2 = c^2$.

Quadrant　The x- and y-axes divide the coordinate plane into four quadrants.

Quadratic equation　In a quadratic equation, the variable in one term is raised to the second power, but no higher. $3x^2 - 5x + 4 = 0$, $x^2 - 49 = 0$, and $6x^2 = 2$ are quadratic equations.

Quadratic formula　The solutions of a quadratic equation of the form $ax^2 + bx + c = 0$ may be found by the formula $x = \dfrac{-b \pm \sqrt{b^2 - 4ac}}{2a}$. The formula is called the quadratic formula.

Quotient　The quotient is the result of a division. In $54 \div 9 = 6$, 6 is the quotient.

Radical equation　In a radical equation, the variable is in the radicand. $\sqrt{2x} = 6$ is a radical equation.

Range of a relation　The range of a relation is the set of all second elements of the ordered pairs in the relation. For the relation $\{(0, 1), (2, -5), (4, 3)\}$, the range is $\{1, -5, 3\}$.

Ratio　The ratio of a to b is the quotient $\dfrac{a}{b}$, or $a:b$. A ratio is a comparison of two numbers by division.

Rationalize the denominator　To rationalize the denominator of a fraction means to write the fraction with no radical in the denominator. To rationalize the denominator of $\dfrac{\sqrt{5}}{\sqrt{3}}$, we multiply by $\dfrac{\sqrt{3}}{\sqrt{3}}$.
$$\frac{\sqrt{5}}{\sqrt{3}} \cdot \frac{\sqrt{3}}{\sqrt{3}} = \frac{\sqrt{15}}{3}.$$

Rational number　A rational number is a number which can be written in the form $\dfrac{a}{b}$, where a and b are integers and $b \neq 0$. $\dfrac{3}{5}, \dfrac{-24}{7}$, 8, and .63 are rational numbers.

Real number　The set of real numbers contains all the rational and all the irrational numbers. {rationals} $\cup$ {irrationals} = {reals}.

Rearrange　In an expression like $9x + 8 - 12x + 7$, we can rearrange the terms to simplify.
$$9x + 8 - 12x + 7 = (9x - 12x) + (8 + 7)$$
$$= -3x + 15$$
In an expression like $7 \cdot x \cdot 5 \cdot y$, we can rearrange the factors to simplify.
$$7 \cdot x \cdot 5 \cdot y = (7 \cdot 5) \cdot (x \cdot y)$$
$$= 35xy$$

Reciprocal　Two numbers are reciprocals (multiplicative inverses) if their product is 1.　5 and $\dfrac{1}{5}$ are reciprocals since $5\left(\dfrac{1}{5}\right) = 1$.

Rectangle　A rectangle is a four-sided figure with opposite sides the same length and four right angles.

Relation　A relation is a set of ordered pairs. $\{(0, 1), (2, -5), (-4, 2)\}$ is a relation.

Relatively prime　Two numbers are relatively prime if their only common factor is 1.

Repeating decimal　A repeating decimal has a digit or a group of digits which repeats forever. The decimal .5858585858..., or .58$\overline{58}$, is a repeating decimal. The bar indicates that the digits repeat forever.

Replacement set　A replacement set is the set of all numbers which may replace the variable in an open sentence or expression.

Right triangle　A right triangle is a triangle with one right angle.

Root   A root of an equation is a solution of the equation.

Satisfy   If a variable in an equation is replaced with a number, and the result is a true statement, then the number satisfies the equation.

Sentence   A mathematical sentence contains either $=$, $\neq$, $>$, $<$, $\geq$, or $\leq$. $4 + 5 = 9$ and $7 \leq x - 3$ are mathematical sentences.

Set   A set is a collection of objects. We use braces $\{ \ \ \}$ to show a set.

Similar   Two figures are similar if the corresponding angles are congruent and the lengths of the corresponding sides have the same ratio.

Simplest radical form   An expression is in simplest radical form if it contains no factor which is a perfect square.

Simplify   To simplify an expression means to replace it with the least complicated equivalent expression.

Sine of an angle   The sine of an acute angle of a right triangle is the ratio of the length of the side opposite the angle to the length of the hypotenuse.

Slope of a line   The slope of a line in a coordinate plane is the slope of any segment on the line. The slope of a horizontal line is zero. The slope of a vertical line is undefined.

Slope of a segment   The slope of a segment in a coordinate plane is $\dfrac{\text{difference of } y\text{-coordinates}}{\text{difference of } x\text{-coordinates}}$.

Solution   A solution of an open sentence is a replacement of the variable which makes the sentence true. In $5x - 3 = 32$, 7 is a solution since $5(7) - 3 = 35 - 3 = 32$.

Solution set   The solution set of an open sentence is the set of all members of the replacement set which are solutions of the sentence.

Solve   To solve an open sentence means to find all of its solutions.

Square   To square a number means to multiply it by itself.

Square of a number   The square of a number is the product of the number and itself.

Square root x is a square root of n if $x \cdot x = n$. 6 is a square root of 36 since $6 \cdot 6 = 36$. Also, -6 is a square root of 36 since $(-6)(-6) = 36$.

Standard form   A quadratic equation is in standard form if the coefficient of the x^2 term is positive, the polynomial is equal to zero, and the terms are arranged in descending order of exponents. $3x^2 - 6x + 1 = 0$ is in standard form. We use $ax^2 + bx + c = 0$ to represent the standard form of a quadratic equation.

Subset   Set B is a subset of set A if every element of B is also in A. $B \subseteq A$ means B is a subset of A.

Substitute   To substitute a value for a variable means to replace the variable with the particular value. For $8y - 9$, we can substitute the value 5 for y.
$$8y - 9$$
$$8(5) - 9$$
$$40 - 9$$
$$31$$

Subtract   To subtract b from a means to add the opposite of b to a. $a - b = a + (-b)$, for all numbers a and b.

Sum   The sum is the result of an addition. In $7 + 8 = 15$, 15 is the sum.

System of equations   Two equations in two variables form a system of equations.
$$\begin{array}{l} 2x + 3y = 6 \\ x - 4y = -3 \end{array} \text{ is a system.}$$

System of inequalities   Two inequalities in two variables form a system of inequalities.
$$\begin{array}{l} 3x - 2y < 8 \\ x - \ y > 4 \end{array} \text{ is a system.}$$

Tangent of an angle   The tangent of an acute angle of a right triangle is the ratio of the length of the side opposite the angle to the length of the side adjacent to the angle.

Terminating decimal A terminating decimal has a finite number of digits.

Terms In $7x - 3y + 8$, the terms are $7x$, $-3y$, and 8. Terms are added.

Theorem A theorem is a property which can be proved.

Triangle A triangle is a three-sided figure.

Trinomial A trinomial is a polynomial with three terms.

Twice Twice a number means two times the number. Twice x means $2x$.

Undefined fraction A fraction is undefined if its denominator is zero.

Union of sets The union of two sets A and B is the set of all elements belonging to set A or to set B or to both sets A and B. $\cup$ is the symbol for union.

Value of a function If (x, y) is an ordered pair in function f, then the value of f at x is y. We read $f(x) = y$ as the value of f at x is y, or as f at x is y.

Variable A variable takes the place of a number. In $5x - 3 = 7$, x is a variable.

Vertical line A vertical line in a coordinate plane is parallel to the y-axis.

Vertical line test A relation is a function if no vertical line crosses its graph in more than one point.

Whole number The numbers 0, 1, 2, 3, . . . are whole numbers.

x-axis The x-axis is the horizontal number line in a coordinate plane.

x-coordinate The x-coordinate of an ordered pair of numbers is the first number in the pair. For $(5, -2)$, 5 is the x-coordinate.

y-axis The y-axis is the vertical number line in a coordinate plane.

y-coordinate The y-coordinate of an ordered pair of numbers is the second number in the pair. For $(5, -2)$, -2 is the y-coordinate.

y-intercept The y-intercept of a line in a coordinate plane is the y-coordinate of the point of intersection of the line with the y-axis. In the equation of a line, $y = mx + b$, b is the y-intercept.

Zero Zero (0) lies between the positive and the negative numbers on a number line. Zero is neither positive nor negative.

Table of Roots and Powers

No.	Sq.	Sq. Root	Cube	Cu. Root	No.	Sq.	Sq. Root	Cube	Cu. Root
1	1	1.000	1	1.000	51	2,601	7.141	132,651	3.708
2	4	1.414	8	1.260	52	2,704	7.211	140,608	3.733
3	9	1.732	27	1.442	53	2,809	7.280	148,877	3.756
4	16	2.000	64	1.587	54	2,916	7.348	157,564	3.780
5	25	2.236	125	1.710	55	3,025	7.416	166,375	3.803
6	36	2.449	216	1.817	56	3,136	7.483	175,616	3.826
7	49	2.646	343	1.913	57	3,249	7.550	185,193	3.849
8	64	2.828	512	2.000	58	3,364	7.616	195,112	3.871
9	81	3.000	729	2.080	59	3,481	7.681	205,379	3.893
10	100	3.162	1,000	2.154	60	3,600	7.746	216,000	3.915
11	121	3.317	1,331	2.224	61	3,721	7.810	226,981	3.936
12	144	3.464	1,728	2.289	62	3,844	7.874	238,328	3.958
13	169	3.606	2,197	2.351	63	3,969	7.937	250,047	3.979
14	196	3.742	2,744	2.410	64	4,096	8.000	262,144	4.000
15	225	3.875	3,375	2.466	65	4,225	8.062	274,625	4.021
16	256	4.000	4,096	2.520	66	4,356	8.124	287,496	4.041
17	289	4.123	4,913	2.571	67	4,489	8.185	300,763	4.062
18	324	4.243	5,832	2.621	68	4,624	8.246	314,432	4.082
19	361	4.359	6,859	2.668	69	4,761	8.307	328,509	4.102
20	400	4.472	8,000	2.714	70	4,900	8.357	343,000	4.121
21	441	4.583	9,261	2.759	71	5,041	8.426	357,911	4.141
22	484	4.690	10,648	2.802	72	5,184	8.485	373,248	4.160
23	529	4.796	12,167	2.844	73	5,329	8.544	389,017	4.179
24	576	4.899	13,824	2.884	74	5,476	8.602	405,224	4.198
25	625	5.000	15,625	2.924	75	5,625	8.660	421,875	4.217
26	676	5.099	17,576	2.962	76	5,776	8.718	438,976	4.236
27	729	5.196	19,683	3.000	77	5,929	8.775	456,533	4.254
28	784	5.292	21,952	3.037	78	6,084	8.832	474,552	4.273
29	841	5.385	24,389	3.072	79	6,241	8.888	493,039	4.291
30	900	5.477	27,000	3.107	80	6,400	8.944	512,000	4.309
31	961	5.568	29,791	3.141	81	6,561	9.000	531,441	4.327
32	1,024	5.657	32,768	3.175	82	6,724	9.055	551,368	4.344
33	1,089	5.745	35,937	3.208	83	6,889	9.110	571,787	4.362
34	1,156	5.831	39,304	3.240	84	7,056	9.165	592,704	4.380
35	1,225	5.916	42,875	3.271	85	7,225	9.220	614,125	4.397
36	1,296	6.000	46,656	3.302	86	7,396	9.274	636,056	4.414
37	1,369	6.083	50,653	3.332	87	7,569	9.327	658,503	4.431
38	1,444	6.164	54,872	3.362	88	7,744	9.381	681,472	4.448
39	1,521	6.245	59,319	3.391	89	7,921	9.434	704,969	4.465
40	1,600	6.325	64,000	3.420	90	8,100	9.487	729,000	4.481
41	1,681	6.403	68,921	3.448	91	8,281	9.539	753,571	4.498
42	1,764	6.481	74,088	3.476	92	8,464	9.592	778,688	4.514
43	1,849	6.557	79,507	3.503	93	8,649	9.644	804,357	4.531
44	1,936	6.633	85,184	3.530	94	8,836	9.695	830,584	4.547
45	2,025	6.708	91,125	3.557	95	9,025	9.747	857,375	4.563
46	2,116	6.782	97,336	3.583	96	9,216	9.798	884,736	4.579
47	2,209	6.856	103,823	3.609	97	9,409	9.849	912,673	4.595
48	2,304	6.928	110,592	3.634	98	9,604	9.899	941,192	4.610
49	2,401	7.000	117,649	3.659	99	9,801	9.950	970,299	4.626
50	2,500	7.071	125,000	3.684	100	10,000	10.000	1,000,000	4.642

Trigonometric Ratios

Angle Measure	Sin	Cos	Tan	Angle Measure	Sin	Cos	Tan
0°	0.000	1.000	0.000	46°	.7193	.6947	1.036
1°	.0175	.9998	.0175	47°	.7314	.6820	1.072
2°	.0349	.9994	.0349	48°	.7431	.6691	1.111
3°	.0523	.9986	.0524	49°	.7547	.6561	1.150
4°	.0698	.9976	.0699	50°	.7660	.6428	1.192
5°	.0872	.9962	.0875	51°	.7771	.6293	1.235
6°	.1045	.9945	.1051	52°	.7880	.6157	1.280
7°	.1219	.9925	.1228	53°	.7986	.6018	1.327
8°	.1392	.9903	.1405	54°	.8090	.5878	1.376
9°	.1564	.9877	.1584	55°	.8192	.5736	1.428
10°	.1736	.9848	.1763	56°	.8290	.5592	1.483
11°	.1908	.9816	.1944	57°	.8387	.5446	1.540
12°	.2079	.9781	.2126	58°	.8480	.5299	1.600
13°	.2250	.9744	.2309	59°	.8572	.5150	1.664
14°	.2419	.9703	.2493	60°	.8660	.5000	1.732
15°	.2588	.9659	.2679	61°	.8746	.4848	1.804
16°	.2756	.9613	.2867	62°	.8829	.4695	1.881
17°	.2924	.9563	.3057	63°	.8910	.4540	1.963
18°	.3090	.9511	.3249	64°	.8988	.4384	2.050
19°	.3256	.9455	.3443	65°	.9063	.4226	2.145
20°	.3420	.9397	.3640	66°	.9135	.4067	2.246
21°	.3584	.9336	.3839	67°	.9205	.3907	2.356
22°	.3746	.9272	.4040	68°	.9272	.3746	2.475
23°	.3907	.9205	.4245	69°	.9336	.3584	2.605
24°	.4067	.9135	.4452	70°	.9397	.3420	2.747
25°	.4226	.9063	.4663	71°	.9455	.3256	2.904
26°	.4384	.8988	.4877	72°	.9511	.3090	3.077
27°	.4540	.8910	.5095	73°	.9563	.2924	3.270
28°	.4695	.8829	.5317	74°	.9613	.2756	3.487
29°	.4848	.8746	.5543	75°	.9659	.2588	3.732
30°	.5000	.8660	.5774	76°	.9703	.2419	4.010
31°	.5150	.8572	.6009	77°	.9744	.2250	4.331
32°	.5299	.8480	.6249	78°	.9781	.2079	4.704
33°	.5446	.8387	.6494	79°	.9816	.1908	5.145
34°	.5592	.8290	.6745	80°	.9848	.1736	5.671
35°	.5736	.8192	.7002	81°	.9877	.1564	6.314
36°	.5878	.8090	.7265	82°	.9903	.1392	7.115
37°	.6018	.7986	.7536	83°	.9925	.1219	8.144
38°	.6157	.7880	.7813	84°	.9945	.1045	9.514
39°	.6293	.7771	.8098	85°	.9962	.0872	11.43
40°	.6428	.7660	.8391	86°	.9976	.0698	14.30
41°	.6561	.7547	.8693	87°	.9986	.0523	19.08
42°	.6691	.7431	.9004	88°	.9994	.0349	28.64
43°	.6820	.7314	.9325	89°	.9998	.0175	57.29
44°	.6947	.7193	.9657	90°	1.000	0.000	
45°	.7071	.7071	1.000				

INDEX

ANSWERS

Page x

3. Turn both hourglasses over and start the egg when the 3-minute hourglass runs out. When the 8-minute hourglass runs out (5 minutes later), turn it over again to get 8 more minutes.

Page 2

1. 25 **3.** 30 **5.** 29 **7.** 35 **9.** 18 **11.** 68
13. 26 **15.** 10 **17.** 73 **19.** 32 **21.** 76
23. 69 **25.** 19 **27.** 79 **29.** 73 **31.** 53
33. 57 **35.** 220 **37.** 1.1835 **39.** .1017

Page 5

1. 13 **3.** 49 **5.** 55 **7.** 18 **9.** 14 **11.** 46
13. 31 **15.** 78 **17.** 73 **19.** 93 **21.** 95
23. 416 **25.** 222

Page 8

1. 77 **3.** 96 **5.** 105 **7.** 1,700 **9.** 1,640
11. 49,000 **13.** Comm. Prop. Add.
15. Assoc. Prop. Add. **17.** Assoc. Prop. Mult.
19. Comm. Prop. Add. **21.** Comm. Prop. Mult.
23. 210 **25.** 600 **27.** 390 **29.** 18,700
31. no; no

Page 11

1. $4 \cdot 6 + 4 \cdot 2$; 32 **3.** $2 \cdot 9 + 2 \cdot 4$; 26
5. $2 \cdot 6 + 9 \cdot 6$; 66 **7.** $98 = 98$ **9.** $6(3) + 6(5)$
11. $3(8) + 3(1)$ **13.** $4(2) + 4(7) + 4(6)$
15. $4(6 + 2)$ **17.** $(5 + 9)6$ **19.** $(3 + 7)8$
21. $5(4 + 2 + 7)$ **23.** $(6 + 4 + 7)8$
25. $4(3 + 7 + 1)$ **27.** $7(8 + 4 + 2)$
29. $7(5) + 7(1) + 7(9) + 7(2)$ **31.** $4(1) + 4(9) + 4(7) + 4(2)$ **33.** $7(8) + 7(4) + 7(3) + 7(5)$
35. $4 \cdot 8 + 4 \cdot 1 + 4 \cdot 3 + 4 \cdot 5 + 4 \cdot 9$
37. $3(8) + 3(9) + 3(1) + 3(4) + 3(6)$
39. $4(7 + 7 + 2 + 7)$ **41.** no **43.** yes

Page 12

1. 3,000 mm **3.** 70,000 dm **5.** .08 m
7. 300 cL **9.** 6,000,000 mL **11.** .008 kL
13. 5,000 mg **15.** 8,000,000 mg
17. .007 kg

Page 15

1. $10x + 3$ **3.** $7y + 9$ **5.** $11a + 9$ **7.** $6z + 12$
9. $9b + 7$ **11.** $9k + 7$ **13.** $5y + 1$ **15.** $11z + 4$
17. $10t + 16$ **19.** $8z + 13$ **21.** $9x + 9y$
23. $7m + 9q$ **25.** $11x + 8y + 1$
27. $16a + 8b + 6$ **29.** $7x + 2y + 5z + 1$
31. 25 **33.** 64 **35.** 54 **37.** 86

Page 17

1. $43y + 7$ **3.** $29m + 36$ **5.** $36c + 14$
7. $29x + 12$ **9.** $42r + 56$ **11.** $27y + 30$
13. $39c + 5$ **15.** $8x + 11$ **17.** $13x + 24$
19. $18c + 11$ **21.** $14x + 26$ **23.** $22r + 29$
25. $38e + 38$ **27.** $170c + 70$ **29.** $87x + 120$

Page 18

1. 22 **3.** 4 **5.** 25 **7.** 65 **9.** 44 **11.** 85
13. 5, $9x$; x; 9 **15.** $8a$, $7b$, $2c$; a, b, c; 8, 7, 2
17. 80 **19.** 4,700 **21.** 8,200 **23.** Assoc. Prop. Mult. **25.** Comm. Prop. Mult. **27.** $6 \cdot 3 + 8 \cdot 3$
29. $8 \cdot 3 + 8 \cdot 7 + 8 \cdot 5$ **31.** $9(8 + 2)$
33. $4(5 + 8 + 3 + 1)$ **35.** $45 = 45$ **37.** $12y + 9$
39. $11p + 14q + 3$ **41.** $20y + 24$
43. $14z + 14$ **45.** $57y + 101$ **47.** $13 + 9y$; 31
49. $4 + 12x + 11y$; 166

Page 20
1. 15°C **3.** 0°C

Page 23
1. +10 **3.** −14 **5.** −10 **7.** +7 **9.** +5
11. −3 **13.** −1 **15.** −9 **17.** −10 **19.** −4
21. −13 **23.** +3 **25.** +5 **27.** −11 **29.** −23
31. +20 **33.** +9 **35.** −7 **37.** +5 **39.** −4
41. +6 **43.** −10 **45.** −2 **47.** +8 **49.** 0
51. 0 **53.** 0 **55.** 0 **57.** −22 **59.** +24
61. +67 **63.** −81 **65.** +8 **67.** −75
69. −131 **71.** 0 **73.** +22 **75.** −787
77. −132 **79.** +994 **81.** Drop the signs;
add the numbers; give a positive sign to the
result. **83.** Drop the signs; subtract the smaller
number from the larger; give the result the
same sign as the larger. **85.** −.83
87. −1.074 **89.** +1.87 **91.** +85.63

Page 25
1. +1 = +1 **3.** −13 = −13 **5.** Comm.
7. Add. Iden. **9.** Add. Iden. **11.** Comm.
13. Assoc. **15.** Add. Inv. **17.** Comm. **19.** −3
21. +2 **23.** −7 **25.** Opposite of neg. is pos.

27.
Expression	Reason
(−9 + +4) + −8	Given
−8 + (−9 + +4)	Comm.
−8 + (+4 + −9)	Comm.
(−8 + +4) + −9	Assoc.

29.
Expression	Reason
(−3 + +5) + +3	Given
(+5 + −3) + +3	Comm.
+5 + (−3 + +3)	Assoc.
+5 + 0	Add. Inv.
+5	Add. Iden.

31.
Expression	Reason
(x + y) + z	Given
(y + x) + z	Comm.
y + (x + z)	Assoc.
y + (z + x)	Comm.
(y + z) + x	Assoc.
(z + y) + x	Comm.

Page 27
1. {H1, H2, H3, H4, H5, H6, T1, T2, T3, T4,
T5, T6} **3.** $\frac{5}{36}$; $\frac{1}{2}$

Page 30
1. +21 **3.** −48 **5.** −45 **7.** −28 **9.** −7
11. −16 **13.** +27 **15.** 0 **17.** −8 **19.** +60
21. +72 **23.** −18 **25.** 0 **27.** +100
29. 0 **31.** −100 **33.** −39 **35.** −120
37. −32 **39.** +72 **41.** +250 **43.** −480
45. −720 **47.** −1,600 **49.** +900 **51.** 0
53. +90 **55.** +144 **57.** +1,512 **59.** −5,040
61. (−4)(+2) = (+2)(−4); (−6)(−5) = (−5)(−6)
63. −8(−6 + +3) = (−8)(−6) + (−8)(+3);
+2(−7 + −9) = (+2)(−7) + (+2)(−9)

Page 32
1. +2 **3.** −5 **5.** +7 **7.** +9 **9.** −9 **11.** 0
13. +6 **15.** +3 **17.** +4 **19.** −3 **21.** +1
23. +5 **25.** −42 **27.** −4 **29.** +7 **31.** −9
33. −8 **35.** +15 **37.** +5 **39.** +6 **41.** −32
43. +1 **45.** +1 **47.** +9 **49.** +1 **51.** −3
53. −5 **55.** −2 **57.** +.0002

Page 34
1. 60 m above sea level **3.** yes **5.** $.62

Page 38
1. −6 **3.** 13 **5.** 0 **7.** −44 **9.** 12 **11.** 7
13. 19 **15.** 10 **17.** 17 **19.** −21 **21.** 5
23. 34 **25.** −126 **27.** −83 **29.** 16
31. −102 **33.** −94 **35.** 0

Page 39
1.
1	12	7	14
8	13	2	11
10	3	16	5
15	6	9	4

Page 41
1. 14 **33.** −2 **5.** 11 **7.** 12 **9.** 63 **11.** 3
13. −32 **15.** −68 **17.** −74 **19.** −41 **21.** 94
23. 71 **25.** −211 **27.** 13x + 36y + 8; 90

Page 43

1. $5y$ **3.** $2b$ **5.** $-2z$ **7.** $-5r$ **9.** $-7r$
11. $-4z - 8$ **13.** $-2q - 9$ **15.** $-9y - 4$
17. $-12x + 1$ **19.** $2x + 6y + 3$
21. $4r - 6s - 6$ **23.** $-14x + 4y + 8$
25. $-10x + 3y - 4$ **27.** $13a - 4c - 16$
29. $-6a + 3b + 1$ **31.** $2x + 6y - 3; -25$
33. $6x + 4y - 4z; -56$ **35.** $-11x + 6y - 6; -2$
37. $1.2x - 1.193y - 4; -7.3425$

Page 45

1. 0 **3.** $3b$ **5.** $12r$ **7.** $-a + 2$ **9.** $c - 1$
11. $-e - 3$ **13.** $-9q + 15$ **15.** $2p - 7$
17. $-5d - 10$ **19.** $-3a + 2$ **21.** $-7z + 16$
23. $14b - 14$ **25.** $2x - 4y - 8; -36$
27. $-x - y + 8z; -28$ **29.** $x - 8y - z; -47$
31. $x - 9y - 6z + 1; -37$ **33.** $.7x + .002y - z;$
-1.98692

Page 47

1. $29x - 16$ **3.** $14y - 14$ **5.** $-8a + 38$
7. $2x - 27$ **9.** $-39a - 63$ **11.** $-29a - 21$
13. $-6x - 11$ **15.** $25c - 27$ **17.** $17x$
19. $-38y - 74$ **21.** $17y - 32; 104$
23. $-37x - 6; 142$ **25.** $10x - 7; -97$
27. $31d - 26; 67$ **29.** $-17x - 1; 16$
31. $-33x + 14$ **33.** $-29y + 33$ **35.** $87z + 19$
37. $-20x - 48$ **39.** $-20x + 2$

Page 49

1. $-11y - 2$ **3.** $-5z - 12$ **5.** $-2c + 8$
7. $3f - 8$ **9.** $9y - 9$ **11.** $8y - 17$
13. $-6e - 13$ **15.** $-6d - 1$ **17.** $4y - 4$
19. $-11z + 6$ **21.** $-19b - 10$ **23.** -12
25. -23 **27.** 39 **29.** -7 **31.** -7
33. $-23y + 33$ **35.** $-4z - 2$ **37.** $9r - 2$
39. $-8x + 10$

Page 51

1. 3 **3.** -2 **5.** -14 **7.** 9 **9.** -18
11. $3b + 8$ **13.** $-x - 12$ **15.** $2y + 17$
17. $-5x + 3$ **19.** $20z + 10$ **21.** $3y - 27$
23. $18z - 6$ **25.** $-3x - 11$

Page 52

1. $+10$ **3.** $+3$ **5.** -18 **7.** -5 **9.** -9 **11.** 8
13. 6 **15.** -9 **17.** -16 **19.** 105 **21.** -75
23. -120 **25.** 7 **27.** -6 **29.** -5 **31.** -27
33. 49 **35.** $-3x$ **37.** $-5p + 20$ **39.** $5a + 16$
41. $-9z - 5$ **43.** $-30k + 16; 166$ **45.** 15
47. $4x + 12$ **49.** $2a - 8$ **51.** Comm.

Page 54

1. Start. Insert first key. Does it work? No: Insert second key. Yes: Stop. Does second key work? No: Insert third key. Yes: Stop.

Page 58

1. 5 **3.** 9 **5.** 5 **7.** 9 **9.** 7 **11.** 4 **13.** 5
15. 7 **17.** 4 **19.** 3 **21.** 4 **23.** 2 **25.** 6
27. 3 **29.** 0 **31.** $\frac{1}{4}$ **33.** -3 **35.** none **37.** $\frac{1}{2}$

Page 62

1. 4 **3.** 6 **5.** -1 **7.** -3 **9.** -2 **11.** -8
13. -1 **15.** -5 **17.** -3 **19.** 1 **21.** -2
23. 0 **25.** $\frac{1}{5}$ **27.** $\frac{1}{6}$ **29.** $\frac{1}{8}$ **31.** $\frac{2}{5}$ **33.** $\frac{1}{4}$ **35.** $\frac{3}{8}$
37. $-.176$ **39.** $.406$

Page 63

1. 7

Page 66

1. 3 **3.** 3 **5.** 8 **7.** 15 **9.** 4 **11.** 7 **13.** -11
15. 6 **17.** 1 **19.** 4 **21.** 5 **23.** 2 **25.** 6
27. 7 **29.** -4 **31.** 1 **33.** 3 **35.** 4 **37.** -3
39. $\frac{1}{4}$ **41.** $\frac{3}{5}$ **43.** $\frac{5}{6}$ **45.** $\frac{5}{4}$ **47.** $-\frac{7}{5}$ **49.** $\frac{3}{2}$
51. $\frac{3}{2}$ **53.** $\frac{5}{2}$ **55.** $.3$ **57.** $.64$

Page 67

1. $x; 2x; 2x + 6; 3x + 6; x + 2; x + 2$

Page 69

1. 7 **3.** -7 **5.** 8 **7.** -6 **9.** 20 **11.** -8
13. 9 **15.** -1 **17.** 10 **19.** 5 **21.** -3
23. -4 **25.** 2 **27.** 2 **29.** -1 **31.** 1 **33.** 11
35. 3 **37.** -2 **39.** 1 **41.** $\frac{16}{5}$ **43.** $\frac{1}{13}$ **45.** $-\frac{1}{6}$
47. $-\frac{3}{19}$ **49.** 2 **51.** 9 **53.** $\frac{42}{11}$ **55.** $-\frac{3}{8}$
57. $-\frac{4}{9}$

Page 71
1. $8 - 5$ **3.** $12 + 6$ **5.** $23 + 2$ **7.** $y + 4$
9. $n - 8$ **11.** $5y + 3$ **13.** $3n - 6$ **15.** $25 - 4n$
17. $4x + 8$ **19.** $14 + 2n$ **21.** $9n - 7$
23. $x + y$ **25.** $7x - 2y$ **27.** $xy + 9$ **29.** $y - 5x$
31. $5 + 7y + 8$, or $7y + 13$ **33.** $5n - 2 + 9$, or
$5n + 7$

Page 74
1. 4 **3.** 3 **5.** 1 **7.** 3 **9.** -2 **11.** -3 **13.** 1
15. -36 **17.** 5 **19.** 7 **21.** -8 **23.** -10
25. 7 **27.** -9 **29.** 1 **31.** -3

Page 78
1. 7, 35   **3.** 39, 11   **5.** 37, 46   **7.** 51, 17
9. $31, $58   **11.** 8, 11, 15   **13.** 9, 12
15. 26, 13

Page 82
1. 3 dimes, 12 nickels   **3.** 1 dime, 3 quarters
5. 7 dimes, 4 quarters   **7.** 14 pennies,
21 nickels   **9.** 502 tickets   **11.** 3 nickels,
18 dimes, 20 pennies   **13.** 44 dimes

Page 83
1. 326 km   **3.** Bus tour is more economical
by $6.

Page 86
1. 13 m; 7 m   **3.** 19 km; 8 km   **5.** 15 cm;
13 cm; 21 cm   **7.** 9 cm; 12 cm; 17 cm
9. 11 m; 11 m   **11.** 16 m   **13.** 18 cm; 9 cm
15. 6 cm; 9 cm

Page 88
1. 7   **3.** 3   **5.** none   **7.** -11 **9.** $-\frac{8}{5}$ **11.** 5
13. 1   **15.** $\frac{23}{2}$ **17.** 3   **19.** 22   **21.** -4
23. -13 **25.** -5 **27.** -3 **29.** 8   **31.** -2
33. $6 + x$ **35.** $n - 3$ **37.** $2y - 5$ **39.** 4   **41.** 5,
22   **43.** 26 cm; 8 cm

Page 90
1. -11, -12, -13 **3.** -3, -3, -3 **5.** .00001,
.000001, .0000001   **7.** 13, 14, 16   **9.** 125, 216,
343   **11.** $\frac{5}{6}$, $\frac{6}{7}$, $\frac{7}{8}$ **13.** 24, 35, 48   **15.** 124, 215,
342

Page 93
1. equal   **3.** not equal   **5.** equal   **7.** finite
9. infinite   **11.** finite   **13.** {1, 2, 3, 4, 5}
15. {-3, -2}   **17.** {7}   **19.** {7}   **21.** {4}
23. {4}   **25.** {9}   **27.** {-1}   **29.** {all numbers}
31. {all numbers}   **33.** {all numbers}

Page 96
1. all points to the left of 3   **3.** 5 and all
points to the left   **5.** -2 and all points to the
left   **7.** all points to the right of 2   **9.** -6 and
all points to the right   **11.** all points to the left
of 2   **13.** all points to the right of 4   **15.** 4 and
all points to the right   **17.** all points to the left
of -3 **19.** 1 and all points to the right
21. -3 and all points to the left   **23.** all points
to the left of -2 **25.** -1 and all points to the
right   **27.** -4 and all points to the left   **29.** all
points to the right of -2 **31.** 2 and all points
to the right   **33.** 1 and all points to the right
35. 5 and all points to the left   **37.** all points to
the right and left of $2\frac{1}{2}$ **39.** all points to the left
of $\frac{5}{4}$ **41.** $\frac{1}{2}$ and all points to the left   **43.** $-\frac{2}{3}$
and all points to the right   **45.** all points to the
right of 5   **47.** all points to the right of -2.5

Page 97
1. -6 **3.** 6

Page 101
1. $10 > 9$ **3.** $-24 < 4$ **5.** $-4 < -1$
7. $-21 < 14$ **9.** $0 > -15$ **11.** $-8 < 4$
13. $-42 < 6$ **15.** $2 \le 3$ **17.** $2 > -2$ **19.** $3 \ge$
-10 **21.** $0 \le 15$ **23.** $7 \le 11$ **25.** $6 > 5$
27. Add -3 **29.** Multiply by -3.   **31.** Add 5.
33. Divide by -3 **35.** Multiply by -3.

Page 104
1. $\{x \mid x > -2\}$ **3.** $\{y \mid y > -1\}$ **5.** $\{x \mid x > 7\}$
7. $\{a \mid a \le 8\}$ **9.** $\{d \mid d < -3\}$ **11.** $\{r \mid r \ge 4\}$
13. $\{x \mid x \le 3\}$ **15.** $\{x \mid x < 4\}$ **17.** $\{x \mid x \le 6\}$
19. $\{y \mid y > 3\}$ **21.** $\{x \mid x \ge 8\}$ **23.** $\{y \mid y > 9\}$
25. $\{x \mid x > 5\}$ **27.** {all numbers}

Page 107

1. $A \nsubseteq B$; $B \subseteq A$　**3.** $A \subseteq B$; $B \nsubseteq A$　**5.** $A \subseteq B$; $B \nsubseteq A$　**7.** $A \subseteq B$; $B \nsubseteq A$　**9.** $A \subseteq B$; $B \subseteq A$
11. $A \nsubseteq B$; $B \nsubseteq A$　**13.** $A \nsubseteq B$; $B \subseteq A$
15. $A \subseteq B$; $B \nsubseteq A$　**17.** $\{1, 2\}$, $\{1\}$, $\{2\}$, ϕ; 4
19. $\{8\}$, ϕ; 2　**21.** $\{-1, 0\}$, $\{-1\}$, $\{0\}$, ϕ; 4
23. $\{3, 5\}$; $\{1, 3, 5\}$　**25.** ϕ; $\{4, 5, 6, 7\}$
27. ϕ; $\{0, 2, 4\}$　**29.** ϕ; $\{-3, -2, -1, 1, 2, 3\}$
31. $\{1, 4, 5\}$; $\{1, 2, 3, 4, 5\}$　**33.** $\{6\}$;
$\{2, 4, 6, 8, 10\}$　**35.** $\{2, 5, 8, 9\}$; $\{2, 5, 8, 9\}$
37. ϕ; $\{0, 1, 2, 3, \ldots\}$　**39.** $\{0, 6, 12, 18, \ldots\}$;
$\{0, 2, 3, 4, 6, 8, 9, 10, 12, \ldots\}$　**41.** $\{0\}$;
{integers}　**43.** {positive integers};
{whole numbers}　**45.** $\{0, 1, 2, 3, 4, 5, 6\}$
47. ϕ　**49.** $\{0, 2, 4\}$

Page 111

1. 4 hr　**3.** 3 hr　**5.** 3 hr　**7.** 48 km　**9.** 5 hr

Page 114

1. $\{x \mid x > -2 \text{ and } x < 5\}$; {all numbers}
3. $\{x \mid x \geq -4 \text{ and } x < 2\}$; {all numbers}
5. $\{x \mid x \geq -1\}$; $\{x \mid x > -3\}$
7. $\{x \mid x \geq -1 \text{ and } x \leq 3\}$; {all numbers}
9. $\{x \mid x < 0\}$; $\{x \mid x < 4\}$　**11.** $\{1\}$; {all numbers}
13. $\{x \mid x > -4\}$; $\{x \mid x > -5\}$
15. $\{x \mid x \leq 2 \text{ and } x > -1\}$; {all numbers}
17. $\{x \mid x > 3\}$; $\{x \mid x \geq 3\}$　**19.** ϕ;
{all numbers}　**21.** ϕ; $\{x \mid x \geq 5\}$
23. $\{x \mid x \geq -3 \text{ and } x \leq 3\}$; {all numbers}
25. $\{-3\}$; $\{x \mid x \leq -3\}$　**27.** $\{x \mid x > 3 \text{ and } x \leq 4\}$;
{all numbers}　**29.** $\{x \mid x > 2\}$; {all numbers}
31. $\{x \mid x \geq 1 \text{ and } x \leq 4\}$
33. $\{x \mid x > -4 \text{ and } x < 3\}$
35. $\{x \mid x \leq -2 \text{ or } x \geq 0\}$
37. $\{x \mid x > 2 \text{ and } x \leq 3\}$　**39.** segment with
endpoints 0 and 5　**41.** all points to the right
of -4

Page 116

1. equal　**3.** not equal　**5.** infinite; the set of all
positive odd integers　**7.** infinite; the set of all
negative integers　**9.** ϕ　**11.** $\{-13\}$
13. all points to the right of -2　**15.** all points
to the right and left of $-\frac{1}{2}$　**17.** all points to the
right of 2　**19.** $1 \geq -3$　**21.** $3 > -6$
23. Add -2.　**25.** $\{x \mid x \leq -2\}$　**27.** $\{x \mid x < 1\}$
29. $A \subseteq B$; $B \nsubseteq A$　**31.** $\{3\}$, ϕ; 2　**33.** $\{9\}$, $\{8\}$,
$\{7\}$, $\{9, 8\}$, $\{9, 7\}$, $\{8, 7\}$, $\{9, 8, 7\}$, ϕ; 8
35. ϕ; $\{1, 2, 3, 4, 5, 6\}$　**37.** $\{x \mid x > 3 \text{ and } x \leq 4\}$;
{all numbers}　**39.** $\{x \mid -4 \leq x \leq 2\}$

Page 120

1. $x \cdot x \cdot x \cdot x \cdot x$　**3.** $a \cdot a \cdot a \cdot a$　**5.** $4 \cdot n \cdot n \cdot n$
7. $-3 \cdot a \cdot a$　**9.** -27　**11.** 16　**13.** -24
15. 64　**17.** 243　**19.** 24　**21.** -27　**23.** -4
25. 64　**27.** 11,664　**29.** 1,048,576　**31.** -216

Page 123

1. $12a^8$　**3.** $6m^{11}$　**5.** $28x^{12}$　**7.** $15a^9$　**9.** $4a^5$
11. $6a^{11}$　**13.** $-8a^8$　**15.** $-8m^8$　**17.** $8a^4$
19. $-15b^8$　**21.** $12a^5b^6$　**23.** $-20m^4n^7$
25. $6a^5b^4$　**27.** a^6　**29.** x^{12}　**31.** z^{30}　**33.** r^{30}
35. g^{45}　**37.** c^{28}　**39.** $16x^8$　**41.** $-8z^{12}$
43. $256x^{12}$　**45.** $9a^4x^6$　**47.** $8m^9n^{12}$
49. $-64a^9m^{12}$　**51.** $8x^3a^6$　**53.** $-243x^5y^{10}m^5$
55. $a^{10}b^{20}c^{15}$　**57.** $27a^9b^6$　**59.** $-27x^9y^{12}z^6$
61. y^{4b}　**63.** x^{6a}　**65.** $2^a x^{5a^2}$

Page 125

1. $3x^2 - 3x - 8$　**3.** $9x^2 + 4x + 5$
5. $5x^2 - 11x + 3$　**7.** $m^2 - 9$　**9.** $7x^3 - 9x^2 + 9x$
11. $-m^3 + 5m$　**13.** $8a^4 + a^2$　**15.** $2a^2 + a - 1$
17. $7b^3 - 2b^2 - b + 8$　**19.** $10a^3 + 2a^2 -$
$12a - 4$　**21.** $3a^4 - 7a^3 + 2a^2 + a - 6$
23. $-22m^9 - m^6 - 3$　**25.** $a^4 + 12a^3 - 10a^2 +$
$13a - 19$

Page 126

1. 6, 8, 10　**3.** $-8, -2, 6, 20$　**5.** Follow the
flow chart on page 126, but change $x > y$ to
$y > x$; or after the question, "Is $x > y$?",
exchange Yes and No branches; so Yes branch
becomes No branch, No branch becomes Yes
branch.

Page 129

1. $3f^4 - 5f^3 + 4f^2$　**3.** $2a^3 - 5a^2 + 4a$
5. $6x^5 - 14x^4$　**7.** $24b^3 - 30b^2$　**9.** $20c^4 - 25c^3$
11. $-4x^2 + 5x$　**13.** $-2x^2 - 5x + 7$
15. $b^2 - 2b$　**17.** $-a^2 + a + 4$
19. $9a^3 + 15a^2 - 6a$　**21.** $-4a^4 + 12a^3 + 16a^2$
23. $m^3 + m^2 + 5m$　**25.** $x^3 + 8x^2 - 12x + 9$
27. $2x^3 + x - 9$　**29.** $x^5 + x^3 - 8x + 7$
31. $3a^2 - 2a - 7$　**33.** $4x^2 - 9x + 17$
35. $6a^2 - 11a$　**37.** $5x^4 - 2x^3 + 4x^2 - 3$
39. $x^4 + x^3 + 3x^2 - 3x + 3$　**41.** $2m^5n^2 -$
$3m^4n^3 + m^3n^4$　**43.** $2a^3b - 6a^2b^2 + 10ab^3$
45. $-2x^3y^2 + x^2y^3 - xy^4$　**47.** $-2a^4c +$
$2a^3c^2 - 2a^2c^3 + 2ac^4$　**49.** $3m^5n^2 - 5m^4n^3 +$
$4m^3n^4$　**51.** $-2x^3y^2 + x^2y^3 - 6xy^4$

Page 131
1. no   **3.** no   **5.** 8,128

Page 133
1. $2 \cdot 2 \cdot 3$ **3.** $3 \cdot 3 \cdot 2$ **5.** $3 \cdot 3 \cdot 5$ **7.** $2 \cdot 13$
9. $5 \cdot 5 \cdot 2$ **11.** $2 \cdot 2 \cdot 11$ **13.** $5 \cdot 2 \cdot 2 \cdot 2 \cdot 2$
15. $3 \cdot 2 \cdot 2 \cdot 2 \cdot 2$ **17.** a^3 **19.** $6m^3$ **21.** $-9x^2$
23. $7x^5$ **25.** $-10x^4$ **27.** b^5 **29.** $-2b$
31. $9a^3b$ **33.** $-8a^2m^2$ **35.** $-ab$ **37.** $-x^2y^4$
39. x **41.** a^{3m} **43.** a^{2m+4}

Page 137
1. $3(x^2 + 9x + 3)$ **3.** $6(b^2 + 3b + 5)$
5. $7(a^2 - 3a + 7)$ **7.** $x^3(x^2 + x - 1)$
9. $a(2a^2 - a + 1)$ **11.** $7a(a - 4)$
13. $4a^2(a + 2)$ **15.** $6a(a - 4)$
17. $4a(a^2 - 3a + 2)$ **19.** $6x(2x^2 - x + 3)$
21. $4(m^2 - 5)$ **23.** $4m^2(m - 8)$
25. $7a^3(a^2 - 5a + 3)$ **27.** $3(a^2 + 4ab + 12b^2)$
29. $9m(2m^3 - 3m^2 - 5m + 4)$

Page 138
1. -8 **3.** 16 **5.** 36 **7.** 64 **9.** 64 **11.** a^{16}
13. $15b^3$ **15.** $-21a^5b^7$ **17.** $16b^2$
19. binomial   **21.** trinomial   **23.** $5a^2 - 2a + 8$
25. $9b^3 + 5b^2 + 5b + 7$
27. $2b^8 + 2b^7 + 2b^6$ **29.** $m^3 + 5m^2 + 2m$
31. $a^4 + 3a^3 - 3a^2 - 11a + 7$
33. $3c^2 + 2c - 1$ **35.** $-3a^4c^2 + 6a^3c^3 - 3a^2c^4 + 3ac^5$ **37.** $-3a^2 - 6a + 5$
39. $2y^3 + 2y^2 - 2y + 4$ **41.** $2 \cdot 2 \cdot 2 \cdot 2 \cdot 2$
43. a^5 **45.** a **47.** $-9ab^4$ **49.** $2(2a^2 - 4a + 3)$
51. $x(4x - 7)$ **53.** $4y(y^2 - 2y + 3)$

Page 140
1. 400   **3.** 26,300,000   **5.** 6.3×10^4
7. 1.75×10^6, or 1,750,000
9. 4.3902×10^8, or 439,020,000

Page 143
1. $6x^2 + 25x + 14$ **3.** $6m^2 + 13m + 5$
5. $8a^2 + 10a - 7$ **7.** $m^2 - 25$ **9.** $4r^2 - 9$
11. $3a^2 - 5a + 2$ **13.** $2y^2 + 3y - 20$
15. $2b^2 - b - 10$ **17.** $3x^2 - 16x - 35$
19. $9y^2 - 1$ **21.** $6a^2 + 7a - 10$
23. $4y^2 + 16my - 9m^2$ **25.** $9y^2 - 30y + 25$
27. $4x^2 + 12x + 9$ **29.** $6x^3 + 10x^2 + 5x - 3$
31. $3x^3 + 20x^2 - 2x + 35$ **33.** $3x^4 - 19x^3 - 5x^2 + 6x$ **35.** $x^2 - 14x + 49$
37. $4m^2 - 4m + 1$

Page 144
1. $a^2 + 5a + 6$ **3.** $x^2 + 7x + 10$

Page 147
1. $(2x + 5)(x + 1)$ **3.** $(5x + 2)(x + 1)$
5. $(3x - 1)(2x - 5)$ **7.** $(x + 3)(x - 2)$
9. $(x + 6)(x - 5)$ **11.** $(3x + 5)(x - 5)$
13. $(x + 5)(x + 2)$ **15.** $(a + 3)(a + 1)$
17. $(m - 5)(m - 4)$ **19.** $(a - 5)(a + 4)$
21. $(a - 9)(a + 2)$ **23.** $(b - 3)(b - 3)$
25. $(2a - 3)(a - 2)$ **27.** $(2a + 1)(a - 4)$
29. $(2a + 3)(a + 5)$ **31.** $(3x - 5)(x + 5)$
33. $(2m - 5)(m - 1)$ **35.** $(3y - 5)(y + 4)$
37. $(2b + 5)(b + 6)$ **39.** $(4y + 1)(3y + 1)$
41. $(2x + 5)(x + 9)$ **43.** $(2a - 5)(a - 10)$
45. $(2b - 5)(b - 12)$ **47.** $(5x + 3)(x - 9)$
49. $(5d - 3)(3d - 2)$ **51.** $(7b + 3)(2b - 3)$
53. $(3a - 2)(3a - 2)$ **55.** $(5x - 3)(3x - 4)$
57. $(6a + 7)(3a - 5)$

Page 149
1. $x = 3$

Page 152
1. $(x - 4)(x + 4)$ **3.** $(b - 5)(b + 5)$
5. $(b - 1)(b + 1)$ **7.** $(m + 8)(m - 8)$
9. $(2b - 7)(2b + 7)$ **11.** $(5a + 6)(5a - 6)$
13. $(7y - 2)(7y + 2)$ **15.** $(5m - 2)(5m + 2)$
17. $(2t - 5)(2t + 5)$ **19.** $(5 + x)(5 - x)$
21. $(9 - t)(9 + t)$ **23.** $(7 + b)(7 - b)$
25. $(1 - y)(1 + y)$ **27.** $(8 - 9c)(8 + 9c)$
29. $(4 - 9y)(4 + 9y)$ **31.** $(12a - 9)(12a + 9)$
33. $(5m - 12)(5m + 12)$ **35.** $(6x + 5)(6x - 5)$
37. $(13p - 4)(13p + 4)$ **39.** $(7 + 15x)(7 - 15x)$
41. $(4t - 15)(4t + 15)$
43. $(15a - 13)(15a + 13)$
45. $(11m - 15)(11m + 15)$

Page 155
1. $2(a-4)(a-1)$ **3.** $2(a+7)(a-5)$
5. $x(3x-2)(x+2)$ **7.** $2x(x+1)(x-1)$
9. $2m(2m+5)(2m-5)$ **11.** $2m(m-9)(m-1)$
13. $4a(a-5)(a+2)$ **15.** $3b(2b-5)(b+2)$
17. $2a(a+3)(a+5)$ **19.** $(2a-1)(a+7)$
21. $(2a+1)(a+1)$ **23.** $3(2x-7)(x+5)$
25. $y^2(3y+5)(y-4)$ **27.** $3a(2a-1)(2a-11)$
29. $3a(3a-2)(a+8)$ **31.** $(x-a)(m+n)$
33. $(r+t)(p-2)$ **35.** $(y+1)(p+5)(p-5)$

Page 157
1. $(a+b)(a+3b)$ **3.** $(c+6d)(c+d)$
5. $5(x-3y)(x+3y)$ **7.** $(2m-5b)(m+2b)$
9. $(2a+b)(a-5b)$ **11.** $(a-2b)(a-b)$
13. $2(a+7b)(a+3b)$ **15.** $2(y+z)(y+9z)$
17. $2(3x+2y)(x-5y)$ **19.** $b(ab-5)(ab+5)$
21. $ab(a+b)(a-b)$ **23.** $3(2x-5y)(x-7y)$
25. $2(2k-5r)(k-8r)$ **27.** $(3a-5b)(a+6b)$
29. $(3a+7b)(2a-3b)$ **31.** $(5x+3y)(2x+3y)$
33. $xy(3x-4y)(2x+5y)$

Page 160
1. $2, 3$ **3.** $1, 8$ **5.** $6, -6$ **7.** $\left\{\frac{1}{2}, -5\right\}$
9. $\left\{\frac{1}{2}, -3\right\}$ **11.** $\left\{\frac{3}{2}, -5\right\}$ **13.** $\left\{\frac{1}{3}, 7\right\}$ **15.** $\left\{\frac{1}{2}, 5\right\}$
17. $\left\{\frac{5}{2}, -\frac{5}{2}\right\}$ **19.** $\left\{\frac{3}{2}, 5\right\}$ **21.** $\left\{0, \frac{5}{3}\right\}$ **23.** $\frac{5}{3}, -7$
25. $\frac{7}{2}, -6$ **27.** $-\frac{7}{2}, -8$ **29.** 10 **31.** $0, 3, -3$
33. $0, 2, -2$ **35.** $0, 7, -7$

Page 161
1. $5{,}625$ **3.** $9{,}025$ **5.** $42{,}025$

Page 164
1. $-3, -5$ **3.** $-4, -8$ **5.** $2, -6$ **7.** $0, -9$
9. $0, -7$ **11.** $\left\{\frac{2}{3}, -\frac{2}{3}\right\}$ **13.** $\{0, -13\}$
15. $\{7, -7\}$ **17.** $\left\{\frac{2}{3}, 1\right\}$ **19.** $\left\{\frac{1}{2}, -1\right\}$
21. $\left\{\frac{1}{3}, -1\right\}$ **23.** $\left\{-\frac{3}{2}, 7\right\}$ **25.** $\left\{\frac{1}{2}, -6\right\}$
27. $\left\{\frac{5}{2}, -\frac{5}{2}\right\}$ **29.** $\frac{3}{5}, \frac{2}{3}$ **31.** $\frac{2}{3}, -\frac{5}{2}$ **33.** $\frac{5}{3}, -\frac{7}{2}$
35. $\frac{7}{2}, -\frac{5}{2}$ **37.** $0, -8$ **39.** $\frac{2}{5}, \frac{5}{2}$ **41.** $3, -3$

Page 167
1. $x+(x+1)+(x+2)=27$ **3.** $x+(x+1)+(x+2)=-15$ **5.** $x(x+2)=35$
7. $x(x+2)(x+4)=48$ **9.** $x+(x+2)+(x+4)+(x+6)=40$ **11.** $2(x+1)+x=35$
13. $2(x+2)+x=19$ **15.** $3(x+2)+2x=46$
17. $x(x+1)(x+2)=8[x+(x+1)+(x+2)]$

Page 170
1. $22, 23$ **3.** $29, 30, 31, 32, 33$ **5.** $7, 8, 9$
7. $37, 39, 41$ **9.** $-4, -3$ or $3, 4$ **11.** $4, 6$ or $-6, -4$ **13.** $7, 9$ or $-9, -7$ **15.** $-3, -2, -1$ or $2, 3, 4$ **17.** $5, 6, 7$ or $-4, -3, -2$
19. $-5, -3$ **21.** $-2, -1, 0, 1$ **23.** $-7, -6, -5, -4$ or $4, 5, 6, 7$

Page 171
1. 38.4 m

Page 172
1. $x^2+8x+15$ **3.** $2x^2+13x+15$
5. $2b^2+5b-12$ **7.** $12z^2-11z+2$
9. $15x^2+7x-4$ **11.** $2x^3+3x^2-17x+12$
13. $9a^2-30a+25$ **15.** $4x^2+12x+9$
17. $(x-3)(x-4)$ **19.** $(2a-1)(a+5)$
21. $(3y+2)(y+5)$ **23.** $(2m-5)(m+4)$
25. $(2x-3)(x-3)$ **27.** $(3x+1)(2x-1)$
29. $(a-2)(a+2)$ **31.** $(2a+5)(2a-5)$
33. $3(x+3)(x+4)$ **35.** $2(a-5)(a+4)$
37. $3k(k+6)(k-5)$ **39.** $6x(x-3)(x-1)$
41. $(x+y)(x+2y)$ **43.** $(a-7b)(a+4b)$
45. $(12x-13y)(12x+13y)$
47. $(3x-7y)(x-8y)$ **49.** $3(2x+3)(2x-3)$
51. $1, 2$ **53.** $-3, 12$ **55.** $4, 6$ **57.** $\{0, 5\}$
59. $\left\{\frac{1}{2}, -5\right\}$ **61.** $\{0, 6\}$ **63.** $8, 9$ or $-9, -8$
65. $7, 8, 9$ or $-2, -1, 0$

Page 178
1. $\frac{1}{7}$ **3.** $\frac{1}{x}$ **5.** $-\frac{1}{3}$; no reciprocal; 1; -1; -5
7. $-\frac{2}{3}$ **9.** $\frac{6}{1}$ **11.** $\frac{12}{3}$ **13.** $-\frac{6}{12}$ **15.** $-\frac{5}{17}$
17. $\frac{a-4}{a+2}$ **19.** 5 **21.** $3, -3$ **23.** $0, 5, -5$
25. $2, -2$

Page 179
1. 1   3. 1   5. $\frac{1}{6}$ 7. $\frac{1}{3}$ 9. 1

Page 183
1. $\frac{6}{48}$ 3. $-\frac{8}{45}$ 5. $\frac{10a^5}{18b^9}$ 7. $-\frac{20a^5}{9b^9}$ 9. $-\frac{x^5}{y^{11}}$

11. $\frac{x^{11}}{y^6}$ 13. $-\frac{2x^2-x-3}{2x^2+7x+6}$

15. $-\frac{2x^2+x-15}{2x^2+15x+25}$ 17. $\frac{10x-5}{x+4}$

19. $\frac{2x^2-11x-21}{x-4}$ 21. $\frac{2a^2+7a-15}{3a-7}$

23. $\frac{x^7}{m^3}$ 25. $\frac{a^2-b^2}{x^2+xy-2y^2}$ 27. $\frac{12r^2-rt-t^2}{r^2+3rt+2t^2}$

29. $-\frac{a^2-4b^2}{x^2-y^2}$ 31. $\frac{9a^2+6ab+b^2}{4a^2+4ab+b^2}$

33. $-\frac{4a^2+11ab-3b^2}{2a^2+ab-b^2}$

35. $\frac{x^3-8x^2+5x+50}{x^3+6x^2-15x-100}$

Page 186
1. $\frac{1}{3}$ 3. $-\frac{5}{12}$ 5. $\frac{a-5}{2a-1}$ 7. $\frac{b+5}{b-2}$ 9. $\frac{1}{4}$

11. $\frac{3}{b-2}$ 13. $\frac{4}{b+3}$ 15. $\frac{y-4}{y}$ 17. $\frac{3(x+2)}{2}$

19. $\frac{b}{b+7}$ 21. $\frac{3p-1}{5}$ 23. $\frac{x+4}{x-4}$ 25. $x+4$

27. $x+5$ 29. $3a-1$ 31. $-11x-3$

33. a^2-a-2

Page 190
1. $-\dfrac{1}{x+4}$ 3. $-\frac{1}{2}$ 5. $\frac{a+5}{4}$ 7. $-(x-4)$

9. -2 11. $-\dfrac{1}{c-2}$ 13. $-(a+2)$ 15. $-\dfrac{a+3}{a+8}$

17. $-\dfrac{y+6}{y+2}$ 19. $-\dfrac{x+2}{x-4}$ 21. $-\dfrac{n-4}{2(n-3)}$

23. $-\dfrac{a-b}{a+2b}$ 25. $-\dfrac{a-b}{2a-b}$ 27. $-\dfrac{a^2-b^2}{a}$

29. $-\dfrac{x^2-5}{x}$ 31. $-(b+3)(b+2)$

Page 193
1. $\dfrac{2m^3}{3n^2}$ 3. $\dfrac{a^5}{2b}$ 5. $-\dfrac{n^2(n-1)}{m^5}$

7. $2a^3b^2(x-2)$ 9. $\dfrac{b-2}{2x}$ 11. $\dfrac{1}{k(a+4)}$

13. $\dfrac{a+2}{n(a-1)}$ 15. $\dfrac{b^3(x+3)}{x-1}$ 17. $\dfrac{a(2x-1)}{b^2(2x-3)}$

19. $\dfrac{y-1}{x^4}$ 21. $\dfrac{x^5}{b+y}$ 23. $\dfrac{x-2}{b^3}$

Page 195
1. $3(x-2)$ 3. $\dfrac{3}{n+2}$ 5. $\dfrac{b+4}{2(b+2)}$ 7. $\dfrac{2b^2}{5x}$

9. $\dfrac{3x^2}{5y}$ 11. $\dfrac{-3a(x+6)}{2b^4}$ 13. $\dfrac{2(b-4)}{b-2}$

15. $\dfrac{b-5}{b-7}$ 17. $\dfrac{a+5}{2}$ 19. $\dfrac{4x}{3y^3(2a+3)}$

21. $\dfrac{3(a+2)}{a+3}$ 23. $\dfrac{6(2x+5)}{x+8}$ 25. $-\dfrac{2(c+1)}{c}$

27. $\dfrac{2(a+2)}{a-4}$ 29. $\dfrac{c}{c+d}$ 31. $\dfrac{2(x+2y)}{a^2b}$

33. $-\dfrac{3(a+3b)}{a-2b}$ 35. $-\dfrac{m+2}{2m+1}$ 37. $-\dfrac{m+1}{2}$

Page 197

1.
```
        573
        219
      5 157
      5 73
     114 6
    125,487
```
3.
```
          384.
    26)9,984
        78
        2 18
        2 08
          104
          104
```

Page 199
1. $\dfrac{x-2}{3(x+6)}$ 3. $2(a-5)$ 5. $\dfrac{5}{3a^2(a+2)}$

7. $\dfrac{-35b^4}{3a^6}$ 9. $-\dfrac{6m(5+m)}{n}$ 11. $\dfrac{5(b-2)}{2(b-3)}$

13. $-\dfrac{x-1}{x+1}$ 15. -1 17. $\dfrac{2y(x+5)}{x^2}$

19. $-\dfrac{m^7(m+1)}{8}$ 21. $\dfrac{a+3}{a+4}$

Page 200

1. $\frac{4}{5}$ **3.** $\frac{3}{2}$ **5.** $\frac{1}{a+7}$ **7.** $\frac{1}{4}$; no reciprocal;

$-\frac{1}{5}$; -3 **9.** 4 **11.** $\frac{20}{63}$ **13.** $\frac{x^2 + 2x - 15}{2x - 3}$

15. $\frac{2}{5}$ **17.** $\frac{b}{2}$ **19.** $x - 2$ **21.** -3 **23.** $-\frac{3a + 5}{a + 7}$

25. $\frac{b - 1}{x}$ **27.** $5(x - 2)$ **29.** $\frac{x^3}{y}$ **31.** $\frac{a - 9}{5(a + 7)}$

33. $-\frac{21b^5}{5a^6}$

Page 204

1. $\frac{2}{3}$ **3.** $\frac{1}{a}$ **5.** $\frac{7y}{y - 3}$ **7.** $\frac{17m}{m + 7}$ **9.** $\frac{1}{6}$

11. $\frac{1}{m - 5}$ **13.** $\frac{1}{a}$ **15.** $\frac{1}{a - 3}$ **17.** $\frac{1}{2}$

19. $\frac{3a + 2b}{7}$ **21.** $\frac{1}{x + 5}$ **23.** $\frac{a + 3}{3a + 5}$

25. $a + 3$ **27.** $4x + 3y$

Page 209

1. Joe 15, Tom 22 **3.** Louis 3, Dorothy 12
5. Sylvia 11, Martin 27 **7.** 4 yr **9.** 6 yr
11. Mona 6, Pedro 12 **13.** 13 yr **15.** 6 yr

Page 213

1. $\frac{3}{2}$ **3.** $\frac{3}{2}$ **5.** $\frac{b}{2}$ **7.** $\frac{23a}{8}$ **9.** $\frac{23a + 10}{12}$

11. $\frac{23m + 21}{28}$ **13.** $\frac{2m - 2}{3m}$ **15.** $\frac{5a + 3}{4a}$

17. $\frac{7}{3}$ **19.** $\frac{31x - 11}{15}$ **21.** $\frac{29a - 2}{6a}$

23. $\frac{23a^2 + 20a - 33}{30a}$

Page 216

1. $\frac{9a + 23}{(a - 4)(a + 4)}$ **3.** $\frac{x + 2}{x}$ **5.** $\frac{3x + 22}{x(x + 5)}$

7. $\frac{2x + 11}{(x - 3)(x + 3)}$ **9.** $\frac{3x + 11}{(x - 8)(x + 2)}$

11. $\frac{9a + 1}{(a - 1)(a + 1)}$ **13.** $\frac{10a + 12}{(2a - 5)(a + 3)}$

15. $\frac{k^2 + 3k - 5}{(k - 3)(k - 2)}$ **17.** $\frac{2m^2 + 5m - 11}{m(2m + 5)}$

Page 217

1. 9; 7 **3.** 25; 25 **5.** 1: comm., not assoc.;
2: not comm., not assoc.; 3: comm., not assoc.

Page 219

1. $\frac{2m + 3}{m}$ **3.** $\frac{3m + 2}{m}$ **5.** $\frac{7x - 10}{(x + 2)(x - 4)}$

7. $\frac{17a + 4}{(a - 3)(2a + 5)}$ **9.** $\frac{7x^2 + 8x + 3}{x^3}$

11. $\frac{7a^2 + 9a + 10}{6a^3}$ **13.** $\frac{5m^2 + 3m + 2}{m^2}$

15. $\frac{a^2 + 2a + 3}{a^2}$ **17.** $\frac{-9b^2 + 50b - 45}{15b^3}$

19. $\frac{6a^3 + 11a^2 + 14a - 2}{12a^3}$ **21.** $\frac{2m^2 + 9m - 2}{m + 5}$

23. $\frac{4x^2 - 3x - 6}{2x - 1}$ **25.** $\frac{3x^2 - 13x - 3}{3x + 2}$

27. $\frac{x^3 - 2x^2 - 14x - 1}{x - 5}$

Page 223

1. $\frac{-2}{a + 5}$ **3.** $\frac{-x^2 + 3x}{x^2 + 5x + 1}$ **5.** $\frac{-3a + 13}{(a - 5)(a - 2)}$

7. $\frac{10x - 3}{2x}$ **9.** $\frac{2a - 11}{a - 2}$ **11.** $\frac{x - 9}{(x - 2)(x - 4)}$

13. $\frac{-2b + 39}{(3b - 1)(2b + 7)}$ **15.** $\frac{9y - 10}{24y^3}$ **17.** $\frac{6}{a - 4}$

19. $\frac{-2a^2 - 2a + 7}{(a + 3)(a + 2)}$ **21.** $\frac{a^2 + 15a - 25}{(2a + 3)(a - 5)}$

23. $\frac{2a^2 - 12a - 6}{a(a - 5)}$ **25.** $\frac{a^2 - 10a + 22}{(2a - 5)(a + 4)}$

27. $\frac{y^2 - 4y - 8}{(y - 4)(2y + 3)}$

Page 226

1. $\frac{3}{x + 7}$ **3.** $\frac{2}{b - 1}$ **5.** $\frac{-b - 5}{(b - 2)(b + 1)}$

7. $\frac{a}{a - 4}$ **9.** $\frac{a}{a + 2}$ **11.** $\frac{8m + 1}{m(m - 1)}$

13. $\frac{-k^2 + 3k + 2}{(k - 6)(k - 2)}$ **15.** $\frac{m}{m - 5}$

17. $\frac{-2m^2 + 7m - 2}{(m - 5)(m - 2)}$ **19.** $\frac{6n^2 - 5n + 9}{(n + 3)(n - 3)}$

21. $\frac{a^2 + 2ab + 2a + 2b - 3b^2 + 7}{(a - b)(a + b)}$

23. $\frac{b^2 + bc + c^2}{(b + c)(b - c)}$

Page 227

1. not a group **3.** not a group

Page 228

1. $\frac{2}{3}$ **3.** $\frac{5}{8}$ **5.** $\frac{7m}{3}$ **7.** $\frac{2b+5}{2b}$ **9.** $\frac{x+6}{x}$

11. $\frac{5a+4}{(a-6)(a+4)}$ **13.** $\frac{35m+4}{5m}$

15. $\frac{-6x^2+35x+3}{14x^3}$ **17.** $\frac{x^2+2x-11}{x-3}$

19. $\frac{-4x+15}{(x-4)(x-3)}$ **21.** $\frac{8}{x-5}$ **23.** $\frac{5}{x+3}$

25. $\frac{m}{m-9}$

Page 232

1. 3 **3.** 6 **5.** 15 **7.** 10 **9.** 7 **11.** 18 **13.** 4, −4
15. 2, −2 **17.** $\frac{18}{5}$ **19.** $\frac{8}{3}$ **21.** $\{x \mid -2 < x < 2\}$
23. $\{x \mid -1 < x < 1\}$ **25.** $\{x \mid x \le -2 \text{ or } x \ge 2\}$

Page 235

1. −1, 7 **3.** 3, −1 **5.** −3, 2 **7.** $\{1, 5\}$
9. $\{3, -11\}$ **11.** $\left\{-\frac{2}{3}, 4\right\}$ **13.** $\left\{\frac{13}{2}, \frac{15}{2}\right\}$ **15.** $\{1, 6\}$
17. 0, 7 **19.** 2, −2

Page 238

1. 4 **3.** 10 **5.** 6 **7.** 18 **9.** 4 **11.** $\frac{5}{6}$ **13.** 3
15. −2

Page 241

1. (1, 3) **3.** (1, 1) **5.** (−2, −3) **7.** (−2, 2)
9. (2, −1) **11.** (4, −3) **13.** (3, 4) **15.** (−3, 1)
17. 1 **19.** 3 **21.** 2

Page 244

1. right 2, up 3 **3.** left 3, down 1 **5.** right 3
7. left 3 **9.** down 7 **11.** right 4, down 1
13. up 3 **15.** left 8 **17.** left $2\frac{1}{2}$, up $4\frac{1}{2}$ **19.** left $1\frac{1}{4}$
21. (−4, 8)

Page 245

1. coefficients of powers of $a + b$ **3.** $a^6 + 6a^5b + 15a^4b^2 + 20a^3b^3 + 15a^2b^4 + 6ab^5 + b^6$;
$a^7 + 7a^6b + 21a^5b^2 + 35a^4b^3 + 35a^3b^4 + 21a^2b^5 + 7ab^6 + b^7$

Page 247

1. x-axis **3.** x-axis **5.** y-axis **7.** x-axis
9. y-axis **11.** 2 **13.** 4 **15.** 3 **17.** 3, 4

Page 250

1. −7 **3.** 1 **5.** −8 **7.** −3 **9.** −11 **11.** 8
13. −6 **15.** −23 **17.** 29 **19.** $-\frac{5}{4}$ **21.** $\frac{13}{6}$
23. $\frac{19}{15}$ **25.** .8 **27.** $-\frac{23}{8}$ **29.** −8a **31.** −3k
33. $-\frac{5m}{6}$

Page 254

1. $\frac{3}{4}$ **3.** $\frac{2}{3}$ **5.** $\frac{3}{10}$ **7.** $-\frac{4}{15}$ **9.** 0 **11.** $-\frac{2t}{7i}$
13. $-\frac{k}{b}$

Page 257

1. undefined; vertical **3.** 0; horizontal
5. $\frac{5}{8}$; up to the right **7.** undefined; vertical
9. 0; horizontal **11.** yes **13.** yes **15.** no
17. no **19.** yes

Page 258

1. 6 **3.** 14 **5.** 7, −7 **7.** 1, $\frac{7}{3}$ **9.** 9 **11.** $-\frac{3}{2}$
13. (5, 1) **15.** (1, −3) **17.** (−4, −1)
19. (−3, 2) **21.** (−2, 0) **23.** 2; left 3, up 2
25. on y-axis; up 3 **27.** y-axis **29.** −5 **31.** 11
33. 5 **35.** 0; horizontal **37.** undefined; vertical
39. yes

Page 263

1. $\frac{10}{3}$ **3.** $\frac{21}{2}$ **5.** $\frac{15}{4}$ **7.** 4 **9.** $\frac{15}{16}$ **11.** 2,310
13. 320 **15.** 8, −8 **17.** 2, 5 **19.** 9, 24
21. 49, 21

Page 267

1. $y = 2x - 1$ **3.** $y = 2x - 5$ **5.** $y = x + 4$
7. $y = 4x - 2$ **9.** $y = -2x - 2$ **11.** $y = 3x + 4$
13. $y = -3x + 4$ **15.** $y = 2x - 8$
17. $-2(-3) - 5 = 1$ **19.** $y = 4x$; $12 = 4(3)$
21. $y = 3x - 5$; $4 = 3(3) - 5$ **23.** $y = 2x + 5$
25. $y = x$

Page 269

1. $y = \frac{3}{2}x + \frac{1}{2}$ **3.** $y = \frac{1}{4}x + \frac{9}{2}$ **5.** $y = -\frac{2}{5}x + \frac{21}{5}$
7. $y = \frac{4}{5}x + \frac{8}{5}$ **9.** $y = \frac{5}{2}x + 5$ **11.** $y = \frac{2}{3}x - 3$; 1
13. $y = \frac{3}{2}x + 2$; -1 **15.** $(-1, -5)$, $(0, -3)$,
$(1, -1)$ **17.** $(-2, -3)$, $(0, -2)$, $(2, -1)$
19. $(-4, 0)$, $(0, -1)$, $(4, -2)$ **21.** $y = \frac{1}{2}x + 5$;
$(-2, 4)$, $(0, 5)$, $(2, 6)$ **23.** $y = \frac{1}{2}x - 6$; $(-2, -7)$,
$(0, -6)$, $(2, -5)$ **25.** $y = \frac{2}{3}x + 1$; $(-3, -1)$,
$(0, 1)$, $(3, 3)$ **27.** $-\frac{1}{2}$ **29.** $-\frac{1}{8}$

Page 271
1. $21.00

Page 275
1. $\frac{1}{2}$; -7 **3.** $-\frac{4}{5}$; 7 **5.** $y = 2x + 4$ **7.** $y = 5x$
9. $(-4, 5)$, $(4, -1)$ **11.** $(0, 1)$, $(1, 4)$
13. $(1, 2)$, $(2, 0)$ **15.** $(1, 1)$, $(2, -3)$
17. $(-3, 7)$, $(3, -3)$ **19.** $(0, 0)$, $(2, 4)$
21. $(-3, 9)$, $(3, -9)$ **23.** $y = -\frac{4}{5}x - 2$; $(0, -2)$,
$(5, -6)$

Page 278
1. $\left(2, \frac{3}{2}\right)$, $\left(4, \frac{9}{2}\right)$ **3.** $(-5, 0)$, $(5, -4)$
5. $(0, 6)$, $(2, 6)$ **7.** $(-3, 2)$, $(3, 6)$ **9.** $(-1, 6)$,
$(1, 2)$ **11.** $(2, 10)$, $(4, 15)$ **13.** $(-1, 2)$, $(1, 4)$
15. $(-1, 2)$, $(1, -2)$ **17.** $\left(-3, -\frac{10}{3}\right)$, $\left(3, \frac{2}{3}\right)$

Page 280
1. $(-2, -1)$, $(-2, 0)$, $(-2, 1)$ **3.** $(-3, -1)$,
$(-3, 0)$, $(-3, 1)$ **5.** $(3, -1)$, $(3, 0)$, $(3, 1)$
7. $(7, -1)$, $(7, 0)$, $(7, 1)$ **9.** $(3, -1)$, $(3, 0)$,
$(3, 1)$ **11.** $(6, -1)$, $(6, 0)$, $(6, 1)$

Page 284
1. $y < -x + 3$ **3.** $y > -x - 3$ **5.** $y > -\frac{3}{2}x$
7. $y < 3x + 4$ (Two points of the boundary line
are given.) **9.** above; $(0, 3)$, $(2, 3)$
11. below and including; $(0, -4)$, $(2, -4)$
13. below; $(0, 0)$, $(1, 3)$ **15.** below and
including; $(0, 0)$, $(2, 2)$ **17.** below and
including; $(0, 5)$, $(2, 7)$ **19.** below; $(0, -3)$,
$(2, -5)$ **21.** below and including; $(0, 1)$, $(2, 5)$
23. to the left of; $(0, 0)$, $(0, 2)$ **25.** below;
$(0, 1)$, $(3, 3)$ **27.** below and including; $(0, 1)$,
$(2, 2)$ **29.** above; $(0, 1)$, $(2, 1)$; $(3, 7)$
31. above; $(0, -6)$, $(2, -4)$; $(3, 8)$ **33.** below
and including; $(0, 1)$, $(2, 7)$; $(3, 0)$ **35.** below;
$(0, 4)$, $(2, 4)$ **37.** below and including; $(0, 0)$,
$(2, 3)$ **39.** above and including; $(0, -3)$, $(2, 0)$
41. below and including; $(0, -2)$, $(3, 2)$
43. above and including; $(0, -3)$, $(5, 0)$
45. above; $\left(0, \frac{1}{2}\right)$, $\left(2, -\frac{7}{2}\right)$ **47.** above and
including; $(0, 3)$, $(4, 6)$ **49.** above $y = 6$;
below and including $y = 9$

Page 286
1. extremes x, 3; means 4, 6; 8 **3.** extremes
$x + 2$, 3; means 4, $x - 5$; 26 **5.** extremes
$2x + 1$, 4; means 5, x; $-\frac{4}{3}$ **7.** extremes x, x;
means 1, 9; 3, -3 **9.** 6,000 **11.** $y = 2x - 5$
13. $y = -2x + 6$ **15.** $y = \frac{1}{3}x + \frac{11}{3}$ **17.** $y = 2x$;
$8 = 2(4)$ **19.** $y = \frac{2}{3}x - 5$ **21.** $y = 3x - 1$
23. $-\frac{4}{5}$; 2; $(-5, 6)$, $(5, -2)$ **25.** 2; 1; $(-1, -1)$,
$(1, 3)$ **27.** 0; -6; $(-1, -6)$, $(1, -6)$
29. $(-1, 3)$, $(1, 5)$ **31.** $(3, 0)$, $(3, 3)$
33. $(-2, 0)(-2, 1)$ **35.** below; $(4, 2)$, $(0, -4)$

Page 291

1. $(2, -3)$ **3.** $(0, 4)$ **5.** $(2, 6)$ **7.** $(2, 5)$
9. $(3, 6)$ **11.** inconsistent **13.** inconsistent
15. 3 **17.** 10

Page 293

For each of the following, the two points given lie on the line. They are not necessarily part of the graph. **1.** to the left of the line containing $(4, 0)$, $(4, 1)$ and above and including the line containing $(0, -2)$, $(1, -2)$; $(3, 1)$ **3.** above and including the line containing $(0, 2)$, $(1, 2)$ and to the left of the line containing $(-5, 0)$, $(-5, 1)$ **5.** above the line containing $(0, 5)$, $(1, 6)$ and to the left of and including the line containing $(2, 0)$, $(2, 1)$ **7.** below the line containing $(1, 1)(2, 2)$ and above and including the line containing $(3, -3)$, $(0, -5)$ **9.** above the line containing $(0, -3)$, $(1, -1)$ and above the line containing $(0, -3)$, $(9, 0)$

Page 296

1. $(3, 6)$ **3.** $(3, 1)$ **5.** $(3, 0)$ **7.** $(2, 0)$
9. $\left(\frac{11}{2}, -\frac{1}{2}\right)$ **11.** $\left(\frac{5}{2}, 5\right)$ **13.** $\left(-1, -\frac{2}{5}\right)$
15. $\left(-3, -\frac{8}{5}\right)$

Page 299

1. $(6, 2)$ **3.** $(2, 2)$ **5.** $(2, 1)$ **7.** $(2, 2)$
9. $(3, 2)$ **11.** $(3, 2)$ **13.** $(3, 6)$ **15.** $(15, 10)$

Page 302

1. $(2, 1)$ **3.** $(2, 2)$ **5.** $(5, 1)$ **7.** $(1, 1)$
9. $(2, 1)$ **11.** $(2, 2)$ **13.** $(-2, 6)$ **15.** $\left(1, \frac{13}{2}\right)$
17. $(3, 2)$ **19.** $(-18, 8)$ **21.** $\left(\frac{58}{27}, \frac{1}{9}\right)$
23. $\left(\frac{4}{5}, -\frac{4}{25}\right)$

Page 305

1. 11 kg; 1,260¢ **3.** $(x + y)$ kg; $(158x + 210y)$¢
5. $(x + y)$ kg; $(4x + 78y)$¢ **7.** $(x + y)$ kg;
$(135x + my)$¢ **9.** $(x + y)$ kg; $(px + qy)$¢

Page 308

1. $x + y = 7$; $90x + 130y = 750$ **3.** $y = x + 2$;
$5x + 15y = 130$ **5.** $x = y - 2$; $230x +$
$170y = 740$ **7.** 5 kg at $.50, 4 kg at $.70
9. 2 at $.15, 9 at $.35 **11.** 4 kg at $1.60,
8 kg at $1.80 **13.** 3 at $.20, 4 at $.15
15. 8 kg at $.80, 5 kg at $1.60 **17.** 5 kg at
$1.20, 2 kg at $1.80

Page 312

1. 10, 40 **3.** 6, 12 **5.** 4, 13 **7.** 5, 17
9. 8, 12 **11.** width 7 m, length 14 m
13. width 10 km, length 68 km

Page 314

1. $(5, 3)$ **3.** $(4,4)$ **5.** inconsistent
7. consistent **9.** $(3, 1)$ **11.** $(5, -1)$ **13.** $(3, 6)$
15. $(6, 0)$ **17.** 3 kg at $1.50, 2 kg at $1.90
19. 2 sheets at $.40, 4 sheets at $.30
21. 16, 24 **23.** 5, 13

Page 316
1. They land at the same time. **3.** 5 seconds

Page 319

1. $\{(-4, 5), (-2, -2), (3, 2), (3, 4), (5, 1)\}$;
$D = \{-4, -2, 3, 5\}$; $R = \{5, -2, 2, 4, 1\}$; no
3. $\{(-1, -3), (0, -2), (2, 0), (3, 1), (4, 2)\}$;
$D = \{-1, 0, 2, 3, 4\}$; $R = \{-3, -2, 0, 1, 2\}$; yes
5. $D = \{3, 4, -1, 0\}$; $R = \{2\}$; yes
7. $D = \{3, -3, 0\}$; $R = \{0, 3, -3\}$; no
9. $D = \{-1, -2, 0, 1, 2\}$; $R = \{-1, -2, 0, 1, 2\}$;
yes **11.** $\{(4, -2), (1, -1), (4, 0)\}$; yes; no
13. $\{(1, -1), (1, -2), (1, 0), (1, 1), (1, 2)\}$; yes;
no **15.** $-6, 6$

Page 321

(Two points belonging to each relation are given.)   **1.** (0, 0), (1, 3); function; linear function
3. (0, 0), (1, 1); function; linear function
5. (−4, 0), (−4, −2)   **7.** (3, 0), (3, 2)
9. (0, −3), (2, 1); function; linear function
11. (−1, 0), (2, 1); function; linear function
13. (0, 0), (2, 0); function; constant function
15. (0, −2), (1, 1); function; linear function
17. (−1, 0), (1, −1); function; linear function
19. (4, 0), (0, 4); function; linear function
21. (4, 0), (4, 2)   **23.** $\left(1, -\frac{3}{4}\right), \left(-2, \frac{3}{4}\right)$;
function; linear function   **25.** (−4, 0), (2, 2);
function; linear function   **27.** (0, −3), (2, −3);
function; constant function   **29.** (0, 5), (−1, 2);
function; linear function   **31.** (−2, 4), (0, 0),
(2, 4); function   **33.** (−1, −2), (0, −3), (1, −2);
function   **35.** (−2, −12), (0, 0), (2, −12);
function   **37.** (4, 2), (0, 0), (4, −2)   **39.** (12, 2),
(0, 0), (12, −2)   **41.** (6, −2), (2, 0), (6, 2)
43. (−2, −8), (−1, −1), (0, 0), (1, 1), (2, 8);
function   **45.** (−2, −24), (−1, −3), (0, 0),
(1, 3), (2, 24); function   **47.** (1, −1), (0, 0),
(1, 1)

Page 324

1. −2   **3.** −8   **5.** −68   **7.** −13   **9.** 35
11. −5   **13.** 11   **15.** 395   **17.** $R = \{-16, 8, 26\}$
19. $R = \{18, 32, 46\}$ **21.** $R = \{131, 101, 75\}$
23. $R = \{-3, 7, 52\}$ **25.** $R = \{5.5, 5.2, 4.9\}$
27. $R = \{25, 49, 81\}$ **29.** $R = \left\{-4\frac{3}{4}, -4\frac{15}{16}\right\}$
31. 20   **33.** 54   **35.** 172   **37.** 151

Page 329

1. 96   **3.** 84   **5.** 93   **7.** 38   **9.** 49   **11.** 72

Page 332

1. 6 or $\frac{1}{6}$ **3.** −4 or $-\frac{1}{4}$ **5.** −2 or $-\frac{1}{2}$ **7.** 14
9. −54   **11.** 437.5 km   **13.** $208.33
15. 10 cups   **17.** $13\frac{1}{3}$ m by $16\frac{2}{3}$ m   **19.** $\frac{135}{4}$
21. 550 m

Page 336

1. 18   **5.** −1   **7.** 4   **9.** 180 cm   **11.** 9 m
13. $4\frac{1}{6}$ hr   **15.** $750   **17.** 24 cm   **19.** $5\frac{1}{3}$ m
21. 2.2 m   **23.** 18

Page 338

1. {(−1, −3), (0, −1), (1, 1), (2, 3), (3, 5)};
$D = \{-1, 0, 1, 2, 3\}$; $R = \{-3, -1, 1, 3, 5\}$; yes
3. {(−4, 1), (−2, −2), (3, 1), (4, −2)};
$D = \{-4, -2, 3, 4\}$; $R = \{-2, 1\}$; yes
5. $D = \{-2, -1, 0, 1, 2\}$; $R = \{1\}$; yes (Two
points of the boundary line are given.)
7. (4, 0), (4, 2)   **9.** (0, −1), (1, 2); function;
linear function   **11.** (0, 1), (2, 9), (−1, 3);
function   **13.** 12   **15.** 39   **17.** $R = \{-2, 1, -5\}$
19. direct variation; 3   **25.** −10   **27.** 150 cm

Page 344

1. −3   **3.** $\frac{5}{4}$ **5.** $\frac{41}{10}$ **7.** $-\frac{10}{9}$ **9.** −84   **11.** {13}
13. {1}   **15.** {1}

Page 345

1. 24.96   **3.** 11.78   **5.** $2.99

Page 348

1. $\frac{27}{2}$ **3.** −19   **5.** $\frac{11}{5}$ **7.** $\left\{\frac{45}{2}\right\}$ **9.** $\left\{\frac{15}{13}\right\}$
11. {11}   **13.** {1, 3}   **15.** −1   **17.** 5

Page 352

1. Jake $\frac{3}{5}$; Bill $\frac{3}{x}$ **3.** Maria $\frac{12}{x}$; Todd $\frac{6}{x}$
5. Lester $\frac{7}{m}$; Jim $\frac{14}{m + 1}$ **7.** Mark $\frac{3}{3m + 1}$;
Stuart $\frac{3}{m - 4}$ **9.** Joan $\frac{5}{7}$; Helene $\frac{2}{7}$
11. Eleanor $\frac{x}{5}$; Ted $\frac{x}{10}$ **13.** Donald $\frac{5}{x}$; Merv $\frac{5}{3x}$

Page 355

1. $1\frac{5}{7}$ hr   **3.** $7\frac{1}{2}$ hr   **5.** $1\frac{1}{3}$ hr   **7.** Josephine
8 hr; Lois 24 hr   **9.** $1\frac{13}{47}$ hr   **11.** $2\frac{2}{5}$ hr
13. 10 hr

Page 356

1. 20%   **3.** 58%   **5.** 50   **7.** $200

Page 360

1. $\frac{20}{3}$ 3. 1,805   5. .31   7. 307.5   9. -140

11. 10.02   13. $\frac{15}{2}$ 15. 5   17. $-296\frac{1}{3}$ 19. .033

Page 363

1. $\frac{-1}{1}$ 3. $\frac{-16}{1}$ 5. $\frac{-24}{36}$ 7. $\frac{-364}{100}$ 9. $\frac{4}{9}$

11. $\frac{34}{45}$ 13. $\frac{32}{9}$ 15. $\frac{16}{99}$ 17. $\frac{83}{99}$ 19. $\frac{98}{99}$

21. $\frac{306,483}{99,900}$

Page 367

1. \$375   3. \$1,200 at 5%, \$600 at 6%
5. \$600 at 4%, \$1,200 at 6%   7. \$500 at 5%,
\$800 at 6%   9. \$6,000 at 5%, \$4,000 at
$4\frac{1}{2}$%   11. \$7,000

Page 370

1. $\frac{14}{5}$ 3. $\frac{5}{11}$ 5. $\frac{5(6a+1)}{2a+3}$ 7. $\frac{12a+1}{6a+1}$

9. $\frac{40a-6a^2}{15a^2+70}$ 11. $\frac{3-5a}{2a+1}$ 13. $x+1$

15. $\frac{1}{m-8}$

Page 373

1. $\frac{2a-1}{6a-18}$ 3. $\frac{3x-2}{9x-34}$ 5. $\frac{2}{7}$ 7. $\frac{a^2+4a-8}{a-4}$

9. $\frac{x^2-6x+10}{x-3}$ 11. $\frac{5x-8}{4x-9}$ 13. $\frac{-3x-2}{7x-6}$

15. $\frac{1}{4}$ 17. $\frac{2}{2x+5}$ 19. $\frac{a+b}{a-b}$

21. $\frac{2x^2+9xy-19y^2}{3x}$

Page 376

1. $x=\frac{2}{a}$ 3. $x=a$ 5. $x=-3a$ 7. $x=4a$

9. $x=\frac{d+c}{2}$ 11. $x=\frac{3b-4a}{2}$ 13. $x=\frac{8}{k+2}$

15. $\frac{b}{2a}$ 17. $x=\frac{3b+c}{2}$ 19. $x=\frac{2ab}{c}$

21. $\frac{p}{4}$; 7   23. $s=\frac{p-b}{2}$; 19   25. $r=\frac{C}{2\pi}$; 2m

27. $h=\frac{V}{lw}$; 4 cm   29. $x=\frac{3c-5a}{2b}$

31. $x=\frac{2d+4c}{a}$ 33. $x=\frac{4b+2}{5b}$ 35. $x=a+2$

37. $x=a+b$ 39. $h=\frac{3V}{\pi r^2}$; 6 km

41. $p=\frac{A}{rt+1}$; 120   43. $a=3A-b-c$; 31

Page 377

1. $\frac{10}{3}\Omega$ 3. $\frac{600}{7}\Omega$

Page 378

1. -1 3. $\frac{-1}{3}$ 5. $-1, -2$ 7. $\frac{45}{4}$ hr   9. $\frac{28}{3}$ mo;

28 mo   11. $\frac{700}{3}$ 13. -230 15. $\frac{0}{1}$ 17. $\frac{42}{9}$

19. $\frac{2}{11}$ 21. $\frac{9+15b}{6b+7}$ 23. $\frac{10a-12}{7}$

25. $\frac{x^2-7x+13}{2x-1}$ 27. $\frac{tr-5a}{m}$ 29. $-a$

31. $\frac{4k}{d^2}$; 7

Page 383

1. R **3.** R **5.** I **7.** R **9.** I **11.** R **13.** I
15. R **17.** R **19.** R **21.** Answers may vary.
23. Answers may vary. **25.** irrational
27. irrational **29.** F **31.** T **33.** T

Page 386

1. 6.1 m **3.** 7.4 m, 14.8 m **5.** 5.5 m,
16.5 m **7.** 5.3 cm **9.** 33.0 m, 6.6 m
11. 2.8 cm

Page 390

1. 5.1 **3.** 6.9 **5.** 9.4 **7.** 4.2 **9.** 7.2 **11.** 3.5
13. 6.1 **15.** 5.7 **17.** 8.2 **19.** 8.4 **21.** 9.1
23. 10.8 **25.** 14.1

Page 393

1. $\sqrt{10}$ **3.** $\sqrt{30}$ **5.** $\sqrt{14}$ **7.** 32 **9.** 35
11. $2\sqrt{3}$ **13.** $3\sqrt{3}$ **15.** $7\sqrt{2}$ **17.** $-4\sqrt{15}$
19. $8\sqrt{2}$ **21.** $5\sqrt{3}$; 8.7 **23.** $-6\sqrt{5}$; -13.4
25. $18\sqrt{5}$; 40.2 **27.** $-14\sqrt{7}$ **29.** $-38\sqrt{5}$
31. $102\sqrt{11}$

Page 395

1. x^4y^2 **3.** cd^4 **5.** $-3y^2$ **7.** $-9ab^3$
9. $-2c^5d$ **11.** $3a^3b^4$ **13.** $a^2b^3c^4$ **15.** $-c^2de^6$
17. $3a^3b^4c$ **19.** $8a^2b^6c^6$ **21.** $6c^4d^5e^6$
23. $5a^6b^5c^2$ **25.** $11c^4d^3e$ **27.** $12a^4bc^8$
29. $-3a^2b^5\sqrt{3}$ **31.** $-4a^3b^6\sqrt{2}$
33. $-4a^5b^6\sqrt{3}$ **35.** $3a^6b^7c\sqrt{5}$
37. $-7a^2b^4c^8\sqrt{2}$ **39.** $-9x^4yz^9\sqrt{3}$
41. $-1.3ab^4c^{10}$ **43.** $\frac{1}{5}x^5yz^6$ **45.** $-\frac{9}{4}ab^{18}c^{50}$

Page 397

1. $x\sqrt{x}$ **3.** $3x^2\sqrt{x}$ **5.** $2x^2\sqrt{2x}$ **7.** $x\sqrt{7x}$
9. $x^2y^3\sqrt{y}$ **11.** $-c^3d\sqrt{d}$ **13.** $x^2y^3\sqrt{xy}$
15. $c\sqrt{cd}$ **17.** $a^2b^4\sqrt{a}$ **19.** $xy^2\sqrt{5x}$
21. $6x\sqrt{y}$ **23.** $x^3y^4\sqrt{6y}$ **25.** $x^2y^4\sqrt{19xy}$
27. $-5mn^2\sqrt{2m}$ **29.** $8yz^3\sqrt{11x}$
31. $12a^2c^6\sqrt{7b}$ **33.** $-c^3d^3e^3\sqrt{d}$
35. $-3xy^3\sqrt{xyz}$ **37.** $-5b^3c^3d^4\sqrt{bc}$
39. $-48x^2y^5\sqrt{2y}$ **41.** xy^3 **43.** $-cd^4$
45. $2ab^3$ **47.** $-4ab^2\sqrt[3]{a}$ **49.** $-2b^2\sqrt[3]{5a^2b^2}$
51. $4x^2z^4\sqrt[3]{3xy}$ **53.** xy^3 **55.** $-2x^2y$
57. $3xy^2\sqrt[5]{x}$ **59.** $-2b\sqrt[5]{3a^2b^2c^3}$
61. $-4acde\sqrt[5]{5de^2}$ **63.** $18xy^2z^2\sqrt[3]{2x^2yz^2}$

Page 398

1. 2.24

Page 401

1. no **3.** no **5.** no **7.** no **9.** $c = 10$
11. $b = 12$ **13.** $a = 4\sqrt{3}$ **15.** $b = 48$
17. $c = 2\sqrt{5}$ **19.** 2.6 m **21.** 5.7 m **23.** 4.2 m

Page 403

1. $9\sqrt{5}$ **3.** $15\sqrt{6}$ **5.** $\sqrt{10}$ **7.** $2\sqrt{6} + 6\sqrt{3}$
9. $12\sqrt{5} - 6\sqrt{7}$ **11.** $8\sqrt{5} - 3\sqrt{2}$
13. $7\sqrt{2}$ **15.** $-5\sqrt{6}$ **17.** $2\sqrt{11}$ **19.** $9\sqrt{a}$
21. $7\sqrt{mn}$ **23.** $-3\sqrt{xy}$ **25.** $4x\sqrt{3z} - x\sqrt{5z}$
27. $-21ab\sqrt{ab}$ **29.** $4\sqrt{3x}$ **31.** cannot
simplify **33.** $-11\sqrt{10x}$ **35.** $8xy\sqrt{5x}$
37. $.6y\sqrt{x}$ **39.** $.22xy\sqrt{x}$ **41.** $3.56ab\sqrt{ab}$

Page 405

1. $40\sqrt{3}$ **3.** $24\sqrt{30}$ **5.** $15\sqrt{30}$ **7.** $2x$ **9.** y
11. $-72y$ **13.** 0 **15.** $-20\sqrt{3} - 60\sqrt{2}$
17. $16 - \sqrt{6}$ **19.** $34 + 24\sqrt{6}$ **21.** 2
23. -30 **25.** $19 + 4\sqrt{21}$ **27.** $26 - 4\sqrt{30}$
29. $62 + 24\sqrt{3}$ **31.** $522 - 72\sqrt{7}$
33. $120 - 80\sqrt{2}$ **35.** $10 + 2\sqrt{6} - 2\sqrt{15} - 2\sqrt{10}$

Page 410

1. $\frac{\sqrt{2}}{2}$ **3.** $\sqrt{5}$ **5.** $2\sqrt{3}$ **7.** $\sqrt{3}$ **9.** $\frac{\sqrt{10}}{2}$
11. $\frac{4\sqrt{x}}{x^3}$ **13.** $\frac{2\sqrt{m}}{m^2}$ **15.** $\frac{6\sqrt{x}}{x}$ **17.** $\frac{3\sqrt{2a}}{2a^3}$
19. $\frac{\sqrt{6x}}{2x}$ **21.** $5y\sqrt{x}$ **23.** $\frac{3\sqrt{y}}{y}$
25. $12x^2y^2\sqrt{xy}$ **27.** $y\sqrt{2y}$ **29.** $\frac{\sqrt{5a}}{5}$
31. $\frac{15 + 5\sqrt{3}}{6}$ **33.** $\frac{\sqrt{30} + 2\sqrt{3}}{6}$ **35.** $-\sqrt{7} - 2$

Page 412

1. $\frac{3}{4}$ **3.** $\frac{10}{9}$ **5.** $\frac{11}{5}$ **7.** $\frac{3\sqrt{6}}{5}$ **9.** $\frac{\sqrt{67}}{9}$ **11.** $\frac{\sqrt{6}}{4}$

13. $\frac{\sqrt{15}}{6}$ **15.** $\frac{\sqrt{110}}{20}$ **17.** $\frac{4\sqrt{x}}{x^2}$ **19.** $\frac{\sqrt{30y}}{5y^2}$

21. $\frac{3\sqrt{6xy}}{y^3}$ **23.** $\frac{\sqrt{2x}}{2x^2}$ **25.** $\frac{\sqrt{3z}}{3xz}$ **27.** $\frac{\sqrt{77}}{7y}$

29. $\frac{y\sqrt{14yz}}{z}$ **31.** $\frac{\sqrt{4x+6}}{2}$ **33.** $\frac{\sqrt{28x+49}}{7}$

35. $\frac{\sqrt{15-25z}}{5}$ **37.** $\frac{\sqrt{6z^2+9}}{3}$ **39.** $\frac{y+3}{y}$

Page 413
1. $340.75

Page 414
1. I **3.** R **5.** I **7.** I **9.** 6.8 cm **11.** 5.9 cm; 11.8 cm **13.** yes; 8.6 **15.** no **17.** yes; 7.9 **19.** 36 **21.** $8a^2b^5$ **23.** $12cd^2e^5$ **25.** $-6x^5y^5\sqrt{3xy}$ **27.** $4xyz^2\sqrt[3]{xy^2}$ **29.** no **31.** yes **33.** $a = 3$ **35.** $-\sqrt{5}$ **37.** $15x - 10\sqrt{x}$ **39.** -2 **41.** $2\sqrt{2}$ **43.** $6y^2\sqrt{2xy}$ **45.** $5x$ **47.** $\frac{\sqrt{12x+6}}{3}$

Page 416
1. $3^2 + 4^2 = 5^2, 5^2 + 12^2 = 13^2, 7^2 + 24^2 = 25^2, 9^2 + 40^2 = 41^2, 11^2 + 60^2 = 61^2$ **3.** 13, 84, 85; 15, 112, 113; 17, 144, 145

Page 419
1. {9} **3.** {20} **5.** $\left\{\frac{1}{16}\right\}$ **7.** {2} **9.** 1 **11.** no solution **13.** $\frac{79}{3}$ **15.** 4 **17.** no solution **19.** 12 **21.** $-3, -2$ **23.** 2 **25.** 25 **27.** 2 **29.** 1 **31.** 4

Page 421
1. {1, −1} **3.** {2, −2} **5.** {7, −7} **7.** {3, −3} **9.** {8, −8} **11.** ϕ **13.** $\{\sqrt{15}, -\sqrt{15}\}$ **15.** $\{\sqrt{13}, -\sqrt{13}\}$ **17.** $\{2\sqrt{6}, -2\sqrt{6}\}$ **19.** $\{3\sqrt{2}, -3\sqrt{2}\}$ **21.** ϕ **23.** $-1, -9$ **25.** $\frac{\sqrt{15}}{3}, -\frac{\sqrt{15}}{3}$ **27.** $\frac{\sqrt{65}}{5}, -\frac{\sqrt{65}}{5}$ **29.** 5, −5 **31.** $-3 + 2\sqrt{2}, -3 - 2\sqrt{2}$ **33.** $-6 + 2\sqrt{7}, -6 - 2\sqrt{7}$ **35.** $7 + 2\sqrt{6}, 7 - 2\sqrt{6}$ **37.** $\left\{\frac{5+2\sqrt{3}}{2}, \frac{5-2\sqrt{3}}{2}\right\}$ **39.** $\left\{\frac{1+\sqrt{5}}{2}, \frac{1-\sqrt{5}}{2}\right\}$

Page 425
1. $\{-8, -2\}$ **3.** $\{-1, -15\}$ **5.** $\{4 + \sqrt{11}, 4 - \sqrt{11}\}$ **7.** $\{-5 + \sqrt{10}, -5 - \sqrt{10}\}$ **9.** $\{7, -3\}$ **11.** {2} **13.** {7, −11} **15.** {2, 14} **17.** {6, 12} **19.** {13, −3} **21.** {−3, −17} **23.** {6, 10} **25.** {21, −1} **27.** $\{-15 + \sqrt{70}, -15 - \sqrt{70}\}$ **29.** {−8, −1} **31.** {5, −10} **33.** {3, −2} **35.** {5, −6} **37.** {3, −4} **39.** {7, −2} **41.** {15, 2} **43.** {7, −8} **45.** {−4, −7} **47.** {12, 7} **49.** {2, 19} **51.** {2, −17} **53.** {20, 5} **55.** $\left\{\frac{-7 \pm \sqrt{37}}{2}\right\}$ **57.** $\left\{\frac{-5 \pm \sqrt{21}}{2}\right\}$ **59.** $\left\{\frac{-5 \pm \sqrt{29}}{2}\right\}$ **61.** $\left\{\frac{1 \pm \sqrt{13}}{2}\right\}$ **63.** $\left\{\frac{-7 \pm \sqrt{33}}{2}\right\}$ **65.** ϕ

Page 429
1. $2x^2 + 6x + 5 = 0; a = 2, b = 6, c = 5$ **3.** $2x^2 - 4x - 8 = 0; a = 2, b = -4, c = -8$ **5.** $x^2 + 2x + 0 = 0; a = 1, b = 2, c = 0$ **7.** $x^2 + 0x - 5 = 0; a = 1, b = 0, c = -5$ **9.** $3x^2 - 6x - 2 = 0; a = 3, b = -6, c = -2$ **11.** $5x^2 - 3x + 0 = 0; a = 5, b = -3, c = 0$ **13.** $-3, -1$ **15.** 1 **17.** 7, −3 **19.** 5, −8 **21.** 4 **23.** {1, −11} **25.** {6, −5} **27.** {−1, −4} **29.** {2, −2} **31.** {2, −1} **33.** {18, −2}

Page 433
1. 3 L **3.** 6 L **5.** 87.5 L **7.** 48 L **9.** 6.5 L **11.** 2 dL **13.** 7.5 dL

1. $\left\{-3, \frac{1}{2}\right\}$ **3.** $\left\{-\frac{1}{2}, \frac{2}{3}\right\}$ **5.** $\left\{\frac{3}{2}, 4\right\}$ **7.** $\left\{-2, \frac{1}{3}\right\}$

9. $\left\{\frac{10}{3}\right\}$ **11.** $\left\{\frac{7 \pm \sqrt{37}}{2}\right\}$ **13.** ϕ

15. $\left\{\frac{-5 \pm \sqrt{37}}{2}\right\}$ **17.** ϕ **19.** ϕ

21. $\{2 \pm \sqrt{14}\}$ **23.** $\{4 \pm \sqrt{13}\}$ **25.** $\left\{-4, \frac{3}{2}\right\}$

27. $\{-2 \pm \sqrt{3}\}$ **29.** $\left\{\frac{7 \pm \sqrt{5}}{2}\right\}$ **31.** $\left\{1, -\frac{5}{2}\right\}$

33. $\left\{\frac{3}{4}\right\}$ **35.** $\left\{\frac{2 \pm \sqrt{29}}{5}\right\}$ **37.** $\{\sqrt{2} \pm 2\}$

39. $\{-3 \pm \sqrt{13}\}$

Page 439

1. $l = 8$ m, $w = 5$ m   **3.** $l = 8$ m, $w = 4$ m
5. $l = 11$ cm, $w = 4$ cm   **7.** $l = 5$ cm, $w = 4$ cm
9. $l = 8.4$ cm, $w = 2.4$ cm   **11.** $l = 7.7$ m,
$w = 5.7$ m   **13.** $l = 12$ cm, $w = 8$ cm
15. $l = 15$ km, $w = 6$ km   **17.** $l = 18$ km,
$w = 4$ km   **19.** $l = 8.1$ m, $w = 3.1$ m
21. $l = 7$, $w = 5$

Page 440

1. yes   **3.** Wednesday

Page 442

1. $\{75\}$ **3.** ϕ **5.** ϕ **7.** $\{10, -10\}$
9. $\{6, -6\}$ **11.** $\{4, -20\}$ **13.** 16   **15.** 1
17. $\frac{25}{4}$ **19.** $\{13, -1\}$ **21.** $\{9, 5\}$ **23.** $\{7, -3\}$
25. $\{-4, -2\}$ **27.** $\{-6, -10\}$
29. $x^2 - x + 6 = 0$; $a = 1$, $b = -1$, $c = 6$
31. $x^2 + 0x - 7 = 0$; $a = 1$, $b = 0$, $c = -7$
33. $5x^2 + 0x - 11 = 0$; $a = 5$, $b = 0$, $c = -11$
35. $7x^2 - 2x + 1 = 0$; $a = 7$, $b = -2$, $c = 1$
37. $\{4, 2\}$ **39.** $\{3, 4\}$ **41.** $\{-2, -5\}$
43. $\{3, -7\}$ **45.** $\{-3, 1\}$ **47.** $\{7, 0\}$
49. $\left\{-2, \frac{1}{3}\right\}$ **51.** $\left\{\frac{1}{2}, -\frac{5}{2}\right\}$ **53.** $\left\{\frac{-1 \pm \sqrt{13}}{3}\right\}$
55. $\left\{\frac{7 \pm \sqrt{5}}{2}\right\}$ **57.** $\left\{\frac{2 \pm 3\sqrt{2}}{2}\right\}$
59. $\left\{\frac{5 \pm \sqrt{17}}{4}\right\}$ **61.** $\left\{\frac{5 \pm \sqrt{97}}{6}\right\}$
63. $l = 5$ m, $w = 4$ m

Page 444

1. 4.5   **3.** 5.6

Page 447

1. 33°, 57°   **3.** 65°, 25°   **5.** 45°   **7.** 16°
9. 15°, 75°   **11.** 75°, 70°, 35°

Page 450

1. $x = 3$, $y = 14$ **3.** $EF = 3\frac{1}{3}$, $DF = 8\frac{2}{3}$
5. $DE = 11\frac{2}{3}$, $EF = 20$ **7.** $CB = 13\frac{1}{3}$, $DF = 15$
9. 6 m   **11.** 9.6 m   **13.** $7\frac{1}{2}$ m

Page 452

1. $\tan A = 1.333$, $\sin A = .800$, $\cos A = .600$,
$\tan B = .750$, $\sin B = .600$, $\cos B = .800$
3. $\tan A = .750$, $\sin A = .600$, $\cos A = .800$,
$\tan B = 1.333$, $\sin B = .800$, $\cos B = .600$
5. $\tan A = .894$, $\sin A = .667$, $\cos A = .745$,
$\tan B = 1.118$, $\sin B = .745$, $\cos B = .667$
7. 1.000   **9.** .707   **11.** $\sin B = \frac{b}{c}$; $\cos A = \frac{b}{c}$;
thus $\sin B = \cos A$
13. $a^2 + b^2 = c^2$, $\dfrac{a^2}{c^2} + \dfrac{b^2}{c^2} = \dfrac{c^2}{c^2} = 1$.

Also, $\dfrac{a^2}{c^2} + \dfrac{b^2}{c^2} = \sin^2 A + \cos^2 A$. By

substitution, $\sin^2 A + \cos^2 A = 1$.   **15.** $\tan A =$
$.775$, $\sin A = .612$, $\cos A = .791$, $\tan B = 1.291$,
$\sin B = .791$, $\cos B = .612$ **17.** Any two
complementary angles may be represented as
the acute angles of a right triangle ABC.

$\sin A = \dfrac{a}{c}$; $\cos B = \dfrac{a}{c}$; thus, $\sin A = \cos B$,

or the sine of an angle is equal to the cosine of
its complement.

Page 457

1. .9613 **3.** .4384 **5.** 57.29 **7.** 2.145
9. .2588 **11.** 8° **13.** 23° **15.** 34° **17.** 49°
19. 77° **21.** 83° **23.** F **25.** T **27.** T **29.** F
31. F **33.** T **35.** F **37.** T **39.** T **41.** Cos A
decreases from 1 to 0. The ratio of b to c
approaches 0.

Page 460

1. $a = 8.9$ **3.** $b = 8.5$ **5.** $c = 9.7$ **7.** $a = 4.7$
9. $c = 18.3$ **11.** $m\angle A = 30$ **13.** $a = 25.7$
15. $m\angle B = 74$, $BC = 5.7$, $AB = 20.8$
17. $m\angle B = 54$, $BC = 10.2$, $AB = 17.3$
19. $m\angle B = 32$, $BC = 15.3$, $AC = 9.5$

Page 463

1. $x = 58.5$ m **3.** $x = 64.7$ km **5.** $x = 342.9$ m
7. $x = 46.6$ m **9.** 216.5 m **11.** 96.0 m
13. 32° **15.** 21,299.3 m **17.** 49.5 km²

Page 464

1. $x = 8$, $y = 10$ **3.** 3.000 **5.** .949 **7.** 72°
9. $c = 20.4$ **11.** $a = 6.9$ **13.** 93.3 m
15. 44°, 44°, 92° **17.** 35°, 55° **19.** 31.3 m

Page 466

1. $BC = 2\sqrt{5}$, $AC = 2\sqrt{5}$